Dreams
and
Inward
Journeys

Dreams and Inward Journeys

A Rhetoric and Reader for Writers

Fourth Edition

Marjorie Ford
Stanford University

Jon Ford
College of Alameda

Longman

New York Boston San Francisco
London Toronto Sydney Tokyo Singapore Madrid
Mexico City Munich Paris Cape Town Hong Kong Montreal

Editor-in-Chief: Joseph Terry
Acquisitions Editor: Lynn M. Huddon
Marketing Manager: Carlise Paulson
Supplements Editor: Donna Campion
Production Manager: Denise Phillip
Project Coordination, Text Design, and Electronic Page Makeup: WestWords, Inc.
Cover Designer/Manager: Nancy Danahy
Cover Image: "Floating Woman" © Roxana Villa/SIS
Photo Researcher: PhotoSearch, Inc.
Senior Manufacturing Buyer: Dennis J. Para
Printer and Binder: R.R. Donnelley & Sons Company
Cover Printers: The Lehigh Press, Inc.

For permission to use copyrighted material, grateful acknowledgment is made to the copyright holders on pp. 571–576, which are hereby made part of this copyright page.

Library of Congress Cataloging-in-Publication Data
Ford, Marjorie (Majorie A.)
    Dreams and inward journeys: a rhetoric and reader for writers / Majorie Ford,
    Jon Ford.—4th ed.
        p.cm
    Includes bibliographical references (p.) and index.
    ISBN 0-321-07624-9
    1. College readers. 2. Report writing--Problems, exercises, etc. 3. English
    language—Rhetoric—Problems, exercises, etc. I. Ford, Jon. II. Title.

    PE1417 .F63 2000
    808'.0427—dc21

Copyright © 2001 by Addison Wesley Longman Inc.

Please visit our websit at http://www.awl.com/englishpages

ISBN 0-321-07624-9

1 2 3 4 5 6 7 8 9 1 0—DOH—0 3 0 2 0 1 0 0

CONTENTS

1 Discovering Ourselves in Writing   1

The Writing Process and Self Discovery   1

The writing process is introduced, including prewriting and journal-keeping techniques.

Stages of the Writing Process | Strategies for Prewriting | Dream Journals | Prewriting and Revising with Computers

Thematic Introduction   9

Writing is presented as a process of self-discovery that is rooted in personal experiences and the unconscious mind, including dreams, childhood memories, and everyday events.

Readings

Student Writing

2 Discovering Ourselves in Reading   66

Readings

5   Obsessions and Transformation   231

Student Writing

6 Journeys in Sexuality and Gender   297

Readings

Student Writing

7 The Double/The Other   369

Readings

Student Writing

9 Visions of Nature   510

Readings

Student Writing

CONTENTS BY STRATEGIES AND MODES

Process Analysis

Example and Illustration

Comparison and Contrast

Classification

Definition

Cause and Effect Analysis

Argument

Interpretation and Evaluation

Research Writing

Myths & Tales

Literary Fiction

Poetry

To THE STUDENT

Nothing said to us, nothing we can learn from others, reaches us so deep as that which we find in ourselves.
Theodore Reik

Each person has a unique definition for the meaning of the word *dream*: the dreams you have while asleep, your day time fantasies, your hopes and aspirations, your belief in the power of your own imagination and creativity. The lyrics of popular songs, the plots of movies and novels, advertisements and travel literature—all speak of the power of dreams and promise fulfillment of fantasies of romance, success, or peace of mind. As you think more about the presence and importance of dreams in your personal life and culture, you will begin to discover even more subtle meanings. Just as everyone dreams while sleeping, each person has a personal dream or vision that guides his or her waking life. Perhaps it is a dream that one is just starting to explore, a dream that one has been working to accomplish, or a dream that has just "come true."

We have designed this text using the concept of the dream as a common meeting ground, one that we hope will encourage you to better understand yourself, your family, friends, college, and professional acquaintances—and the world in which we all live. Dreams and the insights they bring from the inner self, with the universality of their patterns, imagery, and meaning, also provide a central metaphor for the writing process as an inward journey that involves the imagination, creativity, and vision.

Dreams and Inward Journeys: A Reader for Writers, Fourth Edition, is composed of nine chapters. Each chapter presents an aspect of the book's theme as well as a writing strategy that we think will help you to understand yourself and your world while improving your writing fluency and skills. The earlier chapters ask you to reflect on your personal experiences as a reader and as a writer. As you progress through the book, you will be asked to relate your personal and imaginative experiences to the social and cultural realities that also help to shape your identity and values.

In Chapter 1, "Discovering Ourselves in Writing," writing is presented as an often chaotic but powerful and rewarding process that helps the writer to understand himself or herself better and to clarify thoughts and feelings. The writing techniques explained will help you to overcome writing-related anxieties and fears and to get started on your writing. The dream journal project introduced in this chapter will provide you with the opportunity to discover the similarities between the writing process and dreaming—to discover the concerns of your unconscious mind.

In Chapter 2, "Discovering Ourselves in Reading," you will explore the ways in which reading is an active process that encourages a reader to understand and clarify his or her inner resources and values in relation to the values and experiences that have been recorded in a text. Each selection in this chapter presents a unique perspective on the reading process and reflects on the relationships among dreaming, reading, language, and the imagination. The reading strategies introduced discuss techniques for activating and enriching your reading and language experience while emphasizing how reading is closely related to the process of writing.

The readings in Chapter 3, "Memories," explore how early experiences and memories, especially those inner experiences that are rooted in dreams, fantasies, or even obsessions, influence one's sense of self. The readings included in this section also suggest that the stories created and remembered from childhood help to shape personal myths. In this chapter we discuss creative strategies for writing effective description and narratives. These strategies will help you when you write about your dreams and memories.

Chapter 4, "Dreams, Myths, and Fairy Tales," begins to put your inward journey into a broader cultural perspective, encouraging you to see new meanings in your life experiences by suggesting how your self-concept and values have been influenced by ancient and popular myths and fairy tales. Some of the readings in this chapter discuss the similarities and relationships between dreams and myths. Because you will be asked to compare different versions of fairy tales, to contrast an early memory of a favorite childhood book with a more recent reading of that book, or to create and evaluate a personal myth, in this chapter we discuss techniques used in comparison writing as well as approaches to making clear evaluative statements.

The readings included in Chapter 5, "Obsessions and Transformation," reveal situations in which the writer or the main character is overwhelmed by a submerged part of his or her self. Although several of the obsessions presented in the essays and stores are self-destructive, in some selections the unconscious need is transformed positively into greater self-understanding. The thinking and writing strategies presented in this chapter will help you to define and draw distinctions among complex concepts such as those presented in this text: dream, myth, fantasy, fairy tale. We also discuss some common misuses of words and barriers to clear communication as well as the difference between the private and public meanings and associations of words.

Chapter 6, "Journeys in Sexuality and Gender," explores issues of gender and sexuality in both fiction and nonfiction works as they influence an individual's self-concept and role in society. The readings also examine the ways that sexuality is relfected in dreams and emotional life, as well as the way that sexual feelings are channeled through myths and rituals. The writing and thinking strategy presented in this chapter, causal analysis, will help you to analyze and interpret the readings and will provide you with a structure for composing the essays you will be asked to write in response to the readings.

Chapter 7, "The Double/The Other," begins with a discussion of the dual nature of the human personality and presents readings, including a variety of classic stories, many of which are based on dreams or fantasies. These essays and stories reflect different forms of the dualistic struggle within the human mind: the good self as opposed to the evil self, the rational self as opposed to the irrational self. The writing strategies in this chapter focus on how to create a balanced argument through exploring opposing viewpoints, empathizing with your audience, making decisions, and taking a final position of your own.

To what extent have your self-concept and self-image been influenced by the dreams of our mass culture or the prevailing political ideology? What happens to those people who don't choose to fit into, or who feel excluded from, the predominant "dream" of their society? These are some of the questions that are considered in the readings included in Chapter 8, "Society's Dreams." The research writing strategies covered will help you to analyze social issues and to think critically about outside sources of opinion while maintaining your own personal perspective and sense of voice in research-oriented writing.

Often our experiences in nature are powerful and life-affirming; such experiences can become visions that can help us to reshape and rebuild our personal, social, and spiritual worlds. The essays and stories chosen for the final chapter, "Visions of Nature," invite you to reflect on the way nature can inspire and help us reflect on the essential connections between human beings and the natural world. Synthesis and problem solving, the writing strategies presented in this chapter, will help to reinforce your understanding of the chapter's readings and guide you in developing complex, creative essays.

Our experiences as writing teachers continue to confirm the importance of providing students with many opportunities to share their writing with their peers. We have included student essays for you to discuss in class. We hope, too, that you will begin to share your own writing. We believe that you can gain confidence and motivation when you work on your writing with your peers and your instructor.

Although writing is a demanding and challenging activity, it can be a valuable and meaningful experience when you feel you are writing about something vital, something that engages your mind and your feelings. We have worked to provide opportunities for this type of engagement through the materials and activities included in this text. We hope this text will guide and help you to uncover and understand more fully some of your personal and public dreams.

Marjorie Ford
Jon Ford

*T*O THE INSTRUCTOR

Why have many of our greatest writers found inspiration or solved problems in their dreams? What can individuals learn from their dreams that will make their waking lives more rewarding? How does the unconscious mind inform the conscious mind using writing or dreams as a medium? In what ways is the writing process like a dream? These are questions that we have been exploring in our writing classes for almost ten years now. And still they remain as signposts; our search for these answers only grows more compelling.

Throughout this past year, as we have written and revised the Fourth Edition of *Dreams and Inward Journeys*, we have felt very fortunate to have the opportunity to continue following our dream. In this new edition we have built on the pedagogical foundation put in place by the earlier editions. We continue to support a creative approach to teaching writing and reading that acknowledges the role and importance of the unconscious mind, of dreams, of the imagination, of the heart connected to the reasoning mind. Also fundamental to our approach to teaching writing is the value of integrating rather than isolating the teaching of literature and expository writing. We have seen our students' writing develop as they have experimented with different writing projects and genres, from dream journals to arguments and short stories, from practice with the traditional modes such as comparison, causal analysis, and definition to essays that are based on personal experiences or are primarily reflections.

Once again we have enjoyed applying these assumptions in shaping the text around the theme of dreams, a topic that is intriguing, revealing, and challenging. *Dreams and Inward Journeys* presents a rich mixture of essays, stories, poems, and student writings thematically focused on dream-related topics such as writing, reading, memory, myths, obsessions, the double, sexuality, gender roles, technology, popular culture, and visions of nature. Each chapter features rhetorical advice and strategies for writing and thinking. All of the included selections have personal and social meanings that encourage students to think about and develop new ways of seeing and understanding themselves in relationships to fundamental social issues as well as universal human concerns.

Special features of the fourth edition include:

- Thirty-six new readings that continue to develop and update the text's thematic concept with more particular attention to social and political issues.
- A rhetorical advice section that opens each chapter and provides students with one particular writing and thinking strategy.
- Information on keeping a dream journal as well as journal writing prompts before each reading to encourage informal, expressive, and spontaneous thinking and writing.
- Revised and updated introductions to reading and writing.
- A new Chapter 9, "Visions of Nature," which offers visions of the natural world while challenging students to search for creative solutions to problems both personal and global.
- More visuals: professional art work along with student drawings are included to help generate prewriting activities, informal, and formal writing projects.
- Student essays in each chapter present students' perspectives on the topics raised in the chapter and models of the rhetorical strategy outlined at the beginning of each chapter. Four of the student essays in the book are documented research papers.
- Information on keeping a dream journal as well as journal writing prompts before each reading to encourage informal, expressive, and spontaneous thinking and writing.
- Two poems per chapter that explore the chapter's theme in a concrete, expressive, and literary form.
- New "Conections" questions as well as "Questions for Discussion" and "Ideas for Writing."
- "Topics for Research and Writing" questions at the end of each chapter. These questions give students suggestions for research and longer writing assignments, as well as film and URL suggestions for further viewing/reading/research.

Acknowledgments

First, we thank our reviewers around the country whose advice guided us in this revision: John W. Barrett, Richland College; Jacqueline Bush, Hunter College; Dennis Chowenhill, Chabot College; Cynthia Kuhn, University of Denver; Clyde Moneyhun, Youngstown State University; Catherine Packard, Southeastern Illinois College; Katherine Ploeger, California State University, Stanislaus; Cathy Sheeley, Penn Valley Community College; Ruthe Thompson, Southwest State University.

We give special thanks for the editors and staff at Longman: our editors Anne Smith and Lynn Huddon, who continued to develop the creative vision of the book and kept the project on schedule; to Senior Administrative Editorial Assistant, Rebecca Gilpin; and to our project editor, Denise Phillip.

We also want to thank all of our students in the day and evening programs at the College of Alameda, University of California at Berekeley, De Anza College, and Stanford University who have encouraged us through their enthusiasm for the concept as well as through working so hard at improving their writing. We extend particular appreciation to those students who submitted essays, stories, or drawings for this edition.

We thank our children, Michael and Maya, for being fabulous and creating amazingly inspiring dreams for their own lives.

Marjorie Ford
Jon Ford

Dreams
and
Inward
Journeys

Discovering Ourselves in Writing

Writing itself is one of the great, free human activities. . . . For the person who follows what occurs to him with trust and forgiveness, the world remains always ready and deep, an inexhaustible environment, with the combined vividness of an actuality and flexibility of a dream.
WILLIAM STAFFORD
The Way of Writing

[A] writer is someone entranced by the power of language to create a magic show of the imagination, to make the dead sit up and talk, to shine light into the darkness of the great human mysteries.
TIM O'BRIEN
The Magic Show

THE WRITING PROCESS AND SELF-DISCOVERY

William Stafford has said that "writing itself is one of the great, free human activities. There is scope for individuality, and elation, and discovery, in writing." At the same time, a good writer is also a patient craftsperson. Writing makes demands on both the creative and the rational sides of the mind. From the creative and intuitive mind it summons forth details, images, memories, dreams, and feelings; from the rational and logical mind it demands planning, development, evidence, rereading, rethinking, and revision.

Perhaps it is this basic duality associated with the act of writing that can sometimes make it feel like a complex and overwhelming task. Practicing and studying particular writing strategies such as those presented in each chapter of *Dreams and Inward Journeys*, along with drafting, revising, and sharing your writing with your peers and instructor, will help you to develop your self–confidence. As a writer you need to be aware of the feelings and fears of your unconscious self as well as the expectations of your rational mind. Balancing these two sides of your mind—knowing when, for example, to give your creative mind license to explore while controlling and quieting your critical mind—is an important part of the challenge of developing self-confidence and learning to write well.

Stages of the Writing Process

Most professional and student writers benefit from conceptualizing writing as a process with a number of stages. Although these stages do not need to be rigidly separated, an awareness of the different quality of thoughts and feelings that usually occur in each of the stages of writing is useful and will help you create a finished piece of writing that speaks clearly about your own concerns, values, and opinions. The stages of the writing process include the prewriting, drafting, and revision phases. As you become a more experienced and skillful writer, you may find that you want to adapt this process to your own goals, perhaps by spending more time in preliminary reading to collect background information for research essays or possibly by spending less time prewriting if you are working on an essay that must be written in a shorter time frame or during an in-class exam.

As preparation for writing the initial draft of an essay, prewriting allows you to pursue a variety of playful, creative activities that will help you to generate ideas and understand what you want to say about your subject. Drafting is your rapid first "take" on your topic and should be done after you have concentrated on your paper's subject and thought about the thesis or core concept around which you want to center the ideas and examples of your essay. You may find, however, that as you write your first draft, your thesis and focus shift or even change dramatically. Don't be concerned if this happens. Many professional writers have learned that although they begin the drafting phase feeling that they have a focus and thesis, the actual process of writing the draft changes their initial plan. Rewriting is a natural part of the writing process. As you keep returning to your draft and continue to work to shape your thoughts into clear sentences, they will capture your inner feelings and ideas.

While you will need to rewrite to clarify your thinking and ideas, the process of revision can also be approached in stages. They include revising for your paper's overall shape and meaning, which may involve outlining the rough draft; rearranging whole paragraphs or ideas and examples; developing and cutting redundancy within paragraphs; refining and clarifying sentences and individual words; and, finally, proofreading for grammar, spelling, and punctuation. The revision and editing stages of writing have been made more exciting and less tedious since the invention of the computer and word processing software, which usually includes outliners, spelling and grammar checkers, word and paragraph counters, and global search and replace functions that make it easier to correct an aspect of the entire manuscript at the click of a mouse. But revision is still a time–consuming and important element of the writing process, for it is through revision and editing that your essay moves from being an approximate statement of a thought or insight into a well–crafted and moving verbal expression of your thinking.

Strategies for Prewriting

Because writing begins with prewriting, we have chosen to focus on this stage here, at the beginning of your journey as a writer. The prewriting stage is particularly exciting for those who enjoy creative expression, as well as to those who don't have much confidence in themselves as writers, who feel it is hard to get "warmed up" to the task. If you are apprehensive about writing and don't see yourself as a "creative thinker," prewriting activities may help you to discover new or forgotten images, memories, and ideas, as well as to make connections you may never have anticipated. You may find yourself liberating a creative spirit hidden in the recesses of your mind. Only you need to read and evaluate your prewriting; at this stage you determine what seems interesting and relevant.

Prewriting also makes the writing of later drafts easier because it helps you to clarify and organize your thoughts before they are put into a formal format. Drawing, freewriting, invisible writing, brainstorming, clustering, and journal keeping are all effective prewriting techniques that will help you to discover what you really want and need to say. Like the later stages of writing, all of these techniques can be practiced either with a pencil, a pen, or with sophisticated computer software. Although many students feel more comfortable and "natural" prewriting with a pencil, students who are familiar with the computer and have good keyboarding skills often find it helpful to do their prewritings as files that they can save and possibly transform into details, images, and sentences in their drafts.

Drawing   Drawing a picture in response to a topic can help you begin to understand what you think and feel. In the drawings in response to a topic included in this text, students used a computer program to capture their writing processes and responses to readings, but you may feel more comfortable using colored pencils, watercolors, charcoal, or ink. A number of professional writers have spoken of the value of drawing as a way to develop ideas or understand a new text. In *The Nature and Aim of Fiction* Flannery O'Connor maintains, "Any discipline can help your writing. . . particularly drawing. Anything that helps you to see, anything that makes you look." While drawing an image from a complex text you are reading, you will be able to focus your thoughts on the details that may have already unconsciously captured your imagination. This process of drawing about a piece of writing will increase your engagement with it and help you clarify your response as you make that

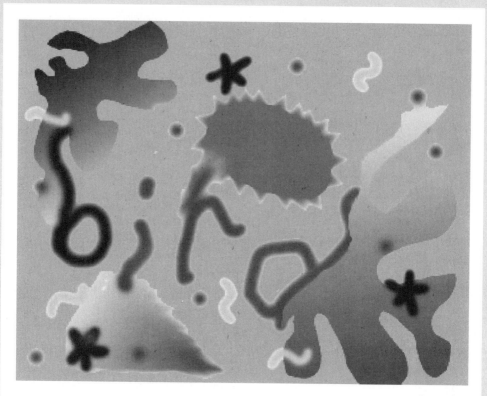

Cori Nelson

I was trying to show how I collect my letters and words from vastly different areas—in writing, I try to bring together the different pieces of my life. I try to bring all the different colors and textures around me together into sentences and paragraphs. I spelled out the word bird because birds inspire a lot of my writing. (This drawing was originally done in color, not in black and white as reproduced here.)

response more tangible. In this edition of *Dreams and Inward Journeys* we have included several examples of drawings that students completed after reading the "Thematic Introduction" of each chapter as an exercise to help them begin thinking about their perspectives on the selections that follow.

Freewriting   A freewrite can start anywhere and usually lasts from five to fifteen minutes. During these brief writing sessions, it is important to continue to write and not to censor any idea or feeling that comes to your mind. If you seem to run out of thoughts, just write, "I have no more to say," or anything you wish until a new thought emerges. After ten minutes of freewriting, read what you have produced and try to sum up the central idea or feeling of the piece. You can then proceed to another freewrite, using the summary state-

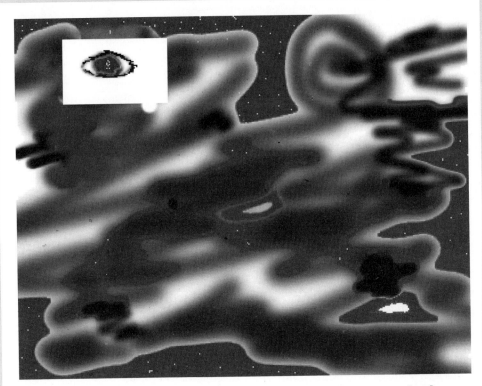

Lori Sunamoto

This picture represents my writing process. I think of my mind as being as open as a midnight sky. And sometimes the clouds that swirl around in my brain part for just a moment allowing me to see the stars and the infinite night. This is when ideas come to me, or perhaps it is more appropriate to say that this is when I am allowed to catch a glimpse of all that is "out there." Writing is almost like trying to pluck the stars from the sky and hold them in your hand.

ment as a new starting point. Writers often do several freewrites before they decide on how to focus their thoughts.

Invisible Writing With invisible writing, the writer creates "invisible" words, or words that can't be seen while the writer is working. Some writers never even look at the words generated in an invisible writing exercise but instead use the exercise as a rehearsal, a building of mental pathways that will make the actual writing of their paper less halting and painful. Many writers find new insights in their thoughts that were produced invisibly. Invisible writing can be done by writing on the back of a piece of carbon paper onto a piece of notebook paper or by keyboarding with a dimmed computer screen. While you are freewriting and doing invisible writing, do not consciously pay attention to central ideas, relationships between ideas, organizational patterns, or grammatical or spelling errors of any kind; concentrate instead on getting your ideas and feelings out in words.

Brainstorming   Brainstorming, which can be done effectively in groups or individually, involves writing a list of all the words, phrases, ideas, descriptions, thoughts, and questions that come to your mind in response to a topic or issue. As in freewriting, it is essential not to stop to censor, judge, or correct any idea or feelings. The process of listing will, itself, bring up new ideas and associations. Ideas will build on one another, leading to thoughts that are original and fresh, while creating a list will help you to see relationships between ideas that may have previously seemed disconnected. When your list is complete, normally in fifteen to twenty minutes, go back to find patterns of thought or main ideas that you have uncovered. Bracketing or circling related ideas and details may help you form an organizational plan. Through brainstorming, you can begin to formulate a rough outline for your essay that will guide you in the drafting phase of writing.

Clustering   Clustering, or mapping, closely reflects the way in which the mind functions in making nonlinear connections between ideas. Combined with brainstorming or freewriting, clustering can also help you to perceive clearer relationships between ideas. Start your cluster by placing the topic to be explored in the center of the page. Draw a circle around it, and then draw lines out from your central circle in different directions to connect it with other circles containing additional ideas, phrases, or clues to experiences. The words in these circles will naturally develop their own offshoots as new associations emerge. The pattern being created by the clustering process continually changes in complex ways because any new idea will relate to all of the ideas already recorded. As in freewriting, clustering should be done without stopping. Once the cluster feels completed to you, write for a few minutes about what you have discovered. Completing a cluster and a related freewrite can help you understand how you want to focus your topic and organize the major relationships between ideas, examples, and details.

Journal Keeping   Daily writing in a notebook or journal will help you to develop a record of your thoughts and feelings. Keeping a journal is similar to the type of prewriting assignments we have just discussed in that it allows you freedom to explore parts of your inner world, knowing that your writing will not be evaluated. Keeping a journal of your responses to the journal topics and study questions in a text, using either a small notebook or computer, is one of the most effective ways to develop your confidence and skills as a writer. Both of the student essays included in this chapter were developed from journal entries that focused on strong inner experiences and images that initially seemed very private but that were clarified and made public through drafting, revising, peer sharing, and more revision.

The Dream Journal   Because this text has been developed around the theme of dreams, and because the process of understanding your dreams may lead you to new insights and images that you may find useful in more formal writing, we recommend that you extend your journal-keeping activity into the night world by writing down your dreams—a process used by many professional writers. Through keeping a dream journal you can improve your ability to recall dreams, and you can begin to capture unconscious images that intrigue or possibly disturb you. Perhaps, too, you will begin to notice more similarities between your dream images and some of the dream-like stories in this text. Your appreciation of metaphors and symbols will increase.

By keeping your dream journal, you will also begin to realize how understanding your writing process is similar to understanding your dreams. The first written draft of your dream is like a prewrite of an essay: a set of strong, if chaotic, images that you can work with thoughtfully and creatively. As you bring form and meaning to a dream through analysis and interpretation, you bring form and meaning to an essay through drafting and revising those first generative ideas that begin the process of writing an essay, story, or poem.

Keep your dream journal at your bedside along with a pen or dark pencil. The best time to write in your dream journal is in the early morning or immediately on awaking from a vivid dream. Some students have even used a tape recorder to capture their "dream voice," its sounds and rhythms. Try to write in your dream journal three or four times a week, even if you have only a dim or fleeting image or impression to record. Write down all the details you can remember, indicating a shift, jump in time, or unclear portion of the dream with a question mark or ellipsis. Try not to censor or "clean up" the dream imagery, even if the thinking seems illogical, chaotic, or even embarrassing to you. Avoid interpreting your dream as you are recording it, although you might list in the margins any associations that immediately come to mind in relation to the images as you record them. Later, as you reread your dream journal entries over a period of several days, you may see patterns and more complex associations emerging and you may want to write about them.

Your Computer: Developing an Important Writing Partnership

More and more students come to their college writing classes with basic computer skills: you may already use e-mail and the Internet on a daily basis. You will also find that your computer will help to facilitate and streamline your writing process. Computers are not just "keyboarding tools," or for printing out text. As mentioned previously, in the later stages of revising and editing, computers are invaluable, making it possible to reorganize your paper easily by moving around large sections of your essay, adding in concise examples and details, fine tuning grammar, syntax, and word choice. The spelling checker on your computer will help you prepare your draft for final presentation, while an on-line dictionary and thesaurus make it possible to find just the right word for precise and powerful expression. Some students find that the flexibility to generate new ideas, experiment, and change sentences, paragraphs, details, examples, and refine major ideas that computers provide helps them to overcome writing blocks.

In fact, all of the strategies for prewriting mentioned here, particularly such techniques as invisible writing, which was really designed with the computer in mind, can be completed on a computer and saved. Other exploratory techniques work only on a computer, such as engaging in an on-line conversation on a subject for writing using a chat program or e-mail, and then saving the conversation for later use. You might decide to copy sections from any of your prewritings into the first or a later draft of your essay; this is much easier to do if you write them on a computer rather than on a piece of paper.

Prewriting strategies are more frequently used in the generative stage of the writing process, but we encourage you to use these techniques whenever you feel yourself getting "blocked" in your work. During the drafting stage of writing, or even after an instructor has returned your paper to you with corrections on it and you are working on a major revision, the exercises discussed here can continue to help you keep in touch with what you really want to say, with your own inner voice.

T H E M A T I C   I N T R O D U C T I O N : D I S C O V E R I N G   O U R S E L V E S I N   W R I T I N G

Writing can be described as an inward journey. The process of discovering what resides within your mind and your spirit begins anew each time you start a writing project. Many people find it difficult to begin, wondering how they will be able to untangle all of their thoughts and feelings and how they will finally decide on the most accurate words and sentence patterns to make their statement clear and compelling. You may feel overwhelmed by the possibilities of all that is waiting to be discovered within you, and at the same time, you may feel a sense of wonder and excitement, anticipating pleasures and rewards of uncovering and expressing new parts of your mind, imagination, and spirit.

The complex feelings often experienced at this stage of the writing process have been eloquently described by many authors whose language, images, and ideas can serve as your guides. They experience writing as a process of self-discovery and self-understanding rooted in the experiences of the unconscious and conscious mind, in the experiences of dreams and of childhood memories, and in everyday events and goals. This chapter's readings begin with Merle Woo's "Poem for the Creative Writing Class, Spring 1982," which explores the potential for freedom and flight of the mind, spirit, and imagination in a classroom of writers who only appear to be caged by their physical space. The next selection is a response to a request for advice about writing. In "A Letter To a Young Poet," poet Rainer Maria Rilke advises a new writer to look within to the "treasure house" of experiences that each of us has ("the images from your dreams, and the objects that you remember") as well as to disregard external critical voices.

In the selection, "A Way of Writing," poet and teacher William Stafford also asks writers to trust themselves. He believes that if writers are receptive to their minds, allowing themselves time to "fish" for ideas in their unconscious minds, and if they do not evaluate their work as it is being produced, they will find an inexhaustible source of ideas and experiences to explore through writing. In "Writing Matters," novelist and essayist Julia Alvarez describes her writing rituals while reflecting on the meaningful role that a writer plays in shaping personal and community values. In "Teaching Two Kinds of Thinking by Teaching Writing," English professor Peter Elbow presents an approach to writing that helps the creative, intuitive unconscious mind to work separately but supportively with the logical, critical mind.

Some writers turn specifically to their dreams for guidance. In the selection, "The Symbolic Language of Dreams," Stephen King discusses the ways in which his dreams have helped him to solve problems that he has had in writing. He compares his writing process to a dream state: "Part of my function as a writer is to dream awake." The meanings of language, like the meanings of dreams, are not always immediately and simply apparent, but through reflection we can understand their messages and apply them in our writing.

In her essay "Mother Tongue," best-selling novelist Amy Tan is critical of achievement tests and the conventional, skills-oriented approach to teaching writing that she encountered in her high school. She claims that she developed her talents by incorporating all that she and her mother, a non-native speaker, knew about language and about life: "what language ability tests can never reveal: her [mother's] intent, her passion, her imagery, the rhythms of her speech and the nature of her thoughts." Also emphasizing non-traditional ways of learning, journalist Jon Katz in "The Tales They Tell in Cyber-Space" argues that on-line chat groups and e-mail interchange encourage individuals to communicate and share in new forms of writing and community.

The final poem in this chapter is also about a journey into the unknown. The speaker in the poem "This Place in the Ways," by Muriel Rukeyser, reflects back on her disappointments with "love and rage," seeing their insignificance in face of the mysteries that the future offers. The speaker's spirit rings as a refrain throughout the poem, reminding us of her unique way of seeing her life's journey.

The two student essays that conclude this chapter give further insights into how writing shapes an individual's inner growth and identity. Joyce Chang, in her essay "Drive Becarefully" (a response to Amy Tan's "Mother Tongue"), discusses her inner struggle to accept her mother's language as fundamental to both their identities. In "Whirling Through: My Writing Process as a Tornado Within," Sheila Chanani explains her writing process using images of a tornado and a flower,

As you read the selections that follow, we think that you will come to better understand how writing is a process of self-discovery, an inward journey, a way of uncovering, creating, and clarifying your relationship to your inner world and the people and communities around you.

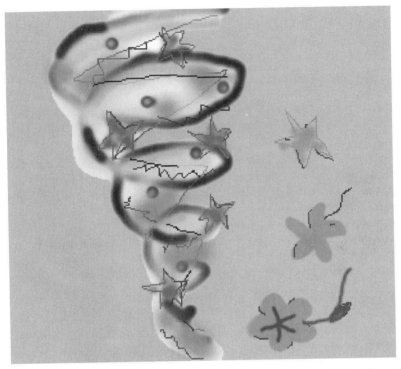

Sheila Chanani
The Tornado Within

In the above drawing, student Sheila Chanani created an image of the beginning of her writing process in the form of an inner tornado, a "swirl of thoughts and words" that she needs to sort through to find what she really wants to say in her essay and give her ideas "substance and shape." See Sheila Chanani's essay at the end of Chapter One, "Whirling Through," for a full explanation of her writing process as represented here in her drawing.

IDEAS FOR DRAWING, WRITING, AND DISCUSSION

1. Do a drawing based on your imagination of your own pre-writing process.
2. Write a brief comment on your drawing and the process of producing it: What did you learn about your feelings about writing and getting started on writing projects from this activity?
3. Working in a small group, share your drawing and commentary with your classmates. What different styles, both of drawing and of attitude towards writing, were found? What common images, themes, and feelings emerged?

Merle Woo

"Poem for the Creative Writing Class, Spring 1982"

Merle Woo (b. 1941) is the daughter of Chinese-Korean immigrants. Her essays, stories, and poems have been included in a number of anthologies, including This Bridge Called My Back: Writings by Radical Women of Color *(1981), and in her own poetry collection,* Yellow Woman Speaks *(1986). Woo is a socialist, feminist, unionist, lecturer on Asian American/Ethnic Studies, and an activist. Believing in the importance of combining her work as teacher, activist, and poet, Woo said "we poets who are outspoken as Asian Americans, women, lesbians/gays, workers, cannot separate ourselves from the reality in which we live. We are freedom fighters with words as our weapons—on the page or on the picket sign." In the poem that follows, Woo encourages students to use their imagination and creates an image of a classroom writing community that promotes freedom of expression.*

JOURNAL

Either write about a writing classroom that felt like a cage or a prison or about a classroom where you felt encouraged to learn and grow.

> The silence in the classroom
> of people I've grown to respect—
> seems like so much potential here:
> men and women
> 5   brown black yellow jewish white
> gay and straight.
>
> Classrooms are ugly,
> cages with beautiful birds in them.
> scraped, peeling walls
> 10   empty bookcase
> an empty blackboard—
> no ideas here.
>
> And one window.
> One writer comes in
> 15   from sitting on the sill,
> three stories up.
> We all want to fly
> and feel the sun on the backs of our wings—
>
> Inhale the breath
> 20   pulling in the energy of

seventeen people around me
and exhale
putting out my ideas, ideas, ideas.
We all want to fly out that window.
25 A breeze comes in once in a while,
we want to go out with it
to where the birds are.

To take flight
using the words
30 that give us wings.

What is language after all
but the touching and uplifting
one to the others:
scenes
35 poems
dreams
our own natural imagery:
coins
a train to El Salvador
40 sleeping, pregnant mothers
menacing garages/ a fist pounding/ voices yelling
a yogi
cops being the bowery boty
roller coasters
45 blood
a girl on a swing
roses
water, streams, rivers, oceans
rise. rise.

50 Who can keep us caged?

QUESTIONS FOR DISCUSSION

1. What point about the writing class does the speaker make in the first stanza? How does the poet link this idea to the image in the second stanza of a classroom as a cage?
2. What different meanings can be read into the image "three stories up"?
3. How does Woo's poem suggest that sharing one's writing is an essential aspect of the creative process?
4. In the poem, the speaker claims that writing can take in the most authentic imagery of self and heritage. Do you think this should be an important function of all writing classes? Why or why not?
5. How would you answer the speaker's final question: "Who can keep us caged?" What features of your education have given you a feeling of being "caged"?

CONNECTION

Compare and contrast Tan's and Woo's critiques of traditional education. How does each deal with the importance of "finding a voice" in one's writing?

IDEAS FOR WRITING

1. Write an essay about a class you took whose members began to function as a family or community. What helped to establish positive communication within the class? What did you learn from this group experience?
2. Develop your journal entry on this poem into an essay that defines your own image of the ideal classroom.

Rainer Maria Rilke

"Letter to a Young Poet"

Rainer Maria Rilke (1875–1926) is one of the greatest modern poets. He was born in Prague and as a teenager was sent to military school, where he was often ill and depressed. After his association with the French sculptor Rodin, Rilke devoted himself exclusively to poetry, traveling throughout Europe and eventually settling in Switzerland after World War I. Rilke's greatest books of poetry are the Duino Elegies *(1923) and the* Sonnets to Orpheus *(1923). In these two works he develops long cycles of dense, mythological poetry that explore death and loss with great artistic complexity and spiritual depth. Mysticism and religious experience remained strong themes in his writing throughout his career, but Rilke came to believe that God could be found within, as well as through an intense contemplation of the things of this world. In addition to writing poetry, Rilke corresponded with many other artists and intellectuals. The* Letters to a Young Poet *(1903–1908) were written in response to a young military student, Franz Kappus, who had sent Rilke some of his poems for criticism. In these sensitive letters to a stranger, Rilke reveals his philosophy of lyrical writing, revealing many of the ideas and images to be found in his great poems.*

JOURNAL

Write about a time when a friend or classmate showed some of his or her writing to you and asked for your opinion of it, or a time when you asked someone whose opinion you respected for an opinion of your writing. Write about your feelings before and after the sharing of opinion.

Paris
February 17, 1903

Dear Sir,

1   Your letter arrived just a few days ago. I want to thank you for the great confidence you have placed in me. That is all I can do. I cannot discuss your verses; for any attempt at criticism would be foreign to me. Nothing touches a work of art so little as words of criticism: they always result in more or less fortunate misunderstandings. Things aren't all so tangible and sayable as people would usually have us believe; most experiences are unsayable, they happen in a space that no word has ever entered, and more unsayable than all other things are works of art, those mysterious existences, whose life endures beside our own small, transitory life.

2   With this note as a preface, may I just tell you that your verses have no style of their own, although they do have silent and hidden beginnings of something personal. I feel this most clearly in the last poem, "My Soul." There, something of your own is trying to become word and melody. And in the lovely poem "To Leopardi" a kind of kinship with that great, solitary figure does perhaps appear. Nevertheless, the poems are not yet anything in themselves, not yet anything independent, even the last one and the one to Leopardi. Your kind letter, which accompanied them, managed to make clear to me various faults that I felt in reading your verses, though I am not able to name them specifically.

3   You ask whether your verses are any good. You ask me. You have asked others before this. You send them to magazines. You compare them with other poems, and you are upset when certain editors reject your work. Now (since you have said you want my advice) I beg you to stop doing that sort of thing. You are looking outside, and that is what you should most avoid right now. No one can advise or help you—no one. There is only one thing you should do. Go into yourself. Find out the reason that commands you to write; see whether it has spread its roots into the very depths of your heart; confess to yourself whether you would have to die if you were forbidden to write. This most of all: ask yourself in the most silent hour of your night: *must* I write? Dig into yourself for a deep answer. And if this answer rings out in assent, if you meet this solemn question with a strong, simple "*I must*," then build your life in accordance with this necessity; your whole life, even into its humblest and most indifferent hour, must become a sign and witness to this impulse. Then come close to Nature. Then, as if no one had ever tried before, try to say what you see and feel and love and lose. Don't write love poems; avoid those forms that are too facile and ordinary: they are the hardest to work with, and it takes a great, fully ripened power to create something individual where good, even glorious, traditions exist in abundance. So rescue yourself from these general themes and write about what your everyday life offers you; describe your sorrows and desires, the thoughts that pass through your mind and your belief in some kind of beauty—describe all these with heartfelt, silent, humble sincerity and, when you express yourself, use the Things around you, the images from your dreams, and the objects that you remember. If your everyday life seems poor, don't blame *it*; blame yourself; admit to yourself that you are not enough of a poet to call

forth its riches; because for the creator there is no poverty and no poor, indifferent place. And even if you found yourself in some prison, whose walls let in none of the world's sounds—wouldn't you still have your childhood, that jewel beyond all price, that treasure house of memories? Turn your attention to it. Try to raise up the sunken feelings of this enormous past; your personality will grow stronger, your solitude will expand and become a place where you can live in the twilight, where the noise of other people passes by, far in the distance.—And if out of this turning-within, out of this immersion in your own world, *poems* come, then you will not think of asking anyone whether they are good or not. Nor will you try to interest magazines in these works: for you will see them as your dear natural possession, a piece of your life, a voice from it. A work of art is good if it has arisen out of necessity. That is the only way one can judge it. So, dear Sir, I can't give you any advice but this: to go into yourself and see how deep the place is from which your life flows; at its source you will find the answer to the question of whether you *must* create. Accept that answer, just as it is given to you, without trying to interpret it. Perhaps you will discover that you are called to be an artist. Then take that destiny upon yourself, and bear it, its burden and its greatness, without ever asking what reward might come from outside. For the creator must be a world for himself and must find everything in himself and in Nature, to whom his whole life is devoted.

4   But after this descent into yourself and into your solitude, perhaps you will have to renounce becoming a poet (if, as I have said, one feels one could live without writing, then one shouldn't write at all). Nevertheless, even then, this self-searching that I ask of you will not have been for nothing. Your life will still find its own paths from there, and that they may be good, rich, and wide is what I wish for you, more that I can say.

5   What else can I tell you? It seems to me that everything has its proper emphasis; and finally I want to add just one more bit of advice: to keep growing, silently and earnestly, through your whole development; you couldn't disturb it any more violently than by looking outside and waiting for outside answers to questions that only your innermost feeling, in your quietest hour, can perhaps answer.

6   It was a pleasure for me to find in your letter the name of Professor Horaček; I have great reverence for that kind, learned man, and a gratitude that has lasted through the years. Will you please tell him how I feel; it is very good of him to still think of me, and I appreciate it.

7   The poems that you entrusted me with I am sending back to you. And I thank you once more for your questions and sincere trust, of which, by answering as honestly as I can, I have tried to make myself a little worthier than I, as a stranger, really am.

Yours very truly,
Rainer Maria Rilke

Questions for Discussion

1. Why does Rilke refuse to criticize the young poet's work? Do you agree with the reasons he gives for his refusal?

2. Although Rilke does not give Kappus a formal critique, he does give the young poet some advice on sending out his work for publication and on the use of traditional forms such as the love poem. What is Rilke's advice, and why does he think it is important?

3. Rilke strongly urges Kappus to "go into [him]self" and seek a deep reason for writing. Do you agree that a writer must have a deep reason to write, so much so that he or she simply "*must*" write?

4. Why does Rilke urge the young poet to draw on his own emotions, fleeting thoughts and experiences ("images from your dreams, and the objects you remember")? Why isn't it possible for a writer simply to make things up, to create non-existent experiences through sheer imagination?

5. Rilke tries to refute objections to his advice about looking within by telling the young poet that no one is poor or wanting in experiences. Do you agree that anyone's past experiences and memories can provide a rich source of writing material?

CONNECTION

Compare and contrast Rilke's advice to a young poet with Stafford's advice to the would-be writer in "A Way of Writing" or with that of professional novelist Stephen King. What do you find most useful in each writer's advice?

IDEAS FOR WRITING

1. Write a letter to Rilke from the perspective of Franz Kappus, the young poet. If you were Kappus, would you find the advice helpful, or would you be annoyed that Rilke had failed to comment directly on your work?

2. Using yourself and your own writing as examples, write about how much (or how little) you typically follow the advice Rilke gives in your own writing efforts. For instance, do you tend to draw on your own past experiences and images from dreams and memory? Do you look deep within when you write, or do you tend to rely on ideas from conversation, books, or the media?

William Stafford

"A Way of Writing"

William Stafford (1914–1993) was born and raised in Kansas, where he worked on farms and in oil refineries. As a conscientious objector, he served time in work camps during World War II. He earned his B.A. and M.A. at the University of Kansas and his Ph.D. at the University of Iowa. Stafford taught creative writing at the University of Iowa and at Lewis and Clark University in Oregon. He won the National Book Award for Traveling through the Dark *(1963). Stafford also wrote nonfic-*

tion, including Writing the Australian Crawl: Views of the Writer's Vocation *(1978). He kept a daily journal and is best known for his personal lyric poetry, which is complex in its perceptions of inner feelings and the social and environmental concerns of rural America. The most recent collection of his work is* The Way It Is: New and Selected Poems *(1998). Stafford's "A Way of Writing," which originally appeared in the Spring 1970 issue of the literary magazine* Field, *expresses his views on the need for receptivity to and trust of one's inner world during the act of writing.*

JOURNAL

Develop an image or draw a picture that captures your creative process as a writer, a painter, a dancer, or a musician. Discuss your creative process as revealed in the image.

1 A writer is not so much someone who has something to say as he is someone who has found a process that will bring about new things he would not have thought of if he had not started to say them. That is, he does not draw on a reservoir; instead, he engages in an activity that brings to him a whole succession of unforeseen stories, poems, essays, plays, laws, philosophies, religions, or—but wait!

2 Back in school, from the first when I began to try to write things, I felt this richness. One thing would lead to another; the world would give and give. Now, after twenty years or so of trying, I live by that certain richness, an idea hard to pin, difficult to say, and perhaps offensive to some. For there are strange implications in it.

3 One implication is the importance of just plain receptivity. When I write, I like to have an interval before me when I am not likely to be interrupted. For me, this means usually the early morning, before others are awake. I get pen and paper, take a glance out of the window (often it is dark out there), and wait. It is like fishing. But I do not wait very long, for there is always a nibble—and this is where receptivity comes in. To get started I will accept anything that occurs to me. Something always occurs, of course, to any of us. We can't keep from thinking. Maybe I have to settle for an immediate impression: it's cold, or hot, or dark, or bright, or in between? Or—well, the possibilities are endless. If I put down something, that thing will help the next thing come, and I'm off. If I let the process go on, things will occur to me that were not at all in my mind when I started. These things, odd or trivial as they may be, are somehow connected. And if I let them string out, surprising things will happen.

4 If I let them string our. . . . Along with initial receptivity, then, there is another readiness: I must be willing to fail. If I am to keep on writing, I cannot bother to insist on high standards. I must get into action and not let anything stop me, or even slow me much. By "standards" I do not mean "correctness"—spelling, punctuation, and so on. These details become mechanical for anyone who writes for a while. I am thinking about such matters as social significance, positive values, consistency, etc. I resolutely disregard these. Something better, greater, is happening! I am following a process that leads so wildly and originally into new territory that no judgment can at the moment be made about values, significance, and so on. I am making something new, something

that has not been judged before. Later others—and maybe I myself—will make judgments. Now, I am headlong to discover. Any distraction may harm the creating.

5   So, receptive, careless of failure, I spin out things on the page. And a wonderful freedom comes. If something occurs to me, it is all right to accept it. It has one justification: it occurs to me. No one else can guide me. I must follow my own weak, wandering, diffident impulses.

6   A strange bonus happens. At times, without my insisting on it, my writings become coherent; the successive elements that occur to me are clearly related. They lead by themselves to new connections. Sometimes the language, even the syllables that happen along, may start a trend. Sometimes the materials alert me to something waiting in my mind, ready for sustained attention. At such times, I allow myself to be eloquent, or intentional, or for great swoops (Treacherous! Not to be trusted!) reasonable. But I do not insist on that; for I know that back of my activity there will be the coherence of my self, and that indulgence of my impulses will bring recurrent patterns and meanings again.

7   This attitude toward the process of writing creatively suggests a problem for me, in terms of what others say. They talk about "skills" in writing. Without denying that I do have experience, wide reading, automatic orthodoxies, and maneuvers of various kinds, I still must insist that I am often baffled about what "skill" has to do with the precious little area of confusion when I do not know what I am going to say and then I find out what I am going to say. That precious interval I am unable to bridge by skill. What can I witness about it? It remains mysterious, just as all of us must feel puzzled about how we are so inventive as to be able to talk along through complexities with our friends, not needing to plan what we are going to say, but never stalled for long in our confident forward progress. Skill? If so, it is the skill we all have, something we must have learned before the age of three of four.

8   A writer is one who has become accustomed to trusting that grace, or luck, or—skill.

9   Yet another attitude I find necessary: most of what I write, like most of what I say in casual conversation, will not amount to much. Even I will realize, and even at the time, that it is not negotiable. It will be like practice. In conversation I allow myself random remarks—in fact, as I recall, that is the way I learned to talk—so in writing I launch many expendable efforts. A result of this free way of writing is that I am not writing for others, mostly; they will not see the product at all unless the activity eventuates in something that later appears to be worthy. My guide is the self, and its adventuring in the language brings about communication.

10   This process-rather-than-substance view of writing invites a final, dual reflection:

1. Writers may not be special—sensitive or talented in any usual sense. They are simply engaged in sustained use of a language skill we all have. Their "creations" come about through confident reliance on stray impulses that will, with trust, find occasional patterns that are satisfying.
2. But writing itself is one of the great, free human activities. There is scope for individuality, and elation, and discovery, in writing. For the person who follows with trust and forgiveness what occurs to him, the world remains always

ready and deep, and inexhaustible environment, with the combined vividness of an actuality and flexibility of a dream. Working back and forth between experience and thought, writers have more than space and time can offer. They have the whole unexplored realm of human vision.

QUESTIONS FOR DISCUSSION

1. What do you think Stafford means when he says that a writer must be receptive? What image does he use to help the reader understand his concept of the creative process?
2. What is Stafford's response to those who talk about the importance of "skills" in writing? Do you agree with his views on the role played by skills in the writer's self-expression?
3. Have you ever used prewriting activities such as freewriting or invisible writing to encourage or allow yourself to write without editing? If you have tried such activities, what was their effect on your writing?
4. Why does Stafford feel that it is important for a writer to be willing to fail? Do you agree with him?
5. Stafford's writing advice comes out of his experiences as a poet. Do you think that his advice will be useful to you in an expository writing course, and if so, how might you apply his ideas to writing an essay?

CONNECTION

Compare Stafford's view of the need for freedom and spontaneity in the writing process to the ideas expressed by Peter Elbow in "Teaching Two Kinds of Thinking by Teaching Writing." Which author's views are closest to your writing practice?

IDEAS FOR WRITING

1. Write an essay that describes your writing process using comparisons or metaphors, as Stafford uses fishing as a metaphor for writing.
2. Develop an essay that responds to Stafford's final comment that writing is one of the "great, free human activities." What does he mean by this statement? Do you agree that writing is really a "free activity"?

Julia Alvarez

"Writing Matters"

Julia Alvarez was born in the Dominican Republic and came to live in Queens, New York, with her family when she was ten. Alvarez was struck by the contrast between the culture of the United States and the oral, story-telling culture of her country of origin. In high school she developed a serious interest in writing, which for her became a way of discovering her evolving identity: "I write to find out who I am." Currently, Alvarez teaches English at Middlebury College in Vermont, where she lives with her family. She has published three novels: How the Garcia Girls Lost their Accents *(1991),* Time of the Butterflies *(1995), and* ¡Yo! *(1997), a series of brief narratives about the life of a writer as seen by the people in her life. She has also published a children's novel and several books of poetry. The following essay about her own writer's life and rituals is from a collection of her essays,* Something to Declare *(1999).*

JOURNAL

Write about a schedule you might develop in order to give yourself the maximum amount of time to devote to the important stages of your writing process.

1   One of the questions that always comes up during question-and-answer periods after readings is about the writing life. The more sophisticated, practiced questioners usually ask me, "Can you tell us something about your process as a writer?" Younger, less self-conscious questioners tend to be more straightforward, "What do you write with? Is it a special kind of pen? What time do you start? How many hours do you spend at the computer? Do you keep a journal?"

2   I always tell my questioners the truth: listen, there are no magic solutions to the hard work of writing. There is no place to put the writing desk that will draw more words out of you. In grade school, I had a friend who claimed that an east-west alignment was the best one for writing. The writing would flow and be more in tune with the positive energies. The north-south alignment would cause blocks as well as bad dreams if your bed was also thus aligned. "Not to mention," she mentioned, "It'll be harder to reach orgasm."

3   See, I tell my questioners, Isn't this silly?

4   But even as I say so, I know I am talking out of both sides of my mouth. I admit that after getting my friend's tip, I lined up my writing desk (and my bed) in the east-west configuration. It wasn't that I thought my writing or my love life would improve, but I am so impressionable that I was afraid that I'd be thinking and worrying about my alignment instead of my line breaks. And such fretting would affect my writing adversely. (My love life was pretty tame already.) Even as recently as this very day, I walk into my study first thing in the morning, and I fill up my bowl of clear water and place it on my desk. And though no one told me to do this, I somehow feel this is the right way to start a writing day.

5   Of course, that fresh bowl of water sits on my desk on good *and* bad writing days. I know these little ceremonies will not change the kind of day before me any more than a funeral service will bring back the dead or a meditation retreat will keep trouble out of my life. The function of ritual is not to control this baffling universe but to render homage to it, to bow to the mystery. Similarly, my daily writing rituals are

small ways in which I contain my dread and affirm my joy and celebrate the mystery and excitement of the calling to be a writer.

6   I use the word *calling* in the old religious sense: a commitment to life connected to deeper, more profound forces (or so I hope) than the market place, or the academy, or the hectic blur of activity, which is what my daily life is often all about. But precisely because it is a way of life, not just a job, the writing life can be difficult to combine with other lives that require that same kind of passion and commitment—the teaching life, the family life, the parenting life, and so on. And since we writers tend to be intense people, whatever other lives we combine with our writing life, we will want to live them intensely, too. Some of us are better at this kind of juggling than others.

7   After twenty-five years of clumsy juggling—marriages, friendships, teaching, writing, community work, political work, caring for young people, one or the other suddenly crashing to the floor because I just couldn't sustain the increased intensity of trying to do them all—I think I've finally figured out what the proper balance is for me. Let me emphasize that this it not a prescription for anyone else. My friend, the novelist, critic, poet, teacher Jay Parini, can juggle six or seven lives successfully at once (write, teach, review, cook, edit, and be a good father, husband, friend), but alas, I'm of the Gerald Ford school of writers who can't chew gum and write iambic pentameter at the same time. (Spondaic chewing throws me off!) I can do two, maybe three intense lives at once: writing and being in a family; writing and teaching and being in a family; writing and teaching and doing political work; but if I try to add a fourth or fifth: writing and being in love and teaching and maintaining a tight friendship and doing political work and taking in the local waif—I fall apart; that is, the writing stops, which for me, is the same thing as saying I fall apart.

8   But still, I'm glad I haven't let such potential breakdowns stop me. I keep juggling, picking up one life and another and another, putting aside the writing from time to time. We only have one life, after all, and we have got to live to many lives with it. (Another reason why the writing life appeals so much is that you can be, at least on paper, all those selves whose lives you can't possibly live out in the one life you've got.) My advice is, if you are sorely tempted to try out a new adventure, go for it! Just don't forget where you are headed, and knowing this will imbue that adventure with even more resonance and richness. (Like going to a party with a lover you know you are going to spend the night with.)

9   Living other lives enriches our writing life. The tension between them can sometimes exhaust us, this is true—but the struggle also makes the hard-won hours at the writing desk all the more precious. And if we are committed to our writing, even if there are what seem impossibly long periods in which we have to put the writing aside in a concerted, focused way while we get our moneymaking careers started or while we raise our very young children, the way we lead our lives can make them lives-in-waiting to be writing lives.

10   What do I mean by the writing life? For me the writing life doesn't just happen when I sit at the writing desk. I mean a life lived with a centering principle, and mine is this, that I will pay close attention to this world I find myself in. "O taste and see that the Lord is good," says one of my favorite psalms. I've always trusted this psalm precisely be-

cause it does not say, "O think and meditate that the Lord is good." Instead we are encouraged to know the sacred by living our lives with all our senses fully engaged.

11   Another way to put it is that writing life is a life lived with all the windows and doors opened. "My heart keeps open house," was the way the poet Theodore Roethke put is in a poem. And rendering what one sees through those opened windows and doors in language is a way of bearing witness to the mystery of what it is to be alive in this world.

12   This is all very high-minded and inspirational, my questioner puts in, fine talk for a reading when we are sitting in a room with other aficionados of the craft. But what about when we are alone at our writing desks, feeling wretchedly anxious, wondering if there is anything in us worth putting down? How about some advice we can take home with us to carry us through the mundane and hard parts of a writing day?

13   Just as my friend took us through the night of losing her husband, as her telling the story helped her survive the experience and helped the rest of us by reminding us of the full journey of our lives, let me take you through the trials and tribulations of a typical writing day. It might help as you also set out onto that blank page, encounter one adventure or mishap after another and wonder—do other writers go through this?

14   The answer is probably yes.

15   Not much has happened at six-twenty or so in the morning when I enter my writing room above the garage. I like it this way. The mind is free of little household details, worries, commitments, voices, problems to solve. In fact, it's probably still rising up from the bottom of a dream. In the summer, the locust trees on the south side make me feel as if I've climbed into a tree house and pulled up the ladder after me. It helps, of course, that I have no children to wake up and feed and pack off to school or drive to day care. I also have a husband who knows how to put his own cereal in his own bowl and who, like me, enjoys having some solitary time in the early morning to read and reflect or putter in his garden before going off to work.

16   My mood entering the room depends on what happened with my writing the day before. If the previous day was a good one, I look forward to the new writing day. If I was stuck or uninspired, I feel apprehensive. Today might be the day when the writing life comes crashing to the floor, and I am shown up for the sham I am. In short, I can't agree more with Hemingway's advice that a writer should always end his writing day knowing where he is headed next. It makes it easier to come back to work.

17   That first entry into the writing room in the early morning is just a brief visit. I fill my writing bowl and say hello to my two old cemíes (stone and wooden Taino deities from the Dominican Republic) and make sure my Virgencita has fresh flowers, if it is summer, or a lit candle, in the winter. Then I head downstairs to the kitchen and my own ministration, a cup of strong Dominican coffee, which Bill* and I bring back by the suitcase. Sometimes I think we plan our trips "home" according to our coffee supply in the deep freeze in the basement.

18   I drink my coffee in the study, reading poetry (Jane Kenyon, George Herbert, Rita Dove, Robert Frost, Elizabeth Bishop, Rhina Espaiuat, Jane Shore, Emily Dickinson. . .). I like to start the day with a poem or two or three or four. This is

the first music I hear, the most essential. Interestingly, I like to follow the reading of poetry with some prose, as if, having been to the heights I need to come back down to earth. (I'm reminded of Frost's wonderful lines about climbing a birch tree, "Earth's the right place for love: / I don't know where it's likely to go better.")

19   I consider this early-morning reading time a combination of pleasure-reading time, when I read the works and authors I most love, and finger-exercise reading time, when I am tuning my own voice to the music of the English language as played by its best writers. That is why I avoid spending my early-morning reading time on magazines and fast-read books and how-to books and newspapers, all of which I enjoy, but all of which use language to provide information, titillation, help, gossip, and in many cases in our consumer culture, to sell something. That's not the chorus I want to hear. I also try never to use this reading time for reading that I must do for teaching or for professional reasons (possible blurbing, book reviewing).

20   Finally, I use this time for reading only in English. I made a discovery one summer when I was reading poetry in Spanish in the early morning. I'd move on to my writing and find myself encountering difficulties, drawing blanks left and right as I tried to express a thought or capture an image or strike the right tone in a passage. I finally figured it out: the whole rhythm of my thinking and writing had switched to my first, native tongue. I was translating into, not writing in, English. I could hear the ropes and pulleys and levers and switches in what I was writing, as if I were unloading the words off a boat that had just come in from another language, far away.

21   Reading for pleasure—I love the phrase, may all my readers read me in this way!—is for me a wonderful way to prepare for doing my own writing. Not all writers feel this way. In fact, some of my writer friends confess that they can't read other writers when they are in the middle of their own novels. They feel they will lose their own voices and start to imitate someone else. But I know that I am stuck with my own voice. I can't write like Michael Ondaatje or Stephen Dixon or Annie Proulx or Toni Morisson any more than I can have their fingerprints. That's not why I invite these writers to say a few words to me in the early morning before I set out on my own journey.

22   There's an old Yiddish story about a rabbi who walks out in a rich neighborhood and meets a watchman walking up and down. "For whom are you working?" the rabbi asks. The watchman tells him, and then in his turn, he asks the rabbi, "And whom are you working for, rabbi?" The words strike the rabbi like a shaft. "I am not working for anybody just yet," he barely manages to reply. Then he walks up and down beside the man for a long time and finally asks him, "Will you be my servant?" The watchman says, "I should like to, but what would be my duties?"

23   "To remind me," the rabbi says.

24   I read my favorite writers to remind me of the quality of writing I am aiming for.

*the author's husband.

25 Now, it's time to set out: pencil poised, I read through the hard copy that I ran off at the end of yesterday's writing day. I used to write everything out by long-hand, and when I was reasonably sure I had a final draft, I'd type it up on my old Selectric. But now, I usually write all my prose drafts right out on the computer, though, for the same reason that I read poetry for its linguistic focus first thing in the morning, I need to write out my poems in longhand, to make each word by hand.

26 This is also true of certain passages of prose and certainly true for times when I am stuck in a novel or story. Writing by hand relieves some of the pressure of seeing something tentative flashed before me on the screen with that authority that print gives to writing. "This is just for me," I tell myself, as I scratch out a draft in pencil. Often, these scribblings turn into little bridges, tendrils, gossamer webs, and nets that take me safely to the other side of silence. When I'm finally on my way, I head back to the computer.

27 But even my hard copies look like they've been written by hand. I once visited a sixth-grade class to talk to them about my writing process. The teacher had asked me to please emphasize revision, as her students were always resisting work-ing on their writing. No problem, I said. I brought in several boxes of folders with ten or twenty drafts of certain stories. The hard copies were heavily marked with my revising pencil. The teacher told me that the day after my visit, she was going over my presentation with her class, and she asked them, "So, what does Julia write with?"

28 "With a pencil!" they all shouted. Obviously, what they remembered were not the hard copies but all the scribblings, jottings, arrows, crossings-out, lists in the margins.

29 With all those emendations, my drafts are almost unreadable. In fact, if I wait several days before transferring these revisions to my computer copy, I can't read them myself. As I revise, I begin to hear the way I want a passage to sound. About the third or fourth draft, if I'm lucky, I start to see the shape of what I am writing, the way an essay will go, a character will react, a poem unfold.

30 Sometimes if Bill and I go on a long car trip, I'll read him what I am working on. This is a wonderful opportunity to hear what I've written. I always end up slashing whole paragraphs and long passages. It reminds me of how my students describe hav-ing their writing workshopped as having it "torn apart." I always imagine a pack of hungry, evil-looking wild dogs when my students use this phrase. Actually, I've found that even if a listener doesn't respond in a negative way, the process of reading my work to someone else does tear apart that beauteous coating of self-love in which my own creation comes enveloped. I start to hear what I've written as it would sound to somebody else. This is not a bad thing if we want to be writers who write not just for ourselves and a few indulgent friends.

31 When I'm done with proofing the hard copy of the story or chapter or poem, I take a little break. This is one of the pleasures of working at home. I can take these refreshing breathers from the intensity of the writing: go iron a shirt or clean out a drawer or wrap up my sister's birthday present. Not so good as "breathers" for me

are activities like answering the phone or making phone calls or engaging with other people in a way that is anything other than brief. Otherwise, I am lured into their lives or into musing on a problem they have presented me with or worrying over some tension between us. And there goes the writing day, down the telephone cable.

32   Admittedly, this makes it hard to have people around when I'm working, and this is where having a home writing room is not such a great idea. I finally caved in and bought one of those machines therapists use that makes white noise. (Now there are fancier models that deliver oceans and rainfalls and cocks crowing in the morning.) Even so, I'm acutely sensitive to the presence of guests and family in the house and the writing day is just not the same as when I have the house to myself. If I had to do it over, I would build a writing space apart from my living space. Of course, it would have to be big enough for an ironing board, shopping bags of wrapping supplies, a small stove for cooking, and all the bureaus I would want to organize.

33   After I've taken a break, I take a deep breath and turn on my computer. What I now do is transcribe all my hand-written revisions on to my computer, before I launch out into the empty space of the next section of the story or essay or the chapter in a novel. This is probably the most intense time of the writing day. I am on my way, and even with the help of the insights from yesterday's run, which I jotted down in my journal, I don't know exactly where it is I am going. But that's why I'm writing, to find out.

34   On the good days, an excitement builds up as I push off into the language, and sentence seems to follow sentence. I catch myself smiling or laughing out loud or sometimes even weeping as I move through a scene or a stanza. "Poetry is a way of thinking with one's feelings," Elizabeth Bishop wrote in a letter to May Swenson, and certainly writing seems to integrate parts of me that are usually at odds. As I write, I feel unaccountably whole; I disappear! That is the irony of this self-absorbed profession: the goal finally is to vanish. "To disappear," the young poet Nicole Cooley says in a poem in the voice of Frida Kahlo, "I paint my portrait again and again."

35   That is why if there is a sudden interruption—a neighbor appears at the door with a petition he wants me to sign, or the UPS man pulls up and honks his horn—they are met with a baffled, startled look. "What's wrong?" the delivery guy with clipboard wants to know. "Aren't you Julia Alvarez?" Honestly, I could say, no, I'm not. She'll be home after two. Why don't you come back then if you want to talk to *her?*

36   In fact, my family is now used to this daily disappearance—though not without occasional resentment. Many a time, a call from one of my sisters begins, "It's so hard to get in touch with you, because of course, I can't call before two." I admit that the comment makes me a little defensive. What if I had "a normal job," what if I were a road worker, jackhammering a hole in the earth, or a surgeon doing fine embroidery stitches on someone's heart? I wouldn't be available at all during the workday. What grates, I think, is the idea that I am home and choosing to ignore them. My mother has joked that she better not die before two in the afternoon. I've learned to tease

back, "No, Mami, please feel free to die any time you want. But have them notify me after two, if you don't mind."

37   Okay, okay, if I heard on the message machine that my mother was dying or that my sister was upset about not getting a certain job or that Bill just heard some sad news about the health of a friend of ours, I'd take the call. But the truth is that when I'm having a good writing day, I "disappear" into the writing. I don't come downstairs to listen to my messages. Many times, especially if the noise machine is on, I don't even hear the phone ring.

38   On bad days, on the other hand, I race downstairs and answer the phone with such a desperate, cheery HELLO! that callers wonder if they've dialed one of those 900 numbers where operators are standing by to render some dubious service. Afterwards, I wander out onto the deck and look longingly south towards the little spire of the Congregational church and wish another life for myself. Maybe I should join some clubs, be a community organizer, have lunch with a friend? I look again and see the peaked roofs of the handsome college on the hill. Maybe I shouldn't have given up tenure? Oh dear, what have I done with my life?

39   I have chosen it, that's what I've done. So I take a deep breath and go back upstairs and sit myself down and work over the passage that will not come. As Flannery O'Connor attested: "Every morning between 9 and 12, I go to my room and sit before a piece of paper. Many times, I just sit for three hours with no ideas coming to me. But I know one thing: if an idea does come between 9 and 12, I am there ready for it." The amazing thing for me is that years later, reading the story or novel or poem, I can't tell the passages that were easy to write, the ones that came forth like "greased lightening" (James Dickey's phrase), from those other passages that made me want to give up writing and take up another life. . . .

40   So it is the end of a good reading, the audience lingers. It's late in Salt Lake City or Portland or Iowa City. Outside the bookstore windows, the sky is dark and star-studded. It's the literary time of day you find in Hemingway's novels and in short stories like "A Clean Well-Lighted Place," when "it was late and everyone had left," and the bookstore people are already mentally pushing the movable bookshelves back in place and trying to remember who is supposed to be on tomorrow night when the next writer on tour rolls into town. Then, that last hand goes up, and someone in the back row wants to know, "So, does writing really matter?"

41   This once really happened to me on a book tour. I felt as if I'd just gotten hit "upside the head," an expression I like so much because it sounds like the blow was so hard, the preposition got jerked around, too. Does writing matter? I sure hope so, I wanted to say. I've "done" sixteen athes. I've published six books. I've spent most of my thinking life, which is now over thirty years, writing. Does writing really matter? It is the hardest, and the best, question I've been asked anywhere.

42   Let's take out the *really*, I said. It makes me nervous. I don't *really* know much of anything, which is why I write, to find things out. Does writing matter?

43   In my darker moods, I want to say, probably not. Has a book ever saved a person's life? Has a novel ever fed the hungry? It is, no doubt, a meaningless human activity

to while the time away before our turn comes to join the great blank page. But that is my three-o'clock-in-the-morning insomniac response, which, when I was an adolescent and then in some of my unhappy thirties, I thought was the "right" time of day when "real" answers came to me. I'm older now. I don't expect "real" answers, and the time of day I prefer for figuring out the meaning of the universe if early morning, after a strong cup of that Dominican coffee. Before dinner with a tall glass of cold white wine is also a good time.

44   It matters, of course, it matters. But it matters in such a small, almost invisible way that is doesn't seem very important. In fact, that's why I trust it, the tiny rearrangements and insights in our hearts that art accomplishes. It's how I, anyhow, learned to see with vision and perplexity and honesty and continue to learn to see. How I keep the windows and doors open instead of shutting myself up inside the things I "believe" and have personally experienced. How I move out beyond the safe, small version of my life to live other lives. "Not only to be one self," the poet Robert Desnos wrote about the power of the imagination, "but to become each one."

45   Back at home, when I'm finally finished with my writing biz or I've put it aside in the growing pile for tomorrow, I head to town to run errands or see a friend or attend a talk at the college. As the fields and farms give way to houses and lawns, I feel as if I'm reentering the world. After having been so intensely a part of a fictional world, I love this daily chance to connect with the small town I live in, to find out how everybody else is doing. Ann at Kinneys wants to know how it's going. Alisa at the College Store fills me in on her dad, the writer. At the post office, the two lovely ladies oblige me by going through their stamp folders to find me a batch of Virgencitas (old Christmas stamps) or butterflies or love swans.

46   How's it going? everyone asks me, as if they really want to know all about my writing day.

47   And this happens not because I'm a writer or, as some questioners put it, "a creative person." I'll bet that even those who aren't writers, those who are concerned with making some sense of this ongoing journey would admit this: that it's by what people have written and continue to write, our stories and creations, that we understand who we are. In a world without any books, we would not be the same kind of critter. "At the moment we are drawn into language, we are as intensely alive as we can be; we create and are created," N. Scott Momaday, the Native American author, claims in his book *The Man Made of Words*. "That existence in a maze of words is our human condition."

48   But one of the characters in Robert Hellenga's *The Sixteen Pleasures* argues the opposite, "Books were my life. But what did I ever learn that I didn't already know in my heart." I admit that this also has the ring of truth for me, but the truth is, that I wouldn't have been conscious of this truth unless I had first read it in Hellenga's book. I don't know what I know in my heart unless somebody—myself included—has put it into words. "Art is not the world," Muriel Rukeyser reminds us, "but a knowing of the world. It prepares us."

49   Prepares us for what? my questioner in the back row wants to know. And again I have to admit that I don't really know what it prepares us for. For our work in the world, I suppose. Prepares us to live our lives more intentionally, ethically, richly. At

this point, a whole phalanx of people stands up to go. A hand shoots up. "You mean to say that if Hitler had read Tolstoy he would have been a better person?"

50   That is a hard one, I admit. Let's say that it would have been worth a try. Let's say that if little Hitler had been caught up in reading Shakespeare or Tolstoy and was moved to the extent that the best books move us, he might not have become who he became. But maybe, Tolstoy or no Tolstoy, Hitler would still have been Hitler. We live, after all, in a flawed world of flawed beings. In fact, some very fine writers who have written some lovely things are not very nice people. I won't mention any names.

51   But I still insist that while writing or entering into the writing of another, they were better people. If for no other reason than they were not out there, causing trouble. Writing is a form of vision, and I agree with that proverb that says, "Where there is no vision, the people perish." The artist keeps that vision alive, cleared of the muck and refuse and junk and little dishonesties that always collect and begin to cloud our view of the world around us.

52   Some time ago, I had a wonderful friend, Carole, who had a way of stringing together a bunch of words that made the lights come on in my head. I'd go on and on about some problem, and Carole would toss out one of her gems. "Hey, babe," she'd say, "put your check mark on the side of light." Or, "You've got too big a soul in too small a personality." Or, "You've got to stop pulling up the little shoots to see if the roots have grown." This last was her take on my habit of second-guessing decisions.

53   Carole spoke, and suddenly I'd feel a tremendous sense of clarity. I could *see* myself. I could *see* other people. See them "in the light of love," another Carolism. It was as if she had turned the switch yet once more on a three-way light, and the world brightened, ever so slightly, but very definitely.

54   This is the way in which I feel writing matters. It clarifies and intensifies, it deepens and connects me to others. "We are," as Jim Harrison says in *Legends of the Fall*, "so largely unimaginable to one another." But writing allows us inside those others and knits us together as a human species. And because writing matters in this way to me, it does something else. It challenges me, not just to read and have that private enjoyment of clarity, but to pass it on.

55   By now a whole phalanx of my audience has fallen asleep on the couches that the bookstore people dragged over from the alcove to give the reading a cozy feel. My questioner in the back of the room has to go home to relieve her babysitter. My readers, who for this brief evening have become real people, come forward to have their books signed and offer some new insight or ask a further question. That they care matters. That they are living fuller versions of themselves and of each one because they have read books matters. The world goes from bright to brilliant to luminous, so that for brief seconds, we see clearly everything that matters.

QUESTIONS FOR DISCUSSION

1. Why does Alvarez frame her essay as a reflection on the questions she has regularly been asked after book reading events? Is this structure effective?

2. Describe Alvarez's "writing ritual." Why does she believe in and follow her ritual? Contrast your writing ritual to hers.
3. What are the stages in Alvarez's writing day? Why is it important for a writer to have a regular schedule for their writing work?
4. What role does reading play in Alvarez's writing day? What does she prefer to read?
5. Why does Alvarez believe that writing is a calling "in the old religious sense"? What ethical assumptions about the role of reading and writing does Alvarez make?
6. How does Alvarez answer the final question posed at the end of a public reading: "So does writing really matter?" What is your response to her answer?

CONNECTION

Compare the role of dreams in Alvarez's writing process with the reliance on dreams in the writing processes of Steven King and Muriel Rukeyser.

IDEAS FOR WRITING

1. Alvarez speaks of the importance of the writer's "bearing witness to the mystery of what it is to be alive in this world." Write an essay in which you give examples of the type of "bearing witness" that you have encountered in the writers you admire and that you try to perform in your own writing. Do you agree with Alvarez that this "bearing witness" is a major part of the writer's responsibility?
2. Alvarez points to the fundamental irony of the writing life: "As I write, I feel unaccountably whole; I disappear! That is the irony of this self-absorbed profession: the goal is finally to vanish." Write an essay in which you explain how you understand this irony. You can refer to you own writing or to artistic experiences such as singing, dancing, or playing an instrument.

Peter Elbow

"Teaching Two Kinds of Thinking by Teaching Writing"

Peter Elbow (b. 1935) was raised in New York and completed his Ph.D. at Brandeis University (1969). Elbow, who has taught at a number of universities including the Massachusetts Institute of Technology and the State University of New

York at Stony Brook, is currently a professor of English at the University Of Mass-achusetts at Amherst. His books about writing include Writing Without Teachers *(1973, 1998),* Writing with Power *(1981, 1998),* Embracing Contraries: Explorations in Learning and Teaching *(1986),* A Community of Writers *(1988, 1994), and* What is English? *(1990). Elbow has contributed numerous articles on the teaching of writing to national English teacher's journals and speaks at many national conferences for writing teachers. His work emphasizes the importance of the development of the student's authentic voice in writing through processes such as freewriting, at the same time, acknowledges revision and critical reflection as essential to the writing process.*

JOURNAL

Discuss activities that have helped you to discover new ideas in your writing. How do you make the transition between such new insights to writing complete essays?

1 When I celebrate freewriting and fast exploratory writing on first drafts—the postponing of vigilance and control during the early stages of writing—it seems to many listeners as though I'm celebrating *holidays* from thinking. Some say "Yes, good, we all need holidays from thinking." Others say, "Horrors! Their vigilance muscles will get flabby and they'll lose their ability to think critically." But I insist that I'm teaching thinking.

2 Or course it's not the only way I teach thinking through writing. I also teach it by teaching careful, conscious, critical revising. Thus I teach two kinds of thinking. I'll call them first-order thinking and second-order thinking.

3 First-order thinking is intuitive and creative and doesn't strive for conscious direction or control. We use it when we get hunches or see gestalts. We use it when we sense analogies or ride on metaphors or arrange the pieces in a collage. We use it when we write fast without censoring and let the words lead us to associations and intuitions we hadn't foreseen. Second-order thinking is conscious, directed, controlled thinking. We steer; we scrutinize each link in the chain. Second-order thinking is committed to accuracy and strives for logic and control: we examine our premises and assess the validity of each inference. Second-order thinking is what most people have in mind when they talk about "critical thinking."

4 Each kind of thinking has its own characteristic strengths and weaknesses. I like to emphasize how second-order thinking often brings our people's worst thinking. If you want to get people to seem dumber than they are, try asking them a hard question and then saying, "Now think carefully." Thinking carefully means trying to examine your thinking while using it too—trying to think about thinking while also thinking about something else—which often leads people to foolishness. This is one of the main reasons why shrewd and sensible students often write essays asserting

things they don't really believe and defending them with wooden reasoning they wouldn't dream of using if they were just talking thoughtfully with a friend.

5   First-order thinking, on the other hand, often heightens intelligence. If you want to get people to be remarkably insightful, try asking them the hard question and then saying, "Don't do any careful thinking yet, just write three or four stories or incidents that come to mind in connection with that question; and then do some fast exploratory freewriting." It turns out that such unplanned narrative and descriptive exploratory writing (or speaking) will almost invariably lead the person spontaneously to formulate *conceptual* insights that are remarkably shrewd. These are fresh insights which are rooted in experience and thus they usually get around the person's prejudices, stock responses, or desires for mere consistency; they are usually shrewder than the person's long-held convictions. (See "The Loop Writing Process" in my *Writing With Power*.) In addition (to bring up a writerly concern), these insights are usually expressed in lively, human, and experienced language. In short, to use Polanyi's terms, we know more tacitly than we do focally. Finally (to raise another writerly concern), when someone really gets going in a sustained piece of generative writing and manages, as it were, to stand out of the way and relinquish planning and control—when someone manages to let the words and images and ideas choose more words, images, and ideas—a more elegant shape or organization often emerges, one more integral to the material than careful outlining or conscious planning can produce. It's not that the rough draft writing will itself be well organized in its totality—though that occasionally happens. What's more common is that the exploratory zigzagging leads finally to a click where the write suddenly sees, "Yes, that's the right handle for this whole issue, now I've go the right point of view, and now I see the right organization or progression of parts. I couldn't find it when I just tried to think, plan, and outline."

6   Yet despite my fascination with the conceptual power of creative intuitive thinking—of what might seem to some like "careless thinking"—I have learned not to forget to tell the other side of the story. That is, we are also likely to be *fooled* by first-order thinking. In first-order thinking we don't reflect on what we are doing and hence we are more likely to be steered by our unaware assumptions, our unconscious prejudices, our unexamined point of view. And often enough, no shape or organization emerges at all—just randomly ordered thoughts. We cannot *count on* first-order thinking to give us something valuable.

7   Thus the two kinds of thinking have the opposite virtues and vices. Second-order thinking is a way to check our thinking, to be more aware, to steer instead of being steered. In particular, we must not trust the fruits of intuitive and experiential first-order thinking unless we have carefully assessed them with second-order thinking. Yet we probably won't *have* enough interesting ideas or hypotheses to assess if we use only our assessing muscles: we need first-order thinking to generate a rich array of insights. And first-order thinking doesn't just give us more; it is faster too. Our early steps in second-order thinking (or our early steps at a higher level of second-order thinking than we are practiced at) are often slow backward steps into wrong-headedness (Bruner, 1966.) Yet this is no argument against the need for second-order thinking. Indeed I suspect that the way we enlarge the penumbra of

our tacit knowledge is by searching harder and further with the beam of our focal knowledge.

8   We are in the habit—in the academic culture anyway—of assuming that thinking is not thinking unless it is wholly logical or critically aware of itself at every step. But I cannot resist calling first-order thinking a bona fide kind of thinking because it is a process of making sense and figuring out: thought not consciously steered or controlled, it is nevertheless purposive and skillful.

9   There is an obvious link between the writing process and these two kinds of thinking. I like first-order intuitive or creative thinking with freewriting and first-draft exploratory writing in which one defers planning, control, organizing, and censoring. I link second-order thinking with slow, thoughtful rewriting or revising where one constantly subjects everything to critical scrutiny.

10   But I'm not content merely to assert a link. The two writing processes enhance the two thinking processes.

11   It is obvious how careful revising enhances second-order thinking. If having any language at all (any "second signaling system") gives us more power over our thinking, it is obvious that a *written* language vastly increases that power. By writing down our thoughts we can put them aside and come back to them with renewed critical energy and a fresh point of view. We can criticize better because writing helps us achieve the perennially difficult task of standing outside our own thinking. Thus outlines are more helpful while revising than at the start of the writing process because finally there's something rich and interesting to outline. Revising is when I use the "X-ray" or "skeleton" exercise—asking both the writer and her readers to isolate the central core of inference in a paper: What is the assertion and what premises and reasons does it rest on? This is the best practice for critical thinking, because instead of being a canned exercise with artificial ingredients unconnected to the student, it is an exercise in assessing and strengthening the thinking which is embodied in one's own or someone else's live discourse. Since we are trying for the tricky goal of thinking about our subject but at the same time thinking about our thinking about it, putting our thoughts on paper gives us a fighting chance. But notice that what most heightens this critical awareness is not so much the writing down of words in the first place, though of course that helps, but the *coming back* to a text and re-seeing it from the outside (in space) instead of just hearing it from the inside (in time).

12   But does freewriting or uncensored, generative writing really enhance creative first-order thinking? You might say that speaking is a better way to enhance creative thinking—either through brainstorming or through the back and forth of discussion or debate. But that only works if we *have* other people available, people we trust, and people skilled at enhancing our creative thinking. Free exploratory writing, on the other hand, though we must learn to use it, is always available. And since the goal in creative thinking is to harness intuition—to get the imagination to take the reins in its own hands—solitary writing for no audience is often more productive than speaking. Speaking is almost invariably to an audience, and an audience puts pressure on us to make sense and avoid inferences we cannot explain.

13   You might also argue that intuitive thinking is better enhanced by silent musing; or going for a walk or sleeping on it or any of a host of other ways to push a question away from focal attention back to the preconscious. But such attempts at nonlinguistic processing often merely postpone thinking instead of actually enriching it. Freewriting and exploratory writing, on the other hand, are almost invariably productive because they exploit the autonomous generative powers of language and syntax themselves. Once you manage to get yourself writing in an exploratory but uncensored fashion, the ongoing string of language and syntax itself becomes a lively and surprising force for generation. Words call up words, ideas call up more ideas. A momentum of language and thinking develops and one learns to nurture it by keeping the pen moving. With a bit of practice, you can usually bring yourself to the place where you can stop and say, "Look at that! I've been led by this unrolling string of words to an insight or connection or structure that I had no premonition of. I could never have proposed it if I were just musing or making an outline. I wasn't steering, I was being taken for a ride." Heuristic prewriting techniques that involve only list-making or diagram-making tend to lack the generative force that comes from the use of actual syntax—speech on paper.

14   I'm not trying to disparage spoken discourse or nonverbal back-burner work. They can be wonderful. But they are not as reliable as writing for enhancing first-order thinking.

15   "Taken for a ride." The metaphor evokes what's good but also what's fearful about first-order thinking and uncensored writing. It is dangerous to be taken for a ride, literally by a horse or metaphorically by a shark. "Eternal vigilance." But the goal of first-order thinking or writing is to *relax* vigilance and be taken on as many rides as possible: *as long as* we remember that this is only half the process. We must assess the results with second-order thinking or revising. In short, by using the writing process in this two-sided way, I can foster contraries: our ability to let go and be taken on surprising rides; yet also our ability critically to assess the resulting views.

16   **Practical Consequences**   I am not concluding from all this that there is only one right way to think or write. We all know too many good thinkers or writers who contradict each other and even themselves in their methods. But his notion of opposite extremes gives a constructive and specific picture of what we're looking for in good thinking and writing. That is, even though there are many good ways to think and write, it seems clear that excellence must involve finding *some* way to be both abundantly inventive yet toughmindedly critical. Indeed this model of conflicting goals suggests why good writers and thinkers are so various in their technique: if they are managing to harness opposites—in particular, opposites that tend to interfere with each other—they are doing something mysterious. Success is liable to take many forms, some of them surprising.

17   As a teacher, it helps me to have these two clear goals in mind when I come across a student about whom I must say, "She clearly *is* a smart person, but why is she so often wrong?" Or "She clearly thinks hard and carefully, but why is she so charac-

teristically uninteresting or unproductive in her work?" I can ask of any person or performance, "Is there enough rich material to build from?" and, "Is there a careful and critical enough assessment of the material?"

18   If I am careful to acknowledge to my students that things are complex and that there is no single best way to think or write—and that excellence in these realms is a mystery that can be mastered in surprising ways—then I may justifiably turn around and stress simplicity by harping on two practical rules of thumb.

19   First, since creative and critical thinking are opposite and involve mentalities that tend to conflict with each other, it helps most people to learn to work on them separately or one at a time by moving back and forth between them. If we are trying to think creatively to write generatively, it usually hinders us if we try at the same time to think critically or to revise it: it makes us reject what we are engaged in thinking before we've really worked it out at all—or to cross out what we've written before we've finished the sentence or paragraph and allowed something to develop. But if we hold off criticism or revising for a while, we can build a safe place for generative thinking or writing. Similarly, if we devote certain times to wholehearted critical thinking or revising, we can be more acute and powerful in our critical assessment.

20   For one of the main things that holds us back from being as creative as we could be is fear of looking silly or being wrong. But that worry dissipates when we know we will soon turn to wholehearted criticism and revising and weed out what is foolish. Similarly, one of the main things that holds us back from being as critical as we could be is fear that we'll have to reject everything and be left with nothing at all. But that worry also dissipates when we know we've already generated an extremely rich set of materials to work on (or if we haven't, we know we can do so quickly whenever we turn to wholehearted generating). In short, even though creative and critical thinking can magically coalesce in the hands of masters and at certain special moments when the rest of us are at our best, it usually helps us to work on them separately so they can flourish yet reinforce each other.

21   Second rule of thumb. It usually helps to *start with* creative thinking and exploratory writing and then engage in critical assessment and revision afterward—after we have gotten ourselves going and there is already lots to assess. It's not that we should necessarily try to force our writing into two self-contained steps (though I aim for this when all goes smoothly). Often I cannot finish all generating or all first-order thinking before I need to do some revising or criticizing—which will sometimes force a new burst of generating. We are never finished with generating—and having generated, we always need to criticize and revise. I used to think that I should try to finish getting my students good at creative generating before I went on to work on revising and being critical. But I've discovered that some students won't let go and allow themselves to be creative till after we do some hard work on critical thinking and revising. They don't feel safe relaxing their vigilance till I demonstrate that I'm also teaching heightened vigilance. Sometimes, early in the semester, I ask students to rethink and revise a paper in order to prove to them that they are not stuck with what they put down in early drafts, and that careful critical thinking can make a big difference.

22   But the fact remains that most people get more and better thinking—and less time-wasting—if they start off generating. My main agenda for the beginning of a semester is always to enforce generating and brainstorming and deferral of criticism in order to build students' confidence and show them that they can quickly learn to come up with a great quantity of words and ideas. Then gradually we progress to a back-and-forth movement between generating and criticizing. I find I help my own writing and thinking and that of my students by consciously training ourselves to start with first-order thinking and generating and to take it on longer and longer rides—to hold off longer and longer the transition to criticizing and logic. Back and forth, yes, but in longer spells so that each mentality has more time to flourish before we move on to its opposite.

23   ***Mutual Reinforcement***   Because the history of our culture is often experienced as a battle between reason and feeling, between rationality and irrationality, between logic and impulse—and because intuitive first-order thinking is indissolubly mixed up with feeling, irrationality, and impulse—we end up with disciplined critical thinking and uncensored creative thinking dug into opposed trenches with their guns trained on each other. Logic and reason have won the battle to be our standard for thinking, but not the battle for hearts and minds, and therefore champions of logic and reason understandably criticize all relaxations of critical vigilance. Similarly, champions of creative first-order thinking sometimes feel they must criticize critical thinking if only to win some legitimacy for themselves. But this is an unfortunate historical and developmental accident. If we would see clearly how it really is with thinking and writing, we would see that the situation isn't either/or, it's both/and: the more first-order thinking, the more second-order thinking; the more generative uncensored writing, the more critical revising; and vice versa. It's a matter of learning to work on opposites one at a time in a generous spirit of mutual reinforcement rather than in a spirit of restrictive combat.

QUESTIONS FOR DISCUSSION

1. Why does Elbow teach "two kinds of thinking"? Why does he consider the intuitive and creative mode "first order" and the critical mode "second order"?
2. Elbow gives examples of each kind of thinking. Why does he believe that we need to engage in both kinds of thinking to produce good writing? Explain why you agree or disagree with him.
3. According to Elbow, why is freewriting preferable to brainstorming aloud or "silent musing" as a way to generate ideas? Do you agree?
4. Discuss the meaning of the metaphor "taken for a ride" in relationship to the two kinds of thinking. What is good and what is "fearful" about this expression in relation to writing? How does Elbow seek to "foster contraries"?

5. What does Elbow expect when he asks us to "work on opposites one at a time in a generous spirit of mutual reinforcement"? Provide an example from your own writing process that supports or refutes his expectation.
6. What is Elbow's most recent position on whether students should begin their writing process with creative generation or with critical thinking and planning? Why has he changed his original position somewhat? What does he continue to believe works best?

CONNECTION

Compare and contrast Elbow's and Julia Alvarez's ideas about the writing process. How does each emphasize a need for a separation between the initial creative impulse and the revision stage of writing?

IDEAS FOR WRITING

1. Using recent writing projects as examples, write an essay that describes how you have attempted to develop a positive interaction between your creative mind and your critical mind. Discuss both successes and problems.
2. Write an essay in response to Elbow's approach to thinking and writing. Discuss the reasons why you agree and/or disagree with his ideas. Develop examples and evidence from your own writing experiences to support your major points.

Stephen King

"The Symbolic Language of Dreams"

Stephen King (b. 1947) is originally from Portland, Maine, where he continues to reside. After graduating from the University of Maine in 1970 with a B.A. in English, King taught high school and worked at odd jobs before finding time to write his first novel Carrie *(1974), a story of the cruelty of adolescence and psychic powers. Carrie was an immediate best seller and was made into a classic horror film, and King has continued to be one of the most popular contemporary writers of horror novels. Some of his best known works include* The Shining *(1977; film version 1980),* Firestarter *(1980; film version 1984),* Misery *(1987; film version 1990),* The Dark Half *(1989),* Desperation *(1996),* Bag of Bones *(1998),* The Girl Who Loved Tom Gordon *(1999), and* Hearts in Atlantis *(1999). King's fiction takes on some serious themes related to writing and creation: the double life of the writer, the responsibility of the writer to his fans, and the role of dreams and early childhood memory in the creative process. In the following essay, King describes some of the ways dreams have helped him with his writing.*

Write about a time when a dream or intuition helped you to solve a writing problem or to understand an issue in your waking life.

1   One of the things that I've been able to use dreams for in my stories is to show things in a symbolic way that I wouldn't want to come right out and say directly. I've always used dreams the way you'd use mirrors to look at something you couldn't see head-on—the way that you use a mirror to look at your hair in the back. To me that's what dreams are supposed to do. I think that dreams are a way that people's minds illustrate the nature of their problems. Or maybe even illustrate the answers to their problems in symbolic language.

2   When we look back on our dreams, a lot of times they decompose as soon as the light hits them. So, you can have a dream, and you can remember very vividly what it's about, but ten or fifteen minutes later, unless it's an extraordinarily vivid dream or an extraordinarily good dream, it's gone. It's like the mind is this hard rubber and you really have to hit it hard to leave an impression that won't eventually just erase.

3   One of the things that we're familiar with in dreams is the sense that familiar or prosaic objects are being put in very bizarre circumstances or situations. And since that's what I write about, the use of dreams is an obvious way to create that feeling of weirdness in the real world. I guess probably the most striking example of using a dream in my fiction was connected to the writing of *Salem's Lot*.

4   Now, I can think of only maybe five or six really horrible nightmares in the course of my life—which isn't bad when you think that that life stretches over forty-four years—but I can remember having an extremely bad dream when I was probably nine or ten years old.

5   It was a dream where I came up a hill and there was a gallows on top of this hill with birds all flying around it. There was a hangman there. He had died, not by having his neck broken, but by strangulation. I could tell because his face was all puffy and purple. And as I came close to him he opened his eyes, reached his hands out and grabbed me.

6   I woke up in my bed, sitting bolt upright, screaming. I was hot and cold at the same time and covered with goosebumps. And not only was I unable to go back to sleep for hours after that, but I was really afraid to turn out the lights for weeks. I can still see it as clearly new as when it happened.

7   Years later I began to work on *Salem's Lot*. Now, I knew that the story was going to be about a vampire that came from abroad to the United States and I wanted to put him in a spooky old house. I got about that far in my thinking and, by whatever way it is that your mind connects things, as I was looking around for a spooky house,

a guy who works in the creative department of my brain said, Well what about that nightmare you had when you were eight or nine years old? Will that work? And I remembered the nightmare and I thought, Yes, it's perfect.

8   I turned the dead man into a guy named Hubie Marston who owned a bad house and pretty much repeated the story of the dream in terms of the way he died.

9   In the story, Hubie Marston hangs himself. He's some sort of black artist of the Aleister Crowley kind—some sort of a dark magician—and I kind of combined him with a stock character in American tabloidism—the wealthy guy who lives and dies in squalor.

10   For me, once the actual act of creation starts, writing is like this high-speed version of the flip books you have when you're a kid, where you mix and match. The cover of the book will say, "You Can Make Thousands of Faces!" You can put maybe six or seven different eyes with different noses. Except that there aren't just thousands of faces, there are literally billions of different events, personalities, and things that you can flip together. And it happens at a very rapid rate. Dreams are just one of those flip strips that you can flip in there. But they also work in terms of advancing the story.

11   Sometimes when I write I can use dreams to have a sort of precognitive effect on the story. Precognitive dreams are a staple of our supernatural folklore. You know, the person who dreamed that flight 17 was going to crash and changed his reservation and sure enough, flight 17 crashed. But it's like those urban fairy tales: you always hear somebody say, "I have a friend that this happened to." I've never actually heard anyone say, "This happened to *me.*"

12   The closest that I can come to a precognitive experience is that I can be in a situation where a really strong feeling of déjà vu washes over me. I'm sure that I've been there before. A lot of times I make the association that, at some point, I had a dream about this place and this series of actions, and forgot it with my conscious mind when I awoke.

13   Every now and then dreams can come in handy. When I was working on *It*— which was this really long book—a dream made a difference.

14   I had a lot of time and a lot of my sense of craft invested in the idea of being able to finish this huge, long book. Now, when I'm working on something, I see books, completed books. And in some fashion that thing is already there. I'm not really making it so much as I am digging it up, the way that you would an artifact, out of the sand. The trick is to get as much of that object as you possibly can, to get the whole thing out, so it's usable, without breaking it. You always break it somewhat— I mean you never get a complete thing—but if you're really careful and if you're really lucky, you can get most of it.

15   When I'm working I never know what the end is going to be or how things are going to come out. I've got an idea what direction I want the story to go in, or hope it will go in, but mostly I feel like the tail on a kite. I don't feel like the kite itself, of like the wind that blows on the kite—I'm just the tail of it. And if I know when I sit down what's happening or what's going to happen, that day and the next day and the day after, I'm happy. But with *It* I got to a point where I couldn't see ahead any

more. And every day I got closer to the place where this young girl, who was one of my people—I don't think of them as good people or bad people, just my people—was going to be and they were going to find her.

16   I didn't know what was going to happen to her. And that made me extremely nervous. Because that's the way books don't get done. All at once you just get to a point where there is no more. It's like pulling a little string out of a hole and all at once it's broken and you don't get whatever prize there was on the end of it.

17   So I had seven, eight hundred pages and I just couldn't stand it. I remember going to bed one night saying, I've got to have an idea. I've got to have an idea! I fell asleep and dreamed that I was in a junk yard, which was where this part of the story was set.

18   Apparently, I was the girl. There was no girl in the dream. There was just me. And there were all these discarded refrigerators in this dump. I opened one of them and there were these things inside, hanging from the various rusty shelves. They looked like macaroni shells and they were all just sort of trembling in a breeze. Then one of them opened up these wings, flew out and landed on the back of my hand. There was a sensation of warmth, almost like when you get a subcutaneous shot of Novocain or something, and this thing started to turn from white to red. I realized it had anesthetized my hand and it was sucking my blood out. Then they all started to fly out of this refrigerator and to land on me. They were these leeches that looked like macaroni shells. And they were swelling up.

19   I woke up and I was very frightened. But I was also very happy. Because then I knew what was going to happen. I just took the dream as it was and put it in the book. Dropped it in. I didn't change anything.

20   In the story "The Body," there's an incident where several boys find themselves covered with leeches. That was something that actually happened to me. There's a lot of stuff in "The Body" that's just simply history that's been tarted up a little bit. These friends and I all went into this pond about a mile and half from the house where I grew up and when we came out we were just covered with those babies. It was awful. I don't remember that I had nightmares about the incident then but of course I had this leech dream years later.

21   I really think what happened with this dream was that I went to sleep and the subconscious went right on working and finally sent up this dream the way that you would send somebody an interoffice message in a pneumatic tube.

22   In the Freudian sense, I don't thing there is any subconscious, any unconscious where things are going on. I think that consciousness is like an ocean. Whether you're an inch below the surface or whether you're down a mile and half deep, it's all water. All H_2O.

23   I think that our minds are the same nutrient bath all the way down to the bottom and different things live at different levels. Some of them are a little bit harder to see because we don't get down that deep. But whatever's going on in our daily lives, our daily thoughts, the things that the surface of our minds are concerned with eddy done—trickle down—and then they have some sort of an influence down there. And the messages that we get a lot of times are nothing more than symbolic rework-

ings of the things that we're concerned with. I don't think they're very prophetic or anything like that. I think a lot of times dreams are nothing more than a kind of mental or spiritual flatulence. They're a way of relieving pressure.

24   One way of looking at this water metaphor might be to talk about jumbo shrimp, everybody's favorite oxymoron. They're the big shrimp that nobody ate in restaurants until 1955 or 1960 because, until then, nobody thought of going shrimping after dark. They were there all the time, living their prosaic shrimp lives, but nobody caught them. So when they finally caught them it was, "Hello! Look at this. This is something entirely new." And if the shrimp could talk they'd say, "Shit, we're not new. We've been around for a couple of thousand years. You were just too dumb to look for us."

25   A slightly different way of looking at this is that there are certain fish that we get used to looking at. There are carp, goldfish, catfish, shad, cod—they're fish that are more or less surface fish. They go down to a depth of maybe fifty, sixty, or a hundred feet. People catch them, and we get used to seeing them. Not only do we see them in aquariums or as pictures in books, we see them on our plates. We cook them. We see them in the supermarket in the fish case. Whereas if you go down in a bathysphere, if you go down real deep, you see all these bright fluorescent, weird, strange things with membranous umbrellas and weird skirts that flare out from their bodies. Those are creatures that we don't see very often because they explode if we bring them up close to the surface. They are to surface fish what dreams are to our surface thoughts. Deep fish are like dreams of surface fish. They change shape, they change form.

26   There are dreams and there are deep dreams. There are dreams where you're able to tap sources that are a lot deeper. I'm sure that if you wanted to extend this metaphor you could say that within the human psyche, within human thought, there really are Mindanao trenches, places that are very very deep, where there are probably some extremely strange things floating around. And what the conscious mind brings up may be the equivalent of an exploded fish. It may just be a mess. It may be something that's gorgeous in its own habitat but when it gets up to the sun it just dries out. And then it's very gray and dull.

27   I remember about six months ago having this really vivid dream.

28   I was in some sort of an apartment building, a cheesy little apartment building. The front door was open and I could see all these black people going back and forth. They were talking and having a wonderful time. Somebody was playing music somewhere. And then the door shut.

29   In the dream I went back and got into bed. I think I must have shut the door myself. My brother was in bed with me, behind me, and he started to strangle me. My brother had gone crazy. It was awful!

30   I remember saying, with the last of my breath, "I think there's somebody out there." And he got up from the bed and went out. As soon as he was out I went up and closed the door and locked it. And then I went back to bed. That is, I started to lie down in this dream.

31   Then I began to worry that I hadn't really locked the door. This is the sort of thing that I'm always afraid of in real life. Did I turn off the burners on the stove?

Did I leave a light on when I left the house? So, I got up to check the door and sure enough it was unlocked. I realized that he was still in there with me. Somewhere.

32   I screamed in the dream, "He's still in the house." I screamed so loud I woke myself up. Except I wasn't screaming when I woke up. I was just sort of muttering it over and over again: He's in the house, he's in the house. I was terrified.

33   Now, I keep a glass of ice water beside the bed where I sleep and the ice cubes hadn't melted yet, so it had happened almost immediately after I fell asleep. That's usually when I have the dreams that I remember most vividly.

34   Part of my function as a writer is to dream awake. And that usually happens. If I sit down to write in the morning, in the beginning of that writing session and the ending of that session, I'm aware that I'm writing. I'm aware of my surroundings. It's like shallow sleep on both ends, when you go to bed and when you wake up. But in the middle, the world is gone and I'm able to see better.

35   Creative imaging and dreaming are just so similar that they've got to be related.

36   In a story like "The Body" or It, which is set around the late fifties or the early sixties, I'm literally able to regress so that I can remember things that I'd forgotten. Time goes by and events pile up on the surface of your mind like snow, and it covers all these other previous layers. But if you're able to put yourself into that sort of semidreaming state—whether you're dreaming or whether you're writing creatively the brainwaves are apparently interchangeable—you're able to get a lot of that stuff back. That might be deep dreaming.

37   I'm aware, particularly in recent years, how precious that state is, I mean the ability to go in there when one is awake. I'm also aware, as an adult, of the vividness of my sleeping dreams when I have them. But I don't have any way of stacking up the number of dreams that I have as opposed to anybody else. My sense is I probably dream a little bit less at night because I'm taking off some of the pressure in the daytime. But I don't have an inherent proof of that.

38   I can remember finding that state for the first time and being delighted. It's a little bit like finding a secret door in a room but not knowing exactly how you got in. I can't remember exactly how I first found that state except that I would sit down to write every day, and I would pretty much do that whether the work went well or the work went badly. And after doing that for a while it was a little bit like having a posthypnotic suggestion.

39   I know that there are certain things that I do if I sit down to write: I have a glass of water or I have a cup of tea. There's a certain time I sit down around eight o'clock—or 8:15 or 8:30—somewhere within that half hour every morning. I have my vitamin pill; I have my music; I have my same seat; and the papers are all arranged in the same places. It's a series of things. The cumulative purpose of doing those things the same way every day seems to be a way of saying to the mind: you're going to be dreaming soon.

40   It's not really any different than a bedtime routine. Do you go to bed a different way every night? Is there a certain side that you sleep on? I mean I brush my teeth. I wash my hands. Why would anybody wash their hands before they go to bed? I don't know. And the pillows: the pillows are supposed to be pointed a certain way. The

open side of the pillowcase is supposed to be pointed *in* toward the other side of the bed. I don't know why.

41   And the sleeping position is the same: turn to the right, turn to the left. I think it's a way of your mind saying to your body, or your body saying to your mind— maybe they're communicating with each other saying—we're gonna go to sleep now. And probably dreaming follows the same pattern if you don't interrupt it with things like drug use, alcohol, or whatever.

42   The dreams that I remember most clearly are almost always early dreams. And they're not always bad dreams. I don't want to give you that impression. I can re- member one very clearly. It was a flying dream. I was over the turnpike and I was fly- ing along wearing a pair of pajama bottoms. I didn't have any shirt on. I'm just buzzing along under overpasses—*kazipp*—and I'm reminding myself in the dream to stay high enough so that I don't get disemboweled by car antennas sticking up from the cars. That's a fairly mechanistic detail but when I woke up from this dream my feeling was not fear or loathing but just real exhilaration, pleasure and happiness.

43   It wasn't an out of control flying dream. I can remember as a kid, having a lot of falling dreams but this is the only flying dream that I can remember in detail.

44   I don't have a lot of repetitive dreams but I do have an anxiety dream: I'm work- ing very hard in a little hot room—it seems to be the room where I lived as a teenager—and I'm aware that there's a madwoman in the attic. There's a little tiny door under the eave that goes to the attic, and I have to finish my work. I have to get that work done or she'll come out and get me. At some point in the dream that door always bursts open and this hideous women—with all this white hair stuck up around her head like a gone-to-seed dandelion—jumps out with a scalpel.

45   And I wake up.

46   I still have that dream when I'm backed up on my work and trying to fill all these ridiculous commitments I've made for myself.

QUESTIONS FOR DISCUSSION

1. King says, "I think that dreams are a way that people's minds illustrate the nature of their problems. Or maybe even illustrate the answers to their problems in symbolic language." How does he develop this insight about dreams through the personal examples provided in the essay?

2. Discuss several different ways in which King uses his dreams in his writ- ing. Which approach seems to have been most productive for him?

3. King is known as a vivid and detailed writer, particularly in the construc- tion of the fantasy scenes in his novels. Give examples of King's use of specific detail and effective choice of language in describing the dreams he refers to in this essay.

4. What conclusions about the way in which the mind functions does King develop through his metaphors of the mind as an ocean, as a nutrient bath, as water? What different roles do the analogies he makes with jumbo shrimp and different kinds of fish play in his explanations?

5. What relationship does King find between his process of writing and his process of dreaming? Why does King believe that "creative imaging and dreaming are just so similar that they've got to be related"? Explain why you agree or disagree with him.

CONNECTION

Compare and contrast how and why King and Rilke value and use their dreams in their writing.

IDEAS FOR WRITING

1. Write down a dream or nightmare that is vivid in your mind but that has never been recorded in words. Then write an analysis of the dream. What do you think it is telling you?
2. King gives us a good sense of the types of dreams that he has, of the impact that his dreams have had on him, and of the detailed fabric of his dreams. Write an essay in which you compare and contrast your dreams to King's dreams. What does this comparison and contrast suggest to you about how dreams might have a significant impact on waking life?

Amy Tan

"Mother Tongue"

Born in Oakland, California, in 1952 to immigrant parents, Amy Tan received an M.A. (1974) from San Jose State University, where she studied linguistics. Her first best-selling novel, The Joy Luck Club *(1989), was inspired by the stories told by Chinese-American women of her mother's generation. Tan has written two other novels,* The Kitchen God's Wife *(1991) and* The One Hundred Secret Senses *(1995); two children's stories,* The Moon Lady *(1992) and* The Chinese Siamese Cat *(1994); as well as a number of essays in which she explores cultural and linguistic issues. As you read the following essay, notice how Tan uses her experiences growing up bilingual in a Chinese-American family to challenge the traditional expectations of academic writing achievement tests.*

JOURNAL

In her essay, Amy Tan states that she is "fascinated by language in daily life." Discuss examples of odd, striking, or creative uses of language that you have noticed in everyday life or conversation.

1   I am not a scholar of English or literature. I cannot give you much more than personal opinions on the English language and its variations in this country or others.

2   I am a writer. And by that definition, I am someone who has always loved language. I am fascinated by language in daily life. I spend a great deal of my time thinking about the power of language—the way it can evoke an emotion, a visual image, a complex idea, or a simple truth. Language is the tool of any trade. And I use them all—all the Englishes I grew up with.

3   Recently, I was made keenly aware of the different Englishes I do use. I was giving a talk to a large group of people, the same talk I had already given to half a dozen other groups. The nature of the talk was about my writing, my life, and my book, *The Joy Luck Club*. The talk was going along well enough, until I remembered one major difference that made the whole talk sound wrong. My mother was in the room. And it was perhaps the first time she had heard me give a lengthy speech, using the kind of English I have never used with her. I was saying things like, "The intersection of memory upon imagination" and "There is an aspect of my fiction that relates to thus-and-thus"—a speech filled with carefully wrought grammatical phrases, burdened, it suddenly seemed to me, with nominalized forms, past perfect tenses, conditional phrases, all the forms of standard English that I had learned in school and through books, the forms of English I did not use at home with my mother.

4   Just last week, I was walking down the street with my mother, and I again found myself conscious of the English I was using, the English I use with her. We were talking about the price of new and use furniture, and I heard myself saying this: "Not waste money that way." My husband was with us as well, and he didn't notice any switch in my English. And then I realized why. It's because over the twenty years we've been together, I've often used that same kind of English with him, and sometimes he even uses it with me. It has become our language of intimacy, a different sort of English that relates to family talk, the language I grew up with.

5   So you'll have some idea of what this family talk I heard sounds like I'll quote what my mother said during a recent conversation which I videotaped and then transcribed. During this conversation, my mother was talking about a political gangster in Shanghai who had the same last name as her family's, Du, and how the gangster in his early years wanted to be adopted by her family, which was rich by comparison. Later, the gangster became more powerful, far richer than my mother's family, and one day showed up at my mother's wedding to pay his respects. Here's what she said in part:

6   "Du Yusong having business like fruit stand. Like off the street kind. He is Du like Du Zong—but not Tsung-ming Island people. The local people call putong, the nier east side, he bolong to that side local people. That man want to ask Du Zong father take him in like become own family. Du Zong father wasn't look down on him, but didn't take seriously, until that man big like become a mafia. Now important person, very hard to inviting him. Chinese way, came only to show respect, don't stay for dinner. Respect for making big celebration, he shows up. Mean gives lots of respect. Chinese custom. Chinese social life that way. If too important won't have to stay

too long. He come to my wedding. I didn't see, I heard it. I gone to boy's side, they have YMCA dinner. Chinese age I was nineteen."

7   You should know that my mother's expressive command of English belies how much she actually understands. She reads the *Forbes* report, listens to *Wall Street Week,* converses daily with her stockbroker, reads all of Shirley MacLaine's books with ease—all kinds of things I can't begin to understand. Yet some of my friends tell me they understand 50 percent of what my mother says. Some say they understand 80 to 90 percent. Some say they understand none of it, as if she were speaking pure Chinese. But to me, my mother's English is perfectly clear, perfectly natural. It's my mother tongue. Her language, as I hear it, is vivid, direct, full of observation and imagery. That was the language that helped shape the way I saw things, expressed things, made sense of the world.

8   Lately, I've been giving more thought to the kind of English my mother speaks. Like others, I have described it to people as "broken" or "fractured" English. But I wince when I say that. It has always bothered me that I can think of no way to describe it other than "broken," as if it were damaged and needed to be fixed, as if it lacked a certain wholeness and soundness. I've heard other terms used, "limited English," for example. But they seem just as bad, as if everything is limited, including people's perceptions of the limited English speaker.

9   I know this for a fact, because when I was growing up, my mother's "limited" English limited my perception of her. I was ashamed of her English. I believed that her English reflected the quality of what she had to say. That is, because she expressed them imperfectly her thoughts were imperfect. And I had plenty of empirical evidence to support me: the fact that people in department stores, at banks, and at restaurants did not take her seriously, did not give her good service, pretended not to understand her, or even acted as if they did not hear her.

10   My mother had long realized the limitations of her English as well. When I was fifteen, she used to have me call people on the phone to pretend I was she. In this guise, I was forced to ask for information or even to complain and yell at people who had been rude to her. One time it was a call to her stockbroker in New York. She had cashed out her small portfolio and it just so happened we were going to go to New York the next week, our very first trip outside California. I had to get on the phone and say in an adolescent voice that was not very convincing, "This is Mrs. Tan."

11   And my mother was standing in the back whispering loudly, "Why he don't send me check, already two weeks late. So mad he lie to me, losing me money."

12   And then I said in perfect English, "Yes, I'm getting rather concerned. You had agreed to send the check two weeks ago, but it hasn't arrived."

13   Then she began to talk more loudly. "What he want, I come to New York tell him front of his boss, you cheating me?" And I was trying to calm her down, make her be quiet, while telling the stockbroker, "I can't tolerate any more excuses. If I don't receive the check immediately, I am going to have to speak to your manager when I'm in New York next week." And sure enough, the following week there we were in front of this astonished stockbroker, and I was sitting there red-faced and quiet, and my mother, the real Mrs. Tan, was shouting at his boss in her impeccable broken English.

14   We used a similar routine just five days ago, for a situation that was far less humorous. My mother had gone to the hospital for an appointment, to find out about a benign brain tumor a CAT scan had revealed a month ago. She said she had spoken very good English, her best English, no mistakes. Still, she said, the hospital did not apologize when they said they had lost the CAT scan and she had come for nothing. She said they did not seem to have any sympathy when she told them she was anxious to know the exact diagnosis, since her husband and son had both died of brain tumors. She said they would not give her any more information until the next time and she would have to make another appointment for that. So she said she would not leave until the doctor called daughter. She wouldn't budge. And when the doctor finally called her daughter, me, who spoke in perfect English—lo and behold—we had assurances the CAT scan would be found, promises that a conference call on Monday would be held, and apologies for any suffering my mother had gone through for a most regrettable mistake.

15   I think my mother's English almost had an effect on limiting my possibilities in life as well. Sociologists and linguists probably will tell you that a person's developing language skills are more influenced by peers. But I do think that the language spoken in the family, especially in immigrant families which are more insular, plays a large role in shaping the language of the child. And I believe that it affected my results on achievements tests, IQ Tests, and the SAT. While my English skills were never judged as poor, compared to math, English could not be considered my strong suit. In grade school I did moderately well, getting perhaps B's, sometimes B-pluses, in English and scoring perhaps in the sixtieth or seventieth percentile on achievement tests. But those scores were not good enough to override the opinion that my true abilities lay in math and science, because in those areas I achieved A's and scored in the ninetieth percentile of higher.

16   This was understandable. Math is precise; there is only one correct answer. Whereas, for me at least, the answers on English tests were always a judgement call, a matter of opinion and personal experience. Those tests were constructed around items like fill-in-the-blank sentence completion, such as "Even though Tom was _____, Mary thought he was _____." And the correct answer always seemed to be the most bland combinations of thoughts, for example, "Even though Tom was shy, Mary thought he was charming," with the grammatical structure "even though" limiting the correct answer to some sort of semantic opposites, so you wouldn't get answers like, "Even though Tom was foolish, Mary thought he was ridiculous." Well, according to my mother, there were very few limitations as to what Tom could have been and what
17 Mary might have thought of him. So I never did well on tests like that.

    The same was true with word analogies, pairs of words in which you were supposed to find some sort of logical, semantic relationship—for example, "*Sunset* is to *nightfall* as _____ is to _____." And here you would be presented with a list of four possible pairs, one of which showed the same kind of relationship: *red* is to *stoplight*, *bus* is to *arrival, chills* is to *fever, yawn* is to *boring*. Well, I could never think that way. I knew what the tests were asking, but I could not block out of my mind the images already created by the first pair "*sunset* is to *nightfall*"—and I would see a burst of colors against a darkening sky, the moon rising, the lowering of a curtain of stars. And all the other pairs of words—red, bus, stoplight, boring—just threw up a mass of confusing images, making it impossible for me to sort out something as logical as saying: "A sunset precedes nightfall" is the same as "a chill precedes a fever." The only way I would have gotten that answer right would have been to imagine an associative situation, for example, my being disobedient and staying out past sunset, catching a chill at night, which turns into feverish pneumonia as punishment, which indeed did happen to me.

18   I have been thinking about all this lately, about my mother's English, about achievement tests. Because lately I've been asked, as a writer, why there are not more Asian Americans represented in American literature. Why are there few Asian Americans enrolled in creative writing programs? Why do so many Chinese students go into engineering? Well, theses are broad sociological questions I can't begin to answer. But I have noticed in surveys—in fact, just last week—that Asian students, as a whole, always do significantly better on math achievement tests than in English. And this makes me think that there are other Asian-American students whose English spoken in the home might also be described as "broken" or "limited." And perhaps they also have teachers who are steering them away from writing and into math and science, which is what happened to me.

19   Fortunately, I happen to be rebellious in nature and enjoy the challenge of disproving assumptions made about me. I became an English major my first year in college, after being enrolled as pre-med. I started writing nonfiction as a freelancer the week after I was told by my former boss that writing was my worst skill and I should hone my talents toward account management.

20   But it wasn't until 1985 that I finally began to write fiction. And at first I wrote using what I thought to be wittily crafted sentences, sentences that would finally prove I had mastery over the English language. Here's an example from the first draft of a story that later made its way into *The Joy Luck Club*, but without this line: "That was my mental quandary in its nascent state." A terrible line, which I can barely pronounce.

21   Fortunately, for reasons I won't get into today, I later decided I should envision a reader for the stories I would write. And the reader I decided upon was my mother, because these were stories about mothers. So with this reader in mind—and in fact she did read my early drafts—I began to write stories using all the Englishes I grew up with: the English I spoke to my mother, which for lack of a better term might be described as "simple"; the English she used with me, which for lack of a better term might be described as "broken"; my translation of her Chinese, which could certainly be described as "watered down"; and what I imagined to be her translation of her Chinese if she could speak in perfect English, her internal language, and for that I sought to preserve the essence, but neither an English nor a Chinese structure. I wanted to capture what language ability tests can never reveal: her intent, her passion, her imagery, the rhythms of her speech and the nature of her thoughts.

22   Apart from what any critic had to say about my writing, I knew I had succeeded where it counted when my mother finished reading my book and gave me her verdict: "So easy to read."

QUESTIONS FOR DISCUSSION

1. Tan discusses her awareness of using language differently when speaking with different audiences and on different occasions. Keep a log for several days that records the situations when you switch the way you use English for a specific group of friends, teachers, relatives, or a work situation. Share your observations and conclusions with your classmates.
2. Why is Tan critical of the descriptive term "limited English"? How did this term influence her perception of her own mother?
3. Why is the article entitled "Mother Tongue"? What do Tan's examples about how she would often speak for her mother suggest?
4. Why is Tan critical of the achievement tests she was given as an adolescent? Do you agree or disagree with her point of view and conclusions?
5. Why does Tan believe that high school teachers encourage Asian students to study math and science rather than writing? How does she explain her success as a writer in spite of the evaluations provided by her teachers and employer?
6. According to Tan, what is the real test of a writer? What advice does Tan offer to the person who aspires to be a successful writer?

CONNECTION

Compare Tan's views on the role of different "Englishes" in her writer's life and in her relationship with her mother with the views of Joyce Chang in her essay "Drive Becarfully."

IDEAS FOR WRITING

1. "I am a writer. And by definition, I am someone who has always loved language. I am fascinated by language in daily life." Develop Tan's ideas on language into an essay, using personal experiences and examples from your reading that illustrate language's complexity and power.
2. Write an essay in which you discuss how your rebellion against a cultural or social myth helped you to develop a skill and talent that is both useful and rewarding.

Jon Katz

"The Tales They Tell in Cyber-Space"

Jon Katz (b. 1938) has had a long writing career as a journalist, playwright, and novelist. He attended Antioch College, City College of New York, and the new school for Social Research. His reviews and critical articles on the media have appeared in Nation,

Rolling Stone, Columbia Journalism Review, *and* New York. *His most recent books include* Virtuous Reality *(1997) and* Media Rants: Postpolitics in the Digital Nation *(1997). Katz has also worked as an "interactive journalist," distributing his reviews and media commentary from his position at HotWired magazine, an on-line publication. In the following article, which appeared in the* New York Times *in 1994, Katz examines the thoughtful and caring exchanges which can occur in on-line discussion groups.*

JOURNAL

Write about a time when you communicated "on-line," either as an e-mail correspondent or as a member of a chat group that shared a common interest. Do you feel your writing improved as a result of this experience?

My daughter has cancer. As some of you know, she is 8. In all the world I never conceived of all the sorrow I would feel at learning this, all the horror at watching her suffer so stoically through test after test. There is not a lot of hope, just a lot of medicine. We are preparing ourselves for the worst, which her doctor has hinted is what we should expect. I've decided to journal you every day, those of you who can bear to read it. Feel free to answer to offer sympathy, encouragement, or whatever else you're feeling. Please feel free to check me if I am too sorry for myself or for her.

We are, as J— herself said, all going to die, and maybe this will help me to bear it. I do not know how to tell her grandparents, or even our friends, for she is much loved, inside and out of the house.

We can start here. She asked me this morning, "Dad, does it get better? It does, doesn't it?" My mouth moved up and down, but nothing came out of it. I could sure use some words.

—Excerpted with permission from the computer
bulletin board Compuserve

1   With a cautionary nod toward technology's drum-beating prophets, we offer an understatement: our creative lives have changed. As happened when the printing press, the telephone, and television were invented, stories and the means by which we tell them will never be the same, not for the people who tell them or for those who take them in. All over the world, the gatekeepers are disintegrating as the few who always decided what stories the rest of us would hear are yielding to the millions telling their stories directly to one another.

2   Of the thousands of potential books, magazine articles, films, or television series, only a tiny fraction ever make it through all the checkpoints. Producers select a dozen or so stories for broadcast each night; book editors say no many more times than yes. As the career-obsessed producer in "The Player" said: "We get fifty thousand pitches a year for movies. We pick twelve."

3   But increasingly, technology is breaking down the notion of few-to-many communications. Some communicators will always be more powerful than others, but the big idea behind cyber-tales is that for the first time the many are talking to the many. Every day, those who can afford the computer equipment and the telephone bills can be their own producers, agents, editors, and audiences. Their stories are becoming more and more idiosyncratic, interactive, and individualistic, told in different forums to diverse audiences in different ways.

4   The roads on which these stories move are the computer bulletin board systems. There are more than thirty-three thousand of them in the United States, and more than eleven million Americans are using them. Above them all hovers the most enormous information entity in history, Internet, the mystic global computer network. It carries more stories, messages, and information each day than otherwise moves around the world in months.

5   "Finding the WELL was like discovering a cozy little world that had been flourishing without me, hidden within the walls of my house; an entire cast of characters welcomed me to the troupe with great merriment a soon as I found the secret door," writes Howard Rheingold in "The Virtual Community: Homesteading on the Electronic Frontier." "Like others who fell into the WELL, I soon discovered that I was audience, performer, and scriptwriter, along with my companions, in an on-going improvisation."

6   The WELL Mr. Rheingold fell into—the Whole Earth 'Lectronic Link, based north of San Francisco—was one of the first and most significant computer bulletin board systems. Small even by cyber-standards (it has eight thousand members, compared with America On-Line's four hundred and fifty thousand), the WELL is the creative and spiritual home of the computer culture, a combination think tank, unofficial legislature, conference center, production company, forum, and village green. Unlike such larger systems as Prodigy and Compuserve, the WELL sells nothing but the ideas, expertise, curiosity, and sometimes the friendship of its members— and their stories, of an astonishing power and range.

7   The WELL, like its electronic sisters around the planet, is helping to redefine what a story is and giving us greater control over the creation and distribution of our own narratives than we have ever had. Ever more quickly and dramatically, the technology is liberating our individual and collective creative visions.

8   I live on the border between the old and the new cultures, between one kind of story and another. As a former editor, I was one of the few whose hands were on the machinery that transmits stories to the many. When I bought a modem last year, I passes thorough the common and predictable stages of panic, frustration, confusion, shock and excitement. Although guided at each step of countless electronic helping hands, I felt incompetent.

9   But it was clear from the beginning—when I first logged on to the WELL, typed "Help!" and was flooded with messages of welcome—that I had transported myself to a place I had read about but had not even begun to imagine.

10   Once I had mastered the machinery, I found myself adrift in a sea of stories, more than I could absorb or measure. They washed over me as the people around me passed back and forth not only literal news of the world, but also debate and information via dozens of growing and evolving electronic conferences—on parenting, poetry, AIDS, sex, religion, aging, virtual reality, feminism, music, psychology. Everyone was telling stories; in fact, everyone was redefining the very form and function of a story. At least that was one way of looking at it.

11   A story was no longer something acquired and distributed by an editor, network, or publisher. A story was an experience, anecdote, musing, or argument that could be tossed off into space for electronic pilgrims to digest, applaud, or ignore. It was never clear where is would land or what might come back as a result. Stories almost always brought a response—sympathy, another story, criticism, laughter. In this sense, they became interactive. The process did not end with the telling. It had only begun.

12   I heard story after story. Once a member of the WELL slipped into a coma in the Far East, was taken home to California through other members' efforts, then tried to recount what being in a coma was like. Another member agonized on line whether to have an elderly diabetic relative's leg amputated, detailing her dilemma and her decision. Families recount tragedies and struggles; multiple-sclerosis victims connect with one another; people look for work, find friends.

13   I realized quickly that technological ignorance matters little. The cyber-towns are not about technology. They are about something much more basic and timeless. People get excited about one another's tales and ideas, not about the means by which they are transmitted. Stories are the heart of it, underlying all the numbing techno-talk. As I wrestled with strange commands, many of which did not work or were not entered properly, with messages that got lost or with prompts that took me places I didn't want to go and couldn't get out of, a friend asked why I was going through it all. For the stories. I wanted to hear theirs; I wanted to tell mine.

14   The stories are told, not written. They lack the structure and form of journalist stories, and the sometimes self-conscious tone of the novel. Since most of the creators are not consciously creating art, their work is generally simple and unadorned. The tellers are preoccupied with the stories themselves, not the manner in which they are presented.

I'm outside of Cleveland, heading for I–80, and I see this bubble in my mirror; and it's a Smokey. "Radar clocked you doing 85," he says, reaching for his ticket book. I'm about to squawk when we hear this horn and this Chevy comes barreling off the road. This man jumps out, screaming that his wife is having a baby, and he says he thinks the baby is choking on the cord. The cop and I are in the car in a flash, pulling the mother out. She's in mid-delivery, and the husband is about to pass out. So the cop turns to me and says, "You up for this?" and I said I was a paramedic in Vietnam, so we lie a blanket down, slide the baby out, unwrap the cord from the baby's neck. It was beautiful and weird. Ambulance comes, husband is very grateful, so is the wife, the cop and I shake hands like we're identical twins, we recap, each of us telling the other what a hero we are and slap each other on the back. I say, "Hey, I'm overdue on this run," and he says, "Good trip, but wait a minute." He finishes writing the ticket. Can you believe cops?

—From Sandy and Eddie's Truckers
computer bulletin board

All of a sudden, this morning I realized that I was old. That's just it. I never noticed it before, not really. I realized that there was no longer any given week in which I didn't have a doctor's appointment. I can't help but notice my diminishing energy. It is more difficult to hear, to see, to endure long walks, the cold, the heat. I have a more difficult time walking my black lab on a leash. I see from my friends that a broken limb is not a small matter. We are not back on our feet in a matter of weeks. Often it is the beginning of a fearful and eternal process— operations, recovery in bed, which weakens our limbs, our muscles, makes us more brittle, nursing or hospital care that clouds our minds, confuses us. My children are angry with me. They want me to be vital, helpful, present, and they simply can't accept that I can't.

—From the computer bulletin board
Prodigy

15   For decades, it was television that tantalized us with the promise of bringing the world into our homes. But it was difficult and expensive to get to stories, to transmit film and to broadcast them. And we rarely got to tell our own. Television was controlled by a handful of companies. So were Hollywood, book publishing, and the other distributors of our culture.

16   By the 80's, cable, VCR's, videocams, satellites, public-access channels and computers began to give ordinary people the chance to tell their own stories via a variety of media. Few of these new creators would define themselves as artists; few critics would define such work as art. But anyone with a home entertainment system and a cable hookup became, in effect, an independent production company, wresting control from network programmers. Anyone with a camcorder became a journalist. On Camnet, the amateur video network shown two days a month in hundreds of thousands of American homes, anyone with a camcorder and a story can tell it and distribute it nationwide. The idea that we could share and shape our own stories in these new media began to grow.

17   All the talk of fiber optics and broadbands, the obsession with the machinery that transmits stories, might make these forms of media seem complex, but the stories themselves are not at all arcane. They are, in fact, familiar, echoing themes and notions that date back to the record birth of produced storytelling.

18   "In drama," writer Daniel Boorstin in *The Creators*, "man found ways to create unique events for delight, reflection, and dismay, and so make experience outlast the actor. The role of spectator, the person who stood outside the action, was not obvious, for the shared communal experience was overwhelming." In ancient Greece, he continues, "we see the slow stages by which man discovered that he need not always be a participant. In a new kind of immortality man could now outlive his time, relive earlier times, foreshadow later times by witnessing actors on a stage."

19   Mr. Boorstin could as well have been writing about cyber-space as the birth of the
spectator in the seventh century B.C. Amid the clacking of keyboards creating and
distributing stories on line, storytellers share the communal experiences of life,
death, work, love, family.

> Do you have any idea what it is like to be gay? To have to hide the most im-
> portant thing about yourself, even though you had no choice about it? To live in
> terror of discovery? To be laughed at, isolated, and beaten up. To live around
> people who hide their children from you? Who wouldn't let you teach them if
> they knew? Because I am a teacher who dreads every call to the principal's office.
> I always wonder if it will be my last. How can you love a country that finds you
> too disgusting to serve? That permits people to attack you and your friends, throw
> things at them from car windows, deny them the right to be married, have fami-
> lies? Can you conceive of that? Does this get through to you on any level at all?
> Two years ago, my lover and I walked through the French Quarter of New
> Orleans. We vacationed there because we knew it to be a tolerant place. We left
> a restaurant just off Bourbon Street, and three men jumped out of their cars. They
> knocked my lover and me down. They kicked us in the face, in the kidneys, in the
> groin. They knocked four of my teeth out, broke my jaw. Then they urinated on
> us. They laughed and said they were soldiers. That they'd love to have us in the
> military. I couldn't tell the police what happened. I was afraid the school district
> might find out back home.
>
> —From the computer bulletin board
> Compuserve

And a reply:

> I was very touched by your message, buddy. What happened to you was horri-
> ble, unsupportable. That's not what I lost three toes for in Vietnam, for scum to
> beat up on people like you and your friend. I fought so you could do whatever
> you wanted so long as you didn't hurt anybody or break the law. You and I have
> no quarrel. But we do have these problems, and I'll be straight with you about it,
> just like you were with me. Do you have any idea what it's like to be in a field or
> jungle or valley with bullets and shells blowing up all around you? With your
> friends being cut down, ripped apart, bleeding, dying right next to you screaming
> for their moms or kids or wives? Do you know how much trust and communica-
> tion it takes to get through that? Do you have any idea what it's like to go through
> that if there's tension among you?
> I'm not saying this can't be worked out. I'm saying, go slow. Don't come in
> here with executive orders and try to change things in a day that should take
> longer. Don't make me into a bigot because I know it takes an unbelievable
> amount of feeling to crawl down there into a valley of death. It takes love of your
> buddy. And that's something both of us can understand, right? But if you hate
> him, or fear him or don't understand him—how can you do it?

20   It is individuals, the cyber-artists—writers and poets—who benefit the most
dramatically from sharing their work in so revolutionary a way. In the cyber-world,

there are no agents to send back your manuscript, no editors to tell you your ideas aren't really what they have in mind, no producers to say your play can't draw an audience. Everyone's stories have an equal shot, if not equal weight. Everyone has an audience. In cyber-space, poets always have audiences.

21   It is not a perfect world. There are cyber-addicts who never seem to get off-line. The pompous and combative can still run amok. The techno-wizards are impossible to keep up with, speaking their own language in their own world. Many people find that no amount of cyber-communication is as satisfying, meaningful, or enduring as personal contact. But the stories pouring over phone lines all over the world all day long can haunt you.

> I don't feel clear much any more. Good luck to everybody. It was really great talking to all of you. I loved hearing about your lives and your work and your kids. I would have loved to have had some, but not in this world. Maybe the next. I loved hearing about your screwed-up personal lives. In comparison, I felt almost normal for the first time in my life, which is weird, considering I was dying. I felt like I had the best, most loving family in the world. Sorry when I got angry, but I couldn't stay angry here for long. Looking forward to a peaceful transition for me, and for all of you. For my sake, I hope there is a God, even though D says if there was, he/she wouldn't have killed me this way.
>
> —From the electronic diary of a computer bulletin board member who died of AIDS

QUESTIONS FOR DISCUSSION

1. According to Katz, how has story-telling become more "democratic" in the era of the Internet and computer bulletin boards? Do you agree?
2. Katz includes a number of stories and testimonies posted on-line. Why does he order them as he does? How do they help illustrate his points?
3. The on-line community, the WELL, is described in the essay as a sort of writer's theater where each member is at the same time "audience, performer, and scriptwriter." Do you think this type of community can be helpful for writers, or might it be for many just a way of killing time, an outlet for gossip and procrastination?
4. How do the WELL members help each other out during hard times? What aspects of traditional society might this kind of electronic interaction help replace?
5. How does Katz's use of comments on ancient drama from Boorstin's *The Creators* clarify the role of the spectator/participant in cyber-space?

CONNECTION

Compare Katz's view of the interaction between writers and audience with the way Julia Alvarez discusses such interactions in her essay "Writing Matters."

IDEAS FOR WRITING

1. Follow a thread of conversation from an on-line discussion group on a serious topic such as AIDS or racism. How do the postings you found compare with those in Katz's essay, and what conclusions might you draw
   from your findings about the quality of critical thought and verbal expression to be found in such discussion groups ?
2. Write an essay in which you respond to Katz's view of the way on-line
   postings are influencing the way people write, publish, and read. What
   kind of influence do you think that the on-line movement will have on
   how people read and write over the next few years?

Muriel Rukeyser

"This Place in the Ways"

*Muriel Rukeyser (1913–1980) was born in New York City and attended Vassar Col-
lege, where she edited an undergraduate journal and covered the Scottsboro trial. The
experience of the trial contributed to her lifelong commitment to social justice that included support of the Spanish loyalists during World War II, protests against the Vietnam War, and struggle against human rights abuses in the United States and abroad.
Rukeyser was a Guggenheim Fellow in 1943. She wrote translations, biography, and
television scripts, as well as many volumes of poetry, including* Speed of Darkness
(1967) and The Gates *(1976). In "This Place in the Ways" (1951), she explores the
process of writing from the perspective of her own concerns and commitments: to love,
to protest against social injustice, and to quiet reflection and personal growth.*

JOURNAL

Write about a time in your life in which you had many new ideas and strong feelings, yet couldn't express yourself in writing, a period of transition and waiting.
What helped you to finally move on and gain (or regain) the ability to express
your insights?

Having come to this place
I set out once again
On the dark and marvelous way
From where I began:

5   Belief in the love of the world,
    Woman, spirit, and man.

    Having failed in all things
    I enter a new age
    Seeing the old ways as toys,
10 The houses of a stage
    Painted and long forgot;
    And I find love and rage.

    Rage for the world as it is
    But for what it may be
15 More love now than last year.
    And always less self-pity
    Since I know in a clearer light
    The strength of the mystery.

    And at this place in the ways
20 I wait for song,
    My poem-hand still, on the paper,
    All night long.
    Poems in throat and hand, asleep,
    And my storm beating strong!

QUESTIONS FOR DISCUSSION

1. What is the "place" referred to in the first stanza, the "new age" in the second stanza, the "mystery" in the third stanza? Why does Rukeyser leave these expressions ambiguous?

2. As the speaker enters the new age, what metaphors does she use to describe the "old ways" she looks back upon? Why does she use this type of language to describe the past?

3. What does the poet continue to believe in and to love, despite her past "failures" and her sense of rage?

4. If the speaker feels a "storm beating strong" within her, why does she continue to "wait for song"? Why doesn't she begin to write?

5. If this is a poem about writing in times of stress and transition, what is the poet's strategy for coping with these concerns? How does she use sleep and dreaming as aids to creation?

CONNECTION

Compare and contrast the way Rukeyser explores the issue of writer's block or obstacles to self-expression with Stafford's advice to the beginning writer in "A Way of Writing." Whose ideas seem most useful to you in your own search for self-expression through writing?

1. Write an essay in which you reflect on a time of transition in your life. How do you perceive reality differently now than you did previously? How have you learned to express your new insights? Have your new perceptions altered the style or voice in which you now wish to express yourself?

2. Rukeyser concludes stanza three with the lines, "Since I know in a clearer light/The strength of the mystery." Write an essay in which you explain what you think she means by this statement and describe similar realizations in your own thought and life. Why is it difficult to write about "the strength of the mystery" of life? What kind of language do you find most effective for such concerns?

Joyce Chang

"Drive Becarefully"

Student writer Joyce Chang (b. 1975) was raised in northern California. Living in a predominantly white neighborhood and growing up in a traditional, close-knit Asian family, Chang struggled to integrate her Chinese heritage with mainstream American culture. In the essay that follows, written originally for an introductory writing class, she explores the problem of coming to terms with her mother's non-standard English in light of reading Amy Tan's essay, "Mother Tongue."

1   ". . . My mother's 'limited' English limited my perception of her. I was ashamed of her English." Amy Tan's self-evaluation in her essay, "Mother Tongue," clung to my conscience as I continued reading. I could have said those words myself. I have definitely thought those words a million times. Like Tan, I too used to be ashamed of my mother's English. I used to shudder whenever I heard an incorrect verb tense, misplaced adverb, or incorrect pronoun come from her lips. Like many people, I couldn't look beyond my mother's incorrect grammar to see the intent and beauty behind her words.

2   My mother immigrated to the United States in the 1970's, speaking only a few words of English. As time went on, she gradually learned more and more words, although her sentence structure remained very basic. As a young working woman and mother of two, my mother didn't have much of a chance to improve her grammar. Taking ESL courses was not one of her immediate concerns—trying to beat rush hour Chicago traffic to get home in time to make dinner was what she worried about. So my mother went on using phrases like: "He go to the store."

3   Since I had the advantage of being born and raised in the United States, my English abilities quickly surpassed those of my mother by the time I was in grade school. I knew all about auxiliary verbs, the subjunctive, and plurals—my mother didn't. I

could form sentences like "He treated her as if she were still a child." For my mother to convey that same idea, she could only say "He treat her like child."

4　　My mother's comprehension of the English language was comparable to her speaking abilities. When I was with her, I learned early on not to try any of the complicated, flowery, descriptive sentences that I had been praised for in school. Anything beyond a simple subject-verb-object construction was poorly received. When I was very young, I did not think much about having to use a different English with my mother. The two Englishes in my life were just different—one was not better than the other. However, that feeling quickly changed in third grade.

5　　My young mind could not always switch between the two Englishes with ease. I usually knew which English belonged in which world, but sometimes my Englishes crossed over. I remember one day in third grade when I was supposed to bring something for a "cultural show-and-tell." It must have been sometime in winter—around Chinese New Year. My mother had given me a "red bag" for show-and-tell. A "red bag" is an envelope that contains money. Chinese people give and receive these envelopes of money as gifts for the new year. As my mother described it to me, "The bag for good fortune. . . you rich for New Year." When I tried to explain the meaning of the red envelope to my class, I used my mother's words, "The bag for good fortune. . . ." I do not think my classmates noticed my grammatical shortcomings, or maybe they did notice but chose not to comment. In any case, my teacher had an alarmed look on her face and sharply demanded, "What did you say?" She seemed to be in complete bewilderment at how one of her students who spoke "good English" could suddenly speak "bad English." Thinking that she just didn't hear me the first time, I innocently repeated the exact same phrase I had said before.

6　　"Where did you learn *that* English?" she questioned. "It's wrong! Please speak correctly!" she commanded.

7　　After her admonishment, it took me a while to continue speaking. When I finally opened my mouth to utter my first word, all I could think of was, "I hope this is correct." I was relieved when I finished with no further interruptions.

8　　Hearing my teacher say that my mother's English was wrong had a lasting impression on me. When I went home that day, all I could think about when my mother spoke was the "wrongness" of her English, and the "wrongness" of her as a person. I took her awkward phrases, sentence fragments, and other incorrect phrases as a sign that she somehow was "incorrect." I became irritated with her when she made grammatical mistakes at home. I became ashamed of her when she made those same mistakes outside of the house.

9　　By the time I entered high school I was tired of being ashamed of my mother's English. I thought I would do her a favor and take on a mission to improve her English. The mission turned out to be a lot more difficult than I thought it would be. No matter how many times I would tell her something that she said was wrong, she would still say the same phrase over and over again. For example, whenever I left the house, my mother would say, "Drive becarefully." After the first time she said that, I told her it was wrong. I would then add, "The correct way to say that is 'drive carefully' or 'be careful driving.'" She would then nod and say good-bye. However, the next day as I headed out the door, mother would come up to me and say "drive be-carefully" again. I would get incredibly frustrated because she never seemed to learn. I was glad, however, that at least I was the only one to hear such an "incorrect" statement.

10   One day, however, a friend of mine was with me as we headed out the door. As usual my mother screamed out "drive becarefully" as we walked toward the car. I immediately rolled my eyes and muttered, "It's 'drive carefully.' Get it right."

11   Later, as I drove my friend back home, she asked me a question that I will never forget. "Is it your mom who wants to improve her English or is it you who wants to 'improve' her?" I was stunned at first by my friend's question. I had no response. After a lot of thinking, I realized my friend was right. My mom was satisfied with her English. She could convey her thoughts and didn't care that she did it in a way that was different from the standard. She had no problem with her use of language— I did.

12   After that conversation, I began to accept the idea that there are many different Englishes and one is not necessarily better that the other. As long as a person is understood, it is not necessary to speak textbook perfect English. Presently, I am very concerned with how people treat others who speak "limited" English. I understand how easy it is to misperceive and mistreat people. In her essay "Mother Tongue," Tan also writes about how people are perceived differently just because of their "limited" English. She describes the problems her mother encounters day to day, "people in department stores, at banks, and at restaurants did not take her seriously, did not give her good service, pretended not to understand her, or even acted as if they did not hear her." Although I am very angry when I read about how a person with "limited" English is mistreated, I still understand how it is all too easy for a person not to take someone seriously when he/she does not speak the same English as that person. It is also easy to assume a person who speaks "broken" English wants someone to help him "fix" it.

13   Now, when I find myself talking with people who speak "another" English, I try to look for the meaning the intent of what they say, and ignore the perhaps awkward structure of their statements. Also when I encounter someone who speaks an English different from my own, I try not to assume that he or she wants to "improve" it.

14   As Tan concludes her essay, the importance of what is spoken lies in a person's ". . . intent,. . . passion,. . . imagery,. . . and nature of . . . thoughts." These are the things I now look for when someone speaks to me. Incorrect verb tenses, misplaced adverbs, and incorrect pronouns are less significant issues. As I begin to realize this more, I feel more comfortable with not only my mom's different English but my own. My mom's English is the one I grew up with at home. It is one of the Englishes I speak.

15   The other day I went home to help my mom run errands.

16   "Go to store," she said.

17   "Buy what?"

18   "Juice and eggs. Drive becarefully!" my mom warned.

19   I couldn't help but to smile. I like hearing that now.

1. How has Chang applied insights and experiences of Amy Tan in "Mother Tongue" to her own relationship with her mother?
2. Could you identify with any aspects of Chang's feelings and attitudes about her mother's English or with her struggle to accept her mother for who she is rather than to "fix her"?
3. Do you agree or disagree with Chang's teacher's attitude and her definition of correct English? Explain your point of view.
4. Do you agree or disagree with Chang's conclusion, "As long as a person is understood, it is not necessary to speak textbook perfect English"?

Sheila Chanani

"Whirling Through: My Writing Process as a Tornado Within"

In the essay that follows, student writer Sheila Chanani explains the drawing she created to express her writing process. She develops the images of the drawing into a series of analogies that communicate her personal view of writing.

1   My head is filled with a tornado of impressions, events, dreams, and ideas that tumble around my every waking moment, getting bigger and bigger. This whirlwind swirl dances about, gathering information from every aspect of my life. Some thoughts remain lucid while others are fragmented, blurred, and submerged in the core. This cyclone carries the intimate pieces, the windblown flowers, of my life. I allow them to be put aside so that I can concentrate on the daily routine of my life. The storm intimidates me and often overwhelms me, because it holds my secrets and fears as well. I push it away, not wanting to be consumed, but knowing that the only way to capture a piece of myself is to be bold and to enter without looking back.

2   I delve into this wild storm attempting to rescue an idea, an obscure flower, from the tempestuous colors, smells, and textures. Being a daydreamer, my best chance to explore this wild segment of my mind is in those hours of complete mind wandering. I can truly reach inward in the peaceful moments when I let go of the present and let the tornado surface. These periods can occur while sitting in my room staring out the window or even while riding with the easy rhythm of a car in motion. In order to release an image, I concentrate, often with pen in hand; sometimes I just "zone out." If luck is on my side, the writing gods smile upon me, and the idea, a hazy undefined shape, emerges easily. Often a glimpse of a mental picture whizzes on by, taunting me (these moments are definitely the most frustrating); some thoughts will just stay hidden in the inner folds of the cyclone.

3   This hazier component of the whirlwind, the core, contains my dreams which are embedded deep within me. Tapping into my dreams has always been a source of ideas for my writing. In the fifth grade, I used a vivid nightmare to write a story about a man who hid in the school bathroom and lured kids in so he could use the showers to boil children. Now, instead of literally using my dreams and nightmares word for word, I use them as a source of insights into those people and events that are most important or that have had the greatest impact on me.

4   Even though my dreams are a fountain for ideas, I am often afraid that to pull out a flower rooted deep within me for all to see would be the ultimate self-exposure and humiliation. My reputation in high school was one of being sarcastic and cynical—I was too insecure to expose the inner buds. In high school, I was given standard formulas that allowed me to write my papers without ever having to involve myself too personally. The rules and formats would guide me rather than my imagination. I wrote analytically without digging deeply into my tornado. Rather than facing the stormy winds of my inner thoughts and finding something original or innovative to say, I took the safe path of the standard format. I found myself doing what was considered "good enough" rather than exceptional, for finding the exceptional meant going beyond the exterior of the whirl to find the perfect petals instead of settling with the first image that surfaced.

5   During my senior year in high school our teacher made us write once a week for an entire period on a topic of choice. This was the most frustrating academic experience of my life. Never having had to write without some kind of a prompt or purpose, I realized that whatever I wrote would be completely and utterly me. Many periods were spent pulling at my hair as I agonized over what to write about. The pieces I ended up writing were sarcastic, mocking, or silly and humorous stories without any depth. A part of me is so afraid of my mysterious whirlwind because, although there is much color and beauty to tap into, I do not always have the confidence to say that this is me, Sheila Kumari Chanani, sprawled out naked on this piece of paper. Being flippant was always easier than exposing my feelings.

6   Although the most difficult part of the writing process for me is unleashing this undeveloped thought from the tornado with the courage to put it on paper, a major villain is my laziness and time constraints. I often leave my writing as the half-formed flower that tumbles out and might blossom if it were nurtured more. The petals for that perfect flower are present; I just need to put the effort into completing the entire process with improvement and refinement.

7   When I do begin writing, with the faint petals in my hand, my problem is that I cannot transform the concept into words that I can actually type onto paper. I find myself unable to put my thoughts into words that clearly define this flower. Often I let my papers ramble, hoping that eventually my point will be made. Many times, I have found as I continue writing pointlessly, that the idea never had any substance at all. The actual writing and rewriting is the most tedious aspect of my process, but it is also the most important. No bud will ever bloom without fertilization and watering. No matter how great an idea I may have pulled from the whorl in my head, without substance and coherence, it will not amount to anything.

8   The final flower, with distinct colors and shape, is the piece that evolves through the entire process of babble and revision—a solid structure. It is aesthetically appealing not only to me but also to my audience. I am always amazed that something from the mess of codes, recipes, calculus formulas, and song lyrics that veil my swirl can come out making any sense at all. As my spiraling mass grows and collects new items with each new experience, I can only hope to master my ability to discover and to extract the flowers whirling through.

QUESTIONS FOR DISCUSSION

1. How clearly does this essay communicate Chanani's writing process? What else would you have liked to know about how she writes?
2. Chanani uses an extended metaphor or analogy of a cyclone/whirlwind to describe her writing process. How does she explain this analogy in the essay? Is her explanation clear? Can you relate to this analogy as you reflect on your writing? How?
3. A second metaphor Chanani uses to describe her writing is that of the flower. How does she develop this metaphor in the final paragraphs of the essay, and what aspects of writing does it represent? Is this a metaphor that would apply to your writing process? Why or why not?
4. What difficulty does Chanani have in doing "topic of choice" writing? Why is it easier for her to be flippant or simply to write on an assigned prompt? Do you find it hard to come up with writing topics?

Topics for Research and Writing

1. Drawing on evidence from the selections in this chapter, outside reading and Internet research, and your own experiences, write an essay that examines the role of dreams and the unconscious mind in the writing process.
2. The authors in this chapter discuss ways in which they have been influenced to become writers. Taking into consideration these writers' experiences as well as those of others you have read about or interviewed, write an essay in which you examine some of the influences that shape a person into a writer.
3. Stafford, King, and Alvarez value writing as a process of self-discovery and healing. Write an essay in which you explore this perspective on writing, taking into account these writers' ideas, those of other writers you read about or interview, as well as your own experiences.
4. Alvarez, Stafford, and other writers discuss the social, ethical, and spiritual values involved in the art of writing. Taking into account their ideas and those of other authors, discuss some of the ways that writing can have a positive influence on beliefs, values, and social behavior.

5. The writers in this chapter all have insights into the nature of creativity and the creative process. After doing some further research into this issue, write an essay in which you present and evaluate several current theories about creative thinking and the creative process.

6. Katz suggests that the wide availability of computers, e-mail, and Internet chat groups are changing the way writers work and relate to their audience. After doing some Internet research into new web-based literary ideas, writers' groups, and on-line publications, write an essay about new directions for writing and interactions of writers and audiences that are arising as a direct result of the cyber-space revolution.

7. See one of the following films, either by yourself or with several of your classmates: *The Postman, Dreamchild, Naked Lunch, Anne Frank Remembered, Misery, The Dark Half, The Color Purple, Shakespeare in Love, You've Got Mail, Muse.* Making reference to such elements of the film as plot, dialogue, voice-over, characters, images, and visual symbolism, write an essay that discusses the ways in which the film explores the inner world of the writer.

8. To learn more about this chapter's themes and for ideas for further research, explore the following Web sites:

COMPUTERS AND COMPOSITION WEB SITE
http://corax.cwrl.utexas.edu/cac/
This site for the journal edited by Gail Hawisher and Cynthia L. Selfe contains on-line articles about computers and writing, indexing both the journals *Computers and Composition* and *College Composition and Communication.*

DREAM JOURNALS AND LUCID DREAMING
http://www.spiritonline.com/dreams/journal.html
This page from the Spirit Online web site provides some helpful questions to ask while keeping a dream journal.

DREAM NETWORK
http://dreamnetwork.net
This is the web site for *Dream Network: A Quarterly Journal.* This on-line publication explores and interprets dreams and gives people a forum to share their ideas on dreams and dream journal keeping.

IMAGE-MAKING WITHIN THE WRITING PROCESS
http://www.unh.edu/ipssr/Lab/ImageM.html
This page from the Laboratory for Interactive Learning at the University of New Hampshire introduces a program for using image-making to enhance students' responses to reading and further their writing process.

JOURNALS AND DIARIES WEB SITE
http://207.158.243.119/html/journals_diaries.html
This personal site from Susan Martin contains helpful tips and techniques for keeping all kinds of journals and diaries, as well as links to other journaling sites.

HYPERTEST WRITER'S GUIDE
http://webserver.maclab.comp.uvic.ca/writersguide/welcome.
html
The Department of English of the University of Victoria, Canada, presents a lengthy alphabetical list and definitions of terms related to writing, grammar, and literature.

WRITING AS CREATIVE DESIGN
http://www.cogs.susx.ac.uk/users/mike/wa/writingdesign.html
In this essay posted on-line, Mike Sharples of the University of Sussex, England presents his ideas on creativity, cognition, and the writing process.

Discovering Ourselves in Reading

A dream which is not understood is like a letter which is not opened.

> The Talmud

Looking back, it's clear to me that I was reading as a creator, bringing myself. . . to a collaboration with the writer in the invention of an alternate world. These books were not collections of abstract symbols called words, printed on paper; they were real events that had happened to me.

> PETE HAMILL
> D'Artagnan on Ninth Street: A
> Brooklyn Boy at the Library

The imagination, which may appear to bear such individual fruit, is rooted in a compost of forgotten books.

> ELIZABETH BOWEN
> Out of a Book

RESPONDING TO READING THROUGH WRITING

When people read, they are concerned with self-discovery just as they are when they write and when they explore their dreams. Reading is a complex process that a reader controls consciously and also experiences unconsciously. In the act of reading, as in a conversation, a dialogue takes place between the voice of the inner self and the voice of the text that is being read. A good conversation with a text can lead to the development and clarification of the reader's values and ideas. At the same time, reading requires a more formal understanding of literary conventions and language codes.

Once absorbed in this complex mental process, a reader often identifies with the characters, the ideas, the emotions, and the cultural and social assumptions of the text. Readers then are able to experience new and different realities vicariously; these encounters can contribute to the reader's personal growth as they present new intellectual and emotional experiences that help readers to build their inner resources. As a person becomes a better reader and develops a richer life through reading, his or her writing may also become more fluent and varied, by way of the reader's becoming more conscious of public values, opinions, and cultures that are different from his or her personal experiences.

One of the most valuable ways to respond to what you read is through writing. Writing about what you read will help you to articulate and clarify your responses and will improve your writing as you develop your writer's voice through connecting to the words and thoughts of others. As with any form of writing, responses to reading can move through a series of phases or stages, each one building upon the next, moving gradually from prereading strategies to interpretation and evaluation.

Prereading/Early Reading

In the "prereading" phase you read "around" what you plan to read more carefully, browsing through titles, subheadings, noting epigraphs, topic sentences, headnotes and footnotes, just as you probably did when you first picked up this textbook. Prereading can be a very helpful process if you combine it with writing down basic questions that you have during this initial "browsing" stage. Does this work seem like fact or fiction? Was it written recently or in the distant past? Is its style experimental or traditional? Is the writer American or is he or she from a different culture and country? Is the writer male or female? Is the subject a familiar one? Do you need more background knowledge to understand the subject? Asking and answering such questions can help you to become involved with the text and can help to put you into a receptive frame of mind. After previewing the work, proceed to the second part of the first stage in reading, the "early reading" phase, in which, as in writing a first draft, you simply "plunge in," reading the work quickly to get an overall sense of its meaning, perhaps noting a few key passages or putting a question mark by an idea or detail that seems unfamiliar or confusing. At this stage of reading, avoid negative preconceptions about the content of the reading; don't tell yourself, "This is an essay or story about a subject in which I have absolutely no interest." Try instead to be open to the reading. Avoid evaluating the text before you give yourself a chance to become engaged with it.

Personal and Interpretive Response

In this second stage, the interpretive response phase, put the reading aside for a moment and write down a few immediate, personal reactions: Is this piece what I expected it to be? Did it make me angry? Sad? Elated? How did the piece challenge me? What didn't I understand after the first reading? Reread your notes and questions before attempting another reading. The second time, read more slowly and reflectively. Try to answer some of your initial questions as well as move toward an overview and interpretation of the piece as a whole—its "meaning," or your view of its meaning at this stage in your reading.

Look for those patterns that support an interpretation or view of the work: metaphors, plot and subplot, character relationships and conflicts, point of view, evolving persona, narrative voice. Mark your book, placing circles around and drawing lines to connect ideas and images that you believe form a pattern of meaning. Ask yourself how much of the work is meant to be responded to literally, and how much is meant to be considered as ironic or symbolic. Record responses to this stage of the reading process in writing, including some particular quotations and references to the text. Also compare your reactions at this stage of reading with your written responses to the first reading of the text. You will probably find that your ideas have deepened considerably and that you have a more complete and interpretive view of the work than you did initially.

Critical and Evaluative Response

For the third stage in your reading/writing process, the "critical" phase, reread the story again more rapidly, after reviewing your second written response and your textual references. Now write a final response, clarifying how this reading confirms, expands on, or causes you to question or revise your earlier readings. Using particular elements in the text that you noticed in your earlier readings as evidence, try to draw some larger evaluative conclusions about the work and your response to it: Is your overall response to the values, ideas, and emotions in the work positive or negative? How do you feel about the unity of the piece, its quality as writing? How do the values of this selection reflect or illuminate issues of concern to you and to your community? Was there something new and special about the experience of reading this work? Did it remind you of or seem to build upon other, similar works with which you are familiar? After finishing the text, did you want to read more by this writer or learn more about the theme of the work by reading related works by other writers? Would you recommend the work to other readers?

"Reading" Non-Print, Multimedia, and On-Line Texts

Although some theorists believe that the traditional act of reading is passé in this electronic age, the perceptual and critical thinking process for decoding, analyzing, interpreting, and evaluating materials that involve images along with printed words or even with no words at all is not as different from book reading as it might seem. Whether you are reading a book, watching a film, viewing a television show, or scrolling through Web pages, you need to pay close attention to all clues for meaning available. You will need to look for patterns of imagery, symbols, significant character interaction, plot-lines, and crucial meaning statements, whether in the form of speeches by characters, key bits of dialogue, or voice-overs (in the case of a film).

Whether reading a book, viewing a film, or examining a Web page, you also need to know something about the author (director/screenwriter, in the case of a film, or, in the case of many Web pages, the organization that has produced the page and its objectives). You need to know how this work builds on other works by the same writer or organization, what cultural assumptions and traditions (of writing, filmmaking, or multimedia) the work issues from.

Finally, whether you are reading a book, watching a film/TV show, or even cruising the Internet, you need to create the opportunity for a second reading/viewing, to get closer to the work through repeated exposure to grasp its full significance and to make interpretations and connections with other similar works. While this is easier and cheaper to do with a book, you can always watch a film a second time, take notes, videotape a TV show, or, in the case of Web pages, bookmark the page or save the text on disk for instant replay later on. Note that in non-print media or multi-media you have to learn to "read" visual images for intellectual suggestions and emotional impact, just as you examine the words in a written text closely for their connotations or shadings of meaning. In multimedia, you need to be alert to a complex interplay between words, images, and even sounds.

What makes a person a good reader, interpreter, and judge of electronic media is precisely the kind of habits of good study that an experienced reader brings to a book. You need to resist the passive mood many people sink into in front of or TV sets or the "surf" mentality that involves clicking rapidly and restlessly from one link to another on the Internet. When studying media, writing can be an especially helpful way to develop critical responses. Try keeping a journal of media you watch and respond actively to the media, using the kind of entries suggested above in the section on the reader's journal: preliminary responses and entries, interpretive entries, and evaluative entries for a repeated viewing of material that looks interesting. In this way, you can become a full reader—sensitive to the world of books as well as an able critic of the electronic media that surround us daily, which may seem at times to overwhelm our abilities to respond or even to take a position.

In reading and writing about the essays, stories, and poems selected for this textbook as well as the different media that you encounter, try to practice the slow, three-stage reading and written response process outlined above, taking time to write down questions and responses in your notebook and in the margins of the text. Give yourself enough time to absorb and think about what you have read and viewed. Your patience will yield you both heightened understanding as well as deeper pleasure in all your learning experiences.

THEMATIC INTRODUCTION: DISCOVERING OURSELVES IN READING

Reading can be an extremely active, intriguing, and creative process. While reading a text, you may notice omitted scenes and transitions or open-ended questions left unanswered by the author. While answering these questions, you are also writing your own text mentally, side by side with the author. As you become a more sophisticated reader, you may begin to use the questions raised by the texts you read as points of departure for your own interpretations of a work. As you continue to read and to reread a text, you will begin to see it from different perspectives, identifying with different characters and ideas, perceiving different elements as more important or dominant. The varying ways in which you respond to what you are reading reflects your growing process of understanding the text and yourself as a reader.

Each of the selections in this chapter presents a unique perspective on the way people read and interpret texts; each reflects on the ways that reading plays a part in the development of the reader's inner life and imagination. In the first selection, a meditative poem by Wallace Stevens, "The House Was Quiet and the World Was Calm," the speaker shows how a reader with a calm mind can come to feel like a part of a book that he or she is reading, suggesting too that meditation is essential to learning from a text. Richard Wright, in "The Library Card," also shares his passion for reading; he speaks of his inner awakening through the knowledge he uncovers in the books of great social writers of his time. Unlike the other writers in this chapter, Wright's struggle to find himself through reading was intensified and shaped by the fact that as a Southern black during the time of segregation, he had to lie in order to check books out from the library.

The three essays that follow present different perspectives on the changing nature of the reading experience in a highly technological age. In "Ruined by Reading: Books and the Movies," novelist Lynne Sharon Schwartz's lifelong fascination with reading fiction compels her to explain her strong reservations about making a great literary work into a film. A critic of the electronic media and a lover of books, English professor Sven Birkerts presents in "States of Reading" his reflections on the impact of the electronic media on the imaginative experience of solitary reading. In contrast, software executive Steven Holtzman argues in "Don't Look Back" that we can't turn our backs on technology, which is already an inextricable part of our lives and has changed our experience of reading and the nature of the book itself

Jorge Luis Borges's postmodernist short story "The Book of Sand" follows these essays on the nature of the reading experience. In this story the main character's obsession with the mysterious and monstrous Book of Sand leads the reader to ask questions about the nature of truth and reality.

Borges's narrator leaves us wondering if knowledge in books is like the sand of our imaginations, constantly shifting. The relationships between reading, imagination, interpretation, and creativity are also explored in the next poem, Denise Levertov's "The Secret." The poem's speaker reflects on the intimate relationship between reader and poet, suggesting that the words in a poem may produce ideas and feelings in the reader that the writer may not have consciously intended.

The two student essays included in this chapter also reflect on the power of reading. In "Hsao-suen: A Chinese Virtue," Caitlin Liu discusses the changing meanings of a Chinese folktale that she first heard as a child when she was taught the virtue of honoring one's parents. Lissy Goralnik's "The Sandstorm of Time and Knowledge" argues that Borges' story is about an inner journey to self-knowledge, which she believes is "the most important goal in life, and should drive us to read, to search, to journey, to converse, and to look in the mirror."

We hope that your journey through the readings in this chapter will help you to reflect on the universal yet changing nature of reading and become an adventure for your mind, your imagination, and your spirit.

Pierre-Auguste Renoir (1841–1919)
"Woman Reading" (1874–76)

Born in Limoges, France, Auguste Renoir was associated with the Impressionist movement in art at the time he painted "Woman Reading," a portrait of a young woman engaged in the act of reading. Renoir uses light in this painting to subtly illuminate both the woman's face and the book she is reading, which also seems to be a source of light through the reflection of the illumination radiating from a lamp or other light sources at the upper left side of the painting. The use of sparkling, yet gentle lighting in this painting is typical of Renoir's work during his Impressionist period, and creates a very relaxed, pleasurable image of the act of reading.

Ideas for Drawing, Writing, and Discussion

1. Do a drawing of yourself or another person reading that tries to capture your feelings about reading and the reading process.
2. Write a brief explanation of your drawing and the emotions brought up in it. Do you see reading as a pleasurable, creative process, or as challenging and possibly frustrating?
3. Divide into small groups and share your drawings and texts with your classmates, taking note of differences and similarities in representation and views of reading.

Wallace Stevens

"The House Was Quiet and the World Was Calm"

One of America's foremost poets of ideas, Wallace Stevens (1879–1955) was educated at Harvard University as a lawyer and spent most of his life working as an executive of the Hartford Accident and Indemnity Company. Stevens published his poetry in reviews, and his first book of poems, Harmonium, came out in 1923. He received national acclaim when he was awarded the Pulitzer Prize for his Collected Poems in 1954. Many of Stevens's poems explore the structured visions of the world provided by the arts. As you read the following poem, notice how it describes and attempts to recreate the kind of calm, meditative state that the reader of a book experiences at times.

JOURNAL

Describe the particular place or type of place where you feel the most comfortable reading.

The house was quiet and the world was calm.
The reader became the book; and summer night
Was like the conscious being of the book.
The house was quiet and the world was calm.

5   The words were spoken as if there was no book,
    Except that the reader leaned above the page,
    Wanted to lean, wanted much most to be
    The scholar to whom his book is true, to whom
    The summer night is like a perfection of thought.
10 The house was quiet because it had to be.
    The quiet was part of the meaning, part of the mind:
    The access of perfection to the page.
    And the world was calm. The truth in a calm world,
    In which there is no other meaning, itself
15 Is calm, itself is summer and night, itself
    Is the reader leaning late and reading there.

Questions for Discussion

1. How are quiet and calm a part of the meaning of the book being read in the poem? For example, if it had been "noisy," would the book have had a different meaning or would it have been read differently?
2. What is Stevens saying in the poem about the relationship between reading and truth? Does Stevens seem to believe there is any absolute truth to be derived from reading, or does he believe that truth through the poem is subjective, changeable?
3. Why is the summer night portrayed in the poem "like perfection of thought"? Have you ever thought of a quiet summer night in this way?
4. In line 5, the speaker says: "The words were spoken as if there was no book." Have you ever had the feeling that the words you read are "coming off the page," that they have begun to take on a life of their own?
5. Poems often contain ambiguities, that is, words, phrases, and lines that can be read in more than one way and which invite the reader to interpret them personally and imaginatively. Give examples of words, phrases, and lines in the poem that you consider ambiguous. Indicate some of the possible meanings you find in them, and discuss how the poem's ambiguity contributes to the comment it is making about the act of reading.

Connection

Compare and contrast the benefits of reading as described by Stevens with Levertov's view of reading in her poem "The Secret." In what ways are both poems concerned with truth, philosophy, and secrets?

IDEAS FOR WRITING

1. Have you ever read a book in the way that Stevens describes in his poem? Write a paper in which you describe your experience of reading a poem or story that is especially meaningful to you.
2. Argue for a different view of the reading experience than Stevens does. Is reading ever an active, noisy, jarring, imperfect, and tentative process?

Richard Wright

"The Library Card"

Richard Wright (1908–1960) grew up in an impoverished area of rural Mississippi. He moved to Chicago, then to New York, and eventually left the United States to live and write in France. Wright, who is best known for his novel Native Son *(1940), was considered the leading black author in the United States after its publication. He influenced James Baldwin and other black writers coming of age in the 1950s. His autobiography,* Black Boy *(1945), tells the story of his childhood in the segregated South of the 1920s and 1930s. In "The Library Card," a selection from his autobiography, Wright recounts his struggles to educate himself through reading books from the public library, to which he was denied access because of his skin color.*

JOURNAL

Write about a book that influenced your life, one that few of your friends bothered to read or even know about. How did it feel to have this special knowledge?

1   One morning I arrived early at work and went into the bank lobby where the Negro porter was mopping. I stood at a counter and picked up the Memphis *Commercial Appeal* and began my free reading of the press. I came finally to the editorial page and saw an article dealing with one H. L. Mencken. I knew by hearsay that he was the editor of the *American Mercury*, but aside from that I knew nothing about him. The article was a furious denunciation of Mencken, concluding with one, hot, short sentence: Mencken is a fool.

2   I wondered what on earth this Mencken had done to call down upon him the scorn of the South. The only people I had ever heard denounced in the South were Negroes, and this man was not a Negro. Then what ideas did Mencken hold that made a newspaper like the *Commercial Appeal* castigate him publicly? Undoubtedly he must be advocating ideas that the South did not like. Were there, then, people other than Negroes who criticized the South? I knew that during the Civil War the South had hated northern whites, but I had not encountered such hate during my

life. Knowing no more of Mencken than I did at that moment, I felt a vague sympathy for him. Had not the South, which had assigned me the role of a non-man, cast
at him its hardest words?

3   Now, how could I find out about this Mencken? There was a huge library near
the riverfront, but I knew that Negroes were not allowed to patronize its shelves any
more than they were the parks and playgrounds of the city. I had gone into the library several times to get books for the white men on the job. Which of them would
now help me to get books? And how could I read them without causing concern to
the white men with whom I worked? I had so far been successful in hiding my
thoughts and feelings from them, but I knew that I would create hostility if I went
about the business of reading in a clumsy way.

4   That afternoon I addressed myself to forging a note. Now, what were the names of
books written by H. L. Mencken? I did not know any of them. I finally wrote what I
thought would be a foolproof note: *Dear Madam: Will you please let this nigger boy*—
I used the word "nigger" to make the librarian feel that I could not possibly be the author of the note—*have some books by H. L. Mencken?* I forged the white man's name.

5   I entered the library as I had always done when on errand for whites, but I felt
that I would somehow slip up and betray myself. I doffed my hat, stood a respectful
distance from the desk, looked as unbookish as possible, and waited for the white patrons to be taken care of. When the desk was clear of people, I still waited. The
white librarian looked at me.

6   "What do you want, boy?"

7   As though I did not possess the power of speech, I stepped forward and simply
handed her the forged note, not parting my lips.

8   "What books by Mencken does he want?" she asked.

9   "I don't know, ma'am," I said, avoiding her eyes.

10   "Who gave you this card?"

11   "Mr. Falk," I said.

12   "Where is he?"

13   "He's at work, at the M—Optical Company," I said. "I've been in here for him
before."

14   "I remember," the woman said. "But he never wrote notes like this."

15   Oh, God, she's suspicious. Perhaps she would not let me have the books? If she
had turned her back at that moment, I would have ducked out the door and never
gone back. Then I thought of a bold idea.

16   "You can call him up, ma'am," I said, my heart pounding.

17   "You're not using these books, are you?" she asked pointedly.

18   "Oh, no, ma'am. I can't read."

19   "I don't know what he wants by Mencken," she said under her breath.

20   I knew now that I had won; she was thinking of other things and the race question had gone out of her mind. She went to the shelves. Once or twice she looked
over her shoulder at me, as though she was still doubtful. Finally she came forward
with two books in her hands.

21   "I'm sending him two books," she said. "But tell Mr. Falk to come in next time, or send me the names of the books he wants. I don't know what he wants to read."

22   I said nothing. She stamped the card and handed me the books. Not daring to glance at them, I went out of the library, fearing that that woman would call me back for further questioning. A block away from the library I opened one of the books and read a title: *A Book of Prefaces*. I was nearing my nineteenth birthday and I did not know how to pronounce the word "preface." I thumbed the pages and saw strange words and strange names. I shook my head, disappointed, looked at the other book; it was called *Prejudices*. I knew what that word meant; I had heard it all my life. And right off I was on guard against Mencken's books. Why would a man want to call a book *Prejudices*? The word was so stained with all my memories of racial hate that I could not conceive of anybody using it for a title. Perhaps I had made a mistake about Mencken? A man who had prejudices must be wrong.

23   When I showed the books to Mr. Falk, he looked at me and frowned.

24   "That librarian might telephone you," I warned him.

25   "That's all right," he said. "But when you're through reading those books, I want you to tell me what you get out of them."

26   That night in my rented room, while letting the hot water run over my can of pork and beans in the sink, I opened *A Book of Prefaces* and began to read. I was jarred and shocked by the style, the clear, clean, sweeping sentences. Why did he write like that? And how did one write like that? I pictured the man as a raging demon, slashing with his pen, consumed with hate, denouncing everything American, extolling everything European or German, laughing at the weaknesses of people, mocking God, authority. What was this? I stood up, trying to realize what reality lay behind the meaning of the words. . . Yes, this man was fighting, fighting with words. He was using words as a weapon, using them as one would use a club. Could words be weapons? Well, yes, for here they were. Then, maybe, perhaps, I could use them as a weapon? No. It frighten me. I read on and what amazed me was not what he said, but how on earth anybody had the courage to say it.

27   Occasionally I glanced up to reassure myself that I was alone in the room. Who were these men about whom Mencken was talking so passionately? Who was Anatole France? Joseph Conrad? Sinclair Lewis, Sherwood Anderson, Dostoevski, George Moore, Gustave Flaubert, Maupassant, Tolstoy, Frank Harris, Mark Twain, Thomas Hardy, Arnold Bennett, Stephen Crane, Zola, Norris, Gorky, Bergson, Ibsen, Balzac, Bernard Shaw, Dumas, Poe, Thomas Mann, O. Henry, Dreiser, H. G. Wells, Gogol, T. S. Eliot, Gide, Baudelaire, Edgar Lee Masters, Stendhal, Turgenev, Huneker, Nietzsche, and scores of others? Were these men real? Did they exist or had they existed? And how did one pronounce their names?

28   I ran across many words whose meanings I did not know, and I either looked them up in a dictionary or, before I had a chance to do that, encountered the word in a context that made its meaning clear. But what strange world was this? I concluded the book with the conviction that I had somehow overlooked something terribly important in life. I had once tried to write, had once reveled in feeling, had let my crude imagination roam, but the impulse to dream had been slowly beaten out of me by ex-

perience. Now it surged up again and I hungered for books, new ways of looking and seeing. It was not a matter of believing or disbelieving what I read, but of feeling something new, of being affected by something that made the look of the world different.

29   As dawn broke I ate my pork and beans, feeling dopey, sleepy. I went to work, but the mood of the book would not die; it lingered, coloring everything I saw, heard, did. I now felt that I knew what the white men were feeling. Merely because I had read a book that had spoken of how they lived and thought, I identified myself with that book. I felt vaguely guilty. Would I, filled with bookish notions, act in a manner that would make the whites dislike me?

30   I forged more notes and my trips to the library became frequent. Reading grew into a passion. My first serious novel was Sinclair Lewis's *Main Street*. It made me see my boss, Mr. Gerald, and identify him as an American type. I would smile when I saw him lugging his golf bags into the office. I had always felt a vast distance separating me from the boss, and now I felt closer to him, though still distant. I felt now that I knew him, that I could feel the very limits of his narrow life. And this had happened because I had read a novel about a mythical man called George F. Babbitt.

31   The plots and stories in the novels did not interest me so much as the point of view revealed. I gave myself over to each novel without reserve, without trying to criticize it; it was enough for me to see and feel something different. And for me, everything was something different. Reading was like a drug, a dope. The novels created moods in which I lived for days. But I could not conquer my sense of guilt, my feeling that the white men around me knew that I was changing, that I had begun to regard them differently.

32   Whenever I brought a book to the job, I wrapped it in newspaper—a habit that was to persist for years in other cities and under other circumstances. But some of the white men pried into my packages when I was absent and they questioned me.

33   "Boy, what are you reading those books for?"

34   "Oh, I don't know, sir."

35   "That's deep stuff you're reading, boy."

36   "I'm just killing time, sir."

37   "You'll addle your brains if you don't watch out."

38   I read Dreiser's *Jennie Gerhardt* and *Sister Carrie* and they revived in me a vivid sense of my mother's suffering; I was overwhelmed. I grew silent, wondering about the life around me. It would have been impossible for me to have told anyone what I derived from these novels, for it was nothing less than a sense of life itself. All my life had shaped me for the realism, the naturalism of the modern novel, and I could not read enough of them.

39   Steeped in new moods and ideas, I bought a ream of paper and tried to write; but nothing would come, or what did come was flat beyond telling. I discovered that more than desire and feeling were necessary to write and I dropped the idea. Yet I still wondered how it was possible to know people sufficiently to write about them? Could I ever learn about life and people? To me, with my vast ignorance, my Jim Crow station in life, it seemed a task impossible of achievement. I now knew what being a Negro meant. I could endure the hunger. I had learned to live with hate. But to feel that

there were feelings denied me, that the very breath of life itself was beyond my reach, that more than anything else hurt, wounded me. I had a new hunger.

40   In buoying me up, reading also cast me down, made me see what was possible, what I had missed. My tension returned, new, terrible, bitter, surging, almost too great to be contained. I no longer *felt* that the world about me was hostile, killing; I *knew* it. A million times I asked myself what I could do to save myself, and there were no answers. I seemed forever condemned, ringed by walls.

41   I knew of no Negroes who read the books I liked and I wondered if any Negroes ever thought of them. I knew that there were Negro doctors, lawyers, newspapermen, but I never saw any of them. When I read a Negro newspaper I never caught the faintest echo of my preoccupation in its pages. I felt trapped and occasionally, for a few days, I would stop reading. But a vague hunger would come over me for books, books that opened up new avenues of feeling and seeing, and again I would forge another note to the white librarian. Again I would read and wonder as only the naïve and unlettered can read and wonder, feeling that I carried a secret, criminal burden about with me each day.

QUESTIONS FOR DISCUSSION

1. Why does Wright want to learn about Mencken? When Wright finally reads Mencken, how is he affected? What does he learn about words and about courage from reading Mencken? How does reading Mencken change his day-to-day life?

2. How does Wright manage to check out books despite the restrictions? How would you feel if, like Wright, you were not allowed to check books out of the public library?

3. As Wright gets more involved in reading, how is his understanding of himself, of his friends and supervisors, of the world in which he lives, changed? Does he seem to be more accepting or less accepting of his life? Why does Wright find reading satisfying?

4. What effect does Wright's reading have on his desire to write? Why is it difficult for him to write, despite the "new ideas and moods" he is exposed to?

5. What is the nature of the "secret criminal burden" that Wright feels he carries around as a result of his reading? What do you think it would take for Wright to ease his burden?

6. Describe the work of a writer whom you felt was "fighting with words. . . using words as a weapon." How did you feel about his or her style?

CONNECTION

Compare and contrast Wright's experience of reading with the experience of reading as described by Birkerts.

IDEAS FOR WRITING

1. Write an essay in which you discuss a writer whose work has had an important impact on your changing self-concept and values.

2. Write an essay about an experience of alienation from your familiar surroundings and associates that came to you through reading. Have you
   ever found that gaining new insights from reading has made you feel
   alienated from the people and community around you? How did you integrate this new awareness into your lifestyle and way of thinking?

Lynne Sharon Schwartz

"Ruined by Reading: Books and the Movies"

*Born in 1939 in Brooklyn, New York, Lynne Sharon Schwartz received a B.A. from
Barnard in 1959, an M.A. from Bryn Mawr College in l961, and worked toward
her Ph.D. at New York University (1967–72). She has taught writing at many col-
leges, including Hunter College, University of Iowa, Columbia University, and the
University of Hawaii. Schwartz has received many awards for her writing: a National
Endowment for the Arts Fellowship, a Guggenheim Fellowship, and a New York
State Foundation for the Arts Fellowship. She is an author of short stories, novels,
and poetry:* Disturbances in the Field *(1983),* Acquainted with the Night and
Other Stories *(1984),* Leaving Brooklyn *(1990),* The Fatigue Artist *(1995),
and* A Lynne Sharon Schwartz Reader: Selected Poetry and Prose *(1992). Her
writing is distinguished for its focus on urban, East Coast family life. The following
selection is drawn from Schwartz's recent memoir,* Ruined by Reading *(1997),
which explores her lifelong fascination with books and the act of reading.*

JOURNAL

Write about a film that you have seen that was based on a book that you read.
Did the film measure up to the book? Did its images stand on their own? Why or
why not?

1   Maybe that early impulse to possess the books I loved by copying them is what
moviemakers feel. Ever more avidly, they have been dusting off old books like
costumes found in the attic, to rip them apart at the seams and redesign them for
their screens. I'm aware that money is a powerful motive here, but I like to think
love plays a part as well. Certainly love, of the reverential kind, inspired the "Masterpiece Theatre" television series, which brought us the likes of Henry James and
Jane Austen in living color, with fatherly Alastair Cooke as mediator: he would explain the subtle points and refresh our memories week to week, like the little summaries heading each serialized novel installment in the women's magazines.
"Masterpiece Theatre" had its charms—Purcell's heraldic trumpet music summoning us to the TV set, the camera panning over those dignified leather bindings, and

the Sunday night time slot, which gave the sense of starting the week on a virtuous note—and yet the aura of pomp made for distance. Great books are best enjoyed as intimates, not decked out in regal trappings. Did *The Golden Bowl* find more readers as a result of its TV excursion? Or did relieved viewers heave a sigh: Well, now I know what that's all about, I don't have to read it. Is it "better" to have seen the televised version than never to have encountered James at all? Assuming, that is, that watching television can in any sense be an encounter with James, the writer.

2   One way or another, "Of making many books there is no end," according to Ecclesiastes, and of making movies out of books there seems no end either. I get a bit edgy whenever I hear of yet another one being remodeled for film. Edgy not so much over what "they" will do to or with it, but rather over what I will do. "Are you going to see *A Little Princess?*" a friend inquires. Certainly not, is my visceral reply, but I pretend to think it over. And while pretending, I do in fact think. Why this intransigence, this unlovely refusal? For I can't bring myself to see the film version of *A Little Princess* any more than I could *Mr. and Mrs. Bridge* or *Housekeeping* or *The Heart Is a Lonely Hunter,* no matter how "faithful" of "sensitive" they are reputed to be. The terse chapters of Evan Connell's *Mr. Bridge* and *Mrs. Bridge,* an accumulation of searing episodes in limpid, uninflected sentences, seem especially uncongenial to movie treatment. Movies are pictures in motion, not designed to shape a patient and dazzling mosaic. And *Housekeeping* stays with me as an underwater dream, not something I would want to see dredged onto solid earth.

3   Least of all could I see *The Heart Is a Lonely Hunter,* which I read as an adolescent. Like *The Little Mermaid,* it turns on the ambiguities of speech, as well as the ramifying issues of human connection—nothing to do with the visual. Together with McCullers's troubled characters, I imagined the silence of Mr. Singer (canny name for a deaf-mute) as richly comprehending, a salvation from loneliness. I had fantasies of telling him my secrets too, and having them finally understood. What a shock to find that his all-embracing acceptance was pure silence—blank and neutral. That all along we had been talking to ourselves. It cast doubt even on those who give us back words: can we ever be understood? Or is language only an elaborate sustaining lie, every sentence a soliloquy? I knew even then I would have to pursue it anyway, but I could never again be quite sure my words weren't falling on deaf ears.

4   Despite all that, I don't much care for my purism about filmed books. Or any purism, for that matter. What is it afraid of? What am I afraid of? The most ready answer is that I want to keep my own images, not have them replaced by a set designer's, nor have the characters take on the forms of actors I've seen before and will see again in other roles. A book's characters are not hollow molds to be filled by living flesh. They have more permanent forms—they are already embodied in words.

5   A commonplace objection, and cogent enough on the face of it, except it doesn't stand up to experience. In unsuccessful books-into-films, the images are usually too weak to do lasting harm. And in the successful ones I've been dragged to see—*Great Expectations, Howards End,* Jean Rhys's *Quartet,* or Waugh's *A Handful of Dust* (obviously I'm not as pure as I'm claiming to be)—the actors for the most part "fit" the characters well. Even so, their images faded fast, leaving the books—my versions of

the books—intact. The only film that has left its actors indelibly fixed in my mind is *Billy Budd,* and not a bad thing, as it turns out. My own imaging apparatus couldn't do better than Terence Stamp as the hapless Billy or Robert Ryan as Claggart (killed, I must constantly remind myself), not to mention Melvyn Douglas as the old Dansker and Peter Ustinov as Captain Vere; I feel quite comfortable with their faces shimmering through Melville's words. Meanwhile, *The Dead,* John Huston's triumph of literal and literary faithfulness, has all but vanished from my memory, leaving only an aura of truth, of Joyceness made visible. And perhaps that is as it should be. What must be conserved, after all, is not the integrity of the reader's vision but of the writer's. And since film is a flight of images through time, it is fitting that they should fly off, leaving the vision that is beyond ordinary imaging.

6   Which makes me wonder if I visualize at all as I read: Terrence Stamp and Robert Ryan have not really replaced anything I can recall. Some readers may run their own private films as each page turns, but I seem to have only spotty fleeting images, a floaty gown, a sofa, a grand ballroom, or a patch of landscape. Language, that is, may lend itself to visual translation, but does not require it. It is its own universe of sound, rhythm, and connotation, which generate the occasional visual flare.

7   Not all books live by language or style, though: a host of other virtues—plot, situation, character, suspense, topical relevance—may keep them afloat. Galsworthy's *Forsyte Saga* or Armistead Maupin's *Tales of the City* fall into that genre and have made spectacular television series; I would have to be absurdly pure not to enjoy them. (*The Forsyte Saga* was so vivid that the actor Eric Porter could travel to remote parts of the world and find himself hailed on the street as Soames Forsyte. When he died recently I felt as if the unhappy Soames had died—a greater tribute, alas, than the actor might have wished.) In yet another genre, these days, are books written with the movie version in mind. But they are not properly books at all, just prefabricated scripts.

8   I've heard a thousand times that ours is a visual age. But I cannot uproot my passion for words for fashion's sake, even if I wanted to. I suppose what I fear is that movies, however ambitious and excellent, can never do for me what a book can do. (I seem, unwillingly or unwittingly, to have worked my way back to my—or my father's—ancient opposition of language and pictures. A picture is not worth a thousand words; it is worth only itself, as are the thousand words.) Films, to grant them their tony name, are an art form, but in my heart a movie is still a movie, an entertainment, a voyage in the dark, a plush seat, a bag of popcorn, Technicolor, air-conditioning, the most luscious of escapes. I do not ask that it feed my soul, only my fancy. When it does feed my soul—more often than I expect—I am surprised and grateful. Still, its words are not crucial or even many; new movies, with their visual elegance and slender scripts, use fewer words than ever. I know I should follow the story through the images, or rather follow the story *of* the images. But where, I keep wondering, is the story of the story?

9   It's clear even to me that my judgment is off the mark: movies are not competing with books but offering something else, a different sort of story. Why can't I appreciate each on its own terms? Because when I've read the book, I stubbornly don't want

anything else. Why should I, when I've had the real thing, as originally conceived? Form and content are inseparable, and Greta Garbo, bewitching as she is, is not the Anna Karenina Tolstoy envisioned. If the form changes, the content must change.

10   Well, so what? Perhaps what I am afraid of is change itself. As if *Anna Karenina* could not withstand an ephemeral change! Can it be that I don't trust the works enough, that I secretly think them too flimsy to survive their adaptations? They are sturdier than I give them credit for. It must be my own responses that are not so sturdy: yes, there is always the danger that *they* might change on seeing an adaptation. So I catch myself out. Unwilling, it seems, to risk a new thought or feeling—like the people who won't read books in the first place, or yank them off the library shelves to protect the innocent.

11   Few, if any, stories are pure invention. Invention needs something to invent from, or with. Stories come from history, or from reality—lived or observed—or, as any quick survey will show, from other stories. But by my petulant logic I would refuse to see Racine's *Phèdre*, and Martha Graham's too. I would have to forswear much of Shakespeare, as well as *West Side Story* and Tennyson's *Ulysses* or Joyce's for that matter, not to mention Tchaikovsky's *Romeo and Juliet* and the host of paintings on classical themes, and on and on to absurdity.

12   Imagination is the refiner's fire; the sensibility of each new generation is the lens. Everything made has been transformed, just as language itself is translation from the inarticulate chaos within. To be a purist about adaptation is to attempt to halt an endlessly evolving process midway.

13   I didn't expect to argue a piece of my mind away. I should repent and repair to the movies. To *A Little Princess*. But will I have the courage?

QUESTIONS FOR DISCUSSION

1. What positive motives does Lynne Sharon Schwartz attribute to those who make novels or short stories into films?

2. Why is Schwartz reluctant to go to films or watch TV adaptations made from books she has read, despite the good intentions of film makers?

3. How does Schwartz differentiate between reading and film viewing? Which process does she value more, and why? Do you agree or disagree with her point of view?

4. Why is Schwartz critical of her own purist position about adaptation of books into films? Why does she conclude with the question about going to see the film version of the *A Little Princess*: "Will I have the courage?"

5. What does Schwartz mean by her comment that "a book's characters are not hollow molds to be filled by living flesh. They have more permanent forms—they are already embodied in words." Do you agree with this perception of the characters in books and films?

6. At the end of the essay, Schwartz seems to have changed her original rejecting position in response to films : "I didn't expect to argue a piece of

my mind away." Is this an effective strategy, or does it weaken the strength of the essay?

CONNECTION

Compare the ways in which Schwartz and Birkerts view the differences between reading books and the "screen" experience so common in modern life. Which writer is more accepting of the newer media?

IDEAS FOR WRITING

1. Read a short novel or a story that has also been made into a movie. After seeing the movie version, compare and contrast the written text and the film version. Did you prefer the film or the text version? Draw on some of Schwartz's insights into the differences between the two media to support your responses.
2. Although Schwartz concedes that books and films are different media, she continues to believe that something vital is always lost in the transition of a book to the screen. Write an essay on this issue. Do you agree with Schwartz, or can the two versions complement one another?

Sven Birkerts

"States of Reading"

Born in 1951 in Michigan, Sven Birkerts earned his B.A. at the University of Michigan in 1973. He worked as a bookstore clerk in Cambridge from 1973–1983 and was a lecturer in expository writing at Harvard University from 1984–1991. Birkerts also has taught at Emerson College and at Mount Holyoke College. Not a follower of academic theories, he began his writing career as an "amateur" literary critic, receiving a citation for excellence in reviewing for the National Book Critics Circle in 1986. His critical essays have been published in New Republic *and* Boston Review, *and his recent books include* American Energies *(1992),* The Gutenberg Elegies *(1994), and* Tolstoy's Dictaphone *(1996). Birkerts has risen to prominence as a critic of electronic technology's impact on our appreciation of books and on the reading process itself. These concerns are evident in the following essay from* Readings *(1999). In "States of Reading," Birkerts describes the reading process as a "collaborative bringing forth of an entire world."*

JOURNAL

Write about your state of mind when you are immersed in and enjoying a novel or long story. How does this mental state differ from ordinary consciousness, or from the frame of mind you are in when watching television or cruising the Internet?

---

1   IN THE opening pages of his coy and crafty novel *If on a Winter's Night a Traveler*, Italo Calvino performs what for any true reader has to feel like a striptease. Or maybe the beginning overtures of what will turn into a full-out seduction. In any event, there is a sense of excited approach, an almost titillating enumeration of the stages by which a reader gets ready to engage a book. "Adjust the light so you won't strain your eyes," he croons. "Do it now, because once you're absorbed in reading there will be no budging you." And: "Try to foresee now everything that might make you interrupt your reading. Cigarettes within reach, if you smoke, and the ashtray. Anything else? Do you have to pee? All right, you know best."

2   Calvino continues, building tension now by tracking back to the moments just after the reader's purchase of the book in question. Familiar sensations: "You are at the wheel of your car, waiting at a traffic light, you take the book out of the bag, rip off the transparent wrapping, start reading the first lines. A storm of honking breaks over you. . . "

3   Then: "Yes, you are in your room, calm; you open the book to page one, no, to the last page, first you want to see how long it is."

4   And: "You turn the book over in your hands, you scan the sentences on the back of the jacket. . . Of course, this circling of the book, too, this reading around it before reading inside it, is part of the pleasure in a new book, but like all preliminary pleasures, it has its optimal duration if you want it to serve as a thrust toward the more substantial pleasure of the consummation of the act, namely, the reading of the book." So Calvino guides his chapter to conclusion, the conclusion being, in effect, the reader's excited haste to turn the page to begin. The paradox is suddenly evident: we are reading about getting ready to read, taking part in the tensions of deferral, even as we breached our own deferral pages ago. All of this is clever and could be shown to be more deeply intriguing, but what interests me is not metafictional self-reflexiveness, but something else: simply that all of this tantalization, this spirited foreplay, is possible only where there exists a shared assumption—that the state we achieve when immersed in a novel is powerful, pleasure-inducing, and very nearly hypnotic. ("Adjust the light," he coaxes, "because once you're absorbed in reading there will be no budging you.")

5   As striptease can work its thrills only on the understanding that the forbidden fruit, the corpora delectable, is right there, under the shimmer of coverings, so Calvino can toy with us in this way only because we know what a transformation of consciousness a successful—that is, *immersed*—reading act accomplishes.

6   Reading—and I will speak of it here in its realized mode—is *not* a continuation of the daily by other means. It is not simply another thing one does, like gathering up the laundry, pondering a recipe, checking the tire pressure, or even talking to a friend on the telephone. Reading is a change of state, a change of state of a very particular sort. And while this can be talked about, it seldom is. Who know why?

7   Several things happen when we move via the first string of words from our quotidian world into the realm of the written. We experience almost immediately a transposition—perhaps an expansion, perhaps a condensation—of our customary perception of reality. We shift our sense of time from our ordinary, sequential, clockface awareness to a quasi-timeless sense of suspension, that sublime forgetting of the grid sometimes called duration. Finally, and no less significantly, we find ourselves instantly and implicitly changing our apprehension of the meaning structure of the world.

8   I would like to explore this transition by looking at the opening passage of Saul Bellow's novel *Humboldt's Gift:*

> The book of ballads published by Von Humboldt Fleisher in the Thirties was an immediate hit. Humboldt was just what everyone had been waiting for. Out in the Midwest I had certainly been waiting eagerly, I can tell you that. An avant-garde writer, the first of a new generation, he was handsome, fair, large, serious, witty, he was learned. The guy had it all. All the papers reviewed his book. His picture appeared in *Time* without insult and in *Newsweek* with praise. I read *Harlequin Ballads* enthusiastically. I was a student at the University of Wisconsin and thought about nothing but literature day and night. Humboldt revealed to me new ways of doing things. I was ecstatic. I envied his luck, his talent, and his fame, and I went east in May to have a look at him—perhaps to get next to him. The Greyhound bus, taking the Scranton route, made the trip in about fifty hours. That didn't matter. The bus windows were open. I had never seen real mountains before. Trees were budding. It was like Beethoven's *Pastorale.* I felt showered by the green, within.

9   Bellow's Charlie Citrine goes on for nearly five hundred pages, but I will stop here—not to make any point about the novel, its characters, or conflicts, but to ask: How is my inwardness, my consciousness, different while I'm reading from whatever it was the instant before I began?

10   Most obviously, the formerly dissipated field of my awareness has been suddenly and dramatically channeled. My attention is significantly, then almost entirely, captured by the voice and what it is telling me. Charlie's confidential tone immediately captures me, replacing whatever cadences I had been thinking in. "An avant-garde writer, the first of a new generation, he was handsome, fair, large, serious, witty, he was learned. The guy had it all." My thought becomes Citrine's, my rhythms and instincts his—I change.

11   With the shift in momentum and focus comes an alteration in time frame. All the divisions and chronologies of the daily present are submerged beneath the timeless awareness of events unfolding as they must. Reading even a few of Bellow's sentences, we feel ourselves entering the duration world of the tale, the same world that fireside listeners stepped into when the tribal teller began to summon up the other place of the narrative.

12   Along with this altered sense of time—bound up with it—comes a condensation of reality. Things are linked each to each through association, not physical or chronological proximity. Months, never mind days, are elided in the space of a

breath: "I envied his luck, his talent, and his fame, and I went east in May to have a look at him—perhaps to get next to him. The Greyhound bus taking the Scranton route . . ." Reality—dull, obstacle-laden reality, which moves all too often at the pace of an intravenous dripper—is reconfigured by the imagination—speeded up, harmonized, made efficient—and served back to us in a far more palatable state, appealing in the extreme.

13   Finally—and my categories are necessarily imprecise—the words, even in so small an excerpt as I cited, change what I call the meaning structure of the world. To follow Citrine fully, as we long to do, we agree to the core requirement of any work of creative literature that we put ourselves in the hands of a self, a sensibility, that will front life with an original and uncorrected passion, that we will allow this self to dictate its understanding of the world to us. We must adopt Citrine's worldview as our own for the duration of the novel. This acceptance on our part is, I believe, the most important and profound consequence of the literary encounter.

14   The meaning structure of the world is, for most of us, experienced as an imprecise and mainly unfocused mingling of thoughts and perceptions. Strands of meaning are as if woven through expanses of seemingly unconnected elements—things observed carefully or obliquely, fitfully attended to or ignored. The upshot, unless we feel a powerful call to something higher and possess the discipline to strive constantly toward it, is that we greet the world outside of our immediate sphere of concern as a chaos essentially beyond our grasp, as an event the meaning of which will be disclosed to us later, if ever. The constant deferral of significance is the operative principle of most lives: tomorrow, next week—I'll think about it, I'll figure it out—not right now.

15   The meaning structure of a novel is absolutely different. Using condensation, moving in an altogether different medium of time, the author creates an artifact that is, in certain striking ways, a semblance of life, but with this exception: *everything* in the novel points toward *meaning*. Every sentence, every meaning observation, every turn of events serves an aesthetic and intellectual purpose. The novel smelts contingency and returns it as meaning.

16   We can see this distinction, between the outer world of reality and the inner world of the text, even in the act of reading, the way we read. In one of the most famous passages in his *Confessions*, Saint Augustine professes his astonishment at seeing Saint Ambrose reading a text without moving his lips. Augustine lived from A.D. 354 to 430, and his simple observation suggests something essential about the evolution of reading. It has gone inward. Reading aloud is common practice these days mainly with children, illiterate adults, or those who cannot, owing to some infirmity, read for themselves. To accompany your reading with silent lip motions is to signal that you may have only the most tenuous grasp on vocabulary and syntax.

17   This transition from exterior vocalizing to silent but perceptible lip movement to an interiority indicated outwardly only by the back and forth shuttling of the eyes signifies a considerable augmentation of the power of the reading act. So long as there are still lip motions, there exists a bridge between the world conjured on the page and the exterior realm. But when those motions cease, then the reader simulta-

neously represents two opposed kinds of presence. One is the physical, the actual—that which occupies space and can be located; the other is the invisible, the unreal—that which happens vividly in the imagination and cannot be fathomed or legislated by any other person. Silent reading, then, is the very signature—the emblem—of subjectivity. The act of reading creates for us a world within a world—indeed, a world within a hollow sphere, the two of them moving not only at different rates, but also, perhaps, counter to one another.

18   The tension between outer and inner is sharpened by the fact that when readers are fully absorbed in a book and the ulterior world it presents, their awareness of solid reality is supplanted by awareness of what the imagination is experiencing. Then, truly, the stubborn surfaces we live among become figments—a paradoxical transformation, since most of the people who discredit the practice of reading, particularly of novels, do so because the contents of the books are seen to be not-real, mere figments. These reading skeptics mistakenly assume that reading attempts to carry on the business of living by other—suspiciously intangible—means. They seldom consider that reading involves a change of state, that it is a sudden, and at times overwhelming, modification of the quotidian.

19   Changes of state. I believe increasingly that this, and mainly this, is the core mission of artistic writing. We go to such writing, engage it, not because it is an adjunct or a supplement to our daily living, but because it allows us the illusion of departure from it. I am not talking merely about bored commuters losing themselves in books by Tom Clancy or John Grisham, but of the somewhat more exalted pattern of departure and return effected by more serious novels. A work of art has done its deeper work when it starts to feel like arrival.

20   Everyone knows that Plato, in the tenth book of his *Republic*, proposed to banish the poets from the ideal State he was envisaging. At the conclusion of his argument he has Socrates say to Glaucon:

> we must remain firm in our conviction that hymns to the gods and praises of famous men are the only poetry which ought to be admitted into our State. For if you go beyond this and allow the honeyed muse to enter, either in epic or lyric verse, not law and the reason of mankind, which by common consent have ever been deeded best, but pleasure and pain will be the rulers in our State.

21   I would agree, I think, that the poet—the artist/writer—poses a threat to the State, at least to the State as Plato thinks of it—which is as a Republic, or "res publica," or "thing of the people"—but not on account of emotional persuasiveness. Rather, the artist is a threat because the effect of art, no matter what its ostensible subject might be, is to alter the relation to experience, to affect a change of state—and the main point of the new relation is not to clarify concrete matters in the here and now, but to propose an understanding that transcends the here and now. The experience is fundamentally asocial, for it directs preoccupation away from the *what* and *how* of daily business toward the *why*, the mere asking of which marks separation from the quotidian, if not yet transcendence. A social order founded on the

question *why*, and the relation to things it implies, would not sustain the headlong consumerism we think of as the only possible option these days.

22   No matter how I try to come at it, my conception of the aesthetic experience—the reading experience—involves, at its core, a transfer between subjectivities; not a simple passing of contents from one subjective "I" to another. Writers are artists precisely to the extent that they use the transformative agency of imagination to surpass personality—the contingent attributes of identity—in order to get at what can be said to exist behind the jumble of appearances: some version of truth that results when the artist has disinterestedly reckoned the forces that underlie psychological, social, or other kinds of relationships.

23   I realize that the critical orthodoxy of our era repudiates this possibility of underlying universals, upholding instead the relativism, the constructedness, of all experience. Yet the reader's self—dare I say, *soul*—and the fact of his engagement with the literary work refutes this version of things. Whether that reader is immersed in Jane Austen, Joseph Conrad, Jane Smiley, or Saul Bellow, the immersion is attained only in part by stylistic power and the presentation of specific situational elements. The true bond is the reader's conviction that beyond all particulars, standing as the very ground and air of the work, is the writer's willing of a supporting world in its entirety. And this willing, which is at the same time an understanding, is achieved only through a complete and possessive act of imagination. It is finally this ability—and determination—to internalize a world that marks the literary artist. Never mind whether it is the world stretching away behind Samuel Beckett's Molloy, Vladimir Nabokov's Pnin, Jane Austen's Emma, or Bellow's Charlie Citrine.

24   When we begin reading *Humboldt's Gift*, or most any other novel, we expend an enormous energy. Only part of this goes toward understanding character, setting, and the details of situation. The rest represents an energy of erasure, of self-silencing. We suspend our sense of the world at large, bracket it off, in order that the author's implicit world may declare itself: "The book of ballads published by Von Humboldt Fleisher in the Thirties was an immediate hit. Humboldt was just what everyone had been waiting for. Out in the Midwest I had certainly been waiting eagerly, I can tell you that." Already it begins. The words make a voice, and the voice begins to sound in our auditory imagination, and as we enter the book we move from hearing the voice to listening to it. And to listen is to surrender self-thoughts, impinging awarenesses, and judgments; to listen is to admit a stance, a vantage, a world other than our own. Of course we do not succeed entirely. Of course the author's world bears a number of features that we project from our own irrepressible sense of things. But the interior transfer is profound nonetheless.

25   Reading, in this very idealized portrayal, is not simply an inscribing of the author's personal subjectivity upon a reader's receptivity. Rather, it is the collaborative bringing forth of an entire world, a world complete with a meaning structure. For hearing completes itself in listening, and listening happens only where there is some subjective basis for recognition. The work is not merely the bridge between author and reader; it is an enabling entity. The text is a pretext. The writer needs the idea

of audition—of readers—in order to begin the creative process that gets him beyond the immediate, daily perception of things. In this one sense, the writer does not bring forth the work so much as the work, the idea of it, brings the writer to imaginative readiness. The finished work, the whole of it, then enables the reader to project a sensible and meaningful order of reality, one that might be initially at odds with the habitual relation to things. Writer and reader make a circuit—complete—outside the entanglements of the social contract.

26   This account of reading is not the majority view. Nor is it in any way self-evident. I don't know if it ever was, but certainly we have trouble thinking this way now. In our time the artistic experience has been compromised on all fronts. For one thing, there is not the belief in art—in literature especially—that existed in previous epochs. We don't, most of us, trust in the transformative power of artistic vision. And lacking the trust, we not only seek it out less, but we are less apt to open ourselves to it when there is a chance.

27   Then, too, there are fewer strong creations—true works of art that arrive on the page for the right reasons, that have not been deformed by the pressures of the marketplace. One can advance all sorts of reasons for this, including prominently the sheer difficulty of creating a world implicitly coherent when our own is so evidently incoherent. True artists—regardless of their subject or its epoch—are still required to grasp the forms and forces that make the reality of the present.

28   Third—and there are many other factors—is the climate of distractedness and envelops us. The world is too much here, too complex, is transected by too many competing signals. We don't believe in sense, in explanatory meaning, in the same way we once did. We are losing our purchase on time—not just the serene leisure required for reading, but also our vestigial awareness of that other time—unstructured duration time—that is the sustaining element of all art. For it is only in the durational mode that we can grasp that noncontingent relation to experience, the perception that used to be called "under the aspect of eternity"— the seeing of life in a way that acknowledges as its foundation the mystery of the *fact* of existence.

29   Then there is the effect that electronic technologies are having on writing and reading. This, while indirect, may be the chief one: that these technologies are, in their capacity as mediating tools, dissolving a sense of time that was until quite recently the human norm. Screen transactions not only make possible a fractured and layered and accelerated relation to time, they *require* it. They train us to a new set of expectations, even as the various complex demands of our living remove us further from the naturally contoured day. Reading of the kind that I have been describing cannot survive in such a climate as we are manufacturing for ourselves. The one hope is that reading will, instead of withering away in the glare of a hundred million screens, establish itself as a kind of preserve, a figurative place where we can go when the self needs to make contact with its sources.

30   It could be, then, that we are just starting to appreciate the potency that reading possesses. It is an interesting speculation: that the cultural threats to reading may be, paradoxically, revealing to us its deeper saving powers. I use the word "saving" intentionally here, not because I want to ascribe to reading some great function of salvation, but

because I want to emphasize one last time the ideas of transformation and change of state. The movement from quotidian consciousness into the consciousness irradiated by artistic vision is analogous to the awakening to spirituality. The reader's aesthetic experience is, necessarily, lowercase, at least when set beside the truly spiritual. But it is marked by similar recognitions, including a changed relation to time, a condensation of the sense of significance, an awareness of a system or structure of meaning, and—most difficult to account for—a feeling of being enfolded by something larger, more profound.

31   Working through these thoughts, I happened upon an essay called "First Person Singular" by Joseph Epstein, wherein he cites Goethe as saying, "A fact of our existence is of value not insofar as it is true, but insofar as it has something to signify." To this Epstein adds concisely, "Only in art do all facts signify." He communicates in seven short words much of what I have been belaboring here: facts signify whenever one believes that existence is intended, that there are reasons that, as Pascal wrote, reason knows nothing of.

32   My depiction of the exalted potential of the text and the no less exalted transformation of the reader by the text draws its main energy from spiritual analogy. But I will end by remarking one way in which the analogy breaks down. In religion there is generally a provision made for the afterlife—that is part of its implicit assurance of purpose, the bait on the hook that would capture the frightened soul. Literature extends no such promise. Quite the reverse. With literature we are always at least subliminally aware of the mocking fact that only the work has a claim to living on, and then most likely through others. Within its borders it achieves the poignant eternity that John Keats accords to one of the figures in his "Ode on a Grecian Urn":

> Fair youth, beneath the trees, thou canst not leave
> Thy song, nor ever can those trees be bare;
>   Bold Lover, never, never canst thou kiss,
> Though winning near the goal—yet, do not grieve;
>   She cannot fade, though thou hast not thy bliss,
> For ever wilt thou love, and she be fair!

33   This is how it is with literary art: though it can give us no afterlife, within its realm of departure we are made plain to ourselves in a way that feels strangely lasting.

QUESTIONS FOR DISCUSSION

1. How do Birkerts and Calvino describe the state of mind we arrive at when reading a long work of fiction such as a novel? In what sense is this state a "transformation of consciousness"?
2. According to Birkerts, how does reading change our perception or relation to reality?
3. How does reading imaginative literature modify our sense of time and change our sense of the meaning of the world?
4. How did the transition to silent reading of texts signify a change in the degree of subjectivity involved in the act of reading?

5. Why does Birkerts agree with Plato that the artist and the aesthetic experience of art work constitute a threat to the State?
6. How does Birkerts compare and contrast the reading experience to spiritual experience?

CONNECTION

Contrast Birkerts' view of the uniqueness of the act of reading books with that of Holtzman. Does Holtzman's presentation of Birkerts' views strike you as accurate or as distorted? What would Birkerts say in response to Holtzman?

IDEAS FOR WRITING

1. Write an essay in which you apply Birkerts' idea of reading as a "collaborative bringing forth of an entire world," using as an example your own reading process in response to a recent literary work you have studied. How did your imaginative and intellectual interaction with this reading help to bring forth a new world for you, one that went beyond just "the words on the page"?
2. Write an essay in response to Birkerts' assertion that certain aspects of the modern world, such as electronic technology, make it difficult to achieve the trust in the "transformative power of the artistic vision" that Birkerts presents in the first part of this essay. Do you believe that electronic technologies such as computers weaken and distract us from the power of reading? Why or why not?

Steven Holtzman

"Don't Look Back"

Steven Holtzman (b. 1947) is interested in computers, philosophy, and creativity. He holds both an undergraduate degree in Western and Eastern philosophy and a Ph.D. in computer science from the University of Edinburgh; he is also founder and Vice President of Optimal Networks in Palo Alto, California. Using computer techniques, he has composed a number of musical works that have been performed in Europe and the United States, some of which can be found on a CD he has produced, Digital Mantras *(Shriek! Records, 1994). He also has written two books that examine the new types of creative expression possible in the age of computers and cyberspace:* Digital Mantras: The Language of Abstract and Virtual Worlds *(1994), and* Digital Mosaics : The Aesthetics of Cyberspace *(1997). Holzman's books are aesthetically appealing as well as intellectually provocative. In the following excerpt from* Digital Mosaics, *he argues that we can't turn our backs on today's digital technology as it is already inextricably a part of our lives.*

JOURNAL

Write about your experience with reading books and other texts on-line: have you found this kind of reading rewarding?

1   For centuries, the book has been the primary vehicle for recording, storing, and transferring knowledge. But it's hard to imagine that paper will be the preferred format in a hundred years. Digital media will marginalize this earlier form of communication, relegating it to a niche just as music CDs have replaced LPs. The book will be forced to redefine itself, just as TV forced radio to redefine itself, and radio and TV together transformed the newspaper's role. The process is survival of the fittest—competition in the market to be a useful medium. Whatever the book's future is, clearly its role will never be the same. The book has lost its preeminence.

2   The print medium of newspaper is also fading. Almost every major newspaper in the United States is experiencing significant declines in circulation. (The exception is USA *Today*—characterized by itself as "TV on paper.") More than 70 percent of Americans under the age of thirty don't read newspapers. And this trend isn't about to change.

3   The powers of the media business today understand this. As part of the frenzied convergence of media, communications, and the digital world, we're witnessing a dizzying tangle of corporate alliances and mega-mergers. Companies are jockeying for position for this epochal change. The list includes many multibillion-dollar companies—AT&T, Bertelsmann, Disney, Microsoft, Time Warner, Viacom—and many, many more small startup technology companies. They all want to position themselves as preeminent new media companies.

Clinging to the Past

4   Members of the literary establishment can also see this imminent change. Yet, for the most part, they take a dim view of these new digital worlds. Beyond the loss of their cherished culture, what disturbs many critics is that they find new digital media like CD-ROMs and the World Wide Web completely unsatisfying.

5   The literacy critic Sven Birkerts eloquently laments that the generation growing up in the digital age is incapable of enjoying literature. Teaching at college has brought Birkerts to despair because his students aren't able to appreciate the literary culture he so values. After only a proudly self-confessed "glimpse of the future" of CD-ROMs, he declares he is "clinging all the more tightly to my books."

6   The disillusionment with the digital experience is summed up by the *New York Times Book Review* critic Sarah Lyall. She complains that multimedia CD-ROMs

> still don't come close to matching the experience of reading a paper-and-print book while curled up in a chair, in bed, on the train, under a tree, in an airplane. . . . After all, the modern book is the result of centuries of trial and error during which people wrote on bark, on parchment, on vellum, on clay, on scrolls, on stone, chiseling characters into surfaces or copying them out by hand.

7   Okay, I thought as I read Birkerts and Lyall, these are members of a dying cultural heritage who—like seemingly every generation—are uncomfortable with new. Unable to shift their perspective, they'll be casualties of change. After all, Birkerts boasts that he doesn't own a computer and still uses only a typewriter.

8   Birkerts clings not to his books, but to the past. I was reminded of a comment by the cultural critic William Irwin Thompson, who is also wary of the consequences of digital technology:

> It is not the literary intelligentsia of *The New York Review of Books* [or *The New York Times,* as the case may be] that is bringing forth this new culture, for it is as repugnant to them as the Reformation was to the Catholic Church. . . . This new cyberpunk, technological culture is brought forth by Top and Pop, electronic science and pop music, and both the hackers and the rockers are anti-intellectual and unsympathetic to the previous Mental level expressed by the genius of European civilization.

9   This helped me dismiss the backlash from those looking in the rearview mirror. But then I came across a book by Clifford Stoll.

Muddier Mud

10   Stoll, who was introduced to computers twenty years ago, is a longtime member of the digerati. In his book *Silicone Snake Oil,* he claims to expose the true emptiness of the digital experience.

11   In opening, Stoll explains that "every time someone mentions MUDs [multi-user dungeons, a type of interactive adventure game] and virtual reality, I think of a genuine reality with muddier mud than anything a computer can deliver." Stoll then nostalgically recounts the story of the first time he went crawling through caves in his college days. "We start in, trailing a string through the muddy tunnel— everything's covered with gunk, as are the six of us crawling behind [the guide]. Not your ordinary slimy, brown, backyard mud, either. This is the goop of inner-earth that works its way into your hair, socks, and underwear."

12   Stoll's general theme: "You're viewing a world that doesn't exist. During that week you spend on-line, you could have planted a tomato garden. . . . While the Internet beckons brightly, seductively flashing an icon of knowledge-as-power, this nonplace lures us to surrender our time on earth."

13   I suppose this excludes any experience that might distract us from the real— a novel, a Beethoven symphony, a movie. (A tomato garden?)

14   And then we get the same theme that Birtkerts and Lyall hit on.

> I've rarely met anyone who prefers to read digital books. I don't want my morning newspaper delivered over computer, or a CD-ROM stuffed with National Geographic photographs. Call me a troglodyte; I'd rather peruse those photos alongside my sweetheart, catch the newspaper on the way to work, and page through a real book. . . . Now, I'm hardly a judge of aesthetics, but of the scores of electronic multimedia productions I've seen, I don't remember any as being beautiful.

A CD-ROM Is Not a Book

15   These laments totally miss the point. No, a CD-ROM isn't a book. Nor is a virtual world—whether a MUD or a simulation of rolling in the mud—the same as the real experience. This is *exactly* the point! A CD-ROM isn't a book; it's something completely new and different. A MUD on the Internet isn't like mud in a cave. A virtual world isn't the real world; it offers possibilities unlike anything we've known before.

16   Birkerts, Lyall, and Stoll dismiss the digital experience to justify staying in the familiar and comfortable worlds of their past. Yet what's exciting to me about these digital worlds is precisely that they're new, they're unfamiliar, and they're our future.

17   It's not that I disagree with the literati's assertions. We will lose part of our literary culture and tradition. Kids today are so attuned to the rapid rhythms of MTV that they're unresponsive to the patient patterns of literary prose. They are indeed so seduced by the flickeringly powerful identifications of the screen as to be deaf to the inner voices of print. Literary culture—like classical music and opera—will become marginalized as mainstream culture pursues a digital path.

18   There never will be a substitute for a book. And today's multimedia CD-ROM—even surfing the World Wide Web—is still for the most part a static and unsatisfying experience. But it's rather early to conclude anything about their ultimate potential.

Patience Is a Virtue

19   It puzzles me that there are people who expect that, in almost no time at all, we'd find great works by those who have mastered the subtleties of such completely new digital worlds. We are seeing the first experiments with a new medium. It took a long time to master the medium of film. Or the book, for that matter. It will also take time to master new digital worlds.

20   It's challenging to create a multimedia digital world today. The enabling technologies that will make radically new digital worlds possible—Java, VRML, and a string of acronymic technologies—are still emerging. Artists, writers, and musicians must also be software programmers. Today, a rare combination of passion, artistry, and technical knowledge is required. Yet, over time, these skills will become common. Even more important than the technical mastery of new digital media, a new conceptual framework and aesthetic must also be established for digital worlds.

21   When this conceptual and technical mastery is achieved, we'll discover the true possibilities of digital expression. In a few decades—or possibly in just five years—we'll look on today's explorations as primitive. Until then, we will continue to explore these new digital worlds and seek to learn their true potential.

Embracing the Digital

22   There will be nothing to replace the reading of a book or newspaper in bed. Curling up by a fireside to read a poem with an electronic tablet won't have the same intimacy as doing so with a book. But curling up by a fireside with an electronic tablet is itself simply an example of substituting electronic technology for an existing medium—extrapolating from today's flat-paneled handheld computers to an "electronic book." We need to develop a new aesthetic—a digital aesthetic. And the emerging backlash from the literati makes clear to me how urgently we need it.

22   When we've mastered digital media, we won't be talking about anything that has much to do with the antiquated form of the book. I imagine myself curled up in bed with laser images projected on my retinas, allowing me to view and travel through an imaginary three-dimensional virtual world. A story about the distant past flashes a quaint image of a young woman sitting and reading a book, which seems just as remote as the idea of a cluster of Navajo Indians sitting around a campfire and listening to a master of the long-lost tradition of storytelling. In a hundred years, we'll think of the book as we do the storyteller today.

23   Will we lose a part of our cultural heritage as we assimilate new media? No doubt. Is this disturbing? Absolutely. Today's traditional media will be further marginalized. Is there much value in decrying an inevitable future? Probably not. The music of *today* is written on electric instruments. Hollywood creates our theater. And soon digital media will be *our* media. Digital technology and new digital media—for better of worse—are here to stay.

24   That's not to say that all things digital are good. Perhaps, like the Luddites in Britain during the first half of the nineteenth century, the literati raise a flag of warning, raise awareness, and create debate, debunking some of the myths of a utopian digital future. But in the end, for better or for worse, the efforts of the Luddites were futile when it came to stopping the industrial revolution.

25   Likewise, today you can't turn off the Internet. Digital technology isn't going away. There are already thousands of multimedia CD-ROMs and hundreds of thousands of sites on the World Wide Web; soon there will be thousands of channels of on-demand digital worlds.

26   Digital technology is part of our lives, a part of our lives that we know will only continue to grow. We can't afford to dismiss it. Rather we must embrace it—not indiscriminately, but thoughtfully. We must seize the opportunities generated by the birth of a new medium to do things we've never been able to do before. Don't look back.

QUESTIONS FOR DISCUSSION

1. Why does Holtzman believe that the power and popularity of books and newspapers are fading? Do you agree?

2. According to William Thompson, why do the members of the "literary intelligentsia" find the "new culture" of CD-ROMs and the Internet to be repugnant? What other reasons for the rejection might there be?

3. What is computer scientist Cliff Stoll's primary reason for rejecting the Internet as a learning experience for children? How does Holtzman attempt to refute Stoll? Is he successful?

4. What features of the book do the traditional critics such as Birkerts consider to be irreplaceable? Do these critics have valid arguments?

5. What do you think Holtzman means by his concluding statement that we must embrace digital media "not indiscriminately, but thoughtfully"? Do you think his essay is a good example of the thoughtful approach he recommends? Why or why not?

Compare Holtzman's view of reading and its significance with Richard Wright's "The Library Card." Would a work of social power and outrage evoke the same powerful response in a person from an oppressed group when viewed on a screen in a computer lab or library as it would if read in privacy, between the covers of a book?

IDEAS FOR WRITING

1. Write an essay in which you compare your own experience with the World Wide Web or a learning program on multimedia CD-ROM disk to reading a regular book or textbook on the same subject. Which experience did you find more useful and worthwhile?
2. Write a comparison of your experience of learning from the physical world through direct experience as opposed to learning about the same subject through using a multimedia CD-ROM or the Internet. Do you agree with Stoll that direct experience is the preferable way to learn? Why or why not?

Jorge Luis Borges

"The Book of Sand"

From a wealthy family in Buenos Aires, Jorge Luis Borges (1899–1986) was the son of a philosophy professor; Borges studied at home in his family's extensive library before traveling abroad to study in Switzerland. He was Director of Buenos Aires's National Library for many years and a professor of literature at the University of Buenos Aires. Although Borges began to write as a young man, he was almost unknown as a writer until he won the International Publishers' Prize (Prix Formentor) in 1961; subsequently, many of his earlier works were translated and published internationally. His story collections include Ficciones *(1962),* Labyrinths *(1962),* The Aleph and Other Stories *(1970), and* The Book of Sand *(1977). Borges's postmodernist stories are often like philosophical puzzles that capture the reader's mind. His fiction explores issues of history, reality, knowledge, mysticism, and imagination in playful ways that often suggest hidden, occult realities. Borges enjoyed inventing imaginary authors, books, and even parallel universes that existed only in his mind and live in the pages of his stories. The intriguing, mysterious, infinite book in his story "The Book of Sand" makes a complex commentary on the act of reading itself.*

JOURNAL

Write about a book that has held a mysterious meaning for you, that has seemed to change or produce a slightly different meaning each time you read it.

. . . thy rope of sands. . .
    —George Herbert

1   The line consists of an infinite number of points; the plane, of an infinite number
    of lines; the volume, of an infinite number of planes; the hypervolume, of an in-
    finite number of volumes. . . . No—this, *more geometrico*, is decidedly not the best
    way to begin my tale. To say that the story is true is by now is now a convention of
    every fantastic tale; mine, nevertheless, *is* true.

2   I live alone, in a fifth-floor apartment on Calle Belgrano. One evening a few
    months ago, I heard a knock at my door. I opened it, and a stranger stepped in. He
    was a tall man, with blurred, vague features, or perhaps my nearsightedness made
    me see him that way. Everything about him spoke of honest poverty: he was dressed
    in gray, and carried a gray valise. I immediately sensed that he was a foreigner. At
    first I thought he was old; then I noticed that I had been misled by his sparse hair,
    which was blond, almost white, like the Scandinavians'. In the course of our con-
    versation, which I doubt lasted more than an hour, I learned that he hailed from
    the Orkneys.

3   I pointed the man to a chair. He took some time to begin talking. He gave off an
    air of melancholy, as I myself do now.

4   "I sell Bibles," he said at last.

5   "In this house," I replied, not without a somewhat stiff, pedantic note, "there are
    several English Bibles, including the first one, Wyclif's. I also have Cipriano de
    Valera's, Luther's (which is, in literary terms, the worst of the lot), and a Latin copy
    of the Vulgate. As you see, it isn't exactly Bibles I might be needing."

6   After a brief silence he replied.

7   "It's not only Bibles I sell. I can show you a sacred book that might interest a man
    such as yourself. I came by it in northern India, in Bikaner."

8   He opened his valise and brought out the book. He laid it on the table. It was a
    clothbound octavo volume that had clearly passed through many hands. I exam-
    ined it; the unusual heft of it surprised me. On the spine was printed *Holy Writ*, and
    then *Bombay*.

9   "Nineteenth century, I'd say," I observed.

10   "I don't know," was the reply. "Never did know."

11   I opened it at random. The characters were unfamiliar to me. The pages, which
    seemed worn and badly set, were printed in double columns, like a Bible. The text
    was cramped, and composed into versicles. At the upper corners of the each page
    were Arabic numerals. I was struck by an odd fact: the even-numbered page would
    carry the number 40,514, let us say, while the odd-numbered page that followed it
    would be 999. I turned the page; the next page bore an eight-digit number. It also
    bore a small illustration, like those one sees in dictionaries: an anchor drawn in pen
    and ink, as though by the unskilled hand of a child.

12   It was at this point that the stranger spoke again.

13   "Look at it well. You will never see it again."

14   There was a threat in the words, but not in the voice.

15   I took note of the page, and then closed the book. Immediately I opened it again. In vain I searched for the figure of the anchor, page after page. To hide my discomfiture, I tried another tack.

16   "This is a version of Scripture in some Hindu language, isn't that right?"

17   "No," he replied.

18   Then he lowered his voice, as though entrusting me with a secret.

19   "I came across this book in a village on the plain, and I traded a few rupees and a Bible for it. The man who owned it didn't know how to read. I suspect he saw the Book of Books as an amulet. He was of the lowest caste; people could not so much as step on his shadow without being defiled. He told me his book was called the Book of Sand because neither sand nor this book has a beginning or an end."

20   He suggest I try to find the first page.

21   I took the cover in my left hand and opened the book, my thumb and forefinger almost touching. It was impossible: several pages always lay between the cover and my hand. It was as though they grew from the very book.

22   "Now try to find the end."

23   I failed there as well.

24   "This can't be," I stammered, my voice hardly recognizable as my own.

25   "It can't be, yet it *is*," the Bible peddler said, his voice little more than a whisper. "The number of pages in this book is literally infinite. No page is the first page; no page is the last. I don't know why they're numbered in this arbitrary way, but perhaps it's to give one to understand that the terms of an infinite series can be numbered any way whatever."

26   Then, as though thinking out loud, he went on.

27   "If space is infinite, we are anywhere, at any point in space. If time is infinite, we are at any point in time."

28   His musings irritated me.

29   "You," I said, "are a religious man, are you not?"

30   "Yes, I'm Presbyterian. My conscience is clear. I am certain I didn't cheat that native when I gave him the Lord's Word in exchange for his diabolic book."

31   I assured him that he had nothing to reproach himself for, and whether he was just passing through the country. He replied that he planned to return to his own country within a few days. It was then that I learned that he was a Scot, and his home was in the Orkneys. I told him I had a great personal fondness for Scotland because of my love for Stevenson and Hume.

32   "And Robbie Burns," he corrected.

33   As we talked I continued to explore the infinite book.

34   "Had you intended to offer this curious specimen to the British Museum, then?" I asked with feigned indifference.

35   "No," he replied, "I am offering it to you," and he mentioned a great sum of money.

36   I told him, with perfect honesty, that such an amount of money was not within my ability to pay. But my mind was working; in a few moments I had devised my plan.

37   "I propose a trade," I said. "You purchased the volume with a few rupees and the Holy Scripture; I will offer you the full sum of my pension, which I have just received, and Wyclif's black-letter Bible. It was left to me by my parents."

38   "A black-letter Wyclif!" he murmured.

39   I went to my bedroom and brought back the money and the book. With a bibliophile's zeal he turned the pages and studied the binding.

40   "Done," he said.

41   I was astonished that he did not haggle. Only later was I to realize that he had entered *my* house already determined to sell the book. He did not count the money, but merely put the bills into his pocket.

42   We chatted about India, the Orkneys, and the Norwegian jarls that had once ruled those islands. Night was falling when the man left. I have never seen him since, nor do I know his name.

43   I thought of putting the Book of Sand in the space left by the Wyclif, but I chose at last to hide it behind some imperfect volumes of the *Thousand and One Nights*.

44   I went to bed but could not sleep. At three or four in the morning I turned on the light. I took out the impossible book and turned its pages. On one, I saw an engraving of a mask. There was a number in the corner of the page—I don't remember now what it was—raised to the ninth power.

45   I showed no one my treasure. To the joy of possession was added the fear that it would be stolen from me, and to that, the suspicion that it might not be truly infinite. Those two points of anxiety aggravated my already habitual misanthropy. I had but few friends left, and those, I stopped seeing. A prisoner of the Book, I hardly left my house. I examined the worn binding and the covers with a magnifying glass, and rejected the possibility of some artifice. I found that the small illustrations were spaced at two-thousand-page intervals. I began noting them down in an alphabetized notebook, which was very soon filled. They never repeated themselves. At night, during the rare intervals spared me by insomnia, I dreamed of the book.

46   Summer was drawing to a close, and I realized that the book was monstrous. It was cold consolation to think that I, who looked upon it with my eyes and fondled it with my ten flesh-and-bone fingers, was no less monstrous than the book. I felt it was a nightmare thing, an obscene thing, and that it defiled and corrupted reality.

47   I considered fire, but I feared that the burning of an infinite book might be similarly infinite, and suffocate the planet in smoke.

48   I remembered reading once that the best place to hide a leaf is in the forest. Before my retirement I had worked in the National Library, which contained nine hundred thousand books; I knew that to the right of the lobby a curving staircase descended into the shadows of the basement, where the maps and periodicals are kept. I took advantage of the librarians' distraction to hide the Book of Sand on one of the library's damp shelves; I tried not to notice how high up, or how far from the door.

49   I now feel a little better, but I refuse even to walk down the street the library's on.

QUESTIONS FOR DISCUSSION

1. What relationship does the narrator establish between infinity and truth in the opening paragraph? While Borges does not expect the reader to accept the story as literally "true," what truth or truths are illuminated through the story?
2. Why is it significant that the Bible salesman is a foreigner from a rather exotic and under-populated place, the Orkney Islands?
3. Why is the book called *The Book of Sand?* Why is it significant that the book is acquired by both the salesman and the narrator in exchange for a Bible?
4. What leads to the narrator's obsession with *The Book of Sand?* What is implied when he hides *The Book of Sand* behind *A Thousand and One Nights?* In what ways are these books compared?
5. Why does the narrator eventually decide that the book is "monstrous"? What does *The Book of Sand* represent to the narrator?
6. Why does the narrator finally abandon the book in the basement of the Argentine National Library? How has his life been changed through his contact with the Book?

CONNECTION

Compare Holtzman's view of the Internet-based reading experience of the future with the infinite, ever-changing quality of *The Book of Sand*. Does a book that is constantly changing seem to you a positive or a negative invention?

IDEAS FOR WRITING

1. Write an essay in which you explore what you think *The Book of Sand* symbolizes or represents in relationship to truth, knowledge, and the act of reading itself.
2. Write a sequel to the Borges story in which a character you create finds the book where the narrator abandoned it and develops an attachment to it.

Denise Levertov

"The Secret"

Born in Ilford, England, Denise Levertov (1923–1998) emigrated to the United States in 1948 after serving as a nurse during World War II. She was active in anti-

Vietnam war protests in the 1960s and taught in the English Department at Stanford University for many years. Levertov published more than eighteen volumes of poetry which explore social, mystical, and natural themes. Some of her better known collections include The Sorrow Dance *(1967),* Freeing the Dust *(1975),* Candles in Babylon *(1982),* Evening Train *(1993), and* Sands of the Well *(1996). Her essays are collected in* New and Selected Essays *(1992). The following work from* Poems 1960–1967 *explores the act of reading from the perspective of both the unsophisticated reader and the writer of a poem.*

| JOURNAL |

Write about a reading experience that helped you to unlock a secret of some kind: a secret about yourself, the world, or about life itself.

Two girls discover
the secret of life
in a sudden line of
poetry.
5 I who don't know the
secret wrote
the line. They
told me
(through a third person)
10 they had found it
but not what it was,
not even
what line it was. No doubt
by now, more than a week
15 later, they have forgotten
the secret,
the line, the name of
the poem. I love them
for finding what
20 I can't find,
and for loving me
for the line I wrote:
and for forgetting it
so that
25 a thousand times, till death
finds them, they may
discover it again, in other
lines,
in other
30 happenings. And for
wanting to know it,

for
assuming there is
such a secret, yes,
35 for that
most of all.

QUESTIONS FOR DISCUSSION

1. The secret that the two young girls have found in a line of the speaker's poetry is never clearly defined in the poem. Why do you think the writer doesn't or isn't able to determine the secret? What does this imply about the act of reading?
2. Why do you think that Levertov indicates that the girls have found what the author can't find? What does this imply about the relationship between authors and the imaginative texts that they write as well as about the relationship between authors and their readers?
3. What does Levertov suggest about the relationship between texts and life experience when she writes that the girls forget the "secret," only to "discover it again, in other lines, in other happenings"?
4. In the last stanzas of the poem, the speaker says she loves the girls most for "wanting to know" the secret of life and for "assuming there is such a secret." What does this suggest about the importance of the values and beliefs that we bring with us to the act of reading?
5. Levertov uses a very short, irregular line and four-line stanzas to organize the thoughts in her poem. How do her ragged lines and stanzas, which seem to jump awkwardly from one to another because of the large spaces between them, help to emphasize the movement of her thinking about the "secret"?

CONNECTION

Compare Levertov's view of the reading experience and the mutable "secrets" to be found in books with the ideas on reading in Borges' "The Book of Sand."

IDEAS FOR WRITING

1. Develop your journal writing into an essay about a "secret" you learned through your reading. Return to the original text and use quotations from it as well as paraphrasing to clarify what you learned from reading it. Indicate also how learning the secret somehow changed you or led you to perceive reality differently or to communicate with people in new ways.

2. Argue for or against the existence of a secret to life. If you do believe there is such a secret, how do you think you can best go about discovering it?

Caitlin Liu

"Hsao-suen: A Chinese Virtue"

Born in Taiwan and raised in El Centro, California, Caitlin Liu was a freshman when she wrote this essay. Concerned about disrespect in modern society for elders, Liu wrote the essay to "provide food for thought for most people of this country." Liu had to work hard to write this essay as she had to present one culture to another, integrate her past with the present, and synthesize tradition with idealism. Liu's essay examines the special meaning a classic Chinese folktale held for her, when she first read it as a child and as she re-reads it again as an adult.

1   As naturally as an American youngster would own a volume of Mother Goose rhymes, I owned a set of books that were common for many Chinese children. The stories in these books bore no resemblance to the highly imaginative English verses about misbehaving children, talking animals, and eloping silverware; rather, they were down-to-earth folklore about the lives of everyday people. If I recall correctly, there were fifty morally instructive stories in this collection, and each one reflected a unique aspect of the morals and values of the Chinese culture. Some of the virtues extolled in these folklores include honesty, courage, and "hsao-suen," a phrase for which a simple and direct English equivalency cannot be assigned. An approximate translation could be "the honoring of one's parents," but even that definition is inadequate. Embodied within these two words are many qualities that allude to their true meaning: the utmost respect, love, and unquestioned obedience to one's parents. Most important of all, one who is "hsao-suen" will place the comfort and well-being of parents above his or her own. The following tale (summarized here and rendered in English) demonstrates one of the most highly esteemed Chinese virtues, "hsao-suen."

2   Two kingdoms of ancient China were at constant war, and the years of unrest had caused a famine throughout the land. A certain boy lived with his mother during this time of hardship. Since food was extremely scarce, the young lad had to gather mulberries for his family's survival. Every morning he would journey into the forest with a basket in each hand. The first basket was usually filled with an assortment of sour red berries. Whenever the boy came across ripe purple berries, however, he would put them into the second basket. Although they were more difficult to find, these were the plump, sweet fruit he wanted his mother to consume.

3   One day while berry-picking, the boy encountered two road bandits. The robbers, after looking over the lad, became curious about the two half-filled baskets of berries he carried, and demanded an explanation. The virtuous boy replied that the sour red berries were for himself, and the sweet purple berries were for his mother to eat. The burly men, touched by the "hsao-suen" of the youth, not only did not take his baskets away from him, but gave him a number of food items, including a leg of lamb. "Take these to your mother, fine young man," the bandits said before riding away.

4   Even though I read this story to myself over thirteen years ago, it still remains vividly etched in my mind. As a child, I had a pampered upbringing. To read about another youngster who had to struggle just to survive sent my imagination soaring; it was such a contrast to my own life. Another aspect of the tale that really impressed my young mind was how "grown-up" the boy was. Not only did he shoulder the adult responsibility of providing food for his family, he was also able to influence the actions of grown men. For me, the boy was both a hero and a role model. As a six-year-old, I must admit that I liked the story most of all because it had a happy ending—the boy was rewarded with food, the bandits had done a good deed, and everyone presumably lived "happily ever after." Now as a "grown-up" nineteen-year-old, I am able to understand the underlying message of the tale that I couldn't see as a child: the importance of being "hsao-suen." The boy loved and respected his mother so much that he wanted only the very best for her, placing her comfort and well-being above his own. The central theme of the story was how "hsao-suen" the boy was to his mother, and how through the strength of his virtue he was able to bring out the good in the bandits also. Because the boy remained true to the virtues he believed in, everyone benefited from the process.

5   I feel that this brief tale I read over a decade ago formed one of the crucial cornerstones in the foundation of my outlook, for I consider "hsao-suen" to be one of the noblest of all human virtues. Also, I believe that there is good in everyone. All it takes to bring out the goodness of another is to have the light of truth and virtue within oneself be visible to others. For no light, whether the flame of a candle or rays of the sun, ever glows without casting an inevitable warm shine upon its surroundings.

QUESTIONS FOR DISCUSSION

1. Does Liu succeed in defining the meaning of "hsao-suen"? Could she have provided other examples?
2. How effectively does the essay use comparison and contrast to develop its major points and ideas? Does the author use a point-by-point or subject-by-subject approach to organizing her ideas and examples?
3. How clearly does Liu contrast her first reading of the story with her more recent reading? Could she have provided more points of distinction?

4. Do you agree with the student that "hsao-suen" is a concept of value for us today? Would American children benefit from practicing the respect and concern for parents implied by this traditional Asian belief?

Lissy Goralnik

"The Sandstorm of Time and Knowledge"

Lissy Goralnik enjoyed playing field hockey in college. She graduated from Stanford University with a B.A. in creative writing. Because writing offers her both an emotional and an intellectual outlet, she enjoyed developing an essay about "The Book of Sand" as the story offers the reader so many possible interpretations. In her essay, she focuses on the way the story explores ideas of eternity, knowledge, and the discovery of one's role in a rapidly changing world.

1   Finding a book of infinite knowledge, the narrator of "The Book of Sand" seems to confront several realizations. Unnerved by the book's endless pages, he faces eternity, seeing there a connection between its continuous invention of information and nature's relentless thriving, as both extend beyond the constraints of definite boundaries. Birth and death, on the other hand, confine and restrict the narrator's mortal existence. The narrator, in the midst of such information, recognizes the restrained capacity of his mind. He will never absorb the full contents of his book before his life ends, and in understanding the influence of these demons of time, nature, and mortality on his life, the narrator must come to admit defeat. These forces, unaffected by his existence, will survive his life, his death, and any attempts he makes to control them. The narrator will never know all that he wants to know. Eventually he will be consumed by the book and the forces it represents.

2   At first excited by the opportunities embodied within the book, by the prospect of total and infinite knowledge, the narrator willingly gazes into its pages. Alarmed at what he sees there, he blames the book for the reflection it provides him. The book serves as a mirror for the narrator, causing him to re-evaluate his place in the world. When he first questions the book's merit, he remarks, " I realized that the book was monstrous. What good did it do to me to think that I, who looked upon the volume with my eyes, who held it in my hands, was any less monstrous?" Here he admits that the book's endless information made him feel that he too should be ever-expanding, like a sponge, to absorb every page, every word, every bit of knowledge it offered. As the knowledge continues to elude him though, as the narrator realizes that he will never see all of the pages, never begin to uncover all of the secrets of the book, he feels like he is nothing in the face of infinity, nothing but a ripple in the water. And for this epiphany, the narrator condemns the book.

3   The narrator, astounded by the vast wealth of knowledge in the book, realizes that he will never be able to attain enough information, and even if he could, to what avail? No one would notice; no one would commend his efforts or applaud his swelling brain. He would learn in a frenzied solitude, die without leaving any sort of mark on the world or on the world's body of knowledge—and life would go on undisturbed. Trying to make order out of such infinite chaos, the narrator organizes a list of the drawings in the text and figures out how frequently they arise. But in a sense, he is only trying to sweep the desert into a tidy little pile in order to calm his inner torment. Such a task would prove impossible.

4   To protect his initially precious possession, the narrator hides his book of knowledge behind "a broken set of *A Thousand and One Nights*." One thousand and one, 1001. This particular number reads the same both forwards and backwards, like a palindrome. Symmetrical, reflected upon itself, and with a mirrored image identical to its original form, one thousand and one represents the ulterior function of *The Book of Sand*. Imposing on the reader a humbling perception of self in alliance with the world, forcing self-reflection, this book allows the narrator first to be consumed by human greed, as he burns to acquire all knowledge, and then causes him to recognize that his capabilities and capacity are both severely limited, as he is not able to digest the vast gifts the book offers. But not any ordinary mirror is this book, for the volumes of *A Thousand and One Nights* composed only an incomplete set, a shattered representation of a solid group. This implies then, as the 1001 is equated with *The Book of Sand* and the book then provides a reflection of the reader, that this broken 1001 stands for a fractured text which reflects a cracked image to the reader. And so when the narrator reveals that, "the book was a nightmarish object, an obscene thing that affronted and tainted reality itself," he articulates Borges' reasoning for hiding this distorted mirror behind the broken set of short stories.

5   Once the narrator recognizes the monstrosity of the text that he tries fanatically to devour, he hopes to hide together both the text and his new awareness gained from it, as he returns to "the forest" to lose the book. As a normal man would try to camouflage himself in a swarming crowd of people to escape the attention of a discerning eye, the narrator feels that he need only hide from the glare of the book to alleviate the shame of representing nothing. A friendless man, only he and the evil text witness his failure. To escape the stigma he feels he now possesses, he need only free himself of the book, a reminder of his new image, and lie to himself. But such a feat of losing awareness would prove impossible, for awareness is a form of knowledge or wisdom, the very qualities which he before looked hungrily to the book to obtain, qualities which cannot be easily unlearned.

6   Through his inner journey the narrator comes to realize that we have no ultimate control over our lives. Time does not allow for infinite endeavors such as the quest for total knowledge, and humans have unknowingly surrendered our very existence to the vices of time. So answering to time and the life cycle it imposes upon us, to boundaries of the mind and personal limitations, to the supremacy of a possible higher being, we cannot shape fate. But rather than accept this path des-

tined for us as a race, the narrator sulks and is disgusted by such a truth. Borges' message is clear and disturbing: the truth evades us and is defined by powers beyond our scope or grasp. We fool ourselves in believing we can take advantage of the system, that we can impose some sort of order on this divine chaos, but really we are just driven by arrogance and greed. The discovery of the narrator, as he realizes his insignificance, his lack of purpose, his hopelessness, prescribes the reality for us all. We will never know everything.

7   Yet the narrator is presented in the story as a flawed seeker of truth. He grouchily admits that his observation skills are distorted by "myopia," which is a disease that leads to "defective vision of distant objects." But the word also means "a lack of foresight or discernment: a narrow view of something" or, in layman's terms, closed-mindedness. Later he also refers to himself as misanthropic, hating and distrusting mankind. Such paranoia and demented vision suggest a maladjusted man, implying that Borges might be showing us a distorted narrator who represents the antithesis of normal human reactions. Possibly, then, a clear image of a cracked man develops through the narrator's experience with the book, rather than a cracked image of a stable man.

8   It seems most likely that Borges is attempting to show us, through a narrator with whom we are not encouraged to sympathize, the necessity and importance of introspection. The narrator admits his solitary life when he says, "I had only few friends left [before I found the book]; I now stopped seeing even them." Willing to abandon any social contact or interactions to be with a book, the narrator lives in a world foreign to most of us. Through portraying this character as withdrawn and possibly mentally unstable, Borges implies that we need not fear fresh glances of ourselves as our narrator did. We need not hide from mirrors or reflective experiences, for they are learning tools so that we may understand ourselves and our niche in this eternal, fluid world.

9   Perhaps knowledge is worth the search, the struggle, the stress. Knowledge may really be the ultimate goal in the trek through the desert and the hike in the forest. Borges wants us to realize that knowledge spins the world, ticks the clocks, propels the humans; for without knowledge, we are unconscious and unfeeling and unaware. Although the quest for knowledge, like a sandstorm, can be dangerous, Borges wants us to understand that big or small, important or unnoticed, we all must make our lives the fullest they can be in the short time we are allotted here, and that expanding our minds through reflection allows us to expand our skills of observation, interaction, and introspection. Self-knowledge, Borges suggests, is the most important goal in life, and should drive us to read, to search, to journey, to converse, and to look in the mirror.

QUESTIONS FOR DISCUSSION

1. According to Goralnik, why does the book come to control the narrator?
2. Why does Goralnik think that the book is a mirror for the narrator? Explain why you agree or disagree with her claim.
3. Compare or contrast your interpretation of the narrator's role in the story to Goralnik's.

4. According to Goralnik, what is Borges's ultimate purpose in telling this story? What evidence from the story does she present? Compare or contrast your interpretation of the story's meaning with Goralnik's.
5. Write about your conflicting attitudes towards knowledge. For what reasons do you value knowledge? For what reasons do you fear knowledge? At what point in your education do you think you may "know enough"?

Topics for Research and Writing

1. Write an essay in which you discuss the importance of established writers as role models for developing writers by referring to selections in this chapter such as "The Library Card," as well as to your own experiences. You might also do some research into community outreach programs such as Writers in the Schools.
2. Write an essay in which you discuss your view of the importance of imagination in reading. Refer to writers in this chapter such as Birkerts and Levertov as well as to outside readings and research.
3. Many people believe that we become better writers through reading, but what exactly is the relationship between reading and writing? How does one influence or build on the other? Do some research into this issue and reflect on your own experience of understanding texts as you write about them. Write an essay in which you discuss your conclusions.
4. Although many in our society take the freedom to read for granted, in some societies access to reading materials is reserved for an elite class because it is believed that knowledge fosters social unrest. Using Wright's "The Library Card" as an example and doing some outside readings of slave narratives and other texts about the struggle to acquire reading materials, show how access to reading has been systematically withheld from oppressed groups.
5. Write an evaluation of a novel or book-length non-fiction work by a professional writer, either an author included in this text or another writer of your choice. You might consider such points as whether the issue taken up in the reading is significant, whether the writer is convincing, whether he or she addresses possible objections, and whether other works or your own experiences seem to contradict or confirm the author's conclusions.
6. Pick a selection from this text and add to it by rewriting it from the point of view of another character in the story or by adding a different ending or a different historical/physical setting. After you have finished your rewrite, comment on the insights into the author's original meaning and your own reading process and creative ability that you discovered from doing the rewrite.

7. After doing some research, present in detail some of the differences of opinion between the "traditionalist" advocates of the book such as Stoll and Birkerts and writers such as Holzman who believe the book will be replaced for most purposes by digital forms of communication. Which position do you find most convincing, and why?

8. Watch a film based on a book you have read or a film that concerns the act and significance of reading. Then write an essay in which you contrast and evaluate the experience of the film and the book, or comment on what the film reveals about the nature and importance of reading. You might choose from the following lists:

   Films made from novels: *Fahrenheit 451, Sense and Sensibility, The Joy Luck Club, One Flew Over The Cuckoo's Nest, The Age of Innocence, Emma, Portrait of a Lady, Washington Square, Beloved, Of Mice and Men, Bladerunner (based on* Phillip K. Dick's *Do Androids Dream of Electric Sheep?)*

   Films about the impact of reading: *Dead Poet's Society, Stanley and Iris, Educating Rita, The Miracle Worker*

9. The following Web sites are for your further research:

   BARTLEBY LIBRARY: GREAT BOOKS ONLINE
   http://www.bartleby.com/
   A very large site of on-line classic texts maintained by Columbia University Library.

   ERIC CLEARINGHOUSE ON READING, ENGLISH, AND COMMUNICATION
   http://www.indiana.edu/~eric_rec/
   This enormous site provides "educational materials, services, and coursework to everyone interested in the language arts." Much of the material concerns the teaching and learning of reading skills, as well as the motivation to read.

   EVALUATING WEB RESOURCES
   http://www2.widener.edu/Wolfgram-Memorial-Library/
   webeval.htm
   This site provides helpful guidelines for evaluating web sites and on-line resources for reading and research.

   HYPERIONS: HYPERTEXT FICTION
   http://www.duke.edu/~mshumate/hyperfic.html
   Hypertext is a new form of writing that takes advantage of the web as a communications medium. This site contains theory and examples of hypertextual works, as well as links to related sites.

LITERARY RESOURCES ON THE NET
http://andromeda.rutgers.edu/~jlynch/Lit/
This site, maintained by Jack Lynch of Rutgers University, contains links to a vast array of literary resources from around the world, including sites on the history of the book and hypertext sites.

ONLINE SYMBOLISM DICTIONARY
http://www.umich.edu/~umfandsf/symbolismproject/symbolism.
html/index.html
This on-line dictionary of symbols in literature, dreams, and the visual arts can be a helpful guide to readers. Browse or search by key word.

PROJECT GUTENBERG OFFICIAL HOME SITE
http://gutenberg.net/index.html
The biggest and oldest index site devoted to on-line texts.

Memories from Childhood

In the New Age the Daughters of Memory shall become the Daughters of Inspiration.

WILLIAM BLAKE

Nothing can be brought to an end in the unconscious; nothing is past or forgotten.

SIGMUND FREUD

Often I felt as though I was in a trance at my typewriter, that the shape of a particular memory was decided not by my conscious mind but by all that is dark and deep within me, unconscious but present.

BELL HOOKS
Writing Autobiography

NARRATION, MEMORY, AND SELF-AWARENESS

You will read a number of narrative accounts of childhood experiences in this chapter. Narratives serve two important functions for a writer: they can bring about a process of self-discovery, and they are fundamental sources and building blocks of both fiction and nonfiction writing. The brief stories or extended examples that develop, illustrate, and support points made in expository and argumentative essays are among the best resources writers have for presenting ideas in a clear, vivid, and convincing manner.

When you create a narrative, you draw on many inner resources and skills: memories of life experiences, dreams, your imagination; the ability to imitate the voices of others; and the skill required to develop a suspenseful plot that will hold your readers' attention. While not everyone likes to entertain friends with a natural story-telling ability, most of us can learn how to write a clear and engaging story.

111

Making Associations

As in other forms of writing, the first phase of narrative writing involves generating ideas and images to write about, experiences from your past that can later be shaped into a story with an overall theme. How do you find ideas and events for your writing, however, if the only memories you have of your early years are vague or sketchy? Notice, for instance, how Corey Okada begins her richly detailed essay "Namesake" with a single image: a memory of a "beautiful photograph" of her great-aunt, propped on a "small coffee table [in] a thick silver frame." You can begin as this student did with whatever you can remember, perhaps only a few basic facts or images: "As a child, I lived for five years on B Street in Sacramento. It was always hot in the summer there."

Writing strategies such as drawing, freewriting, invisible writing, brainstorming, and clustering can help you to generate details, images, and ideas associated with a particular time and place in your life. For example, you could start with a significant part of an address and do a cluster or ten-minute freewrite around it, letting one detail lead to another: "B Street, hot, barren, dusty, fire hydrant out front turned on in the summer, the ice cream wagon's jingle. . . ." If you follow this process long enough, you will begin to remember a number of details you thought you had forgotten, and you will have begun to gather the words, thoughts, and images that you can later shape into an essay.

Focusing and Concentration: The Inner Screen

In developing your narrative it is also important to try to focus on the most significant aspect of your memory. For example, you might visualize a particular room or the backyard of your house on a summer day when something significant happened to you: a fateful accident, a moment of serious conflict, an unexpected gift, a moment of friendship or intimacy. Close your eyes and try to visualize all the objects, colors, forms, people, and expressions associated with that place and a particular time there. Then try to visualize the movements within the scene. How did the people walk? What gestures did they make? What activities did they perform? What did they say to one another? After visualizing and naming specific colors, try to recall other sensations: textures, warmth or coolness, smells, tastes, sounds. Take notes as you begin to remember sensations, forms, and movements.

Dialogue and Characters

While not all people have vivid auditory memories, including some conversation in your narrative will help to bring it to life. Focus on the way each person in your scene speaks; jot down some of the typical brief exchanges that the group could have had, and then try to understand each character more fully through role-playing. Imagine that you have become each person in the scene, one at a time. As you role-play, speak out loud in the voice of each person, then write down a paragraph in which you try to capture their typical concerns and rhythms of speech. Finally, try to construct a conversation between the people in the scene.

Main Idea or Dominant Impression

Now you should be ready to write about the strong ideas or feelings that underlie or dominate your scene. Brainstorm or cluster around key details in your notes. Which emotions does the remembered moment call up for you? What ideas, what "lessons" does it suggest? Develop a statement that you can later clarify and qualify: "That evening was one of waiting and apprehension"; "The morning was a joyful one for my family, yet tinged by regret." Writing this type of dominant impression statement will guide you in adding more details and bits of dialogue and in selecting and ordering your material. A central idea for your narrative will help you to achieve a sense of focus and purpose that will help you to engage your readers' interest; most importantly, it will help you clarify what you have gained from the experience. The process of writing the narrative will contribute to your personal growth and self-awareness.

Drafting and Shaping the Narrative

Using your central idea or dominant impression as a guide in selecting and ordering details and events, write a rapid first draft, including what is relevant from the notes you generated in your preliminary brainstorming. Leave out any details or events that introduce a tone or feeling that conflicts, detracts, or clashes with the one you want to emphasize. Relevant but not particularly interesting events and periods of time do not need to be narrated in detail and can be summed up in a sentence or two: "For hours I played with my dog, waiting eagerly for my father to return from work."

Try to order the events of your narrative to emphasize your main idea as well. Although most writers use a chronological sequence in shaping a narrative, your dominant idea may demand withholding a key event for purposes of suspense or creating a powerful conclusion, as Maya Angelou does with the powerful fantasy in "The Angel of the Candy Counter," included in this chapter. You might also consider the use of flashbacks; you might begin with a brief scene that occurs at the end of the action and then tell the sequence of events leading up to the initially described event. Any order is acceptable as long as you clarify shifts of time for the reader with transitions and make sure that your order serves the overall purpose of your story. While writing different drafts of your narrative, don't hesitate to experiment with rearranging the parts of the story or essay until you find a clear, comfortable fit between the structure and meaning of your work. This rearrangement process is made much easier if you are revising on a computer, as the cut and paste functions of your word processor make it easy to see how different sequences work. You might try saving different versions of your narrative with different file names, each using a different sequence of events, printing each out and reading them over to see more clearly what may be the advantages of each version.

Revising the Narrative: Point of View and Style

Point of View   As you move from the early stages into the final drafting of your narrative, pay special attention to your point of view and style. Your narrative will probably use the first-person "I" pronoun, unless you are writing about someone else's experience. As is the case with the essays in this chapter, narrative essays are most frequently told from the perspective of an adult looking back on the past and are known as memoir narratives. Be sure to maintain a consistent point of view. If you decide to move into your mind as a young person, indicate this shift with a clear transition ("Then I thought to myself . . . "), after which you could write in language that is typical of the younger "you."

Word Choice   Narratives are seldom written in highly formal, abstract, or generalized language, so try to sound natural as you try to capture the mood and feeling of the event being revealed and the characters involved. In refining the style of your narrative, ask yourself some questions about your word and sentence choices: For instance, have you used specific, concrete nouns, adjectives, verbs, and adverbs? Wherever possible, try to avoid "generic" words that fail to communicate vivid images and emotions. Always search for the word that best fits your meaning and mood. A thesaurus (paper or on-line) can be very helpful in finding specific replacements for tired, imprecise, general terms. When it seems as though no word exists to communicate your exact sensory impression or mood, try using literal or figurative comparisons: she looked like _____; it was as dark as _____; I felt as sick as _____. Notice how an implied comparison between skin and paper in Corey Okada's essay helps to create a vivid picture of a sick relative: "Observing her thin, papery skin made me wince sadly for her fragility." Comparisons can add a lively and imaginative flavor to your writing, but take your time to find the right, original comparison. Clichés like "she looked like an angel" or "it was as dark as a dungeon" can tarnish the original impression that you are trying to create.

Sentence Patterns   Your writing style is also created through the way you put words together. Thus, your sentence patterns are a vital part of your narrative, as they should be in everything you write. Vary your sentence length for emphasis, using short sentences to slow down the action and to emphasize climactic moments. Try, too, to capture the voice rhythms of your characters through your punctuation. Remember that you can use a number of different sentence patterns (simple, compound, complex) as well as different ordering possibilities for the parts of your sentences. Again, in writing on your computer, try saving different versions of key sentences with different strategies for combination and punctuation; print them out and decide which works best in context. Consult your grammar text repeatedly to review the range of sentence patterns and punctuation strategies; experiment to heighten the dramatic effects of your writing.

Writing an engaging narrative is a challenge. It can also be a fulfilling writing experience that will bring you in closer touch with your past experiences, feelings, values, and identity.

THEMATIC INTRODUCTION: MEMORIES

Self-concept, imagination, dreams, and memories—all are born in childhood. A person's identity as a writer begins there, too. Through writing about your memories, you will begin to rediscover yourself through the places, the people, the events, and the stories that are still alive in your mind. These formative memories may have kindled your dreams while creating the foundation of your self-concept. Because writing is a process of self-discovery that has its roots in childhood, we have included poems, essays, and stories that address issues of childhood identity in relationship to dreams and fantasies, expectations, and goals. In the selections that follow, essayists and fiction writers create vividly narrated moments, some positive and some painful, from their earliest remembered experiences.

The chapter begins with Michele Murray's "Poem To My Grandmother in Her Death." Twelve years after her grandmother's death, the speaker in this poem reflects on the depth of her grandmother's love; even though many of the speaker's memories of her grandmother are fading, she realizes that her grandmother still lives within her.

The next three selections present turning-point narrative memories of family life. In "Tío Ramón," novelist Isabel Allende recalls her memories of her step father, a diplomat who taught her how to use her imagination, think critically, and be resourceful. In "The Angel of the Candy Counter," taken from Maya Angelou's autobiography, *I Know Why the Caged Bird Sings*, the reader comes to understand Angelou's great respect for her grandmother and how a childhood fantasy of revenge helped her to overcome her anger and humiliation at a white dentist's cruel and prejudiced refusal to grant her grandmother's request to pull Maya's aching tooth. Finally, in "Silent Dancing," Judith Ortiz Cofer, who was born in Puerto Rico and raised in New Jersey, explores how her childhood memories of her Puerto Rican culture and relatives continue to have a powerful influence on her understanding and fears about her life in the United States.

The next selections focus on how and why memories that may remain dream-like in our minds continue to influence our self-concepts. Memoirist bell hooks writes about how she looks first to her memories as the cornerstone of her writer's identity. In "Writing Autobiography," she presents writing as a way of accepting one's past and of revealing forgotten secrets of pain, growth, and celebration. In "The Dream of Authority," English professor Jane Tompkins explores memories of authority figures from her elementary school days to conclude that learning as an adult how to recognize and face her fears has helped her to control the power they once held over her. In the next essay, "Remembering," psychologist Naomi Remen shows how through patience, concern and listening she helped a patient to free herself from self-hatred that developed from traumatic memories that had previously dominated her spirit.

Do our memories represent the deepest truth, or cloud and distort our pasts? In "Muller Bros. Moving & Storage," acclaimed scientist and writer Stephen Jay Gould reflects on his own relationship with his grandfather as he asks his readers to think about why people continue to cherish memories of the past, despite the fact that these memories often do not represent the truth. Poet Li-Young Lee, in "For a New Citizen of These United States," sees the double-edged quality of memories for the immigrant, memories that remind us of painful past experiences and that sometimes interfere with our bonding with the new society we have decided to call home. Yet these memories also give life a fullness and depth that can easily be lost in making the difficult transition into a new culture.

The chapter closes with two student essays, each exploring an issue of memory. Corey Okada's "Namesake" reflects on her memories of an aunt with whom she shared a name, but whom Okada rejected as a child because of her aunt's disability. In "Enter Dragon," Tin Le, a Vietnamese-American student, presents disturbing memories of a childhood in which his fantasies of power and revenge gave him courage in the face of the prejudice and bullying of his classmates.

Although most people mature and learn to function in the rational world, the dreams and ghosts of their childhoods continue to shape, to haunt, and to inspire their waking lives. Writing about the past can be one of the best ways to face and come to terms with the ghosts of memory. This type of writing can then help us begin to formulate and construct realistic and positive dreams for the future.

Edward Hopper (1882–1967)
"Nighthawks" (1942)

The mood of Edward Hopper's classic American painting of a late-night, deserted street and a few late-night patrons in an old-fashioned diner leads us to reflect our own memories to find similar scenes of isolation from our earlier years, or even from old photographs kept by our parents or grandparents. Critic Robert Hughes has said of Hopper's work that "Hopper gives us a created world, not one that is merely recorded. Everything in it is shaped by memory, sympathy, distance and formal imperatives."

Ideas for Drawing, Writing, and Discussion

1. Create a picture (a painting or drawing) that expresses a memory from your past called up by looking at Hopper's "Nighthawks."
2. Describe the memory that you tried to capture in your picture. How does describing in words differ from the original visual version? How do both add to your perceptions of the original memory?
3. Share your memory picture and your accompanying writing with the students in your group. Discuss the different kinds of memories that people chose to express, and how expressing the memories in different media changes and adds to them.

Michele Murray

"Poem to My Grandmother in Her Death"

Michele Murray (1933–1974) was born in Brooklyn and graduated from the New School for Social Research in New York and the University of Connecticut. Murray held teaching positions in English for a number of years, primarily in schools in the Washington, D.C. area. She wrote children's books and poems, the latter collected posthumously in The Great Mother *(1974). She also edited the ground-breaking anthology* A House of Good Proportion: Images of Women in Literature *(1973). Michele Murray's work often explores her memories of relatives, as in the following selection, "Poem to my Grandmother in Her Death" (1974).*

JOURNAL

Write a letter to a relative or friend you have not seen for many years. Examine how and why certain memories of this person continue to live on in your mind.

After a dozen years of death
even love wanders off, old faithful
dog tired of lying on stiff marble.

In any case you would not understand
5   this life, the plain white walls
& the books, a passion lost on you.

I do not know what forced your life
through iron years into a shape of giving—
an apple, squares of chocolate, a hand.

10 There should have been nothing left
   after the mean streets, foaming washtubs,
   the wild cries of births at home.

   Never mind. It's crumbling in my hands,
   too, what you gave. I've jumped from ledges
15 & landed oddly twisted, bleeding internally.

   Thus I learn how to remember your injuries—
   your sudden heaviness as fine rain fell,
   or your silence over the scraped bread board.

   Finding myself in the end is finding you
20 & if you are lost in the folds of your silence
   then I find only to lose with you those years

   I stupidly slung off me like ragged clothes
   when I was ashamed to be the child
   of your child. I scramble for them now

25 In dark closets because I am afraid.
   I have forgotten so much. If I could meet you
   again perhaps I could rejoin my own flesh.

   And not lose whatever you called love.
   I could understand your silences & speak them
30 & you would be as present to me as your worn ring.

   In the shadows I reach for the bucket of fierce dahlias
   you bought without pricing, the coat you shook
   free of its snow, the blouse that you ironed.

   There's no love so pure it can thrive
35 without its incarnations. I would like to know you
   once again over your chipped cups brimming with tea.

QUESTIONS FOR DISCUSSION

1. What does the first stanza of the poem say about memory through the
   metaphor of the dog "lying on the stiff marble" and about the nature of
   and the endurance of love?
2. How does the narrator contrast her current lifestyle and attitudes with her
   grandmother's life? How does the narrator come to understand the "injuries" her grandmother suffered?
3. What conflict did the narrator have with her mother? Does the conflict
   seem to be a typical one, or a major breakdown in relations?

4. In the last three stanzas, the narrator refers to several items she has retained, in reality or in memory, which evoke for her qualities of her grandmother. What do these symbols of memory suggest to you about the grandmother's values and personality?
5. What is meant by the statement in the last stanza of the poem, "There's no love so pure it can thrive / without its incarnations"? Do you agree or disagree with this concept of remembered love?
6. Do you think that the narrator has been successful in her efforts to revive the connection she once felt with her grandmother through writing about it, or is this primarily a poem about the inevitability of loss and change?

CONNECTION

Compare the way Murray focuses on physical objects as a means to reconnect with a vanished past to Isabel Allende's effort to recall her life in Beirut through describing objects such as Tío Ramón's three-sectioned wardrobe.

IDEAS FOR WRITING

1. Write a reflective essay in which you select several objects that belonged to an absent or deceased friend or relative. Describe each briefly and discuss what memories and values are entwined with the objects.
2. Write an essay about memory in which you consider what causes certain early memories to stay in the mind while others are quickly forgotten. You might provide examples related to the role of keepsakes, mementos, and photographs, as well as family stories.

Isabel Allende

"Tío Ramón"

Born in 1943 in Lima, Peru, Isabel Allende graduated at sixteen from a private high school in Chile. She grew up in a powerful political family: her father was a Chilean diplomat, and her uncle, Chilean President Salvador Allende, was assassinated in 1973, after which her family was forced to flee to Venezuela. Allende moved to the United States in 1988, and currently lives in Marin county in Northern California. She began her career in Chile as a journalist and television interviewer, but after leaving Chile she began to write novels. Her first novel, The House of Spirits (1982; 1985 in English translation), won the award for the Best Novel of the Year in Chile. The books that followed have all been popular both in Latin America and the United States: Love and Shadows (1984; 1987), The Stories of Eva Luna (1990; 1991),

The Infinite Plan *(1991; 1993), and* Daughter of Fortune *(1999). Allende also wrote a memoir,* Paula *(1994), an elegy to her daughter who died of a rare, lingering illness. The following excerpt from* Paula *describes the attempt of her stepfather to instruct and to discipline Allende during their life in exile in Lebanon.*

JOURNAL

Write about a family member, relative, or adult who taught you an important lesson about life.

1   We lived in Lebanon for three surreal years, which allowed me to learn some French and to travel to most of the surrounding countries—including the Holy Land and Israel, which in the decade of the fifties, as now, existed in a permanent state of war with the Arabs. Crossing the border by car, as we did more than once, was a sobering experience. We lived in a large, ugly, modern apartment. From the terrace, we could look down on a market and the Guard Headquarters that played important roles later when the violence began. Tío Ramón set aside one room for the consulate, and hung the shield and flag of Chile on the front of the building. None of my new friends had ever heard of that country; they thought I came from China. In general, in that time and in that part of the world, girls were confined to house and school until the day of their marriage—if they had the misfortune to marry—the moment at which they exchanged a paternal prison for a conjugal one. I was shy, and kept very much to myself. Elvis Presley was already fat before I ever saw him in a film. Our family life was not smooth; my mother did not adapt well to the Arab culture, the hot climate, or Tío Ramón's authoritarianism; she suffered headaches, allergies, and sudden hallucinations. Once we packed our suitcases to return to my grandfather's house in Santiago because she swore that an Orthodox priest in full liturgical vestments was spying on her bath through a transom. My stepfather missed his own children but had little contact with them; communications with Chile could be delayed for months, contributing to the feeling that we lived at the end of the world. Finances were extremely tight; money was laboriously stretched out in weekly accountings, and then, if anything was left over, we went to the movies or to an indoor ice-skating rink, the only luxuries we could allow ourselves. We lived decently, but on a level different from that of other members of the diplomatic corps or the social circle we frequented, for whom private clubs, winter sports, the theater, and vacations in Switzerland were the norm. My mother made herself a long silk dress for gala receptions; she transformed it in miraculous ways with a brocade train, lace sleeves, or velvet bow at the waist. I suspect that people focused on her face, however, not her clothes. She became expert in the supreme art of keeping up appearances; she prepared inexpensive dishes, disguised them with sophisticated sauces of her own invention, and served them on her famous silver trays;

she made the living room and dining room elegant with paintings from my grandfather's house and tapestries bought on credit on the docks of Beirut, but everything else was at best modest. Tío Ramón's unbending optimism never flagged. With all the problems my mother had, I have often wondered what kept them together during that time, and the only answer that comes to me is, the tenacity of a passion born of distance, nourished with love letters, and fortified by a veritable Everest of obstacles. They are very different, and it is not unusual for them to argue to the point of exhaustion. Some of their battles were of such magnitude that they were dubbed with a name of their own and given a place in the family archive of anecdotes. I admit that I did nothing to facilitate their living together; when I realized that my stepfather had arrived in our lives to stay, I declared all-out war. Today it shames me to recall all the times I plotted horrible ways to kill him. His role was not easy; I cannot imagine how he was able to rear the three Allende children who fell into his lap. We never called him Papa, because that word brought back bad memories, but he earned his avuncular title, Tío Ramón, as a symbol of admiration and confidence. Today, at seventy-five, hundreds of persons scattered across five continents—including no few government officials and members of Chile's diplomatic corps—call him Tío Ramón for the same reason.

2   In an attempt to provide continuity to my education, I was sent to an English school for girls whose objective was to build character through trials of rigor and discipline—none of which much impressed me because it was not for nothing I had emerged unscathed from my uncles' famous Ruffin games. The goal of that teaching was for all students to memorize the Bible. "Deuteronomy, chapter five, verse three," Miss St. John would intone, and we had to recite it without stopping to think. In this way, I learned a little English, and also perfected to absurdity the stoic sense of life already implanted by my grandfather in the big old house with swirling currents of air. Both the English language and stoicism in the face of adversity have been beneficial; most of what other skills I possess Tío Ramón taught me by example and a methodology that modern psychology would consider brutal. He acted as consul general for several Arab countries, using Beirut as his base, a magnificent city that was considered the Paris of the Middle East: traffic was tied up by camels and sheikhs' Cadillacs with gold bumpers, and Muslim women, draped in black with only a peephole for their eyes, shopped in the souks elbow to elbow with scantily clad foreigners. On Saturdays, some of the housewives in the North American colony liked to wash their cars wearing shorts and bare midriff tops. Those Arab men who rarely saw women without veils came from remote villages, harrowing journeys by burro, to attend the spectacle of the half-naked foreign women. The locals rented chairs and sold coffee and syrupy sweets to the spectators lined up in rows on the opposite side of the street.

3   Summers were as hot and humid as a Turkish bath, but my school was ruled by norms imposed by Queen Victoria in a foggy, late-nineteenth-century England. Our uniform was a medieval cassocklike affair of coarsely woven cloth that closed with ties because buttons were considered frivolous; we wore orthopedic-looking shoes and a pith helmet-style hat pulled down to our eyebrows, an outfit that would take

the wind out of anyone's sails. Food was fodder for shaping character; every day we were served unsalted rice, and twice a week it was burned; on Monday, Wednesday, and Friday, it was accompanied by vegetables, Tuesday, by yogurt, and Thursday, by boiled liver. It was months before I could refrain from gagging when I saw those pieces of gray organs floating in tepid water, but in the end I found them delicious, and eagerly awaited Thursday lunch. Since then, I have never met a meal I cannot eat, including English food. The girls came from many regions, and almost all were boarding students. Shirley was the prettiest girl in the school; she looked good even in our uniform hat. She came from India, had blue-black hair, made up her eyes with a pearly powder, and walked with the gravity-defying step of a gazelle. Behind closed bathroom doors, she taught me to belly dance, an accomplishment that has not done me much good since I have never had enough nerve to seduce a man by shaking and grinding. One day, soon after her fifteenth birthday, Shirley was removed from the school and taken back to her country to be wed to a fifty-year-old merchant her parents had chosen for her, a man she had never seen but knew only from a hand-tinted studio portrait. Eliza, my best friend, was straight out of a novel: an orphan, she was raised like a servant by sisters who had stolen her share of their inheritance; she sang like an angle and had plans to run away to America. Thirty-five years later, we met in Canada. She had fulfilled her dreams of independence; she owned her own business, had a fine mansion, a car with a telephone, four fur coats, and two spoiled dogs, but she still weeps when she remembers her childhood in Beirut. While Eliza was saving her pennies to flee to the New World, and the beautiful Shirley was fulfilling her destiny in an arranged marriage, the rest of us were studying the Bible and whispering about a certain Elvis Presley, whom none of us had seen or heard but who was said to create havoc with his electric guitar and rotating pelvis. I rode the school bus every day, the first to be picked up in the morning and the last to be left off in the afternoon. I spent hours circling around the city, an arrangement I liked because I didn't much want to go home. When I was eventually delivered, I often found Tío Ramón sitting in his undershirt beneath the ceiling fan, trying to move more air with a folded newspaper and listening to boleros.

4 "What did the nuns teach you today?" he would ask.

5 I particularly remember one day replying, sweating, but phlegmatic and dignified in my dreadful uniform, "They're not nuns, they're Protestant ladies. And we talked about Job."

6 "Job? That idiot God tested by sending every calamity known to mankind?"

7 "He wasn't an idiot, Tío Ramón, he was a saintly man who never denied the Lord, no matter how much he suffered."

8 "Does that seem right? God makes a bet with Satan, punishes poor Job unmercifully, and wants to be loved by him besides. That is a cruel, unjust, and frivolous God. A master who treated his servants that way would deserve neither loyalty nor respect, much less adoration."

9 Tío Ramón, who had been educated by Jesuits, was intimidatingly emphatic and implacably logical—the same skills he used in squabbles with my mother—as he set out to prove the stupidity of the biblical hero whose attitude, far from setting a

praiseworthy example, demonstrated a personality disorder. In less than ten minutes of oratory, he had demolished all Miss St. John's virtuous teachings.

10   "Are you convinced that Job was a numskull?"

11   "Yes, Tío Ramón."

12   "Will you swear to that in writing?"

13   "Yes."

14   The consul of Chile crossed the couple of yards that separated us from his office and composed on letterhead paper a document with three carbons saying that I, Isabel Allende Llona, fourteen years old, a Chilean citizen, attested that Job, he of the Old Testament, was a dolt. He made me sign it, after reading it carefully—"because you must never sign anything blindly"—then folded it and put it in the consulate safe. He went back to his chair beneath the ceiling fan and, heaving a weary sigh, said:

15   "All right, child, now I shall prove that you were correct in the first place, and that Job was a holy man of God. I shall give you the arguments you should have used had you known how to think. Please understand that I am doing this only to teach you how to debate, something that will be very helpful in life." And he proceeded to dismantle his previous arguments and convince me of what I had firmly believed in the first place. In a very few minutes, I was again defeated, and this time on the verge of tears.

16   "Do you accept that Job was right to remain faithful to his God despite his misfortunes?"

17   "Yes, Tío Ramón."

18   "Are you absolutely sure?"

19   "Yes."

20   "Would you sign a document?"

21   And he composed a second statement that said that I, Isabel Allende Llona, fourteen years old, a Chilean citizen, was retracting my earlier opinion and instead agreeing that Job acted correctly. He handed me his pen, but just as I was about to sign my name at the bottom of the page he stopped me with a yell.

22   "No! How many times have I told you not to let anyone twist your arm? The most important thing in winning an argument is not to vacillate even if you have doubts, let alone if you are wrong!"

23   That is how I learned to defend myself, and years later in Chile I participated in an intermural debate between our girls' school and San Ignacio, which was represented by five boys with the mien of criminal lawyers, and two Jesuit priests whispering instructions to them. The boys' team arrived with a load of books they consulted to support their arguments and intimidate their opponents. My only resource was the memory of those afternoons with Job and my Tío Ramón in Lebanon. I lost, of course, but at the end my team paraded me around on their shoulders as our macho rivals retreated haughtily with their cartload of arguments. I do not know how many statements with three carbons I signed in my adolescence on topics as wildly diverse as biting my fingernails and the threatened extinction of whales. I believe that for a few years Tío Ramón kept some of them—for example, the one in which I swear that it is his fault that I will never meet any men and will end up an old maid. That was in Bolivia, when at age eleven I threw a tantrum because he did not let me go to a party

where I thought I would see my beloved Big Ears. Three years later I was invited to a different party, this one in Beirut at the home of the U.S. ambassador and his wife. That time I had the good sense not to want to go because the girls had to play the part of passive sheep; I was sure that no boy in his right mind would ask me to dance, and I could not think of a worse humiliation than being a wallflower. That time my stepfather forced me to attend because, he said, if I did not overcome my complexes I would never have any success in life. The day before the party, he closed the consulate and dedicated the afternoon to teaching me to dance. With single-minded tenacity, he made me sway to the rhythm of the music, first holding the back of a chair, then a broom, and finally him. In several hours I learned everything from the Charleston to the samba. Then he dried my tears and drove me to buy a new dress. As he left me at the party, he offered a piece of unforgettable advice, one I have followed at crucial moments of my life: *Remember that all the others are more afraid than you.* He added that I should not sit down for a second, but should take up a position near the record player. . . oh, and not eat anything, because it takes tremendous courage for a boy to cross a room and go up to a girl anchored like a frigate in her chair and with a plate of cake in her hand. Besides, the few boys who know how to dance are the same ones who change the records, so you want to be near the player. At the entrance to the embassy, a cement fortress in the worst fifties style, there was a cage of huge black birds that spoke English with a Jamaican accent. I was greeted by the ambassador's wife—in some sort of admiral get-up and with a whistle around her neck for giving instructions to the guests—and led to an enormous room swarming with tall, ugly adolescents with pimply faces, all chewing gum, eating french fries, and drinking Coca-Cola. The boys were wearing plaid jackets and bow ties, and the girls had on circle skirts and angora sweaters that left a flurry of hair in the air but revealed enviable protuberances on their chest. I, on the other hand, had nothing to put in a brassiere. They were all wearing bobby socks. I felt totally alien; my dress was a disaster of taffeta and velvet, and I didn't know a soul there. Panic-stricken, I stood and fed cake crumbs to the black birds until I remembered Tío Ramón's instructions. Trembling, I removed my shoes and headed toward the record player. Soon I saw a male hand stretched in my direction and, unable to believe my luck, was borne off to dance a sugary tune with a boy who had flat feet and braces on his teeth and was not half as graceful as my stepfather. It was the time when everyone danced cheek-to-cheek, a feat usually denied me even today, since my face comes about to a normal man's breastbone; at this party, barely fourteen and not wearing my shoes, my head was at the level of my partner's belly button. After that first ballad, they played a whole record of rock 'n' roll. Tío Ramón had never even heard of that, but all I had to do was watch the others for a few minutes and apply what I had learned the afternoon before. For once, my size and my limber joints were a plus; it was a breeze for my partners to toss me toward the ceiling, twirl me through the air like an acrobat, and catch me just before I broke my neck on the floor. I found myself performing arabesques, lifted, dragged, whipped around, and bounced by a variety of youths who by this point had shed their plaid jackets and bow ties. I had no complaint. I was not a wallflower that night, as I had dreaded, but danced until I raised blisters on my feet, in the process acquiring the assurance that it is not so difficult to meet men after all, and that certainly I would not be an old maid. I did not, however, sign a document to that effect. I had learned not to let anyone twist my arm.

24   Tío Ramón had a three-sectioned wardrobe that could be taken apart when we moved, in which he locked his clothes and treasures: a collection of erotic magazines, cartons of cigarettes, boxes of chocolates, and liquor. My brother Juan discovered a way to open it with a bent wire, and we became expert sneak thieves. If we had taken only a few chocolates or cigarettes, he would have noticed, but we would sneak an entire layer of chocolates and reseal the box so perfectly it looked unopened, and we filched entire cartons of cigarettes, never a few, or a pack. Tío Ramón first became suspicious in La Paz. He called us in, one by one, and tried to get us either to confess or to inform on the guilty party. Neither gentle words nor threats were any good: we thought that to admit to the crime would be stupid and, in our moral code, betrayal among siblings was unpardonable. One Friday afternoon when we got back from school, we found Tío Ramón and a man we didn't know waiting for us in the living room.

25   "I have no patience with your disregard for the truth; the least I can expect is not to be robbed in my own home. This gentleman is a police detective. He will take your fingerprints, compare them with the evidence on my wardrobe, and we will know who the thief is. This is your last chance to confess the truth."

26   Pale with terror, my brothers and I stared at the floor and clamped our jaws shut.

27   "Do you know what happens to criminals? They rot in jail," Tío Ramón added.

28   The detective pulled a tin box from his pocket. When he opened it, we could see the black inkpad inside. Slowly, with great ceremony, he pressed each of our fingers to the pad, then rolled them onto a prepared cardboard.

29   "Have no worry, Señor Consul. Monday you will have the results of my investigation," the man assured Tío Ramón as he left.

30   Saturday and Sunday were days of moral torture; hidden in the bathroom and the most private corners of the garden, we whispered about our black future. None of us was free of guilt; we would all end up in a dungeon on foul water and dry bread crusts, like the Count of Monte Cristo. The following Monday, the ineffable Tío Ramón called us into his office.

31   "I know exactly who the thief is," he announced, wiggling thick, satanic eyebrows. "Nevertheless, out of consideration for your mother, who has interceded in your behalf, I shall not incarcerate anyone this time. The culprit knows I know who he or she is. It will remain between the two of us. I warn all of you that on the next occasion I shall not be so softhearted. Do I make myself clear?"

32   We stumbled from the room, grateful, unable to believe such magnanimity. We did not steal anything for a long time, but a few years later in Beirut I thought about it again, and was struck by the suspicion that the purported detective was actually an embassy chauffeur—Tío Ramón was quite capable of playing such a trick. Bending a wire of my own, I again opened the wardrobe. This time, in addition to the predictable treasures, I found four red leather-bound volumes of *A Thousand*

and One Nights. I deduced that there must be some powerful reason these books were under lock and key, and that made them much more interesting than the bonbons, cigarettes, or erotic magazines with women in garter belts. For the next three years, every time Tío Ramón and my mother were at some cocktail party or dinner, I read snatches of the tales, curled up inside the cabinet with my faithful flashlight. Even though diplomats necessarily suffer an intense social life, there was never enough time to finish those fabulous stories. When I heard my parents coming, I had to close the wardrobe in a wink and fly to my bed and pretend to be asleep. It was impossible to leave a bookmark between the pages and I always forgot my place; worse yet, entire sections fell out as I searched for the dirty parts, with the results that innumerable new versions of the stories were created in an orgy of exotic words, eroticism, and fantasy. The contrast between the puritanism of my school, where work was exalted and neither bodily imperatives nor lightning flash of imagination allowed, and the creative idleness and enveloping sensuality of those books branded my soul. For decades I wavered between those two tendencies, torn apart inside and awash in a sea of intermingled desires and sins, until finally in the heat of Venezuela, when I was nearly forty years old, I at last freed myself from Miss St. John's rigid precepts. Just as in my childhood I hid in the basement of Tata's house to read my favorite books, so in full adolescence, just as my body and mind were awakening to the mysteries of sex, I furtively read *A Thousand and One Nights.* Deep in that dark wardrobe, I lost myself in magical tales of princes on flying carpets, genies in oil lamps, and appealing thieves who slipped into the sultan's harem disguised as old ladies to indulge in marathon love fests with forbidden women with hair black as night, pillowy hips and breasts like apples, soft women smelling of musk and eager for pleasure. On those pages, love, life, and death seemed like a gambol; the descriptions of food, landscapes, palaces, markets, smells, tastes, and textures were so rich that after them the world has never been the same to me.

QUESTIONS FOR DISCUSSION

1. Why is Allende's family living in Beirut? How do they survive their three difficult years there?
2. Allende characterizes Tío Ramón as a brutal teacher. Why does she respect him? Do you think he is an effective teacher?
3. What does Tío Ramón teach Isabel about signing her name to legal documents? How does he help her to be a success at the dance?
4. Why does Tío Ramón hide the *A Thousand and One Nights* in his wardrobe? What does Isabel learn from this book?
5. What does Tío Ramón's three sectioned wardrobe symbolize?
6. Contrast what Allende learns at school with what she learns at home.
7. How does reading this selection help you speculate about why we remember certain people and incidents in our lives?

CONNECTION

Compare and contrast what Allende learns from her stepfather to what Angelou learns from her grandmother. Contrast the "teaching methods" of each.

IDEAS FOR WRITING

1. Write an essay based on your journal entry about a family member who taught you something of value.
2. Write an essay that explains the three most important lessons that Tío Ramón taught Isabel. Quote from the text to support your main ideas. In conclusion, explain why you think that he was or was not a good teacher.

Maya Angelou

"The Angel of the Candy Counter"

Maya Angelou (b. 1928) grew up in Stamps, Arkansas, where she spent her childhood with her grandmother, a storekeeper and leader in the African-American community of Stamps. Currently she is a professor of American Studies at Wake Forest University. Angelou has worked as a dancer, actress, teacher, and screenwriter. She has lectured all over the world, speaking as an advocate of civil rights. Angelou's most recent works include Wouldn't Take Nothing for My Journey Now *(1993),* The Challenge of Creative Leadership *(1996), and* Even the Stars Look Lonesome *(1997). Her autobiographical writings reflect on the impact of poverty on and racism toward the black community, as well as on those moments of joy, insight, and creative expression that sometimes can ease the pain of oppression. In the following selection excerpted from the first book of her memoir,* I Know Why the Caged Bird Sings *(1970), Angelou remembers the fierce courage and determination of her grandmother.*

JOURNAL

Write about a time in your childhood when you retreated into fantasy to help protect yourself from feelings of rejection or loss. How did the fantasy help you to cope with your situation ?

1   The Angel of the candy counter had found me out at last, and was exacting excruciating penance for all the stolen Milky Ways, Mounds, Mr. Goodbars and Hersheys with Almonds. I had two cavities that were rotten to the gums. The pain was beyond the bailiwick of crushed aspirins or oil of cloves. Only one thing could help me, so I prayed earnestly that I'd be allowed to sit under the house and have the building collapse on my left jaw. Since there was no Negro dentist in Stamps, nor doctor either, for that matter, Momma had dealt with previous toothaches by

pulling them out (a string tied to the tooth with the other end looped over her fist), pain killers and prayer. In this particular instance the medicine had proved ineffective; there wasn't enough enamel left to hook a string on, and the prayers were being ignored because the Balancing Angel was blocking their passage.

2   I lived a few days and nights in blinding pain, not so much toying with as seriously considering the idea of jumping in the well, and Momma decided I had to be taken to a dentist. The nearest Negro dentist was in Texarkana, twenty-five miles away, and I was certain that I'd be dead long before we reached half the distance. Momma said we'd go to Dr. Lincoln, right in Stamps, and he'd take care of me. She said he owed her a favor.

3   I knew that there were a number of whitefolks in town that owed her favors. Bailey and I had seen the books which showed how she had lent money to Blacks and whites alike during the Depression, and most still owed her. But I couldn't aptly remember seeing Dr. Lincoln's name, nor had I ever heard of a Negro's going to him as a patient. However, Momma said we were going, and put water on the stove for our baths. I had never been to a doctor, so she told me that after the bath (which would make my mouth feel better) I had to put on freshly starched and ironed underclothes from inside out. The ache failed to respond to the bath, and I knew then that the pain was more serious than that which anyone had ever suffered.

4   Before we left the Store, she ordered me to brush my teeth and then wash my mouth with Listerine. The idea of even opening my clamped jaws increased the pain, but upon her explanation that when you go to a doctor you have to clean yourself all over, but most especially the part that's to be examined, I screwed up my courage and unlocked my teeth. The cool air in my mouth and the jarring of my molars dislodged what little remained of my reason. I had frozen to the pain, my family nearly had to tie me down to take the toothbrush away. It was no small effort to get me started on the road to the dentist. Momma spoke to all the passers by, but didn't stop to chat. She explained over her shoulder that we were going to the doctor and she'd "pass the time of day" on our way home.

5   Until we reached the pond the pain was my world, an aura that haloed me for three feet around. Crossing the bridge into whitefolks' country, pieces of sanity pushed themselves forward. I had to stop moaning and start walking straight. The white towel, which was drawn under my chin and tied over my head, had to be arranged. If one was dying, it had to be done in style if the dying took place in whitefolks' part of town.

6   On the other side of the bridge the ache seemed to lessen as if a whitebreeze blew off the whitefolks and cushioned everything in their neighborhood—including my jaw. The gravel road was smoother, the stones smaller and the tree branches hung down around the path and nearly covered us. If the pain didn't diminish then, the familiar yet strange sights hypnotized me into believing that it had.

7   But my head continued to throb with the measured insistence of a bass drum, and how could a toothache pass the calaboose, hear the songs of the prisoners, their blues and laughter, and not be changed? How could one or two or even a mouthful of angry tooth roots meet a wagonload of powhitetrash children, endure their idiotic snobbery and not feel less important?

8   Behind the building which housed the dentist's office ran a small path used by servants and those tradespeople who catered to the butcher and Stamps' one restaurant. Momma and I followed that lane to the backstairs of Dentist Lincoln's office. The sun was bright and gave the day a hard reality as we climbed up the steps to the second floor.

9   Momma knocked on the back door and a young white girl opened it to show surprise at seeing us there. Momma said she wanted to see Dentist Lincoln and to tell him Annie was there. The girl closed the door firmly. Now the humiliation of hearing Momma describe herself as if she had no last name to the young white girl was equal to the physical pain. It seemed terribly unfair to have a toothache and a headache and have to bear at the same time the heavy burden of Blackness.

10   It was always possible that the teeth would quiet down and maybe drop out of their own accord. Momma said we would wait. We leaned in the harsh sunlight on the shaky railings of the dentist's back porch for over an hour.

11   He opened the door and looked at Momma. "Well, Annie, what can I do for you?"

12   He didn't see the towel around my jaw or notice my swollen face.

13   Momma said, "Dentist Lincoln. It's my grandbaby here. She got two rotten teeth that's giving her a fit."

14   She waited for him to acknowledge the truth of her statement. He made no comment, orally or facially.

15   "She had this toothache purt' near four days now, and today I said, 'Young lady, you going to the Dentist.'"

16   "Annie?"

17   "Yes, sir, Dentist Lincoln."

18   He was choosing words the way people hunt for shells. "Annie, you know I don't treat nigra, colored people."

19   "I know, Dentist Lincoln. But this here is just my little grandbaby, and she ain't gone be no trouble to you . . . "

20   "Annie, everybody has a policy. In this world you have to have a policy. Now, my policy is I don't treat colored people."

21   The sun had baked the oil out of Momma's skin and melted the Vaseline in her hair. She shone greasily as she leaned out of the dentist's shadow.

22   "Seem like to me, Dentist Lincoln, you might look after her, she ain't nothing but a little mite. And seems like maybe you owe me a favor or two."

23   He reddened slightly. "Favor or no favor. The money has all been repaid to you and that's the end of it. Sorry, Annie." He had his hand on the doorknob. "Sorry." His voice was a bit kinder on the second "Sorry," as if he really was.

24   Momma said, "I wouldn't press on you like this for myself but I can't take No. Not for my grandbaby. When you come to borrow my money you didn't have to beg. You asked me, and I lent it. Now, it wasn't my policy. I ain't no moneylender, but you stood to lose this building and I tried to help you out."

25   "It's been paid, and raising your voice won't make me change my mind. My policy . . ." He let go of the door and stepped nearer Momma. The three of us were

crowded on the small landing. "Annie, my policy is I'd rather stick my hand in a dog's mouth than in a nigger's."

26   He had never once looked at me. He turned his back and went through the door into the cool beyond. Momma backed up inside herself for a few minutes. I forget everything except her face which was almost a new one to me. She leaned over and took the doorknob, and in her everyday soft voice she said, "Sister, go on downstairs. Wait for me. I'll be there directly."

27   Under the most common of circumstances I knew it did no good to argue with Momma. So I walked down the steep stairs, afraid to look back and afraid not to do so. I turned as the door slammed, and she was gone.

28   *Momma walked in that room as if she owned it. She shoved that silly nurse aside with one hand and strode into the dentist's office. He was sitting in his chair, sharpening his mean instruments and putting extra sting into his medicines. Her eyes were blazing like live coals and her arms had doubled themselves in length. He looked up at her just before she caught him by the collar of his white jacket.*

29   *"Stand up when you see a lady, you contemptuous scoundrel." Her tongue had thinned and the words rolled off well enunciated. Enunciated and sharp like little claps of thunder.*

30   *The dentist had no choice but to stand at R.O.T.C. attention. His head dropped after a minute and his voice was humble. "Yes, ma'am, Mrs. Henderson."*

31   *"You knave, do you think you acted like a gentleman, speaking to me like that in front of my granddaughter?" She didn't shake him, although she had the power. She simply held him upright.*

32   *"No, ma'am, Mrs. Henderson."*

33   *"No, ma'am, Mrs. Henderson, what?" Then she did give him the tiniest of shakes, but because of her strength the action set his head and arms to shaking loose on the ends of his body. He stuttered much worse than Uncle Willie. "No, ma'am. Mrs. Henderson, I'm sorry."*

34   *With just an edge of her disgust showing, Momma slung him back in his dentist's chair. "Sorry is as sorry does, and you're about the sorriest dentist I ever laid my eyes on." (She could afford to slip into the vernacular because she had such eloquent command of English.)*

35   *"I didn't ask you to apologize in front of Marguerite, because I don't want her to know my power, but I order you, now and herewith. Leave Stamps by sundown."*

36   *"Mrs. Henderson, I can't get my equipment . . ." He was shaking terribly now.*

37   *"Now, that brings me to my second order. You will never again practice dentistry. Never! When you get settled in your next place, you will be a veterinarian caring for dogs with the mange, cats with the cholera and cows with the epizootic. Is that clear?"*

38   *The saliva ran down his chin and his eyes filled with tears. "Yes, ma'am. Thank you for not killing me. Thank you, Mrs. Henderson."*

39   *Momma pulled herself back from being ten feet tall with eight-foot arms and said, "You're welcome for nothing, you varlet, I wouldn't waste a killing on the likes of you."*

40   *On her way out she waved her handkerchief at the nurse and turned her into a crocus sack of chicken feed.*

41   Momma looked tired when she came down the stairs, but who wouldn't be tired if they had gone through what she had. She came close to me and adjusted the towel under my jaw (I had forgotten the toothache; I only knew that she made her hands gentle in order not to awaken the pain). She took my hand. Her voice never changed. "Come on, Sister."

42   I reckoned we were going home where she would concoct a brew to eliminate the pain and maybe give me new teeth too. New teeth that would grow overnight out of my gums. She led me toward the drugstore, which was in the opposite direction from the Store. "I'm taking you to Dentist Baker in Texarkana."

43   I was glad after all that I had bathed and put on Mum and Cashmere Bouquet talcum powder. It was a wonderful surprise. My toothache had quieted to solemn pain, Momma had obliterated the evil white man, and we were going on a trip to Texarkana, just the two of us.

44   On the Greyhound she took an inside seat in the back, and I sat beside her. I was so proud of being her granddaughter and sure that some of her magic must have come down to me. She asked if I was scared. I only shook my head and leaned over on her cool brown upper arm. There was no chance that a dentist, especially a Negro dentist, would dare hurt me then. Not with Momma there. The trip was uneventful, except that she put her arm around me, which was very unusual for Momma to do.

45   The dentist showed me the medicine and the needle before he deadened my gums, but if he hadn't I wouldn't have worried. Momma stood right behind him. Her arms were folded and she checked on everything he did. The teeth were extracted and she bought me an ice cream cone from the side window of a drug counter. The trip back to Stamps was quiet, except that I had to spit into a very small empty snuff can which she had gotten for me and it was difficult with the bus humping and jerking on our country roads.

46   At home, I was given a warm salt solution, and when I washed out my mouth I showed Bailey the empty holes, where the clotted blood sat like filling in a pie crust. He said I was quite brave, and that was my cue to reveal our confrontation with the peckerwood dentist and Momma's incredible powers.

47   I had to admit that I didn't hear the conversation, but what else could she have said than what I said she said? What else done? He agreed with my analysis in a lukewarm way, and I happily (after all, I'd been sick) flounced into the Store. Momma was preparing our evening meal and Uncle Willie leaned on the door sill. She gave her version.

48   "Dentist Lincoln got right uppity. Said he'd rather put his hand in a dog's mouth. And when I reminded him of the favor, he brushed it off like a piece of lint. Well, I sent Sister downstairs and went inside. I hadn't never been in his office before, but I found the door to where he takes out teeth, and him and the nurse was in there thick as thieves. I just stood there till he caught sight of me." Crash bang the pots on the stove. "He jumped just like he was sitting on a pin. He said, 'Annie, I done tole you, I ain't gonna mess around in no niggah's mouth.' I said, 'Somebody's got to do it then,' and he said, 'Take her to Texarkana to the colored dentist' and that's when I

said, 'If you paid me my money I could afford to take her.' He said, 'It's all been paid.' I tole him everything but the interest had been paid. He said, 'Twasn't no interest.' I said, ''Tis now. I'll take ten dollars as payment in full.' You know, Willie, it wasn't no right thing to do, 'cause I lent that money without thinking about it.

49   "He tole that little snippity nurse of his'n to give me ten dollars and make me sign a 'paid in full' receipt. She gave it to me and I signed the papers. Even though by rights he was paid up before, I figger, he gonna be that kind of nasty, he gonna have to pay for it."

50   Momma and her son laughed and laughed over the white man's evilness and her retributive sin.

51   I preferred, much preferred, my version.

Questions for Discussion

1. Why does Momma think that the white dentist, Dr. Lincoln, will pull Maya's tooth? What type of woman is Maya's grandmother?
2. Angelou contrasts the physical pain of her toothache with the painful realization of the doctor's prejudice. Which pain do you think was more hurtful for Maya? Why?
3. Contrast the types of discrimination against blacks in the South and elsewhere in this country today to the discrimination that Angelou describes in her story.
4. What does Maya learn about Momma on her trip to Dr. Lincoln's?
5. What does Maya's revenge fantasy reveal about her self-concept and self-esteem? Why does she prefer her version?
6. Point out instances of effective dialogue, dialect, setting, details, and imagery that help make this an especially moving memoir.

Connection

Compare Angelou's presentation of her painful childhood experience with that presented in bell hooks' essay. How does each writer use the memory in a unique way? How do the memories presented have a different long-term impact on the women involved?

Ideas for Writing

1. Develop your journal entry into an essay that discusses what you have learned from living through situations when you were discriminated against, humiliated, or rejected unjustly.
2. Write about a childhood fantasy that helped you to overcome feelings of inadequacy and rejection and develop courage and inner strength. Develop observations about the role that you think childhood fantasies of

power and heroism play in helping children to make the transition into adulthood.

Judith Ortiz Cofer

"Silent Dancing"

Born in Puerto Rico in 1952, Judith Ortiz Cofer came to New Jersey with her family when she was a child. After receiving an M.A. from Florida Atlantic University, Cofer taught English and Spanish at the University of Miami and currently teaches at the University of Georgia. Cofer's works include the novel Line of the Sun *(1989),* Silent Dancing: A Partial Remembrance of a Puerto Rican Childhood *(1990),* Latin Deli: Prose and Poetry *(1993), and* Island Like You: Stories of the Barrio *(1995). In the following selection from* Silent Dancing, *Cofer recalls memories of a childhood spent in two stikingly different cultures.*

JOURNAL

Write about a photograph or a home movie that evokes memories of your childhood.

1   *We have a home movie of this party. Several times my mother and I have watched it together, and I have asked questions about the silent revellers coming in and out of focus. It is grainy and of short duration but a great visual aid to my first memory of life in Paterson at that time. And it is in color—the only complete scene in color I can recall from those years.*

2   We lived in Puerto Rico until my brother was born in 1954. Soon after, because of economic pressures on our growing family, my father joined the United States Navy. He was assigned to duty on a ship in Brooklyn Yard, New York City—a place of cement and steel that was to be his home base in the States until his retirement more than twenty years later. He left the Island first, tracking down his uncle who lived with his family across the Hudson River, in Paterson, New Jersey. There he found a tiny apartment in a huge apartment building that had once housed Jewish families and was just being transformed into a tenement by Puerto Ricans overflowing from New York City. In 1955 he sent for us. My mother was only twenty years old, I was not quite three, and my brother was a toddler when we arrived at *El Building*, as the place had been christened by its new residents.

3   My memories of life in Paterson during those first few years are in shades of gray. Maybe I was too young to absorb vivid colors and details, or to discriminate between the slate blue of the winter sky and the darker hues of the snow-bearing clouds, but the single color washes over the whole period. The building we lived in was gray, the

streets were gray with slush the first few months of my life there, the coat my fa-ther had bought for me was dark in color and too big. It sat heavily on my thin frame.

4   I do remember the way the heater pipes banged and rattled, startling all of us out of sleep until we got so used to the sound that we automatically either shut it out or raised our voices above the racket. The hiss from the valve punctuated my sleep, which has always been fitful, like a nonhuman presence in the room—the dragon sleeping at the entrance of my childhood. But the pipes were a connection to all the other lives being lived around us. Having come from a house made for a single family back in Puerto Rico—my mother's extended-family home—it was curious to know that strangers lived under our floor and above our heads, and that the heater pipe went through everyone's apartment. (My first spanking in Paterson came as a result of playing tunes on the pipes in my room to see if there would be an answer.) My mother was as new to this concept of beehive life as I was, but had been given strict orders by my father to keep the doors locked, the noise down, ourselves to ourselves.

5   It seems that Father had learned some painful lessons about prejudice while searching for an apartment in Paterson. Not until years later did I hear how much resistance he had encountered with landlords who were panicking at the influx of Latinos into a neighborhood that had been Jewish for a couple of generations. But it was the American phenomenon of ethnic turnover that was changing the urban core of Paterson, and the human flood could not be held back with an accusing finger.

6   "You Cuban?" the man had asked my father, pointing a finger at his name tag on the Navy uniform—even though my father had the fair skin and light brown hair of his northern Spanish family background and our name is as common in Puerto Rico as Johnson is in the U.S.

7   "No," my father had answered looking past the finger into his adversary's angry eyes, "I'm Puerto Rican."

8   "Same shit." And the door closed. My father could have passed as European, but we couldn't. My brother and I both have our mother's black hair and olive skin, and so we lived in El Building and visited our great-uncle and his fair children on the next block. It was their private joke that they were the German branch of the fam-ily. Not many years later that area too would be mainly Puerto Rican. It was as if the heart of the city map were being gradually colored in brown—café-con-leche brown. Our color.

9   *The movie opens with a sweep of the living room. It is "typical" immigrant Puerto Rican decor for the time: the sofa and chairs are square and hard-looking, upholstered in bright colors (blue and yellow in this instance, and covered in the transparent plastic) that furniture salesmen then were adept at making women buy. The linoleum on the floor is light blue, and if it was subjected to the spike heels as it was in most places, there were dime-sized indentations all over it that cannot be seen in this movie. The room is full of people dressed in mainly two colors: dark suits for the men, red dresses for the women. I have asked my mother why most of the women are in red that night, and she*

shrugs, "I don't remember. Just a coincidence." She doesn't have my obsession for as-signing symbolism to everything.

10   The three women in red sitting on the couch are my mother, my eighteen-year-old cousin, and her brother's girlfriend. The "novia" is just up from the Island, which is apparent in her body language. She sits up formally, and her dress is carefully pulled over her knees. She is a pretty girl but her posture makes her look insecure, lost in her full skirted red dress which she has carefully tucked around her to make room for my gorgeous cousin, her future sister-in-law. My cousin has grown up in Paterson and is in her last year of high school. She doesn't have a trace of what Puerto Ricans call "la mancha" (literally, the stain: the mark of the new immigrant—something about the posture, the voice, or the humble demeanor making it obvious to everyone that that person has just arrived on the mainland; has not yet acquired the polished look of the city dweller). My cousin is wearing a tight red-sequined cocktail dress. Her brown hair has been light-ened with peroxide around the bangs, and she is holding a cigarette very expertly be-tween her fingers, bringing it up to her mouth in a sensuous arc of her arm to her as she talks animatedly with my mother, who has come up to sit between the two women, both only a few years younger than herself. My mother is somewhere halfway between the poles they represent in our culture.

11   It became my father's obsession to get out of the barrio, and thus we were never permitted to form bonds with the place or with the people who lived there. Yet the building was a comfort to my mother, who never got over yearning for la isla. She felt surrounded by her language: the walls were thin, and voices speaking and argu-ing in Spanish could be heard all day. Salsas blasted out of radios turned on early in the morning and left on for company. Women seemed to cook rice and beans per-petually—the strong aroma of red kidney beans boiling permeated the hallways.

12   Though Father preferred that we do our grocery shopping at the supermarket when he came home on weekend leaves, my mother insisted that she could cook only with products whose labels she could read, and so, during the week, I accompa-nied her and my little brother to La Bodega—a hole-in-the-wall grocery store across the street from El Building. There we squeezed down three narrow aisles jammed with various products. Goya and Libby's—those were the trademarks trusted by her Mamá, and so my mother bought cans of Goya beans, soups and condiments. She bought little cans of Libby's fruit juices for us. And she bought Colgate toothpaste and Palmolive soap. (The final e is pronounced in both those products in Spanish, and for many years I believed that they were manufactured on the Island. I remem-ber my surprise at first hearing a commercial on television for the toothpaste in which Colgate rhymed with "ate.") We would linger at La Bodega, for it was there that mother breathed best, taking in the familiar aromas of the foods she knew from Mamá's kitchen, and it was also there that she got to speak to the other women of El Building without violating outright Father's dictates against fraternizing with our neighbors.

13   But he did his best to make our "assimilation" painless. I can still see him carrying a Christmas tree up several flights of stairs to our apartment, leaving a trail of aro-

matic pine. He carried it formally, as if it were a flag in a parade. We were the only ones in El Building that I knew of who got presents on both Christmas Day and on *Día de Reyes*, the day when the Three Kings brought gifts to Christ and to Hispanic children.

14   Our greatest luxury in El Building was having our own television set. It must have been a result of Father's guilty feelings over the isolation he had imposed on us, but we were one of the first families in the barrio to have one. My brother quickly became an avid watcher of Captain Kangaroo and Jungle Jim. I loved all the family series, and by the time I started first grade in school, I could have drawn a map of Middle America as exemplified by the lives of characters in "Father Knows Best," "The Donna Reed Show," "Leave It to Beaver," "My Three Sons," and (my favorite) "Bachelor Father," where John Forsythe treated his adopted teenage daughter like a princess because he was rich and had a Chinese houseboy to do everything for him. Compared to our neighbors in El Building, we were rich. My father's Navy check provided us with financial security and a standard of life that the factory workers envied. The only thing his money could not buy us was a place to live away from the barrio—his greatest wish and Mother's greatest fear.

15   *In the home movie the men are shown next, sitting around a card table set up in one corner of the living room, playing dominoes. The clack of the ivory pieces is a sound familiar. I heard it in many houses on the Island and in many apartments in Paterson. In "Leave It to Beaver," the Cleavers played bridge in every other episode; in my childhood, the men started every social occasion with a hotly debated round of dominoes: the women would sit around and watch, but they never participated in the games.*

16   *Here and there you can see a small child. Children were always brought to parties and, whenever they got sleepy, put to bed in the host's bedrooms. Babysitting was a concept unrecognized by the Puerto Rican women I knew: a responsible mother did not leave her children with any stranger. And in a culture where children are not considered intrusive, there is no need to leave children at home. We went where our mother went.*

17   Of my pre-school years I have only impressions: the sharp bite of the wind in December as we walked with our parents towards the brightly lit stores downtown, how I felt like a stuffed doll in my heavy coat, boots and mittens; how good it was to walk into the five-and-dime and sit at the counter drinking hot chocolate.

18   On Saturdays our whole family would walk downtown to shop at the big department stores on Broadway. Mother bought all our clothes at Penny's and Sears, and she liked to buy her dresses at the women's specialty shops like Lerner's and Diana's. At some point we would go into Woolworth's and sit at the soda fountain to eat.

19   We never ran into other Latinos at these stores or eating out, and it became clear to me only years later that the women from El Building shopped mainly at other places—stores owned either by other Puerto Ricans, or by Jewish merchants who had philosophically accepted our presence in the city and decided to make us their good customers, if not neighbors and friends. These establishments were located not

downtown, but in the blocks around our street, and they were referred to generically as *La Tienda, El Bazar, La Bodega, La Botánica.* Everyone knew what was meant. These were the stores where your face did not turn a clerk to stone, where your money was as green as anyone else's.

20   On New Year's Eve we were dressed up like child models in the Sears catalogue— my brother in a miniature man's suit and bow tie, and I in black patent leather shoes and a frilly dress with several layers of crinolines underneath. My mother wore a bright red dress that night, I remember, and spike heels; her long black hair hung to her waist. Father, who usually wore his Navy uniform during his short visits home, had put on a dark civilian suit for the occasion: we had been invited to his uncle's house for a big celebration. Everyone was excited because my mother's brother, Hernán—a bachelor who could indulge himself in such luxuries—had bought a movie camera which he would be trying out that night.

21   Even the home movie cannot fill in the sensory details such a gathering left imprinted in a child's brain. The thick sweetness of women's perfume mixing with the ever-present smells of food cooking in the kitchen: meat and plantain *pasteles*, the ubiquitous rice dish made special with pigeon peas—*gandules*—and seasoned with the precious *sofrito* sent up from the island by somebody's mother or smuggled in by a recent traveler. *Sofrito* was one of the items that women hoarded, since it was hardly ever in stock at La Bodega. It was the flavor of Puerto Rico.

22   The men drank Palo Viejo rum and some of the younger ones got weepy. The first time I saw a grown man cry was at a New Year's Eve party. He had been reminded of his mother by the smells in the kitchen. But what I remember most were the boiled *pasteles*—boiled plantain or yucca rectangles stuffed with corned beef or other meats, olives, and many other savory ingredients, all wrapped in banana leaves. Everyone had to fish one out with a fork. There was always a "trick" pastel— one without stuffing—and whoever got that one was the "New Year's Fool."

23   There was also the music. Long-playing albums were treated like precious china in these homes. Mexican recordings were popular, but the songs that brought tears to my mother's eyes were sung by the melancholic Daniel Santos, whose life as a drug addict was the stuff of legend. Felipe Rodríguez was a particular favorite of couples. He sang about faithless women and broken-hearted men. There is a snatch of a lyric that has stuck in my mind like a needle on a worn groove: "De piedra ha de ser mi cama, de piedra la cabecera . . . la mujer que a mí me quiera . . . ha de quererme de veras. Ay, Ay, corazón, ¿por qué no amas . . . ?" I must have heard it a thousand times since the idea of a bed made of stone, and its connection to love, first troubled me with its disturbing images.

24   The five-minute home movie ends with people dancing in a circle. The creative filmmaker must have asked them to do that so that they could file past him. It is both comical and sad to watch silent dancing. Since there is no justification for the absurd movements that music provides for some of us, people appear frantic, their faces embarrassingly intense. It's as if you were watching sex. Yet for years, I've had dreams in the form of this home movie. In a recurring scene, familiar faces push themselves forward into my mind's eye, plastering their features into distorted close-

ups. And I'm asking them: "Who is she? Who is the woman I don't recognize? Is she an aunt? Somebody's wife? Tell me who she is. Tell me who these people are."

25   "No, see the beauty mark on her cheek as big as a hill on the lunar landscape of her face—well, that runs in the family. The women on your father's side of the family wrinkle early; it's the price they pay for that fair skin. The young girl with the green stain on her wedding dress is *La Novia*—just up from the island. See, she lowers her eyes as she approaches the camera like she's supposed to. Decent girls never look you directly in the face. *Humilde*, humble, a girl should express humility in all her actions. She will make a good wife for your cousin. He should consider himself lucky to have met her only weeks after she arrived here. If he married her quickly, she will make him a good Puerto Rican-style wife; but if he waits too long, she will be corrupted by the city, just like your cousin there."

26   "She means me. I do what I want. This is not some primitive island I live on. Do they expect me to wear a black *mantilla* on my head and go to mass every day? Not me. I'm an American woman and I will do as I please. I can type faster than anyone in my senior class at Central High, and I'm going to be a secretary to a lawyer when I graduate. I can pass for an American girl anywhere—I've tried it—at least for Italian, anyway. I never speak Spanish in public. I hate these parties, but I wanted the dress. I look better than any of these *humildes* here. My life is going to be different. I have an American boyfriend. He is older and has a car. My parents don't know it, but I sneak out of the house late at night sometimes to be with him. If I marry him, even my name will be American. I hate rice and beans. It's what makes these women fat."

27   "Your *prima* is pregnant by that man she's been sneaking around with. Would I lie to you? I'm your great-uncle's common-law wife—the one he abandoned on the island to marry your cousin's mother. I was not invited to this party, but I came anyway. I came to tell you that story about your cousin that you've always wanted to hear. Remember that comment your mother made to a neighbor that has always haunted you? The only thing you heard was your cousin's name and then you saw your mother pick up your doll from the couch and say: 'It was as big as this doll when they flushed it down the toilet.' This image has bothered you for years, hasn't it? You had nightmares about babies being flushed down the toilet, and you wondered why anyone would do such a horrible thing. You didn't dare ask your mother about it. She would only tell you that you had not heard her right and yell at you for listening to adult conversations. But later, when you were old enough to know about abortions, you suspected. I am here to tell you that you were right. Your cousin was growing an *Americanito* in her belly when this movie was made. Soon after she put something long and pointy into her pretty self, thinking maybe she could get rid of the problem before breakfast and still make it to her first class at the high school. Well, Niña, her screams could be heard downtown. Your aunt, her Mamá, who had been a midwife on the Island, managed to pull the little thing out. Yes, they probably flushed it down the toilet, what else could they do with it—give it a Christian burial in a little white casket with blue bows and ribbons? Nobody wanted that baby—least of all the father, a teacher at her school with a house in

West Paterson that he was filling with real children, and a wife who was a natural blond.

28   "Girl, the scandal sent your uncle back to the bottle. And guess where your cousin ended up? Irony of ironies. She was sent to a village in Puerto Rico to live with a relative on her mother's side: a place so far away from civilization that you have to ride a mule to reach it. A real change in scenery. She found a man there. Women like that cannot live without male company. But believe me, the men in Puerto Rico know how to put a saddle on a woman like her. *La Gringa*, they call her. ha, ha. ha. *La Gringa* is what she always wanted to be . . . "

29   The old woman's mouth becomes a cavernous black hole I fall into. And as I fall, I can feel the reverberations of her laughter. I hear the echoes of her last mocking words: *La Gringa, La Gringa!* And the conga line keeps moving silently past me. There is no music in my dream for the dancers.

30   When Odysseus visits Hades asking to see the spirit of his mother, he makes an offering of sacrificial blood, but since all of the souls crave an audience with the living, he has to listen to many of them before he can ask questions. I, too, have to hear the dead and the forgotten speak in my dream. Those who are still part of my life remain silent, going around and around in their dance. The others keep pressing their faces forward to say things about the past.

31   My father's uncle is last in line. He is dying of alcoholism, shrunken and shriveled like a monkey, his face is a mass of wrinkles and broken arteries. As he comes closer I realize that in his features I can see my whole family. If you were to stretch that rubbery flesh, you could find my father's face, and deep within *that* face—mine. I don't want to look into those eyes ringed in purple. In a few years he will retreat into silence, and take a long, long time to die. *Move back, Tío,* I tell him. *I don't want to hear what you have to say. Give the dancers room to move, soon it will be midnight. Who is the New Year's Fool this time?*

QUESTIONS FOR DISCUSSION

1. Of what cultural and lifestyle differences was Cofer most conscious when she first arrived in Paterson? What prejudice did her family encounter there?
2. What do the television programs that she watches teach Cofer about American family life and how to adapt to it?
3. How do Cofer's father and mother relate differently to their neighborhood environment? With whose values does Cofer identify?
4. How does Cofer respond to the La Gringa story? Why does she respond in this way? What dream continues to haunt her?
5. What dream-like images and symbols does Cofer use in her narrative? How do these images contribute to the story and its power?
6. Interpret the meaning of the title, "Silent Dancing." Why is the dancing "silent"?

CONNECTION

Compare and contrast Cofer and Li-Young Lee's ways of adjusting to a new life in America and dealing with memories of the culture left behind.

IDEAS FOR WRITING

1. Write an essay in which you discuss a conflict that you or a close friend experienced because you or your friend was not a member of the dominant cultural group in your community. What did you learn from this conflict and how did it help shape your perceptions and expectations of the world?
2. Develop your journal entry into an essay. You might discuss a series of photographs or two or three films or videos made over a period of years. What do these images reveal to you about you and your family's evolving values and concerns?

bell hooks

"Writing Autobiography"

Gloria Watkins (b. 1952) uses the pen name bell hooks for her writing. She earned a Ph.D. at Stanford University and has taught English and African-American Literature at City University of New York, Yale University, and Oberlin College in Ohio. She has written many books including Ain't I a Woman *(1981) and essay collections* Talking Back, Thinking Feminist, Thinking Black *(1989),* Yearning: Race, Gender, and Cultural Politics *(1990),* Black Looks: Race and Representation *(1992), and* Killing Rage *(1995). Her most recent works have focused on issues memory and passion:* Bone Black *(1996),* Wounds Of Passion *(1997), and* Remembered Rapture *(1999). In writing about cultural and gender issues, hooks always reflects deeply on her own experiences. As you read the following selection from* Talking Back, *notice how hooks emphasizes the role that pain and memory play in the writing process, as well as how writing can be a healing experience.*

JOURNAL

Write about an important memory that you have never written about. How was your understanding of the memory changed by writing about it?

1 To me, telling the story of my growing up years was intimately connected with the longing to kill the self I was without really having to die. I wanted to kill that self in writing. Once that self was gone—out of my life forever—I could more

easily become the me of me. It was clearly the Gloria Jean of my tormented and anguished childhood that I wanted to be rid of, the girl who was always wrong, always punished, always subjected to some humiliation or other, always crying, the girl who was to end up in a mental institution because she could not be anything but crazy, or so they told her. She was the girl who sat a hot iron on her arm pleading with them to leave her alone, the girl who wore her scar as a brand marking her madness. Even now I can hear the voices of my sisters saying "mama make Gloria stop crying." By writing the autobiography, it was not just this Gloria I would be rid of, but the past that had a hold on me, that kept me from the present. I wanted not to forget the past but to break its hold. This death in writing was to be liberatory.

2   Until I began to try and write an autobiography, I thought that it would be a simple task this telling of one's story. And yet I tried year after year, never writing more than a few pages. My inability to write out the story I interpreted as an indication that I was not ready to let go of the past, that I was not ready to be fully in the present. Psychologically, I considered the possibility that I had become attached to the wounds and sorrows of my childhood, that I held to them in a manner that blocked my efforts to be self-realized, whole, to be healed. A key message in Toni Cade Bambara's novel *The Salteaters*, which tells the story of Velma's suicide attempt, her breakdown, is expressed when the healer asks her "are you sure sweetheart, that you want to be well?"

3   There was very clearly something blocking my ability to tell my story. Perhaps it was remembered scoldings and punishments when mama heard me saying something to a friend or stranger that she did not think should be said. Secrecy and silence—these were central issues. Secrecy about family, about what went on in the domestic household was a bond between us—was part of what made us family. There was a dread one felt about breaking that bond. And yet I could not grow inside the atmosphere of secrecy that had pervaded our lives and the lives of other families about us. Strange that I had always challenged the secrecy, always let something slip that should not be known growing up, yet as a writer staring into the solitary space of paper, I was bound, trapped in the fear that a bond is lost or broken in the telling. I did not want to be the traitor, the teller of family secrets—and yet I wanted to be a writer. Surely, I told myself, I could write a purely imaginative work—a work that would not hint at personal private realities. And so I tried. But always there were the intruding traces, those elements of real life however disguised. Claiming the freedom to grow as an imaginative writer was connected for me with having the courage to open, to be able to tell the truth of one's life as I had experienced it in writing. To talk about one's life—that I could do. To write about it, to leave a trace—that was frightening.

4   The longer it took me to begin the process of writing autobiography, the further removed from those memories I was becoming. Each year, a memory seemed less and less clear. I wanted not to lose the vividness, the recall and felt an urgent need to begin the work and complete it. Yet I could not begin even though I had begun to confront some of the reasons I was blocked, as I am blocked just now in writing this

piece because I am afraid to express in writing the experience that served as a catalyst for that block to move.

5   I had met a young black man. We were having an affair. It is important that he was black. He was in some mysterious way a link to this past that I had been struggling to grapple with, to name in writing. With him I remembered incidents, moments of the past that I had completely suppressed. It was as though there was something about the passion of contact that was hypnotic, that enabled me to drop barriers and thus enter fully, rather re-enter those past experiences. A key aspect seemed to be the way he smelled, the combined odors of cigarettes, occasionally alcohol, and his body smells. I thought often of the phrase "scent of memory," for it was those smells that carried me back. And there were specific occasions when it was very evident that the experience of being in his company was the catalyst for this remembering.

6   Two specific incidents come to mind. One day in the middle of the afternoon we met at his place. We were drinking cognac and dancing to music from the radio. He was smoking cigarettes (not only do I not smoke, but I usually make an effort to avoid smoke). As we held each other dancing those mingled odors of alcohol, sweat, and cigarettes led me to say, quite without thinking about it, "Uncle Pete." It was not that I had forgotten Uncle Pete. It was more that I had forgotten the childhood experience of meeting him. He drank often, smoked cigarettes, and always on the few occasions that we met him, he held us children in tight embraces. It was the memory of those embraces—of the way I hated and longed to resist them—that I recalled.

7   Another day we went to a favorite park to feed ducks and parked the car in front of tall bushes. As we were sitting there, we suddenly heard the sound of an oncoming train—a sound which startled me so that it evoked another long-suppressed memory: that of crossing the train tracks in my father's car. I recalled an incident where the car stopped on the tracks and my father left us sitting there while he raised the hood of the car and worked to repair it. This is an incident that I am not certain actually happened. As a child, I had been terrified of just such an incident occurring, perhaps so terrified that it played itself out in my mind as though it had happened. These are just two ways this encounter acted as a catalyst breaking down barriers enabling me to finally write this long-desired autobiography of my childhood.

8   Each day I sat at the typewriter and different memories were written about in short vignettes. They came in a rush, as though they were a sudden thunderstorm. They came in a surreal, dreamlike style which made me cease to think of them as strictly autobiographical because it seemed that myth, dream, and reality had merged. There were many incidents that I would talk about with my siblings to see if they recalled them. Often we remembered together a general outline of an incident but the details were different for us. This fact was a constant reminder of the limitations of autobiography, of the extent to which autobiography is a very personal story telling—a unique recounting of events not so much as they had happened but as we remember and invent them. One memory that I would have sworn was "the truth and nothing but the truth" concerned a wagon that my brother and I shared as a child. I remembered that

we played with this toy only at my grandfather's house, that we shared it, that I would ride it and my brother would push me. Yet one facet of the memory was puzzling, I remembered always returning home with bruises or scratches from this toy. When I called my mother, she said there had never been any wagon, that we had shared a red wheelbarrow, that it had always been at my grandfather's house because there were sidewalks on that part of town. We lived in the hills where there were no sidewalks. Again I was compelled to face the fiction that is a part of all retelling, remembering. I began to think of the work I was doing as both fiction and autobiography. It seemed to fall in the category of writing that Audre Lorde, in her autobiographically-based work *Zami*, calls bio-mythography. As I wrote, I felt that I was not as concerned with accuracy of detail as I was with evoking in writing the state of mind, the spirit of a particular moment.

9   The longing to tell one's story and the process of telling is symbolically a gesture of longing to recover the past in such a way that one experiences both a sense of reunion and a sense of release. It was the longing for release that compelled the writing but concurrently it was the joy of reunion that enabled me to see that the act of writing one's autobiography is a way to find again that aspect of self and experience that may no longer be an actual part of one's life but is a living memory shaping and informing the present. Autobiographical writing was a way for me to evoke the particular experience of growing up southern and black in segregated communities. It was a way to recapture the richness of southern black culture. The need to remember and hold to the legacy of that experience and what it taught me has been all the more important since I have since lived in predominately white communities and taught at predominately white colleges. Black southern folk experience was the foundation of the life around me when I was a child; that experience no longer exists in many places where it was once all of life that we knew. Capitalism, upward mobility, assimilation of other values have all led to rapid disintegration of black folk experience or in some cases the gradual wearing away of that experience.

10   Within the world of my childhood, we held onto the legacy of a distinct black culture by listening to the elders tell their stories. Autobiography was experienced most actively in the art of telling one's story. I can recall sitting at Baba's (my grandmother on my mother's side) at 1200 Broad Street—listening to people come and recount their life experience. In those days, whenever I brought a playmate to my grandmother's house, Baba would want a brief outline of their autobiography before we would begin playing. She wanted not only to know who their people were but what their values were. It was sometimes an awesome and terrifying experience to stand answering these questions or witness another playmate being subjected to the process and yet this was the way we would come to know our own and one another's family history. It is the absence of such a tradition in my adult life that makes the written narrative of my girlhood all the more important. As the years pass and these glorious memories grow much more vague, there will remain the clarity contained within the written words.

11   Conceptually, the autobiography was framed in the manner of a hope chest. I remembered my mother's hope chest, with its wonderful odor of cedar and thought

about her taking the most precious items and placing them there for safekeeping. Certain memories were for me a similar treasure. I wanted to place them somewhere for safekeeping. An autobiographical narrative seemed an appropriate place. Each particular incident, encounter, experience had its own story, sometimes told from the first person, sometimes told from the third person. Often I felt as though I was in a trance at my typewriter, that the shape of a particular memory was decided not by my conscious mind but by all that is dark and deep within me, unconscious but present. It was the act of making it present, bringing it into the open, so to speak, that was liberating.

12   From the perspective of trying to understand my psyche, it was also interesting to read the narrative in its entirety after I had completed the work. It had not occurred to me that bringing one's past, one's memories together in a complete narrative would allow one to view them from a different perspective, not as singular isolated events but as part of a continuum. Reading the completed manuscript, I felt as though I had an overview not so much of my childhood but of those experiences that were deeply imprinted in my consciousness. Significantly, that which was absent, left out, not included also was important. I was shocked to find at the end of my narrative that there were few incidents I recalled that involved my five sisters. Most of the incidents with siblings were with me and my brother. There was a sense of alienation from my sisters present in childhood, a sense of estrangement. This was reflected in the narrative. Another aspect of the completed manuscript that is interesting to me is the way in which the incidents describing adult men suggest that I feared them intensely, with the exception of my grandfather and a few old men. Writing the autobiographical narrative enabled me to look at my past from a different perspective and to use this knowledge as a means of self-growth and change in a practical way.

13   In the end I did not feel as though I had killed the Gloria of my childhood. Instead I had rescued her. She was no longer the enemy within, the little girl who had to be annihilated for the woman to come into being. In writing about her, I reclaimed that part of myself I had long ago rejected, left uncared for, just as she had often felt alone and uncared for as a child. Remembering was part of a cycle of reunion, a joining of fragments, "the bits and pieces of my heart" that the narrative made whole again.

QUESTIONS FOR DISCUSSION

1. "To me, telling the story of my growing up years was intimately connected with the longing to kill the self I was without really having to die." What was your initial response to hooks's opening sentence? After reading the entire essay, go back and reinterpret the meaning of the statement.

2. Why is it difficult for hooks to write her autobiography? What helps her to get beyond her writer's block? Do you think her technique might help you in your own writing? Why or why not?

3. How does hooks experience the recollection of her memories? What specific events, sensations, and images in the present helped her to recall past

memories? Have you experienced the recollection of memories in similar ways? What helps you to get in touch with your memories?

4. Why does hooks believe that autobiography involves invention and imagination as well as the reporting of events? Do you agree with her? Why or why not?

5. Hooks writes, "Often I felt as though I was in a trance at my typewriter, that the shape of a particular memory was decided not by my conscious mind but by all that is dark and deep within me, unconscious but present." Have you ever experienced writing in this way?

6. Hooks describes the influence that the legacy of African-American oral storytelling had on her ability to frame her past experiences in writing. Was there a similar type of legacy in your own family? If so, do you think that you could draw on it as a source for your writing?

CONNECTION

Compare bell hooks' discussion of the reasons for distortion and gaps in her memories with Stephen Jay Gould's insights into his own childhood memories.

IDEAS FOR WRITING

1. Write about an incident from your past about which you still have mixed feelings, a part of the past you still don't quite understand or to which you don't yet feel reconciled. Compare your experiences of self-understanding with those that hooks experienced in writing her autobiography. How did your feelings toward the material you were writing about change in the course of doing the writing? What did you learn about the event and yourself in the writing process?

2. Hooks discusses her writer's block and how she works through it. Develop an essay that explores the topic of writer's block. Present some strategies for overcoming the problem that have worked for you or other writers.

Jane Tompkins

"The Dream of Authority"

Jane Tompkins (b. 1940) was born in New York City, where she attended Public School 98 and was considered a gifted student. She received a B.A. from Bryn Mawr College, graduating Magna Cum Laude. After receiving her Ph.D. in English at Yale University, she began her academic career as a professor at Temple Univer-

sity, Philadelphia (1970–83); since 1985 she has served as a professor of English at Duke University in North Carolina. Tompkins has edited literary casebooks and an anthology of reader-response criticism; her books of criticism include Sensational Designs: The Cultural Work of American Fiction, 1790–1850 *and* West of Everything: The Inner Life of Westerns (1992). *The following selection on the long-term impact of her childhood experiences as a student, "The Dream of Authority," is from her memoir,* A Life in School: What the Teacher Learned (1996).

JOURNAL

Write about a dream or memory that expresses or reflects upon your fear and/or defiance of authority.

---

1   *I'm in front of the class on the first day of school, and for some reason, I'm totally unprepared. (How did this happen?) Throat tight, I fake a smile, grab for words, tell an anecdote, anything to hold their attention. But the strangers in rows in front of me aren't having any. They start to shuffle and murmur; they turn their heads away. Then chairs scrape back, and I realize it's actually happened. The students are walking out on me. I have finally gotten what I deserve.*

2   This dream in one form or another is dreamed by thousands of teachers before the beginning of the fall semester. Some dream that they can't find their classrooms and are racing frantically through darkened halls; others that they are pontificating in nasal tones on subjects they know nothing about; others see themselves turning to write on the blackboard and feel the class leaving behind their backs. The dream is so common that most people I know discount it. "Oh, everybody has that dream," they say, dismissing the subject. But the dream is not discountable. It is about the fear of failure—the failure of one's authority—and it points to the heart of what it means to be a teacher.

3   When I had this dream, I'd been teaching for over fifteen years. I was a full professor at a reputable university, regarded as good teacher and a productive scholar. So why was I having a nightmare about my students walking out on me? Where did the doubt and insecurity come from? The answer lies in another dream; in this one, I'm a student.

4   *I am studying for my Ph.D. exams and am about to take them. Suddenly I realize I haven't studied at all. I've been doing some vague research on topics that interest me, but they aren't the right ones. I've never even cracked the surveys of English literature I'd relied on in graduate school. Why haven't I touched these books? I have twenty-five minutes before the exam. Maybe I can cram at the last minute. But instead I get myself a cup of coffee, find a good place to read, go back for my jacket, and so on, until there's no time left.*

5   *I realize then they're going to fail me. (This is all taking place at the university where I currently teach; it comes to me that this is the chance the older faculty have been waiting for to show me up for what I am.) It's a ten-hour written exam with an oral component. I've*

learned from a colleague I consider more learned than myself that the exam has short-answer questions such as "Who were the Fugitives?" (Do I know who the Fugitives were? I'm not sure.)

6   *Then comes the familiar moment of recognition: I already have a Ph.D.! I decide in a frenzy of rebellion that I won't take this exam. I will not subject myself to the humiliation of failure. I'm walking up the stairs now toward the exam room; there's no time left. What will I do?*

7   In this dream I appear as a student in an institution where I'm a full professor. I'm almost fifty, dreaming of being in the position of a twenty-four-year-old. Here, as in the other dream, I'm a fraud, someone who's supposed to know things she doesn't actually know. It's the same situation, really; only this time instead of being humiliated and rejected by students, I'm going to be humiliated and rejected by teachers, people in authority over me. The old fear, the exam fear, never goes away. As you go through life, it just gets projected onto other situations. If you become a teacher, the fear is projected onto your students. They don't have the power over you that your teachers once had, but your internalized fear gives them the power.

8   Terror is like a ball that bounces back and forth between two walls of a small room. Once you throw it hard at one wall, it rebounds to the other and then back against the first, and so on until it loses momentum and gravity pulls it to the floor. With terror, though, I'm not sure what stops the ball, or whether in some instances it doesn't pick up speed and bounce harder. The walls in this metaphor are teachers and students, and the ball is the fear they pass back and forth.

9   Looking back, I now see that because of these fears, I developed, over the years, a good-cop/bad-cop routine in the classroom. In order to win my students' love, I would try to divest myself of authority by constant self-questioning, by deference to students' opinions; through disarming self-revelation, flattery, jokes, criticizing school authorities; by accepting late papers, late attendance, and nonperformance of various kinds. Meanwhile, in order to establish and maintain my authority, I would almost invariably come to class overprepared, allowing no deviations from the plan for the day, making everything I said as complex, high level, and idiosyncratic as possible lest the students think I wasn't as smart as they were. I would pile on the work, grade hard, and—this must have confused them—tell them that all I cared about was their individual development.

10   It's easy, though, to caricature the devices I'd stoop to in order to both yield and keep hold of authority. It's easy to criticize. If I alternately intimidated and placated the students it's because I was threatened and felt afraid, afraid of my students, and afraid of the authorities who had stood in judgment on me long ago.

11   The image of authority is embodied for me in teachers. Mrs. Colgan in 1B, standing tense and straight in a black dress with little white spots that droops on her figure. Her lips are pursed, her hair is in a hairnet, her black eyes snap with intensity, and her whole thin being radiates the righteous authority she exercises over us; it is mixed with wrath. She is scolding, holding a small book in front of her flat, draped chest. Mrs. Colgan has to exert all the energy she has to maintain this stance. Most of the time she spoke to us in a soft, gentle voice; she liked to be soft and gentle with

the children. Only when someone really stepped out of line did she become her steely, purse-lipped self. Because I saw this, I was only afraid of Mrs. Colgan, not terrified of her. I saw in her the two faces of authority: the desire to lead gently, to be kind and affectionate, to love; and the necessity to instill fear, the desperation of having to beat back the enemy by whatever means.

12   It's the second image that tends to remain in people's memories. The teacher, the one who stands in front, who stands while others sit, the one whom you must obey, the one who exacts obedience. For obedience is the basis for everything else that happens in school; unless the children obey, nothing can be taught. That is what I learned. Obedience first. Or rather, fear first, fear of authority, yielding obedience, then, everything else.

13   There was a boy in the second or third grade who symbolized the need for the kind of authority I hated. I'll call him Louis Koslowski. He was always bad. Nothing the teachers could do or say ever shut Louis up. He could be temporarily quelled, but sooner or later he always came back for more. I was terrified of being spoken to and about the way the teachers spoke to and about Louis Koslowski, for he brought out the worst in them: shouting, name-calling, intimidation; every form of sarcasm and ridicule they could command, every threat, every device of shaming. If there had been stocks in P.S. 98, Louis Koslowski would have been in them.

14   Louis, though, like Mrs. Colgan, had two sides. He was terrible, we were told; he was the universal troublemaker without whom everything would have been fine. And surely he caused us to suffer through hours of yelling, and hours of leftover bad feeling spilling over from the teacher onto us, and oozing out from us into the corners of the room. But he was cute, his energy was exciting; he was an appealing figure in a rough-and-tumble way. Sometimes I thought the teachers were right, but sometimes I thought he was being picked on unfairly. Why make such a fuss? I mean, we were supposed to sit all day, hands folded on our desks, legs crossed (if you were a girl), silent, staring forward in our rows. Looking back on it now, it seems that much of the time in school, the only interest or action lay in the power struggle between the teachers, whose reign of terror enforced the rules, and the students like Louis K., whose irrepressible energy contested them.

15   But the struggle was not for me.

16   I have another image of a boy in third grade—his name was Steven Kirschner— a pretty blond child with sky blue eyes and a soft-as-doeskin nature. He is standing at attention next to his seat, being dressed down by the teacher for some slight. I don't remember what it was, but I knew he didn't deserve such treatment. He stands there, stiffly, hands at his sides, in brown corduroy pants. His china blue eyes brim with the tears he's trying to hold back. He is the very picture of innocence abused, yet the lash, metaphorically, fell on him just the same. And it fell on me, too, for strange as it may seem, I did not distinguish between myself and the unhappy scapegoat for the teacher's wrath. And so when Mrs. Garrity, the worst one of all, with her brown suit and red face made red by perennial anger, was heard screaming horribly and interminably in the hall at some unlucky person, it seemed to me entirely an accident that that person had not yet been me; when Mrs. Seebach, of the enormous

bosom and enormous behind, bellowed at us in gym class, seized by demonic rage over a student's failure properly to execute grand right and left, I trembled. I could have made the same mistake. Once Mrs. Seebach did ridicule me in front of the class because I didn't know how to tie a knot at the end of a piece of thread; there was no knowing when it would happen again.

17   It was executioner and victim in my scenario, and the victims had better watch out. For above these harridans were other authorities even more august. Mr. Rothman, the new principal, and (holy of holies) Mr. Zimmerman, superintendent of schools: presences so terrible no one dared, not even the Louis Koslowskis, to so much as breathe naturally as we stood in rigid rows for their inspection. When I look back on my early years in school, it's Steven Kirschner standing helpless next to his desk whom I identify with, not Louis Koslowski rolling a spitball under his, and certainly not with the teachers.

18   You would think that with experiences like these so vivid in my mind, I would have avoided school, but no. I became a teacher. I *joined*. The teachers I consciously modeled myself on were not the ones I've been describing but teachers I had later in junior high and high school, teachers who never used the metaphoric whip, but inspired, encouraged, and praised. Still, the older models remain; the deeper stratum lies underneath, its breath of ancient terror haunting me. Unless I perform for the authorities, unless I do what I'm told, I will be publicly shamed.

19   My own early and repeated exposure to authorities who terrified me absolutely helps to explain my habit of alternate rebellion against and submission to the authority figures in my life. And it accounts at least in part for my contradictory behavior toward my students: wanting to control and not to control, wanting to be loved—and obeyed.

20   The pedagogy that produces oppression starts early and comes from traditions of childrearing like those Alice Miller describes in *For Your Own Good*, where she writes: "Child-rearing is basically directed not toward the *child's* welfare but toward satisfying the parents' need for power and revenge." This need, in its turn, is created by abuse suffered and forgotten. "It is precisely those events that have never been come to terms with that must seek an outlet," says Miller. "The jubilation characteristic of those who declare war is the expression of the revived hope of finally being able to avenge earlier debasement, and presumably also of relief at finally being permitted to hate and shout."

21   I do not know what earlier debasements the teachers at P.S. 98 were avenging when they screamed at us in the halls, but I know they must have been the object of someone's vengefulness. Their hatred and shouting are still echoing in my mind, and I'm sure I cannot be the only one.

22   Eventually, I became aware that childhood experiences of authority had controlled, without my knowing it, the way I exercised and failed to exercise authority as an adult, and that it was the reality of what had happened at P.S. 98, more than my present one, that had been dictating the terms of my university life, day to day. Fear was the underside of that life. Much of my behavior had been ruled by it. The fear stayed buried, controlling me secretly, because, though I became learned, was

taught four languages, three literatures, and many other things beside, I'd not been taught how to recognize and face my fear. Learning this for myself has been frightening and discouraging and a long study. But for me, it seems, there was no other way.

QUESTIONS FOR DISCUSSION

1. Why does Tompkins begin her narrative with her dream about being in front of the class "totally unprepared"? How else does she integrate her dreams into this essay? Is this technique effective?
2. What does Tompkins learn about authority from Mrs. Colgan, as well as from Louis Koslowski, Steven Kirschner, Mrs. Garrity, and Mrs. Seebach? Why does she identify with Stephen Kirschner?
3. Why is the "good-cop/bad-cop " approach to authority a self-defeating strategy? How does Tompkins believe that a teacher establishes authority in her/his classroom? Explain why you agree or disagree with her point of view.
4. Why does Tompkins believe that childhood memories and fears of authority rule her adult behavior? How does she use the ideas of psychologist Alice Miller to help explain the long-term effects of early childhood oppression?
5. If Tompkins was so horrified by the oppression she encountered in school, why does she join the teaching profession? From the tone of her essay, do you think she made a mistake?
6. How do you think Tompkins would want to establish rules and authority in her classroom? Do you think you would like to be a student in one of her classes? Explain.

CONNECTION

Compare Tompkins' memories of authority figures such as Mrs. Seebach and Mrs. Colgan and how they influenced her to Isabel Allende's memories of Tío Ramón, an important mentor in her early life.

IDEAS FOR WRITING

1. As Jane Tompkins does, develop an essay about the teachers who embodied both positive and negative authority in your life. Draw conclusions about how they influenced your sense of self and your ability to act as an authority figure.
2. Develop an essay in which you narrate a frightening dream or dreams of a teacher or other authority figure. Explain how understanding these dreams has helped you to understand yourself better in terms of your attitudes toward classroom situations.

Rachel Naomi Remen

"Remembering"

Nationally known for her leadership in the mind-body health movement, Rachel Naomi Remen, M.D. is the co-founder and medical director of the Commonweal Cancer Help Program in Bolinas, California. Formerly on the faculty of the Stanford Medical School, she is currently a clinical professor of family and community medicine at the University of California at San Francisco School of Medicine. Her books include The Masculine Principle, the Feminine Principle, and Humanistic Medicine *(1975),* The Human Patient *(1980), and* Kitchen Table Wisdom *(1996). In her private practice, she has worked as a psycho-oncologist for more than twenty years. Her particular blend of caring and wisdom has developed through her professional life as a physician and her experience of living with a chronic illness for more than forty years. In the following selection from* Kitchen Table Wisdom, *Remen reflects on the power of memory to shape identity and to heal.*

JOURNAL

Write about a time in your life when resolving issues from your past helped you feel better about yourself.

1   What we do to survive is often different from what we may need to do in order to live. My work as a cancer therapist often means helping people to recognize this difference, to get off the treadmill of survival, and to refocus their lives. Of the many people who have confronted this issue, one of the most dramatic was an Asian woman of remarkable beauty and style. Through our work together I realized that some things which can never be fixed can still heal.

2   She was about to begin a year of chemotherapy for ovarian cancer, but this is not what she talked about in our first meeting. She began our work together by telling me she was a "bad" person, hard, uncaring, selfish, and unloving. She delivered this self-indictment with enormous poise and certainty. I watched the light play across her perfect skin and the polish of her long black hair and thought privately that I did not believe her. The people I had known who were truly selfish were rarely aware of it—they simply put themselves first without doubt or hesitation.

3   In a voice filled with shame, Ana began to tell me that she had no heart, and that her phenomenal success in business was a direct result of this ruthlessness. Most important, she felt that it was not possible for her to become well, as she had earned her cancer through her behavior. She questioned why she had come seeking help. There was a silence in which we took each other's measure. "Why not start from the beginning?" I said.

4   It took her more than eight months to tell her story. She had not been born here. She had come to this country at ten, as an orphan. She had been adopted by a good family, a family that knew little about her past. With their support she had built a life for herself.

5   In a voice I could barely hear, she began to speak of her experiences as a child in Vietnam during the war. She began with the death of her parents. She had been four years old the morning the Cong had come, small enough to hide in the wooden box that held the rice in the kitchen. The soldiers had not looked there after they had killed the others. When at last they had gone and she ventured from hiding she had seen that her family had been beheaded. That was the beginning. I was horrified.

6   She continued on. It had been a time of brutality, a world without mercy. She was alone. She had starved. She had been brutalized. Hesitantly at first, and then with growing openness, she told story after story. She had become one of a pack of homeless children. She had stolen, she had betrayed, she had hated, she had helped kill. She had seen things beyond human endurance, done things beyond imagination. Like a spore, she had become what was needed to survive.

7   As the weeks went by, there was little I could say. Over and over she would tell me that she was a bad person, "a person of darkness." I was filled with horror and pity, wishing to ease her anguish, to offer comfort. Yet she had done these things. I continued to listen.

8   Over and over a wall of silence and despair threatened to close us off from each other. Over and over I would beat it back, insisting that she tell me the worst. She would weep and say, "I do not know if I can," and hoping that I would be able to hear it, I would tell her that she must. And she would begin another story. I often found myself not knowing how to respond, unable to do anything but stand with her here, one foot in this peaceful calm office on the water, the other in a world beyond imagination. I had never been orphaned, never been hunted, never missed a meal except by choice, never violently attacked another person. But I could recognize the whisper of my darkness in hers and I stood in that place in myself to listen to her, to try to understand. I wanted to jump in, I wanted to soothe, I wanted to make sense, yet none of this was possible. Once, in despair myself, I remember thinking, "I am her first witness."

9   Over and over she would cry out, "I have such darkness in me." At such times it seemed to me that the cancer was actually helping her make sense of her life; offering the relief of a feared but long-awaited punishment.

10   At the close of one of her stories, I was overwhelmed by the fact that she had actually managed to live with such memories. I told her this and added, "I am in awe." We sat looking at each other. "It helps me that you say that. I feel less alone." I nodded and we sat in silence. I *was* in awe of this woman and her ability to survive. In all the years of working with people with cancer, I had never met anyone like her. I ached for her. Like an animal in a trap that gnaws off its own leg, she had survived— but only at a terrible cost.

11   Gradually she began to shorten the time frame of her stories, to talk of more recent events: her ruthless business practices, how she used others, always serving her

own self-interest. She began to talk about her contempt, her anger, her unkindness, her distrust of people, and her competitiveness. It seemed to me that she was completely alone. "Nothing has really changed," I thought. Her whole life was still organized around her survival.

12   Once, at the close of a particularly painful session, I found myself reviewing my own day, noticing how much of the time I was focused on surviving and not on living. I wondered if I too had become caught in survival. How much had I put off living today in order to do or say what was expedient? To get what I thought I needed. Could survival become a habit? Was it possible to live so defensively that you never got to live at all?

13   "You have survived, Ana," I blurted out. "Surely you can stop now." She looked at me, puzzled. But I had nothing further to say.

14   One day, she walked in and said, "I have no more stories to tell."

15   "Is it a relief?" I asked her. To my surprise she answered, "No, it feels empty."

16   "Tell me." She looked away. "I am afraid I will not know how to survive now." Then she laughed. "But I could never forget," she said.

17   A few weeks after this she brought in a dream, one of the first she could remember. In the dream, she had been looking in a mirror, seeing herself reflected there to the waist. It seemed to her that she could see through her clothes, through her skin, through to the very depths of her being. She saw that she was filled with darkness and felt a familiar shame, as intense as that she had felt on the first day she had come to my office. Yet she could not look away. Then it seemed to her as if she were moving, as if she had passed through into the mirror, into her own image, and was moving deeper and deeper into her darkness. She went forward blindly for a long time. Then, just as she was certain that there was no end, no bottom, that surely this would go on and on, she seemed to see a tiny spot far ahead. As she moved closer to it, she was able to recognize what it was. It was a rose. A single, perfect rosebud on a long stem.

18   For the first time in eight months she began to cry softly, without pain. "It's very beautiful," she told me. "I can see it very clearly, the stem with its leaves and its thorns. It is just beginning to open. And its color is indescribable: the softest, most tender, most exquisite shade of pink."

19   I asked her what this dream meant to her and she began to sob. "It's mine," she said. "It is still there. All this time it is still there. It has waited for me to come back for it."

20   The rose is one of the oldest archetypical symbols for the heart. It appears in both the Christian and the Hindu traditions and in many fairy tales. It presented itself now to Ana even though she had never read these fairy tales or heard of these traditions. For most of her life, she had held her darkness close to her, had used it as her protection, had even defined herself through it. Now, finally, she had been able to remember. There was a part she had hidden even from herself. A part she had kept safe. A part that had not been touched.

21   Even more than our experiences, our beliefs became our prisons. But we carry our healing with us even into the darkest of our inner places. A Course in Miracles says,

"When I have forgiven myself and remembered who I am, I will bless everyone and everything I see." The way to freedom often lies through the open heart.

QUESTIONS FOR DISCUSSION

1. Why does Ana believe that she is a bad person and that her cancer is a punishment? Do you think Ana recovers from her cancer? Why doesn't Remen tell us?
2. Why do you think that Remen values memory? What is unique about her perspective on memory?
3. How and why is Remen able to help Ana? What has Remen learned from listening to Ana's struggle? What have you learned?
4. What is the significance of Ana's dream?
5. Why does Remen believe that "something which can never be fixed can still heal"? Explain why you agree or disagree with Remen?
6. How does Remen's discussion of Ana support her conclusion that freedom can begin only after one can forgive him or herself and have an open heart? Do you agree with Remen?

CONNECTION

How do Remen's insights into the need for an immigrant to integrate traumatic memories rather than to deny their impact help you to understand Li-Young Lee's poem, "To A New Citizen"?

IDEAS FOR WRITING

1. Explain Remen's claim, "What we do to survive is often different from what we may need to do in order to live." Develop the idea into an essay, using examples drawn from personal experience and observation.
2. Write an essay that supports or refutes Remen's implied premise hat people's beliefs about themselves affect their ability to live a healthy life and recover from an illness. Can a person remain healthy if he or she feels consumed by self-hatred and guilt?

Stephen Jay Gould

"Muller Bros. Moving & Storage"

A professor of biology, geology, and the history of science at Harvard University, Stephen Jay Gould (b. 1941) is well known for his views on evolution, creationism, and race. He is widely read by thinkers in many different disciplines as his works often point out relationships between scientific and humanistic thought, making technical subjects understandable to nonscientific readers. Gould has been the recipient of a number of distinguished awards, including grants from the National Science Foundation and the MacArthur Foundation. He has written many essays; his most recent collections are Panda's Thumb *(1991),* Dinosaur in a Haystack *(1996),* Questioning the Millennium *(1997),* Leonardo's Mountain of Clams and the Diet of Worms: Essays On Natural History *(1998), and* Rocks Of Ages: Science and Religion In the Fullness of Life *(1999). As you read the following essay, which first appeared in* Natural History Magazine *(1990), notice how Gould shows his readers the limitations of factual recall in memories while illustrating the emotional power that recollections of the past can have in shaping an individual's values.*

JOURNAL

Write about a possession a relative gave you that you cherish for the memories it embodies.

1   I own many old and beautiful books, classics of natural history bound in leather and illustrated with hand-colored plates. But no item in my collection comes close in personal value to a modest volume, bound in gray cloth and published in 1892: "Studies of English Grammar," by J.M. Greenwood, superintendent of schools in Kansas City. The book belonged to my grandfather, a Hungarian immigrant. He wrote on the title page, in an elegant European hand: "Prop. of Joseph A. Rosenberg, New York." Just underneath, he added in pencil the most eloquent of all possible lines: "I have landed. Sept. 11, 1901."

2   Papa Joe died when I was 13, before I could properly distill his deepest experiences, but long enough into my own ontogeny for the precious gifts of extensive memory and lasting influence. He was a man of great artistic sensibility and limited opportunity for expression. I am told that he sang beautifully as a young man, although increasing deafness and a pledge to the memory of his mother (never to sing again after her death) stilled his voice long before my birth.

3   He never used his remarkable talent for drawing in any effort of fine arts, although he marshaled these skills to rise from cloth-cutting in the sweatshops to middle-class life as a brassiere and corset designer. (The content of his chosen expression titillated me as a child, but I now appreciate the primary theme of economic emancipation through the practical application of artistic talent.)

4   Yet, above all, he expressed his artistic sensibilities in his personal bearing—in elegance of dress (a bit on the foppish side, perhaps), grace of movement, beauty of handwriting, ease of mannerism.

5   I well remember one manifestation of this rise above the ordinary—both because we repeated the act every week and because the junction of locale and action seemed so incongruous, even to a small child of 5 or 6. Every Sunday morning, Papa Joe and I

would take a stroll to the corner store on Queens Boulevard to buy the paper and a half dozen bagels. We then walked to the great world-class tennis stadium of Forest Hills, where McEnroe and his ilk still cavort. A decrepit and disused side entrance sported a rusty staircase of three or four steps.

6   With his unfailing deftness, Papa Joe would take a section of the paper that we never read and neatly spread several sheets over the lowermost step (for the thought of a rust flake or speck of dust in contact with his trousers filled him with horror). We would then sit down and have the most wonderful man-to-man talk about the latest baseball scores, the rules of poker, or the results of the Friday night fights.

7   I retain a beautiful vision of this scene: The camera pans back and we see a tiny staircase, increasingly dwarfed by the great stadium. Two little figures sit on the bottom step—a well-dressed, elderly man gesturing earnestly; a little boy listening with adoration.

8   Certainty is both a blessing and a danger. Certainty provides warmth, solace, security—an anchor in the unambiguously factual events of personal observation and experience. I know that I sat on those steps with my grandfather because I was there, and no external power of suggestion has ever played havoc with this most deeply personal and private experience. But certainty is also a great danger, given the notorious fallibility—and unrivaled power—of the human mind. How often have we killed on vast scales for the "certainties" of nationhood and religion; how often have we condemned the innocent because the most prestigious form of supposed certainty —eyewitness testimony—bears all the flaws of our ordinary fallibility.

9   Primates are visual animals *par excellence*, and we therefore grant special status to personal observation—to being there and seeing directly. But all sights must be registered in the brain and stored somehow in its intricate memory. And the human mind is both the greatest marvel of nature and the most perverse of all tricksters; Einstein and Loge inextricably combined.

10   This special (but unwarranted) prestige accorded to direct observation has led to a serious popular misunderstanding about science. Since science is often regarded as the most objective and truth-directed of human enterprises, and since direct observation is supposed to be the favored route to factuality, many people equate respectable science with visual scrutiny—just the facts, ma'am, and palpably before my eyes.

11   But science is a battery of observational and inferential methods, all directed to the testing of propositions that can, in principle, be definitely proved false. A restriction of compass to matters of direct observation would stymie the profession intolerably. Science must often transcend sight to win insight. At all scales, from smallest to largest, quickest to slowest, many well-documented conclusions of science lie beyond the limited domain of direct observation. No one has ever seen an electron or a black hole, the events of picosecond or a geological eon.

12   One of the phoniest arguments raised for rhetorical effect by "creation scientists" tried to deny scientific status to evolution because its results take so much time to unfold and therefore can't be seen directly. But if science required such

immediate vision, we could draw no conclusion about any subject that studies the past—no geology, no cosmology, no human history (including the strength and influence of religion), for that matter.

13   We can, after all, be reasonably sure that Henry V prevailed at Agincourt even though no photos exist and no one has survived more than 500 years to tell the tale. And dinosaurs really did snuff it tens of millions of years before any conscious observer inhabited our planet. Evolution suffers no special infirmity as a science because its grandest-scale results took so long to unfold during an unobservable past. (The small-scale results of agriculture and domestication have been recorded, and adequate evidence survives to document the broader events of a distant past.) The sciences of history rely on our ability to infer the past from signs of ancestry preserved in modern structures—as in the "panda's thumb" principle of current imperfection preserved as a legacy of ancestral inheritances originally evolved for different purposes.

14   Moreover, eyewitness accounts do not deserve their conventional status as ulti-mate arbiters even when testimony of direct observation can be marshaled in abun-dance. In her sobering book, *"Eyewitness Testimony"* (Harvard University Press, 1979), Elizabeth Loftus debunks, largely in a legal context, the notion that visual ob-servation confers some special claim for veracity. She identifies three levels of poten-tial error in supposedly direct and objective vision: misperception of the event itself and the two great tricksters of passage through memory before later disgorgement—retention and retrieval.

15   In one experiment, for example, Loftus showed forty students a three-minute videotape of a classroom lecture disrupted by eight demonstrators (a relevant sub-ject for a study from the early 1970s!). She gave the students a questionnaire and asked half of them: "Was the leader of the twelve demonstrators . . . a male?" and the other half, "Was the leader of the four demonstrators . . . a male?" One week later, in a follow-up questionnaire, she asked all the students: "How many demon-strators did you see entering the classroom?" Those who had previously received the question about twelve demonstrators reported seeing an average of 8.9 people; those told of four demonstrators claimed an average of 6.4. All had actually seen eight, but compromised later judgment between their actual observation and the largely subliminal power of suggestion in the first questionnaire.

16   People can even be induced to "see" totally illusory objects. In another experiment, Loftus showed a film of an accident, followed by a misleading question: "How fast was the white sports car going when it passed the barn while traveling along the country road?" (The film showed no barn, and a control group received a more accurate question: "How fast was the white sports car going while traveling along the country road?") A week later, 17 percent of the students in the first group stated that they had seen the nonexistent barn; only 3 percent of the control group reported a barn.

17   Thus, we are easily fooled on all fronts of both eye and mind: seeing, storing and recalling. The eye tricks us badly enough; the mind is infinitely more perverse. What remedy can we possibly have but constant humility, and eternal vigilance and scrutiny? Trust your memory as you would your poker buddy (one of my grandfather's mottoes from the steps).

18   With this principle in mind, I went searching for those steps last year after more than thirty years of absence from my natal turf. I exited the subway at 67th Avenue, walked to my first apartment at 98–50, and then set off on my grandfather's route for Queens Boulevard and the tennis stadium.

19   I was walking in the right direction, but soon realized that I had made a serious mistake. The tennis stadium stood at least a mile down the road, too far for those short strolls with a bag of bagels in one hand and a five-year-old boy attached to the other. In increasing puzzlement, I walked down the street and, at the very next corner, saw the steps and felt the jolt and flood of memory that drives our *recherches du temps perdus*.

20   My recall of the steps was entirely accurate—three modest flagstone rungs, bordered by rusty iron railings. But the steps are not attached to the tennis stadium; they form the side entrance to a modest brick building, now crumbling, padlocked, and abandoned, but still announcing its former use with a commercial sign, painted directly on the brick in the old industrial style: "Muller Bros. Inc. Moving & Storage"—with a telephone number below from the age before all-digit dialing: Illinois 9–9200.

21   Obviously, I had conflated the most prominent symbol of my old neighborhood, the tennis stadium, with an important personal place—and had constructed a juxtaposed hybrid for my mental image. Yet even now, in the face of conclusive correction, my memory of the tennis stadium soaring above the steps remains strong.

22   I might ask indulgence on the grounds of inexperience and relative youth for my failure as an eyewitness at the Muller Bros. steps. After all, I was only an impressionable lad of five or so, when even a modest six-story warehouse might be perceived as big enough to conflate with something truly important.

23   But I have no excuses for a second story. Ten years later, at a trustable age of fifteen, I made a western trip by automobile with my family; I have specially vivid memories of an observation at Devils Tower, Wyoming (the volcanic plug made most famous as a landing site for aliens in "Close Encounters of the Third Kind"). We approach from the east. My father tells us to look out for the tower from tens of miles away, for he has read in a guidebook that it rises, with an awesome near-verticality, from the dead-flat Great Plains—and that pioneer families used the tower as a landmark and beacon on their westward trek.

24   We see the tower, first as a tiny projection, almost square in outline, at the horizon. It gets larger as we approach, assuming its distinctive form and finally revealing its structure as a conjoined mat of hexagonal basalt columns. I have never forgotten the two features that inspired my rapt attention: the maximal rise of verticality from flatness, forming a perpendicular junction; and the steady increase in size from a bump on the horizon to a looming, almost fearful giant of a rock pile.

25   Now I know, I absolutely *know*, that I saw this visual drama, as described. The picture in my mind of that distinctive profile, growing in size, is as strong as any memory I possess. I see the tower as a little dot in the distance, as a mid-sized monument, as a full field of view. I have told the story to scores of people, comparing this natural reality with a sight of Chartres as a tiny toy tower twenty miles from Paris, growing to the overarching symbol and skyline of its medieval city.

26   In 1987, I revisited Devils Tower with my family—the only return since my first close encounter thirty years before. I planned the trip to approach from the east, so that they would see the awesome effect—and I told them my story, of course.

27   In the context of this essay, my denouement will be anticlimactic in its predictability, however acute my personal embarrassment. The terrain around Devils Tower is mountainous; the monument cannot be seen from more than a few miles away in any direction. I bought a booklet on pioneer trails westward, and none passed anywhere near Devils Tower. We enjoyed our visit, but I felt like a perfect fool. Later, I checked my old logbook for that high-school trip. The monument that rises from the plain, the beacon of the pioneers, is Scotts Bluff, Nebraska—not nearly so impressive a pile of stone as Devils Tower.

28   And yet I still see Devils Tower in my mind when I think of that growing dot on the horizon. I see it as clearly and as surely as ever, although I now know that the memory is false.

29   This has been a long story for a simple moral. Papa Joe, the wise old peasant in a natty and elegant business suit, told me on those steps to be wary of all blandishments and to trust nothing that cannot be proved. We must extend his good counsel to our own interior certainties, particularly those we never question because we regard eyewitnessing as paramount in veracity.

30   Of course we must treat the human mind with respect—for nature has fashioned no more admirable instrument. But we must also struggle to stand back and to scrutinize our own mental certainties. This last line poses an obvious paradox, if not an outright contradiction—and I have no solution to offer. Yes, step back and scrutinize your own mind. But with what?

QUESTIONS FOR DISCUSSION

1. Why is *Studies in English Grammar* Gould's most valued possession? Why was this book also cherished by Gould's grandfather?
2. Why does Gould remember his Sunday morning breakfasts with Papa Joe? Why does Gould admire his grandfather?
3. Gould is skeptical of the accuracy of direct visual observation. What evidence and descriptions does he present to support his point of view?
4. Gould is also skeptical of the accuracy of memory. Why do the subjects in the experiments he discusses come to different conclusions about what they saw and what they remembered?
5. When Gould goes back after thirty years to the place where he and Papa Joe had breakfast, what does Gould realize about his memory? Why does he still value his memory, despite its distortions? How does Gould's inaccurate recall of Devil's Tower support the premise developed in his earlier example?
6. How does Gould effectively relate his personal experiences to broader scientific issues involving the past and observation?

CONNECTION

Compare and contrast how Gould and Michele Murray reflect on the way memories of grandparents are embodied in objects and are changed over time.

IDEAS FOR WRITING

1. Develop your journal assignment into an essay in which you discuss how the memory you have of a relative is connected to and influenced by a physical possession that you keep to remind yourself of the relative. What feelings and values do you associate with the possession?

2. Write an essay in which you discuss the implications of the paradox Gould presents at the end of the essay: "Step back and scrutinize your own mind. But with what?" How can people become better at reflecting on and clarifying the memories and perceptions that they bring with them from their pasts?

Li-Young Lee

"To A New Citizen of These United States"

Born in 1957 in Jakarta, Indonesia, Li-Young Lee is from an aristocratic Chinese family; his father was a Christian minister who was forced to leave China during the Maoist regime. In 1959, after spending a year as political prisoners, Lee's family fled from Indonesia, traveling in Hong Kong, Macau, and Japan, before finally arriving in America in 1964. Currently residing in Chicago, Lee studied at several universities and has taught at the University of Iowa and at Northwestern. He has been featured in Bill Moyers' public television program, Voices of Memory, *and has published two collections of his work:* Rose *(1986) and* The City in Which I Love You *(1990), as well as a memoir* The Winged Seed *(1995). Lee's poetry is characterized by a focus on language, memory, and imagination, as can be seen in the poem that follows, "To a New Citizen," from* The City in Which I Love You. *Directed to immigrants who feel they must put aside their culture and their memories of homeland, this poem employs the kind of strong emotion and rich sensory imagery which make Lee's poetry so intriguing.*

JOURNAL

Write about a time when you "migrated," either from country to country or from one state, city, or neighborhood to another. What did you have to forget? What do you continue to remember from your "past life"?

Forgive me for thinking I saw
the irregular postage stamp of death;
a black moth the size of my left
thumbnail is all I've trapped in the damask.
5   There is no need for alarm. And

there is no need for sadness, if
the rain at the window now reminds you
of nothing; not even of that
parlor, long like a nave, where cloud-shadow,
10 wing-shadow, where father-shadow
continually confused the light. In flight,
leaf-throng and, later, soldiers and
flags deepened those windows to submarine.

But you don't remember, I know,
15 so I won't mention that house where Chung hid,
Lin wizened, you languished, and Ming—
Ming hush-hushed us with small song. And since you
don't recall the missionary
bells chiming the hour, or those words whose sounds
20 alone exhaust the heart—*garden,
heaven, amen*—I'll mention none of it.

After all, it was just our life,
merely years in a book of years. It was
1960, and we stood with
25 the other families on a crowded
railroad platform. The trains came, then
the rains, and then we got separated.

And in the interval between
familiar faces, events occurred, which
30 one of us faithfully pencilled
in a day-book bound by a rubber band.

But birds, as you say, fly forward.
So I wont show you letters and the shawl
I've so meaninglessly preserved.
35 And I won't hum along, if you don't, when
our mothers sing *Nights in Shanghai*.
I won't, each Spring, each time I smell lilac,
recall my mother, patiently
stitching money inside my coat lining,
40 if you don't remember your mother
preparing for your own escape.

After all, it was only our
life, our life and its forgetting.

QUESTIONS FOR DISCUSSION

1. From whom does Lee's narrator ask forgiveness and for what reason?
2. What is the significance of the "irregular postage stamp of death"? What has died, or is about to die?
3. Would you consider that the speaker is being ironic when he says "there is need for alarm . . . no need for sadness"? What is there to be sad about?
4. What specific images are provided as examples of forgetting? How are these images and examples connected to the heroic struggle of many immigrants?
5. Why does the poem focus on language, story-telling, and writing as ways of preserving memories? Why is the preservation of these records seen by the narrator as a "meaningless" act?
6. Evaluate the ironic message of the poem's final lines: "After all, it was only our/ life, our life and its forgetting." What, if anything, does the poem suggest will be provided for the new citizen in exchange for "our life and its forgetting"?

CONNECTION

Contrast and compare this poem about forgetting of images from the distant past with a similar theme in Michele Murray's "Poem to My Grandmother in her Death."

IDEAS FOR WRITING

1. Develop your journal entry into a longer narrative essay about the experience of migration and the impact it has had on your memories of your past.
2. Write an essay designed as a response to the advice given by the speaker in this poem. What advice would you have for the new citizen? For instance, is it possible for the citizen to maintain a former cultural identity and sense of vital memory of the past while still taking an active role in the cultural life of "these United States"?

Corinne Kiku Okada

"Namesake"

Originally from Manhattan Beach, California, Corey Okada was a design major with an interest in writing and designing children's books when she wrote this essay. Okada chose to write about her early memories of the name that she shared with her great-aunt because she "knew it would force [her] to be honest about something very personal" that she had had difficulty dealing with directly in the past. Okada went through several drafts of this essay, using a silver-framed photograph of her great-aunt to help keep the paper focused. For Okada, writing is an "exciting challenge to . . . express and preserve moments, feelings, and ideas on paper. It is a challenge that never lessens and never grows dull."

1 It was always the first thing I went to look at when I entered her apartment, and it was always the last thing I glanced at when I left. On a small coffee table, a thick silver frame propped it up towards me. It was a beautiful photograph of my Great-Aunt Corinne, taken when she was a young woman. Her face in the photograph somehow always struck me as unusual. A gentle wave of thick black hair contrasted stunningly with her fair face, and her smile was strangely happy and melancholy at the same time. What I found disturbing about the photograph was a contrast greater than that between her dark hair and her fair face, a contrast that was harsh and unkind.

2 The discrepancy was between the Aunt Corinne I knew and the Aunt Corinne in the photograph. The Aunt Corinne I knew had short, greasy, black hair pinned back upon a pale, balding head. Her smile was almost toothless, gaping, childish. She seemed retarded because of a brain tumor that had spread as she grew from a young girl to adulthood. Since her family was poor, they could not afford any medical attention for her other than glasses for her failing vision.

3 My name is also Corinne. I have never used it until recently. All my life I have been called "Corey," and I have corrected others when they did not use my nickname. I have done this not only because I like the name Corey, but also because I have not wanted to be associated with my great aunt in such an intimate way. Identity and individuality are tightly woven into our names, especially when we are seven or so. When I was this age, I feared that I, too, might develop a deteriorating mental condition like that of my great aunt just because we shared the same name. More importantly I did not want to use the name Corinne because I was embarrassed at the bond the name created with this person whom I considered pathetic and incomplete, whose greatest tragedy was the loss of a healthy mind. This frightening change was tangible to me in the silver-framed picture of my great aunt.

4 I rarely saw that haunting picture, for my family seldom visited Corinne, who lived far away. When we did visit, I tried to conceal my reluctance and fear. While I did not want to be reminded of the bond I had to this woman, a member of my family never failed to tell me how happy Corinne would be to see me and how honored she was that I was named after her. At the time, I could not understand why I was her namesake. Why name your daughter after a mentally deficient aunt—out of pity? That was all I could think of. When we entered her apartment, time slowed down; even the air-conditioner seemed to drone more quietly and slowly. The air was still and calm. Either Corinne or her mother, my great grandmother, would welcome us into the tiny living room. I could not tell which was older; to me, they both were simply very old. Then I would see it: the dreaded and admired woman gazing

up from the silver frame. The two-dimensional eyes never focused on anything in the room. From an age only captured in browning photographs, those eyes gazed through ours and peacefully into the distance.

5   Although the two women never offered us any refreshments on our visits, I would not have wanted to eat, for I was thoughtfully absorbing my surroundings and my great aunt with special care and silence. Observing her thin, papery skin made me wince sadly for her fragility, and when she grasped my hand with her swollen fingers, I could not help but feel warmth for her. Her eyes were bright and glistened with the damp glaze that always covered them. The long, fine, black hairs above her lip, graceful in contrast to her chewed words, quivered ever so slightly as she talked. When I was with her, my discomfort at being related to her seemed to go away, exposing a rawer discomfort underneath, an embarrassment for ever reproaching her and her name.

6   After what seemed like neither hours nor minutes—time somehow had been lost among those fine black hairs—we would hug and say goodbye to the two women. As we left I would take one last look at the photograph on the coffee table. When I told Corinne how pretty it was, she would smile proudly and gaze at it with affection. She never looked at it with sorrow for that which had been lost forever, but with simple acceptance and joy for that which she once was.

7   Aunt Corinne died when I was in eighth grade. I remember the ride home from school when my mother told me that she had passed away. An emptiness swelled up within me, and I suddenly felt that I had lost a part of myself. In a basic way, I had found security in the bond of our shared name; it was as if she was my physical tie to the world before I existed. That day on the ride home from school I was very sad for Corinne, for both of us.

8   Corinne—when I hear this name now and when I sign my checks with this name, I often think of her, my great aunt. But sometimes when I hear the name I do not think of her at all because the name Corinne is more comfortable to me now. After all, it is my name, too.

QUESTIONS FOR DISCUSSION

1. How does Okada use the framed photograph of her great-aunt as a structuring device for her essay? What other images and details help to convey her feelings about her great-aunt and their relationship?
2. Why does Okada feel embarrassed and ashamed when visiting her great-aunt?
3. How does the student use contrasts to develop the ambivalent feelings she has about her great-aunt and their relationship?
4. How do the writer's changing feelings about her name parallel both changes in her attitude toward her great-aunt and the growth of her own self-awareness? What did Okada learn about herself from analyzing her relationship with her great-aunt?

Tin Le

"Enter Dragon"

Tin Le was born in Vietnam and has many pleasant memories of his childhood there. In 1985, his brother, mother, and Le reunited with his father in the United States after six years of separation. Le has a special love of nature and photography; he enjoys taking pictures of landscapes and animals. Le wrote the following essay in response to a question that asked him to narrate an experience similar to Maya Angelou's in "Angel of the Candy Counter," in which a childhood memory of discrimination is countered by a fantasy of power.

1   Have you ever been harassed or even physically abused by your schoolmates or other people you encountered just because you were different from the "average" person in your school or community? This happened to me when I came to America in 1985, an immigrant from Vietnam, and was placed in a seventh grade classroom in Redwood City. It was a small school in a quiet community, but also a place where I had a stormy life for about a year. It was the most horrible experience that I ever had in my life. Kids at that age can be very mean to each other, and I was unfortunate to be on the receiving end of the cruelty.

2   I went to a school that did not have a lot of Asians. Because I was Asian, my schoolmates often teased me. Some of them, influenced by Japanese ninjas and Chinese martial art fighters in movies, often challenged me to fights because they thought that I was one of "them," the Asian martial arts fighters. When I refused to fight, they taunted me, calling me chicken. They also called me weak and a nerd because I wore glasses. For a whole year in seventh grade I suffered from their harassment.

3   I especially remember one day when a classmate came to me on the playground and asked if I knew Karate. When I answered, "No," he acted surprised and remarked, "All Chinese know Kung Fu; aren't you one of them? You're supposed to know some Karate. Let's fight and see who is better." Although I ignored him and walked away, he followed me and started to push me around. The more I yielded, the more he attacked me, yet I could do nothing because he was so much bigger than I was. Eventually he seemed to achieve his goal because other students started to gather around us and cheer for him. He became the hero, the macho guy, and I became the laughing-stock of the school. From then on, they labeled me chicken and a weak Chinese, even though I am actually Vietnamese. In my classmates' eyes, all Asians were the same; there were no distinctions.

4   After this episode, many students hit me or pushed me around whenever they felt like it, because they knew that I would not fight back. For example, often at lunch time, several of them would pretend that they did not see me and would walk right into me, spilling my milk or anything else on my tray; then they would say, "Sorry." However, saying sorry solved nothing and did not replace my lunch.

5   The worst part about this experience was that I did not have anyone to turn to for help. I did not have the courage to share my problem with my parents, for I was afraid that worrying about my problem would just contribute to their own burdens. My parents had to work long hours every day so they could provide a happy life for my brother and me. Once they came home, they were very tired and they needed to rest. Furthermore, I wanted them to feel proud of me as they always had.

6   Fortunately, like Maya Angelou in "The Angel of the Candy Counter," I found a way to resolve my problem by developing a fantasy to endure the pain. I fantasized that I had Bruce Lee's fighting skill (he was the greatest movie star martial arts fighter; his skill even surpassed that of Chuck Norris). I imagined that I fixed up a date after school to settle my unfinished business with the guy who started my nightmare. The moment for our showdown came, and with just one roundhouse kick, I knocked him down to the ground in front of hundreds of schoolmate spectators. He begged me to let him go and promised that he would not pick on anyone anymore. In my fantasy world, from that point on, my friends began to respect me and even to move aside wherever I went. I also imagined that I would disguise myself in black clothes like those of the ninjas and rescue other victims from bullies in the school, disappearing from the scene as soon as everything was over.

7   Even though the fantasy did not actually solve my problem, it helped me to escape and forget about the bitter reality that I was in, allowing me to enter a world of my own. The fantasy was very helpful to me because it brought joy and a feeling of victory into my harsh experience at school. As a recent immigrant, it was hard for me to try to cope with the language and cultural barriers, and, at the same time, to deal with the bullying and abuse from the students at my school. I still cannot understand how human beings could be so cruel to one another. I realize now that people use fantasies all the time as defense mechanisms to release them from the stress and abuse they must endure in daily life. I wish that people could get to a stage where they would not have to use these compensatory fantasies, a stage in which people could accept one another for who they are, despite differences in physical character, race, and culture.

QUESTIONS FOR DISCUSSION

1. The theme and structure of Le's essay are modeled after Maya Angelou's autobiographical piece included in this chapter. How are Le's experiences and the insights he draws from them similar to Angelou's experience at the dentist? How does Le's perspective differ from hers?
2. What comment does the essay make about racially motivated bullying and its influence on Asian immigrant youth? Have you witnessed behavior similar to that described in the essay? What was your response to this harassment?
3. Le's essay concludes by stating that he cannot "understand how human beings can be so cruel to one another." What would be your response to

this statement? What do you believe causes human cruelty such as that described in the essay?

4. Comment on Le's use of narrative examples to support his comments on
racial harassment. How does his use of narrative help to support the major points he makes in the essay?

Topics for Research and Writing

1. As Naomi Remen does in her essay "Remembering," many psychologists
have written of the importance of recapturing buried and traumatic memories of the distant past—sometimes using controversial therapies such as
hypnosis for enhanced recall—in order to free oneself and to heal psychologically. Do some research into this issue and write an essay about the
importance—and controversy—over the use of buried memories in the
healing process.

2. Write an essay in which you discuss how the readings in this chapter as
well as outside readings and research have affected your understanding of
the importance of memories as a rich source for writing material.

3. Li-Young Lee and Naomi Remen explore the impact of immigrants' memories, and how these memories are often at odds with the lives of American citizens. Do some research into an immigrant group such as
Holocaust survivors or Vietnam War refugees, and write about the legacy
of traumatic memories of persecution that continue to influence these immigrants and their families.

4. Do some reading about the nature of memory: What causes a person to
have a "good memory," even a "photographic" memory while another
person is "forgetful" and remembers the past only vaguely? Can we improve our memories of recent and past events, or is memory simply a
"given" quality that we can do nothing about? Write an essay that presents your point of view on this topic.

5. Gould explores the reliability of memories of the past, questioning the extent to which the past and "history" are said to truly exist outside of what
we recall and recreate through memory and imagination. Do some further
research into the reliability of early memories, and draw some conclusions. Is there an "objective" past, or does each person or group of people
invent a version of history? If so, what are our "versions" most often
based upon? Write up your conclusions in an essay.

6. Write an essay that explores your family's legacy by giving an account of
several memories that have been crucial to your family's sense of identity
and values. If possible, interview different family members, including extended family such as grandparents, uncles, aunts, and cousins.

7. Write about a film that focuses on the importance of memories and/or
the reliability of memory, referring to elements such as dreams of charac-

ters, flashback sequences, and other cinematic devices for showing remembered scenes. Films to consider include *Wild Strawberries, Fried Green Tomatoes, Prince of Tides, Avalon, To Sleep with Anger, Stand By Me, Cinema Paradiso, The Joy Luck Club, Lone Star,* and *The Governess.*

8. The following list of URLs is presented to help you get started with Internet research into the subject of memory:

EXPOSING THE NERVE: NOTES ON MEMORY, HYPERTEXT, AND POETRY
http://bmarsh.dtai.com/works/essays/hypertext/expos/exposing.html
Hypterext site from Bill Marsh includes comments on capturing memories through hypertext and poetry.

FORSYTH'S MEMORY AND COGNITION PAGE
http://www.vcu.edu/hasweb/psy/psy101/forsyth/zmemory.htm
Donelson Forsyth's page from VCU on memory and cognition covers memory-related issues such as stress, trauma, sleep and consciousness, sensation and perception.

HOLOCAUST ACTIVITIES: DIARIES AND MEMOIRS
http://fcit.coedu.usf.edu/holocaust/activity/plans1/diaries.htm
Site provides information and activities on reading and keeping diaries and memoir writing, with a focus on the Holocaust.

LOOKSMART.COM—GENERAL INFORMATION ON MEMORY DISORDERS
http://www.looskmart.com/eus1/eus317837/eus317920/eus53948/eus273036/eus273805/eus273810/eus274205/eus532430/r?1&
Looksmart.com's memory disorder page presents links which examine the connection between memory loss and Alzheimer's Disease, as well as information on how memory works and how to improve it.

MEMOIRS, JOURNALS, DIARIES, STORIES
http://www.wizard.net/~loiselle/story_2.html
Dawnelle Loiselle's site provides some interesting activities for journal entries as well as a bibliography of books on journal/diary keeping and links to on-line diaries and other web sites on the subject.

SIDRAN FOUNDATION ONLINE
http://www.sidran.org/index.html
This organization provides on-line links and articles devoted to "education, advocacy and research related to the early recognition and treatment of trauma-related stress in children and the understanding and treatment of adults suffering from trauma-generated disorders." See especially on-line articles on the influence of early trauma on memory.

4

Dreams, Myths, and Fairy Tales

"Myths are public dreams, dreams are private myths."
                    JOSEPH CAMPBELL
                    Hero With a Thousand Faces

"Fantasy is the core of all writing for children, as I think it is for the writing of any book, for any creative act, perhaps for the act of living."
                    MAURICE SENDAK

The ancient Pueblo vision of the world was inclusive. . . . Pueblo oral tradition necessarily embraced all levels of human experience. . . .
                    LESLIE MARMON SILKO
                    Landscape, History and the Pueblo Imagination

COMPARING AND CONTRASTING: STRATEGIES FOR THINKING AND WRITING

The readings selected for this chapter encourage you to think comparatively. You will find that dreams are compared to myths, myths to fairy tales, traditional tales to modern forms of literature; also included are different versions of the same basic myths from various cultures. We have designed the chapter in this way because comparing and contrasting are related and essential aspects of reading and writing and are crucial as well to the way the mind thinks and organizes experiences.

When you compare and contrast, you explore relationships between subjects that, despite apparent distinctions, have qualities in common. In this chapter, for example, Carl Jung uses comparison and contrast to emphasize the differences between his own ideas on dream analysis. Comparative writing

170

demands sophisticated, analytical thinking and organization of ideas. Although everyone naturally makes comparisons while thinking, the structure of comparative writing is more balanced and complex than what one normally does when making comparisons in daily life. Prewriting is especially useful for gathering insights and details to use for comparison.

Prewriting for Comparison

You can begin to do prewriting for a comparison paper by using any of the techniques discussed in Chapter 1, such as freewriting or clustering. For example, to use brainstorming begin by dividing a piece of paper down the middle; then create brainstorming lists of points or qualities you perceive in the subjects of your analysis. A student who wanted to develop a comparison between fairy tales and elementary school readers took the following notes:

Fairy Tales	*Elementary School Readers*
imaginative	seem written by "formula"
engage interest and feelings	don't involve students deeply
teach living skills & heroism	teach "basic reading skills"
encourage imagination	encourage conformity
raise some disturbing issues	avoid controversial issues

You can see some striking contrasts in the lists above. After eliminating some items and grouping the related points, the student could move from the list to a general, clearly worded thesis statement such as the following: "Fairy tales engage the feelings and minds of the child, while primary school texts often fail to attract the interests of children, and thus may actually turn children off to reading." In a very short time, this student writer has found several major points of contrast for possible development and a good central idea to unify a paragraph or essay.

Outlining and Transition

Use of an outline helps to structure extended comparison/contrast papers. An outline will help you to achieve a balanced treatment of each subject and major point in your paper. In preparing an outline, consider the kind of organization you want to use. Comparisons can be structured around points of similarity or difference; use details to clarify and to add interest to the comparison. In subject-by-subject comparing, points are made about two subjects in separate paragraphs or sections of a paper, bringing the two subjects together in the conclusion for a final evaluation or summary of major points. In writing your comparison essay, make the basic points of your comparison clear to your readers through transitional statements. As you move from one comparative issue to another, use expressions such as "in comparison to," "similarly," and "likewise." If the differences between your subjects seem more striking than the similarities, use contrast as your major strategy for examining and noting distinctions, emphasizing your points with transitional expressions such as "in contrast to" and "another point of distinction." As student writer Josh Groban does in his comparison essay in this chapter between the Yao myth of creation and the story of Genesis in the Bible, you need to be careful that you order and develop your points with care, distinguishing between similarities and differences so as to avoid confusion and to retain a clear sense of the overall purpose of your comparison: to understand complex realities, to evaluate, to make a choice.

Evaluation

Evaluating involves making a judgment based on a standard that you hold about a subject or issue. In the prewriting exercise above, the student who contrasted fairy tales with primary school textbooks made an evaluation of each based on personal likes and dislikes: the student liked fairy tales and disliked textbooks. Although the student writer didn't discuss her standards for judging children's literature, we can assume that she likes reading that is entertaining and engaging and is bored by writing that exists simply as a tool for learning. In fact, the student might have thought more critically about the standards that are appropriate for school readers. If she had, she might have considered the problems that schools have in selecting and judging materials for different types of learners. Regardless of your subject of comparison, by establishing guidelines for comparing your standards with those of other people, you can come closer to seeing whether your values are realistic guides for belief and behavior.

Logical Fallacies of Comparison and Contrast

When you begin to think and write comparatively, you may find yourself falling into misleading patterns of thought. A common problem involving comparison and contrast is the drawing of rigid distinctions that force a choice between artificially opposed positions. Often a contrastive statement will imply that one position is a "bad" choice: "America, Love it or leave it"; "A person is either a God-fearing Christian or a sinful atheist"; "You're either a real he-man or a spineless sissy." Such statements employ both an incorrect use of contrast and an inappropriate use of evaluation by setting up an either/or dilemma. In fact, there are occasions when any comparison oriented to evaluating may seem inappropriate. In comparing and contrasting the myths from different cultures included in the portfolio in this chapter, for instance, you may note that each myth of creation involves very different sets of images and values relative to the act and purpose of creation. When thinking about radically different cultures and values, it is more useful simply to make relevant distinctions than to attempt to evaluate one culture as superior or inferior to another.

In the faulty analogy, another common error in comparing, a person attempts to create a connection between two subjects when there are few strong points of similarity, such as arguing that, because life is dreamlike in certain ways, a person should go through life passively, accepting whatever happens just as one might in a dream. Analogies and imaginative, nonliteral comparisons, known as metaphors and similes, can be useful in writing, giving a sense of unexpected and imaginative connections, making descriptions clearer, bringing new insights. On the other hand, taking a metaphorical statement, such as "Life is a dream," and applying it too literally as a standard for conduct ignores real distinctions between the waking world and the sleeping world.

The section on dialogic argument in Chapter 7 discusses ways in which flexible stances in argument can allow you to move beyond overly rigid, unexamined standards of comparison and evaluation. For now, you should feel ready to use the strategy of comparison more systematically and productively to help you to perceive clear relationships between the public world and your inner world.

THEMATIC INTRODUCTION: DREAMS, MYTHS AND FAIRY TALES

Once you begin to understand how your memories of particular child-hood events have shaped and continue to influence your identity and the direction of your life, you may begin to enjoy relating your personal history to myths and fairy tales. These universal stories have helped to connect humans to one another, despite their historical and cultural differences. Myths are patterned stories that present the reader with ideal heroes and heroines acting through dream-like plots and settings, representing the fundamental values of a society. Fairy tales satisfy the needs of younger people, and adults as well, for dangerous adventures where happiness and justice ultimately prevail. Both forms provide ethical lessons that help readers to discriminate between creative and destructive or good and evil behavior. Although our culture often encourages us to doubt the imaginative world of the mythical, asking us instead to seek out practical, logical solutions to problems, myths continue to live on as cornerstones of traditional belief and to help people to uncover meaning, order, and hope in a world that sometimes seems chaotic. The fundamental adventure and quest patterns of stories and legends are continually being transformed and adapted according to the values of each new age. Today's popular myths provide readers with revised values and reflections on changing cultural norms.

This chapter begins with two fictional portraits that reveal the power of myths in the lives of individuals and in communal existence. The first selection, "ego-tripping (there may be a reason why)," is a poem by the African-American writer Nikki Giovanni. In this poem speaker imagines herself living through the myths of her heritage as she realizes that identification with these myths protects her and gives her power. Gabriel García Marquez's modern tale, "The Handsomest Drowned Man in the World: A Tale for Children," chronicles the creation of a peasant myth about the redemption brought by a drowned man in a remote seaside village.

The next two selections present theoretical perspectives on the meaning and importance of dreams and myths. In "The Four Functions of Mythology," a scholar of world mythology, Joseph Campbell, describes the way in which myths help individuals to reconcile their awareness of good and evil, provide images of the universe that validate social order, and offer spiritual meanings. In the next selection, taken from the opening chapter of *Man and His Symbols*, psychologist Carl Jung concludes that it is through symbol-laden dreams that the unconscious mind speaks, helping people to get more closely in touch with their inner selves. Jung sees dreams with their universal symbolism as vital creations in themselves and as internal representations of myths.

In order to provide concrete examples of imaginatively charged mythical stories, we have included a selection of creation myths. These myths celebrate the mystery of creation and embody core values and beliefs about the origins of the world, its creatures, and human beings. We have included myths from the Western tradition (The Book of Genesis), as well as the African and Native American cultural traditions.

Just as dreams and myths give us clues to our unconscious selves and our connections to universal human concerns, fairy tales, a particular class of myths that have been adapted for the entertainment and enlightenment of children as well as to reflect on the darker side of human nature. In the next selection, "Fairy Tales and the Existential Predicament," Bruno Bettelheim asserts that children in our modern world need to read classic fairy tales, which present the good and the bad sides of human nature and the conscious and unconscious needs and impulses of humans. To help you to understand and reflect on the different ways in which a single fairy tale can be interpreted and transformed by particular cultures and historical periods, we have included four versions of the Cinderella myth: the Brothers Grimm's "Aschenputtel," a Native American version of the tale, "The Algonquin Cinderella," and a satirical retelling of the Cinderella story by journalist James Finn Garner, "The Politically Correct Cinderella." Garner pokes fun at those who believe that traditional fairy tales are not suitable for young children because they support traditional gender roles. Finally, poet Olga Broumas envisions the Cinderella story in the form of a feminist sequel: the unhappy and isolated Cinderella yearns to return to her home to start a new life among her "sisters."

Two student essays conclude the readings selected for this chapter. In the first, Joshua Groban compares the meanings of two creation myths to show the different values and beliefs held by the two cultures that produced the myths. The next student essay focuses on the Cinderella story. In "Cinderella: Politically Incorrect?" Liz Scheps analyses the use of language and social satire in Garner's "The Politically Correct Cinderella," comparing this modern re-telling to the more traditional version by the Brothers Grimm.

Thinking about myths and fairy tales from different cultures can help you to gain new insights into your own culture, as you begin to see your world in a broader perspective of diverse values, emotional needs, and spiritual concerns. Through drawing comparisons between versions of myths and fairy tales, you will also be better able to see how these universal forms can change and yet endure; perhaps they will help you to make sense of your contemporary world and to see its connection to the past. Reflecting on and writing about the implications of your dreams and myths as well as the dreams and myths of others is an essential path on your inward journey toward better self-understanding and a deeper appreciation of the world in which you live.

Linda Lomahaftewa (1947–)
"Starmakers" (1990)

Linda Lomahaftewa, an art instructor at the Institute of American Indian Art in Santa Fe, N.M., is from a Hopi/Choctaw background and is one of the leading contemporary Native American Artists. Her works, which have appeared in many exhibits around the country, often display a whimsical sensibility while exploring elements of traditional Native myth and ritual. The vibrant painting "Starmakers" depicts the Hopi myth of the creation of the evening star.

IDEAS FOR DRAWING, WRITING, AND DISCUSSION

1. Do a drawing based either on one of the creation stories in this chapter or on your own idea of the story of the creation of the world.
2. Do a brief writing in which you explain the myth that lies behind your drawing. What idea of creation does it reflect?
3. Working in a group, share your drawings and explanations of creation stories. How were the accounts both distinct and similar in their view of creation?

Nikki Giovanni

"ego-tripping (there may be a reason why)"

Nikki Giovanni (b. 1943) has written children's fiction, memoir, and essays; she is best known for her poetry. Giovanni's poetry, which she frequently has read aloud on television and records, has been a significant influence on younger African-American writers and poets, especially the new rap poets and musicians. Giovanni won a Ford Foundation grant and has received awards from the National Endowment for the Arts and the Harlem Cultural Council. Her first book, Black Feeling, Black Talk, *appeared in 1968. Her recent publications include* Racism 101 (1994), Selected Poems (1996), Love Poems (1997), *and* Blues: for all the Changes: New Poems (1999). *Currently Giovanni teaches at Virginia Polytechnic Institute and State University. As you read her poem "ego-tripping" (1973), notice how she is able to capture the cultural myths and historical realities that can be a source of pride for African Americans.*

JOURNAL

Imagine yourself as related to the larger-than-life heroes and/or heroines you admire. Begin each sentence of your freewrite with "I"; exaggerate and have fun!

I was born in the congo
I walked to the fertile crescent and built
   the sphinx
I designed a pyramid so tough that a star
5   that only glows every one hundred years falls
   into the center giving divine perfect light
I am bad

I sat on the throne
   drinking nectar with allah
10 I got hot and sent an ice age to europe
   to cool my thirst
My oldest daughter is nefertiti
   the tears from my birth pains
   created the nile
15 I am a beautiful woman

I gazed on the forest and burned
   out the sahara desert
   with a packet of goat's meat
   and a change of clothes
20 I crossed it in two hours
I am a gazelle so swift
   so swift you can't catch me

For a birthday present when he was three
I gave my son hannibal an elephant
25   He gave me rome for mother's day
My strength flows ever on

My son noah built new/ark and
I stood proudly at the helm
   as we sailed on a soft summer day
30 I turned myself into myself and was
   jesus
   men intone my loving name

   All praises All praises
I am the one who would save
35 I sowed diamonds in my back yard
My bowels deliver uranium
   the filings from my fingernails are
   semi-precious jewels
   On a trip north
40 I caught a cold and blew
My nose giving oil to the arab world
I am so hip even my errors are correct
I sailed west to reach east and had to round off
   the earth as I went
45   The hair from my head thinned and gold was
   laid across three continents

I am so perfect so divine so ethereal so surreal
I cannot be comprehended
   except by my permission

50 I mean . . . I . . . can fly
   like a bird in the sky . . .

QUESTIONS FOR DISCUSSION

1. To emphasize her pride in her African descent, Giovanni's narrator invokes a number of African cultures, mythologies, places, and historical figures. Identify several of the African references in the poem and explain how the narrator finds pride and power through these references and comparisons.

2. Giovanni's poem combines African references with African-American expressions. Identify slang words and phrases in the poem and explain how such expressions add to the power of the poem.

3. In addition to its references to the African-Egyptian cultural tradition, the poem also alludes to biblical characters and mythologies. Point out any references to the Old or New Testament of the Bible, and discuss how you

think such references and implied comparisons help to develop the poem's tone and meaning.

4. Although the poem has a boisterous, buoyant feeling, at times it seems as if Giovanni may be questioning the narrator's boastfulness. Explain how expressions such as "ego tripping" and "even my errors are correct" could be read as criticisms of the narrator. Why do you think the poet built this self-critical perspective into the poem?

5. What does this poem suggest to you about the functions and power of myth in literature as well as in the inner life of the individual?

CONNECTION

Interpret the dreams and fantasies in GIovanni's poem using some of the ideas on dreams and symbols in the essay by Carl Jung in this chapter.

IDEAS FOR WRITING

1. Try developing your ego-tripping freewriting into your own "rap" or "boast" poem. Refer to myths and cultural traditions that are familiar to you.

2. The speaker in Giovanni's poem seems to gain a sense of personal empowerment through making a series of mythical comparisons. Write an essay in which you argue for or against the importance of comparing oneself to and identifying with characters and situations in myths to gain a sense of pride and self-respect. Use examples of myths you or other people you know believe in that could help to develop a sense of self-esteem.

Gabriel García Marquez

"The Handsomest Drowned Man in the World: A Tale for Children"

Gabriel García Marquez (b. 1928) grew up in a small town in Colombia, the eldest of twelve children in a poor family. In 1947 he entered the National University in Bogota, continuing his studies at the University of Cartagena, where he began to write a daily newspaper column. His first book of stories, Leaf Storm and Other Stories *(1955), which includes "The Handsomest Drowned Man in the World," confirmed his commitment to politics and social change. From 1959 to 1961, he traveled extensively while working for a Cuban news agency. After the Cuban revolution, Marquez returned to Central America to encourage other revolutionary causes. With the publication of his novel* One Hundred Years of Solitude *(1967), he was recognized as one of the most talented writers of Latin America. Among his*

other widely read novels are The Autumn of the Patriarch *(1975) and* Love in
the Time of Cholera *(1988); his short story collections include* Collected Stories
(1984) and Strange Pilgrims *(1993). He received the Nobel Prize for Literature in
1982. Marquez's work combines the realistic and the fantastic, and he often uses
peasant fables as the basis of his stories, as in the tale that follows.*

JOURNAL

Write about a local hero in your community or neighborhood who achieved
larger-than-life, "mythical" status after his or her death.

---

1   The first children who saw the dark and slinky bulge approaching through the sea
    let themselves think it was an empty ship. Then they saw it had no flags or
masts and they thought it was a whale. But when it washed up on the beach, they removed the clumps of seaweed, the jellyfish tentacles, and the remains of fish and
flotsam, and only then did they see that it was a drowned man.

2   They had been playing with him all afternoon, burying him in the sand and digging
him up again, when someone chanced to see them and spread the alarm in the village.
The men who carried him to the nearest house noticed that he weighed more than any
dead man they had ever known, almost as much as a horse, and they said to each other
that maybe he'd been floating too long and the water had got into his bones. When
they laid him on the floor they said he'd been taller than all other men because there
was barely enough room for him in the house, but they thought that maybe the ability
to keep on growing after death was part of the nature of certain drowned men. He had
the smell of the sea about him and only his shape gave one to suppose that it was the
corpse of a human being, because the skin was covered with a crust of mud and scales.

3   They did not even have to clean off his face to know that the dead man was a
stranger. The village was made up of only twenty-odd wooden houses that had stone
courtyards with no flowers and which were spread about on the end of a desertlike
cape. There was so little land that mothers always went about with the fear that the
wind would carry off their children and the few dead that the years had caused
among them had to be thrown off the cliffs. But the sea was calm and bountiful and
all the men fit into seven boats. So when they found the drowned man they simply
had to look at one another to see that they were all there.

4   That night they did not go out to work at sea. While the men when to find out if
anyone was missing in neighboring villages, the women stayed behind to care for the
drowned man. They took the mud off with grass swabs, they removed the underwater stones entangled in his hair, and they scraped the crust off with tools used for
scaling fish. As they were doing that they noticed that the vegetation on him came
from faraway oceans and deep water and that his clothes were in tatters, as if he had
sailed through laybrinths of coral. They noticed too that he bore his death with
pride, for he did not have the lonely look of other drowned men who came out of

the sea or that haggard, needy look of men who drowned in rivers. But only when they finished cleaning him off did they become aware of the kind of man he was and it left them breathless. Not only was he the tallest, strongest, most virile, and best built man they had ever seen, but even though they were looking at him there was no room for him in their imagination.

5   They could not find a bed in the village large enough to lay him on nor was there a table solid enough to use for his wake. The tallest men's holiday pants would not fit him, nor the fattest ones' Sunday shirts, nor the shoes of the one with the biggest feet. Fascinated by his huge size and his beauty, the women then decided to make him some pants from a large piece of sail and a shirt from some bridal Brabant linen so that he could continue through his death with dignity. As they sewed, sitting in a circle and gazing at the corpse between stitches, it seemed to them that the wind had never been so steady nor the sea so restless as on that night and they supposed that the change had something to do with the dead man. They thought that if that magnificent man had lived in the village, his house would have had the widest doors, and highest ceiling, and the strongest floor; his bedstead would have been made from a midship frame held together by iron bolts, and his wife would have been the happiest woman. They thought that he would have had so much authority that he could have drawn fish out of the sea simply by calling their names and that he would have put so much work into his land that springs would have burst forth from among the rocks so that he would have been able to plant flowers on the cliffs. They secretly compared him to their own men, thinking that for all their lives theirs were incapable of doing what he could do in one night, and they ended up dismissing them deep in their hearts as the weakest, meanest, and most useless creatures on earth. They were wandering through that maze of fantasy when the oldest woman, who as the oldest had looked upon the drowned man with more compassion than passion, sighed:

6   "He has the face of someone called Esteban."

7   It was true. Most of them had only to take another look at him to see that he could not have any other name. The more stubborn among them, who were the youngest, still lived for a few hours with the illusion that when they put his clothes on and he lay among the flowers in patent leather shoes his name might be Lautaro. But it was a vain illusion. There had not been enough canvas, the poorly cut and worse sewn pants were too tight, and the hidden strength of his heart popped the buttons on his shirt. After midnight the whistling of the wind died down and the sea fell into its Wednesday drowsiness. The silence put an end to any last doubts: he was Esteban. The women who had dressed him, who had combed his hair, had cut his nails and shaved him were unable to hold back a shudder of pity when they had to resign themselves to his being dragged along the ground. It was then that they understood how unhappy he must have been with that huge body since it bothered him even after death. They could see him in life, condemned to going through doors sideways cracking his head on crossbeams, remaining on his feet during visits, not knowing what to do with his soft pink, sealion hands while the lady of the house looked for her most resistant chair and begged him, frightened to death, sit here, Esteban, please, and he, leaning against the wall, smiling,

don't bother, ma'am, I'm fine where I am, his heels raw and his back roasted from having done the same thing so many times whenever he paid a visit, don't bother ma'am, I'm fine where I am to avoid the embarrassment of breaking up the chair, and never knowing perhaps that the one who said don't go, Esteban, at least wait till the coffee's ready, were the ones who later on would whisper the big boob finally left, how nice, the handsome fool has gone. That was what the women were thinking beside the body a little before dawn. Later, when they covered his face with a handkerchief so that the light would not bother him, he looked so forever dead, so defenseless, so much like their men that the first furrows of tears opened in their hearts. It was one of the younger ones who began the weeping. The others, coming to, went from sighs to wails, and the more they sobbed the more they felt like weeping, because the drowned man was becoming all the more Esteban for them, and so they wept so much, for he was the most destitute, most peaceful, and most obliging man on earth, poor Esteban. So when the men returned with the news that the drowned man was not from the neighboring villages either, the women felt an opening of jubilation in the midst of their tears.

8   "Praise the Lord," they sighed, "he's ours!"

9   The men thought the fuss was only womanish frivolity. Fatigued because of the difficult nighttime inquiries, all they wanted was to get rid of the bother of the newcomer once and for all before the sun grew strong on that arid, windless day. They improvised a litter with the remains of foremasts and gaffs, tying it together with rigging so that it would bear the weight of the body until they reached the cliffs. They wanted to tie the anchor from a cargo ship to him so that he would sink easily into the deepest waves, where the fish are blind and divers die of nostalgia, and bad currents would not bring him back to shore, as had happend with other bodies. But the more they hurried, the more the women thought of ways to waste time. They walked about like startled hens, pecking with the sea charms on their breasts, some interfering on one side to put a scapular of the good wind on the drowned man, some on the other side to put a wrist compass on him, and after a great deal of *get away from there woman, stay out of the way, look, you almost made me fall on top of the dead man*, the men began to feel mistrust in their livers and started grumbling about why so many main-altar decorations for a stranger, because no matter how many nails and holywater jars he had on him, the sharks would chew him all the same, but the women kept on piling on their junk relics, running back and forth, stumbling, while they released in sighs what they did not in tears, so that the men finally exploded with *since when has there ever been such a fuss over a drifting corpse, a drowned nobody, a piece of cold Wednesday meat*. One of the women, mortified by so much lack of care, then removed the handkerchief from the dead man's face and the men were left breathless too.

10   He was Esteban. It was not necessary to repeat it for them to recognize him. If they had been told Sir Walter Raleigh, even they might have been impressed with his gringo accent, the macaw on his shoulder, his cannibal-killing blunderbuss, but there could be only one Esteban in the world and there he was, stretched out like a sperm whale, shoeless, wearing the pants of an undersized child, and with those stony nails that had to be cut with a knife. They had only to take the handkerchief off his face to see that he was ashamed, that it was not his fault that he was so big or

so heavy or so handsome, and if he had known that his was going to happen, he would have looked for a more discreet place to drown in; seriously, I even would have tied the anchor off a galleon around my neck and staggered off a cliff like someone who doesn't like things in order not to be upsetting people now with this Wednesday dead body, as you people say, in order not to be bothering anyone with this fithy piece of cold meat that doesn't have anything to do with me. There was so much truth in his manner that even the most mistrustful men, the ones who felt the bitterness of endless nights at sea fearing that their women would tire of dreaming about them and begin to dream of drowned men, even they and others who were harder still shuddered in the marrow of their bones at Esteban's sincerity.

11   That was how they came to hold the most splendid funeral they could conceive of for an abandoned drowned man. Some women who had gone to get flowers in the neighboring villages returned with other women who could not believe what they had been told, and those women went back for more flowers when they saw the dead man, and they brought more and more until there were so many flowers and so many people that it was hard to walk about. At the final moment it pained them to return him to the waters as an orphan and they chose a father and mother from among the best people, and aunts and uncles and cousins, so that through him all the inhabitants of the village became kinsmen. Some sailors who heard the weeping from a distance went off course, and people heard of one who had himself tied to the manmast, remembering ancient fables about sirens. While they fought for the privilege of carrying him on their shoulders along the steep escarpment by the cliffs, men and women became aware for the first time of the desolation of their streets, the dryness of their courtyards, the narrowness of their dreams as they faced the splendor and beauty of their drowned man. They let him go without an anchor so that he could come back if he wished and whenever he wished, and they all held their breath for the fraction of centuries the body took to fall into the abyss. They did not need to look to one another to realize that they were no longer all present, that they would never be. But they also knew that everything would be different from then on, that their houses would have wider doors, higher ceilings, and stronger floors so that Esteban's memory could go everywhere without bumping into beams and so that no one in the future would dare whisper the big boob finally died, too bad, the handsome fool has finally died, because they were going to paint their house fronts gay colors to make Esteban's memory eternal and they were going to break their backs digging for springs among the stones and planting flowers on the cliffs so that in future years at dawn the passengers on great liners would awaken, suffocated by the smell of gardens on the high seas, and the captain would have to come down from the bridge in his dress uniform, with his astrolabe, his pole star, and his row of war medals and, pointing to the promontory of roses on the horizon, he would say in fourteen languages, look there, where the wind is so peaceful now that it's gone to sleep beneath the beds, over there, where the sun's so bright that the sunflowers don't know which way to turn, yes, over there, that's Esteban's village.

Translated by Gregory Rabassa

QUESTIONS FOR DISCUSSION

1. What is revealed through the initial description of the drowned man? Why was "there . . . no room for him in their [the villagers'] imagination"?
2. Why and how does the drowned man make the women happy and the sea peaceful? Why does the community of women finally agree that this man must be Esteban?
3. How did the women feel about Esteban when he was alive? How do they feel about him now that he is dead?
4. Do the men of the village change their attitude toward the drowned man once they realize he is Esteban? Why or why not?
5. What is the significance of the villagers' making their island into a beautiful shrine dedicated to Esteban's size and beauty?
6. Why is the story subtitled "A Tale for Children"? What warnings and hope does the story offer?

CONNECTION

Compare this story about the origins of a myth with Joseph Campbell's "Four Functions of Mythology." Which of the four functions would this myth fulfill?

IDEAS FOR WRITING

1. Write an essay that examines the way the story weaves together realistic details and fantasy. How does this style help to emphasize and build the mythical quality of the story and its central character, Esteban?
2. Write an essay that interprets the myth and moral of "Handsomest Drowned Man." What truth and values are revealed in this portrait of a society in the process of creating a new myth?

Joseph Campbell

"The Four Functions of Mythology"

Joseph Campbell (1904–1987) was born in New York and studied Medieval Literature at Columbia University. He dropped out of his doctoral program there after learning that mythology would not be an acceptable subject for his dissertation. Campbell taught mythological studies at Sarah Lawrence College for many years before retiring to Hawaii and pursuing his interests in writing and lecturing. In later life, he became a popular figure in contemporary culture, inspiring George Lucas's Star Wars films and doing a number of interviews with Bill Moyers on public television. Campbell shared Carl Jung's belief in the archetypal patterns of symbolism in myths and dreams. He was author and editor of many books on world mythology, including The Hero With a Thousand Faces *(1949) and the four-volume* The Masks of God *(1962). In the following selection from "Mythological Themes in Creative Literature and Art," an essay included in the collection* Myths, Dreams, and Religion *(1970), Campbell explores what he considers to be the major functions of mythology in the life of individuals, cultures, and societies.*

JOURNAL

Write a definition of "myth" or "mythology" based on your personal associations with the terms. List as many qualities and functions of myths or mythology as you know.

1   Traditional mythologies serve, normally, four functions, the first of which might be described as the reconciliation of consciousness with the preconditions of its own existence. In the long course of our biological prehistory, living creatures had been consuming each other for hundreds of millions of years before eyes opened to the terrible scene, and millions more elapsed before the level of human consciousness was attained. Analogously, as individuals, we are born, we live and grow, on the impulse of organs that are moved independently of reason to aims antecedent to thought—like beasts: until, one day, the crisis occurs that has separated mankind from the beasts: the realization of the monstrous nature of this terrible game that is life, and our consciousness recoils. In mythological terms: we have tasted the fruit of the wonder-tree of the knowledge of good and evil, and have lost our animal innocence. Schopenhauer's scorching phrase represents the motto of this fallen state: "Life is something that should not have been!" Hamlet's state of indecision is the melancholy consequence: "To be, or not to be!" And, in fact, in the long and varied course of the evolution of the mythologies of mankind, there have been many addressed to the aims of an absolute negation of the world, a condemnation of life, and a backing out. These I have termed the mythologies of "The Great Reversal." They have flourished most prominently in India, particularly since the Buddha's time (sixth century B.C.), whose First Noble Truth, "All life is sorrowful," derives from the same insight as Schopenhauer's rueful dictum. However, more general, and certainly much earlier in the great course of human history, have been the mythologies and associated rites of redemption through affirmation. Throughout the primitive world, where direct confrontations with the brutal bloody facts of life are inescapable and unremitting, the initiation ceremonies to which growing youngsters are subjected are frequently horrendous, confronting them in the most appalling, vivid terms, with experiences—both optically and otherwise—of this monstrous thing that is life: and always with the requirement of a "yea," with no sense of either personal or collective guilt, but gratitude and exhilaration.

2   For there have been, finally, but three attitudes taken toward the awesome mystery in the great mythological traditions; namely, the first, of a "yea"; the second, of a "nay"; and the last, of a "nay," but with a contingent "yea," as in the great complex of messianic cults of the late Levant: Zoroastrianism, Judaism, Christianity, and Islam. In these last, the well-known basic myth has been, of an originally good creation corrupted

by a fall, with, however, the subsequent establishment of a supernaturally endowed society, through the ultimate world dominion of which a restoration of the pristine state of the good creation is to be attained. So that, not in nature but in the social order, and not in all societies, but in this, the one and only, is there health and truth and light, integrity and the prospect of perfection. The "yea" here is contingent therefore on the ultimate world victory of this order.

3   The second of the four functions served by traditional mythologies—beyond this of redeeming human consciousness from its sense of guilt in life—is that of formulating and rendering an image of the universe, a cosmological image in keeping with the science of the time and of such kind that, within its range, all things should be recognized as parts of a single great holy picture, an icon as it were: the trees, the rocks, the animals, sun, moon, and stars, all opening back to mystery, and thus serving as agents of the first function, as vehicles and messengers of the teaching.

4   The third traditional function, then, has been ever that of validating and maintaining some specific social order, authorizing its moral code as a construct beyond criticism or human emendation. In the Bible, for example, where the notion is of a personal god through whose act the world was created, that same god is regarded as the author of the Tablets of the Law; and in India, where the basic idea of creation is not of the act of a personal god, but rather of a universe that has been in being and will be in being forever (only waxing and waning, appearing and disappearing, in cycles ever renewed), the social order of caste has been traditionally regarded as of a piece with the order of nature. Man is not free, according to either of these mythic views, to establish for himself the social aims of his life and to work, then, toward these through institutions of his own devising; but rather, the moral, like the natural order, is fixed for all time, and if times have changed (as indeed they have, these past six hundred years), so that to live according to the ancient law and to believe according to the ancient faith have become equally impossible, so much the worse for these times.

5   The first function served by a traditional mythology, I would term, then, the mystical, or metaphysical, the second, the cosmological, and the third, the sociological. The fourth, which lies at the root of all three as their base and final support, is the psychological: that, namely, of shaping individuals to the aims and ideals of their various social groups, bearing them on from birth to death through the course of a human life. And whereas the cosmological and sociological orders have varied greatly over the centuries and in various quarters of the globe, there have nevertheless been certain irreducible psychological problems inherent in the very biology of our species, which have remained constant, and have, consequently, so tended to control and structure the myths and rites in their service that, in spite of all the differences that have been recognized, analyzed, and stressed by sociologists and historians, there run through the myths of all mankind the common strains of a single symphony of the soul. Let us pause, therefore, to review briefly in sequence the order of these irreducible psychological problems.

6   The first to be faced derives from the fact that human beings are born some fourteen years too soon. No other animal endures such a long period of dependency on its parents. And then, suddenly, at a certain point in life, which varies, according to the culture, from, say, twelve to about twenty years of age, the child is expected to become an

adult, and his whole psychological system, which has been tuned and trained to dependency, is now required to respond to the challenges of life in the way of responsibility. Stimuli are no longer to produce responses either of appeal for help or of submission to parental discipline, but of responsible social action appropriate to one's social role. In primitive societies the function of the cruel puberty rites has been everywhere and always to effect and confirm this transformation. And glancing now at our own modern world, deprived of such initiations and becoming yearly more and more intimidated by its own intransigent young, we may diagnose a neurotic as simply an adult who has failed to cross this threshold to responsibility: one whose response to every challenging situation is, first, "What would Daddy say? Where's Mother?" and only then comes to realize, "Why gosh! *I'm* Daddy, I'm forty years old! Mother is now my wife! It is *I* who must do this thing!" Nor have traditional societies ever exhibited much sympathy for those unable or unwilling to assume the roles required. Among the Australian aborigines, if a boy in the course of his initiation seriously misbehaves, he is killed and eaten*—which is an efficient way, of course, to get rid of juvenile delinquents, but deprives the community, on the other hand, of the gifts of original thought. As the late Professor A. R. Radcliffe-Brown of Trinity College, Cambridge, observed in his important study of the Andaman Island pygmies: "A society depends for its existence on the presence in the minds of its members of a certain system of sentiments by which the conduct of the individual is regulated in conformity with the needs of the society. . . . The sentiments in question are not innate but are developed in the individual by the action of the society upon him."† In other words: the entrance into adulthood from the long career of infancy is not, like the opening of a blossom, to a state of naturally unfolding potentialities, but to the assumption of a social role, a mask or "persona," with which one is to identify. In the famous lines of the poet Wordsworth:

Shades of the prison-house begin to close
Upon the growing Boy.‡

A second birth, as it is called, a social birth, is effected, and, as the first had been of Mother Nature, so this one is of the Fathers, Society, and the new body, the new mind, are not of mankind in general but of a tribe, a caste, a certain school, or a nation.

7   Whereafter, inevitably, in due time, there comes a day when the decrees of nature again break forth. That fateful moment at the noon of life arrives when, as Carl Jung reminds us, the powers that in youth were in ascent have arrived at their apogee and the return to earth begins. The claims, the aims, even the interests of society, begin to fall away and, again as in the lines of Wordsworth:

Our noisy years seem moments in the being
Of the eternal Silence: truths that wake,
    To perish never:

*Géza Róheim, *The Eternal Ones of the Dream* (New York: International Universities Press, 1945), p. 232, citing K. Langloh Parker, *The Euahlayi Tribe* (London: A. Constable & Co., 1905), pp 72–73.
†A. R. Radcliffe-Brown, *The Andaman Islanders* (Cambridge: The University Press, 1933), pp. 233–234.
‡William Wordsworth, *Intimations of Immortality from Recollections of Early Childhood* II. 64–65.

Which neither listlessness, nor mad endeavour,
Nor Man nor Boy,
　Nor all that is at enmity with joy,
Can utterly abolish or destroy!

Hence in a season of calm weather
　Though inland far we be,
Our Souls have sight of that immortal sea
　Which brought us hither,
Can in a moment travel thither,
And see the Children sport upon the shore,
And hear the mighty waters rolling evermore.*

8　　Both the great and the lesser mythologies of mankind have, up to the present, always served simultaneously, both to lead the young from their estate in nature, and to bear the aging back to nature and on through the last dark door. And while doing all this, they have served, also, to render an image of the world of nature, a cosmological image as I have called it, that should seem to support the claims and aims of the local social group; so that through every feature of the experienced world the sense of an ideal harmony resting on a dark dimension of wonder should be communicated. One can only marvel at the integrating, life-structuring force of even the simplest traditional organization of mythic symbols.

QUESTIONS FOR DISCUSSION

1. As the title indicates, Campbell describes four functions of mythology. What are the functions and how do they differ from one another? Do you agree with this division? Would you have included other functions?
2. Why does Campbell believe that "our consciousness recoils" at the awareness of the "terrible game" of life? What is terrible or sorrowful about life? How does this awareness involve a loss of innocence similar to the tasting of the apple in the Book of Genesis? How does Christianity offer an answer to the sorrow and loss of innocence that is the nature of life?
3. Campbell believes that traditional mythology presents "an image of the universe," a sense of the order of created things. What image of the universe does traditional Judeo-Christian religion present in the Book of Genesis, for example?
4. Why do the mythic views of both the Bible and the tradition of India tell us that humans are not free? What prevents individual freedom from occurring, according to these traditional mythological views? Can you give examples of other mythic stories and classical works that contain a moral or pattern that implies there is no individual freedom of choice and action?

*Ibid., II. 158–171.

5. How do traditional religions and mythological systems pattern our psychological growth and development as we move toward adulthood, reducing the kind of "neurotic" fixations at a certain maturity level that are so common in our own society? How do mythologies help one to create a "persona" as a social being and prepare us emotionally to come to terms with aging and death?
6. Although Campbell approaches his topic from a general perspective, he makes his ideas more concrete through the use of quotations and references to mythologies familiar to his readers, such as the Book of Genesis from the Bible. What other examples might he have used?

CONNECTION

Compare Campbell's ideas on the function of myths with Bruno Bettelheim's ideas on the role of fairy tales in the life of the child. What common views of myths and tales are shared by these writers?

IDEAS FOR WRITING

1. Elsewhere in the longer essay from which this selection is excerpted, Campbell states that both the cosmological and social functions of mythology have been weakened through modern advances in science and technology. Write an essay in which you present several examples that either support or refute Campbell's assertion that the reliance on science and technology have diminished the power of the human spirit that myths embody.
2. Write an essay in which you discuss a myth that you are familiar with that fulfills one of the four functions that Campbell discusses in his essay. Include a copy or detailed description of the myth with your essay. In what ways is this myth woven into the cultural and social assumptions and values that form the basis of your beliefs and lifestyle?

Carl Jung

"The Importance of Dreams"

A Swiss physician and analyst, Carl Jung (1875–1961) was a follower of Sigmund Freud but later rejected Freud's psychoanalytic method and his views on the purpose and meaning of dreams. In the 1920s, Jung traveled extensively, studying the myths, dreams, values, and religions of preliterate peoples. Eventually Jung developed the concept of the collective unconscious to explain the archetypal patterns of imagery and symbolism that he believed could be found in dreams, literature, and world religions. His Collected Works include twenty volumes of his essays and correspondence.

Jung's best-known works include Modern Man in Search of a Soul *(1933) and his autobiography,* Memories, Dreams, Reflections *(1961). The following selection, which is excerpted from his last work,* Man and His Symbols *(1964), explores Jung's ideas about the place of symbols in dreams and myths.*

Which of the images or symbols that occur in your dreams might also appear in other people's dreams or in dreams of people from other cultures? What is it about these images that make them "universal"?

1   Man uses the spoken or written word to express the meaning of what he wants to convey. His language is full of symbols, but he also often employs signs or images that are not strictly descriptive. Some are mere abbreviations or strings of initials, such as UN, UNICEF, or UNESCO; others are familiar trade marks, the names of patent medicines, badges, or insignia. Although these are meaningless in themselves, they have acquired a recognizable meaning through common usage or deliberate intent. Such things are not symbols. They are signs, and they do no more than denote the objects to which they are attached.

2   What we call a symbol is a term, a name, or even a picture that may be familiar in daily life, yet that possesses specific connotations in addition to its conventional and obvious meaning. It implies something vague, unknown, or hidden from us. Many Cretan monuments, for instance, are marked with the design of the double adze. This is an object that we know, but we do not know its symbolic implications. For another example, take the case of the Indian who, after a visit to England, told his friends at home that the English worship animals, because he had found eagles, lions, and oxen in old churches. He was not aware (nor are many Christians) that these animals are symbols of the Evangelists and are derived from the vision of Ezekiel, and that this in turn has an analogy to the Egyptian sun god Horus and his four sons. There are, moreover, such objects as the wheel and the cross that are known all over the world, yet that have a symbolic significance under certain conditions. Precisely what they symbolize is still a matter for controversial speculation.

3   Thus a word or an image is symbolic when it implies something more than its obvious and immediate meaning. It has a wider "unconscious" aspect that is never precisely defined or fully explained. Nor can one hope to define or explain it. As the mind explores the symbol, it is led to ideas that lie beyond the grasp of reason. The wheel may lead our thoughts toward the concept of a "divine" sun, but at this point reason must admit its incompetence; man is unable to define a "divine" being. When, with all our intellectual limitations, we call something "divine," we have merely given it a name, which may be based on a creed, but never on factual evidence.

4   Because there are innumerable things beyond the range of human understanding, we constantly use symbolic terms to represent concepts that we cannot define or

fully comprehend. This is one reason why all religions employ symbolic language or images. But this conscious use of symbols is only one aspect of a psychological fact of great importance: Man also produces symbols unconsciously and spontaneously, in the form of dreams.

5　　It is not easy to grasp this point. But the point must be grasped if we are to know more about the ways in which the human mind works. Man, as we realize if we reflect for a moment, never perceives anything fully or comprehends anything completely. He can see, hear, touch, and taste; but how far he sees, how well he hears, what his touch tells him, and what he tastes depend upon the number and quality of his senses. These limit his perception of the world around him. By using scientific instruments he can partly compensate for the deficiencies of his senses. For example, he can extend the range of his vision by binoculars or of his hearing by electrical amplification. But the most elaborate apparatus cannot do more than bring distant or small objects within range of his eyes, or make faint sounds more audible. No matter what instruments he uses, at some point he reaches the edge of certainty beyond which conscious knowledge cannot pass.

6　　There are, moreover, unconscious aspects of our perception of reality. The first is the fact that even when our senses react to real phenomena, sights, and sounds, they are somehow translated from the realm of reality into that of the mind. Within the mind they become psychic events, whose ultimate nature is unknowable (for the psyche cannot know its own psychical substance). Thus every experience contains an indefinite number of unknown factors, not to speak of the fact that every concrete object is always unknown in certain respects, because we cannot know the ultimate nature of matter itself.

7　　Then there are certain events of which we have not consciously taken note; they have remained, so to speak, below the threshold of consciousness. They have happened, but they have been absorbed subliminally, without our conscious knowledge. We can become aware of such happenings only in a moment of intuition or by a process of profound thought that leads to a later realization that they must have happened; and though we may have originally ignored their emotional and vital importance, it later wells up from the unconscious as a sort of afterthought.

8　　It may appear, for instance, in the form of a dream. As a general rule, the unconscious aspect of any event is revealed to us in dreams, where it appears not as a rational thought but as a symbolic image. As a matter of history, it was the study of dreams that first enabled psychologists to investigate the unconscious aspect of conscious psychic events.

9　　It is on such evidence that psychologists assume the existence of an unconscious psyche—though many scientists and philosophers deny its existence. They argue naïvely that such an assumption implies the existence of two "subjects," or (to put it in a common phrase) two personalities within the same individual. But this is exactly what it does imply—quite correctly. And it is one of the curses of modern man that many people suffer from this divided personality. It is by no means a pathological symptom; it is a normal fact that can be observed at any time and everywhere. It is not merely the neurotic whose right hand does not know what the left hand is

doing. This predicament is a symptom of a general unconsciousness that is the unde-
niable common inheritance of all mankind.

10   Man has developed consciousness slowly and laboriously, in a process that took
untold ages to reach the civilized state (which is arbitrarily dated from the invention
of script in about 4000 B.C.). And this evolution is far from complete, for large areas
of the human mind are still shrouded in darkness. What we call the "psyche" is by no
means identical with our consciousness and its contents.

11   Whoever denies the existence of the unconscious is in fact assuming that our present knowledge of the psyche is total. And this belief is clearly just as false as the assumption that we know all there is to be known about the natural universe. Our
psyche is part of nature, and its enigma is as limitless. Thus we cannot define either
the psyche or nature. We can merely state what we believe them to be and describe,
as best we can, how they function. Quite apart, therefore, from the evidence that
medical research has accumulated, there are strong grounds of logic for rejecting
statements like "There is no unconscious." Those who say such things merely express an age-old "misoneism"—a fear of the new and the unknown.

12   There are historical reasons for this resistance to the idea of an unknown part of
the human psyche. Consciousness is a very recent acquisition of nature, and it is still
in an "experimental" state. It is frail, menaced by specific dangers, and easily injured.
As anthropologists have noted, one of the most common mental derangements that
occur among primitive people is what they call "the loss of a soul"—which means, as
the name indicates, a noticeable disruption (or, more technically, a dissociation) of
consciousness.

13   Among such people, whose consciousness is at a different level of development
from ours, the "soul" (or psyche) is not felt to be a unit. Many primitives assume that a
man has a "bush soul" as well as his own, and that this bush soul is incarnate in a wild
animal or a tree, with which the human individual has some kind of psychic identity.
This is what the distinguished French ethnologist Lucien Lévy-Brühl called a "mystical participation." He later retracted this term under pressure of adverse criticism, but I
believe that his critics were wrong. It is a well-known psychological fact that an individual may have such an unconscious identity with some other person or object.

14   This identity takes a variety of forms among primitives. If the bush soul is that of
an animal, the animal itself is considered as some sort of brother to the man. A man
whose brother is a crocodile, for instance, is supposed to be safe when swimming a
crocodile-infested river. If the bush soul is a tree, the tree is presumed to have something like parental authority over the individual concerned. In both cases an injury
to the bush soul is interpreted as an injury to the man.

15   In some tribes, it is assumed that a man has a number of souls; this belief expresses
the feeling of some primitive individuals that they each consist of several linked but
distinct units. This means that the individual's psyche is far from being safely syn-
thesized; on the contrary, it threatens to fragment only too easily under the onslaught of unchecked emotions.

16   While this situation is familiar to us from the studies of anthropologists, it is not
so irrelevant to our own advanced civilization as it might seem. We too can become

dissociated and lose our identity. We can be possessed and altered by moods, or become unreasonable and unable to recall important facts about ourselves or others, so that people ask: "What the devil has got into you?" We talk about being able "to control ourselves," but self-control is a rare and remarkable virtue. We may think we have ourselves under control; yet a friend can easily tell us things about ourselves of which we have no knowledge.

17   Beyond doubt, even in what we call a high level of civilization, human consciousness has not yet achieved a reasonable degree of continuity. It is still vulnerable and liable to fragmentation. This capacity to isolate part of one's mind, indeed, is a valuable characteristic. It enables us to concentrate upon one thing at a time, excluding everything else that may claim our attention. But there is a world of difference between a conscious decision to split off and temporarily suppress a part of one's psyche, and a condition in which this happens spontaneously, without one's knowledge or consent and even against one's intention. The former is a civilized achievement, the latter a primitive "loss of a soul," or even the pathological cause of a neurosis.

18   Thus, even in our day the unity of consciousness is still a doubtful affair; it can too easily be disrupted. An ability to control one's emotions that may be very desirable from one point of view would be a questionable accomplishment from another, for it would deprive social intercourse of variety, color, and warmth.

19   It is against this background that we must review the importance of dreams—those flimsy, evasive, unreliable, vague, and uncertain fantasies. To explain my point of view, I would like to describe how it developed over a period of years, and how I was led to conclude that dreams are the most frequent and universally accessible source for the investigation of man's symbolizing faculty.

20   Sigmund Freud was the pioneer who first tried to explore empirically the unconscious background of consciousness. He worked on the general assumption that dreams are not a matter of chance but are associated with conscious thoughts and problems. This assumption was not in the least arbitrary. It was based upon the conclusion of eminent neurologists (for instance, Pierre Janet) that neurotic symptoms are related to some conscious experience. They even appear to be split-off areas of the conscious mind, which, at another time and under different conditions, can be conscious.

21   Before the beginning of this century, Freud and Josef Breuer had recognized that neurotic symptoms—hysteria, certain types of pain, and abnormal behavior—are in fact symbolically meaningful. They are one way in which the unconscious mind expresses itself, just as it may in dreams; and they are equally symbolic. A patient, for instance, who is confronted with an intolerable situation may develop a spasm whenever he tries to swallow: He "can't swallow it." Under similar conditions of psychological stress, another patient has an attack of asthma: He "can't breathe the atmosphere at home." A third suffers from a peculiar paralysis of the legs: He can't walk, i.e., "he can't go on any more." A fourth, who vomits when he eats, "cannot digest" some unpleasant fact. I could cite many examples of this kind, but such physical reactions are only one form in which the problems that trouble us unconsciously may express themselves. They more often find expression in our dreams.

22   Any psychologist who has listened to numbers of people describing their dreams knows that dream symbols have much greater variety than the physical symptoms of neurosis. They often consist of elaborate and picturesque fantasies. But if the analyst who is confronted by this dream material uses Freud's original technique of "free association," he finds that dreams can eventually be reduced to certain basic patterns. This technique played an important part in the development of psychoanalysis, for it enabled Freud to use dreams as the starting point from which the unconscious problem of the patient might be explored.

23   Freud made the simple but penetrating observation that if a dreamer is encouraged to go on talking about his dream images and the thoughts that these prompt in his mind, he will give himself away and reveal the unconscious background of his ailments, in both what he says and what he deliberately omits saying. His ideas may seem irrational and irrelevant, but after a time it becomes relatively easy to see what it is that he is trying to avoid, what unpleasant thought or experience he is suppressing. No matter how he tries to camouflage it, everything he says points to the core of his predicament. A doctor sees so many things from the seamy side of life that he is seldom far from the truth when he interprets the hints that his patient produces as signs of an uneasy conscious. What he eventually discovers, unfortunately, confirms his expectations. Thus far, nobody can say anything against Freud's theory of repression and wish fulfillment as apparent causes of dream symbolism.

24   Freud attached particular importance to dreams as the point of departure for a process of "free association." But after a time I began to feel that this was a misleading and inadequate use of the rich fantasies that the unconscious produces in sleep. My doubts really began when a colleague told me of an experience he had during the course of a long train journey in Russia. Though he did not know the language and could not even decipher the Cyrillic script, he found himself musing over the strange letters in which the railway notices were written, and he fell into a reverie in which he imagined all sorts of meanings for them.

25   One idea led to another, and in his relaxed mood he found that this "free association" had stirred up many old memories. Among them he was annoyed to find some long-buried disagreeable topics—things he had wished to forget and had forgotten *consciously*. He had in fact arrived at what psychologists would call his "complexes"—that is, repressed emotional themes that can cause constant psychological disturbances or even, in many cases, the symptoms of a neurosis.

26   This episode opened my eyes to the fact that it was not necessary to use a dream as the point of departure for the process of "free association" if one wished to discover the complexes of a patient. It showed me that one can reach the center directly from any point of the compass. One could begin from Cyrillic letters, from meditations upon a crystal ball, a prayer wheel, or a modern painting, or even from casual conversation about some trivial event. The dream was no more and no less useful in this respect than any other possible starting point. Nevertheless, dreams have a particular significance, even though they often arise from an emotional upset in which the habitual complexes are also involved. (The habitual complexes are the tender spots of

the psyche, which react most quickly to an external stimulus or disturbance.) That is why free association can lead one from any dream to the critical secret thoughts.

27   At this point, however, it occurred to me that (if I was right so far) it might reasonably follow that dreams have some special and more significant function of their own. Very often dreams have a definite, evidently purposeful structure, indicating an underlying idea or intention—though, as a rule, the latter is not immediately comprehensible. I therefore began to consider whether one should pay more attention to the actual form and content of a dream, rather than allowing "free" association to lead one off through a train of ideas to complexes that could as easily be reached by other means.

28   This new thought was a turning-point in the development of my psychology. It meant that I gradually gave up following associations that led far away from the text of a dream. I chose to concentrate rather on the associations to the dream itself, believing that the latter expressed something specific that the unconscious was trying to say.

29   The change in my attitude toward dreams involved a change of method; the new technique was one that could take account of all the various wider aspects of a dream. A story told by the conscious mind has a beginning, a development, and an end, but the same is not true of a dream. Its dimensions in time and space are quite different; to understand it you must examine it from every aspect—just as you may take an unknown object in your hands and turn it over and over until you are familiar with every detail of its shape.

30   Perhaps I have now said enough to show how I came increasingly to disagree with "free" association as Freud first employed it: I wanted to keep as close as possible to the dream itself, and to exclude all the irrelevant ideas and associations that it might evoke. True, these could lead one toward the complexes of a patient, but I had a more far-reaching purpose in mind than the discovery of complexes that cause neurotic disturbances. There are many other means by which these can be identified: The psychologist, for instance, can get all the hints he needs by using word-association tests (by asking the patient what he associates to a given set of words, and by studying his responses). But to know and understand the psychic life-process of an individual's whole personality, it is important to realize that his dreams and their symbolic images have a much more important role to play.

31   Almost everyone knows, for example, that there is an enormous variety of images by which the sexual act can be symbolized (or, one might say, represented in the form of an allegory). Each of these images can lead, by a process of association, to the idea of sexual intercourse and to specific complexes that any individual may have about his own sexual attitudes. But one could just as well unearth such complexes by day-dreaming on a set of indecipherable Russian letters. I was thus led to the assumption that a dream can contain some message other than the sexual allegory, and that it does so for definite reasons. To illustrate this point:

32   A man may dream of inserting a key in a lock, of wielding a heavy stick, or of breaking down a door with a battering ram. Each of these can be regarded as a sexual allegory. But the fact that his unconscious for its own purposes has chosen one of these specific images—it may be the key, the stick, or the battering ram—is also of major significance.

The real task is to understand *why* the key has been preferred to the stick, or the stick to the ram. And sometimes this might even lead one to discover that it is not the sexual act at all that is represented, but some quite different psychological point.

33   From this line of reasoning, I concluded that only the material that is clearly and visibly part of a dream should be used in interpreting it. The dream has its own limitation. Its specific form itself tells us what belongs to it and what leads away from it. While "free" association lures one away from that material in a kind of zigzag line, the method I evolved is more like a circumambulation whose center is the dream picture. I work all round the dream picture and disregard every attempt that the dreamer makes to break away from it. Time and time again, in my professional work, I have had to repeat the words: "Let's go back to your dream. What does the *dream* say?"

34   For instance, a patient of mine dreamed of a drunken and disheveled vulgar woman. In the dream, it seemed that this woman was his wife, though in real life his wife was totally different. On the surface, therefore, the dream was shockingly untrue, and the patient immediately rejected it as dream nonsense. If I, as his doctor, had let him start a process of association, he would inevitably have tried to get as far away as possible from the unpleasant suggestion of his dream. In that case, he would have ended with one of his staple complexes—a complex, possibly, that had nothing to do with his wife—and we should have learned nothing about the special meaning of this particular dream.

35   What then, was his unconscious trying to convey by such an obviously untrue statement? Clearly it somehow expressed the idea of a degenerate female who was closely connected with the dreamer's life; but since the projection of this image on to his wife was unjustified and factually untrue, I had to look elsewhere before I found out what this repulsive image represented.

36   In the Middle Ages, long before the physiologists demonstrated that by reason of our glandular structure there are both male and female elements in all of us, it was said that "every man carries a woman within himself." It is this female element in every male that I have called the "anima." This "feminine" aspect is essentially a certain inferior kind of relatedness to the surroundings, and particularly to women which is kept carefully concealed from others as well as from oneself. In other words, though an individual's visible personality may seem quite normal, he may well be concealing from others—or even from himself—the deplorable condition of "the woman within."

37   That was the case with this particular patient: His female side was not nice. His dream was actually saying to him: "You are in some respects behaving like degenerate female," and thus gave him an appropriate shock. (An example of this kind, of course, must not be taken as evidence that the unconscious is concerned with "moral" injunctions. The dream was not telling the patient to "behave better," but was simply trying to balance the lopsided nature of his conscious mind, which was maintaining the fiction that he was a perfect gentleman throughout.)

38   It is easy to understand why dreamers tend to ignore and even deny the message of their dreams. Consciousness naturally resists anything unconscious and unknown. I have already pointed out the existence among primitive people of what anthropologists call "misoneism," a deep and superstitious fear of novelty. The primitives

manifest all the reactions of the wild animal against untoward events. But "civilized" man reacts to new ideas in much the same way, erecting psychological barriers to protect himself from the shock of facing something new. This can easily be observed in any individual's reaction to his own dreams when obliged to admit a surprising thought. Many pioneers in philosophy, science, and even literature have been victims of the innate conservatism of their contemporaries. Psychology is one of the youngest of the sciences; because it attempts to deal with the working of the unconscious, it has inevitably encountered misoneism in an extreme form.

QUESTIONS FOR DISCUSSION

1. How does Jung define a symbol? Why does he believe that people need to use symbols to express themselves?
2. What relationships does Jung establish among symbols, dreams, and the unconscious?
3. According to Jung, why does the presence of the unconscious support the modern perception that people have divided selves? Why does Jung think that it is natural to have a divided self?
4. Why does Jung believe that primitive people often feel an unconscious identification with another object or person? In what way is this characteristic of primitive people relevant to modern people and their identity issues?
5. Jung states that "dreams are the most frequent and universally accessible source for the investigation of man's symbolizing faculty." What evidence does Jung provide to support his claim?
6. What relationships does Jung see between dreams and myths?

CONNECTION

In his attempt to understand man's unconscious, Jung extends Sigmund Freud's interpretations of the meaning of dreams. Contrast Freud's ideas with Jung's theories as they are presented in this selection and in Freud's essay "Erotic Wishes and Dreams" (included in Chapter 6 of this text). Which approach to interpreting dreams and myths do you find more useful? Why?

IDEAS FOR WRITING

1. Write an essay in which you discuss several reasons why you think that understanding the symbols presented in dreams can be important. Develop examples that illustrate how you have used dreams and dream interpretation to help solve problems and to understand your inner world.
2. Write an essay in which you compare a particular dream you have had to a fundamental myth or story with which you are familiar; study and interpret your dream using the principles suggested in Jung's essay. Through completing this assignment, what did you learn about dream symbolism and about how your mind functions?

Portfolio of Creation Myths

We have selected the following myths from cultures around the world to encourage you to compare different fundamental beliefs and assumptions about reality through the mythological stories that are central to a people. Preceding each myth is a note about the culture that produced it; following the portfolio is a set of questions for thought and writing.

JOURNAL

Discuss a creation myth or an experience of creating something very special to you. Try to develop imaginative comparisons and vivid details.

Genesis 2:4–23 (Old Testament of the Hebrew Bible)

This is the second account of creation in the book of Genesis. Genesis 2 is thought to come from a different, less formal writing tradition (the "J," or Jehovah, tradition) from that of Genesis 1 and reveals an intimate relationship between God and his natural and human creations. The following passage portrays the God Jehovah in an agricultural role, creating and watering the Garden of Eden, then creating animals, a man to till the fields, and finally a female helper for "the man." As you read the following selection, consider the impact that the Book of Genesis has had on Western cultural assumptions and traditions.

1   (2:4) In the day that the Lord God made the earth and the heavens, (5) when no plant of the field was yet in the earth and no herb of the field had yet sprung up—for the Lord God had not caused it to rain upon the earth, and there was no man to till the ground; (6) but a mist went up from the earth and watered the whole face of the ground—(7) then the Lord God formed man of dust from the ground, and breathed into his nostrils the breath of life; and man became a living being. (8) And the Lord God planted a garden in Eden, in the east; and there he put the man whom he had formed. (9) And out of the ground the Lord God made to grow every tree that is pleasant to the sight and good for food, the tree of life also in the midst of the garden, and the tree of the knowledge of good and evil.

2   (10) A river flowed out of Eden to water the garden, and there it divided and became four rivers. (11) The name of the first is Pishon; it is the one which flows around the whole land of Hav'ilah, where there is gold; (12) and the gold of that land is good; bdellium and onyx stone are there. (13) The name of the second river is Gihon; it is the one which flows around the whole land of Cush. (14) And the name of the third river is Tigris, which flows east of Assyria. And the fourth river is the Euphrates.

3   (15) The Lord God took the man and put him in the Garden of Eden to till it and keep it. (16) And the Lord God commanded the man, saying, "You may freely eat of every tree of the garden; (17) but of the tree of the knowledge of good and evil you shall not eat, for in the day that you eat of it you shall die."

4   (18) Then the Lord God said, "It is not good that the man should be alone; I will make him a helper fit for him." (19) So out of the ground the Lord God formed every beast of the field and every bird of the air, and brought them to the man to see what he would call them; and whatever the man called every living creature, that was its name. (20) The man gave names to all cattle, and to the birds of the air, and to every beast of the field; but for the man there was not found a helper fit for him. (21) So the Lord God caused a deep sleep to fall upon the man, and while he slept took one of his ribs and closed up its place with flesh; (22) and the rib which the Lord God had taken from the man he made into a woman and brought her to the man. (23) Then the man said,

This at last is bone of my bones
   and flesh of my flesh;
she shall be called Woman,
   because she was taken out of Man.

The Chameleon Finds (Yao-Bantu, African)

"The Chameleon Finds" is a creation myth of the Yao, a Bantu tribe living by Lake Nyasa in Mozambique, Africa. Expressive of a close relationship with nature, this Yao myth, with a clever Chameleon and a helper Spider as the creator-god's assistants, takes a critical view of human beings. The unnatural and destructive culture of the humans causes the animals to flee and the gods to retreat from the earth. As you read this creation story, compare the critical view of human culture held by the Yao with that of the other myths in this section.

1   At first there were no people. Only Mulungu and the decent peaceful beasts were in the world. One day Chameleon sat weaving a fish-trap, and when he had finished he set it in the river. In the morning he pulled the trap and it was full of fish, which he took home and ate. He set the trap again. In the morning he pulled it out and it was empty: no fish.

2   "Bad luck," he said, and set the trap again.

3   The next morning when he pulled the trap he found a little man and woman in it. He had never seen any creatures like this.

4   "What can they be?" he said. "Today I behold the unknown." And he picked up the fish-trap and took the two creatures to Mulungu.

5   "Father," said Chameleon, "see what I have brought."

6   Mulungu looked. "Take them out of the trap," he said. "Put them down on the earth and they will grow."

7   Chameleon did this. And the man and woman grew. They grew until they became as tall as men and women are today.

8   All the animals watched to see what the people would do. They made fire. They rubbed two sticks together in a special way and thus made fire. The fire caught in the bush and roared through the forest and the animals had to run to escape the flames. The people caught a buffalo and killed it and roasted it in the fire and ate it. The next day they did the same thing. Every day they set fires and killed some animal and ate it.

9   "They are burning up everything!" said Mulungu. "They are killing my people!"

10   All the beasts ran into the forest as far away from mankind as they could get. Chameleon went into the high trees.

11   "I'm leaving!" said Mulungu. He called to Spider. "How do you climb on high?" he said.

12   "Very nicely," said Spider. And Spider spun a rope for Mulungu and Mulungu climbed the rope and went to live in the sky.

13   Thus the gods were driven off the face of the earth by the cruelty of man.

The Yauelmani Yokut Creation

The Yaulemani Yokuts were a small tribe from the southern San Joachin Valley in California with their own unique language and customs. The following creation myth demonstrates the cooperative, non-hierarchical values of this tribal group; it is similar to many other Native American creation stories in that a group of animals and birds, as opposed to men or gods, perform the creation. The animals work together persistently despite deaths, failed efforts, and earthquakes to perform the work of creating the world from a primal ocean.

1   At first there was water everywhere. A tree grew up out of the water to the sky. On the tree there was a nest. Those who were inside did not see any earth. There was only water to be seen. The eagle was the chief of them. With him were the wolf, Coyote, the panther, the prairie falcon, the hawk called *po´yon*, and the condor. The eagle wanted to make the earth. He thought, "We will have to have land." Then he called *k´uik´ui*, a small duck. He said to it: "Dive down and bring up the earth." The duck dived, but did not reach the bottom. It died. The eagle called another kind of duck. He told it to dive. This duck went far down. It finally reached the bottom. Just as it touched the mud there it died. Then it came up again. Then the eagle and the other six saw a little dirt under its fingernail. When the eagle saw this he took the dirt from its nail. He mixed it with *telis* and *pele* seeds and ground them up. He put water with the mixture and made dough. This was in the morning. Then he set it in the water and it swelled and spread everywhere, going out from the middle. (These seeds when ground and mixed with water swell.) In the evening the eagle told his companions: "Take some earth." They went down and took a little earth up in the tree with them. Early in the morning, when the morning star came, the eagle said to the wolf: "Shout." The wolf

shouted and the earth disappeared, and all was water again. The eagle said: "We will make it again," for it was for this purpose that they had taken some earth with them into the nest. Then they took *telis* and *pele* seeds again, and ground them with the earth, and put the mixture into the water, and it swelled out again. Then early next morning when the morning star appeared, the eagle told the wolf again: "Shout!" and he shouted three times. The earth was shaken by the earthquake, but it stood. Then Coyote said: "I must shout too." He shouted and the earth shook a very little. Now it was good. Then they came out of the tree on the ground. Close to where this tree stood there was a lake. The eagle said: "We will live here." Then they had a house there and lived there.

Spider Woman Creates the Humans (Hopi, Native American)

The Hopis, who reside in several villages in Northern Arizona, have kept themselves separate from other cultures and have maintained their native traditions and myths. The following myth of creation is only a brief selection from the much longer Hopi Emergence Story, which uses birth imagery to explain a complex sequence of transformations in the act of creation. In the Hopi culture, the Emergence Story is told to the tribal initiates on the last evening of the year, after which the young men ascend a ladder to emerge from the kiva (Hopi dwelling) as full-fledged adult members of the Hopi community.

"Spider Woman Creates the Humans" is unique because of its use of a female creator who functions as mother-goddess, singer, and artist, molding the original people from multicolored clay while singing them the Creation Song.

1 So Spider Woman gathered earth, this time of four colors, yellow, red, white, and black; mixed with tuchvala, the liquid of her mouth; molded them; and covered them with her white-substance cape which was the creative wisdom itself. As before, she sang over them the Creation Song, and when she uncovered them these forms were human beings in the image of Sotuknang. Then she created four other beings after her own form. They were wuti, female partners, for the first four male beings.

2 When Spider Woman uncovered them the forms came to life. This was at the time of the dark purple light, Qoyangnuptu, the first phase of the dawn of Creation, which first reveals the mystery of man's creation.

3 They soon awakened and began to move, but there was still a dampness on their foreheads and a soft spot on their heads. This was at the time of the yellow light, Sikangnuqua, the second phase of the dawn of Creation, when the breath of life entered man.

4 In a short time the sun appeared above the horizon, drying the dampness on their foreheads and hardening the soft spot on their heads. This was the time of the red light, Talawva, the third phase of the dawn of Creation, when man, fully formed and firmed, proudly faced his Creator.

5   "That is the Sun," said Spider Woman. "You are meeting your Father the Creator for the first time. You must always remember and observe these three phases of your Creation. The time of the three lights, the dark purple, the yellow, and the red reveal in turn the mystery, the breath of life, and warmth of love. These comprise the Creator's plan of life for you as sung over you in the Song of Creation."

QUESTIONS FOR DISCUSSION

1. What different images of the creator gods are presented in the various myths? How clearly described is the primary god in each ? What powers and limits does the god have? Does the god operate alone or with other helping beings? What conclusions about the culture that produced each myth can you draw from these differences?

2. In the myths that present a clear picture of the physical world of the creation, how is the world described? How orderly and sequential is the act of creating the different elements and beings of the world? What conclusions can you draw from the varied presentation in these creation myths about the values of the culture that produced each myth?

3. Creation myths make significant comments on the roles and status of the sexes in various cultures. Compare and contrast the roles of sex and gender in the different creation myths included.

4. Another issue presented in some creation myths is the relation of men and women to their creator. How do the humans in the various myths relate to the creator gods? How worshipful of God are the humans in the various myths?

5. Compare the ways that the different myths show the relationship between humans and nature. How harmonious a part of nature or how much at odds with nature do humans seem in the various myths? How are animals involved in the act of creation? Does part of the natural world need to be destroyed for creation to be completed?

6. Creation myths differ in tone. They can be imaginative and dream-like, solemn and serious, philosophical, or even comical and mocking in tone. Compare the tone and attitude toward creation presented in each of the myths; then draw some conclusions about the values of each culture.

IDEAS FOR WRITING

1. Write your own creation myth, using characters, description, and narration to illustrate the relationship between different aspects of creation: gods, animals, people, and the earth. At the end of your myth, comment on the values and ideas about the creative process and the world that your myth is designed to illustrate.

2. Develop an essay in the form of an extended comparison between two or three creation myths, each of which illustrates fundamental values and beliefs about gods, humans, and the natural world.

Bruno Bettelheim

"Fairy Tales and the Existential Predicament"

Born in Vienna and educated at the University of Vienna, Bruno Bettelheim (1903–1991) was imprisoned in a Nazi concentration camp for a time before immigrating to the United States. After settling in Chicago, he worked with autistic children, serving as Director of the University of Chicago Orthogenic School from 1944 to 1973. Bettelheim's books, such as On Learning to Read *(1981) and* A Good Enough Parent *(1987), focus on the relationships between reading, parenting, and raising emotionally healthy children. The following selection from* The Uses of Enchantment *(1976) presents a psychological perspective on the impact on children of traditional fairy tales. As you read the selection, think about whether you agree with Bettelheim's theories about the role that fairy tales play in creating healthy children.*

JOURNAL

Narrate the fairy tale that you remember most vividly from your childhood. Why do you think you remember it? Would you share (or have you shared) this tale with your own children? Why or why not?

1   In order to master the psychological problems of growing up—overcoming narcissistic disappointments, oedipal dilemmas, sibling rivalries; becoming able to relinquish childhood dependencies; gaining a feeling of selfhood and of self-worth, and a sense of moral obligation—a child needs to understand what is going on within his conscious self so that he can also cope with that which goes on in his unconscious. He can achieve this understanding, and with it the ability to cope, not through rational comprehension of the nature and content of his unconscious, but by becoming familiar with it through spinning out daydreams—ruminating, rearranging, and fantasizing about suitable story elements in response to unconscious pressures. By doing this, the child fits unconscious content into conscious fantasies, which then enable him to deal with that content. It is here that fairy tales have unequaled value, because they offer new dimensions to the child's imagination which would be impossible for him to discover as truly on his own. Even more important, the form and structure of fairy tales suggest images to the child by which he can structure his daydreams and with them give better direction to his life.

2   In child or adult, the unconscious is a powerful determinant of behavior. When the unconscious is repressed and its content denied entrance into awareness, then eventually the person's conscious mind will be partially overwhelmed by derivatives of these unconscious elements, or else he is forced to keep such rigid, compulsive control over them that his personality may become severely crippled. But when unconscious

material *is* to some degree permitted to come to awareness and worked through in imagination, its potential for causing harm—to ourselves or others—is much reduced; some of its forces can then be made to serve positive purposes. However, the prevalent parental belief is that a child must be diverted from what troubles him most: his formless, nameless anxieties, and his chaotic, angry, and even violent fantasies. Many parents believe that only conscious reality or pleasant and wish-fulfilling images should be presented to the child—that he should be exposed only to the sunny side of things. But such one-sided fare nourishes the mind only in a one-sided way, and real life is not all sunny.

3   There is a widespread refusal to let children know that the source of much that goes wrong in life is due to our very own natures—the propensity of all men for acting aggressively, asocially, selfishly, out of anger and anxiety. Instead, we want our children to believe that, inherently, all men are good. But children know that *they* are not always good; and often, even when they are, they would prefer not to be. This contradicts what they are told by their parents, and therefore makes the child a monster in his own eyes.

4   The dominant culture wishes to pretend, particularly where children are concerned, that the dark side of man does not exist, and professes a belief in an optimistic meliorism. Psychoanalysis itself is viewed as having the purpose of making life easy— but this is not what its founder intended. Psychoanalysis was created to enable man to accept the problematic nature of life without being defeated by it, or giving in to escapism. Freud's prescription is that only by struggling courageously against what seem like overwhelming odds can man succeed in wringing meaning out of his existence.

5   This is exactly the message that fairy tales get across to the child in manifold form: that a struggle against severe difficulties in life is unavoidable, is an intrinsic part of human existence—but that if one does not shy away, but steadfastly meets unexpected and often unjust hardships, one masters all obstacles and at the end emerges victorious.

6   Modern stories written for young children mainly avoid these existential problems, although they are crucial issues for all of us. The child needs most particularly to be given suggestions in symbolic form about how he may deal with these issues and grow safely into maturity. "Safe" stories mention neither death or aging, the limits to our existence, nor the wish for eternal life. The fairy tale, by contrast, confronts the child squarely with the basic human predicaments.

7   For example, many fairy stories begin with the death of a mother or father; in these tales the death of the parent creates the most agonizing problems, as it (or the fear of it) does in real life. Other stories tell about an aging parent who decides that the time has come to let the new generation take over. But before this can happen, the successor has to prove himself capable and worthy. The Brothers Grimm's story "The Three Feathers" begins: "There was once upon a time a king who had three sons. . . . When the king had become old and weak, and was thinking of his end, he did not know which of his sons should inherit the kingdom after him." In order to decide, the king sets all his sons a difficult task; the son who meets it best "shall be king after my death."

8   It is characteristic of fairy tales to state an existential dilemma briefly and pointedly. This permits the child to come to grips with the problem in its most essential

form, where a more complex plot would confuse matters for him. The fairy tale sim-plifies all situations. Its figures are clearly drawn; and details, unless very important, are eliminated. All characters are typical rather than unique.

9   Contrary to what takes place in many modern children's stories, in fairy tales evil is as omnipresent as virtue. In practically every fairy tale good and evil are given body in the form of some figures and their actions, as good and evil are omnipresent in life and the propensities for both are present in every man. It is this duality which poses the moral problem, and requires the struggle to solve it.

10   Evil is not without its attractions—symbolized by the mighty giant or dragon, the power of the witch, the cunning queen in "Snow White"—and often it is temporarily in the ascendancy. In many fairy tales a usurper succeeds for a time in seizing the place which rightfully belongs to the hero—as the wicked sisters do in "Cinderella." It is not that the evildoer is punished at the story's end which makes immersing one-self in fairy stories an experience in moral education, although this is part of it. In fairy tales, as in life, punishment or fear of it is only a limited deterrent to crime. The conviction that crime does not pay is a much more effective deterrent, and that is why in fairy tales the bad person always loses out. It is not the fact that virtue wins out at the end which promotes morality, but that the hero is most attractive to the child, who identifies with the hero in all his struggles. Because of this identification the child imagines that he suffers with the hero his trials and tribulations, and tri-umphs with him as virtue is victorious. The child makes such identifications all on his own, and the inner and outer struggles of the hero imprint morality on him.

11   The figures in fairy tales are not ambivalent—not good and bad at the same time, as we all are in reality. But since polarization dominates the child's mind, it also dominates fairy tales. A person is either good or bad, nothing in between. One brother is stupid, the other is clever. One sister is virtuous and industrious, the oth-ers are vile and lazy. One is beautiful, the others are ugly. One parent is all good, the other evil. The juxtaposition of opposite characters is not for the purpose of stressing right behavior, as would be true for cautionary tales. (There are some amoral fairy tales where goodness or badness, beauty or ugliness play no role at all.) Presenting the polarities of character permits the child to comprehend easily the difference be-tween the two, which he could not do as readily were the figures drawn more true to life, with all the complexities that characterize real people. Ambiguities must wait until a relatively firm personality has been established on the basis of positive identi-fications. Then the child has a basis for understanding that there are great differ-ences between people, and that therefore one has to make choices about who one wants to be. This basic decision, on which all later personality development will build, is facilitated by the polarizations of the fairy tale.

12   Furthermore, a child's choices are based, not so much on right versus wrong, as on who arouses his sympathy and who his antipathy. The more simple and straightfor-ward a good character, the easier it is for a child to identify with it and to reject the bad other. The child identifies with the good hero not because of his goodness, but be-cause the hero's condition makes a deep positive appeal to him. The question for the

child is not "Do I want to be good?" but "Who do I want to be like?" The child decides this on the basis of projecting himself wholeheartedly into one character. If this fairy-tale figure is a very good person, then the child decides that he wants to be good, too.

13   Amoral fairy tales show no polarization or juxtaposition of good and bad persons; that is because these amoral stories serve an entirely different purpose. Such tales or type figures as "Puss in Boots," who arranges for the hero's success through trickery, and Jack, who steals the giant's treasure, build character not by promoting choices between good and bad, but by giving the child the hope that even the meekest can succeed in life. After all, what's the use of choosing to become a good person when one feels so insignificant that he fears he will never amount to anything? Morality is not the issue in these tales, but rather, assurance that one can succeed. Whether one meets life with a belief in the possibility of mastering its difficulties or with the expectation of defeat is also a very important existential problem.

14   The deep inner conflicts originating in our primitive drives and our violent emotions are all denied in much of modern children's literature, and so the child is not helped in coping with them. But the child is subject to desperate feelings of loneliness and isolation, and he often experiences mortal anxiety. More often than not, he is unable to express these feelings in words, or he can do so only by indirection: fear of the dark, of some animal, anxiety about his body. Since it creates discomfort in a parent to recognize these emotions in his child, the parent tends to overlook them, or he belittles these spoken fears out of his own anxiety, believing this will cover over the child's fears.

15   The fairy tale, by contrast, takes these existential anxieties and dilemmas very seriously and addresses itself directly to them: the need to be loved and the fear that one is thought worthless; the love of life, and the fear of death. Further, the fairy tale offers solutions in ways that the child can grasp on his level of understanding. For example, fairy tales pose the dilemma of wishing to live eternally by occasionally concluding: "If they have not died, they are still alive." The other ending—"And they lived happily ever after"—does not for a moment fool the child that eternal life is possible. But it does indicate that which alone can take the sting out of the narrow limits of our time on this earth: forming a truly satisfying bond to another. The tales teach that when one has done this, one has reached the ultimate in emotional security of existence and permanence of relation available to man; and this alone can dissipate the fear of death. If one has found true adult love, the fairy story also tells, one doesn't need to wish for eternal life. This is suggested by another ending found in fairy tales: "They lived for a long time afterward, happy and in pleasure."

16   An uninformed view of the fairy tale sees in this type of ending an unrealistic wish-fulfillment, missing completely the important message it conveys to the child. These tales tell him that by forming a true interpersonal relation, one escapes the separation anxiety which haunts him (and which sets the stage for many fairy tales, but it's always resolved at the story's ending). Furthermore, the story tells, this ending is not made possible, as the child wishes and believes, by holding on to his mother eternally. If we try to escape separation anxiety and death anxiety by desperately keeping our grasp on our parents, we will only be cruelly forced out, like Hansel and Gretel.

17   Only by going out into the world can the fairy-tale hero (child) find himself there; and as he does, he will also find the other with whom he will be able to live happily ever after; that is, without ever again having to experience separation anxiety. The fairy tale is future-oriented and guides the child—in terms he can understand in both his conscious and his unconscious mind—to relinquish his infantile dependency wishes and achieve a more satisfying independent existence.

18   Today children no longer grow up within the security of an extended family, or of a well-integrated community. Therefore, even more than at the times fairy tales were invented, it is important to provide the modern child with images of heroes who have to go out into the world all by themselves and who, although originally ignorant of the ultimate things, find secure places in the world by following their right way with deep inner confidence.

19   The fairy-tale hero proceeds for a time in isolation, as the modern child often feels isolated. The hero is helped by being in touch with primitive things—a tree, an animal, nature—as the child feels more in touch with those things than most adults do. The fate of these heroes convinces the child that, like them, he may feel outcast and abandoned in the world, groping in the dark, but, like them, in the course of his life he will be guided step by step, and given help when it is needed. Today, even more than in past times, the child needs the reassurance offered by the image of the isolated man who nevertheless is capable of achieving meaningful and rewarding relations with the world around him.

QUESTIONS FOR DISCUSSION

1. What does Bettelheim consider to be the primary positive psychological value of fairy tales? Do you agree?

2. According to Bettelheim, how do fairy tales help a child to control his or her destructive unconscious impulses? How does the polarization of good and evil in fairy tales help children?

3. Why does Bettelheim believe that children benefit more from reading traditional versions of fairy tales than from the modern popular type of children's stories?

4. How do fairy-tale endings help children to accept their isolation, their "existential predicament," while at the same time encouraging them to believe in the possibility of creating meaningful relationships in their own world?

5. Why does Bettelheim believe that it is important for fairy tales to have happy endings? Do you agree with him? Why or why not?

6. What examples does Bettelheim give to support his ideas? What other examples might he have provided?

CONNECTION

After reading The Brothers Grimms' version of Cinderella, included in this chapter, consider what place Bettelheim would see for this story within the theories he sets forth in "Fairy Tales and the Existential Predicament."

IDEAS FOR WRITING

1. Write a defense or refutation of Bettelheim's theory about the value of fairy tales for children. Refer specifically to both Bettelheim's ideas and to your own ideas and experiences as a child reader or as an adult parenting or teaching young children.

2. Develop your journal entry into an essay. Expand on it by showing how your interpretation of the meaning of the fairy tale has changed as you have matured, contrasting the way you understand it now with the way you interpreted it as a child.

FOUR VERSIONS OF CINDERELLA

Common tales are shared throughout the world in similar yet subtly distinct versions and are retold, generation after generation, over a period of many centuries. Following are four versions of the popular fairy tale "Cinderella": the classic Grimm Brothers fairy tale, "Aschenputtel"; the Native American "Algonquin Cinderella"; James Finn Garner's satire "The Politically Correct Cinderella"; and "Cinderella," a feminist poem by Olga Broumas. In addition, one of the student essays in this chapter, Liz Scheps' "Cinderella: Politically Incorrect?" responds critically to Garner' s satirical story.

JOURNAL

Write down a fairy tale that you remember from your childhood. Why was this story an important one to you when you were a child? What meaning does the story have for you today?

The Brothers Grimm
"Aschenputtel"

Jacob Grimm (1785–1863) and his brother Wilhelm Grimm (1786–1859) were scholars of the German language and of folk culture; they collected oral narratives that embodied the cultural values of the German peasant and reflected on universal human concerns. The Grimms' tales have been translated into more than seventy different languages. "Aschenputtel," a version of the Cinderella story, appears here in a version translated by Lucy Crane. As you read this tale, consider how it differs from the less violent version more familiar to American readers through the Disney films and picture books.

1   There was once a rich man whose wife lay sick, and when she felt her end drawing near she called to her only daughter to come near her bed, and said,

2   "Dear child, be pious and good, and God will always take care of you, and I will look down upon you from heaven, and will be with you."

3   And then she closed her eyes and expired. The maiden went everyday to her mother's grave and wept, and was always pious and good. When the winter came the snow covered the grave with a white covering, and when the sun came in the early spring and melted it away, the man took to himself another wife.

4   The new wife brought two daughters home with her, and they were beautiful and fair in appearance, but at heart were black and ugly. And then began very evil times for the poor stepdaughter.

5   "Is the stupid creature to sit in the same room with us?" said they; "those who eat food must earn it. Out upon her for a kitchen-maid!"

6   They took away her pretty dresses, and put on her an old gray kirtle, and gave her wooden shoes to wear.

7   "Just look now at the proud princess, how she is decked out!" cried they laughing, and then they sent her into the kitchen. There she was obliged to do heavy work from morning to night, get up early in the morning, draw water, make the fires, cook, and wash. Besides that, the sisters did their utmost to torment her—mocking her, and strewing peas and lentils among the ashes, and setting her to pick them up. In the evenings, when she was quite tired out with her hard day's work, she had no bed to lie on, but was obliged to rest on the hearth among the cinders. And as she always looked dusty and dirty, they named her Aschenputtel.

8   It happened one day that the father went to the fair, and he asked his two stepdaughters what he should bring back for them.

9   "Fine clothes!" said one.

10 "Pearls and jewels!" said the other.

11 "But what will you have, Aschenputtel?" said he.

12 "The first twig, father, that strikes against your hat on the way home; that is what I should like you to bring me."

13 So he bought for the two stepdaughters fine clothes, pearls, and jewels, and on his way back, as he rode through a green lane, a hazel-twig struck against his hat; and he broke it off and carried it home with him. And when he reached home he gave to the stepdaughters what they had wished for, and to Aschenputtel he gave the hazel-twig. She thanked him, and went to her mother's grave, and planted this twig there, weeping so bitterly that the tears fell upon it and watered it, and it flourished and became a fine tree. Aschenputtel went to see it three times a day, and wept and prayed, and each time a white bird rose up from the tree, and if she uttered any wish the bird brought her whatever she had wished for.

14 Now it came to pass that the king ordained a festival that should last for three days, and to which all the beautiful young women of that country were bidden, so

that the king's son might choose a bride from among them. When the two step-daughters heard that they too were bidden to appear, they felt very pleased, and they called Aschenputtel, and said,

15   "Comb our hair, brush our shoes, and make our buckles fast, we are going to the wedding feast at the king's castle."

16   Aschenputtel, when she heard this, could not help crying, for she too would have liked to go to the dance, and she begged her stepmother to allow her.

17   "What, you Aschenputtel!" said she, "in all your dust and dirt, you want to go to the festival! you that have no dress and no shoes! you want to dance!"

18   But as she persisted in asking, at last the stepmother said,

19   "I have strewed a dish-full of lentils in the ashes, and if you can pick them all up again in two hours you may go with us."

20   Then the maiden went to the back-door that led into the garden, and called out,

"O gentle doves, O turtle-doves,
And all the birds that be,
The lentils that in ashes lie
Come and pick up for me!
  The good must be put in the dish,
  The bad you may eat if you wish."

21   Then there came to the kitchen-window two white doves, and after them some turtle-doves, and at last a crowd of all the birds under heaven, chirping and flutter-ing, and they alighted among the ashes; and the doves nodded with their heads, and began to pick, peck, pick, peck, and then all the others began to pick, peck, pick, peck, and put all the good grains into the dish. Before an hour was over all was done, and they flew away. Then the maiden brought the dish to her stepmother, feeling joyful, and thinking that now she should go to the feast; but the stepmother said,

22   "No, Aschenputtel, you have no proper clothes, and you do not know how to dance, and you would be laughed at!"

23   And when Aschenputtel cried for disappointment, she added,

24   "If you can pick two dishes full of lentils out of the ashes, nice and clean, you shall go with us," thinking to herself, "for that is not possible." When she had strewed two dishes full of lentils among the ashes the maiden went through the backdoor into the garden, and cried,

"O gentle doves, O turtle-doves,
And all the birds that be,
The lentils that in ashes lie
Come and pick up for me!
  The good must be put in the dish,
  The bad you may eat if you wish."

25   So there came to the kitchen-window two white doves, and then some turtle-doves, and at last a crowd of all the other birds under heaven, chirping and flutter-ing, and they alighted among the ashes, and the doves nodded with their heads and

began to pick, peck, pick, peck, and then all the others began to pick, peck, pick, peck, and put all the good grains into the dish. And before half-an-hour was over it was all done, and they flew away. Then the maiden took the dishes to the stepmother, feeling joyful, and thinking that now she should go with them to the feast; but she said "All this is of no good to you; you cannot come with us, for you have no proper clothes, and cannot dance; you would put us to shame."

26   Then she turned her back on poor Aschenputtel, and made haste to set out with her two proud daughters.

27   And as there was no one left in the house, Aschenputtel went to her mother's grave, under the hazel bush, and cried,

"Little tree, little tree, shake over me,
That silver and gold may come down and cover me."

28   Then the bird threw down a dress of gold and silver, and a pair of slippers embroidered with silk and silver. And in all haste she put on the dress and went to the festival. But her stepmother and sisters did not know her, and thought she must be a foreign princess, she looked so beautiful in her golden dress. Of Aschenputtel they never thought at all, and supposed that she was sitting at home, and picking the lentils out of the ashes. The King's son came to meet her, and took her by the hand and danced with her, and he refused to stand up with any one else, so that he might not be obliged to let go her hand; and when any one came to claim it he answered,

29   "She is my partner."

30   And when the evening came she wanted to go home, but the prince said he would go with her to take care of her, for he wanted to see where the beautiful maiden lived. But she escaped him, and jumped up into the pigeon-house. Then the prince waited until the father came, and told him the strange maiden had jumped into the pigeon-house. The father thought to himself,

31   "It cannot surely be Aschenputtel," and called for axes and hatchets, and had the pigeon-house cut down, but there was no one in it. And when they entered the house there sat Aschenputtel in her dirty clothes among the cinders, and a little oil-lamp burnt dimly in the chimney; for Aschenputtel had been very quick, and had jumped out of the pigeon-house again, and had run to the hazel bush; and there she had taken off her beautiful dress and laid it on the grave, and her bird had carried it away again, and then she had put on her little gray kirtle again, and had sat down in the kitchen among the cinders.

32   The next day, when the festival began anew, and the parents and stepsisters had gone to it, Aschenputtel went to the hazel bush and cried,

"Little tree, little tree, shake over me,
That silver and gold may come down and cover me."

33   Then the bird cast down a still more splendid dress than on the day before. And when she appeared in it among the guests every one was astonished at her beauty. The prince had been waiting until she came, and he took her hand and danced with her alone. And when any one else came to invite her he said,

34   "She is my partner."

35   And when the evening came she wanted to go home, and the prince followed her, for he wanted to see to what house she belonged; but she broke away from him, and ran into the garden at the back of the house. There stood a fine large tree, bearing splendid pears; she leapt as lightly as a squirrel among the branches, and the prince did not know what had become of her. So he waited until the father came, and then he told him that the strange maiden had rushed from him, and that he thought she had gone up into the pear-tree. The father thought to himself, "It cannot surely be Aschenputtel," and called for an axe, and felled the tree, but there was no one in it. And when they went into the kitchen there sat Aschenputtel among the cinders, as usual, for she had got down the other side of the tree, and had taken back her beautiful clothes to the bird on the hazel bush, and had put on her old gray kirtle again.

36   On the third day, when the parents and the stepchildren had set off, Aschenputtel went again to her mother's grave, and said to the tree,

"Little tree, little tree, shake over me,
That silver and gold may come down and cover me."

37   Then the bird cast down a dress, the like of which had never been seen for splendour and brilliancy, and slippers that were of gold.

38   And when she appeared in this dress at the feast nobody knew what to say for wonderment. The prince danced with her alone, and if any one else asked her he answered,

39   "She is my partner."

40   And when it was evening Aschenputtel wanted to go home, and the prince was about to go with her, when she ran past him so quickly that he could not follow her. But he had laid a plan, and had caused all the steps to be spread with pitch, so that as she rushed down them the left shoe of the maiden remained sticking in it. The prince picked it up, and saw that it was of gold, and very small and slender. The next morning he went to the father and told him that none should be his bride save the one whose foot the golden shoe should fit. Then the two sisters were very glad, because they had pretty feet. The eldest went to her room to try on the shoe, and her mother stood by. But she could not get her great toe into it, for the shoe was too small; then her mother handed her a knife, and said,

41   "Cut the toe off, for when you are queen you will never have to go on foot." So the girl cut her toe off, squeezed her foot into the shoe, concealed the pain, and went down to the prince. Then he took her with him on his horse as his bride, and rode off. They had to pass by the grave, and there sat the two pigeons on the hazel bush, and cried,

"There they go, there they go!
There is blood on her shoe;
The shoe is too small,
—Not the right bride at all!"

42   Then the prince looked at her shoe, and saw the blood flowing. And he turned his horse round and took the false bride home again, saying she was not the right

one, and that the other sister must try on the shoe. So she went into her room to do so, and got her toes comfortably in, but her heel was too large. Then her mother handed her the knife, saying, "Cut a piece off your heel; when you are queen you will never have to go on foot."

43 So the girl cut a piece off her heel, and thrust her foot into the shoe, concealed the pain, and went down to the prince, who took his bride before him on his horse and rode off. When they passed by the hazel bush the two pigeons sat there and cried,

"There they go, there they go!
There is blood on her shoe;
The shoe is too small,
—Not the right bride at all!"

44 Then the prince looked at her foot, and saw how the blood was flowing from the shoe, and staining the white stocking. And he turned his horse round and brought the false bride home again.

45 "This is not the right one," said he, "have you no other daughter?"

46 "No," said the man, "only my dead wife left behind her a little stunted Aschenputtel; it is impossible that she can be the bride." But the King's son ordered her to be sent for, but the mother said,

47 "Oh no! she is much too dirty, I could not let her be seen."

48 But he would have her fetched, and so Aschenputtel had to appear.

49 First she washed her face and hands quite clean, and went in and curtseyed to the prince, who held out to her the golden shoe. Then she sat down on a stool, drew her foot out of the heavy wooden shoe, and slipped it into the golden one, which fitted it perfectly. And when she stood up, and the prince looked in her face, he knew again the beautiful maiden that had danced with him, and he cried,

50 "This is the right bride!"

51 The stepmother and the two sisters were thunderstruck, and grew pale with anger; but he put Aschenputtel before him on his horse and rode off. And as they passed the hazel bush, the two white pigeons cried,

"There they go, there they go!
No blood on her shoe;
The shoe's not too small,
The right bride is she after all."

And when they had thus cried, they came flying after and perched on Aschenputtel's shoulders, one on the right, the other on the left, and so remained.

52 And when her wedding with the prince was appointed to be held the false sisters came, hoping to curry favour, and to take part in the festivities. So as the bridal procession went to the church, the eldest walked on the right side and the younger on the left, and the pigeons picked out an eye of each of them. And as they returned the elder was on the left side and the younger on the right, and the pigeons picked

out the other eye of each of them. And so they were condemned to go blind for the rest of their days because of their wickedness and falsehood.

The Algonquin Cinderella

This Native American version of the Cinderella story was anthologized by Idries Shah, a student of world folklore and Sufism, in World Tales *(1979). As you read the tale, notice its emphasis on the spiritual power of beauty and vision.*

1   There was once a large village of the MicMac Indians of the Eastern Algonquins, built beside a lake. At the far end of the settlement stood a lodge, and in it lived a being who was always invisible. He had a sister who looked after him, and everyone knew that any girl who could see him might marry him. For that reason there were very few girls who did not try, but it was very long before anyone succeeded.

2   This is the way in which the test of sight was carried out: at evening-time, when the Invisible One was due to be returning home, his sister would walk with any girl who might come down to the lakeshore. She, of course, could see her brother, since he was always visible to her. As soon as she saw him, she would say to the girls:

3   "Do you see my brother?"

4   "Yes," they would generally reply—though some of them did say "No."

5   To those who said that they could indeed see him, the sister would say:

6   "Of what is his shoulder strap made?" Some people say that she would enquire:

7   "What is his moose-runner's haul?" or "With what does he draw his sled?"

8   And they would answer:

9   "A strip of rawhide" or "a green flexible branch," or something of that kind.

10   Then she, knowing that they had not told the truth, would say:

11   "Very well, let us return to the wigwam!"

12   When they had gone in, she would tell them not to sit in a certain place, because it belonged to the Invisible One. Then, after they had helped to cook the supper, they would wait with great curiosity, to see him eat. They could be sure that he was a real person, for when he took off his moccasins they became visible, and his sister hung them up. But beyond this they saw nothing of him, not even when they stayed in the place all the night, as many of them did.

13   Now there lived in the village an old man who was a widower, and his three daughters. The youngest girl was very small, weak and often ill: and yet her sisters, especially the elder, treated her cruelly. The second daughter was kinder, and sometimes took her side: but the wicked sister would burn her hands and feet with hot cinders, and she was covered with scars from this treatment. She was so marked that people called her *Oochigeaskw*, the Rough-Faced-Girl.

14   When her father came home and asked why she had such burns, the bad sister would at once say that it was her own fault, for she had disobeyed orders and gone near the fire and fallen into it.

15   These two elder sisters decided one day to try their luck at seeing the Invisible One. So they dressed themselves in their finest clothes, and tried to look their prettiest. They found the Invisible One's sister and took the usual walk by the water.

16   When he came, and when they were asked if they could see him, they answered: "Of course." And when asked about the shoulder strap or sled cord, they answered: "A piece of rawhide."

17   But of course they were lying like the others, and they got nothing for their pains.

18   The next afternoon, when the father returned home, he brought with him many of the pretty little shells from which wampum was made, and they set to work to string them.

19   That day, poor Little Oochigeaskw, who had always gone barefoot, got a pair of her father's moccasins, old ones, and put them into water to soften them so that she could wear them. Then she begged her sisters for a few wampum shells. The elder called her a "little pest," but the younger one gave her some. Now, with no other clothes than her usual rags, the poor little thing went into the woods and got herself some sheets of birch bark, from which she made a dress, and put marks on it for decoration, in the style of long ago. She made a petticoat and a loose gown, a cap, leggings and a handkerchief. She put on her father's large old moccasins, which were far too big for her, and went forth to try her luck. She would try, she thought, to discover whether she could see the Invisible One.

20   She did not begin very well. As she set off, her sisters shouted and hooted, hissed and yelled, and tried to make her stay. And the loafers around the village, seeing the strange little creature, called out "Shame!"

21   The poor little girl in her strange clothes, with her face all scarred, was an awful sight, but she was kindly received by the sister of the Invisible One. And this was, of course, because this noble lady understood far more about things than simply the mere outside which all the rest of the world knows. As the brown of the evening sky turned to black, the lady took her down to the lake.

22   "Do you see him?" the Invisible One's sister asked.

23   "I do, indeed—and he is wonderful!" said Oochigeaskw.

24   The sister asked:

25   "And what is his sled-string?"

26   The little girl said:

27   "It is the Rainbow."

28   "And, my sister, what is his bow-string?"

29   "It is The Spirit's Road—the Milky Way."

30   "So you *have* seen him," said his sister. She took the girl home with her and bathed her. As she did so, all the scars disappeared from her body. Her hair grew again, as it was combed, long, like a blackbird's wing. Her eyes were now like stars: in all the world there was no other such beauty. Then, from her treasures, the lady gave her a wedding garment, and adorned her.

31   Then she told Oochigeaskw to take the *wife's* seat in the wigwam: the one next to where the Invisible One sat, beside the entrance. And when he came in, terrible and beautiful, he smiled and said:

32   "So we are found out!"
33   "Yes," said his sister. And so Oochigeaskw became his wife.

James Finn Garner

"The Politically Correct Cinderella"

An author, radio personality, and improvisational theater artist, James Finn Garner (b. 1960) has lived most of his life in the Chicago area. He earned his B.A. at the University of Michigan. Garner is best known for his Politically Correct Bedtime Stories *(1994) and a sequel,* Politically Correct Holiday Stories *(1995), both of which include re-written versions of classical fairy tales. In the selection that follows, Garner satirizes the politically correct approach to reading materials that would consider the original story to be classist, sexist, and even "speciesist."*

1 **Introduction**   When they were first written, the stories on which the following tales are based certainly served their purpose—to entrench the patriarchy, to estrange people from their own natural impulses, to demonize "evil" and to "reward" an "objective" "good." However much we might like to, we cannot blame the Brothers Grimm for their insensitivity to women's issues, minority cultures, and the environment. Likewise, in the self-righteous Copenhagen of Hans Christian Andersen, the inalienable rights of mermaids were hardly given a second thought.

2   Today, we have the opportunity—and the obligation—to rethink these "classic" stories so they reflect more enlightened times. To that effort I submit this humble book. While its original title, *Fairy Stories for a Modern World,* was abandoned for obvious reasons (kudos to my editor for pointing out my heterosexualist bias), I think the collection stands on its own. This, however, is just a start. Certain stories, such as "The Duckling That Was Judged on Its Personal Merits and Not on Its Physical Appearance," were deleted for space reasons. I expect I have volumes left in me, and I hope this book sparks the righteous imaginations of other writers and, of course, leaves an indelible mark on our children.

3   If, through omission or commission, I have inadvertently displayed any sexist, racist, culturalist, nationalist, ageist, lookist, ableist, sizeist, speciesist, intellectualist, socioeconomicist, ethnocentrist, phallocentrist, heteropatriarchalist, or other type of bias as yet unnamed, I apologize and encourage your suggestions for rectification. In the quest to develop meaningful literature that is totally free from bias and purged from the influences of its flawed cultural past, I doubtless have made some mistakes.

4 **Cinderella**   There once lived a young woman named Cinderella, whose natural birthmother had died when Cinderellas was but a child. A few years after, her father married a widow with two older daughters. Cinderella's mother-of-step treated her

very cruelly, and her sisters-of-step made her work very hard, as if she were their own personal unpaid laborer.

5   One day an invitation arrived at their house. The prince was celebrating his exploitation of the dispossessed and marginalized peasantry by throwing a fancy dress ball. Cinderella's sisters-of-step were very excited to be invited to the palace. They began to plan the expensive clothes they would use to alter and enslave their natural body images to emulate an unrealistic standard of feminine beauty. (It was especially unrealistic in their case, as they were differently visaged enough to stop a clock.) Her mother-of-step also planned to go to the ball, so Cinderella was working harder than a dog (an appropriate if unfortunately speciesist metaphor).

6   When the day of the ball arrived, Cinderella helped her mother- and sisters-of-step into their ball gowns. A formidable task: It was like trying to force ten pounds of processed nonhuman animal carcasses into a five-pound skin. Next came immense cosmetic augmentation, which it would be best not to describe at all. As evening fell, her mother- and sisters-of-step left Cinderella at home to finish her housework. Cinderella was sad, but she contented herself with her Holly Near records.

7   Suddenly there was a flash of light, and in front of Cinderella stood a man dressed in loose-fitting, all-cotton clothes and wearing a wide-brimmed hat. At first Cinderella thought he was a Southern lawyer or a bandleader, but he soon put her straight.

8   "Hello, Cinderella, I am your fairy godperson, or individual deity proxy, if you prefer. So, you want to go to the ball, eh? And bind yourself into the male concept of beauty? Squeeze into some tight-fitting dress that will cut off your circulation? Jam your feet into high-heeled shoes that will ruin your bone structure? Paint your face with chemicals and makeup that have been tested on nonhuman animals?"

9   "Oh yes, definitely," she said in an instant. Her fairy godperson heaved a great sigh and decided to put off her political education till another day. With his magic, he enveloped her in a beautiful, bright light and whisked her away to the palace.

10   Many, many carriages were lined up outside the palace that night; apparently, no one had ever thought of carpooling. Soon, in a heavy, gilded carriage painfully pulled by a team of horse-slaves, Cinderella arrived. She was dressed in a clinging gown woven of silk stolen from unsuspecting silkworms. Her hair was festooned with pearls plundered from hard-working, defenseless oysters. And on her feet, dangerous though it may seem, she wore slippers made of finely cut crystal.

11   Every head in the ballroom turned as Cinderella entered. The men stared at and lusted after this wommon who had captured perfectly their Barbie-doll ideas of feminine desirability. The womyn, trained at an early age to despise their own bodies, looked at Cinderella with envy and spite. Cinderella's own mother- and sisters-of-step, consumed with jealousy, failed to recognize her.

12   Cinderella soon caught the roving eye of the prince, who was busy discussing jousting and bear-baiting with his cronies. Upon seeing her, the prince was struck with a fit of not being able to speak as well as the majority of the population. "Here," he thought, "is a woman that I could make my princess and impregnate with the

progeny of our perfect genes, and thus make myself the envy of every other prince for miles around. And she's blond, too!"

13   The prince began to cross the ballroom towad his intended prey. His cronies also began to walk toward Cinderella. So did every other male in the ballroom who was younger than 70 and not serving drinks.

14   Cinderella was proud of the commotion she was causing. She walked with head high and carried herself like a wommon of eminent social standing. But soon it became clear that the commotion was turning into something ugly, or at least socially dysfunctional.

15   The prince had made it clear to this friends that he was intent on "possessing" the young wommon. But the prince's resoluteness angered his pals, for they too lusted after her and wanted to own her. The men began to shout and push each other. The prince's best friend, who was a large if cerebrally constrained duke, stopped him halfway across the dance floor and insisted that *he* was going to have Cinderella. The prince's response was a swift kick to the groin, which left the duke temporarily inactive. But the prince was quickly seized by other sex-crazed males, and he disappeared into a pile of human animals.

16   The womyn were appalled by this vicious display of testosterone, but try as they might, they were unable to separate the combatants. To the other womyn, it seemed that Cinderella was the cause of all the trouble, so they encircled her and began to display very unsisterly hostility. She tried to escape, but her impractical glass slippers made it nearly impossible. Fortunately for her, none of the other womyn were shod any better.

17   The noise grew so loud that no one heard the clock in the tower chime midnight. When the bell rang the twelfth time, Cinderella's beautiful gown and slippers disappeared, and she was dressed once again in her peasan'ts rags. Her mother- and sisters-of-step recognized her now, but kept quiet to avoid embarrassment.

18   The womyn grew silent at this magical transformation. Freed from the confinements of her gown and slippers, Cinderella sighed and stretched and scratched her ribs. She smiled, closed her eyes and said, "Kill me now if you want, sisters, but at least I'll die in comfort."

19   The womyn around her again grew envious, but this time they took a different approach: Instead of exacting vengeance on her, they stripped off their bodices, corsets, shoes, and every other confining garment. They danced and jumped and screeched in sheer joy, comfortable at last in their shifts and bare feet.

20   Had the men looked up from their macho dance of destruction, they would have seen many desirable woman dressed as if for the boudoir. But they never ceased pounding, punching, kicking, and clawing each other until, to the last man, they were dead.

21   The womyn clucked their tongues but felt no remorse. The palace and realm were theirs now. Their first official act was to dress the men in their discarded dresses and tell the media that the fight arose when someone threatened to expose the crossdressing tendencies of the prince and his cronies. Their second was to set up a clothing co-op that produced only comfortable, practical clothes for womyn. Then

they hung a sign on the castle advertising CinderWear (for that was what the new clothing was called), and [through self-determination and clever marketing], they all—even the mother and sisters-of-step—lived happily ever after.

Olga Broumas

"Cinderella"

OIga Broumas was born in Greece in 1949 and came to the United States in 1967. After studying at the University of Pennsylvania and the University of Oregon (MFA, 1973), Broumas taught English, creative writing, and women's studies at a number of universities. She also has worked as a body work therapist and was a founder and long-time faculty member of Freehand, a community of women photographers and writers in Provincetown, Massachusetts. Broumas has received a number of awards for her writing, and has produced seven volumes of poetry, including Beginning With O *(1977), from which the following poem is taken;* Pastoral Jazz *(1983);* Perpetua *(1989); and (with T. Begley),* Sappho's Gymnasium *(1994). Broumas often explores gender issues in her poetry, emphasizing the need for a sense of community among women, as can be seen in her modern sequel to the Cinderella story that follows.*

. . . *the joy that isn't shared*
I heard, dies young.
Anne Sexton, 1928–1974

Apart from my sisters, estranged
from my mother, I am a woman alone
in a house of men
who secretly
5 call themselves princes, alone
with me usually, under cover of dark. I am the one allowed in

to the royal chambers, whose small foot conveniently
fills the slipper of glass. The woman writer, the lady
umpire, the madam chairman, anyone's wife.
10 I know what I know.
And I once was glad

of the chance to use it, even alone
in a strange castle, doing overtime on my own, cracking
the royal code. The princes spoke
15 in their fathers' language, were eager to praise me
my nimble tongue. I am a woman in a state of siege, alone

as one piece of laundry, strung on a windy clothesline a

mile long. A woman co-opted by promises: the lure
of a job, the ruse of a choice, a woman forced
20 to bear witness, falsely
against my kind, as each
other sister was judged inadequate, bitchy, incompetent,
jealous, too thin, too fat. I know what I know.
What sweet bread I make

25 for myself in this prosperous house
is dirty, what good soup I boil turns
in my mouth to mud. Give
me my ashes. A cold stove, a cinder-block pillow, wet
canvas shoes in my sisters', my sisters' hut. Or I swear

30 I'll die young
like those favored before me, hand-picked each one
for her joyful heart.

Questions for Discussion

1. What aspects of each tale help you to identify it as a Cinderella story?
2. How do you feel about rereading the original Grimm's tale as an adult? Does the Cinderella story hold a different meaning for you today than it did when it was first told to you? Why?
3. Contrast the tone and theme of the four versions of the story. What different attitudes toward nature and the material world are expressed in each tale?
4. Were you surprised or shocked by the violent and punitive ending of the Grimms' version? Do you think the Native American version is more suitable for children? Why do you think that the popular fairy tales that most parents today read to their children are less violent than the Grimms' version?
5. Comment on the theme of alienation and its resolution in the various versions of Cinderella. What set of values is implied by each resolution?
6. Compare Broumas' portrait of a modern, feminist Cinderella with that of Garner in his "Politically Correct Cinderella." Does Garner's conclusion seem at all feasible as a solution to Cinderella's estrangement as portrayed by Broumas? What would Broumas' response be to Garner?
7. Which of the four versions did you prefer, and why?

Ideas for Writing

1. Write an essay that discusses how the Cinderella story helps to shape values for young women. Do you consider this story in its classic version to be sexist, or do you think it still had relevant meanings to convey ? Explain your response.

2. Do a close comparison of any two of the Cinderella versions. You can consider such issues as nature, materialism, class dominance, and feminism.

Joshua Groban

"Two Myths"

Joshua Groban, who grew up in an artistic and literary family, has always been interested in mythology and issues related to creativity. In his freshman English class, Groban wrote a research paper comparing a number of different Native American accounts of the creation and was fascinated by the imagination and diversity of the visions he encountered in his reading. The following essay is Groban's comparative response to the two accounts of creation from the casebook of myths presented in this chapter.

1   An individual growing up in today's society is quickly indoctrinated into believing the predominant myth about creation. Our church, our parents, our teachers, and the media all reinforce such concepts as Adam and Eve and the Garden of Eden. However, every culture has its own unique myth to explain the birth of the planet and its inhabitants. By comparing the Bible's depiction of creation to that of the Yao myth, "The Chameleon Finds," one is reminded of the many different and imaginative ways people have presented such fundamental issues as gender relations, our connection with and responsibility to the environment, and the relationship of human beings to God.

2   First, we are struck by the different views of women in the two accounts of creation, the Bible's narration of creation depicts women as secondary to and subservient to men. In the Book of Genesis, "the cattle," "all the birds of the air," and "every beast of the field" are created before women. This order of creation gives the impression that the beasts are more central to life on earth than women, and thus are created first. But, despite the abundance of these beasts, "there was not found a helper fit for him [man]." Genesis makes it clear that women are given life not as man's equal, but as his "helper" or assistant. When God finally creates females, they are divested from any sense of individuality; they are not created in the image of God, as man is, but from the rib of man. Thus, women are presented as owing their very existence to men. Genesis 2:4 concludes by emphasizing this idea, explaining that "she shall be called Woman, because she was taken out of man." The Bible ties not only a woman's existence, but even her name to men. In this way, this creation myth clearly establishes women as subservient to men and lacking an equivalent sense of identity.

3   The Yao creation myth presents a different and more favorable portrayal of women. Women are not created as an afterthought in "The Chameleon Finds," to function as a helper to men, as they are in the Bible. Instead, men and women come into the world together, as companions. Males and females are given life when The

Creator plucks them from the river in his trap. The myth says, "The next morning when he pulled the trap he found a little man and woman in it. He had never seen any creatures like this." In this way, the two sexes begin their existence in equality. Females do not come from males and are not granted life after men, cattle, birds, and beasts. The myth creates men and women together, and thus suggests that the two sexes should live their lives in this state of equality as well.

4   A juxtaposition of the Genesis and Yao stories in regards to their view of nature reveals a similar divergence. In the Bible, man dominates nature in much the same way as he dominates women. Both the environment and females are presented in Genesis as subservient "helpers" to man. Genesis 2:4 professes, "and out of the ground the Lord God made to grow every tree that is pleasant to the sight and good for food. . . ." Nature exists to serve and to help man; trees have life only to serve mankind by being "pleasant to the sight and good for food." Like women, the role of nature is to serve man rather than exist in equality with him. The Bible reads, "The Lord God took the man and put him in the garden of Eden to till and keep it." Man does not exist in the garden to co-exist with the plants and animals of the garden. Instead, he is to "keep it," as if the earth were a possession.

5   The Yao story of creation sees humans as irresponsible and destructive in their relation to the earth. In the Yao tale, the first man and woman set fire to the vegetation and kill animals that inhabit the earth. Their creator is appalled by this behavior: "They are burning up everything," he exclaims. "They are killing my people." He is so disturbed by the way humans treat the earth that He decides to leave the planet. A spider makes him a ladder and He goes to live in the sky. The story ends, "Thus the gods were driven off the face of the earth by the cruelty of man." This myth, in contrast to the Bible, sets clear expectations about the consequences of man's mistreatment of the earth. In "The Chameleon Finds," nature, like women, has rights that should never be usurped. Genesis ignores these universal rights, affording them only to God and to man.

6   This contrast also exists in the way the two myths portray man's relationship to God. In Genesis, God is a distant, autocratic deity; he speaks and the act is performed. In this story, God "took" the man and "put him" in the garden of Eden. Later, He "commands" man never to eat from the tree of good and evil. Humans are pawns controlled by this distant deity. They make no decisions in Genesis 2:4, but are instead "taken," "put," and "commanded." The Bible's God is one that controls humans and merely speaks in order to create.

7   The Yao Creator is an entirely different, more human sort of figure. This God is not presented as an all-powerful deity that merely speaks to create life. He unknowingly discovers humans in his trap, and no indication is given that He created them at all. This Creator does not command humans to do as He wants them to do. When humans destroy the earth, no punishment comes from a distant deity, as in the Bible. Instead, the Creator leaves the earth, leaving humans free to make their own decisions and choose their own destiny. This contrast impacts both man's relationship with God and his view of himself. In the Bible, The Creator is a force that has complete control over humans. He creates by merely speaking, commands humans,

and punishes them. In contrast, the Yao Creator does not control every human action. He creates people not by speaking, but by discovering them. He does not command or punish, but leaves people to make their own choices about life on earth. This divergent approach functions to empower humans. The Yao myth enables people to feel in control of their life because no distant, supreme being controls them. Consequently, this fosters a heightened sense of morality and responsibility. "The Chameleon Finds" does not allow the individual to blame God or rely upon him. Instead, this creator diety, having set the world in motion and established His ideology, now leaves the decisions in the hands of humans, whose punishment for their crimes against nature is abandonment by the creator.

8   It would be misguided to contend that the discrepancy between the Bible and other myths on gender issues, the environment, and man's relationship with God proves that the Bible is responsible for the social ills of today. Religion does not create society; rather society creates religion. The Bible did not cause sexism or environmental disaster, and is not at the root of today's societal evils. However, comparing the account of The Creation in Genesis to similar myths from other cultures is of value in reminding the individual that there are no absolute truths. Every society has to define its origins and values as it sees fit. The dominance of Judeo-Christian thinking in our society does not make it more correct. There are alternative stories, such as "The Chameleon Finds," that present different visions of creation. This process of comparison can lead to an appreciation of a contrasting ideology; however, the appreciation of other religions and their view of creation comes only when someone begins to think about the validity of their own religion rather than blindly accepting it. The comparison of different creation myths is not antithetical to religion; it represents a reasoned approach to looking at God and creation and thus defines what true religious conviction really is.

QUESTIONS FOR DISCUSSION

1. What are the main points of comparison and contrast around which Groban structures his essay? Do they seem appropriate to the myths he studied, or would you have selected others?

2. How effectively does Groban use details and references to the two myths he contrasts to support his conclusions about their differences? Are there other details he might have used or different inferences he might have drawn based on the details he selects?

3. Although Groban states in some parts of his essay that all creation myths have validity, since "there are no absolute truths," he seems quite critical of the Biblical version of Creation. Do you think that some views of creation are "better" than others, or is each version a product of the culture that produced it?

4. What seem to be the criteria that Groban uses in his evaluation of the two myths he is comparing? Do his criteria seem appropriate, or would you substitute others? How would you set up criteria for evaluating myths of creation, if you believe that it is possible to do so?

Liz Scheps

"Cinderella: Politically Incorrect?"

Liz Scheps was a college senior when she wrote the following essay. She majored in linguistics and history, and her interests include popular culture, adolescent studies, earth and space science, and ice skating. The best part about writing this essay for Scheps as a linguistic major was being given the opportunity to take an in-depth look at the language in the "Politically Correct Cinderella." In the essay that follows, Scheps critiques Garner's version of the Cinderella tale by comparing and contrasting it to the original Grimms' version.

1   In today's politically correct society, people may be vertically-challenged, hair-deprived, or differently-abled; they are rarely short, bald, or handicapped. While the political correctness movement is meant, in the eyes of its supporters, to remove through changes in language and ideology the prejudice towards and denigration of various types of people who do not fit the societal ideal, many critics find this social and linguistic doctoring laughable or even offensive. James Finn Garner makes hyperbolic use of the language and doctrines of the politically correct ideology in order to ridicule political correctness in his retelling of the classic Cinderella tale.

2   The original Cinderella story, written by the Brothers Grimm in the early nineteenth century, is not the sweet tale of fairy godmothers and singing mice that Disney has made common knowledge. The original is a darker story, in which promises are broken, deception is encouraged, and harsh revenge is exacted. The reader is instructed from the outset that Cinderella's stepsisters are "at heart black and ugly"; there is no hope for their redemption in the Grimms' tale. Similarly, it becomes clear that the stepmother is also inherently evil; she informs Cinderella that she may go to the prince's ball if she is able to pick lentils out of the ashes precisely because she believes it will be impossible for Cinderella to complete the task; when Cinderella does accomplish this feat, the stepmother simply informs her that she is too dirty and under-dressed to attend. When the prince comes to their house in search of the maiden whose foot will fit the slipper, the stepmother instructs the eldest daughter to "'[c]ut the toe off, for when you are queen you will never have to go on foot.'" In the end, the stepsisters both pay for their "wickedness and falsehood" by losing their sight to the doves who are allies of Cinderella. Throughout the tale, the values of honesty, piety, goodness, resourcefulness, and closeness to nature are emphasized; the message sent is that if one is genuinely good, he or she will eventually be rewarded; if one inflicts pain on others or lies, he or she will lose out in the end.

3   The Grimms' tale is certainly not the most familiar Cinderella story for most people. Today, many children and adults alike look to the dream-like ball and fairy godmother of the Disney animated version as the true essence of the Cinderella tale; far from being a sinister story of revenge and triumph of good over evil, the Disney movie focuses on

the transformation of Cinderella from a kind but simple working girl into a beautiful and glamorous princess. The huge popularity of the 1998 Drew Barrymore movie *Ever After* has given many people a glimpse of the darker tone of the Grimm version, but it still preserves the fantasy-based qualities of the Disney tale. More than any one of these stories, the tale of Cinderella has become a part of society's collective imagination and cultural knowledge.

4   Garner's Cinderella tale uses a parody of the myth of Cinderella to satirize politically correct language and behavior. The stepmother and stepsisters become "mother-of-step" and "sisters-of-step" respectively; this tongue in cheek labeling flouts the negative connotations that the traditional names "stepmother" and "stepsister" connote, due in large part to the legacy of the original Cinderella tale. It might also be a comment on the increasingly complex familial situations which have become common in our society; as divorce and remarriage lead to intricate webs of half-brothers, stepsisters, and so forth, the labeling patterns of these family members has become more and more nebulous in order to downplay the lack of blood relation between members of the same family. Furthermore, the multi-word label "sisters-of-step" is in keeping with the politically correct tradition of creating long convoluted names for originally blunt terms, such as hair-deprived for bald.

5   One of the most controversial and most publicized features of politically correct language is the movement to eliminate the word "man" from the term "woman" in order to lessen the subordinate status of the word "woman," as well as of the group that it represents. Garner plays on this notion throughout the Cinderella tale by referring to a single female as a "wommon" and a group of them as "womyn." The traditional fairy godmother is replaced, interestingly, by a man, who informs Cinderella that he is her "fairy godperson, or individual deity proxy." By replacing the fairy godmother with a male figure, Garner plays upon the challenge presented by the politically correct, particularly by feminists, to make all occupations open to both genders. Since a fairy is traditionally female in the popular conception, Garner is able to make fun of the politically correct agenda by placing a male in this fairy tale career. However, what is interesting about Garner's use of a male fairy godperson is that the role that this character plays switches as well. In the Disney-like story, the fairy godmother is a nurturing figure who aids Cinderella; in Garner's version, the godperson (who is really a godman) seems to be elevated above Cinderella; he laments her desire to conform to societal standards of beauty and finally reconciles himself to teaching her political values at a later time.

6   In addition to using politically correct language to refer to gender differences, Garner employs politically correct stereotypes and critiques of societally-determined gender roles throughout the Cinderella tale. In the Grimm original, gender is not especially important on a literal level, but many women have complained that what young girls who read fairy tales like this learn is that they should simply be good and beautiful; Cinderella gets the chance to go to the ball because she is good, but she wins the heart of the prince because she is beautiful and well-proportioned: the prince does not search for the woman who dazzled his mind, but rather for the

woman who will fit a silver slipper. Garner exaggerates the politically correct critique of gender roles throughout the tale; he apparently does this to show just how much this critique ruins the charming fairy tale ideology which is a foundation of western culture. For instance, instead of having fun spending the day getting ready for the ball, the sisters-of-step "began to plan the expensive clothes they would use to alter and enslave their natural body images to emulate an unrealistic standard of feminine beauty." By thus drawing mock-critical attention to the thin supermodel look which so many feminists have attacked as being unattainable and a cause of eating disorders, low self-esteem, and other problems of women in American society, Garner ridicules the feminist position as puritanical and exaggerated: of course, he seems to say, women don't knowingly and actively enslave their bodies every time they get dressed—they just want to dress up, look good, and have some fun!

7   Garner portrays Cinderella as undergoing a transition not from working girl to princess, as in the original tale, but from politically incorrect to politically correct; through the course of the story she changes from a woman who wants to be beautiful and is proud of the effect her appearance has on men to a "wommon" who is independent and has no need of beauty and the attention of men; instead of tight dresses that might be bad for her health, she wears "comfortable, practical clothing" and runs her own business through "self-determination and clever marketing." Thus, Cinderella has attained the supposed goal of the politically correct and/or feminist movements, but because of Garner's sarcastic tone, she does not seem at all desirable as a heroine the way that the honest, loyal and courageous Grimms' Aschenputel is; rather she conforms to the popular media's negative stereotype of the conniving female capitalist—and she's a frump, at that! Garner holds the new, supposedly progressive Cinderella up to ridicule, reinstilling the politically incorrect notion that beauty is more important than anything else. Furthermore, the fact that "they all—even the mother- and sisters-of-step—lived happily ever after" suggests that good and evil are irrelevant in a politically correct world—no one receives their just desserts for what they have done throughout the tale. In fact, the womyn succeed because the men self-destruct sooner, forcing them to join together in bonds of feminine sisterhood, which Garner portrays as phony, just another politically correct pose.

8   Garner also uses his tale to ridicule the politically correct critique of men as overly competitive, drawn to women primarily for reasons of sexual conquest. In the original tale, the prince and the father are portrayed as good, civilized characters. The prince is portrayed as a young gentleman willing to do anything to find the woman who has stolen his heart. In Garner's version, the men are reduced to animalistic, sex-crazed fools. The men at the ball lust after Cinderella because she fits the Barbie-doll image which the politically correct suggest that men press onto women. The prince's first thought upon seeing her is of sex and continuing his own lineage; he ponders the idea that Cinderella "'is a wommon that I could make my princess and impregnate with the progeny of our perfect genes, and thus make myself the envy of every other prince for miles around. And she's blond too!'" These lines ridicule the guerrilla-feminist position, which claims that men simply react with the animalistic instinct to reproduce with the most fit female available, as well as the more commonly accepted female

stereotype of men who revel in having sex and impregnating women and then relate their exploits to friends in order to appear super-masculine.

9   As the men at the ball all gaze upon Cinderella, the commotion grows until it becomes "socially dysfunctional," and gradually a pile of "sex-crazed males" dissolves into a pile of "human animals" who are so busy ripping each other to shreds that they take no notice of the women stripping off their confining clothing; this of course is ironic since getting the women's clothes off is presumably all the men wanted in the first place. At the end of the tale, the womyn tell to the media that the men died because the prince wished to keep his cross-dressing a secret; this plays upon the politically correct notion of men as needing to be undeniably macho because of their underlying sexual insecurity or closeted deviance. Overall, Garner depicts the men in the story as an extreme, ridiculous version of how the politically correct movement has often depicted them: as aggressive, testosterone-driven, and drawn to women for their looks rather than their intelligence.

10   The original Grimm's Cinderella, like the Disney version, shows Cinderella as a character from a pre-industrial, agrarian age who draws what power she has through living in harmony with nature, in touch with familiar spirits of mice, birds, and growing things. Garner seems unaware of the natural quality of the original tale, creating his Cinderella as someone who moves from a non-politically correct attitude towards nature to a heavily parodied kind of environmental consciousness. The environmental movement, as Garner perceives it, advocates great responsibility towards animals; thus it is politically incorrect to test cosmetics on animals, to log forests, or to wear fur or synthetic fibers which cause pollution. Garner takes this awareness to a ridiculous level, placing blame on people for every involvement they have with animals and characterizing the animals as profoundly hurt by the actions and even the casual verbal expressions of people. Thus, after Cinderella is said to be working "harder than a dog," Garner apologizes that this is "an appropriate if unfortunately speciesist metaphor." The row of carriages outside the palace is singled out as an example of the environmental irresponsibility displayed by the citizens of the kingdom in not carpooling, while everything Cinderella wears is environmentally incorrect: her dress is silk stolen from "unsuspecting" silkworms and her hair is decorated with pearls "plundered from hard-working, defenseless oysters." It is not until the end of the story, when the womyn supposedly shed the constraints of materialistic society, that they become environmentally conscious and thus politically correct. However, this development too has its ironies: they succeed not because of their social consciousness but because of their "clever marketing" of "natural" clothing—which simply reinforces materialism.

11   Garner clearly wishes to condemn and ridicule the politically correct agenda in his version of the Cinderella tale. By choosing to retell a classic fairy tale through the hyperbolic language of the politically correct movement, he seeks to expose the repressive, rule-bound society and overly euphemistic language usage that would result from living under a politically correct regime. His main point seems to be that the original tale and the values it connotes, no matter how old-fashioned or misogynistic they might seem, are no worse than the convoluted notions of the political

correctness movement. By exaggerating the politically correct viewpoint to a laugh-able degree, Garner creates a tale designed to entice and entertain people of all out-looks, while at the same time providing a strong and stinging critique of political correctness, and especially of feminism.

12   However, it is clear from Garner's retelling that he uses the Cinderella story as a transparent vehicle for his own agenda; rather than being a cleverly subtle and witty tweaking of a well-known tale in order to make a point, the "Politically Correct Cinderella" is a wildly concocted diatribe which is exaggerated to the point of absur-dity. Garner draws only loosely on any version of the Cinderella tale, and he spends most of the story creating outlandish scenarios which have little to do with the any of the original versions and serve only to ridicule political correctness. Though Gar-ner's version of the Cinderella tale is at times amusing, its heavy-handed plotting and lack of insight into the historic roots of environmentalism and feminism weaken his critique of the politically correct movement. The story must be taken primarily as light entertainment for politically conservative readers rather than as a serious social commentary.

QUESTIONS FOR DISCUSSION

1. Why does Scheps begin her essay with a summary of the original Cin-derella tale? How does this help readers to better understand her critique of Garner's version?

2. What main points of contrast does Scheps make between the original story and the Garner version? How well does each of these points support her overall critique? Could she have made other points?

3. As a linguistics major, Scheps was particularly interested in the parody of "politically correct" language in the Garner version of Cinderella. How effectively does Scheps analyze the significance of made-up words and phrases in Garner's story?

4. What conclusions does Scheps draw about the failings of Garner's story in her final paragraph? Do you agree with her evaluation here? Why or why not?

Topics for Research and Writing

1. Write an essay that presents your definition of a myth. Draw on your per-sonal experiences and the readings in this chapter as well as outside re-search into the nature of myths and mythology. How does a myth differ from a lie or falsehood?

2. Write your own myth, based on your view of yourself as a hero or hero-ine. Then write an analysis of your myth, comparing the "ideal" self that

emerges in the story you have written to your "real" self. How does your myth reflect the concerns of your generation and your own values? In what ways is your myth traditional? Make connections between your myth and other hero myths that you read about in your research.

3. Over five hundred different versions of the Cinderella tale are told in cultures around the world. Do some research to find two interesting versions from different cultures; then write a comparison paper of these two versions. What did you learn about the cultures that produced each story? See particularly *Cinderella: A Folklore Casebook* by Alan Dundes (Garland, 1992).

4. Compare and contrast a traditional myth or tale with a modern retelling of that myth, perhaps in a popular culture format such as a TV show or comic book. Reflect on how and why the original myth has been changed. Which of the two versions do you prefer and why?

5. In what important ways do you think that myths function in people's lives and in society? Write an essay in which you do some research into this issue and discuss several ways that myths serve people; support each main point you make with an example. (See particularly the essay by Joseph Campbell in this chapter as well as other works by Campbell such as *Hero with a Thousand Faces*.)

6. See one of the following films or one that you choose that explores the role of myth, either by yourself or with several of your classmates. Write analysis of the film that discusses the ways in which the film explores the nature and meaning of myths or fairy tales and their relationship to dreams and the imagination. *The Endless Journey, Disney's Cinderella, Black Orpheus, The Neverending Story, The Adventures of Baron Münchausen, Star Wars, The Princess Bride, The First Knight, Monty Python's Holy Grail, The Fisher King, Ever After.*

7. The following URLs can be useful in beginning your research into myths, tales, and their social and psychological significance.

Fairy Tale Links
http://www.darkgoddess.com/fairy/links.htm
This set of links from the Dark Goddess Web Site provides access to original texts and interpretations of a wide range of legends, myths, folk tales, and fairy tales, including resources on the Cinderella story.

Fairy Tale Resource Page
http://www.ualberta.ca/~mshane/title.htm
This resource page for teachers and librarians includes ideas for teaching, links to listservs and "alternative" fairy tales.

Jungian Articles and Authors
http://www.cgjung.com/cgjung/authors.html

Jungian resources web site maintained by Donald Williams and Dolores Brien provides a bibliography with many articles and on-line sources on and by Carl Jung as well as other criticism and authors influenced by him. Contains interesting Jungian-influenced film criticism.

MYTHING LINKS / CREATION MYTHS
http://mythinglinks.org/ct~creation.html
Creation myth links from an *Annotated & Illustrated Collection of Worldwide Links to Mythologies, Fairy Tales & Folklore, Sacred Arts & Traditions* by Kathleen Jenks, Ph.D.

MYTHS OF CREATION, GREEK MYTHOLOGY LINKS
http://hsa.brown.edu/~maicar/MythsOfCreation.html
This site, written and maintained by Carlos Parada, presents on-line information and images on Greek mythology, particularly the classical myths of creation.

SOURCES FOR THE ANALYSIS AND INTERPRETATION OF FOLK AND FAIRY TALES
http://shoga.wwa.com/~callison/
Links, bibliographies, and Internet resources on folk and fairy tale interpretation, including psychological, feminist, and Marxist views.

5

Obsessions and Transformation

True!—nervous—very, very dreadfully nervous I had been and am;
but why will you say that I am mad?
>   EDGAR ALLAN POE
>   The Tell-Tale Heart

Yes indeed, I realized, looking into the mirror. There was a world
in my eye. And I saw that it was possible to love it: that in fact, for all
it had taught me of shame and anger and inner vision, I did love it.
>   ALICE WALKER
>   Beauty: When the Other Dancer is
>   the Self

A fallen man, I climb out of my fear.
The mind enters itself, and God the mind,
And one is One, free in the tearing wind.
>   THEODORE ROETHKE
>   In a Dark Time

DEFINITION: WORD BOUNDARIES OF THE SELF

Definition involves clarifying a term's meaning through precise use of language and through distinguishing between several words that may be difficult to use appropriately because they have similar or overlapping meanings. Definitions, both short and more fully expanded, can be used not only as a way of clarifying the denotative or dictionary meanings of the crucial words and abstract terminology that you use in your writing, but also as a way of exploring personal definitions of terms, feelings, values, and language.

Public Meanings and Formal Definition

In essay writing, definition is most often used as a method for clarifying meaning for your readers. If, for example, you are writing an essay on obsessions, you would first want to define what is meant by obsession. Although you would first turn to a dictionary, an encyclopedia, or another reliable authority for a definition of this basic term, you would also need to use your own words to create your statement of meaning. Your own words will help you get control over the direction of your paper and capture your reader's interest. Begin by placing the term within a formal pattern. First, state the word you will be defining, in this case, "obsession"; then put the term in a larger class or group: "An obsession is a strong emotional response." Next, you will need one or more details or qualifying phrases to distinguish your term from others in the larger group of strong emotions: "An obsession is an emotional response or preoccupation that is compulsive and highly repetitive, a response over which a person often has little or no control and which can have destructive consequences." If this definition still seems inadequate, you could add more details and develop the definition further with a typical example: "Overeating can be an obsessive form of behavior."

In writing an extended definition of a key term, carefully construct the initial definition. If you place the term in too large a class, do not distinguish it from others in the class, or merely repeat your original term or a form of the term, you will have difficulty developing your ideas clearly and will confuse your reader. You also need to decide how you plan to use your definition: what will its purpose be?

Once you have created the initial definition, you can proceed to develop your paragraph or essay using other analytical writing strategies such as process analysis, discussion of cause and effect, or comparative relationships. For example, you could discuss several of the qualities of a typical obsession, provide an ordered exploration of the "stages" of the obsession, or examine the kinds of human growth and interactions with which the obsession can interfere, as Sharon Slayton does in her essay on the obsession with being "good." For clarity, reader interest, and development, examples and illustrations can be used effectively with any of the larger analytical structures that you might wish to take advantage of in your essay: examples from personal experience, friends, or your reading of fictional or fact-based sources.

Stipulative and Personal Definitions

Sometimes writers decide to develop a personal definition. This form of definition, referred to as a stipulative definition, is based on the writer's personal ideals and values. In this case, you still need to be clear in making crucial distinctions. For example, if you are writing a paper on your own personal dream, you might begin with a dictionary definition of "dream" to contrast the qualities of your personal dream to the traditional connotations associated with the term as stated in the dictionary.

Freewriting and clustering will help you clarify what the term you are defining really means to you and to discover the term's deeper personal levels of meaning. Comparative thinking can also be useful. Try writing a series of sentences beginning with the words "My dream is . . ." or "My dream is like. . . ." Make as many different associations with concrete objects or events as you can. Examine the associations you have made and construct a personal definition that is qualified with expressions such as "my," "to me," or "in my opinion" and that includes several personal distinguishing qualities, too.

A stipulative definition is often supported by personal experiences that help the reader understand the origins and basis of your views. You may decide to provide contrasts with qualities others may associate with the term. For example, other people may believe that a dream as you have defined it is just "wishful thinking," an exercise in escapism. You could argue that, to the contrary, it is necessary to have a dream as a high ideal or aspiration; otherwise, one may too readily accept a version of reality that is less than what it could be and lose faith in the imagination that is necessary to solve problems and to move confidently into the future. Thus, a stipulative definition can become a type of argument, an advocacy of one's perspective on life.

Contradiction

In developing your definition, be careful not to create contradictions. Contradiction or equivocation occurs when you begin by defining a term in one way and then shift the definition to another level of meaning. To base an argument intentionally on a contradiction is at best confusing and at worst dishonest and propagandistic. For example, if you begin your paper with a definition of "myth" as the cultural and social stories that bind a people together and then shift in the body of your paper to a discussion of private dreams and personal mythology, you will confuse your reader by violating the logic of your definition, and your essay will lose much of its credibility. A better strategy for dealing with the real complexity of certain words is to concede from the start (in your thesis) that this is an expression with seemingly contradictory or ironic shades of meaning (as in the case of the word "good" in Slayton's essay in this chapter)—and then spell out the complexity clearly in your definition. Read your paper carefully before turning it in, checking to see that your definition and the arguments and examples that are developed in it are consistent. If not, your paper needs a revision, and you may want to modify your initial definition.

Writing objective and personal definitions will help you clarify your thoughts, feelings, and values. As you work to find the qualities, distinctions, and personal experiences that give a complex concept a meaning that reflects your inner self as well as the consensus of the public world, you will also be moving forward on your inward journey.

THEMATIC INTRODUCTION: OBSESSIONS AND TRANSFORMATION

Dreams and fantasies can be healthy; they can serve as a means for escape from trivial or tedious routines and demands. Popular entertainment, for example, often provides us with simple escapist fantasies that encourage us to identify with an idealized hero or heroine. We can become strong, beautiful, courageous, or very wise, and for some moments we may be able to forget the realities of our own lives. When our minds return from a fantasy, we may feel more refreshed, more capable of handling daily responsibilities. Often fantasies provide more than just possibilities of short-term escape; they can also offer insights that will lead to deeper self-understanding and psychological, spiritual transformation. Each individual has unique dreams and fantasies; when these messages from our unconscious minds, from our dream worlds, are understood and interpreted, they can help us have more fulfilling and rewarding lives.

Sometimes, however, fantasies can become overwhelming and painful; they may grow into obsessions and compulsions which lead to behavior that can be limiting and become repetitive, sometimes even self-destructive or destructive to others. In such cases, the obsession controls the individual rather than the individual controlling the fantasy. What causes some people to have these types of obsessions? Why, for instance, does a woman's one-night stand with a married man grow into a destructive fascination, as in the popular film *Fatal Attraction*? Why does a scientist's interest in understanding human nature develop into an obsession to create a perfect man, as in the classic Gothic horror novel *Frankenstein*? Why do some people become possessed by their fantasies and obsessions to the point of madness, whereas others can maintain their psychological equilibrium and learn about themselves through their interests and dreams? How do people's unconscious obsessions influence their day-to-day life and decision-making processes? The essays, stories, and poems included in this chapter provide you with a range of perspectives that will help you begin to consider these and other issues related to our inner lives, dreams, obsessions, and nightmares.

In this chapter's first selection, "Fog-Horn" by W. S. Merwin, the poem's speaker reflects on the power of the forgotten, unconscious world; the foghorn becomes a symbol of the hidden inner self and of secret fears and nightmares, acting as a constant reminder that we cannot escape the powers of the unconscious forces that shape our lives and exist beyond the realm of our rational control. In the next selection, "Nightmares: Terrors of the Night," dream researchers Franklin Galvin and Ernest Hartmann offer a scientific perspective on what types of people are most likely to have nightmares.

In William Styron's "The Roots of Depression," a Pulitzer Prize-winning novelist reflects on his own struggle against depression to show that his writing had warned him through his unconscious mind of his own suicidal tendencies. Through the presentation of his own struggle and examples of the lives of other well-known artists and writers, Styron introduces the well-documented but not well-understood connection between creative genius and depression or manic depression.

In Edgar Allan Poe's classic story, "The Tell-Tale Heart," the narrator's depression and obsession finally lead him to an act of senseless murder. Destructive depression and obsession are also issues for the narrator of Charlotte Perkins Gilman's short story "The Yellow Wallpaper." In defiance of her husband, who has forbidden her to write, this story's narrator grows obsessed with writing about the wallpaper patterns in the room where she is confined to bed, finally imagining that there are women behind the shapes in the wallpaper, struggling to be free. The complex symbolism developed in this story asks the reader to reflect on the relationships between self-understanding, creativity, writing, obsessive fantasies, and madness.

While the first selections in this chaper present observations about and examples of the power of nightmares and obsessions, the next three works focus on how obsessive behavior can be transformed through writing, reflection, and love. In "Beauty: When the Other Dancer Is the Self," Alice Walker shows how she is transformed through her own poetry writing and through her daughter's love and understanding; finally, she comes to value herself and see beauty in a scar that had haunted her since her own childhood. The next selection, Anne Lamott's "Hunger," shares her struggle to overcome her eating disordent. For Lamott, "learning to eat was about learning how to live—and deciding to live." The chapter's final poem, "In a Dark Time" by Theodore Roethke, reveals the speaker's reflective mind as it comes face to face with a crisis of spirit and climbs out of obsessive fear to embrace the exhilerating freedom of life.

The two student writings that conclude this chapter also explore the power of obsession and transformation. In her humorous narrative "I'll Tell It You Called," Adine Kernberg develops a personality for her answering machine, which takes control of her social life. The narrator's relationship to her machine warns readers not to become totally dependent on time-saving technological devices at the expense of human communication. Sharon Slayton, in her essay "The Good Girl," attempts to define the obsession with being well-behaved and pleasing to others, a form of behavior that can have negative consequences, as the "good girl" can never relax, can never do anything just to please herself.

All of the works in this chapter ask readers to look within, to listen to the questions and fears in their hearts and spirits. When we can see such experiences as portrayed in the readings in perspective, as reflections of archetypal patterns of human development and as potential sources of creative inspiration and love, then these different forms of obsession can also be seen as having the power to bring transformation and spiritual growth.

Vincent Van Gogh (1853–1890)
"Starry Night" Saint-Remy, June 1889

Dutch painter Vincent Van Gogh, one of the most famous modern artists, was a depressive who took his own life only one year after painting one of his greatest works, "Starry Night." Van Gogh's expressionistic painting of a night time sky reminds us of how we transform the world as we view it through our own inner "lenses" of obsession, suffering, or joy.

Ideas for Drawing, Writing, and Discussion

1. Close your eyes and allow your imagination to create a picture of something very important to you. Then draw or paint a picture of your vision. How has the act of realizing the vision made you feel?
2. Now do a description in words of your vision, your drawing, and the feelings this process of creation has brought up for you.
3. Share your picture with your group. How did explaining and sharing your vision change your understanding of it?

W. S. Merwin

Fog-Horn

*W. S. Merwin (b. 1927) was raised in Pennsylvania. After graduating from Princeton in 1947, he lived for several years in London, translating French and Spanish classics for the British Broadcasting Corporation. Merwin, who has published many collections of poems and translations, explores myths, cultural contrasts, and ecology. His style is often discontinuous, mysterious, wavering between waking and sleeping states, and creating a dialogue between the conscious and the unconscious mind. Merwin's work often creates strong emotional responses. Some of his more widely read books include Se-*lected Translations: 1948–1969 *(1969),* The Compass Flower *(1977),* Opening the Hand *(1983),* The Lost Upland *(1992), and* The Vixen *(1996). "Fog-Horn" was included in* The Drunk in the Furnace *(1958). As you read the poem, try to recreate the sound and image of the foghorn in your own imagination.*

JOURNAL

Write about a warning that came to you from your unconscious, a warning that might have taken the form of a dream, a fantasy, a minor accident, or a psychosomatic illness.

Surely that moan is not the thing
That men thought they were making, when they
Put it there, for their own necessities.
That throat does not call to anything human
5 But to something men had forgotten,
That stirs under fog. Who wounded that beast
Incurably, or from whose pasture
Was it lost, full grown, and time closed round it
With no way back? Who tethered its tongue
10 So that its voice could never come
To speak out in the light of clear day,
But only when the shifting blindness
Descends and is acknowledged among us,
As though from under a floor it is heard,
15 Or as though from behind a wall, always
Nearer than we had remembered? If it
Was we that gave tongue to this cry
What does it bespeak in us, repeating
And repeating, insisting on something
20 That we never meant? We only put it there
To give warning of something we dare not

Ignore, lest we should come upon it
Too suddenly, recognize it too late,
As our cries were swallowed up and all hands lost.

QUESTIONS FOR DISCUSSION

1. How does Merwin personify the foghorn, bringing it to life, making it more than just an object? Refer to specific details that you think are particularly effective.
2. What does the cry of the foghorn signify? What is its warning?
3. What words, images, and phrases make the poem seem like a dream or a nightmare?
4. Why can't the voice of the foghorn "speak out in the light of clear day"?
5. Why does the voice of the foghorn "call" to something "forgotten"? What parts of ourselves are we most likely to forget or ignore? What helps us to remember what we want to forget?
6. What is your interpretation of the poem? What state of mind is the poet attempting to define?

CONNECTION

Compare the obsessive symbol of the foghorn in Merwin's poem with the heart in the "Tell-Tale Heart" by Edgar Allan Poe in this chapter. How does each symbol help to focus themes of psychic repression and denial, as well as insights into the destructive consequences of obsessive behavior?

IDEAS FOR WRITING

1. Write an essay in which you define and clarify with examples and comparisons the positive role that you think the unconscious mind can play in helping one to create a balanced and fulfilling life. Refer to the poem in shaping your response.
2. Write a narrative or a poem in which you use an object or an animal as a comparison to or as a way of defining and understanding the unconscious mind. Try to emphasize how the unconscious mind communicates with the conscious mind.

Franklin Galvin and Ernest Hartmann

Nightmares: Terrors of the Night

Franklin Galvin was a doctoral candidate in Clinical Psychology at Boston University and conducted research at the Lemuel Shattuck Hospital Sleep Laboratory when he co-authored this article with Ernest Hartmann, M.D. (b. 1934), a Professor of Psychiatry at the Tufts University School of Medicine. Hartmann is the director of the Sleep Research Laboratory, West-Ros Park Mental Health Center at Lemuel Shattuck Hospital and the director of the Sleep Disorders Center, Newton-Wellesley Hospital. He has written many books related to dreams and nightmares, including The Nightmare: The Psychology and Biology of Terrifying Dreams *(1984),* Boundaries in the Mind: A New Psychology of Personality *(1991), and* Dreams and Nightmares: The New Theory on the Origin and Meaning of Dreams *(1998). In the following essay the authors define and make distinctions between nightmares and night terrors, while examining some of the causes and treatments for both.*

JOURNAL

Record a nightmare that you remember from your childhood or recent times. How does your nightmare help to define your inner world and the issues that are important to you?

1   To Sigmund Freud, the nightmare was an annoyance, a stumbling block to his development of a theory of dreams as wish fulfillments. He first tried to include nightmares in his general view by suggesting that they represent the fulfillment of superego wishes—wishes for punishment. Freud was not satisfied with this view, however, and he later suggested that certain nightmares, especially traumatic nightmares, represent a repetition compulsion—a primitive tendency of the mind to repeat what has been experienced. Theodore Lidz, when studying traumatic nightmares, proposed that these dreams could be understood as a wish for punishment, as Freud first suggested, but also as an "ambivalent wish for death": both the wish for death and the wish to escape it.

2   The manifest fear of death figured prominently in a childhood dream of Freud's. It is the first of three dreams we present to illustrate how the nightmare has heralded momentous change in the lives of three noted dreamworkers.

3   In his discussion of anxiety dreams near the end of *The Interpretation of Dreams*, Freud presented us with the only dream from his childhood to be found in his published works and letters. "A true anxiety-dream," he called it, "from my seventh or eighth year." This dating is of special import in Freud's life because it "starts—spiritually—the gestation period of a new and original thought." Of this dream, Freud wrote:

> It was a very vivid one, and in it I saw my beloved mother, with a peculiarly peaceful, sleeping expression on her features, being carried into the room by two (or three) people with birds' beaks and laid upon the bed. I awoke in tears and screaming, and interrupted my parents' sleep. . . . I remember that I suddenly grew calm when I saw my mother's face, as though I had needed to be reassured that she was not dead. . . . I was not anxious because I had dreamt that my mother was dying. . . . The anxiety can be traced back, when repression is taken into account,

to an obscure and evidently sexual craving that had found appropriate expression in the visual content of the dream.

4   Some thirty years after he dreamed this, Freud submitted the dream to interpretation. Through the associations he presented, it appears that he revealed both his incestuous wishes toward his mother and his fear of castration as a consequence of sexual excitement aroused by witnessing the primal scene. A related fear was that his mother would bleed and die as a result of sexual relations. The "obscure and evidently sexual craving" giving rise to this dream was, it seems, the essence of Freud's own Oedipus complex. The dream heralded a startlingly new psychological theory.

5   The second dream is from the first chapter of Carl Jung's autobiography, *Memories, Dreams, Reflections*. The earliest dream that Jung remembered was one from between ages three and four, "a dream which was to preoccupy me all my life," he recorded. In the dream, he "was paralyzed with terror" and "awoke sweating and scared to death." It was a dream of encountering a huge phallus standing on a magnificent throne in an underground chamber of hewn stone and hearing his mother's voice call out: "Yes, just look at him. That is the man-eater!" For many nights afterwards the young Jung was afraid to go to sleep. The dream haunted him for years, and in old age he wrote:

> Through this childhood dream I was initiated into the secrets of the earth. What happened then was a kind of burial in the earth, and many years were to pass before I came out again. Today I know that it happened in order to bring the greatest possible amount of light into the darkness. It was an initiation into the realm of darkness. My intellectual life had its unconscious beginnings at that time.

6   The third terrifying dream was recorded in a modern sleep laboratory, and it heralded scientific change in the entire community of dreamworkers. This dream helped to establish the link between rapid eye movements and dreaming—a link that launched the scientific investigation of dreams in the early 1950s. As a graduate student in Nathaniel Kleitman's laboratory at the University of Chicago, Eugene Aserinsky observed the rapid eye movements made by infants during sleep. In pursuing this phenomenon, he attempted to find correlations between these movements and both physiological and psychological functions. He spoke years later about this early period in a follow-up discussion on somnambulism and stated:

> For a long time I was not sure whether those eye movements were associated with dreaming. Finally, one night when the polygraph pens showed deflections indicating either eye movements or instrument generated artifacts, I decided that the time was proper to make a direct visual observation of the subject's eyes. However, all of a sudden the pens practically went wild and almost went off the carriage. Well, I dashed into the sleeping chamber to see what had happened, turned on the lights, and saw the subject, a medical student, lying there, making some mumbling noises while his eyes, although closed, were moving vigorously, violently in all directions. I awakened him and he told me that he had a nightmare from which he felt he couldn't awaken. . . . Well now, this episode more or less

convinced me that dreaming, or at least this nightmare, was associated with rapid eye movements.

7   *Distinguishing Nightmares from Night Terrors*   Based on the pioneering work of Kleitman, Aserinsky, and William Dement, other researchers have established that there are two important and very different phenomena that can wake us in a fright during the night: the *night terror* and the *nightmare*.

8   The night terror is an abrupt awakening early in the night, most often within the first hour or two of sleep, and usually occurring during stage three or four (deep, slow-wave) sleep. This awakening is most often accompanied by sweating, body movements, and a sudden scream or cry for help as the sleeper wakes in terror. Particularly with children, the physical movements may become intense and even continue into a sleepwalking episode. When night terrors were observed in the sleep laboratory, pulse and respiratory rates sometimes doubled during the thirty seconds or so involved in these awakenings. The night terror has been called a *disorder of arousal* and can be considered a minor abnormality in the brain's sleep-wake mechanisms.

9   When asked about the experience, the sleeper either does not remember the night terror or simply recalls waking in fright, heart pounding, and not knowing what to make of it. Occasionally the person will be aware of a single frightening image—"Something was crushing me and I couldn't breathe." The night terror also has been called *pavor nocturnus* or an "incubus attack" because of this sensation of suffocation, as if an incubus—a kind of demon or goblin that was supposed to produce nightmares—was actually sitting on the sleeper's chest. Yet the terrifying episode is generally not described as a dream.

10   The nightmare—sometimes called *REM-nightmare* or *dream anxiety attack*—is a quite different experience from the night terror. Usually occurring late during the night in the last three hours of sleep, the nightmare is a long, frightening dream that awakens the sleeper. Laboratory recordings show that it occurs during REM sleep, often during a long REM period of twenty to thirty minutes. Pulse and blood pressure may show some increase but not as much as in a night terror, and there are neither gross body movements nor sleepwalking, because during REM sleep the arms, legs, and trunk are temporarily paralyzed.

11   The person awakened by a nightmare almost always remembers very distinctly a long, intense, and vivid dream, ending with a frightening sequence. The nightmare is a very detailed, colorful, lifelike dream experience involving some of the earliest, most profound anxieties and the most thoroughly terrifying fears to which we are all subject. The nightmare often includes sensations and perceptions other than vision—even including pain, which is very rarely felt in dreams. For example: "It was a wartime scene. I could *hear* awful noises: bombs bursting around me, screams. Something hit me in the shoulder; I could *feel the pain* and the blood flowing down my arm."

12   When a person reports having frightening sleep interruptions, the answer to one simple question—"Are these experiences dreams?"—usually will indicate whether the events are night terrors or nightmares. The nightmare sufferers will answer, "Yes, of course," whereas those who have night terrors will reply, "Definitely not." They know

what they experience is something other than a dream. The two are very different events physiologically and psychologically and seldom occur in the same individual.

13   An occasional person suffers from what are called hypnagogic nightmares—terrifying nightmarish fantasies experienced upon just falling asleep. Also, some persons have a condition called nocturnal myoclonus—many jerking muscle movements during the night. Sometimes these persons will report a nightmarelike occurrence when awakened by muscle jerks.

14   Lastly, people troubled with chronic post-traumatic stress disorder experience repetitive nightmares depicting the traumatic episode long after the event. These repeated experiences share characteristics of both nightmares and night terrors and may occur in various stages of sleep. Prominent in this group are combat veterans and victims of exceptionally violent accidents or crimes.

15   It is evident from the above descriptions that the experiences of the medical student observed by Eugene Aserinsky in the laboratory, that of the young Carl Jung, and that of the young Sigmund Freud were all true nightmares and not night terrors or other nightmarelike events.

16 NIGHTMARE INCIDENCE   Nightmares are far more common than night terrors. Almost everyone has had a nightmare on occasion, most likely in childhood. Although people tend to forget their childhood nightmares, some have had particularly frequent or especially vivid ones that are remembered clearly throughout their lives.

17   Nightmares are definitely more frequent in children than in adults and are particularly common at ages three through six. Evidence suggests that they probably occur as early as age one. While they become less frequent after age six, their incidence may increase again in adolescence between ages thirteen to eighteen. The incidence of nightmares generally decreases with age and in healthy adults is relatively low.

18   Based on many survey studies, sleep researchers estimate that approximately 50 percent of the adult population have no nightmares at all, though they may have had them as children. Most others remember an occasional nightmare, and the average is perhaps one or two per year. Between 5 and 10 percent of the population report nightmares once a month or more. Only a small percentage have nightmares that are frequent enough or severe enough to be significantly disturbing to their lives. Men are probably as likely to have nightmares as often as women, but they tend to be much more reluctant to mention them.

19 WHAT PRODUCES NIGHTMARES?   For centuries the word *nightmare* has been used loosely to mean anything that wakes one up in fright, a creature that produces such terror, the frightening dream itself, or the actual awakening. Most scholars now agree that the root *mare* derives from the Old English and Old German root *mara*, meaning "an incubus or succubus," and not from *myre*, meaning "a female horse." The folklore of peoples' experiences during the night inspired the eighteenth-century Swiss artist Henry Fuseli to depict both images in his well-known painting *The Nightmare*.

20   We no longer believe that demons or evil spirits produce nightmares, nor is there any solid evidence that eating something disagreeable will cause them. Recent evidence also contradicts another widely held view that a lack of oxygen gives rise to nightmares. Obstructive sleep apnea is a disorder in which air does not get through the throat to the lungs of the sleeper because of some obstruction at the back of the throat. This may happen 100 or more times in one night. The chest and abdomen of the sleeper heave but no air gets through, and after ten to twenty seconds there is a brief awakening, allowing normal breathing to resume. Sleep-apnea sufferers very rarely report nightmares, indicating that a lack of oxygen is not causally related to nightmares.

21   One factor that does appear to precipitate nightmares is physical illness, although it is unclear whether illness itself or the stress that accompanies it is more important. Children who do not otherwise have nightmares report them during times of illness, particularly febrile illness. Adults, too, seem to have more nightmares during high fever or around the time of an operation. In addition, certain neurological disorders sometimes have been associated with nightmares—notably epilepsy and postencephalitic parkinsonism.

22   Mental illness is often associated with nightmares. In certain individuals nightmares occur at the onset of psychosis, especially schizophrenic episodes. Depression can also be associated with an increase of nightmares.

23   Stressful events seem to be causally related to frequent and severe nightmares in susceptible persons. Stressful periods in adulthood, such as times of examinations, job changes, moves, or the loss of significant persons, may produce or increase nightmares.

24   The one generalization that seems to hold true for nightmare sufferers is that their nightmares almost always involve feelings of helplessness, most often helplessness dating from childhood. The most frequent situations in their nightmares involve being chased, attacked, thrown off a cliff, or generally feeling at the mercy of others. Almost invariably it is the dreamer who is in danger and utterly powerless—not someone else. A decrease or sometimes a cessation of adult nightmares usually occurs as the dreamer feels more confident, more mature, and thus less close to the helpless feelings of childhood.

25 **PROFILE OF THE NIGHTMARE SUFFERER**   Recent in-depth studies carried out at Ernest Hartmann's sleep laboratory at the Shattuck Hospital in Boston have provided information about the personalities of people clearly reporting nightmares rather than night terrors. Using newspaper ads, subjects were recruited who had frequent nightmares as a long-term condition. One study examined thirty-eight adults reporting nightmares at least once per week for at least one year and beginning in childhood. A second study compared another twelve frequent nightmare sufferers with twelve people who reported vivid dreams but no nightmares and twelve others who reported neither nightmares nor vivid dreams. All the subjects were interviewed and given a battery of psychological tests including the Rorschach Inkblot Technique and several personality inventories; some were also monitored in the sleep laboratory.

26   Individuals in the nightmare groups from both of these studies were no different in intelligence from those in the comparison groups, and likewise there were no clearcut physical differences in appearance distinguishing the groups. The nightmare subjects were different in having jobs or lifestyles related to the arts or other creative pursuits; they ranged from painters, poets, and musicians to craftspersons, teachers, and nontraditional therapists. No blue-collar workers or white-collar executives or office personnel were found who had frequent nightmares, but there were many such workers in the comparison groups.

27   The artistic and creative interest of the nightmare subjects was a lifelong characteristic. These subjects felt themselves to be in some way unusual for as long as they could remember and often described themselves as sensitive in various ways. Some were sensitive to bright light or loud sound, most could be easily hurt emotionally, and some were quite empathic or sensitive to others' feelings. However, no extreme trauma could be discerned in their histories.

28   More commonly than in the comparison groups, those with nightmares described their adolescence as stormy and difficult, often with bouts of depression and thoughts of suicide. They tended to rebel by using drugs and alcohol, fighting with parents, or running away. From adolescence on, the nightmare sufferers appeared to be extremely open and trusting people—perhaps too trusting, making them defenseless and vulnerable. They often became quickly involved in difficult, entangling friendships and love relationships from which they could not easily escape.

29   However, these nightmare sufferers were *not* especially anxious, angry, or depressed people. Some were vulnerable to mental illness: 70 percent of them had been in psychotherapy, and 15 percent had previously been admitted to mental hospitals; but at the time of the interviews, as a group they were functioning quite well in life.

30   Hartmann and his associates described the creative, sensitive, and vulnerable nightmare subjects as having "thin boundaries" in many different senses. They had thin interpersonal boundaries—that is, they became involved with others very quickly; thin ego boundaries, being extremely aware of their inner wishes and fears; and thin sexual boundaries—they easily imagined being of the opposite sex, and many fantasized or engaged in bisexual activity. They also had thin group boundaries, for they did not strongly identify themselves with a single community or ethnic group. Their sleep-wakefulness boundaries were thin, for they often experienced in-between states of consciousness, unsure whether they were awake, asleep, or dreaming. Some would awaken from one dream only to find themselves in another.

31 **TREATMENT OF NIGHTMARES**   Treatment is not usually required for nightmares. Parents of children ages three through six, when nightmares are most common, should be aware that the occurrence of nightmares is not abnormal. Talking with these children and allowing them to express any fearful feelings may be helpful, as is checking the children's environment at home and school for any potential sources of fear or anxiety.

32   Most of the adult subjects with frequent nightmares in the above-mentioned studies had never sought treatment specifically for their nightmares, though many had sought it for other conditions, such as stress or depression. The majority had accepted their terrifying dreams as part of themselves and sometimes made use of them in their creative endeavors. However, some sufferers wanted treatment specifically for their nightmares. Judging from published accounts of case reports and a few controlled studies, a variety of therapeutic techniques have been used with success.

33   In a recent review of psychological therapies for nightmares, psychologist Gordon Halliday suggested four distress-producing features of the nightmare and proposed that treatment may reduce the distress by altering any of these features: the nightmare's uncontrollability, its perceived sense of reality, the dreadful and anxiety-producing story line, and the nightmare's believed importance. He categorized treatment techniques into these classes: desensitization and related behavioral procedures, psychoanalytic and cathartic techniques, story-line alteration procedures, and "face [the danger] and conquer" *approaches*.

34   Desensitization and related behavioral procedures first identify the fear-generating components of the nightmares and then desensitize the dreamer to those elements through relaxation procedures, invoking pleasant imagery, or repeated exposure of those elements to the dreamer in a therapeutic setting. Psychoanalytic and cathartic techniques attempt to convey to dreamers an understanding of their nightmares in the context of their life situations and developmental histories, to allow suppressed or repressed emotion to be appropriately released, and to strengthen their adaptive mechanisms. Story-line alteration procedures try to change the nightmares through imagination or hypnotic suggestion by rehearsing different endings, confronting the nightmare figures, or modifying some detail. The "face and conquer" approaches consist of instructions to the dreamer to face and confront the nightmare figures when the dreamer is next experiencing an actual nightmare dream state. Several other methods that have been used clinically but not yet reported in the case literature including teaching dreamers, especially children, to call upon a "dream friend" for help and restaging the nightmares in collages or drawings.

35   We are currently investigating a "face and conquer" treatment procedure that attempts to teach frequent nightmare subjects to attain a lucid dream state in order to reduce the frequency and severity of their terrifying dreams. A lucid dream is one in which the sleeper is aware *during the dream* that he or she is dreaming and feels to be in full possession of mental functions as if awake. This awareness permits the dreamer to make choices as the dream occurs. For example, the dreamer may be walking through an unusual landscape, realize that the experience is a dream, and decide to fly into the air to see the dream landscape from a new perspective.

36   In nonlucid dreams, which are more common, there is generally a sense of the dream experience happening *to* the dreamer with little feeling of choice about what occurs. Thus, when confronted by a threatening figure in a nightmare, the dreamer usually tries to run away from it. By becoming lucid in the nightmare, the dreamer could then choose to turn and face the threatening figure and possibly master what is feared.

37   In nearly all of the published reports, clinical accounts, and first-person descriptions of utilizing the lucid dream state to deal with nightmares, the actual dreamers perceived and felt their encounters to be positive, enriching, and empowering experiences both during and after their dreams. However, given that most of these persons are from a normal population, it is possible that these observations may not generalize to a population of frequent nightmare sufferers. Also, though such a treatment has therapeutic potential, it does involve some risk, because there are isolated accounts of negative lucid dream experience.

38   The lucid-dream treatment approach has the potential to alter three of the four distress-producing aspects of the nightmare suggested by Halliday. Once one achieves lucidity within a nightmare, the nightmare's uncontrollability can be altered, because the dreamer can choose and act to change his or her response to the threatening images; the nightmare's perceived sense of reality can be altered, because the dreamer understands that the experience is a dream rather than part of everyday physical external reality; and the nightmare's dreadful and anxiety-producing story line can be altered as a result of the changed response of the dreamer. Other dreamworkers, such as Stephen LaBerge, may contend that the fourth distress-producing aspect, the believed importance of the nightmare, also may be altered, because lucid dreamers "realize that they themselves contain, and thus transcend, the entire dream world and all of its contents, because they know that their imaginations have created the dream."

39   The major limitation cited by Halliday in utilizing the lucid dream state as a treatment modality for nightmares is that it is not yet known how to reliably induce this experience. Psychologist Joseph Dane has developed a posthypnotic suggestion technique for inducing the lucid dream state in hypnotically susceptible women. Using this technique, seven of the eight women in one group of his study succeeded in having verified lucid dreams. This is a promising approach for frequent nightmare sufferers, because there is evidence that they have higher hypnotizability scores than others.

40   Two recent studies indicate that learning lucid dreaming could be a viable treatment method for frequent nightmare sufferers. The first is a study of boundary characteristics by Franklin Galvin, which matched forty spontaneous lucid dreamers with forty frequent nightmare dreamers and forty nonlucid and relatively nightmare-free dreamers (ordinary dreamers). In comparison to the ordinary dreamers, both the lucid dreamers and the nightmare dreamers were shown to have "thin boundaries." In addition, a number of the spontaneous lucid dreamers stated that they had first developed lucidity during frightening dreams.

41   The second is a case study by Andrew Brylowski, which related the treatment of a thirty-five-year-old woman, Ms. D., with a history of major depression and a diagnosis of borderline personality disorder. She reported one to four nightmares per week and had a history of recurrent nightmares of variable frequency and intensity since age ten. The treatment focused on alleviating her nightmares using lucid dreaming. Within the first four weekly sessions, the introduction of lucidity into

the patient's dream life coincided with a decrease in the frequency and intensity of her nightmares.

42   The report of a dream by Ms. D. seven weeks into the treatment illustrates her ability to avert a potential nightmare by using lucidity to convert a threat into a learning experience.

> Ms. D. was walking up huge grey stone stairs leading to a fortress or castle. Looking down she saw a colleague and felt thrilled. The stairs then extended over a moat. She stopped to look at the water and a vicious grey shark with big white teeth surfaced. It propelled itself along the stairs toward her. Ms. D. was frozen with fear and couldn't move. She then realized that she had been having a good dream until the shark appeared; then she thought: "It is a dream!" She was unable to do anything but stare at the shark. The shark changed into a huge whale that smiled and was no longer terrorizing. She awakened in peace.

43   Though she had previously thought of things she might do when she became lucid in a frightening dream, at the moment of fear she could only stare and not run. When she stood her ground and faced the terror rather than attempting to flee, the threatening image was transformed into an acceptable figure positively acknowledging her. Facing the fear in her dream enabled her to wake in peace. Altering her nightmares also facilitated Ms. D. in making positive changes to deal with her waking emotions.

44   The skills Ms. D. learned in lucid dreaming extended into areas of her waking life. After another nine weeks of treatment, she reported a dream in which she was working on a painting with two colors, each scintillating. Upon realizing it was a dream, she created a third color by blending the first two. With this new color she added depth and dimension to the painting. This accomplishment in her dream prompted Ms. D. to complete other art projects in her waking life that she had left unfinished.

45   As Sigmund Freud's nightmare was able to retain "its imperishable value. . . by becoming a driving force in the making of a genius," and as Carl Jung was initiated into the secrets of the earth by a nightmare and later brought light into this realm of darkness, so too have the nightmares of others heralded some meaningful change in their lives. For those with frequent nightmares, the use of the lucid dream state could offer a unique opportunity to begin such a change.

QUESTIONS FOR DISCUSSION

1. How do the authors use the examples of Freud, Jung, and case histories recorded in Nathaniel Kleitman's laboratory as background for their theory about the differences between nightmares and night terrors?

2. How do the authors distinguish the night terror from the nightmare? How are the experiences different psychologically and physiologically? Why do they seldom occur in the same individuals?

3. According to the essay, what causes nightmares in children and adults? Why do adults have fewer nightmares than children?
4. What are the personality traits of the nightmare sufferer and of the night terror sufferer? How have adult sufferers from nightmares been treated effectively?
5. How do the authors define lucid dreaming? How can nightmares become sources of power and creativity?
6. How convincing is the authors' use of research data and accounts of successful treatment programs to support their definitions and theories about nightmares and night terrors? Would any other type of research or experimental data have made the essay clearer and more persuasive?

CONNECTION

Compare the definition and description of nightmares and night terrors presented in this essay with the hallucinatory experiences presented in Charlotte Perkins Gilman's "The Yellow Wallpaper," in this chapter. Does Gilman's narrator seem to be suffering from a repeated nightmare similar to those described in this essay? If so, how could the advice in the essay have helped her?

IDEAS FOR WRITING

1. Develop your journal entry into an essay in which you explore the way your nightmares help to define your inner life and preoccupations.
2. Do some research into a topic discussed in this article: sleep, lucid dreaming, nightmares, or night terrors. Write a definition essay that explores the subject that you have selected to research.

William Styron

The Roots of Depression

William Styron (b. 1925) was born in Newport News, Virginia. He served in the Marine Corps during World War II and received his B.A. from Duke University in 1947. Styron was awarded the Pulitzer Prize in 1968 for The Confessions of Nat Turner, *which he developed from a slave narrative and turned into "a meditation on history." His novel,* Sophie's Choice (1979), *which focuses on the life of a concentration camp survivor, was also made into a film; his most recent book is a collection of stories,* A Tide Water Morning (1993). *Styron's memoir,* Darkness Visible:*

A Memoir Of Madness (1990), is a personal account of his struggle with depression from which the selection below is excerpted.

Do you think that creative/artistic people are more vulnerable to depression than other people?

1   By far the great majority of the people who go through even the severest depression survive it, and live ever afterward at least as happily as their unafflicted counterparts. Save for the awfulness of certain memories it leaves, acute depression inflicts few permanent wounds. There is a Sisyphean torment in the fact that a great number—as many as half—of those who are devastated once will be struck again; depression has the habit of recurrence. But most victims live through even these relapses, often coping better because they have become psychologically tuned by past experience to deal with the ogre. It is of great importance that those who are suffering a siege, perhaps for the first time, be told—be convinced, rather—that the illness will run its course and that they will pull through. A tough job, this; calling "Chin up!" from the safety of the shore to a drowning person is tantamount to insult, but it has been shown over and over again that if the encouragement is dogged enough—and the support equally committed and passionate—the endangered one can nearly always be saved. Most people in the grip of depression at its ghastliest are, for whatever reason, in a state of unrealistic hopelessness, torn by exaggerated ills and fatal threats that bear no resemblance to actuality. It may require on the part of friends, lovers, family, admirers, an almost religious devotion to persuade the sufferers of life's worth, which is so often in conflict with a sense of their own worthlessness, but such devotion has prevented countless suicides.

2   During the same summer of my decline, a close friend of mine—a celebrated newspaper columnist—was hospitalized for severe manic depression. By the time I had commenced my autumnal plunge my friend had recovered (largely due to lithium but also to psychotherapy in the aftermath), and we were in touch by telephone nearly every day. His support was untiring and priceless. It was he who kept admonishing me that suicide was "unacceptable" (he had been intensely suicidal), and it was also he who made the prospect of going to the hospital less fearsomely intimidating. I still look back on his concern with immense gratitude. The help he gave me, he later said, had been a continuing therapy for him, thus demonstrating that, if nothing else, the disease engenders lasting fellowship.

3   After I began to recover in the hospital it occurred to me to wonder—for the first time with any really serious concern—why I had been visited by such a calamity. The psychiatric literature on depression is enormous, with theory after theory concerning the disease's etiology proliferating as richly as theories about the death of the dinosaurs or the origin of black holes. The very number of hypotheses is testimony to the malady's all but impenetrable mystery. As for that initial triggering mechanism—what I have

called the manifest crisis—can I really be satisfied with the idea that abrupt withdrawal from alcohol started the plunge downward? What about other possibilities—the dour fact, for instance, that at about the same time I was smitten I turned sixty, that hulking milestone of mortality? Or could it be that a vague dissatisfaction with the way in which my work was going—the onset of inertia which has possessed me time and time again during my writing life, and made me crabbed and discontented—had also haunted me more fiercely during that period than ever, somehow magnifying the difficulty with alcohol? Unresolvable questions, perhaps.

4   These matters in any case interest me less than the search for earlier origins of the disease. What are the forgotten or buried events that suggest an ultimate explanation for the evolution of depression and its later flowering into madness? Until the onslaught of my own illness and its denouement, I never gave much thought to my work in terms of its connection with the subconscious—an area of investigation belonging to literary detectives. But after I had returned to health and was able to reflect on the past in the light of my ordeal, I began to see clearly how depression had clung close to the outer edges of my life for many years. Suicide has been a persistent theme in my books—three of my major characters killed themselves. In rereading, for the first time in years, sequences from my novels—passages where my heroines have lurched down pathways toward doom—I was stunned to perceive how accurately I had created the landscape of depression in the minds of these young women, describing with what could only be instinct, out of a subconscious already roiled by disturbances of mood, the psychic imbalance that led them to destruction. Thus depression, when it finally came to me, was in fact no stranger, not even a visitor totally unannounced; it had been tapping at my door for decades.

5   The morbid condition proceeded, I have come to believe, from my beginning years—from my father, who battled the gorgon for much of his lifetime, and had been hospitalized in my boyhood after a despondent spiraling downward that in retrospect I saw greatly resembled mine. The genetic roots of depression seem now to be beyond controversy. But I'm persuaded that an even more significant factor was the death of my mother when I was thirteen; this disorder and early sorrow—the death or disappearance of a parent, especially a mother, before or during puberty—appears repeatedly in the literature on depression as a trauma sometimes likely to create nearly irreparable emotional havoc. The danger is especially apparent if the young person is affected by what has been termed "incomplete mourning"—has, in effect, been unable to achieve the catharsis of grief, and so carries within himself through later years an insufferable burden of which rage and guilt, and not only dammed-up sorrow, are a part, and become the potential seeds of self-destruction.

6   In an illuminating new book on suicide, *Self-Destruction in the Promised Land*, Howard I. Kushner, who is not a psychiatrist but a social historian, argues persuasively in favor of this theory of incomplete mourning and uses Abraham Lincoln as an example. While Lincoln's hectic moods of melancholy are legend, it is much less well known that in his youth he was often in a suicidal turmoil and came close more than once to making an attempt on his own life. The behavior seems directly linked to the

death of Lincoln's mother, Nancy Hanks, when he was nine, and to unexpressed grief exacerbated by his sister's death ten years later. Drawing insights from the chronicle of Lincoln's painful success in avoiding suicide, Kushner makes a convincing case not only for the idea of early loss precipitating self-destructive conduct, but also, auspiciously, for that same behavior becoming a strategy through which the person involved comes to grips with his guilt and rage, and triumphs over self-willed death. Such reconciliation may be entwined with the quest for immortality—in Lincoln's case, no less than that of a writer of fiction, to vanquish death through work honored by posterity.

7   So if this theory of incomplete mourning has validity, and I think it does, and if it is also true that in the nethermost depths of one's suicidal behavior one is still subconsciously dealing with immense loss while trying to surmount all the effects of its devastation, then my own avoidance of death may have been belated homage to my mother. I do know that in those last hours before I rescued myself, when I listened to the passage from the *Alto Rhapsody*—which I'd heard her sing—she had been very much on my mind.

8   Near the end of an early film of Ingmar Bergman's, *Through a Glass Darkly*, a young woman, experiencing the embrace of what appears to be profound psychotic depression, has a terrifying hallucination. Anticipating the arrival of some transcendental and saving glimpse of God, she sees instead the quivering shape of a monstrous spider that is attempting to violate her sexually. It is an instant of horror and scalding truth. Yet even in this vision of Bergman (who has suffered cruelly from depression) there is a sense that all of his accomplished artistry has somehow fallen short of a true rendition of the drowned mind's appalling phantasmagoria. Since antiquity—in the tortured lament of Job, in the choruses of Sophocles and Aeschylus—chroniclers of the human spirit have been wrestling with a vocabulary that might give proper expression to the desolation of melancholia. Through the course of literature and art the theme of depression has run like a durable thread of woe—from Hamlet's soliloquy to the verses of Emily Dickinson and Gerard Manley Hopkins, from John Donne to Hawthorne and Dostoevski and Poe, Camus and Conrad and Virginia Woolf. In many of Albrecht Dürer's engravings there are harrowing depictions of his own melancholia; the manic wheeling stars of Van Gogh are the precursors of the artist's plunge into dementia and the extinction of self. It is a suffering that often tinges the music of Beethoven, of Schumann and Mahler, and permeates the darker cantatas of Bach. The vast metaphor which most faithfully represents this fathomless ordeal, however, is that of Dante, and his all-too-familiar lines still arrest the imagination with their augury of the unknowable, the black struggle to come:

Nel mezzo del cammin di nostra vita
Mi ritrovai per una selva oscura,
Ché la diritta via era smarrita.

In the middle of the journey of our life
I found myself in a dark wood,
For I had lost the right path.

9   One can be sure that these words have been more than once employed to conjure the ravages of melancholia, but their somber foreboding has often overshadowed the last lines of the best-known part of that poem, with their evocation of hope. To most of those who have experienced it, the horror of depression is so overwhelming as to be quite beyond expression, hence the frustrated sense of inadequacy found in the work of even the greatest artists. But in science and art the search will doubtless go on for a clear representation of its meaning, which sometimes, for those who have known it, is a simulacrum of all the evil of our world: of our everyday discord and chaos, our irrationality, warfare and crime, torture and violence, our impulse toward death and our flight from it held in the intolerable equipoise of history. If our lives had no other configuration but this, we should want, and perhaps deserve, to perish; if depression had no termination, then suicide would, indeed, be the only remedy. But one need not sound the false or inspirational note to stress the truth that depression is not the soul's annihilation; men and women who have recovered from the disease—and they are countless—bear witness to what is probably its only saving grace: it is conquerable.

10   For those who have dwelt in depression's dark wood, and known its inexplicable agony, their return from the abyss is not unlike the ascent of the poet, trudging upward and upward out of hell's black depths and at last emerging into what he saw as "the shining world." There, whoever has been restored to health has almost always been restored to the capacity for serenity and joy, and this may be indemnity enough for having endured the despair beyond despair.

E quindi uscimmo a riveder le stelle.

And so we came forth, and once again beheld the stars.

QUESTIONS FOR DISCUSSION

1. Why does Styron believe that close friends and relatives are crucial to the recovery of persons suffering from depression?
2. After Styron's battle against depression, what relationship does he come to discover between his writing and his subconscious concerns?
3. What factors contributed to Styron's depression?
4. Why does Styron believe that an ungrieved loss in childhood can be a cause of depression and suicide? Is the example from Lincoln's life effective? Why or why not?
5. What effect does Styron's reference to some of the greatest artists, musicians, scientists, and writers as sufferers of depression have on your understanding of the illness?
6. What does Styron imply that those who suffer from depression learn How is personal depression a reflection of the dark side of human nature and society?

CONNECTION

Compare Styron's account of his descent into madness with that contained in Charlotte Perkins Gilman's "The Yellow Wallpaper." What allowed him to succeed in overcoming insanity while Gilman's narrator seemingly does not?

IDEAS FOR WRITING

1. Write an essay defining the disease of depression. Are there different types of depression? Different theories of its origins?
2. Present a case history of a writer or artist who suffered from depression. How did the depression influence his or her work and personal life?

Edgar Allan Poe

The Tell-Tale Heart

Edgar Allan Poe (1809–1849) is respected internationally as one of the originators of modern story forms, including fantasy, science fiction, horror, and the modern detective story. During his lifetime he was best known as a talented writer of magazine fiction and book reviews. Born to a family of traveling actors and orphaned at two, Poe was adopted along with his sister and raised in the home of a wealthy Virginia merchant, John Allan. His adopted father died in 1834 but left Poe none of his fortune; consequnetly, Poe was forced to try to make a living from his writing and editing of periodicals. Between 1838 and 1846, Poe had his most productive years, publishing Tales of the Grotesque and Arabesque *(1840), in which "The Tell-Tale Heart" is included, and his popular narrative poem, "The Raven" (1845). With the death of his wife in 1847, Poe fell into a depression and wrote little, attempting suicide several times and indulging in heavy drinking. Two years later, Poe died in a delirium on the streets of Baltimore.*

JOURNAL

Write about a repeated nightmare or obsessive fantasy that you have had.

1   True!—nervous—very, very dreadfully nervous I had been and am; but why *will* you say that I am mad? The disease had sharpened my senses—not destroyed—not dulled them. Above all was the sense of hearing acute. I heard all things in the heaven and in the earth. I heard many things in hell. How, then, am I mad? Hearken! and observe how healthily—how calmly I can tell you the whole story.

2   It is impossible to say how first the idea entered my brain; but once conceived, it haunted me day and night. Object there was none. Passion there was none. I loved the old man. He had never wronged me. He had never given me insult. For his gold I had no desire. I think it was his eye! yes, it was this! One of his eyes resembled that of a vulture—a pale blue eye, with a film over it. Whenever it fell upon me, my blood ran cold; and so by degrees—very gradually—I made up my mind to take the life of the old man, and thus rid myself of the eye for ever.

3   Now this is the point. You fancy me mad. Madmen know nothing. But you should have seen *me*. You should have seen how wisely I proceeded—with what caution—with what foresight—with what dissimulation I went to work! I was never kinder to the old man than during the whole week before I killed him. And every night, about midnight, I turned the latch of his door and opened it—oh, so gently! And then, when I had made an opening sufficient for my head, I put in a dark lantern, all closed, closed, so that no light shone out, and then I thrust in my head. Oh, you would have laughed to see how cunningly I thrust it in! I moved it slowly—very, very slowly, so that I might not disturb the old man's sleep. It took me an hour to place my whole head within the opening so far that I could see him as he lay upon his bed. Ha!—would a madman have been so wise as this? And then, when my head was well in the room, I undid the lantern cautiously—oh, so cautiously—cautiously (for the hinges creaked)—I undid it just so much that a single thin ray fell upon the vulture eye. And this I did for seven long nights— every night just at midnight—but I found the eye always closed; and so it was impossible to do the work; for it was not the old man who vexed me, but his Evil Eye. And every morning, when the day broke, I went boldly into the chamber, and spoke courageously to him, calling him by name in a hearty tone, and inquiring how he had passed the night. So you see he would have been a very profound old man, indeed, to suspect that every night, just at twelve, I looked in upon him while he slept.

4   Upon the eighth night I was more than usually cautious in opening the door. A watch's minute hand moves more quickly than did mine. Never before that night had I *felt* the extent of my own powers—of my sagacity. I could scarcely contain my feelings of triumph. To think that there I was, opening the door, little by little, and he not even to dream of my secret deeds or thoughts. I fairly chuckled at the idea; and perhaps he heard me; for he moved on the bed suddenly, as if startled. Now you may think that I drew back—but no. His room was as black as pitch with the thick darkness (for the shutters were close fastened, through fear of robbers), and so I knew that he could not see the opening of the door, and I kept pushing it on steadily, steadily.

5   I had my head in, and was about to open the lantern, when my thumb slipped upon the tin fastening, and the old man sprang up in the bed, crying out—"Who's there?"

6   I kept quite still and said nothing. For a whole hour I did not move a muscle, and in the meantime I did not hear him lie down. He was still sitting up in the bed

listening;—just as I have done, night after night, hearkening to the death watches in the wall.

7   Presently I heard a slight groan, and I knew it was the groan of mortal terror. It was not a groan of pain or of grief—oh, no!—it was the low stifled sound that arises from the bottom of the soul when overcharged with awe. I knew the sound well. Many a night, just at midnight, when all the world slept, it has welled up from my own bosom, deepening, with its dreadful echo, the terrors that distracted me. I say I knew it well. I knew what the old man felt, and pitied him, although I chuckled at heart. I knew that he had been lying awake ever since the first slight noise, when he had turned in the bed. His fears had been ever since growing upon him. He had been trying to fancy them causeless, but could not. He had been saying to himself—"It is nothing but the wind in the chimney—it is only a mouse crossing the floor," or "it is merely a cricket which has made a single chirp." Yes, he has been trying to comfort himself with these suppositions; but he had found all in vain. *All in vain;* because Death, in approaching him, had stalked with his black shadow before him, and enveloped the victim. And it was the mournful influence of the unperceived shadow that caused him to feel—although he neither saw nor heard—to *feel* the presence of my head within the room.

8   When I had waited a long time, very patiently, without hearing him lie down, I resolved to open a little—a very, very little crevice in the lantern. So I opened it— you cannot imagine how stealthily, stealthily—until, at length, a single dim ray, like the thread of a spider, shot from out the crevice and full upon the vulture eye.

9   It was open—wide, wide open—and I grew furious as I gazed upon it. I saw it with perfect distinctness—all a dull blue, with a hideous veil over it that chilled the very marrow in my bones; but I could see nothing else of the old man's face or person: for I had directed the ray as if by instinct, precisely upon the damned spot.

10   And now have I not told you that what you mistake for madness is but over- acuteness of the senses?—now, I say, there came to my ears a low, dull, quick sound, such as a watch makes when enveloped in cotton. I knew *that* sound well too. It was the beating of the old man's heart. It increased my fury, as the beating of a drum stimulates the soldier into courage.

11   But even yet I refrained and kept still. I scarcely breathed. I held the lantern mo- tionless. I tried how steadily I could maintain the ray upon the eye. Meantime the hellish tattoo of the heart increased. It grew quicker and quicker, and louder and louder every instant. The old man's terror *must* have been extreme! It grew louder, I say, louder every moment!—do you mark me well? I have told you that I am ner- vous: so I am. And now at the dead hour of the night, amid the dreadful silence of that old house, so strange a noise as this excited me to uncontrollable terror. Yet, for some minutes longer I refrained and stood still. But the beating grew louder, louder! I thought the heart must burst! And now a new anxiety seized me—the sound would be heard by a neighbor! The old man's hour had come! With a loud yell, I threw open the lantern and leaped into the room. He shrieked once—once only. In an in- stant I dragged him to the floor, and pulled the heavy bed over him. I then smiled

gaily, to find the deed so far done. But, for many minutes, the heart beat on with a muffled sound. This, however, did not vex me; it would not be heard through the wall. At length it ceased. The old man was dead. I removed the bed and examined the corpse. Yes, he was stone, stone dead. I placed my hand upon the heart and held it there many minutes. There was no pulsation. He was stone dead. His eye would trouble me no more.

12   If still you think me mad, you will think so no longer when I describe the wise precautions I took for the concealment of the body. The night waned, and I worked hastily, but in silence. First of all I dismembered the corpse. I cut off the head and the arms and the legs.

13   I then took up three planks from the flooring of the chamber, and deposited all between the scantlings. I then replaced the boards so cleverly, so cunningly, that no human eye—not even *his*—could have detected anything wrong. There was nothing to wash out—no stain of any kind—no blood-spot whatever. I had been too wary for that. A tub had caught all—ha! ha!

14   When I had made an end of these labors, it was four o'clock—still dark as midnight. As the bell sounded the hour, there came a knocking at the street door. I went down to open it with a light heart—for what had I *now* to fear? There entered three men, who introduced themselves, with perfect suavity, as officers of the police. A shriek had been heard by a neighbor during the night; suspicion of foul play had been aroused; information had been lodged at the police office, and they (the officers) had been deputed to search the premises.

15   I smiled—for *what* had I to fear? I bade the gentlemen welcome. The shriek, I said, was my own in a dream. The old man, I mentioned, was absent in the country. I took my visitors all over the house. I bade them search—search *well*. I led them, at length, to *his* chamber. I showed them his treasures, secure, undisturbed. In the enthusiasm of my confidence, I brought chairs into the room, and desired them *here* to rest from their fatigues, while I myself, in the wild audacity of my perfect triumph, placed my own seat upon the very spot beneath which reposed the corpse of the victim.

16   The officers were satisfied. My *manner* had convinced them. I was singularly at ease. They sat, and while I answered cheerily, they chatted familiar things. But, ere long, I felt myself getting pale and wished them gone. My head ached, and I fancied a ringing in my ears: but still they sat and still they chatted. The ringing became more distinct—it continued and became more distinct: I talked more freely to get rid of the feeling: but it continued and gained definitiveness—until, at length, I found that the noise was *not* within my ears.

17   No doubt I now grew *very* pale—but I talked more fluently, and with a heightened voice. Yet the sound increased—and what could I do? It was *a low, dull, quick sound—much such a sound as a watch makes when enveloped in cotton.* I gasped for breath—and yet the officers heard it not. I talked more quickly—more vehemently; but the noise steadily increased. I arose and argued about trifles, in a high key and with violent gesticulations, but the noise steadily increased. Why *would* they not be

gone? I paced the floor to and fro with heavy strides, as if excited to fury by the observation of the men—but the noise steadily increased. Oh God! what *could* I do? I foamed—I raved—I swore! I swung the chair upon which I had been sitting, and grated it upon the boards, but the noise arose over all and continually increased. It grew louder—louder—*louder*! And still the men chatted pleasantly, and smiled. Was it possible they heard not? Almighty God!—no, no! They heard!—they suspected!—they *knew*!—they were making a mockery of my horror!—this I thought, and this I think. But any thing was better than this agony! Any thing was more tolerable than this derision! I could bear those hypocritical smiles no longer! I felt that I must scream or die!—and now—again!—hark! louder! louder! louder! *louder*!—

18   "Villains!" I shrieked, "dissemble no more! I admit the deed!—tear up the planks!—here, here!—it is the beating of his hideous heart!"

QUESTIONS FOR DISCUSSION

1. This is a story about what the French call an *idée fixe*—a fixed idea that takes possession of a person and drives them to an act of madness. How does Poe's plot develop the *idée fixe* of the narrator?
2. One of the pleasures of reading this story by Poe is in the discovery that the narrator, although he thinks himself perfectly sane and rational in his perceptions and decisions, is in fact perfectly mad. Discuss incidents of the distortions in the narrator's perceptions and the irrationality of his decisions that demonstrate his insanity.
3. Poe was a master of the sharply observed descriptive detail. Why does Poe's description of the "evil eye" of the old man seem so compelling? Do you feel the narrator is telling the truth when he blames the eye for his obsession and his crime?
4. Compare the image of the lantern the narrator uses to shine into the old man's room with the "vulture eye" of the man. What effect and significance is achieved by juxtaposing these two "eyes," one mechanical, one natural? What does each come to symbolize?
5. Why is the sound of the old man's heart particularly disturbing to the narrator? How does he describe it, both before and after the killing? Why does he compare its sound to that of a watch?
6. What do you think Poe intended to accomplish by writing this story? What insights does Poe have into the nature of obsessive behavior?

CONNECTION

Compare the *idée fixe* of the narrator in "The Tell-Tale Heart" with that of Charlotte Perkins Gilman's narrator in "The Yellow Wall Paper." How do the characters differ in terms of the causes of and their response to their obsessions?

IDEAS FOR WRITING

1. Write an essay in which you trace the narrator's mental deterioration and descent into madness. How do the descriptive details and metaphors he uses help to reveal his insanity? Why does he go insane?
2. Write a story using a first person narrator who gradually goes insane, although he or she tries to appear to be "in control."

Charlotte Perkins Gilman

The Yellow Wallpaper

A *feminist and economist, Charlotte Perkins Gilman (1860–1935) was born in Hartford, Connecticut, and attended the Rhode Island School of Design. Her best known work is* Women and Economics *(1898); she also wrote* Herland *(1915), a feminist utopia. Gilman's "The Yellow Wallpaper" (1892), which was originally published as a ghost story, became popular with the rebirth of the feminist movement in the 1970s. The story is a fictionalized account of Gilman's severe depression after the birth of her daughter. While "The Yellow Wallpaper" gives us insights into the role of women at the turn of the century, many readers today can still identify with the struggles that the narrator in the story faces.*

JOURNAL

Describe a place about which you have dreamed or fantasized that embodies or symbolizes one of your fears or obsessions.

1   It is very seldom that mere ordinary people like John and myself secure ancestral halls for the summer.

2   A colonial mansion, a hereditary estate, I would say a haunted house and reach the height of romantic felicity—but that would be asking too much of fate!

3   Still I will proudly declare that there is something queer about it.

4   Else, why should it be let so cheaply? And why have stood so long untenanted?

5   John laughs at me, of course, but one expects that.

6   John is practical in the extreme. He has no patience with faith, an intense horror of superstition, and he scoffs openly at any talk of things not to be felt and seen and put down in figures.

7   John is a physician, and *perhaps*—(I would not say it to a living soul, of course, but this is dead paper and a great relief to my mind)—*perhaps* that is one reason I do not get well faster.

8   You see, he does not believe I am sick! And what can one do?

9   If a physician of high standing, and one's own husband, assures friends and relatives that there is really nothing the matter with one but temporary nervous depression—a slight hysterical tendency—what is one to do?

10   My brother is also a physician, and also of high standing, and he says the same thing.

11   So I take phosphates or phosphites—whichever it is—and tonics, and air and exercise, and journeys, and am absolutely forbidden to "work" until I am well again.

12   Personally, I disagree with their ideas.

13   Personally, I believe that congenial work, with excitement and change, would do me good.

14   But what is one to do?

15   I did write for a while in spite of them; but it *does* exhaust me a good deal—having to be so sly about it, or else meet with heavy opposition.

16   I sometimes fancy that in my condition, if I had less opposition and more society and stimulus—but John says the very worst thing I can do is to think about my condition, and I confess it always makes me feel bad.

17   So I will let it alone and talk about the house.

18   The most beautiful place! It is quite alone, standing well back from the road, quite three miles from the village. It makes me think of English places that you read about, for there are hedges and walls and gates that lock, and lots of separate little houses for the gardeners and people.

19   There is a *delicious* garden! I never saw such a garden—large and shady, full of box-bordered paths, and lined with long grape-covered arbors with seats under them.

20   There were greenhouses, but they are all broken now.

21   There was some legal trouble, I believe, something about the heirs and co-heirs; anyhow, the place has been empty for years.

22   That spoils my ghostliness, I am afraid, but I don't care—there is something strange about the house—I can feel it.

23   I even said so to John one moonlight evening, but he said what I felt was a draught, and shut the window.

24   I get unreasonably angry with John sometimes. I'm sure I never used to be so sensitive. I think it is due to this nervous condition.

25   But John says if I feel so I shall neglect proper self-control; so I take pains to control myself—before him, at least, and that makes me very tired.

26   I don't like our room a bit. I wanted one downstairs that opened onto the piazza and had roses all over the window, and such pretty old-fashioned chintz hangings! But John would not hear of it.

27   He said there was only one window and not room for two beds, and no near room for him if he took another.

28   He is very careful and loving, and hardly lets me stir without special direction.

29   I have a schedule prescription of each hour in the day; he takes all care from me, and so I feel basely ungrateful not to value it more.

30   He said he came here solely on my account, that I was to have perfect rest and all the air I could get. "Your exercise depends on your strength, my dear," said he, "and your food somewhat on your appetite; but air you can absorb all the time." So we took the nursery at the top of the house.

31   It is a big, airy room, the whole floor nearly, with windows that look all ways, and air and sunshine galore. It was nursery first, and then playroom and gymnasium, I should judge, for the windows are barred for little children, and there are rings and things in the walls.

32   The paint and paper look as if a boys' school had used it. It is stripped off—the paper—in great patches all around the head of my bed, about as far as I can reach, and in a great place on the other side of the room low down. I never saw a worse paper in my life. One of those sprawling, flamboyant patterns committing every artistic sin.

33   It is dull enough to confuse the eye in following, pronounced enough constantly to irritate and provoke study, and when you follow the lame uncertain curves for a little distance they suddenly commit suicide—plunge off at outrageous angles, destroy themselves in unheard-of contradictions.

34   The color is repellent, almost revolting: a smouldering unclean yellow, strangely faded by the slow-turning sunlight. It is a dull yet lurid orange in some places, a sickly sulphur tint in others.

35   No wonder the children hated it! I should hate it myself if I had to live in this room long.

36   There comes John, and I must put this away—he hates to have me write a word.

37   We have been here two weeks, and I haven't felt like writing before, since that first day.

38   I am sitting by the window now, up in this atrocious nursery, and there is nothing to hinder my writings as much as I please, save lack of strength.

39   John is away all day, and even some nights when his cases are serious.

40   I am glad my case is not serious!

41   But these nervous troubles are dreadfully depressing.

42   John does not know how much I really suffer. He knows there is no reason to suffer, and that satisfies him.

43   Of course it is only nervousness. It does weigh on me so not to do my duty in any way!

44   I meant to be such a help to John, such a real rest and comfort, and here I am a comparative burden already!

45   Nobody would believe what an effort it is to do what little I am able—to dress and entertain, and order things.

46   It is fortunate Mary is so good with the baby. Such a dear baby!

47   And yet I *cannot* be with him, it makes me so nervous.

48   I suppose John never was nervous in his life. He laughs at me so about this wallpaper!

49   At first he meant to repaper the room, but afterward he said that I was letting it get the better of me, and that nothing was worse for a nervous patient than to give way to such fancies.

50 He said that after the wallpaper was changed it would be the heavy bedstead, and then the barred windows, and then that gate at the head of the stairs, and so on.

51 "You know the place is doing you good," he said, "and really, dear, I don't care to renovate the house just for a three months' rental."

52 "Then do let us go downstairs," I said. "There are such pretty rooms there."

53 Then he took me in his arms and called me a blessed little goose, and said he would go down cellar, if I wished, and have it whitewashed into the bargain.

54 But he is right enough about the beds and windows and things.

55 It is as airy and comfortable a room as anyone need wish, and, of course, I would not be so silly as to make him uncomfortable just for a whim.

56 I'm really getting quite fond of the big room, all but that horrid paper.

57 Out of one window I can see the garden—those mysterious deep-shaded arbors, the riotous old-fashioned flowers, and bushes and gnarly trees.

58 Out of another I get a lovely view of the bay and a little private wharf belonging to the estate. There is a beautiful shaded lane that runs down there from the house. I always fancy I see people walking in these numerous paths and arbors, but John has cautioned me not to give way to fancy in the least. He says that with my imaginative power and habit of story-making, a nervous weakness like mine is sure to lead to all manner of excited fancies, and that I ought to use my will and good sense to check the tendency. So I try.

59 I think sometimes that if I were only well enough to write a little it would relieve the press of ideas and rest me.

60 But I find I get pretty tired when I try.

61 It is so discouraging not to have any advice and companionship about my work. When I get really well, John says we will ask Cousin Henry and Julia down for a long visit; but he says he would as soon put fireworks in my pillow-case as to let me have those stimulating people about now.

62 I wish I could get well faster.

63 But I must not think about that. This paper looks to me as if it *knew* what a vicious influence it had!

64 There is a recurrent spot where the pattern lolls like a broken neck and two bulbous eyes stare at you upside down.

65 I get positively angry with the impertinence of it and the everlastingness. Up and down and sideways they crawl, and those absurd unblinking eyes are everywhere. There is one place where two breadths didn't match, and the eyes go all up and down the line, one a little higher than the other.

66 I never saw so much expression in an inanimate thing before, and we all know how much expression they have! I used to lie awake as a child and get more entertainment and terror out of blank walls and plain furniture than most children could find in a toy-store.

67 I remember what a kindly wink the knobs of our big old bureau used to have, and there was one chair that always seemed like a strong friend.

68 I used to feel that if any of the other things looked too fierce I could always hop into that chair and be safe.

69   The furniture in this room is no worse than inharmonious, however, for we had to bring it all from downstairs. I suppose when this was used as a playroom they had to take the nursery things out, and no wonder! I never saw such ravages as the children have made here.

70   The wallpaper, as I said before, is torn off in spots, and it sticketh closer than a brother—they must have had perseverance as well as hatred.

71   Then the floor is scratched and gouged and splintered, the plaster itself is dug out here and there, and this great heavy bed, which is all we found in the room, looks as if it had been through the wars.

72   But I don't mind it a bit—only the paper.

73   There comes John's sister. Such a dear girl as she is, and so careful of me! I must not let her find me writing.

74   She is a perfect and enthusiastic housekeeper, and hopes for no better profession. I verily believe she thinks it is the writing which made me sick!

75   But I can write when she is out, and see her a long way off from these windows.

76   There is one that commands the road, a lovely shaded winding road, and one that just looks off over the country. A lovely country, too, full of great elms and velvet meadows.

77   This wallpaper has a kind of subpattern in a different shade, a particularly irritating one, for you can only see it in certain lights, and not clearly then.

78   But in the places where it isn't faded and where the sun is just so—I can see a strange, provoking, formless sort of figure that seems to skulk about behind that silly and conspicuous front design.

79   There's sister on the stairs!

80   Well, the Fourth of July is over! The people are all gone, and I am tired out. John thought it might do me good to see a little company, so we just had Mother and Nellie and the children down for a week.

81   Of course I didn't do a thing. Jennie sees to everything now.

82   But it tired me all the same.

83   John says if I don't pick up faster he shall send me to Weir Mitchell in the fall.

84   But I don't want to go there at all. I had a friend who was in his hands once, and she says he is just like John and my brother, only more so!

85   Besides, it is such an undertaking to go so far.

86   I don't feel as if it was worthwhile to turn my hand over for anything, and I'm getting dreadfully fretful and querulous.

87   I cry at nothing, and cry most of the time.

88   Of course I don't when John is here, or anybody else, but when I am alone.

89   And I am alone a good deal just now. John is kept in town very often by serious cases, and Jennie is good and lets me alone when I want her to.

90   So I walk a little in the garden or down that lovely lane, sit on the porch under the roses, and lie down up here a good deal.

91   I'm getting really fond of the room in spite of the wallpaper. Perhaps *because* of the wallpaper.

92   It dwells in my mind so!

93   I lie here on this great immovable bed—it is nailed down, I believe—and follow that pattern about by the hour. It is as good as gymnastics, I assure you. I start, we'll say, at the bottom, down in the corner over there where it has not been touched, and I determine for the thousandth time that I *will* follow that pointless pattern to some sort of a conclusion.

94   I know a little of the principle of design, and I know this thing was not arranged on any laws of radiation, or alternation, or repetition, or symmetry, or anything else that I ever heard of.

95   It is repeated, of course, by the breadths, but not otherwise.

96   Looked at in one way, each breadth stands alone; the bloated curves and flourishes—a kind of "debased Romanesque" with dilirium tremens go waddling up and down in isolated columns of fatuity.

97   But, on the other hand, they connect diagonally, and the sprawling outlines run off in great slanting waves of optic horror, like a lot of wallowing seaweeds in full chase.

98   The whole thing goes horizontally, too, at least it seems so, and I exhaust myself trying to distinguish the order of its going in that direction.

99   They have used a horizontal breadth for a frieze, and that adds wonderfully to the confusion.

100   There is one end of the room where it is almost intact, and there, when the crosslights fade and the low sun shines directly upon it, I can almost fancy radiation after all—the interminable grotesque seems to form around a common center and rush off in headlong plunges of equal distraction.

101   It makes me tired to follow it. I will take a nap, I guess.

102   I don't know why I should write this.

103   I don't want to.

104   I don't feel able.

105   And I know John would think it absurd. But I *must* say what I feel and think in some way—it is such a relief!

106   But the effort is getting to be greater than the relief.

107   Half the time now I am awfully lazy, and lie down ever so much. John says I mustn't lose my strength, and has me take cod liver oil and lots of tonics and things, to say nothing of ale and wines and rare meat.

108   Dear John! He loves me very dearly, and hates to have me sick. I tried to have a real earnest reasonable talk with him the other day, and tell him how I wish he would let me go and make a visit to Cousin Henry and Julia.

109   But he said I wasn't able to go, nor able to stand it after I got there; and I did not make out a very good case for myself, for I was crying before I had finished.

110   It is getting to be a great effort for me to think straight. Just this nervous weakness, I suppose.

111   And dear John gathered me up in his arms, and just carried me upstairs and laid me on the bed, and sat by me and read to me till it tired my head.

112   He said I was his darling and his comfort and all he had, and that I must take care of myself for his sake, and keep well.

113   He says no one but myself can help me out of it, that I must use my will and self-control and not let any silly fancies run away with me.

114   There's one comfort—the baby is well and happy, and does not have to occupy this nursery with the horrid wallpaper.

115   If we had not used it, that blessed child would have! What a fortunate escape! Why, I wouldn't have a child of mine, an impressionable little thing, live in such a room for worlds.

116   I never thought of it before, but it is lucky that John kept me here after all; I can stand it so much easier than a baby, you see.

117   Of course I never mention it to them any more—I am too wise—but I keep watch for it all the same.

118   There are things in the wallpaper that nobody knows about but me, or ever will.

119   Behind that outside pattern the dim shapes get clearer every day.

120   It is always the same shape, only very numerous.

121   And it is like a woman stooping down and creeping about behind that pattern. I don't like it a bit. I wonder—I begin to think—I wish John would take me away from here!

122   It is so hard to talk with John about my case, because he is so wise, and because he loves me so.

123   But I tried it last night.

124   It was moonlight. The moon shines in all around just as the sun does.

125   I hate to see it sometimes, it creeps so slowly, and always comes in by one window or another.

126   John was asleep and I hated to waken him, so I kept still and watched the moonlight on that undulating wallpaper till I felt creepy.

127   The faint figure behind seemed to shake the pattern, just as if she wanted to get out.

128   I got up softly and went to feel and see if the paper *did* move, and when I came back John was awake.

129   "What is it, little girl?" he said. "Don't go walking about like that—you'll get cold."

130   I thought it was a good time to talk, so I told him that I really was not gaining here, and that I wished he would take me away.

131   "Why, darling!" said he. "Our lease will be up in three weeks, and I can't see how to leave before."

132   "The repairs are not done at home, and I cannot possibly leave town just now. Of course, if you were in any danger, I could and would, but you really are better, dear, whether you can see it or not. I am a doctor, dear, and I know. You are gaining flesh and color, your appetite is better, I feel really much easier about you."

133   "I don't weigh a bit more," said I, "nor as much; and my appetite may be better in the evening when you are here but it is worse in the morning when you are away!"

134   "Bless her little heart!" said he with a big hug. "She shall be as sick as she pleases! But now let's improve the shining hours by going to sleep, and talk about it in the morning!"

135   "And you won't go away?" I asked gloomily.

136   "Why, how can I, dear? It is only three weeks more and then we will take a nice little trip for a few days while Jennie is getting the house ready. Really, dear, you are better!"

137   "Better in body perhaps—" I began, and stopped short, for he sat up straight and looked at me with such a stern, reproachful look that I could not say another word.

138   "My darling," said he, "I beg you, for my sake and for our child's sake, as well as for your own, that you will never for one instant let that idea enter your mind! There is nothing so dangerous, so fascinating, to a temperament like yours. It is a false and foolish fancy. Can you trust me as a physician when I tell you so?"

139   So of course, I said no more on that score, and we went to sleep before long. He thought I was asleep first, but I wasn't, and lay there for hours trying to decide whether that front pattern and the back pattern really did move together or separately.

140   On a pattern like this, by daylight, there is a lack of sequence, a defiance of law, that is a constant irritant to a normal mind.

141   The color is hideous enough, and unreliable enough, and infuriating enough, but the pattern is torturing.

142   You think you have mastered it, but just as you get well under way in following, it turns a back-somersault and there you are. It slaps you in the face, knocks you down, and tramples upon you. It is like a bad dream.

143   The outside pattern is a florid arabesque, reminding one of a fungus. If you can imagine a toadstool in joints, an interminable string of toadstools, budding and sprouting in endless convolutions—why, that is something like it.

144   That is, sometimes!

145   There is one marked peculiarity about this paper, a thing nobody seems to notice but myself, and that is that it changes as the light changes.

146   When the sun shoots in through the east window—I always watch for that first long, straight ray—it changes so quickly that I never can quite believe it.

147   That is why I watch it always.

148   By moonlight—the moon shines in all night when there is a moon—I wouldn't know it was the same paper.

149   At night in any kind of light, in twilight, candlelight, lamplight, and worst of all by moonlight, it becomes bars! The outside pattern, I mean, and the woman behind it is as plain as can be.

150   I didn't realize for a long time what the thing was that showed behind, that dim subpattern, but now I am quite sure it is a woman.

151   By daylight she is subdued, quiet. I fancy it is the pattern that keeps her so still. It is so puzzling. It keeps me quiet by the hour.

152   I lie down ever so much now. John says it is good for me, and to sleep all I can.

153   Indeed he started the habit by making me lie down for an hour after each meal.

154   It is a very bad habit, I am convinced, for you see, I don't sleep.

155   And that cultivates deceit, for I don't tell them I'm awake—oh, no!

156   The fact is I am getting a little afraid of John.

157   He seems very queer sometimes, and even Jennie has an inexplicable look.

158   It strikes me occasionally, just as a scientific hypothesis, that perhaps it is the paper!

159   I have watched John when he did not know I was looking, and come into the room suddenly on the most innocent excuses, and I've caught him several times *looking at the paper!* And Jennie too. I caught Jennie with her hand on it once.

160   She didn't know I was in the room, and when I asked her in a quiet, a very quiet voice, and the most restrained manner possible, what she was doing with the paper, she turned around as if she had been caught stealing, and looked quite angry—asked me why I should frighten her so!

161   Then she said that the paper stained everything it touched, that she had found yellow smooches on all my clothes and John's and she wishes we would be more careful!

162   Did not that sound innocent? But I know she was studying that pattern, and I am determined that nobody shall find it out but myself!

163   Life is very much more exciting now than it used to be. You see, I have something more to expect, to look forward to, to watch. I really do eat better, and am more quiet than I was.

164   John is so pleased to see me improve! He laughed a little the other day, and said I seemed to be flourishing in spite of my wallpaper.

165   I turned it off with a laugh. I had no intention of telling him it was *because* of the wallpaper—he would make fun of me. He might even want to take me away.

166   I don't want to leave now until I have found it out. There is a week more, and I think that will be enough.

167   I'm feeling so much better!

168   I don't sleep much at night, for it is so interesting to watch developments; but I sleep a good deal during the daytime.

169   In the daytime it is tiresome and perplexing.

170   There are always new shoots on the fungus, and new shades of yellow all over it. I cannot keep count of them, though I have tried conscientiously.

171   It is the strangest yellow, that wallpaper! It makes me think of all the yellow things I ever saw—not beautiful ones like buttercups, but old, foul, bad yellow things.

172   But there is something else about that paper—the smell! I noticed it the moment we came into the room, but with so much air and sun it was not bad. Now we have had a week of fog and rain, and whether the windows are open or not, the smell is here.

173   It creeps all over the house.

174   I find it hovering in the dining-room, skulking in the parlor, hiding in the hall, lying in wait for me on the stairs.

175   It gets into my hair.

176   Even when I go to ride, if I turn my head suddenly and surprise it—there is that smell!

177   Such a peculiar odor, too! I have spent hours in trying to analyze it, to find what it smelled like.

178   It is not bad—at first—and very gentle, but quite the subtlest, most enduring odor I ever met.

179   It used to disturb me at first. I thought seriously of burning the house—to reach the smell.

180   But now I am used to it. The only thing I can think of that it is like is the *color* of the paper! A yellow smell.

181   There is a very funny mark on this wall, low down, near the mopboard. A streak that runs round the room. It goes behind every piece of furniture, except the bed, a long straight, even *smooch*, as if it had been rubbed over and over.

182   I wonder how it was done and who did it, and what they did it for. Round and round and round—round and round and round—it makes me dizzy!

183   I really have discovered something at last.

184   Through watching so much at night, when it changes so, I have finally found out.

185   The front pattern *does* move—and no wonder! The woman behind shakes it!

186   Sometimes I think there are a great many women behind, and sometimes only one, and she crawls around fast, and her crawling shakes it all over.

187   Then in the very bright spots she keeps still, and in the very shady spots she just takes hold of the bars and shakes them hard.

188   And she is all the time trying to climb through. But nobody could climb through that pattern—it strangles so; I think that is why it has so many heads.

189   They get through and then the pattern strangles them off and turns them upside down, and makes their eyes white!

190   If those heads were covered or taken off it would not be half so bad.

191   I think that woman gets out in the daytime!

192   And I'll tell you why—privately—I've seen her!

193   I can see her out of every one of my windows!

194   It is the same woman, I know, for she is always creeping, and most women do not creep by daylight.

195   I see her in that long shaded lane, creeping up and down. I see her in those dark grape arbors, creeping all round the garden.

196   I see her on that long road under the trees, creeping along, and when a carriage
197 comes she hides under the blackberry vines.

       I don't blame her a bit. It must be very humiliating to be caught creeping by daylight!

198   I always lock the door when I creep by daylight. I can't do it at night, for I know John would suspect something at once.

199   And John is so queer now that I don't want to irritate him. I wish he would take another room! Besides, I don't want anybody to get that woman out at night but myself.

200   I often wonder if I could see her out of all the windows at once.

201   But, turn as fast as I can, I can only see out of one at one time.

202   And though I always see her, she *may* be able to creep faster than I can turn! I have watched her sometimes away off in the open country, creeping as fast as a cloud shadow in a wind.

203   If only that top pattern could be gotten off from the under one! I mean to try it, little by little.

204   I have found out another funny thing, but I shan't tell it this time! It does not do to trust people too much.

205   There are only two more days to get this paper off, and I believe John is beginning to notice. I don't like the look in his eyes.

206 And I heard him ask Jennie a lot of professional questions about me. She had a very good report to give.

207 She said I slept a good deal in the daytime.

208 John knows I don't sleep very well at night, for all I'm so quiet!

209 He asked me all sorts of questions too, and pretended to be very loving and kind.

210 As if I couldn't see through him!

211 Still, I don't wonder he acts so, sleeping under this paper for three months.

212 It only interests me, but I feel sure John and Jennie are affected by it.

213 Hurrah! This is the last day, but it is enough. John is to stay in town over night, and won't be out until this evening.

214 Jennie wanted to sleep with me—the sly thing; but I told her I should undoubtedly rest better for a night all alone.

215 That was clever, for really I wasn't alone a bit! As soon as it was moonlight and that poor thing began to crawl and shake the pattern, I got up and ran to help her.

216 I pulled and she shook. I shook and she pulled, and before morning we had peeled off yards of that paper.

217 A strip about as high as my head and half around the room.

218 And then when the sun came and that awful pattern began to laugh at me, I declared I would finish it today!

219 We go away tomorrow, and they are moving all my furniture down again to leave things as they were before.

220 Jennie looked at the wall in amazement, but I told her merrily that I did it out of pure spite at the vicious thing.

221 She laughed and said she wouldn't mind doing it herself, but I must not get tired.

222 How she betrayed herself that time!

223 But I am here, and no person touches this paper but Me—not *alive*!

224 She tried to get me out of the room—it was too patent! But I said it was so quiet and empty and clean now that I believed I would lie down again and sleep all I could, and not to wake me even for dinner—I would call when I woke.

225 So now she is gone, and the servants are gone, and the things are gone, and there is nothing left but that great bedstead nailed down, with the canvas mattress we found on it.

226 We shall sleep downstairs tonight, and take the boat home tomorrow.

227 I quite enjoy the room, now it is bare again.

228 How those children did tear about here!

229 This bedstead is fairly gnawed!

230 But I must get to work.

231 I have locked the door and thrown the key down into the front path.

232 I don't want to go out, and I don't want to have anybody come in, till John comes.

233 I want to astonish him.

234 I've got a rope up here that even Jennie did not find. If that woman does get out, and tries to get away, I can tie her!

235 But I forgot I could not reach far without anything to stand on!

236 This bed will *not* move!

237 I tried to lift and push it until I was lame, and then I got so angry I bit off a little piece at one corner—but it hurt my teeth.

238 Then I peeled off all the paper I could reach standing on the floor. It sticks horribly and the pattern just enjoys it! All those strangled heads and bulbous eyes and waddling fungus growths just shriek with derision!

239 I am getting angry enough to do something desperate. To jump out of the window would be admirable exercise, but the bars are too strong even to try.

240 Besides I wouldn't do it. Of course not. I know well enough that a step like that is improper and might be misconstrued.

241 I don't like to *look* out of the windows even—there are so many of those creeping women, and they creep so fast.

242 I wonder if they all come out of that wallpaper as I did!

243 But I am securely fastened now by my well-hidden rope—you don't get *me* out in the road there!

244 I suppose I shall have to get back behind the pattern when it comes night, and that is hard!

245 It is so pleasant to be out in this great room and creep around as I please!

246 I don't want to go outside. I won't, even if Jennie asks me to.

247 For outside you have to creep on the ground, and everything is green instead of yellow.

248 But here I can creep smoothly on the floor, and my shoulder just fits in that long smooch around the wall, so I cannot lose my way.

249 Why, there's John at the door!

250 It is no use, young man, you can't open it!

251 How he does call and pound!

252 Now he's crying to Jennie for an axe.

253 It would be a shame to break down that beautiful door!

254 "John, dear!" said I in the gentlest voice. "The key is down by the front steps, under a plantain leaf!"

255 That silenced him for a few moments.

256 Then he said, very quietly indeed, "Open the door, my darling!"

257 "I can't," said I. "The key is down by the front door under a plantain leaf!" And then I said it again, several times, very gently and slowly, and said it so often that he had to go and see, and he got it of course, and came in. He stopped short by the door.

258 "What is the matter?" he cried. "For God's sake, what are you doing!"

259 I kept on creeping just the same, but I looked at him over my shoulder.

260 "I've got out at last," said I, "in spite of you and Jane. And I've pulled off most of the paper, so you can't put me back!"

261 Now why should that man have fainted? But he did, and right across my path by the wall, so that I had to creep over him every time!

Activity:
The drawings that follow were created by students using a computer drawing program. The students were asked to draw an image of the yellow wallpaper that for

them was representative of the story's meaning. Try doing your own drawing of the wallpaper and write a paragraph explaining your response.

Vera Shimsky

My picture of "The Yellow Wallpaper" is a rather literal representation of the wallpaper as described in the story. The woman behind the bars is both the women imagined by the narrator and the narrator herself. She is shaking the bars, just as in the story, the narrator and the woman in the wallpaper try to free the woman from the image she has to put on for society, the bars on the wallpaper. Imagine a greenish tint to the wallpaper as the different view of it that comes with the change of the time of day. This tint is one of the things the narrator hates most about the paper. The upside-down faces with the eyes are portrayed here as circles with two glowing spots—the eyes.

Drawing this picture helped me understand even more intimately how much the narrator is the woman behind the wallpaper. In fact, the entire process of her growing more and more connected with the paper demonstrates the deterioration of her mental state. The eyes that stare at her from the wallpaper are the eyes of her husband and Jennie, as well as the rest of society who are watching her and observing whether or not she is improving. The confusing pattern of the wallpaper that the narrator cannot seem to figure out or follow all the way through represents the confusion and the struggle within her mind. The bars are what she is struggling against, both her mental condition and the pressures of the society put upon her that, instead of helping her, are making her worse. Having to visualize the wallpaper and put it into an image helped me transcend the story into a true understanding of the narrator's state of mind.

Shanney Yu

"The Yellow Wallpaper" is a story about one woman's struggle with postpartum depression. She is confined to a bedroom in order to regain her strength. The yellow wallpaper in this bedroom becomes the focal point of her attentions as its convoluted pattern slowly drives her to the brink of insanity.

The narrator describes the design of the wallpaper:

> Looked at in one way, each breadth stands alone; the bloated curves and flourishes—a kind of "debased Romanesque" with delirium tremens go waddling up and down in isolated columns of fatuity . . . they connect diagonally . . . in great slanting waves of optic horror . . . . The whole thing goes horizontally, too . . . and I exhaust myself trying to distinguish the order of its going in that direction.

The narrator is also convinced that the twisted design of the wallpaper is the prison of one or more women. She feels as if the eyes of these women follow her every move. ". . . those absurd unblinking eyes are everywhere . . . I can see a strange, provoking, formless sort of figure that seems to skulk about behind that sill and conspicuous front design."

I tried to incorporate all of these elements into my drawing. I started by drawing vertical bars that run across the entire drawing, creating a sort of prison effect. In the tangled web of the pattern, I drew two "unblinking" eyes. The swirls around the eyes make up the face of a trapped woman and the swirls beneath this face are her arms. Her hands grasp the bars as she struggles to be freed. The circular swirls I drew next serve two purposes: to make the design all the more hypnotic as well as to represent the other "unblinking" eyes that taunt the narrator.

QUESTIONS FOR DISCUSSION

1. Why are John and the narrator spending their summer at the colonial mansion? In what ways are the room's former function, the peculiarities of its location and decoration, and the objects left behind in it significant to the story's meaning? What is causing the narrator to be sick?
2. Characterize John and then contrast him to the narrator. Who is in control? Why? How does their relationship change as the story develops?
3. Why doesn't John think that the narrator should write? Why does she want to write?
4. Describe the yellow wallpaper. Why does it fascinate the narrator? Why and how does the yellow wallpaper change? What do the wallpaper and its changes signify about the narrator? How do you feel about the narrator's response to the yellow wallpaper? Can you identify with her struggle and her obsession with it?
5. Why does John faint in the final scene? Is this scene comic or tragic? Do you assume that the narrator is insane or on the verge of an important discovery. What do you think will happen to the narrator? What perspectives on the causes of mental illness does this story present?
6. Do you think the story makes a feminist statement? Why or why not?

CONNECTION

Compare the narrator's obsession with the wallpaper and the trapped women behind it to Anne Lamott's obsession with thinness and eating in "Hunger." Which work takes a more feminist position in response to the obsession and its transformation into meaningful action?

IDEAS FOR WRITING

1. Write an essay in which you discuss the relevance of several issues presented in the story about the ways that men and women communicate with one another or try to control one another's behavior.
2. Write an essay in which you discuss the symbol of the wallpaper in the story, taking into consideration the student drawings and interpretations on pages 270-271.

Alice Walker

Beauty: When the Other Dancer Is the Self

Born in Eatonton, Georgia, Alice Walker (b. 1944) attended Spelman College for one year and completed a B.A. at Sara Lawrence College in 1967. Walker was involved with the civil rights movement of the 1960s and has lived for many years in San Francisco and in rural Mendocino County in Northern California. Walker's writing explores the concerns of African- American and African women, as well as ecological and spiritual concerns. Her novel The Color Purple *(1982) won the Pulitzer Prize and was made into a film by Steven Speilberg. Other works by Walker include* In Love & Trouble: Stories of Black Women *(1973),* Living by the Word: Selected Writings, 1973–1987 *(1988),* The Temple of My Familiar *(1989),* Anything We Love Can Be Saved: A Writer's Activism *(1997), and* By the Light Of My Father's Smile: A Novel *(1998). The following selection, "Beauty: When the Other Dancer Is the Self," which is collected in* In Search of Our Mothers' Gardens *(1983), focuses on an accident that caused the loss of her eyesight in one eye and led to an obsession with her appearance, loss of self-esteem, and ultimately to a deeper sense of self-awareness.*

JOURNAL

Discuss a time when you were obsessed with your appearance or when someone you knew had such an obsession.

1   It is a bright summer day in 1947. My father, a fat, funny man with beautiful eyes and a subversive wit, is trying to decide which of his eight children he will take with him to the country fair. My mother, of course, will not go. She is knocked out from getting most of us ready: I hold my neck stiff against the pressure of her knuckles as she hastily completes the braiding and then beribboning
2   of my hair.

   My father is the driver for the rich old white lady up the road. Her name is Miss Mey. She owns all the land for miles around, as well as the house in which we live. All I remember about her is that she once offered to pay my mother thirty-five cents for cleaning her house, raking up piles of her magnolia leaves, and washing her family's clothes, and that my mother—she of no money, eight children, and a chronic earache—refused it. But I do not think of this in 1947. I am two and a half years old. I want to go everywhere my daddy goes. I am excited at the prospect of riding in a car. Someone has told me fairs are fun. That there is room in the car for only three of us doesn't faze me at all. Whirling happily in my starchy frock, showing off my biscuit-polished patent-leather shoes and lavender socks, tossing my head in a way that makes my ribbons bounce, I stand, hands on hips, before my father. "Take me, Daddy," I say with assurance; "I'm the prettiest!"

3   Later, it does not surprise me to find myself in Miss Mey's shiny black car, sharing the back seat with the other lucky ones. Does not surprise me that I thoroughly enjoy the fair. At home that night I tell the unlucky ones all I can remember about the merry-go-round, the man who eats live chickens, and the

teddy bears, until they say: that's enough, baby Alice. Shut up now, and go to sleep.

4   It is Easter Sunday, 1950. I am dressed in a green, flocked, scalloped-hem dress (handmade by my adoring sister, Ruth) that has its own smooth satin petticoat and tiny hot-pink roses tucked into each scallop. My shoes, new T-strap patent leather, again highly biscuit-polished. I am six years old and have learned one of the longest Easter speeches to be heard that day, totally unlike the speech I said when I was two: "Easter lilies / pure and white / blossom in / the morning light." When I rise to give my speech I do so on a great wave of love and pride and expectation. People in the church stop rustling their new crinolines. They seem to hold their breath. I can tell they admire my dress, but it is my spirit, bordering on sassiness (womanishness), they secretly applaud.

5   "That girl's a little *mess,*" they whisper to each other, pleased.

6   Naturally I say my speech without stammer or pause, unlike those who stutter, stammer, or, worst of all, forget. This is before the word "beautiful" exists in people's vocabulary, but "Oh, isn't she the *cutest* thing!" frequently floats my way. "And got so much sense!" they gratefully add. . . for which thoughtfull addition I thank them to this day.

7   *It was great fun being cute. But then, one day, it ended.*

8   I am eight years old and a tomboy. I have a cowboy hat, cowboy boots, check-ered shirt and pants, all red. My playmates are my brothers, two and four years older than I. Their colors are black and green, the only difference in the way we are dressed. On Saturday nights we all go to the picture show, even my mother; Westerns are her favorite kind of movie. Back home, "on the ranch," we pretend we are Tom Mix, Hopalong Cassidy, Lash LaRue (we've even named one of our dogs Lash LaRue); we chase each other for hours rustling cattle, being outlaws, delivering damsels from distress. Then my parents decide to buy my brothers guns. These are not "real" guns. They shoot "BBs," copper pellets my brothers say will kill birds. Because I am a girl, I do not get a gun. Instantly I am relegated to the position of Indian. Now there appears a great distance between us. They shoot and shoot at everything with their new guns. I try to keep up with my bow and arrows.

9   One day while I am standing on top of our makeshift "garage"—pieces of tin nailed across some poles—holding my bow and arrow and looking out towards the fields, I feel an incredible blow in my right eye. I look down just in time to see my brother lower his gun.

10   Both brothers rush to my side. My eye stings, and I cover it with my hand. "If you tell," they say, "we will get a whipping. You don't want that to happen do you?" I do not. "Here is a piece of wire," says the older brother, picking it up from the roof; "say you stepped on one end of it and the other flew up and hit you." The pain is begin-ning to start. "Yes," I say. "Yes, I will say that is what happened." If I do not say this

is what happened, I know my brothers will find ways to make me wish I had. But now I will say anything that gets me to my mother.

11 Confronted by our parents we stick to the lie agreed upon. They place me on a bench on the porch and I close my left eye while they examine the right. There is a tree growing from underneath the porch that climbs past the railing to the roof. It is the last thing my right eye sees. I watch as its trunk, its branches, and then its leaves are blotted out by the rising blood.

12 I am in shock. First there is intense fever, which my father tries to break using lily leaves bound around my head. Then there are chills: my mother tries to get me to eat soup. Eventually, I do not know how, my parents learn what has happened. A week after the "accieent" they take me to see a doctor. "Why did you wait so long to come?" he asks, looking into my eye and shaking his head. "Eyes are sympathetic," he says. "If one is blind, the other will likely become blind too."

13 This comment of the doctor's terrifies me. But it is really how I look that bothers me most. Where the BB pellet struck there is a glob of whitish scar tissue, a hideous cataract, on my eye. Now when I stare at people—a favorite pastime, up to now— they will stare back. Not at the "cute" little girl, but at her scar. For six years I do not stare at anyone, because I do not raise my head.

14 Years later, in the throes of a mid-life crisis, I ask my mother and sister whether I changed after the "accident." "No," they say, puzzled, "What do you mean?"

15 *What do I mean?*

16 I am eight, and, for the first time, doing poorly in school, where I have been something of a whize since I was four. We have just moved to the place where the "accident" occurred. We do not know any of the people around us because this is a different county. The only time I see the friends I knew is when we go back to our old church. The new school is the former state penitentiary. It is a large stone building, cold and drafty, crammed to overflowing with boisterous, ill-disciplined children. On the third floor there is a huge circular imprint of some partition that has been torn out.

17 "What used to be here?" I ask a sullen girl next to me on our way past it to lunch.

18 "The electric chair," says she.

19 At night I have nightmares about the electric chair, and about all the people reputedly "fried" in it. I am afraid of the school, where all the students seem to be budding criminals.

20 "What's the matter with your eye?" they ask, critically.

21 When I don't answer (I cannot decide whether it was an "accident" or not), they shove me, insist on a fight.

22 My brother, the one who created the story about the wire, comes to my rescue. But then brags so much about "protecting" me, I become sick.

23 After months of torture at the school, my parents decide to send me back to our old community, to my old school. I live with my grandparents and the teacher they board. But there is no room for Phoebe, my cat. By the time my grandparents decide

there is room, and I ask for my cat, she cannot be found. Miss Yarborough, the boarding teacher, takes me under her wing, and begins to teach me to play the piano. But soon she marries an African—a "prince," she says—and is whisked away to his continent.

24   At my old school there is at least one teacher who loves me. She is the teacher who "knew me before I was born" and bought my first baby clothes. It is she who makes life bearable. It is her presence that finally helps me turn on the one child at the school who continually calls me "one-eyed bitch." One day I simply grab him by his coat and beat him until I am satisfied. It is my teacher who tells me my mother is ill.

25   My mother is lying in bed in the middle of the day, something I have never seen. She is in too much pain to speak. She has an abscess in her ear. I stand looking down on her, knowing that if she dies, I cannot live. She is being treated with warm oils and hot bricks held against her cheek. Finally a doctor comes. But I must go back to my grandparents' house. The weeks pass but I am hardly aware of it. All I know is that my mother might die, my father is not so jolly, my brothers still have their guns, and I am the one sent away from home.

26   "You did not change," they say.

27   *Did I imagine the anguish of never looking up?*

28   I am twelve. When relatives come to visit I hide in my room. My cousin Brenda, just my age, whose father works in the post office and whose mother is a nurse, comes to find me. "Hello," she says. And then she asks, looking at my recent school picture, which I did not want taken, and on which the "glob," as I think of it, is clearly visible, "You still can't see out of that eye?"

29   "No," I say, and flop back on the bed over my book.

30   That night, as I do almost every night, I abuse my eye. I rant and rave at it, in front of the mirror. I plead with it to clear up before morning. I tell it I hate it and despise it. I do not pray for sight. I pray for beauty.

31   "You did not change," they say.

32   I am fourteen and baby-sitting for my brother Bill, who lives in Boston. He is my favorite brother and there is a strong bond between us. Understanding my feelings of shame and ugliness he and his wife take me to a local hospital, where the "glob" is removed by a doctor named O. Henry. There is still a small bluish crater where the scar tissue was, but the ugly white stuff is gone. Almost immediately I become a different person from the girl who does not raise her head. Or so I think. Now that I've raised my head I win the boyfriend of my dreams. Now that I've raised my head I have plenty of friends. Now that I've raised my head classwork comes from my lips as faultlessly as Easter speeches did, and I leave high school as valedictorian, most popular student, and *queen,* hardly believing my luck. Ironically, the girl who was voted most beautiful in our class (and was) was later shot twice through the chest by a male companion, using a "real" gun, while she was pregnant. But that's another story in itself. Or is it?

33   "You did not change," they say.

34   It is now thirty years since the "accident." A beautiful journalist comes to visit and to interview me. She is going to write a cover story for her magazine that focuses on my latest book. "Decide how you want to look on the cover," she says. "Glamorous, or whatever."

35   Never mind "glamorous," it is the "whatever" that I hear. Suddenly all I can think of is whether I will get enough sleep the night before the photography session: if I don't my eye will be tired and wander, as blind eyes will.

36   At night in bed with my lover I think up reasons why I should not appear on the cover of a magazine. "My meanest critics will say I've sold out," I say. "My family will now realize I write scandalous books."

37   "But what's the real reason you don't want to do this?" he asks.

38   "Because in all probability," I say in a rush, "my eye won't be straight."

39   "It will be straight enough," he says. Then, "Besides, I thought you'd made your peace with that."

40   And I suddenly remember that I have.

41   I *remember*:

42   I am talking to my brother Jimmy, asking if he remembers anything unusual about the day I was shot. He does not know I consider that day the last time my father, with his sweet home remedy of cool lily leaves, chose me, and that I suffered and raged inside because of this. "Well," he says, "all I remember is standing by the side of the highway with Daddy, trying to flag down a car. A white man stopped, but when Daddy said he needed somebody to take his little girl to the doctor, he drove off."

43   I *remember*:

44   I am in the desert for the first time. I fall totally in love with it. I am so overwhelmed by its beauty, I confront for the first time, consciously, the meaning of the doctor's words years ago: "Eyes are sympathetic. If one is blind, the other will likely become blind too." I realize I have dashed about the world madly, looking at this, looking at that, storing up images against the fading of the light. *But I might have missed seeing the desert!* The shock of that possibility—and gratitude for over twenty-five years of sight—sends me literally to my knees. Poem after poem comes—which is perhaps how poets pray.

   ### On Sight
   I am so thankful I have seen
   The Desert
   And the creatures in the desert
   And the desert Itself.

5 The desert has its own moon
   Which I have seen
   With my own eye.

There is no flag on it.

Trees of the desert have arms
10 All of which are always up
   That is because the moon is up
   The sun is up
   Also the sky
   The stars
15 Clouds
   None with flags.

If there *were* flags, I doubt
the trees would point.
Would you?

45   *But mostly, I remember this:*

46   I am twenty-seven, and my baby daughter is almost three. Since her birth I have worried about her discovery that her mother's eyes are different from other people's. Will she be embarrassed? I think. What will she say? Eery day she watches a television program called "Big Blue Marble." It begins with a picture of the earth as it appears from the moon. It is bluish, a little battered-looking, but full of light, with whitish clouds swirling around it. Every time I see it I weep with love, as if it is a picture of Grandma's house. One day when I am putting Rebecca down for her nap, she suddenly focuses on my eye. Something inside me cringes, gets ready to try to protect myself. All children are cruel about physical differences, I know from experience, and that they don't always mean to be is another matter. I assume Rebecca will be the same.

47   But no-o-o-o. She studies my face intently as we stand, her inside and me outside her crib. She even holds my face maternally between her dimpled little hands. Then, looking every bit as serious and lawyerlike as her father, she says, as if it may just possibly have slipped my attention: "Mommy, there's a *world* in your eye." (As in, "Don't be alarmed, or do anything crazy.") And then, gently, but with great interest: "Mommy, where did you *get* that world in your eye?"

48   For the most part, the pain left then. (So what, if my brothers grew up to buy even more powerful pellet guns for their sons and to carry real guns themselves. So what, if a young "Morehouse man" once nearly fell off the steps of Trevor Arnett Library because he thought my eyes were blue.) Crying and laughing I ran to the bathroom, while Rebecca mumbled and sang herself off to sleep. Yes indeed, I realized, looking into the mirror. There *was* a world in my eye. And I saw that it was possible to love it: that in fact, for all it had taught me of shame and anger and inner vision, I *did* love it. Even to see it drifting out of orbit in boredom, or rolling up out of fatigue, not to mention floating back at attention in excitement (bearing witness, a friend has called it), deeply suitable to my personality, and even characteristic of me.

49   That night I dream I am dancing to Stevie Wonder's song "Always" (the name of the song is really "As," but I hear it as "Always"). As I dance, whirling and joyous, happier than I've ever been in my life, another bright-faced dancer joins me. We

dance and kiss each other and hold each other through the night. The other dancer has obviously come through all right, as I have done. She is beautiful, whole and free. And she is also me.

QUESTIONS FOR DISCUSSION

1. Why does Walker keep the facts about her accident secret? What are the most painful parts of Walker's adjustment to living with her damaged "glob" eye?
2. Why doesn't Walker's family believe that Alice was changed by the accident? Do you think that they are right?
3. In what ways is Walker's painful adjustment related to her transformation into an adolescent? How does Walker change when the "glob" is removed from her eye?
4. Why does Walker fall in love with the desert? In what ways does the meaning of the poem "On Sight" support the themes of the essay?
5. How does Walker's daughter help her to make peace with her damaged eye? What does her daughter mean when she says, "Mommy, there's a world in your eye?"
6. Explain the meaning of the essay's title. How has Walker's understanding and definition of beauty changed through her experiences? What part of herself has she come to accept?

CONNECTION

Compare Walker's self-transforming experience at the end of this essay with Anne Lamott's in "Hunger."

IDEAS FOR WRITING

1. Write an essay or a short story that presents your definition of beauty.
2. Like Walker, write about a realization that helped you to accept a part of yourself that you had previously been ashamed of.

Anne Lamott

"Hunger"

Anne Lamott (b. 1954) grew up in Marin County, north of San Francisco, where she still lives. After attending two years of Goucher College from 1971–1973, Lamott began her career as a writer. To help support herself, she has also worked as an editor, a restaurant critic, a lecturer, and writing teacher. Hard Laughter *(1980), about her father's struggle with brain cancer, was her first widely acclaimed book.* Operating Instructions: A Journal of My Son's First Year *(1993), humorously presents her experiences adjusting to her new life as a single mother. In* Bird by Bird *(1994) Lamott explores the crucial human connections between writing and life. In 1997 Lamott's novel,* Crooked Little Heart, *became a best seller immediately after its publication. The following selection, "Hunger," about her personal obsession with food and eating, is from her most recent collection of essays,* Traveling Mercies *(l998).*

JOURNAL

Explore your thoughts and feelings about eating disorders. You might want to write about the causes or the effects or your observations of people who have had eating disorders.

1 This is the story of how, at the age of thirty-three, I learned to feed myself.

2 To begin with, here's what I did until then: I ate, starved, binged, purged, grew fat, grew thin, grew fat, grew thin, binged, purged, dieted, was good, was bad, grew fat, grew thin, grew thinner.

3 I had been a lean and energetic girl, always hungry, always eating, always thin. But I weighed 100 pounds at thirteen, 130 at fourteen. For the next ten years, I dieted. It is a long, dull story. I had lots of secrets and worries about me and food and my body. It was very scary and obsessive, the way it must feel for someone who is secretly and entirely illiterate.

4 One week after my father was diagnosed with brain cancer, I discovered bulimia. I felt like I'd discovered the secret to life, because you could eat yourself into a state of emotional numbness but not gain weight. Then I learned how to do it more effectively by reading articles in women's magazines on how to stop doing it. I barfed, but preferred laxatives. It was heaven: I lost weight.

5 All right, OK: there were some problems. I was scared all the time, full of self-loathing, and my heart got funky. When you've lost too much water and electrolytes, your muscular heart cramps up; it races like a sewing machine. Sometimes it would skip beats, and other times there would be a terrible feeling of vacuum, as if there were an Alhambra water tank in my heart and a big bubble had just burbled to the surface.

6 I would try to be good, in the puritanical sense, which meant denying my appetites. Resisting temptation meant I was good—strong, counter-animal—and I'd manage to resist fattening foods for a while. But then the jungle drums would start beating again.

7   I looked fine on the outside: thin, cheerful, even successful. But on the inside, I was utterly obsessed. I went into a long and deep depression after seeing some photos of people on a commune, working with their hands and primitive tools and workhorses, raising healthy food. I could see that they were really tuned to nature, to the seasons, to a direct sense of bounty, where you plant something and it grows and you cut it down or pick it and eat it, savoring it and filling up on it. But I was a spy in the world of happy eating, always hungry, or stuffed, but never full.

8   Luckily I was still drinking at the time.

9   But then all of a sudden I wasn't. When I quit in 1986, I started getting healthier in almost every way and I had all these women helping me, and I told them almost every crime and secret I had, because I believed them when they said that we are as sick as our secrets. My life got much sweeter right away, and less dramatic; the pond inside me began to settle, and I could see through the water, which was the strangest sensation because for all those years I'd been taking various sticks—desperate men, financial drama, impossible deadlines—and stirring that pond water up. So now I was noticing beautiful little fish and dreamy underwater plants, and shells lying in the sand. I started getting along with myself pretty well for the first time in my life. But I couldn't or wouldn't tell anyone that for the last ten years I had been bingeing and purging, being on a diet, being good, getting thin, being bad, getting fat.

10   I remember hanging out with these people, letting their stories wash over me, when all of a sudden the thing inside would tap me on the shoulder and whisper, "OK, honey, let's go." And I'd cry out inwardly, No! No! "Sorry," it would say, "time to go shopping." And silently I'd cry out, Please don't make me go shopping! I'm not even hungry! "Shh, shh," it would whisper, "Let's go."

11   I felt that when I got sober, God had saved me from drowning, but now I was going to get kicked to death on the beach. It's so much hipper to be a drunk than a bulimic. Drunks are like bikers or wrestlers; bulimics are baton twirlers, gymnasts. The voice would say how sorry it was, but then glance down at its watch, tap its foot and sigh, and I'd sigh loudly too, and get up, and trudge behind it to the store.

12   It was actually more painful than that. It reminded me of the scene in Kazantzakis's *The Last Temptation of Christ*, when Jesus is walking along in the desert, really wanting to spend his life in a monastery praying, secluded and alone with God. Only of course God has different plans for him and, to get his attention, sends eagles down to wrap their talons around Jesus' heart, gripping him so that he falls to the sand in pain.

13   I did not feel eagle talons, but I felt gripped in the heart by a presence directing me to do exactly what it said. It said it was hungry and we had to go to the store.

14   So that voice and I would go buy the bad things—the chocolates, the Chee•tos, the Mexican food—and big boxes of Epsom salts and laxatives. I grew weaker and more desperate until finally, one day in 1987, I called a woman named Rita Groszmann, who was listed in the Yellow Pages as a specialist in eating disorders. I told

her what was going on and that I had no money, and she said to come in anyway, because she was afraid I was going to die. So I went in the next day.

15   I sat in her office and explained how I'd gotten started and that I wasn't ready to stop but that I was getting ready to be ready to stop. She said that was fine. I said that in fact I was going to go home that very night and eat chocolates and Mexican food and then purge. She said fine. I said, "Don't try to stop me." She said, "OK." I said, "There's nothing you can do to stop me, it's just the way it is," and we did this for half an hour or so, until she finally said very gently that she was not going to try to take my bulimia away from me. That she in fact was never going to take anything away from me, because I would try to get it back. But she said that I had some choices.

16   They were ridiculous choices. She proposed some, and I thought, This is the angriest person I've ever met. I'll give you a couple of examples. If I was feeling lonely and overwhelmed and about to binge, she said I could call someone up and ask them if they wanted to meet me for a movie. "Yeah," I said, "right." Or here's another good one: If I was feeling very *other*, sad and scared and overwhelmed, I could invite someone over for a meal, and then see if he or she felt like going for a walk. It is only because I was raised to be Politeness Person that I did not laugh at her. It was like someone detoxing off heroin, who's itching to shoot up, being told to take up macramé.

17   She asked if I was willing to make one phone call after I ate and buy time. I could always purge if I needed to, but she wanted me to try calling one person and see what happened. Now I'm not stupid. I knew she was up to something.

18   But I was really scared by the power the bad voice had over me, and I felt beaten up and out of control, scared of how sick I had somehow become, how often my pulse raced and my heart skipped beats, scared that one time when the eagle talons descended, they would grip too hard and pop me open. So I agreed. I got home, ate a more or less regular meal, called a friend, made contact, and didn't purge. The next day, I ate a light breakfast and lunch, and then a huge dinner, rooting around the fridge and cupboards like a truffle pig. But then I called my younger brother. He came over. We went for a walk.

19   Several weeks later, during one of our sessions, Rita asked me what I'd had for breakfast. "Cereal," I said.

20   "And were you hungry when you ate?"

21   "What do you mean?" I asked.

22   "I mean, did you experience hunger, and then make breakfast?"

23   "I don't really understand what you're asking," I said.

24   "Let me put it this way," she said. "Why did you have breakfast?"

25   "Oh! I see," I said. "I had breakfast because it was breakfast time."

26   "But were you hungry?"

27   I stared at her a moment. "Is this a trick question?" I asked.

28   "No," she said. "I just want to know how you know it's time to eat."

29   "I know it's time to eat because it's mealtime," I said. "It's morning, so I eat breakfast, or it's midday, so I eat lunch. And so on."

30   To make a long story ever so slightly shorter, she finally asked me what it felt like when I was hungry, and I could not answer. I asked her to explain what it felt like when she was hungry, and she described a sensation in her stomach of emptiness, an awareness of appetite.

31   So for the next week, my assignment was to notice what it felt like when I was hungry. It was so strange. I was once again the world's oldest toddler. I walked aroung peering down as if to look inside my stomach, as if it was one of those old-fashioned front-loading washing machines with a window through which you could see the soapy water swirling over your clothes. And I paid attention until I was able to isolate this feeling in my stomach, a gritchy kind of emptiness, like a rat was scratching at the door, wanting to be let in.

32   "Wonderful," Rita said, and then gave me my next assignment: first, to notice when I was hungry, and then—this blew my mind—to feed myself.

33   I practiced, and all of a sudden I was Helen Keller after she breaks the code for "water," walking around touching things, learning their names. Only in my case, I was discovering which foods I was hungry for, and what it was like to eat them. I felt a strange loneliness at first, but then came upon a great line in one of Geneen Roth's books on eating, which said that awareness was about learning to keep yourself company. So I'd feel the scratchy emptiness in my belly, and I'd mention to myself that I seemed hungry. And then I'd ask myself, in a deeply maternal way, what I felt like eating.

34   "Well, actually, I feel like some Chee•tos," I might say. So I'd go and buy a bag of Chee•tos, put some in a bowl, and eat them. God! It was amazing. Then I'd check in with myself: "Do you want some more?" I'd ask.

35   "No," I'd say. "But don't throw them out."

36   I had been throwing food out or wetting it in the sink since I was fourteen, ever since my first diet. Every time I broke down and ate forbidden foods, I would throw out or wet what I'd left uneaten, because each time I was about to start over and be good again.

37   "I'm hungry," I'd say to myself. "I'd like some frosting."

38   "OK."

39   "And some Chee•tos."

40   So I'd have some frosting and some Chee•tos for breakfast. I'd eat for a while. Then I'd check in with myself, kindly: "More?"

41   "Not now," I'd say. "But don't wet them. I might want some more later."

42   I ate frosting and Chee•tos for weeks. Also, cookies that a local bakery made with M&M's instead of chocolate chips. I'd buy half a dozen and keep them on the kitchen counter. It was terrifying; it was like knowing there were snakes in my kitchen. I'd eat a little, stop when I was no longer hungry. "Want one more cookie?" I'd ask.

43   "No, thanks," I'd say. "But maybe later. Don't wet them."

44   I never wet another bag of cookies. One day I woke up and discovered that I also felt like having some oranges, then rice, then sautéed bell peppers. Maybe also some days the random pound of M&M's. But from then on I was always able at least to

keep whatever I ate down—or rather, in my case, up. I went from feeling like a Diane Arbus character, viewed through the lens of her self-contempt, to someone filmed by a friendly cousin, someone who gently noted the concentration on my face as I washed a colander of tiny new potatoes.

45   Over the years, my body has not gotten firmer. Just the opposite in fact. But when I feel fattest and flabbiest and most repulsive, I try to remember that gravity speaks; also, that no one needs that plastic-body perfection from women of age and substance. Also, that I do not live in my thighs or in my droopy butt. I live in joy and motion and cover-ups. I live in the nourishment of food and the sun and the warmth of the people who love me.

46   It is, finally, so wonderful to have learned to eat, to taste and love what slips down my throat, padding me, filling me up, that I'm not uncomfortable calling it a small miracle. A friend who does not believe in God says, "Maybe not a miracle, but a little improvement," but to that I say, Listen! You must not have heard me right: I couldn't *feed* myself! So thanks for your input, but I know where I was, and I know where I am now, and you just can't get here from there. Something happened that I had despaired would ever happen. It was like being a woman who has despaired of ever getting to be a mother but now who cradles a baby. So it was either a miracle—Picasso said, "Everything is a miracle; it's a miracle that one does not dissolve in one's bath like a lump of sugar"—or maybe it was more of a gift, one that required some assembly. But whatever it was, learning to eat was about learning to live—and deciding to live; and it is one of the most radical things I've ever done.

QUESTIONS FOR DISCUSSION

1. Lamott writes in the first person about her own eating disorder. How does this influence the meaning of the essay for you? Do you think a more clinical or statistical approach to the subject would have been more or less effective? Explain your response.
2. After Lamott stops drinking, she says, "The pond inside me began to settle, and I could see through the water." What can she see? Why is she still unable to reveal her secret eating disorder? Why does she think it is harder to recover from alcohol addiction than from eating-disordered behavior?
3. What do the eagle talons symbolize? Why does Lamott finally call Rita Grossman to ask for help with her eating disorder? How do Rita and the choices she offers help Lamott ?
4. What does Lamott's food wetting ritual symbolize?
5. Why does she need to relearn what it feels like to be hungry and feed herself? What allows her to take this responsibility for herself? How does she accomplish this simple but challenging task?
6. Why does Lamott conclude that deciding to feed herself and live was "one of the most radical things I've ever done"?

CONNECTION

Compare Lamott's obsession with her eating disorder with the depressed state of mind described by William Styron. Does eating disorder seem to you to be a symptom of depression?

IDEAS FOR WRITING

1. Write an essay in which you discuss the positive aspects of Lamott's struggle to overcome her eating disorder. Consider how her obsession and struggle transform her life.
2. Write a paper on the causes and/or effects of eating disorders.

Theodore Roethke

In a Dark Time

Theodore Roethke (1908–1963) grew up in Saginaw, Michigan, where he spent much of his time in his father's large commercial greenhouses. Even as a young man, Roethke had a sense that he would become a poet; he began to write and study the craft of poetry before attending the University of Michigan and Harvard. For most of his life, Roethke supported himself and his family as a creative writing teacher at the University of Washington. Roethke's poetry often celebrates his students, for whom he cared deeply. His intense and emotional nature is also reflected in his love for nature and his interest in understanding the spiritual world. Commenting on his first volume of poems, Open House *(1941), Roethke shared his "intention to use himself as the material for his art." Roethke explores his inner world and reflects on the natural mysteries of life in volumes such as* The Lost Son *(1948) and* Words for the Wind *(1957).* On the Poet and His Selected Prose *(1966) gives readers insight into his writing process. In the poem that follows, Roethke explores his thoughts about the kind of positive illumination and transformation that can come out of times of confusion and despondency.*

JOURNAL

Write about a crisis in your life, an experience through which you grew or experienced a feeling of transformation.

In a dark time, the eye begins to see,
I meet my shadow in the deepening shade;
I hear my echo in the echoing wood—

A lord of nature weeping to a tree.
5   I live between the heron and the wren,
    Beasts of the hill and serpents of the den.

What's madness but nobility of soul
At odds with circumstances? The day's on fire!
I know the purity of pure despair,
10 My shadow pinned against a sweating wall.
    That place among the rocks—is it a cave,
    Or winding path? The edge is what I have.

A steady storm of correspondences!
A night flowing with birds, a ragged moon,
15 And in broad day the midnight comes again!
    A man goes far to find out what he is—
    Death of the self in a long, tearless night,
    All natural shapes blazing unnatural light.

Dark, dark my light, and darker my desire.
20 My soul, like some heat-maddened summer fly,
    Keeps buzzing at the sill. Which I is *I*?
    A fallen man, I climb out of my fear.
    The mind enters itself, and God the mind,
    And one is One, free in the tearing wind.

QUESTIONS FOR DISCUSSION

1. How would you interpret the poem's opening line, "In a dark time, the eye begins to see." What does this line suggest about the positive outcome of states of mind such as loss and depression?
2. What is the speaker's mood at the beginning of the poem? How has the poem's tone changed by the final line?
3. What is the "steady storm of correspondences" the speaker experiences ? What do these correspondences indicate about his relationship with nature as a source of inspiration and renewal?
4. In what sense does the speaker die during the night?
5. In what sense is the speaker reborn? How has the speaker changed through his "rebirth"? What new sense of identity does the speaker discover ?
6. In what ways is this a religious poem? If it is an account of a religious experience, what do you think will be the outcome of this experience?

CONNECTION

Compare the spiritual transformation of the narrator at the end of Roethke's poem with the transformation experienced by Styron in his essay in this chapter, "The Roots of Depression."

1. Develop your journal entry into an essay. Discuss how you came to change and grow, working and struggling through your personal crisis.
2. Write an essay about the meaning of the word "transformation" or "rebirth" in terms of psychological or spiritual experience. Use examples drawn from Roethke's poem, other readings, and/or personal experiences.

Adine Kernberg

I'll Tell It You Called

Adine Kernberg of Scarsdale, New York, studied graphic design in college and has a special interest in literature and the social sciences. She wrote the following essay to clarify her feelings about the way that luxuries can become necessities and to better understand her special relationship with a cranky answering machine. Kernberg prefers reading drafts of her papers aloud to friends, pausing to observe their responses to her work. She had some difficulty in finding the right language and voice for this light, entertaining story, and finally followed a friend's advice to write it in the way she actually speaks rather than using a more formal, academic diction.

JOURNAL

Write about an important object in your life that you sometimes treat as if it were a person.

1   It finally arrived. Within this ordinary postal box lay the key to another world, the key to a richer and more fulfilling existence. At last I would be freed from the oppression of perpetual wonder, emancipated from the eternal sea of uncertainty. I would possess the wisdom of the omnipresent. Now I would know—who called while I was out.

2   I ripped open the brown carton, causing a minor styrofoam eruption. I reached inside the now half-empty box and suddenly felt the streamlined form underneath my fingertips. It was a phone with a built-in answering machine—the ultimate in telecommunications. I ran upstairs and immediately connected all of the wires and cords. Eventually the bright red "messages" light greeted me with its fiery glow while the green "personal memo" light pulsated eagerly.

3   Every day when I came home, I would rush into my room to see if the red light was flashing. Long-distance messages always gave me the greatest satisfaction. "Just think, if I didn't have an answering machine I wouldn't have known that he called!" I would say this to myself almost every day, along with, "How did I ever live without one?" I became so infatuated with the whole concept of answering machines that I began to lose my patience with people who didn't have one. "I'm sorry Robin, but I just think it's savage. What the hell do you expect me to do—just sit around and listen to it ring? Really." Now my life had a whole new dimension. . . and there was no going back.

4   One of my favorite features was "Remote Message Retrieval." This mechanism allows one to "play, replay, and save messages from a remote telephone." Not many people will freely admit this, but there is a certain kind of pleasure that can only be derived from Remote Message Retrieval. It lets you pretend, for just a few minutes, that you are an internationally renowned surgeon whose messages are simply too important to let wait. Of course, my messages usually consisted only of "Hi, it's so and so. Give me a call sometime"—but the other people at the pay phone would never have to know that.

5   Then one day I tried to call for my messages, but there was no answer. I let my phone ring ten times, which is supposed to turn my machine on in case one forgets to do so (another essential feature for the answering machine connoisseur), but even that didn't work. I knew I would never willingly disconnect my favorite appliance, so I quickly drove home.

6   "That's strange. I don't remember leaving it on the floor," I said, when suddenly the phone rang.

7   "Hello?" I said.

8   "Uh, hello?. . . Adine?. . . Is that you?. . . It's Sean."

9   "Yeah, Hi! You know, for a second you almost sounded disappointed."

10   "I was so excited to leave a funny message—"

11   "Well you can still tell me can't you? After all I am the one who listens to the messages. . . ."

12   "No, forget it. . . it won't be as funny this way." I thought his sudden lack of enthusiasm was a bit strange, but I didn't give the conversation much thought afterwards.

13   Then, when Michelle informed me that my machine told her where she could find Rich, I began to wonder.

14   "Was it just playing back my messages by accident? Machines do that sometimes, you know. You probably heard that eternal one my dad left about the car registration and insurance, and let's see what else. . . ."

15   "No, I just heard the part of Rich's where he said he'd be at the diner. It was so funny because I was calling to ask you if you knew where he was! That's one great machine—why don't you ask it to take the Calc final for you?" Michelle, who proceeded to tell answering machine jokes throughout the conversation, obviously found all this very amusing. A few days later, my answering machine seemed to be the focus of conversation among my close friends.

16   "You know, I talk to your machine more than I talk to you!" said Robin.

17   "Yeah, but tell me Adine's machine isn't the greatest friend! It's always there for you; it always listens to what you have to say, and on a good day, it will even cheer you up by playing funny messages!" giggled Diana.

18   "Oh my god! Did you hear the message her mom left when she found out that Adine dented the car! I was dying! Her mom, yelling in her Spanish accent was the most hysterical thing ever!" Robin and Diana went on for what seemed like an eternity with "And did you hear this one?" and "Or how about that one?" Some of the messages really were funny, but I couldn't help but feel uncomfortable about people hearing things they shouldn't have heard. I tried to share my frustration with them but they seemed to be much more concerned with the discrepancies between Steve and Christy's recorded explanations of their breakup.

19   As the weeks passed, my machine grew less and less cooperative. It would play my greeting instead of my messages and play my messages in place of my greeting. When it did take a message, it would only record fragments of it—that is, if I was lucky. Sometimes the machine would disappear altogether and return the following morning. I finally decided to rope it to my refrigerator. I thought that would be the end of all of these bizarre occurrences. Then I came home one day and caught it trying on my clothes.

20   "WHAT DO YOU THINK YOU'RE DOING! I HAVEN'T EVEN WORN THAT YET!" I shouted.

21   "Which do you think looks better? The tweed or cotton?" Ignoring my outrage, it spoke to me in a rather unusual voice. It sounded as if it had spliced my friends' messages together and rearranged their words to form sentences. I was so perplexed by this that I almost overlooked the fact that machines should not be able to create sentences at will. My machine wasn't even supposed to have a will—but it did.

22   "Listen, if I had wanted a fashion-conscious machine I would have—Wait a second. . . You're not even supposed to be able to talk! What's going on? Why aren't you answering my calls?"

23   "For the same reason that you don't answer them. I'm going out."

24   "And where do you think you're going?"

25   "Out to grab a beer at the "Fore 'n' Aft" with Michelle and Diana. Don't wait up for me. . . I'm meeting Sean later on. Just let me know if anyone calls—"

26   "You can't do that! You can't just go out with my friends!"

27   "But as you always say"—now it spoke in what seemed to be a mimicking tone— "if I hadn't been here, you wouldn't have known that they called!"

28   Before I realized what I was doing, I found my hands in a strangling position around the neck of the receiver. Just as I was reaching to pull out the cassette and throw it away, the machine managed to utter a few more cutting remarks.

29   "I don't see why you're so upset. You know as well as I do that I am putting in overtime for you—you've gotten so lazy you don't even pick up the phone when you are home! The day you began selectively screening your calls was the day I decided

to take a stand—for myself and for your friends. You expect your friends to do all the work. You seem to think that just because you have me you don't need to make an effort to contact them. Sure you call them back eventually, but only when you feel you have the time. I know I wouldn't want a friend who felt she had to squeeze me into her schedule! I'm no ordinary appliance you know! You didn't expect me to just sit back like some docile toaster-oven and take your abuse, did you?" All of a sudden, sparks began to fly from out of the speaker. Soon the machine was surrounded by smoke and entangled in the slick strands of its own regurgitated tape ribbon.

30   I had no choice. I had to dismantle it. It was destroying my social life—and my sanity. I never thought I'd lose my perspective to the point where I would actually argue with an appliance. Now it sits in hundreds of innocuous pieces in a small brown box, while I am forced to take part in the barbaric ritual of answering my own calls.

QUESTIONS FOR DISCUSSION

1. Characterize the diction of the narrative. Does Adine Kernberg succeed in her attempts to use a natural speaking voice? Does the "voice" in the story sound authentic and personal?
2. Comment on the use of humor in the story. What is comic about the story? Is the laughter directed at the situation, at the people in the story, or both?
3. What points does the story make about friendship and responsibility? Does the humor help or hinder the author's efforts to make these points?
4. Can the answering machine be seen as a symbol for the dehumanizing, obsessive consequences of technology, or does the story just seem like a light fantasy? Defend your response with specific references to the story.

Sharon Slayton

The Good Girl

After growing up in Florida and spending several years in Denver working in the computer field, Sharon Slayton moved to California to complete her education. When she wrote this essay, she was a part-time student in psychology with plans to transfer to a four-year university and eventually became a lawyer. Slayton enjoys writing and has contributed several articles to small-business newsletters. The following essay was written in response to a question posed in her critical thinking class that asked her to define a form of obsessive or addictive behavior about which she had personal knowledge.

1   Most people who meet me today see a very strong and confident individual. They see a young woman who has accomplished a great deal in a short time. They see a very responsible and reliable person who can be counted on to get a job done with skill and competency. Typically, I am spokesperson for any group of which I become part. I am looked to for leadership and guidance among my friends and colleagues. I am quite proud of my reputation; however, I wish that I had come by it through some other means. You see, all of these admirable characteristics were developed over the past 25 years through an obsession with being good.

2   Maybe I should rephrase that, because merely being "good" has never quite been "good" enough for me—not since I was six years old and my parents failed to believe me about the most important issue in my life. I went to them for protection against a child molester, and they refused to believe that such a thing could be happening in their world. Those things do not happen to "nice" people, to "good" people. Those things could not happen to *their* child. My parents defended themselves the only way they knew how, by denying the reality of my perceptions and telling me that I was "bad" for telling such stories. Their choice of the word "bad" affected everything I was ever to do afterwards. From that time on I understood only one thing, that I must be "good."

3   "Good" soon came to encompass everything in my world: school, friends, home, work, society. I had to be good; and, if at all possible, I had to be great. Every deed at which I excelled, every recognition I received, every honor bestowed meant that I was one step closer to no longer being "bad." As the years passed, I forgot why I was trying so hard and lost touch with the reasoning that had started this quest—yet I pursued my goal with a diligence and devotion that can only be termed as obsessive.

4   I knew just about everyone at school, but I never made many friends. I didn't have time to be bothered with people, except superficially, because I was totally preoccupied with my grades; I had to get all "As." Nothing less would do. When I wasn't studying, I was deeply involved in clubs and organizations. I decided, while still in elementary school, when I saw my first high school yearbook, that I would have the longest senior listing in my high school class when I graduated. Out of a class of almost eight hundred students, I got what I wanted. I had hoped my parents would be proud, but they hardly seemed to notice.

5   By the time I was fifteen I was looking for more ways to show "them" that I could do anything, and do it well. I was a junior in high school and started working full time while attending classes all day. My day began at 7:20 A.M. when the first bell rang and ended around 1:00 A.M. when I arrived home from work. Neither I nor my family needed extra money, but for me, there was no other way: I always had to do more. I kept this schedule up until I graduated. Of course, I was an honor student; I

was also a student council representative, vice president of two clubs, treasurer of one. I attended and received top awards in state foreign language competitions in two languages and was a member of two choral groups which gave concerts state-wide and which participated in state-level competitions. No one ever seemed to notice or to care.

6   What I didn't notice was that my parents were immensely proud of me. They often bragged about me to their friends and relatives, but I wasn't paying attention. I was after something that they could never give. My "badness" no longer existed for them, and probably had not since about an hour after that episode when I was six— but it was very much a part of me. I picked everything apart, thinking that everything could always use improvement, that nothing was "good" enough as it was. My grades were good, but some of the subjects weren't as "easy" for me as I wished. I was popular, but there were always some people I didn't know. I was working, but I had to be the best at my job, the fastest, the most knowledgeable. I actually learned stock numbers and prices to over two hundred items of inventory by heart so I could impress my manager with how good I was.

7   Was I getting tired? Maybe. But I was also getting plenty of recognition for my accomplishments. I fed off of it; I lived for it; I required it. I needed every reward or approval I got to reinforce me in my feeling that I was on the right track, that I was getting better and better. I was no longer consciously aware of what I was seeking. The obsession had taken over my behavior, almost completely; being constantly challenged was now a way of life. Never resting, never relaxing, always striving, always achieving—these things were second nature to me by the time I was twenty.

8   My relationships were disastrous. My constant need for approval and recognition was very difficult for anyone to supply. Likewise, no matter how much praise I was given, I never felt like it was enough. I felt that people patronized me, so I had to prove to them that I could always do more than anyone else. I criticized anyone who was willing to settle for less than I. If someone told me that they loved me, I would pick it apart, frequently arguing with the people I was involved with: "How can you say you love me? If you loved me, then you would stop making me feel like nothing I ever do is good enough."

9   When I was twenty-three I started my own business, which was quite successful for a time. I had moved two thousand miles away from my family, determined that I would be a great success. I was really going to make them proud this time, but my plans went awry as moving away from my family helped dim the constant need to impress them. Because of distance, they were no longer privy to my life and to daily events. Lacking the "audience" for my constant efforts to prove myself, I began to lose the motivation to excel, to be the "good one." Slowly, I began to lose interest in my business, lacking the drive to devote myself utterly to something that was unrecognized by my family. I began to realize what I might never have discovered if I had stayed close to home. Without parental recognition and approval, my business success meant little.

10   In fact, I began to realize that I had been so damned "good" all my life that I had missed out on a great deal of fun. Suddenly my life began to change. I was involved in many things, but I derived little pleasure now from activities I had thoroughly enjoyed in the past. At twenty-seven years of age I knew nothing about myself. I had no idea what I really liked and had no concept of happiness. I only knew what I was capable of accomplishing. I set about enjoying myself with the same devotion that I had given to everything else, and for the next few years my life became a set of extremes. Struggling constantly with a desire to be good and a need to be "bad," I would go out drinking with friends and get very drunk, but I was always the one who forced myself to try to act sober. I was always the one responsible for making sure that everyone else got home. I thought I was enjoying the first freedom that I had ever experienced in my life, but I had really only broadened my obsession to include being bad as well. Whatever mood I was in, whatever my particular focus was for the hour, whether being good or being bad, I accomplished either with an abandon and passion hard to match. And I was very, very unhappy.

11   What was the point? Did I really enjoy anything I was doing? No. I had no idea what I wanted, yet I demanded attention and recognition. If I couldn't get enough recognition from my family, then I would get it from everyone else. But that had proved unsatisfying as well. What could I do now? What was I after and what did I want? The only thing I really knew was that I didn't want to go on living like I was anymore. With the help of one of the few friends I had managed to make along the way, I started psychiatric counseling. The results of that counseling you see in what you have just read.

12   So, here I am today, thirty-two years old and just beginning to discover myself as a person who exists outside of the obsession to be good. Actually, I think I have an advantage over a lot of people my age in that I covered a lot of ground when I was young. Driven by an obsession for goodness, I tested my limits and discovered what many people never learn: that I really could accomplish anything to which I put my mind. In going from one subject to another to prove I could do it all, I was exposed to a wide variety of experiences and activities, some of which I have rejected, some of which I have made a part of my current life-style. Either way, the experiences I have picked up along the way have made my life rich and varied. My obsessive past has given me a strength with which to confront the future; I just wish I had arrived here by some other way.

Questions for Discussion

1. Despite feeling pride about her achievements, why does Slayton now wish she "had arrived here by some other way"? Do you agree with her?

2. How did Slayton's parents respond to her story about a molestation? Does their response seem understandable? Would parents today be as likely to respond as Slayton's parents did in the early 1960s?

3. This essay is an example of what is known as an extended definition. What qualities make up Slayton's definition of the "good girl" obsession? Is her definition of the essay's key terms a clear one?

4. To develop her definition essay, Slayton uses her own case history and a number of examples from her life at different stages. What are the key incidents that Slayton emphasizes? Are there any that seem to need more development or detail? Do all of the incidents she mentions seem relevant to her definition?

Topics for Research and Writing

1. Write an extended definition of one of the following terms: *dream, obsession, fantasy, memory.* Provide examples from your research and contrasts to indicate how your sense of the term differs from the dictionary meaning, how readings in this text have influenced your current definition, and how your personal experiences have helped you to understand the term's meaning.

2. Using the essay by Garvin and Hartmann as a starting point, research the concept of lucid dreaming as an alternative to being overwhelmed by frightening nightmares. Write a paper in which you define this expression and explore the causes and effects of the lucid dreaming process. Do you consider lucid dreaming valid as a way of controlling dreams and finding a way to use their power for creative thinking?

3. Poe's short story "The Tell-Tale Heart" has long fascinated students of criminology because of its chilling portrait of an obsessed, irrational murderer. Do some research into the obsessive fantasies that can lead to the seemingly random murder of a stranger or even to serial killings. Write a paper that defines the mind of the murderer and its motivation.

4. Gilman's "The Yellow Wallpaper" is a famous story about a 19th-century woman's obsession and nervous breakdown after childbirth. How were young women who suffered from "nervous disorders" or mental illness treated in 19th-century medicine? Research this aspect of medical history and draw some conclusions. How do modern treatment approaches differ?

5. Using Lamott's essay "Hunger" as a point of departure, do some research and write an essay defining the nature and origins of eating disorders such as anorexia and bulimia. What social, psychological, or chemical factors can lead to an eating disorder?

6. Both Roethke's narrator in "In A Dark Time" and Lamott in "Hunger" escape from their depression and obsession through a form of spiritual transformation (Note: see also Hanh's essay "Love in Action," in Chapter 9).

Do some research into spiritual dimensions of mental healing and draw some conclusions about the efficacy of such approaches, in contrast to more traditional forms of therapy or medications.

7. See one of the following films that explores the relationship between nightmares and obsessions, either by yourself or with several of your classmates. Write an individual or collaborative analysis of the film, focusing on the definition the film provides for the type of obsession it examines and whether it regards the obsession as a primarily negative or potentially positive state of mind.

   Fatal Attraction, Field of Dreams, The Piano, House of Games, Jacob's Ladder, Spellbound, Death Becomes Her, Crumb, Unstrung Heroes, Disclosure, Tom and Viv, Shall We Dance?, Beloved, Seven Years in Tibet, Permanent Midnight, What Dreams May Come

8. Explore the following URLs for Web pages that provide information and definitions related to common obsessions as well as methods of personal healing and transformation:

   ACADEMY FOR EATING DISORDERS WEB SITE
   http://www.acadeatdis.org/
   The site of the Academy for Eating Disorders, a "multidisciplinary professional organization focusing on Anorexia Nervosa, Bulimia Nervosa, Binge Eating Disorder, and related disorders," presents information and links related to such disorders, their causes, consequences, and treatment.

   CENTER ON ADDICTION AND SUBSTANCE ABUSE
   http://www.casacolumbia.org/
   This web site from The National Center on Addiction and Substance Abuse at Columbia University provides helpful links resources programs, publications, and other on-line resources on substance abuse and addiction.

   DEPRESSION.COM HOME PAGE
   http://www.depression.com/
   This site contains links to information on definitions, coping with, and treatments for various kinds of depression.

   OBSESSIVE-COMPULSIVE DISORDER
   http://noah.cuny.edu/illness/mentalhealth/cornell/conditions/ocd.html
   This fact sheet from the Department of Psychiatry of the New York Hospital Cornell Medical Center provides some fundamental information and advice about Obsessive-Compulsive Disorder (OCD).

   MANIC DEPRESSION (BIPOLAR) AND CREATIVITY
   http://www.schizophrenia.com/ami/cnsmr/creative.html
   A page in the web site maintained by the organization NAMI/NYC presents Kay Redfield Jamison's research and writing on the relationship between

Manic-Depressive Illness and Creativity. See also NAMI/NYC's full web site on families and schizophrenia.

SLEEP DISORDERS
http://sleepdisorders.about.com/health/sleepdisorders/?REDIR_404=yes
This page from the health section of About.com provides a list of links to information on sleep disorders such as narcolepsy, insomnia, and nightmares.

WEB OF ADDICTIONS
http://www.well.com/user/woa/new.htm
This site, maintained by Andrew L. Homer, Ph.D. and Dick Dillon, provides information and frequent updates on different kinds of addictions and treatments.

6

Journeys in Sexuality and Gender

No one who accepts the view that the censorship is the chief reason for dream distortion will be surprised to learn from the results of dream interpretation that most of the dreams of adults are traced back by analysis to erotic wishes.

SIGMUND FREUD
Erotic Wishes and Dreams

She obeyed him; she always did as she was told.

MAXINE HONG KINGSTON
No Name Woman

No, it wasn't easy for any of us, girls and boys, as we forced our beautiful, free-flowing child-selves into those narrow, constricting cubicles labeled female and male.

JULIUS LESTER
Being a Boy

CAUSALITY AND THE INWARD JOURNEY

What causes people to have certain kinds of dreams or to remember a particular dream? Do people's gender concerns influence their dreams? How do dreams and sexual fantasies influence an individual's waking life and personal relationships? Why can certain people use their dreams to make their lives richer while others are overwhelmed by their unconscious fears? All of these questions, central to the issues raised in Dreams and Inward Journeys, are also issues of causality.

As you reflect on your dreams and emotions, working to understand what you read and to create clear, focused arguments, causal analysis will be a fundamental part of your thinking process. Causal analysis can help you to understand your inner life, to interpret your relationship to the public world, and to explain how and why things happen the way they do. Finding Connections that exist between one event and another event, understanding how one event led to or produced another event, and speculating about the consequences of earlier events—all involve causal reasoning.

Observing and Collecting Information

People naturally search for solutions to mental dilemmas and physical problems, wanting to be able to explain why something occurred and how they can improve the situation. In most cases, the more confident we are about our explanations of any event, the better we feel. Being observant and collecting information about both your inner and outer world will increase your chances of making accurate causal connections and inferences about the sources and meanings of your dreams and the public events that are influencing you. For example, if you are keeping a dream journal, you may find that after writing down your dreams for a while you notice repeated images or situations that may reflect your psychological concerns and may help you to draw more accurate inferences about your inner needs. Similarly, keeping a media journal of newspaper clippings or stories downloaded from the Internet will help you become more alert to issues of cause and effect in the external world: immediate and long-term causes for our country's attack on another nation, for instance, or the effects of a series of "strategic" bombing raids on the ecological system, rate of global pollution and disease, and the flow of refugees out of and into various countries in a region of the world.

Whether you are studying dreams, literature, or current events, you need to be sure that the causal connections you make are sound ones. You should observe carefully and consider all possible causes, not simply the obvious, immediate ones. For example, student writer Julie Bordner Apodaca began her preparation to write "Gay Marriage: Why the Resistance?" included in this chapter with her own personal observations of biased comments about gay relationships, comments that had come up in conversations she had with other students and people in her community. These comments led her to consider some of the deeper, underlying causes for homophobia. She searched for information about the causes through further conversations and interviews with students and with her own mother, who is a psychotherapist. Apodaca also read a number of books and magazine articles on the subject, some of which are referred to in the bibliography that accompanies her essay. Ultimately, Apodaca found so many causes of bias that she chose to classify them into several different categories: religious, sociopolitical, and medical.

In writing a causal analysis, whether of a dream, a short story, or a social issue, it is also essential that you provide adequate evidence, of both a factual and a logical nature, for the conclusions that you draw. You may believe that you understand the causes involved quite clearly, but perceiving these connections for yourself is not enough; you must recreate for your reader, in clear and specific language, the mental process you went through to arrive at your conclusions. Methodically and carefully questioning your own thought process will help you to clarify your insights, to generate new ideas and evidence that can be used to support your analysis, and to avoid logical fallacies.

Causal Logical Fallacies

People create connections between events or personal issues about which they feel strongly, often rushing their thinking process to a hasty conclusion. One of the most common causal errors, the post hoc fallacy ("after this, therefore because of this"), mistakenly attempts to create a causal connection between unrelated events that follow each other closely in time. But a sequence in time is not at all the same thing as a causal sequence. In fact, much "magical" or superstitious thinking relative to dreams and daily life is based on faulty causal analysis of sequences in time. For instance, people may carry a burden of guilt because of accidental sequential parallels between their inner thoughts and outer events, such as a dream of the death of a loved one and a subsequent death or accident.

Another common problem in thinking and writing about causality is causal oversimplification, in which a person argues that one thing caused something to happen, when in fact a number of different elements worked together to produce a major effect or outcome. For example, one's dream of flying may have been inspired in part by watching a television program about pilots the night before; yet other causes may also be present: one's love for performing or "showing off" or one's joy about a recent accomplishment. When trying to apply a broad theory to explain many individual cases, thinkers often become involved in causal oversimplification. We can ask, for example, if Freud's theories about the sexual content and sources of dreams really explain the entire range of dream stories and imagery. What other causes and sources might he have neglected to consider? Asking about other possible causal relations not covered by a causal thesis will help you to test the soundness of your analysis.

The "slippery slope" fallacy is also of particular relevance to the issues explored in this text. In the slippery slope fallacy, a reasoned analysis of causes and effects is replaced by a reaction of fear, in which a person might argue that if one seemingly insignificant event is allowed to happen, there will be serious consequences. Of course, in some cases this may be true: if one isn't careful about sexually transmitted diseases, there is the possibility that a person may get AIDS and eventually die. In most cases, however, theorizing about dreadful future events can become a way of validating irrational fears, can become a way of providing an excuse for maintaining the status quo. Recognizing the slippery slope fallacies both in others' thinking and within one's own thinking can help you to free yourself from irrational fears and develop better critical thinking skills.

Good causal reasoning can lead you closer to understanding and developing theories and explanations for the multiple causes and effects of the issues and events you encounter in your reading and in your own life. With an awareness of the complexities of causal thinking, you should be able to think and write more critically, clearly, and persuasively.

THEMATIC INTRODUCTION: SEXUALITY AND GENDER

People in all cultures define themselves in relationship to their sexuality and sex roles. Gender roles supported by social values and customs influence each person's inner and public life, helping to determine the extent to which a person assumes positions of power and leadership or accepts the role of a nurturer. In the same way, the extent to which a person's sexual orientation is accepted by family and peers also plays a major role in an individual's ability to find peace and contentment. Furthermore, the shifting social definitions of acceptable gender role behavior have led many people to feel confused about their gender identity and about what constitutes appropriate behavior toward the "opposite sex" or toward individuals with sexual orientations different from their own.

Each of the readings selected for this chapter relates to a particular issue of controversy related to sexuality and gender. The first group of readings focuses on a major problem in relationships, the way we recreate the people we meet in terms of our own fantasies and values, rather than letting them "be themselves." We begin with a poem by Walt Whitman, "To a Stranger." The speaker in this poem sees a stranger and develops a fantasy that he has known the person before, has shared a life with the stranger, and will meet the stranger again at the right moment; he must only wait patiently. Next we have juxtaposed the classical version of the Pygmalion myth, in which a sculptor creates a perfect woman out of marble and falls in love with his creation, to John Updike's short story "Pygmalion," a tale of modern marriage, manipulation, and divorce.

The next selections explore repression and the impact of control of erotic feelings, psychologically and through rigid social channeling. The essay "Erotic Wishes and Dreams" presents the ideas of Sigmund Freud, the founder of modern psychiatry, on dream symbol interpretation and the real content of our dreams, which Freud believed to be sexual desire and erotic wish fulfillment. Next, Maxine Hong Kingston in her story "No Name Woman" portrays a culture driven by repressed erotic desire and sexual taboo, a society where women are limited—and sometimes destroyed—by rigid expectations of gender role and conduct. In contrast, Julius Lester's "Being a Boy" offers first hand accounts of what it was like to grow up as a boy, concentrating on his adolescent awkwardness and inability to act sufficiently masculine to meet his own standards and those of his peers.

The next two selections are stories; they explore the intense conflicts that the main characters, both unmarried couples, have about the consequences of their sexuality and gender roles. Ernest Hemingway's "Hills Like White Elephants" a dialogue between a young couple having drinks at a train station reveals that each has different expectations about relationships and love. In "The Two," Gloria Naylor shows how partners in a stable lesbian relationship have conflicts that are similar to those experienced in a traditional marriage, while experiencing the added stress of gossip and hostility in their immediate community because of the non-traditional nature of their relationship.

The next three selections examine ways that our perceptions of gender identity are being redefined. In "Swinging," biographer Diane Wood Middlebrook traces the transformation of a cross-dressing jazz musician from a young woman attracted to members of her own sex to an adult who passed successfully as a male, marrying and raising a family. Columnist Holly Brubach in the "The Age of the Female Icon" offers a positive interpretation of the current popularity of the female media icons who have a strong influence on young people's expectations and ideas about gender identity. In the next selection, "Virtual Sex," psychologist Sherry Turkle examines the influence of the electronic media on gender identity among those who engage in on-line sexual relationships.

For contrast, the final poem, Chitra Divakaruni's "Nargis' Toilette," provides insights into a very traditional form of ritual designed to channel sexuality and gender identity along socially and religiously sanctioned lines. The poem seems to pose the question of what we gain and lose when we discard such rituals and definitions. Divakaruni's poem is set in the world of a veiled Muslim bride-to-be, and reveals the joy of the women who help prepare the bride for her arranged marriage; the bride is seen only as "a black candle." Her feelings are opaque to us, and perhaps also to herself.

The two student essays that close this chapter also explore issues of gender. In "On Not Being a Girl," Rosa Contreras responds critically to Julias Lester's essay, discussing the difficulties she faced growing up in a Mexican-American family that expected her to follow the gender roles of her traditional-culture immigrant family while also expecting her to attend college. In "Gay Marriage: Why the Resistance?," Julie Bordner Apodaca writes about the political and social struggles for gay relationships to be recognized as legitimate family units and considers some of the reasons why it is difficult for such relationships to gain acceptance.

As we enter the new millennium, issues of gender identity and sexuality only promise to become more complex. We hope that the readings in this chapter can give you some insights into the customs of the past and guidance toward the ways of the future in these areas.

Marc Chagall (1887–1985)
"Birthday" (1915)

Painted less than a year after Russian-born painter Marc Chagall's arrival in Paris, "Birthday" reveals the romantic, bohemian influence of the artist's life in the city. This painting is also typical of Chagall's work in its rejection of realism and the visual logic of traditional painting for a kind of art that creates its own rules in order to reveal the reality of dreams, the passions, and the spirit.

Ideas for Drawing, Writing, and Discussion

1. Do a drawing in which you represent in an imaginative, playful way some of your ideas on love and the relationship between the sexes.
2. Write an interpretation of the scene you portrayed in your drawing, indicating why you chose certain characters, images, and symbols.
3. Share your drawing with some classmates. What different views of love and gender relations were found in the drawings? Did male students perceive gender issues differently from female students? What common themes and issues were represented?

Walt Whitman

To a Stranger

Walt Whitman (1819–1892) was born in a farmhouse on Long Island, New York. He moved to Brooklyn with his family as a young child, and he was largely self-educated.

*When he was twelve he began a series of jobs in the New York area, working as a type-
setter, schoolteacher, journalist, and house builder. During the Civil War, Whitman
served as a nurse, an experience that, along with the death of Abraham Lincoln, had a profound impact on him. In 1855, Whitman published the first edition of his life work of
poetry, the collection Leaves of Grass, which kept evolving to its final edition of
1891–1892. Leaves of Grass is a declaration of literary independence, a broad,
bold, and comprehensive book. As Whitman put it, it presents readers with "poems
of freedom . . . democracy and the New World."*

JOURNAL

Write about meeting a stranger with whom you felt an instant bond or a sense of
strong attraction.

Passing stranger! You do not know how longingly I look upon you,
You must be he I was seeking, or she I was seeking (it comes to me as of a dream,)
I have somewhere surely lived a life of joy with you,
5   All is recall'd as we flit by each other, fluid, affectionate, chaste, matured,
You grew up with me, were a boy with me or a girl with me,
I ate with you and slept with you, your body has become not yours only nor left my
  body mine only,
You give me the pleasure of your eyes, face, flesh, as we pass, you take of my beard,
  breast, hands, in return,
I am not to speak to you, I am to think of you when I sit alone or wake at night
  alone,
10 I am to wait, I do not doubt I am to meet you again,
I am to see to it that I do not lose you.

QUESTIONS FOR DISCUSSION

1. What do you think the speaker means when he says "you must be he I
  was seeking, or she I was seeking?" How does the speaker know that this
  stranger is "the one"?
2. Does the gender of the speaker in the poem matter? Why are the genders
  of speaker and stranger left ambiguous?
3. In the third line, the speaker recalls "memories" of the stranger: "I have . . .
  surely lived a life of joy with you." What is the basis of these recollections
  ("All is recall'd")? Are they pure fantasies, or do they have a deeper source?
4. In the tenth line, the speaker mentions the pleasure given to him by the encounter with the stranger, and an exchange of pleasure to the stranger from
  him: "you/take of my beard, breast, hands, in return." What do you make
  of this exchange of pleasure? Is this the speaker's fantasy? Can merely *looking*
  at another person bring the deep type of pleasure described here?
5. Why does the speaker choose not to speak to the stranger, but to wait and
  think, confident that he is "to meet you [the stranger] again"? In what
  sense will they "meet again"? Have they ever met?

6. In the poem's final line, the speaker vows that he will see to it that he "will not lose you." How can someone not lose a person they have never formally met?

CONNECTION

Compare Whitman's poem to the Pygmalion stories in this chapter. How does each of these works reveal the active creation of an imaginary ideal of a lover that may differ radically from the "real" person?

IDEAS FOR WRITING

1. Write an essay about an imaginary relationship or a "crush" you once had on a stranger. How was the crush resolved? What do you think the imaginary relationship represented for you?
2. Write an essay about the role that imagination and fantasy play in selecting a lover and entering into a relationship. What are the advantages and disadvantages of such fantasies?

Two Versions of Pygmalion

Pygmalion was a character in ancient mythology who created a statue of a perfect woman and asked the gods to bring her to life. Ever since, the name Pygmalion has been associated with manipulative people who try to remake their partner in a relationship into a representation of their own values and ideals. The following two versions of Pygmalion are from very different temporal and cultural backgrounds; the first is from the Roman era and the second is from our current American literature.

JOURNAL

Write about a relationship that you were in or one that you observed when one person in the relationship tried to change the other person.

Thomas Bulfinch

Pygmalion

Thomas Bulfinch (1796–1867) was born in Boston and taught at Harvard College. His retellings of myths from the classical age were first collected in The Age of the Fable *(1855). The original source of the Pygmalion story told here is a poem from the* Metamorphoses *of the Roman poet Ovid (43 B.C.–A.D. 17).*

1   Pygmalion saw so much to blame in women that he came at last to abhor the sex, and resolved to live unmarried. He was a sculptor, and had made with wonderful skill a statue of ivory, so beautiful that no living woman came anywhere near it. It was indeed the perfect semblance of a maiden that seemed to be alive, and only prevented from moving by modesty. His art was so perfect that it concealed itself, and its product looked like the workmanship of nature. Pygmalion admired his own work and at last fell in love with the counterfeit creation. Oftentimes he laid his hand upon it as if to assure himself whether it were living or not, and could not even then believe that it was only ivory. He caressed it and gave it presents such as young girls love—bright shells and polished stones, little birds and flowers of various hues, beads and amber. He put raiment on its limbs, and jewels on its fingers, and a necklace about its neck. To the ears he hung ear-rings, and strings of pearls upon the breast. Her dress became her, and she looked not less charming than when unattired. He laid her on a couch spread with cloths of Tyrian dye, and called her his wife, and put her head upon a pillow of the softest feathers, as if she could enjoy their softness.

2   The festival of Venus was at hand—a festival celebrated with great pomp at Cyprus. Victims were offered, the altars smoked, and the odor of incense filled the air. When Pygmalion had performed his part in the solemnities, he stood before the altar and timidly said, "Ye gods, who can do all things, give me, I pray you, for my wife"—he dared not say "my ivory virgin," but said instead—"one like my ivory virgin." Venus, who was present at the festival, heard him and knew the thought he would have uttered; and as an omen of her favor, caused the flame on the altar to shoot up thrice in a fiery point into the air. When he returned home, he went to see his statue, and leaning over the couch, gave a kiss to the mouth. It seemed to be warm. He pressed its lips again, he laid his hand upon the limbs; the ivory felt soft to his touch and yielded to his fingers like the wax of Hymettus. While he stands astonished and glad, though doubting, and fears he may be mistaken, again and again with a lover's ardor, he touches the object of his hopes. It was indeed alive! The veins when pressed yielded to the finger and again resumed their roundness. Then at last the votary of Venus found words to thank the goddess, and pressed his lips upon lips as real as his own. The virgin felt the kisses and blushed, and opening her timid eyes to the light, fixed them at the same moment on her lover. Venus blessed the nuptials she had formed, and from this union Paphos was born, from whom the city, sacred to Venus, received its name.

John Updike

Pygmalion

John Updike (b. 1932) was raised in Shillington, Pennsylvania, and completed his B.A. at Harvard in 1954, graduating summa cum laude. After studying art at the Ruskin School in Oxford, England, he returned to New York where he joined the staff of the New Yorker. *In 1959, Updike published his first novel,* The Poorhouse Fair. *At this time he moved with his family to Ipswich, Massachusetts, and made writing his full-time career. Updike is best known for his sequence of novels about Harry "Rabbit" Angstrom, who lives in suburbia and continually thinks back to his life as a high school athlete:* Rabbit Run *(1960);* Rabbit Redux *(1971);* Rabbit Is Rich *(1981); and* Rabbit at Rest *(1990), which won the Pulitzer Prize in 1991. Updike has written a number of other best-selling novels;* The Witches of Eastwick *(1984) was made into a popular film starring Jack Nicholson. Some of his short story collections include* Pigeon Feathers *(1962),* Problems *(1979),* Trust Me *(1987), and* The Afterlife and Other Stories *(1994). His most recent novels are* Toward the End of Time *(1997) and* Bech At Bay *(1998). Updike is a social satirist and an intellectual who enjoys examining contemporary ideas and social trends through his writing, as can be seen in the following story about divorce and remarriage.*

1   What he liked about his first wife was her gift of mimicry; after a party, theirs or another couple's, she would vivify for him what they had seen, the faces, the voices, twisting her pretty mouth into small contortions that brought back, for a dazzling instant, the presence of an absent acquaintance. "Well, if I reawy—how does Gwen talk?—if I *re*-awwy cared about conservation—" And he, the husband, would laugh and laugh, even though Gwen was secretly his mistress and would become his second wife. What he liked about *her* was her liveliness in bed, and what he disliked about his first wife was the way she would ask to have her back rubbed and then, under his laboring hands, night after night, fall asleep. For the first years of the new marriage, after he and Gwen had returned from a party, he would wait, unconsciously, for the imitations, the recapitulation, to begin. He would even prompt: "What did you make of our hostess's brother?"

2   "Oh," Gwen would simply say, "he seemed very pleasant." Sensing with feminine intuition that he expected more, she might add, "Harmless. Maybe a little stuffy." Her eyes flashed as she heard in his expectant silence an unvoiced demand, and with that touching, childlike impediment of hers she blurted out, "What are you reawy after?"

3   "Oh, nothing. Nothing. It's just—Marguerite met him once a few years ago and she was struck by what a pompous nitwit he was. That way he has of sucking his pipestem and ending every statement with 'Do you follow me?'"

4   "I thought he was perfectly pleasant," Gwen said frostily, and turned her back to remove her silvery, snug party dress. As she wriggled it down over her hips she turned her head and defiantly added, "He had a *lot* to say about tax shelters."

5   "I bet he did," Pygmalion scoffed feebly, numbed by the sight of his wife frontally advancing, nude, toward him as he lay on their marital bed. "It's awfully late," he warned her.

6   "Oh, come on," she said, the lights out.

7   The first imitation Gwen did was of Marguerite's second husband, Marvin; they had all unexpectedly met at a Save the Whales benefit ball, to which invitations had been sent out indiscriminately. "Oh-ho-*ho*," she boomed in the privacy of their bedroom afterwards, "so you're my noble predecessor!" In an aside she added, "Noble, my ass. He hates you so much you turned him on."

8   "I did?" he said. "I thought he was perfectly pleasant, in what could have been an awkward encounter."

9   "Yes, in*deedy*," she agreed, imitating hearty Marvin, and for a dazzling second she allowed the man's slightly glassy and slack expression of forced benignity to invade her own usually petite and rounded features. "Nothing awkward about *us*, ho-ho," she went on, encouraged by her husband's laughter. "And tell me, old chap, why *is* it your childsupport check is never on time anymore?"

10   He laughed and laughed, entranced to see his bride arrive at what he conceived to be a proper womanliness—a plastic, alert sensitivity to the human environment, a susceptible responsiveness tugged this way and that by the currents of Nature herself. He could not know the world, was his fear, unless a woman translated it for him. Now, when they returned from a gathering, and he asked what she had made of so-and-so, Gwen would stand in her underwear and consider, as if onstage. "We-hell, my dear," she would announce in sudden, fluting parody, "if it weren't for Portugal there *rally* wouldn't be a *bear*able country left in Europe!"

11   "Oh, come on," he would protest, delighted at the way her pretty features distorted themselves into an uncanny, snobbish horsiness.

12   "How did she do it?" Gwen would ask, as if professionally intent. "Something with the chin, sort of rolling it from side to side without unclenching the teeth."

13   "You've got it!" he applauded.

14   "Of course you *knoaow*," she went on in the assumed voice, "there *used* to be Greece, but now all these dreadful Arabs . . ."

15   "Oh, yes, yes," he said, his face smarting from laughing so hard, so proudly. She had become perfect for him.

16   In bed she pointed out, "It's awfully late."

17   "Want a back rub?"

18   "Mmmm. That would be reawy nice." As his left hand labored on the smooth, warm, pliable surface, his wife—that small something in her that was all her own—sank out of reach; night after night, she fell asleep.

QUESTIONS FOR DISCUSSION

1. In what ways does Updike pattern his story after the myth? In what ways does the myth differ from the story? Which tale is more romantic and affirmative?
2. How are the motifs of statue and transformation used in both versions?
3. Both versions have erotic elements. Which tale is more erotic? Why?
4. If myths reveal assumptions about our culture, what does Updike suggest about modern marriage through his retelling of the ancient story of Pygmalion?
5. Discuss modern stories that are built on the Pygmalion myth. Why do you think that this myth has continued to be so popular?

IDEAS FOR WRITING

1. Write a comparison/contrast essay of the two Pygmalion stories, focusing on a comparison between the relative dominance of males in relation to females in the two societies. In which society do women have a clearer position, one in which they are respected?
2. Write a story based on some of the ideas in the Pygmalion tale.

Sigmund Freud

Erotic Wishes and Dreams

Known as the founder of the psychoanalytic method and of concepts such as the uncon-scious mind and the Oedipus complex, Sigmund Freud (1856–1939) was also a pio-neer in the scientific study of dreams and human sexuality. Freud spent most of his life in Vienna, where he practiced psychoanalysis and published many important studies on psychology and dream interpretation as well as on cultural studies that focus on psycho-logical interpretations of art and history. His works include Interpretation of Dreams *(1900),* Totem and Taboo, *and* Leonardo da Vinci: A Study in Psychosexuality. *In "Erotic Wishes and Dreams," from his explanation of dream theory,* On Dreams *(1901), Freud presents his ideas on dream symbolism and expresses his conviction that dreams focus on erotic wishes and fantasies, although sometimes in a disguised form.*

JOURNAL

Write about a dream you have had that you consider explicitly or implicitly sex-ual in its content. Did you consider the dream to be a form of wish fulfillment, or could there have been some other explanation of the dream and its images?

1   No one who accepts the view that the censorship is the chief reason for dream dis-tortion will be surprised to learn from the results of dream interpretation that most of the dreams of adults are traced back by analysis to *erotic wishes*. This assertion is not aimed at dreams with an *undisguised* sexual content, which are no doubt familiar to all dreamers from their own experience and are as a rule the only ones to be described as "sexual dreams." Even dreams of this latter kind offer enough surprises in their choice of the people whom they make into sexual objects, in their disregard of all the limitations which the dreamer imposes in his waking life upon his sexual desires, and by their many strange details, hinting at what are commonly known as "perversions." A great many other dreams, however, which show no sign of being erotic in their manifest content, are revealed by the work of interpretation in analysis as sexual wish fulfillments; and, on the other hand, analysis proves that a great many of the thoughts left over from the

activity of waking life as "residues of the previous day" only find their way to representation in dreams through the assistance of repressed erotic wishes.

2   There is no theoretical necessity why this should be so; but to explain the fact it
may be pointed out that no other group of instincts has been submitted to such far-
reaching suppression by the demands of cultural education, while at the same time
the sexual instincts are also the ones which, in most people, find it easiest to escape
from the control of the highest mental agencies. Since we have become acquainted
with infantile sexuality, which is often so unobtrusive in its manifestations and is always overlooked and misunderstood, we are justified in saying that almost every civilized man retains the infantile forms of sexual life in some respect or other. We can
thus understand how it is that repressed infantile sexual wishes provide the most frequent and strongest motive forces for the construction of dreams.*

3   There is only one method by which a dream which expresses erotic wishes can
succeed in appearing innocently nonsexual in its manifest content. The material
of the sexual ideas must not be represented as such, but must be replaced in the
content of the dream by hints, allusions and similar forms of indirect representation. But, unlike other forms of indirect representation, that which is employed
in dreams must not be immediately intelligible. The modes of representation
which fulfill these conditions are usually described as "symbols" of the things
which they represent. Particular interest has been directed to them since it has
been noticed that dreamers speaking the same language make use of the same
symbols, and that in some cases, indeed, the use of the same symbols extends beyond the use of the same language. Since dreamers themselves are unaware of the
meaning of the symbols they use, it is difficult at first sight to discover the source
of the connection between the symbols and what they replace and represent. The
fact itself, however, is beyond doubt, and it is important for the technique of
dream interpretation. For, with the help of a knowledge of dream symbolism, it is
possible to understand the meaning of separate elements of the content of a
dream or separate pieces of a dream or in some cases even whole dreams, without
having to ask the dreamer for his associations. Here we are approaching the popular ideal of translating dreams and on the other hand are returning to the technique of interpretation used by the ancients, to whom dream interpretation was
identical with interpretation by means of symbols.

4   Although the study of dream symbols is far from being complete, we are in a position to lay down with certainty a number of general statements and a quantity of special information on the subject. There are some symbols which bear a single meaning
almost universally: thus the Emperor and Empress (or the King and Queen) stand for
the parents, rooms represent women and their entrances and exits the openings of
the body. The majority of dream symbols serve to represent persons, parts of the body
and activities invested with erotic interest; in particular, the genitals are represented
by a number of often very surprising symbols, and the greatest variety of objects are

*See my *Three Essays on the Theory of Sexuality* (1905) [Author's note].

employed to denote them symbolically. Sharp weapons, long and stiff objects, such as tree trunks and sticks, stand for the male genital; while cupboards, boxes, carriages or ovens may represent the uterus. In such cases as these the *tertium comparationis*, the common element in these substitutions, is immediately intelligible; but there are other symbols in which it is not so easy to grasp the connection. Symbols such as a staircase or going upstairs, representing sexual intercourse, a tie or cravat for the male organ, or wood for the female one, provoke our unbelief until we can arrive at an understanding of the symbolic relation underlying them by some other means. Moreover a whole number of dream symbols are bisexual and can relate to the male or female genitals according to the context.

5   Some symbols are universally disseminated and can be met with in all dreamers belonging to a single linguistic or cultural group; there are others which occur only within the most restricted and individual limits, symbols constructed by an individual out of his own ideational material. Of the former class we can distinguish some whose claim to represent sexual ideas is immediately justified by linguistic usage (such, for instance, as those derived from agriculture, e.g., "fertilization" or "seed") and others whose relation to sexual ideas appears to reach back into the very earliest ages and to the most obscure depths of our conceptual functioning. The power of constructing symbols has not been exhausted in our own days in the case of either of the two sorts of symbols which I have distinguished at the beginning of this paragraph. Newly discovered objects (such as airships) are, as we may observe, at once adopted as universally available sexual symbols.

6   It would, incidentally, be a mistake to expect that if we had a still profounder knowledge of dream symbolism (of the "language of dreams") we could do without asking the dreamer for his associations to the dream and go back entirely to the technique of dream interpretation of antiquity. Quite apart from individual symbols and oscillations in the use of universal ones, one can never tell whether any particular element in the content of a dream is to be interpreted symbolically or in its proper sense, and one can be certain that the *whole* content of a dream is not to be interpreted symbolically. A knowledge of dream symbolism will never do more than enable us to translate certain constituents of the dream content, and will not relieve us of the necessity for applying the technical rules which I gave earlier. It will, however, afford the most valuable assistance to interpretation precisely at points at which the dreamer's associations are insufficient or fail altogether.

7   Dream symbolism is also indispensable to an understanding of what are known as "typical" dreams, which are common to everyone, and of "recurrent" dreams in individuals.

8   If the account I have given in this short discussion of the symbolic mode of expression in dreams appears incomplete, I can justify my neglect by drawing attention to one of the most important pieces of knowledge that we possess on this subject. Dream symbolism extends far beyond dreams: it is not peculiar to dreams, but exercises a similar dominating influence on representation in fairy tales, myths and legends, in jokes and in folklore. It enables us to trace the intimate connections between dreams and these latter productions. We must not suppose that dream symbolism is a creation of the dream work; it is in all probability a characteristic of the

unconscious thinking which provides the dream work with the material for condensation, displacement and dramatization.

QUESTIONS FOR DISCUSSION

1. Why does Freud believe that "repressed infantile sexual wishes" are the strongest motivation behind dreams and their primary content? Does he provide convincing evidence for this belief?
2. How might a dream express erotic wishes and at the same time appear innocent of sexual content? What might cause this apparent contradiction?
3. How does Freud define "symbols" as they appear in dreams? What examples does he provide? Do these seem like sexual symbols to you?
4. How does Freud compare traditional, culturally universal dream symbols with more modern symbols based on technological inventions? Can you think of modern dream symbols that have sexual implications?
5. According to Freud, why is it always a mistake to create dream interpretations without investigating the dreamer's own associations with the symbols from his or her dreams? Do you agree with Freud that popular books which list the "meanings" of dream symbols are basically worthless? Explain your position.
6. What is the relationship between dream symbolism, the unconscious mind, and more literary works such as fairy tales, myths, and legends? Do you agree with Freud's comparison and analysis?

CONNECTION

Compare Freud's view of sexuality, gender, dreams, and fantasy to Sherry Turkle's observations in her essay in this chapter, "Virtual Sex." How would Freud respond to Turkle's essay?

IDEAS FOR WRITING

1. Apply Freud's theory about the content and symbolism of dreams to a dream you have had; then write an interpretive essay about your dream. Did Freud's ideas help you to understand your dream and its causes more clearly? What else might have influenced the imagery and events in your dream?
2. Because Freud's theories about the repressed erotic content and symbolism in dreams can also be applied to fantasy literature such as myths and fairy tales, many critics have attempted "Freudian" analyses of imaginative literature. Using a "Freudian" or sexual-symbol approach, try to interpret the characters, symbolism, and events of one of the stories or myths in this text. Did you find this approach satisfactory? Why or why not?

Maxine Hong Kingston

No Name Woman

Maxine Hong Kingston (b. 1940) is from Stockton, California, where she grew up listening to the stories her mother would tell about Chinese village life. Hong Kingston graduated from the University of California at Berkeley and taught high school and college English in Hawaii for a number of years before returning to the San Francisco Bay Area. Books by Hong Kingston include a personal memoir, The Woman Warrior: Memories of a Childhood among Ghosts *(1976); a historical account of Chinese-American life,* China Men *(1980); and a novel,* Tripmaster Monkey: His Fake Book *(1989). The following selection from* The Woman Warrior *reflects on one of the stories Hong Kingston's mother told her about an aunt in China whose sexual indiscretion leads her to become a "no name woman" and to lose her place in the life of the community.*

JOURNAL

Retell a story that you heard from a family member when you were a child which warned you of the dangers of adult life and sexuality.

1   "You must not tell anyone," my mother said, "what I am about to tell you. In China your father had a sister who killed herself. She jumped into the family well. We say that your father has all brothers because it is as if she had never been born.

2   "In 1924 just a few days after our village celebrated seventeen hurry-up weddings—to make sure that every young man who went 'out on the road' would responsibly come home—your father and his brothers and your grandfather and his brothers and your aunt's new husband sailed for America, the Gold Mountain. It was your grandfather's last trip. Those lucky enough to get contracts waved good-bye from the decks. They fed and guarded the stowaways and helped them off in Cuba, New York, Bali, Hawaii. 'We'll meet in California next year,' they said. All of them sent money home.

3   "I remember looking at your aunt one day when she and I were dressing; I had not noticed before that she had such a protruding melon of a stomach. But I did not think, 'She's pregnant,' until she began to look like other pregnant women, her shirt pulling and the white tops of her black pants showing. She could not have been pregnant, you see, because her husband had been gone for years. No one said anything. We did not discuss it. In early summer she was ready to have the child, long after the time when it could have been possible.

4   "The village had also been counting. On the night the baby was to be born the villagers raided our house. Some were crying. Like a great saw, teeth strung with lights, files of people walked zigzag across our land, tearing the rice. Their lanterns doubled in the disturbed black water, which drained away through the broken

bunds. As the villagers closed in, we could see that some of them, probably men and women we knew well, wore white masks. The people with long hair hung it over their faces. Women with short hair made it stand up on end. Some had tied white bands around their foreheads, arms, and legs.

5   "At first they threw mud and rocks at the house. Then they threw eggs and began slaughtering our stock. We could hear the animals scream their deaths—the roosters, the pigs, a last great roar from the ox. Familiar wild heads flared in our night windows; the villagers encircled us. Some of the faces stopped to peer at us, their eyes rushing like searchlights. The hands flattened against the panes, framed heads, and left red prints.

6   "The villagers broke in the front and the back doors at the same time, even though we had not locked the doors against them. Their knives dripped with the blood of our animals. They smeared blood on the doors and walls. One woman swung a chicken, whose throat she had slit, splattering blood in red arcs about her. We stood together in the middle of our house, in the family hall with the pictures and tables of the ancestors around us, and looked straight ahead.

7   "At that time the house had only two wings. When the men came back, we would build two more to enclose our courtyard and a third one to begin a second courtyard. The villagers rushed through both wings, even your grandparents' rooms, to find your aunt's, which was also mine until the men returned. From this room a new wing for one of the younger families would grow. They ripped up her clothes and shoes and broke her combs, grinding them underfoot. They tore her work from the loom. They scattered the cooking fire and rolled the new weaving in it. We could hear them in the kitchen breaking our bowls and banging the pots. They over-turned the great waist-high earthenware jugs; duck eggs, pickled fruits, vegetables burst out and mixed in acrid torrents. The old woman from the next field swept a broom through the air and loosed the spirits-of-the-broom over our heads. 'Pig.' 'Ghost.' 'Pig,' they sobbed and scolded while they ruined our house.

8   "When they left, they took sugar and oranges to bless themselves. They cut pieces from the dead animals. Some of them took bowls that were not broken and clothes that were not torn. Afterward we swept up the rice and sewed it back up into sacks. But the smells from the spilled preserves lasted. Your aunt gave birth in the pigsty that night. The next morning when I went for the water, I found her and the baby plugging up the family well.

9   "Don't let your father know that I told you. He denies her. Now that you have started to menstruate, what happened to her could happen to you. Don't humiliate us. You wouldn't like to be forgotten as if you had never been born. The villagers are watchful."

10   Whenever she had to warn us about life, my mother told stories that ran like this one, a story to grow up on. She tested our strength to establish realities. Those in the emigrant generations who could not reassert brute survival died young and far from home. Those of us in the first American generations have had to figure out how the invisible world that the emigrants built around our childhoods fit in solid America.

11   The emigrants confused the gods by diverting their curses, misleading them with crooked streets and false names. They must try to confuse their offspring as well,

who, I suppose, threaten them in similar ways—always trying to get things straight, always trying to name the unspeakable. The Chinese I know hide their names; sojourners take new names when their lives change and guard their real names with silence.

12   Chinese-Americans, when you try to understand what things in you are Chinese, how do you separate what is peculiar to childhood, to poverty, insanities, one family, your mother who marked your growing with stories from what is Chinese? What is Chinese tradition and what is the movies?

13   If I want to learn what clothes my aunt wore, whether flashy or ordinary, I would have to begin, "Remember Father's drowned-in-the-well sister?" I cannot ask that. My mother has told me once and for all the useful parts. She will add nothing unless powered by Necessity, a riverbank that guides her life. She plants vegetable gardens rather than lawns; she carries the odd-shaped tomatoes home from the fields and eats food left for the gods.

14   Whenever we did frivolous things, we used up energy; we flew high kites. We children came up off the ground over the melting cones our parents brought home from work and the American movie on New Year's Day—*Oh, You Beautiful Doll* with Betty Grable one year, and *She Wore a Yellow Ribbon* with John Wayne another year. After the one carnival ride each, we paid in guilt; our tired father counted his change on the dark walk home.

15   Adultery is extravagance. Could people who hatch their own chicks and eat the embryos and the heads for delicacies and boil the feet in vinegar for party food, leaving only the gravel, eating even the gizzard lining—could such people engender a prodigal aunt? To be a woman, to have a daughter in starvation time was a waste enough. My aunt could not have been the lone romantic who gave up everything for sex. Women in the old China did not choose. Some man had commanded her to lie with him and be his secret evil. I wonder whether he masked himself when he joined the raid on her family.

16   Perhaps she encountered him in the fields or on the mountain where the daughters-in-law collected fuel. Or perhaps he first noticed her in the marketplace. He was not a stranger because the village housed no strangers. She had to have dealings with him other than sex. Perhaps he worked an adjoining field, or he sold her the cloth for the dress she sewed and wore. His demand must have surprised, then terrified her. She obeyed him; she always did as she was told.

17   When the family found a young man in the next village to be her husband, she stood tractably beside the best rooster, his proxy, and promised before they met that she would be his forever. She was lucky that he was her age and she would be the first wife, an advantage secure now. The night she first saw him, he had sex with her. Then he left for America. She had almost forgotten what he looked like. When she tried to envision him, she only saw the black and white face in the group photograph the men had had taken before leaving.

18   The other man was not, after all, much different from her husband. They both gave orders: she followed. "If you tell your family, I'll beat you. I'll kill you. Be here

again next week." No one talked sex, ever. And she might have separated the rapes from the rest of living if only she did not have to buy her oil from him or gather wood in the same forest. I want her fear to have lasted just as long as rape lasted so that the fear could have been contained. No drawn-out fear. But women at sex hazarded birth and hence lifetimes. The fear did not stop but permeated everywhere. She told the man, "I think I'm pregnant." He organized the raid against her.

19　On nights when my mother and father talked about their life back home, sometimes they mentioned an "outcast table" whose business they still seemed to be settling, their voices tight. In a commensal tradition, where food is precious, the powerful older people made wrongdoers eat alone. Instead of letting them start separate new lives like the Japanese, who could become samurais and geishas, the Chinese family, faces averted but eyes glowering sideways, hung on to the offenders and fed them leftovers. My aunt must have lived in the same house as my parents and eaten at an outcast table. My mother spoke about the raid as if she had seen it, when she and my aunt, a daughter-in-law to a different household, should not have been living together at all. Daughters-in-law lived with their husbands' parents, not their own; a synonym for marriage in Chinese is "taking a daughter-in-law." Her husband's parents could have sold her, mortgaged her, stoned her. But they had sent her back to her own mother and father, a mysterious act hinting at disgraces not told me. Perhaps they had thrown her out to deflect the avengers.

20　She was the only daughter; her four brothers went with her father, husband and uncles "out on the road" and for some years became western men. When the goods were divided among the family, three of the brothers took land, and the youngest, my father, chose an education. After my grandparents gave their daughter away to her husband's family, they had dispensed all the adventure and all the property. They expected her alone to keep the traditional ways, which her brothers, now among the barbarians, could fumble without detection. The heavy, deep-rooted women were to maintain the past against the flood, safe for returning. But the rare urge west had fixed upon our family, and so my aunt crossed boundaries not delineated in space.

21　The work of preservation demands that the feelings playing about in one's guts not be turned into action. Just watch their passing like cherry blossoms. But perhaps my aunt, my forerunner, caught in a slow life, let dreams grow and fade and after some months or years went toward what persisted. Fear at the enormities of the forbidden kept her desires delicate, wire and bone. She looked at a man because she liked the way the hair was tucked behind his ears, or she liked the question-mark line of a long torso curving at the shoulder and straight at the hip. For warm eyes or a soft voice or a slow walk—that's all—a few hairs, a line, a brightness, a sound, a pace, she gave up family. She offered us up for a charm that vanished with tiredness, a pigtail that didn't toss when the wind died. Why, the wrong lighting could erase the dearest thing about him.

22　It could very well have been, however, that my aunt did not take subtle enjoyment of her friend, but, a wild woman, kept rollicking company. Imagining her free with sex doesn't fit, though. I don't know any women like that, or men either. Unless I see her life branching into mine, she gives me no ancestral help.

23   To sustain her being in love, she often worked at herself in the mirror, guessing at the colors and shapes that would interest him, changing them frequently in order to hit on the right combination. She wanted him to look back.

24   On a farm near the sea, a woman who tended her appearance reaped a reputation for eccentricity. All the married women blunt-cut their hair in flaps about their ears or pulled it back in tight buns. No nonsense. Neither style blew easily into heart-catching tangles. And at their weddings they displayed themselves in their long hair for the last time. "It brushed the backs of my knees," my mother tells me. "It was braided, and even so, it brushed the backs of my knees."

25   At the mirror my aunt combed individuality into her bob. A bun could have been contrived to escape into black streamers blowing in the wind or in quiet wisps about her face, but only the older women in our picture album wear buns. She brushed her hair back from her forehead, tucking the flaps behind her ears. She looped a piece of thread, knotted into a circle between her index fingers and thumbs, and ran the double strand across her forehead. When she closed her fingers as if she were making a pair of shadow geese bite, the string twisted together catching the little hairs. Then she pulled the thread away from her skin, ripping the hairs out neatly, her eyes watering from the needles of pain. Opening her fingers, she cleaned the thread, then rolled it along her hairline and the tops of her eyebrows. My mother did the same to me and my sisters and herself. I used to believe that the expression "caught by the short hairs" meant a captive held with a depilatory string. It especially hurt at the temples, but my mother said we were lucky we didn't have to have our feet bound when we were seven. Sisters used to sit on their beds and cry together, she said, as their mothers or their slave removed the bandages for a few minutes each night and let the blood gush back into their veins. I hope that the man my aunt loved appreciated a smooth brow, that he wasn't just a tits-and-ass man.

26   Once my aunt found a freckle on her chin, at a spot that the almanac said predestined her for unhappiness. She dug it out with a hot needle and washed the wound with peroxide.

27   More attention to her looks than these pullings of hairs and pickings at spots would have caused gossip among the villagers. They owned work clothes and good clothes, and they wore good clothes for feasting the new seasons. But since a woman combing her hair hexes beginnings, my aunt rarely found an occasion to look her best. Women looked like great sea snails—the corded wood, babies, and laundry they carried were the whorls on their backs. The Chinese did not admire a bent back; goddesses and warriors stood straight. Still there must have been a marvelous freeing of beauty when a worker laid down her burden and stretched and arched.

28   Such commonplace loveliness, however, was not enough for my aunt. She dreamed of a lover for the fifteen days of New Year's, the time for families to exchange visits, money, and food. She plied her secret comb. And sure enough she cursed the year, the family, the village, and herself.

29   Even as her hair lured her imminent lover, many other men looked at her. Uncles, cousins, nephews, brothers would have looked, too, had they been home between journeys. Perhaps they had already been restraining their curiosity, and they left, fearful that their glances, like a field of nesting birds, might be startled and caught. Poverty hurt, and that was their first reason for leaving. But another, final reason for leaving the crowded house was the never-said.

30   She may have been unusually beloved, the precious only daughter, spoiled and mirror gazing because of the affection the family lavished on her. When her husband left, they welcomed the chance to take her back from the in-laws; she could live like the little daughter for just a while longer. There are stories that my grandfather was different from other people, "crazy ever since the little Jap bayoneted him in the head." He used to put his naked penis on the dinner table, laughing. And one day he brought home a baby girl, wrapped up inside his brown western-style greatcoat. He had traded one of his sons, probably my father, the youngest, for her. My grandmother made him trade back. When he finally got a daughter of his own, he doted on her. They must have all loved her, except perhaps my father, the only brother who never went back to China, having once been traded for a girl.

31   Brothers and sisters, newly men and women, had to efface their sexual color and present plain miens. Disturbing hair and eyes, a smile like no other, threatened the ideal of five generations living under one roof. To focus blurs, people shouted face to face and yelled from room to room. The immigrants I know have loud voices, unmodulated to American tones even after years away from the village where they called their friendships out across the fields. I have not been able to stop mother's screams in public libraries or over telephones. Walking erect (knees straight, toes pointed forward, not pigeon-toed, which is Chinese-feminine) and speaking in an inaudible voice, I have tried to turn myself American-feminine. Chinese communication was loud, public. Only sick people had to whisper. But at the dinner table, where the family members came nearest one another, no one could talk, not the outcasts nor any eaters. Every word that falls from the mouth is a coin lost. Silently they gave and accepted food with both hands. A preoccupied child who took his bowl with one hand got a sideways glare. A complete moment of total attention is due everyone alike. Children and lovers have no singularity here, but my aunt used a secret voice, a separate attentiveness.

32   She kept the man's name to herself throughout her labor and dying; she did not accuse him that he be punished with her. To save her inseminator's name she gave silent birth.

33   He may have been somebody in her own household, but intercourse with a man outside the family would have been no less abhorrent. All the village were kinsmen, and the titles shouted in loud country voices never let kinship be forgotten. Any man within visiting distance would have been neutralized as a lover—"brother," "younger brother," "older brother"—one hundred and fifteen relationship titles. Parents researched birth charts probably not so much to assure good fortune as to circumvent incest in a population that has but one hundred surnames. Everybody has eight million relatives. How useless then sexual mannerisms, how dangerous.

34   As if it came from an atavism deeper than fear, I used to add "brother" silently to boys' names. It hexed the boys, who would or would no ask me to dance, and made them less scary and as familiar and deserving of benevolence as girls.

35   But, of course, I hexed myself also—no dates. I should have stood up, both arms waving, and shouted out across libraries, "Hey, you! Love me back." I had no idea, though, how to make attraction selective, how to control its direction and magnitude. If I made myself American-pretty so that the five or six Chinese boys in the class fell in love with me, everyone else—the Caucasian, Negro, and Japanese boys—would too. Sisterliness, dignified and honorable, made much more sense.

36   Attraction eludes control so stubbornly that whole societies designed to organize relationships among people cannot keep order, not even when they bind people to one another from childhood and raise them together. Among the very poor and the wealthy, brothers married their adopted sisters, like doves. Our family provided some romance, paying adult brides' prices and providing dowries so that their sons and daughters could marry strangers. Marriage promises to turn strangers into friendly relatives—a nation of siblings.

37   In the village structure, spirits shimmered among the live creatures, balanced and held in equilibrium by time and land. But one human being flaring up into violence could open up a black hole, a maelstrom that pulled in the sky. The frightened villagers, who depended on one another to maintain the real, went to my aunt to show her a personal, physical representation of the break she had made in the "roundness." Misallying couples snapped off the future, which was to be embodied in true offspring. The villagers punished her for acting as if she could have a private life, secret and apart from them.

38   If my aunt had betrayed the family at a time of large grain yields and peace, when many boys were born, the wings were being built on many houses, perhaps she might have escaped such severe punishment. But the men—hungry, greedy, tired of planting in dry soil, cuckolded—had had to leave the village in order to send food-money home. There were ghost plagues, bandit plagues, wars with the Japanese, floods. My Chinese brother and sister had died of an unknown sickness. Adultery, perhaps only a mistake during good times, became a crime when the village needed food.

39   The round moon cakes and round doorways, the round tables of graduated size that fit one roundness inside another, round windows and rice bowls—these talismans had lost their power to warn this family of the law: a family must be whole, faithfully keep the descent line by having sons to feed the old and the dead, who in turn look after the family. The villagers came to show my aunt and her lover-in-hiding a broken house. The villagers were speeding up the circling of events because she was too short-sighted to see that her infidelity had already harmed the village, that waves of consequences would return unpredictably, sometimes in disguise, as now, to hurt her. This roundness had to be made coin-sized so that she would see its circumference: punish her at the birth of her baby. Awaken her to the inexorable. People who refused fatalism because they could invent small resources insisted on culpability. Deny accidents and wrest fault from the stars.

40   After the villagers left, their lanterns now scattering in various directions toward home, the family broke their silence and cursed her. "Aiaa, we're going to die. Death is coming. Death is coming. Look what you've done. You've killed us. Ghost! Dead ghost! Ghost! You've never been born." She ran out into the fields, far enough from the house so that she could no longer hear their voices, and pressed herself against the earth, her own land no more. When she felt the birth coming, she thought that she had been hurt. Her body seized together. "They've hurt me too much," she thought. "This is gall, and it will kill me." With forehead and knees against the earth, her body convulsed and then relaxed. She turned on her back, lay on the ground. The black well of sky and stars went out and out and out forever; her body and her complexity seemed to disappear, without home, without a companion, in eternal cold and silence. An agoraphobia rose in her, speeding higher and higher, bigger and bigger; she would not be able to contain it; there would be no end to fear.

41   Flayed, unprotected against space, she felt pain return, focusing her body. This pain chilled her—a cold, steady kind of surface pain. Inside, spasmodically, the other pain, the pain of the child, heated her. For hours she lay on the ground, alternately body and space. Sometimes a vision of normal comfort obliterated reality: she saw the family in the evening gambling at the dinner table, the young people massaging their elder's backs. She saw them congratulating one another, high joy on the mornings the rice shoots came up. When these pictures burst, the stars drew yet further apart. Black space opened.

42   She got to her feet to fight better and remembered that old-fashioned women gave birth in their pigsties to fool the jealous, pain-dealing gods, who do not snatch piglets. Before the next spasms could stop her, she ran to the pigsty, each step a rushing out into emptiness. She climbed over the fence and knelt in the dirt. It was good to have a fence enclosing her, a tribal person alone.

43   Laboring, this woman who had carried her child as a foreign growth that sickened her every day, expelled it at last. She reached down to touch the hot, wet, moving mass, surely smaller than anything human, and could feel that it was human after all—fingers, toes, nails, nose. She pulled it up on to her belly, and it lay curled there, butt in the air, feet precisely tucked one under the other. She opened her loose shirt and buttoned the child inside. After resting, it squirmed and thrashed and she pushed it up to her breast. It turned its head this way and that until it found her nipple. There, it made little snuffling noises. She clenched her teeth at its preciousness, lovely as a young calf, a piglet, a little dog.

44   She may have gone to the pigsty as a last act of responsibility: she would protect this child as she had protected its father. It would look after her soul, leaving supplies on her grave. But how would this tiny child without family find her grave when there would be no marker for her anywhere, neither in the earth nor the family hall? No one would give her a family hall name. She had taken the child with her into the wastes. At its birth the two of them had felt the same raw pain of separation, a wound that only the family pressing tight could close. A child with no descent line would not

soften her life but only trail after her, ghost-like, begging her to give it purpose. At dawn the villagers on their way to the fields would stand around the fence and look.

45   Full of milk, the little ghost slept. When it awoke, she hardened her breasts against the milk that crying loosens. Toward morning she picked up the baby and walked to the well.

46   Carrying the baby to the well shows loving. Otherwise abandon it. Turn its face into the mud. Mothers who love their children take them along. It was probably a girl; there is some hope of forgiveness for boys.

47   "Don't tell anyone you had an aunt. Your father does not want to hear her name. She has never been born." I have believed that sex was unspeakable and words so strong and fathers so frail that "aunt" would do my father mysterious harm. I have thought that my family, having settled among immigrants who had also been their neighbors in the ancestral land, needed to clean their name, and a wrong word would incite the kinspeople even here. But there is more to this silence: they want me to participate in her punishment. And I have.

48   In the twenty years since I heard this story I have not asked for details nor said my aunt's name; I do not know it. People who can comfort the dead can also chase after them to hurt them further—a reverse ancestor worship. The real punishment was not the raid swiftly inflicted by the villagers, but the family's deliberately forgetting her. Her betrayal so maddened them, they saw to it that she would suffer forever, even after death. Always hungry, always needing, she would have to beg food from other ghosts, snatch and steal it from those whose living descendants give them gifts. She would have to fight the ghosts massed at crossroads for the buns a few thoughtful citizens leave to decoy her away from village and home so that the ancestral spirits could feast unharassed. At peace, they could act like gods, not ghosts, their descent lines providing them with paper suits and dresses, spirit money, paper houses, paper automobiles, chicken, meat, and rice into eternity— essences delivered up in smoke and flames, steam and incense rising from each rice bowl. In an attempt to make the Chinese care for people outside the family, Chairman Mao encourages us now to give our paper replicas to the spirits of out- standing soldiers and workers, no matter whose ancestors they may be. My aunt re- mains forever hungry. Goods are not distributed evenly among the dead.

49   My aunt haunts me—her ghost drawn to me because now, after fifty years of ne- glect, I alone devote pages of paper to her, though not origamied into houses and clothes. I do not think she always means me well. I am telling on her, and she was a spite suicide, drowning herself in the drinking water. The Chinese are always very frightened of the drowned one, whose weeping ghost, wet hair hanging and skin bloated, waits silently by the water to pull down a substitute.

QUESTIONS FOR DISCUSSION

1. Why is this a "story to grow on"? What lesson is it designed to teach? Does the daughter, Maxine, accept her mother's purpose in telling the story, or does she interpret the story to create a new meaning from it?

2. What possible reasons for the aunt's pregnancy and suicide does the narrator propose? What do these different reasons suggest about the status of women in the Chinese family and about the double standard for male and female behavior in Chinese culture prior to World War II? Do you think that in today's Chinese families men and women are treated equally?
3. Why was it so important for Chinese family members to "efface their sexual color" and to remain silent at meals? How is this ritual reflective of their culture's values?
4. What relationship exists between the individual and the community in the Chinese village of the "No Name Woman"? How is this relationship between the individual and the community different from the one in your neighborhood?
5. Why did the aunt's killing of her infant, combined with her suicide, reflect "signs of loving"? Why was the infant "probably a girl"?
6. Why does the aunt's ghost continue to "haunt" the narrator? What perspective on gender roles do they seem to share? In what ways are the two women different from one another?

CONNECTION

Compare the traditional status of women as seen in "No Name Woman " with that of the Muslim bride in "Nargis' Toilette" in this chapter.

IDEAS FOR WRITING

1. Write about a relative who continues to haunt your family or a relative about whom there is a family legend because of his or her sexual life. What does the legacy of this ghost-like figure reflect about your family's values? What impact has it had on your own values?
2. Write about a value or tradition related to gender role or sexuality that your grandparents or parents accepted that you have rebelled against. What do you think caused you to believe in values different from those that were accepted by your parents and grandparents? How does this generation gap influence the functioning of your family?

Julius Lester

Being a Boy

Born in 1939 in Saint Louis, Julius Lester came from a religious family; his father was a Christian minister. Lester attended Fisk University and after graduation worked as a folk singer, radio talk show host, college teacher, and writer. Lester has taught since 1971 at the University of Massachusetts, where he has been a Professor of African-American studies as well as Near Eastern and Judaic studies. Lester has written children's stories, novels, memoirs, and books of social and cultural analysis. His books include The Long Journey Home: Stories from Black History *(1972),* Do Lord Remember Me *(1984),* Lovesong: Becoming A Jew *(1988),* Fallen Pieces of the Broken Sky *(1990), and* And All Our Wounds Forgiven *(1994). In the following article, originally written for* Ms. *magazine in 1973, Lester reflects on his childhood experiences as he explores the impact of stereotypes of "masculine" and "feminine" behavior on the consciousness of the adolescent.*

JOURNAL

Write about a time when you felt subjected by parental or peer pressure to conform to very traditional standards of "masculine" or "feminine" behavior.

---

1   As boys go, I wasn't much. I mean, I tried to be a boy and spent many childhood hours pummeling my hardly formed ego with failure at cowboys and Indians, baseball, football, lying, and sneaking out of the house. When our neighborhood gang raided a neighbor's pear tree, I was the only one who got sick from the purloined fruit. I also failed at setting fire to our garage, an art at which any five-year-old boy should be adept. I was, however, the neighborhood champion at getting beat up. "That Julius can take it, man," the boys used to say, almost in admiration, after I emerged from another battle, tears brimming in my eyes but refusing to fall.

2   My efforts at being a boy earned me a pair of scarred knees that are a record of a childhood spent falling from bicycles, trees, the tops of fences, and porch steps; of tripping as I ran (generally from a fight), walked, or simply tried to remain upright on windy days.

3   I tried to believe my parents when they told me I was a boy, but I could find no objective proof for such an assertion. Each morning during the summer, as I cuddled up in the quiet of a corner with a book, my mother would push me out the back door and into the yard. And throughout the day as my blood was let as if I were a patient of 17th-century medicine, I thought of the girls sitting in the shade of porches, playing with their dolls, toy refrigerators and stoves.

4   There was the life, I thought! No constant pressure to prove oneself. No necessity always to be competing. While I humiliated myself on football and baseball fields, the girls stood on the sidelines laughing at me, because they didn't have to do anything except be girls. The rising of each sun brought me to the starting line of yet another day's Olympic decathlon, with no hope of ever winning even a bronze medal.

5   Through no fault of my own I reached adolescence. While the pressure to prove myself on the athletic field lessened, the overall situation got worse—because now I had to prove myself with girls. Just how I was supposed to go about doing this was beyond me, especially because, at the age of fourteen, I was four foot nine and weighed seventy-eight pounds. (I think there may have been one ten-year-old girl

in the neighborhood smaller than I.) Nonetheless, duty called, and with my ninth-grade gym-class jockstrap flapping between my legs, off I went.

6   To get a girlfriend, though, a boy had to have some asset beyond the fact that he was alive. I wasn't handsome like Bill McCord, who had girls after him like a cop-killer has policemen. I wasn't ugly like Romeo Jones, but at least the girls noticed him: "That ol' ugly boy better stay 'way from me!" I was just there, like a vase your grandmother gives you at Christmas that you don't like or dislike, can't get rid of, and don't know what to do with. More than ever I wished I were a girl. Boys were the ones who had to take the initiative and all the responsibility. (I hate responsi-bility so much that if my heart didn't beat of itself, I would now be a dim memory.)

7   It was the boy who had to ask the girl for a date, a frightening enough prospect until it occurred to me that she might say no! That meant risking my ego, which was about as substantial as a toilet-paper raincoat in the African rainy season. But I had to thrust that ego forward to be judged, accepted, or rejected by some girl. It wasn't fair! Who was she to sit back like a queen with the power to create joy by her con-sent or destruction by her denial? It wasn't fair—but that's the way it was.

8   But if (God forbid!) she should say Yes, then my problem would begin in earnest, because I was the one who said where we would go (and waited in terror for her ap-proval of my choice). I was the one who picked her up at her house where I was in-spected by her parents as if I were a possible carrier of syphilis (which I didn't think one could get from masturbating, but then again, Jesus was born of a virgin, so what did I know?). Once we were on our way, it was I who had to pay the bus fare, the price of the movie tickets, and whatever she decided to stuff her stomach with after-ward. (And the smallest girls are all stomach.) Finally, the girl was taken home where once again I was inspected (the father looking covertly at my fly and the mother examining the girl's hair). The evening was over and the girl had done noth-ing except honor me with her presence. All the work had been mine.

9   Imagining this procedure over and over was more than enough: I was a sopho-more in college before I had my first date.

10   I wasn't a total failure in high school, though, for occasionally I would go to a party, determined to salvage my self-esteem. The parties usually took place in some-body's darkened basement. There was generally a surreptitious wine bottle or two being passed furtively among the boys, and a record player with an insatiable ap-petite for Johnny Mathis records. Boys gathered on one side of the room and girls on the other. There were always a few boys and girls who'd come to the party for the sole purpose of grinding away their sexual frustrations to Johnny Mathis's falsetto, and they would begin dancing to their own music before the record player was plugged in. It took a little longer for others to get started, but no one matched my talent for standing by the punch bowl. For hours, I would try to make my legs do what they had been doing without effort since I was nine months old, but for some reason they would show all the symptoms of paralysis on those evenings.

11   After several hours of wondering whether I was going to die ("Julius Lester, a sixteen-year-old, died at a party last night, a half-eaten Ritz cracker in one hand and a potato chip dipped in pimiento-cheese spread in the other. Cause of death: failure

to be a boy"), I would push my way to the other side of the room where the girls sat like a hanging jury. I would pass by the girl I wanted to dance with. If I was going to be refused, let it be by someone I didn't particularly like. Unfortunately, there weren't many in that category. I had more crushes than I had pimples.

12   Finally, through what surely could only have been the direct intervention of the Almighty, I would find myself on the dance floor with a girl. And none of my prior agony could compare to the thought of actually dancing. But there I was and I had to dance with her. Social custom decreed that I was supposed to lead, because I was the boy. Why? I'd wonder. Let her lead. Girls were better dancers anyway. It didn't matter. She stood there waiting for me to take charge. She wouldn't have been worse off if she'd waited for me to turn white.

13   But, reciting "Invictus" to myself, I placed my arms around her, being careful to keep my armpits closed because, somehow, I had managed to overwhelm a half jar of deodorant and a good-size bottle of cologne. With sweaty armpits, "Invictus," and legs afflicted again with polio, I took her in my arms, careful not to hold her so far away that she would think I didn't like her, but equally careful not to hold her so close that she could feel the catastrophe which had befallen me the instant I touched her hand. My penis, totally disobeying the lecture I'd given it before we left home, was as rigid as Governor Wallace's jaw would be if I asked for his daughter's hand in marriage.

14   God, how I envied girls at that moment. Wherever *it* was on them, it didn't dangle between their legs like an elephant's trunk. No wonder boys talked about nothing but sex. That thing was always there. Every time we went to the john, there *it* was, twitching around like a fat little worm on a fishing hook. When we took baths, it floated in the water like a lazy fish and God forbid we should touch it! It sprang to life like lightning leaping from a cloud. I wished I could cut it off, or at least keep it tucked between my legs, as if it were a tail that had been mistakenly attached to the wrong end. But I was helpless. It was there, with a life and mind of its own, having no other function than to embarrass me.

15   Fortunately, the girls I danced with were discreet and pretended that they felt nothing unusual rubbing against them as we danced. But I was always convinced that the next day they were all calling up their friends to exclaim: "Guess what, girl? Julius Lester got one! I ain't lyin'!"

16   Now, of course, I know that it was as difficult being a girl as it was a boy, if not more so. While I stood paralyzed at one end of a dance floor trying to find the courage to ask a girl for a dance, most of the girls waited in terror at the other, afraid that no one, not even I, would ask them. And while I resented having to ask a girl for a date, wasn't it also horrible to be the one who waited for the phone to ring? And how many of those girls who laughed at me making a fool of myself on the baseball diamond would have gladly given up their places on the sidelines for mine on the field?

17   No, it wasn't easy for any of us, girls and boys, as we forced our beautiful, free-flowing child-selves into those narrow, constricting cubicles labeled *female* and *male*. I tried, but I wasn't good at being a boy. Now, I'm glad, knowing that a man is nothing but the figment of a penis's imagination, and any man should want to be something more than that.

QUESTIONS FOR DISCUSSION

1. How does Lester describe himself as a boy? Was he perceived by others as "manly"? How did his own perceptions differ from those of his peers?
2. Why did Lester envy girls when he was a young boy? Did you share his feelings about the advantages that the "opposite sex" had when you were an adolescent?
3. How did the pressures on Lester change as he reached adolescence? Which pressures lessened and which increased? Do you think Lester's experiences are typical of adolescent expectations and pressures?
4. What frightened Lester most about the prospect of asking girls for dates or to dance? Do you think his fears are typical ones among adolescent males?
5. What was particularly embarrassing to Lester when he danced with girls? Why does he conclude from this that girls had less reason for sexual anxiety than boys? Do you agree?
6. How does Lester's view of the differences between girls and boys change as he becomes a man? What is he now "glad" about?

CONNECTION

Compare young Lester's view of women and their place in society with the response by student Rosa Contreras in this chapter.

IDEAS FOR WRITING

1. Based on your own adolescent experiences write an essay about the typical fears and sexual anxiety experienced by someone of your gender or sexual orientation.
2. Write an essay in which you consider the cultural factors that might cause adolescence to be such a difficult period in the sexual life of a young person. You might consider the role of stereotypes of rigidly masculine and feminine behavior that come to adolescents from the mass media, religion, and family tradition.

Ernest Hemingway

Hills Like White Elephants

Ernest Hemingway (1899–1961) is remembered for his adventurous life as well as for his novels and stories. Born in Oak Park, Illinois, as a boy he often went hunting and fishing with his father. After he finished high school, Hemingway began to work as a newspaper reporter for the Kansas City Star *and the Toronto* Star. *Hemingway went on to be a foreign correspondent, meeting expatriate writers in Paris and covering World War I. His war experiences and contacts with the expatriate community formed the basis for much of his early fiction, as well as the novels* The Sun Also Rises *(1926) and* A Farewell to Arms *(1929). He was awarded the Nobel Prize in 1954. Influenced by his journalistic experience, Hemingway saw himself primarily as a realist whose seemingly simple style was designed to strip away inauthentic language: "When you have read something by me you actually experience the thing." "Hills Like White Elephants," a story about a conflict between lovers, appeared in his story collection* In Our Time *(1925).*

JOURNAL

Describe a verbal conflict you had with a member of the opposite gender. In what ways was your conflict related to your different values, especially those connected to your gender identity? Explain why you think the two of you were unable to communicate with one another.

1   The hills across the valley of the Ebro were long and white. On this side there was no shade and no trees and the station was between two lines of rails in the sun. Close against the side of the station there was the warm shadow of the building and a curtain, made of strings of bamboo beads, hung across the open door into the bar, to keep out flies. The American and the girl with him sat at a table in the shade, outside the building. It was very hot and the express from Barcelona would come in forty minutes. It stopped at this junction for two minutes and went on to Madrid.

2   "What should we drink?" the girl asked. She had taken off her hat and put it on the table.

3   "It's pretty hot," the man said.

4   "Let's drink beer."

5   "*Dos cervezas,*" the man said into the curtain.

6   "Big ones?" a woman asked from the doorway.

7   "Yes. Two big ones."

8   The woman brought two glasses of beer and two felt pads. She put the felt pads and the beer glasses on the table and looked at the man and the girl. The girl was looking off at the line of hills. They were white in the sun and the country was brown and dry.

9   "They look like white elephants," she said.

10   "I've never seen one," the man drank his beer.

11   "No, you wouldn't have."

12   "I might have," the man said. "Just because you say I wouldn't have doesn't prove anything."

13   The girl looked at the bead curtain. "They've painted something on it," she said. "What does it say?"

14   "Anis del Toro. It's a drink."

15   "Could we try it?"

16   The man called "Listen" through the curtain. The woman came out from the bar.

17   "Four reales."

18   "We want two Anis del Toro."

19   "With water?"

20   "Do you want it with water?"

21   "I don't know," the girl said. "Is it good with water?"

22   "It's all right."

23   "You want them with water?" asked the woman.

24   "Yes, with water."

25   "It tastes like licorice," the girl said and put the glass down.

26   "That's the way with everything."

27   "Yes," said the girl. "Everything tastes of licorice. Especially all the things you've waited so long for, like absinthe."

28   "Oh, cut it out."

29   "You started it," the girl said. "I was being amused. I was having a fine time."

30   "Well, let's try and have a fine time."

31   "All right. I was trying. I said the mountains looked like white elephants. Wasn't that bright?"

32   "That was bright."

33   "I wanted to try this new drink: That's all we do, isn't it—look at things and try new drinks?"

34   "I guess so."

35   The girl looked across at the hills.

36   "They're lovely hills," she said. "They don't really look like white elephants. I just meant the coloring of their skin through the trees."

37   "Should we have another drink?"

38   "All right."

39   The warm wind blew the bead curtain against the table.

40   "The beer's nice and cool," the man said.

41   "It's lovely," the girl said.

42   "It's really an awfully simple operation, Jig," the man said. "It's not really an operation at all."

43   The girl looked at the ground the table legs rested on.

44   "I know you wouldn't mind it, Jig. It's really not anything. It's just to let the air in."

45   The girl did not say anything.

46   "I'll go with you and I'll stay with you all the time. They just let the air in and then it's all perfectly natural."

47   "Then what will we do afterward?"

48   "We'll be fine afterward. Just like we were before."

49   "What makes you think so?"

50   "That's the only thing that bothers us. It's the only thing that's made us unhappy."

51   The girl looked at the bead curtain, put her hand out, and took hold of two of the strings of beads.

52   "And you think then we'll be all right and be happy."

53   "I know we will. You don't have to be afraid. I've known lots of people that have done it."

54   "So have I," said the girl. "And afterward they were all so happy."

55   "Well," the man said, "if you don't want to you don't have to. I wouldn't have you do it if you didn't want to. But I know it's perfectly simple."

56   "And you really want to?"

57   "I think it's the best thing to do. But I don't want you to do it if you don't really want to."

58   "And if I do it you'll be happy and things will be like they were and you'll love me?"

59   "I love you now. You know I love you."

60   "I know. But if I do it, then it will be nice again if I say things are like white elephants, and you'll like it?"

61   "I'll love it. I love it now but I just can't think about it. You know how I get when I worry."

62   "If I do it you won't ever worry?"

63   "I won't worry about that because it's perfectly simple."

64   "Then I'll do it. Because I don't care about me."

65   "What do you mean?"

66   "I don't care about me."

67   "Well, I care about you."

68   "Oh, yes. But I don't care about me. And I'll do it and then everything will be fine."

69   "I don't want you to do it if you feel that way."

70   The girl stood up and walked to the end of the station. Across, on the other side, were fields of grain and trees along the banks of the Ebro. Far away, beyond the river, were mountains. The shadow of a cloud moved across the field of grain and she saw the river through the trees.

71   "And we could have all this," she said. "And we could have everything and every day we make it more impossible."

72   "What did you say?"

73   "I said we could have everything."

74   "We can have everything."

75   "No, we can't."

76   "We can have the whole world."

77   "No, we can't."

78   "We can go everywhere."

79   "No, we can't. It isn't ours any more."

80   "It's ours."

81   "No, it isn't. And once they take it away, you never get it back."

82   "But they haven't taken it away."

83   "We'll wait and see."

84   "Come on back in the shade," he said. "You mustn't feel that way."

85   "I don't feel any way," the girl said. "I just know things."

86   "I don't want you to do anything that you don't want to do—"

87   "Nor that isn't good for me," she said. "I know. Could we have another beer?"

88   "All right. But you've got to realize—"

89   "I realize," the girl said. "Can't we maybe stop talking?"

90   They sat down at the table and the girl looked across at the hills on the dry side of the valley and the man looked at her and at the table.

91   "You've got to realize," he said, "that I don't want you to do it if you don't want to. I'm perfectly willing to go through with it if it means anything to you."

92   "Doesn't it mean anything to you? We could get along."

93   "Of course it does. But I don't want anybody but you. I don't want any one else. And I know it's perfectly simple."

94   "Yes, you know it's perfectly simple."

95   "It's all right for you to say that, but I do know it."

96   "Would you do something for me now?"

97   "I'd do anything for you."

98   "Would you please please please please please please please stop talking?"

99   He did not say anything but looked at the bags against the wall of the station. There were labels on them from all the hotels where they had spent nights.

100   "But I don't want you to," he said, "I don't care anything about it."

101   "I'll scream," the girl said.

102   The woman came out through the curtains with two glasses of beer and put them down on the damp felt pads. "The train comes in five minutes," she said.

103   "What did she say?" asked the girl.

104   "That the train is coming in five minutes."

105   The girl smiled brightly at the woman, to thank her.

106   "I'd better take the bags over to the other side of the station," the man said. She smiled at him.

107   "All right. Then come back and we'll finish the beer."

108   He picked up the two heavy bags and carried them around the station to the other tracks. He looked up the tracks but could not see the train. Coming back, he walked through the barroom, where people waiting for the train were drinking. He drank an Anis at the bar and looked at the people. They were all waiting reasonably for the train. He went out through the bead curtain. She was sitting at the table and smiled at him.

109   "Do you feel better?" he asked.

110   "I feel fine," she said. "There's nothing wrong with me. I feel fine."

QUESTIONS FOR DISCUSSION

1. What mood is created through setting the story in a train-station bar in a foreign country with a view of the "long and white" hills across the Ebro River valley? Why does Jig admire the view of the mountains, the field of grain, and the river?

2. Why does Jig remark that the hills remind her of "white elephants"? What symbolism is suggested by the expression "a white elephant"?
3. What is the subject of the disagreement between the American and Jig? How are their personalities and outlooks on life contrasted through their positions in the disagreement?
4. Point out lines in the dialogue that seem to have a double or oblique meaning. For example, when Jig remarks, "Everything tastes of licorice. Especially the things you've waited so long for, like absinthe," what motivates her remark and to what is she actually referring? What does she mean when she says "It isn't ours any more"?
5. What is ironic about the American's line, "They just let the air in and then it's perfectly natural"? Give other examples of irony in the American's comments. Do you think the American intends to be ironic?
6. Do you think that the characters' attitudes about what is important in a relationship are typical of male/female conflicts? Could you identify with one of the character's points of view, or were you sympathetic to both?

CONNECTION

Compare the American's attempt to mold Jig into his "ideal" girlfriend with Pygmalion's attempt to mold Gwen into his ideal wife in John Updike's story in this chapter. Why and how do both efforts fail?

IDEAS FOR WRITING

1. Write an essay in which you interpret the meaning of Jig's final remark in the story, "I feel fine," based on evidence from the conversation between the couple earlier in the story.
2. Write a story involving a conflict between two characters using the type of brief dialogue and simple, unadorned description that characterizes Hemingway's "Hills Like White Elephants."

Gloria Naylor

The Two

Gloria Naylor (b. 1950) was raised in New York City; her parents were originally from Mississippi. After high school she spent seven years as a missionary for the Jehovah's Witnesses but then turned from religion to a strong belief in feminism. Naylor attended Brooklyn College of the City University of New York where she earned a

B.A. in 1981. She went on to study at Yale and completed her M.A. in African-American studies in 1983. Naylor has taught at a number of universities, including Princeton, New York University, Boston University, and the University of Pennsylvania. Her novel, The Women of Brewster Place: A Novel in Seven Stories (1982), in which "The Two" appears, won the American Book Award for the best first novel and was later made into a television mini-series. Naylor won a National Endowment for the Arts Fellowship in 1985 and a Guggenheim Fellowship in 1988. Her subsequent novels, such as Mama Day (1988), Children of the Night (1985), and The Men of Brewster Place (1998), reflect Naylor's belief in the importance of courage, community, and cultural identity.

JOURNAL

Write about a person who was judged differently once people learned that he or she did not follow traditional sex roles.

1   At first they seemed like such nice girls. No one could remember exactly when they had moved into Brewster. It was earlier in the year before Ben was killed—of course, it had to be before Ben's death. But no one remembered if it was in the winter or spring of that year that the two had come. People often came and went on Brewster Place like a restless night's dream, moving in and out in the dark to avoid eviction notices or neighborhood bulletins about the dilapidated condition of their furnishings. So it wasn't until the two were clocked leaving in the mornings and returning in the evenings at regular intervals that it was quietly absorbed that they now claimed Brewster as home. And Brewster waited, cautiously prepared to claim them, because you never knew about young women, and obviously single at that. But when no wild music or drunken friends careened out of the corner building on weekends, and especially, when no slightly eager husbands were encouraged to linger around that first-floor apartment and run errands for them, a suspended sigh of relief floated around the two when they dumped their garbage, did their shopping, and headed for the morning bus.

2   The women of Brewster had readily accepted the lighter, skinny one. There wasn't much threat in her timid mincing walk and the slightly protruding teeth she seemed so eager to show everyone in her bell-like good mornings and evenings. Breaths were held a little longer in the direction of the short dark one—too pretty, and too much behind. And she insisted on wearing those thin Qiana dresses that the summer breeze molded against the maddening rhythm of the twenty pounds of rounded flesh that she swung steadily down the street. Through slitted eyes, the women watched their men watching her pass, knowing the bastards were praying for a wind. But since she seemed oblivious to whether these supplications went answered, their sighs settled around her shoulders too. Nice girls.

3   And so no one even cared to remember exactly when they had moved into Brewster Place, until the rumor started. It had first spread through the block like a sour odor

that's only faintly perceptible and easily ignored until it starts growing in strength from the dozen mouths it had been lying in, among clammy gums and scum-coated teeth. And then it was everywhere—lining the mouths and whitening the lips of everyone as they wrinkled up their noses at its pervading smell, unable to pinpoint the source or time of its initial arrival. Sophie could—she had been there.

4   It wasn't that the rumor had actually begun with Sophie. A rumor needs no true parent. It only needs a willing carrier, and it found one in Sophie. She had been there—on one of those August evenings when the sun's absence is a mockery because the heat leaves the air so heavy it presses the naked skin down on your body, to the point that a sheet becomes unbearable and sleep impossible. So most of Brewster was outside that night when the two had come in together, probably from one of those air-conditioned movies downtown, and had greeted the ones who were loitering around their building. And they had started up the steps when the skinny one tripped over a child's ball and the darker one had grabbed her by the arm and around the waist to break her fall. "Careful, don't wanna lose you now." And the two of them had laughed into each other's eyes and went into the building.

5   The smell had begun there. It outlined the image of the stumbling woman and the one who had broken her fall. Sophie and a few other women sniffed at the spot and then, perplexed, silently looked at each other. Where had they seen that before? They had often laughed and touched each other—held each other in joy or its dark twin—but where had they seen *that* before? It came to them as the scent drifted down the steps and entered their nostrils on the way to their inner mouths. They had seen that—done that—with their men. That shared moment of invisible communion reserved for two and hidden from the rest of the world behind laughter or tears or a touch. In the days before babies, miscarriages, and other broken dreams, after stolen caresses in barn stalls and cotton houses, after intimate walks from church and secret kisses with boys who were now long forgotten or permanently fixed in their lives—that was where. They could almost feel the odor moving about in their mouths, and they slowly knitted themselves together and let it out into the air like a yellow mist that began to cling to the bricks on Brewster.

6   So it got around that the two in 312 were *that* way. And they had seemed like such nice girls. Their regular exits and entrances to the block were viewed with a jaundiced eye. The quiet that rested around their door on the weekends hinted of all sorts of secret rituals, and their friendly indifference to the men on the street was an insult to the women as a brazen flaunting of unnatural ways.

7   Since Sophie's apartment windows faced theirs from across the air shaft, she became the official watchman for the block, and her opinions were deferred to whenever the two came up in conversation. Sophie took her position seriously and was constantly alert for any telltale signs that might creep out around their drawn shades, across from which she kept a religious vigil. An entire week of drawn shades was evidence enough to send her flying around with reports that as soon as it got dark they pulled their shades down and put on the lights. Heads nodded in knowing unison—a definite sign. If doubt was voiced with a "But I pull my shades down at night too," a whispered "Yeah, but you're not *that* way" was argument enough to win them over.

8   Sophie watched the lighter one dumping their garbage, and she went outside and opened the lid. Her eyes darted over the crushed tin cans, vegetable peelings, and empty chocolate chip cookie boxes. What do they do with all them chocolate chip cookies? It was surely a sign, but it would take some time to figure that one out. She saw Ben go into their apartment, and she waited and blocked his path as he came out, carrying his toolbox.

9   "What ya see?" She grabbed his arm and whispered wetly in his face.

10   Ben stared at her squinted eyes and drooping lips and shook his head slowly. "Uh, uh, uh, it was terrible."

11   "Yeah?" She moved in a little closer.

12   "Worst busted faucet I seen in my whole life." He shook her hand off his arm and left her standing in the middle of the block.

13   "You old sop bucket," she muttered, as she went back up on her stoop. A broken faucet, huh? Why did they need to use so much water?

14   Sophie had plenty to report that day. Ben had said it was terrible in there. No, she didn't know exactly what he had seen, but you can imagine—and they did. Confronted with the difference that had been thrust into their predictable world, they reached into their imaginations and, using an ancient pattern, weaved themselves a reason for its existence. Out of necessity they stitched all of their secret fears and lingering childhood nightmares into this existence, because even though it was deceptive enough to try and look as they looked, talk as they talked, and do as they did, it had to have some hidden stain to invalidate it—it was impossible for them both to be right. So they leaned back, supported by the sheer weight of their numbers and comforted by the woven barrier that kept them protected from the yellow mist that enshrouded the two as they came and went on Brewster Place.

15   Lorraine was the first to notice the change in the people on Brewster Place. She was a shy but naturally friendly woman who got up early, and had read the morning paper and done fifty sit-ups before it was time to leave for work. She came out of her apartment eager to start her day by greeting any of her neighbors who were outside. But she noticed that some of the people who had spoken to her before made a point of having something else to do with their eyes when she passed, although she could almost feel them staring at her back as she moved on. The ones who still spoke only did so after an uncomfortable pause, in which they seemed to be peering through her before they begrudged her a good morning or evening. She wondered if it was all in her mind and she thought about mentioning it to Theresa, but she didn't want to be accused of being too sensitive again. And how would Tee even notice anything like that anyway? She had a lousy attitude and hardly ever spoke to people. She stayed in that bed until the last moment and rushed out of the house fogged-up and grumpy, and she was used to being stared at—by men at least—because of her body.

16   Lorraine thought about these things as she came up the block from work, carrying a large paper bag. The group of women on her stoop parted silently and let her pass.

17   "Good evening," she said, as she climbed the steps.

18   Sophie was standing on the top step and tried to peek into the bag. "You been shopping, huh? What ya buy?" It was almost an accusation.

19   "Groceries." Lorraine shielded the top of the bag from view and squeezed past her with a confused frown. She saw Sophie throw a knowing glance to the others at the bottom of the stoop. What was wrong with this old woman? Was she crazy or something?

20   Lorraine went into her apartment. Theresa was sitting by the window, reading a copy of *Mademoiselle*. She glanced up from her magazine. "Did you get my chocolate chip cookies?"

21   "Why good evening to you, too, Tee. And how was my day? Just wonderful." She sat the bag down on the couch. "That little Baxter boy brought in a puppy for show-and-tell, and the damn thing pissed all over the floor and then proceeded to chew the heel off my shoe, but, yes, I managed to hobble to the store and bring you your chocolate chip cookies."

22   Oh, Jesus, Theresa thought, she's got a bug up her ass tonight.

23   "Well, you should speak to Mrs. Baxter. She ought to train her kid better than that." She didn't wait for Lorraine to stop laughing before she tried to stretch her good mood. "Here, I'll put those things away. Want me to make dinner so you can
24   rest? I only worked half a day, and the most tragic thing that went down was a broken fingernail and that got caught in my typewriter."

      Lorraine followed Theresa into the kitchen. "No, I'm not really tired, and fair's
25   fair, you cooked last night. I didn't mean to tick off like that; it's just that . . . well, Tee, have you noticed that people aren't as nice as they used to be?"

      Theresa stiffened. Oh, God, here she goes again. "What people, Lorraine? Nice in what way?"

26   "Well, the people in this building and on the street. No one hardly speaks anymore. I mean, I'll come in and say good evening—and just silence. It wasn't like that when we first moved in. I don't know, it just makes you wonder; that's all. What are they thinking?"

27   "I personally don't give a shit what they're thinking. And their good evenings don't put any bread on my table."

28   "Yeah, but you didn't see the way that woman looked at me out there. They must feel something or know something. They probably—"

29   "They, they, they!" Theresa exploded. "You know, I'm not starting up with this again, Lorraine. Who in the hell are they? And where in the hell are we? Living in some dump of a building in this God-forsaken part of town around a bunch of ignorant niggers with the cotton still under their fingernails because of you and your theys. They knew something in Linden Hills, so I gave up an apartment for you that I'd been in for the last four years. And then they knew in Park Heights, and you made me so miserable there we had to leave. Now these mysterious theys are on Brewster Place. Well, look out the window, kid. There's a big wall down that block, and this is the end of the line for me. I'm not moving anymore, so if that's what you're working yourself up to—save it!"

30   When Theresa became angry she was like a lump of smoldering coal, and her fierce bursts of temper always unsettled Lorraine.

31   "You see, that's why I didn't want to mention it." Lorraine began to pull at her fingers nervously. "You're always flying up and jumping to conclusions—no one said anything about moving. And I didn't know your life has been so miserable since you met me. I'm sorry about that," she finished tearfully.

32   Theresa looked at Lorraine, standing in the kitchen door like a wilted leaf, and she wanted to throw something at her. Why didn't she ever fight back? The very softness that had first attracted her to Lorraine was now a frequent cause for irritation. Smoked honey. That's what Lorraine had reminded her of, sitting in her office clutching that application. Dry autumn days in Georgia woods, thick bloated smoke under a beehive, and the first glimpse of amber honey just faintly darkened about the edges by the burning twigs. She had flowed just that heavily into Theresa's mind and had stuck there with a persistent sweetness.

33   But Theresa hadn't known then that this softness filled Lorraine up to the very middle and that she would bend at the slightest pressure, would be constantly seeking to surround herself with the comfort of everyone's goodwill, and would shrivel up at the least touch of disapproval. It was becoming a drain to be continually called upon for this nurturing and support that she just didn't understand. She had supplied it at first out of love for Lorraine, hoping that she would harden eventually, even as honey does when exposed to the cold. Theresa was growing tired of being clung to—of being the one who was leaned on. She didn't want a child—she wanted someone who could stand toe to toe with her and be willing to slug it out at times. If they practiced that way with each other, then they could turn back to back and beat the hell out of the world for trying to invade their territory. But she had found no such sparring partner in Lorraine, and the strain of fighting alone was beginning to show on her.

34   "Well, if it was that miserable, I would have been gone a long time ago," she said, watching her words refresh Lorraine like a gentle shower.

35   "I guess you think I'm some sort of a sick paranoid, but I can't afford to have people calling my job or writing letters to my principal. You know I've already lost a position like that in Detroit. And teaching is my whole life, Tee."

36   "I know," she sighed, not really knowing at all. There was no danger of that ever happening on Brewster Place. Lorraine taught too far from this neighborhood for anyone here to recognize her in that school. No, it wasn't her job she feared losing this time, but their approval. She wanted to stand out there and chat and trade makeup secrets and cake recipes. She wanted to be secretary of their block association and be asked to mind their kids while they ran to the store. And none of that was going to happen if they couldn't even bring themselves to accept her good evenings.

37   Theresa silently finished unpacking the groceries. "Why did you buy cottage cheese? Who eats this stuff?"

38   "Well, I thought we should go on a diet."

39   "If *we* go on a diet, then you'll disappear. You've got nothing to lose but your hair."

40   "Oh, I don't know. I thought that we might want to try and reduce our hips or something." Lorraine shrugged playfully.

41   "No, thank you. We are very happy with our hips the way they are," Theresa said, as she shoved the cottage cheese to the back of the refrigerator. "And even when I

lose weight, it never comes off there. My chest and arms just get smaller, and I start looking like a bottle of salad dressing."

42   The two women laughed, and Theresa sat down to watch Lorraine fix dinner. "You know, this behind has always been my downfall. When I was coming up in Georgia with my grandmother, the boys used to promise me penny candy if I would let them pat my behind. And I used to love those jawbreakers—you know, the kind that lasted all day and kept changing colors in your mouth. So I was glad to oblige them, because in one afternoon I could collect a whole week's worth of jawbreakers."

43   "Really. That's funny to you? Having some boy feeling all over you."

44   Theresa sucked her teeth. "We were only kids, Lorraine. You know, you remind me of my grandmother. That was one straight-laced old lady. She had a fit when my brother told her what I was doing. She called me into the smokehouse and told me in this real scary whisper that I could get pregnant from letting little boys pat my butt and that I'd end up like my cousin Willa. But Willa and I had been thick as fleas, and she had already given me a step-by-step summary of how she'd gotten into her predicament. But I sneaked around to her house that night just to double-check her story, since that old lady had seemed so earnest. 'Willa, are you sure?' I whispered through her bedroom window. 'I'm tellin' ya, Tee,' she said. 'Just keep both feet on the ground and you home free.' Much later I learned that advice wasn't too biologically sound, but it worked in Georgia because those country boys didn't have much imagination."

45   Theresa's laughter bounced off of Lorraine's silent, rigid back and died in her throat. She angrily tore open a pack of the chocolate chip cookies. "Yeah," she said, staring at Lorraine's back and biting down hard into the cookie," "it wasn't until I came up north to college that I found out there's a whole lot of things that a dude with a little imagination can do to you even with both feet on the ground. You see, Willa forgot to tell me not to bend over or squat or—"

46   "Must you!" Lorraine turned around from the stove with her teeth clenched tightly together.

47   "Must I what, Lorraine? Must I talk about things that are as much a part of my life as eating or breathing or growing old? Why are you always so uptight about sex or men?"

48   "I'm not uptight about anything. I just think it's disgusting when you go on and on about—"

49   "There's nothing disgusting about it, Lorraine. You've never been with a man, but I've been with quite a few—some better than others. There were a couple who I still hope to this day will die a slow, painful death, but then there were some who were good to me—in and out of bed."

50   "If they were so great, then why are you with me?" Lorraine's lips were trembling.

51   "Because—" Theresa looked steadily into her eyes and then down at the cookie she was twirling on the table. "Because," she continued slowly, "you can take a chocolate chip cookie and put holes in it and attach it to your ears and call it an earring, or hang it around your neck on a silver chain and pretend it's a necklace—but it's still a cookie. See—you can toss it in the air and call it a Frisbee or even a flying saucer, if the mood hits you, and it's still just a cookie. Send it spinning on a

table—like this—until it's a wonderful blur of amber and brown light that you can imagine to be a topaz or rusted gold or old crystal, but the law of gravity has got to come into play, sometime, and it's got to come to rest—sometime. Then all the spinning and pretending and hoopla is over with. And you know what you got?"

52 "A chocolate chip cookie," Lorraine said.

53 "Uh-huh." Theresa put the cookie in her mouth and winked. "A lesbian." She got up from the table. "Call me when dinner's ready, I'm going back to read." She stopped at the kitchen door. "Now, why are you putting gravy on that chicken, Lorraine? You know it's fattening."

QUESTIONS FOR DISCUSSION

1. How does the sentence, "They seemed like such nice girls," set the tone for the story? How often is this phrase repeated? When does it become ironic?
2. Describe Brewster Place and the people who live there. Why are they such gossips and rumor spreaders? What is their first impression of Lorraine and Theresa? Why does their attitude toward the women change?
3. What is the connection between the story's theme and the shift in point of view midway through the story? Why did the author wait to present the women's perspective and names?
4. Contrast Lorraine and Theresa's attitudes about their neighbors. How do their different attitudes reflect deeper differences in their personalities and within their relationship?
5. In what ways does the chocolate chip cookie symbolize and clarify Theresa's point about her sexual orientation? Does Lorraine see the cookie in the same way as Theresa does? How do you think their relationship will develop? Will it survive the social pressures the couple must endure?
6. With which of the main characters were you most sympathetic? Why?

CONNECTION

Compare the attitude of the tenants towards "The Two" with the villagers' response to the pregnant woman in "No Name Woman."

IDEAS FOR WRITING

1. Write an essay that compares the two sections of the story, the first part that reflects the perspective of the neighbors and the second part that involves a dialogue between Lorraine and Theresa. How does this contrasting structure help to emphasize the values reflected in the story?
2. Write an essay in which you analyse the story in terms of what it reveals about popular attitudes that are based on a lack of knowledge and understanding of lesbians or women who live together in non-traditional relationships.

Diane Wood Middlebrook

Swinging

Diane Middlebrook (b.1939) was born in Pocatello, Idaho, and attended the University of Washington to earn her B.A. in 1961, completing her Ph.D. at Yale in 1968. Middlebrook has been a member of the English Department at Stanford University since 1966, where she specializes in teaching 20th-Century American Poetry. She edited Coming to Light: American Women Poets in the 20th Century *(1985), and is best known for her groundbreaking biography* Anne Sexton: A Biography *(1991). The following selection, "Swinging" is from her latest book* Suits Me *(1998), about a successful jazz musician, Billy Tipton, who lived most of her life as a man, marrying several women and raising children. In this selection, which takes place in the World War II era in Joplin, Missouri, Tipton makes a transition in her life from lesbian-like relationships to a lifestyle in which she came to totally conceal her feminine identity and pose as a man even to her most intimate associates and lovers.*

JOURNAL

What are your views on "cross dressing"? Do you find it acceptable, amusing, or offensive and disturbing when men dress up as women or women as men?

Bill Tipton is just 5 feet, 4 1/2 inches tall, but every fraction of an inch is packed with talent . . . His wife is a talented vocalist.

—The Dial, March 1944

1   Saturday afternoon in the late autumn of 1943: a dressed-up young couple walks purposefully down Main Street in Joplin, Missouri. She is diminutive, small-boned as a bird; he holds her lightly by the elbow, possessive. He's wearing a fedora and a double-breasted suit, somewhat threadbare but fastidiously brushed and pressed. She has hung an unbuttoned polo coat over her shoulders like a cape, partially revealing a knee-length dress with a gored skirt. On her feet are platform shoes, and she has applied pancaked makeup to her shapely legs; fashion, contributing to the war effort, dictates raised hemlines, to save fabric, though hosiery is hard to get. The street is crowded with buses depositing load after load of soldiers and a few women in WAC uniforms, up from Camp Crowder for the weekend. The couple's civvies stand out amid the khaki. Is that why they stare straight ahead, meeting no one's eyes? They are headed for afternoon drinks and people-watching at the Rendezvous Lounge in the grand old Connor Hotel, where a jazz ensemble plays in the afternoon. Then they will go on to drinks at a lounge in the Keystone Hotel called the Glass Hat, where the customers sit as if arranged on display behind the plate-glass windows.

2   This is Billy Tipton and his new wife, June, who had married each other, they said, in October. June was eye-catching, "oh so hip and so cool!" according to a mu-

sician who was just seventeen when he first laid eyes on her. Women recall that she had clean-cut, small features set off by a short pageboy hairstyle and that she was "tiny," "very slight," "petite," well proportioned. Men say that she had great legs and, despite her small size, a buxom figure. And a good voice. Though June was not really a professional singer and had no regular job with a band, she was sometimes billed as a torch singer, as in "carrying a torch," as in "tortured." Her style evoked comparisons with some of the best jazz vocalists, such as Anita O'Day and Ella Fitzgerald. One musician who backed her occasionally during the late 1940s recalled, "June could sing up a storm. She did a lot of the jazz things, not quite as bluesy as Billie Holiday or Sarah Vaughan, but certainly capable. Very, very talented, and very nice. I was just young, a kid, and not married. If it hadn't been for her being older than I was—which I don't think was much of a roadblock to me at that age—and if she hadn't been attached to Billy, I think I would have chased her."

3   Joplin's history as the place "to go out for a little action" fostered tolerance of a different kind from that in Oklahoma City. According to a former fire chief, Harry Guinn, wartime Joplin was a haven for lesbians and gay men. He observed that "a lot of Gladys's clientele might have been that way—she was kind of known for that." Guinn had opportunity to observe this firsthand, since his fire station was directly across the road from the Heidelberg Inn. But, he added, the Heidelberg was not their only hangout. "There were a lot of places. Seems like [lesbians] were around quite a bit during the war," some wearing men's clothes. In the 1940s, when Gladys Stewart was Billy Tipton's landlady, her nightclub "was a beehive," said one of her friends, a gathering place for every sort of customer. "Gladys had a lot of friends. I guess you could say she was a liberal. If entertainers came through town and they were broke, she put them up there, and the kind of people that went there were kind of an oddball bunch. Don't know about Gladys, but she was probably the sort that did everything once. I don't mean that in a bad way. I liked Gladys. Liked her kids. She raised some good kids."

4   Gladys's son indicated that growing up around his mother's clubs made him savvy about a lot of things other people might not notice. Consequently, he was able to see through Billy's disguise as Billy went around with June on his arm. "Billy dressed like a man but had little boys' shoes on," he said. "There were some of us kids that were streetwise that knew she was a lesbian, but nobody ever made any mention of it. Billy never caused any trouble with anyone, and I guess it's obvious that he wasn't a fighter. He didn't talk like a woman, not like they do now. He looked a little funny, but I guess people just figured they were show people and didn't pay much attention to them."

5   Guessing Billy's secret, Clark Stewart observed that Billy and June were very discreet in public, "never did smooch or anything, never held hands. I remember they'd come down the street walking with their heads up, just looking straight ahead, arms hooked, like you were escorting someone into a dance." Stewart's sister, who had not guessed their secret, remembered rather wistfully that Billy was very much in love with June and "spoiled her to death. He was that kind of person, sympathetic and understanding. If he loved you, he spoiled you." Nor did Billy's musician friends observe anything at all unusual about this couple. A comment by Jerry Seaton, one

of Billy's cronies, is typical: "Why, we all played our different jobs around the clubs, then we'd all meet downtown at the Horseshoe Cafe, just off Fourth and Main. We'd eat, sit around and unwind, just talk. Didn't stay very long, sometimes an hour, then all go our different directions. And June would almost always accompany Billy. She was singing, or sometimes she'd just go with him. I don't know that I ever knew much about where she came from."

6   By the end of 1946, Billy and June were no longer together. Billy had a double identity, and quite possibly June had fallen in love with only half of it. "Why not take all of me?" was such stuff as songs were made of, but marriages needed firmer ground, and Billy's desire to pass as a married man placed the relationship on a fault line. What June alone knew could always be used against him.

7   In any case, when Billy and June separated, their parting was called a divorce by the people who remember it, and Billy got custody of their dog, Troubles. One musician remembers something else, as well: "Now this woman named June that he married, she circulated a story after they broke up and supposedly got a divorce—I don't know that they ever really got married, but they claimed they did—but she later circulated the story that he was a *hermorphadite*, had both sexes. She'd wiggle her little finger up and down, you know, like Billy was the size of a pinkie."

8   This memory raises a number of questions about the years when Billy went from cross-dressing to passing. What did June know about Billy's body when she became his wife? She may have been using the term "hermaphrodite" as a euphemism. Sometimes rather poetically mispronounced "hermorphadite" (a woman morphed, as we might say), this was common parlance for "lesbian," as was evident in the way people phrased their recollections of Buck Thomason, the radio announcer. Was June a closeted lesbian, like Billy? Or was "hermaphrodite" Billy's term, an improvised explanation meant to allay the outrage June might have felt upon discovering that she had been deceived?

9   What actually was Billy's biological sex? As we have seen, certain aspects of Billy's body were commented on by people who knew him as a man. Paul Jensen observed, with reference to the strength of Billy's piano playing that he "had arms big around as some people's waists almost. Real strong-looking arms." Another musician said that Billy's large buttocks earned him the nickname Pear Shape, after a male character in the comic strip *Dick Tracy*, though to female observers this feature looked female. Among the many reasons we can summon to explain Billy's choice to live as a man, was there a biological reason?

10   The social conventions by which we recognize only two sexes and call them "opposite" conceal a number of biological actualities. Sex difference is defined at several bodily sites. Outside lie the genitals and, after puberty, the secondary sex characteristics: breasts and hips on a woman, Adam's apple and facial and body hair on a man. Inside lie the gonads (ovaries in the female, testes in the male), which direct sexual development through the production of estradiol for female development, testosterone for male. Yet male and female bodies synthesize variable amounts of both sex hormones, and the complexity of the interactions of the hormones results in so much variation that sex difference is best understood as a spectrum or continuum. One contemporary biologist has claimed that there are actually five discernibly different and biologically

coherent human sexes. Female and male are two of the five. The others are mixtures. "Herms," or true hermaphrodites, possess one testis and one ovary; female pseudohermaphrodites, or "ferms," have ovaries and some aspects of the male genitalia but lack testes; male pseudohermaphrodites, or "merms," have testes and some aspects of the female genitalia but lack ovaries. "Each of these categories is in itself complex," the biologist Anne Fausto-Sterling observes. "The percentage of male and female characteristics, for instance, can vary enormously among members of the same subgroup." In the medical literature, the hermaphroditic types are classed together as "intersexes." The condition is thought to occur in possibly 4 percent of newborns.

11   The external sex organs in human beings are visibly as different as a pair of gloves, one turned inside out: what is extended in one is concealed in the other. Yet in a newborn, the clitoris can be long, the penis abbreviated, the scrotum similar to labia. Such ambiguity is well known to pediatric endrocrinologists, the usual referees when a baby's sex is not immediately obvious. Until very recently, medical treatment with hormones or surgery was often undertaken immediately, to insure that the external and internal sex organs matched up and gave one clear message at puberty. The treatment would be done early to help the child develop a secure pyschological gender identity—the conviction, which is thought to form by age three, that one is a girl or a boy. Such medical intervention has grown controversial in the wake of recent reassessments of the notion that gender identity is an either-or proposition.

12   This brings us back to Billy. Evidence from the autopsy performed on Billy's corpse indicates that she was not a herm, for she possessed no testes. Was she a ferm? June's memorable finger-waggle suggests that she possessed an unusually large clitoris with some of the characteristics of a penis, but the autopsy report—a better source than hearsay—does not support this conjecture. "The body habitus is that of a normally developed, adult female (despite the name and past history of male identity)," the report says. "The genitalia are those of a normal adult female."

13   Yet as people remember and as photographs confirm, from time to time beginning in the 1940s, Billy sported a trim little mustache. At least two explanations are possible. The mustache could have been a cosmetically assisted feature of a normal woman's facial hair pattern, or it could have been the result of elevated levels of androgens. Billy's chromosomes were not examined during the autopsy to learn whether her cells carried the Y chromosome, which would make her male, or two X chromosomes, which would make her female. A Y chromosome might have caused an increased production of androgens if she had androgen insensitivity syndrome, a genetic disorder that prevents the full development of masculine traits in males. Another possibility is that Billy had a condition, not uncommon in females, called polycystic ovary syndrome, an enzymatic defect in the ovaries that causes them to produce too much testosterone, the steroid hormone that stimulates the production of male sex characteristics. Billy's chunky upper body, tendency to obestiy, relatively undefined waistline, facial hair, and masculine walk could have been the developmental outcome of a flood of testosterone from polycystic ovary disease. Another result would have been a reduction in the number and strength of menstrual periods, a great convenience in Billy's way of life. Neither the presence of

the Y chromosome in Billy's cells nor the effect of polycystic ovary disease would have made her any less than the biologically normal female described in the autopsy report. "Normal" is a very capacious category. Conceivably, though, Billy's fortitude got a little biochemical lift from testosterone.

14   As far as Billy's relationship with June and other women is concerned, we can assume that after she separated from June, being Billy full-time solved the psychological and social difficulties presented by Dorothy's strong masculine gender identification and her sexual desire for women, quite aside from solving the problem of achieving professional status in a man's world. Billy wanted to be happy, and for Billy it was easier to be happy as a man than as a lesbian. Confiding in sexual partners therefore became both unwise and unnecessary.

15   This decision inaugurated the final phase in the development of the persona of Billy Tipton, and it can be attached to a photograph of Billy with Reggie and Lynn Fullenwider at the Green Frog Café in Abilene, Texas. The nightclub's photographer captured them in their finery that night. Both men are in coats and ties, and Reggie wears a hat with a veil and a triple string of pearls. The spine of a matchbook on the table reads "Merry Christmas," so the occasion is quite possibly a celebration of Billy's birthday, 29 December. Possibly the year is 1944, when Billy was working in Corpus Christi. Billy turned thirty that year.

16   At least three prints of this photograph were made. One, nicely framed in ivory leather and covered with protective glass, was found among Billy's scrapbooks and memorabilia after his death. Another print was pasted into Reggie's photo album, probably by Reggie herself. This one has been trimmed of Billy, all except the hands, and has become a picture of Reggie and Lynn in a nightclub with some anonymous third party who is fiddling with a cigarette lighter. The third print, framed in silvery metal, always traveled with Billy. In this print, the figure of Lynn has been trimmed away, leaving Billy alone with his mother.

17   This keepsake in its three versions seems to be a record of the permanent transfer of Billy's secret into Reggie's keeping, for Reggie's album preserved portraits only of a daughter. From now on, Reggie alone held the part that once was her daughter's heart, the part now fully masked for everybody else by the professional persona of Billy. "Dorothy was my mother's daughter," Dorothy's brother often remarked, and Reggie's photo album seems to have served as the repository of the identity.

18   In Billy's show copy of the photograph, which he took on the road with him, Reggie's personal history has been scissored away, probably to improve her usefulness as a prop. Reggie's presence gives this birthday party its authenticity, so to speak. Mother and son are out on the town, with a popping flashbulb confirming his celebrity and her pride in it. This is the only image of Reggie that any of the other women in Billy's life would ever see.

19   Billy's private copy of the full, uncensored print is the most interesting of all, for it shows that by age thirty, she had won acceptance not only from Reggie but within the family life that Reggie formed with Lynn Fullenwider. The same private filing cabinet that preserved the photograph also contained a rather long

letter from Lynn, dated 1961. The letter thanks "Dot" for a Father's Day present and invites her for a visit. "I hope you can make it to Okla this year. Both of us would love so much to see you," Lynn wrote. "Thank you again Dear for the swell Father's Day rememberances. With lots of love." This suggests that Billy continued to put a good deal of effort into the preservation of her role as a member of the family, and that this effort was successful in spite of the potentially humiliating difficulties that her charade presented to those who loved her and had to play along. In 1944, Lynn was there as stepfather to celebrate the birthday of a successful entertainer whose public persona was masculine, and he continued to affirm their relationship as Billy extended the disguise. For Billy did not choose to live alone after he and June parted company in 1946. He had already met the next woman he would call his wife.

QUESTIONS FOR DISCUSSION

1. What do you learn about Billy and June as a couple in the opening paragraphs? What do their friends think about their relationship? How was Gladys' son able to see through Billy's disguise?
2. What does Middlebrook suggest may have led to the eventual breakup of Billy and June? What other factors may have played a part?
3. How does Middlebrook explain the stages of change through which Billy/Dot came eventually to live as a man and to conceal her biological sexual identity even from the women with whom she was intimately involved? What evidence exists to support this speculation?
4. After their breakup, June suggested that Billy may have been a "hermorphadite." What medical and biological evidence does Middlebrook cite to suggest that gender identity is not necessarily an either/or proposition?
5. What is the significance of the three prints of the photograph of Lynn and Reggie Fullenwider with Billy at the Green Frog Café? What do the different versions of the photograph kept by the parties involved reveal about the complex, shifting gender identity and social façades of Billy/Dot ?
6. What is revealed about Billy's complex gender identity in the letter from Lynn dated 1961 in which he thanks Billy for a recent Father's Day present and refers to him/her affectionately as "Dot" and "Dear"?

CONNECTION

Compare the life of Billy to the lives of those who engage in on-line gender bending and gender deception as portrayed in Sherry Turkle's article on "Virtual Sex" in this chapter. Which approach, if either, seems more acceptable, from an ethical/moral perspective?

IDEAS FOR WRITING

1. Write an essay that explores the ways that the information about Billy's life provided in this essay has given you a different perspective on the relationship between sexuality and gender identity. Provide examples from the essay and from your own observations.
2. Write an essay that explains why you think that Billy would be more or less comfortable living today. Would the disguise have been necessary? Have our ideas about the acceptability of "non-traditional" gender identities changed that much since the 1940s? Provide examples.

Holly Brubach

The Age of the Female Icon

Holly Brubach (b. 1953) studied to become a dancer and, after leaving her native Pittsburgh, moved to New York to dance professionally with experimental choreographers in New York. In New York she has worked as a choreographer, advertising copywriter, and TV script writer. After an injury forced her early retirement from dance, Brubach began writing reviews about dance as well as essays and book reviews on the popular arts, fashion, and travel. Her reviews and columns have appeared in Mademoiselle, Saturday Review, New York Times Book Review, *and* New York Times Magazine, *where she currently has a weekly column. The following essay on today's female cultural icons was published in a special 1996 issue of* New York Times Magazine *that focused on female icons and role models.*

JOURNAL

Write about a figure in public life or the media of the same gender as yourself who has been a "role model" for you.

1   It's the 90s, and the pantheon we've built to house the women in our minds is getting crowded. Elizabeth Taylor, Eleanor Roosevelt, Oprah Winfrey, Alanis Morissette, Indira Gandhi, Claudia Schiffer, Coco Chanel, Doris Day, Aretha Franklin, Jackie Onassis, Rosa Parks—they're all there, the dead and the living side by side, contemporaneous in our imaginations. On television and in the movies, in advertising and magazines, their images are scattered across the landscape of our everyday lives. Their presence is sometimes decorative, sometimes uplifiting, occasionally infuriating. The criteria for appointment to this ad hoc hall of fame that takes up so much space in our thoughts and in our culture may at first glance appear to be utterly random. In fact, irrespective of their achievements, most of these women have been apotheosized primarily on the basis of their ability to appeal to our fantasies.

2   An icon is a human sound bite, and individual reduced to a name, a face and an idea: Dale Evans, the compassionate cowgirl. In some cases, just the name and an idea suffice. Few people would recognize Helen Keller in a photograph, but her name has become synonymous with being blind and deaf to such an extent that she has inspired an entire category of jokes. Greta Garbo has gone down in the collective memory as an exalted enigma with a slogan about being alone. Asking a man if that's a gun in his pocket is all it takes to invoke Mae West. Catherine Deneuve's face, pictured on a stamp, is the emblem of France. Virginia Woolf has her own T-shirt. Naomi Campbell has her own doll. Celebrity being the engine that drives our culture, these women have been taken up by the media and made famous, packaged as commodities and marketed to a public eager for novelty and easily bored.

3   Many worthy women are acknowledged for their accomplishments but never take on the status of an icon. . . . The sheer number of icons now in circulation makes any attempt to catalogue them all impossible. . . . Our icons are by no means exclusively female, but the male ones are perhaps less ubiquitous and more accessible. The pedestals we put them on are lower; the service they are called on to perform is somewhat different.

4   Like women, men presumably look to icons for tips that they can take away and apply to their lives. The men who are elevated to the status of icons are the ones who are eminently cool, whose moves the average guy can steal. They do not prompt a fit of introspection (much less of self-recrimination), as female icons often do in women. What a male icon inspires in other men is not so much the desire to be him as the desire to be accepted by him—to be buddies, to shoot pool together, to go drinking. I have all this on good authority from a man of my acquaintance who insists that, though regular guys may envy, say, Robert Redford for his ability to knock women dead, what they're thinking as they watch him in a movie is not "Hey, I wonder if I have what it takes to do that, too," but "I wonder if Redford would like to hang out with me."

5   Whereas women may look at an icon like Raquel Welch, whose appeal is clearly to the male half of humanity, and ask themselves, "If that's what's required to appeal to a man, have I got it, or can I get it?" (The thought of hanging out with Welch— going shopping together or talking about boyfriends—would, I think it's safe to say, never cross most women's minds.)

6   An entire industry, called fashion, has grown up around the business of convincing women that they need to remake themselves in someone else's image: makeup and clothes and other products are presented not as alterations but as improvements. The notion of appearance and personality as a project to be undertaken is inculcated early on. A man may choose to ignore certain male icons; a woman has no such luxury where the great majority of female icons are concerned. She must come to terms with them, defining herself in relation to them—emulating some, rejecting others. In certain cases, a single icon may exist for her as both an example and a reproach.

7   Our male icons are simply the latest entries in a tradition of long standing, broad enough in any given era to encompass any number of prominent men. But the current array of female icons is a recent phenomenon, the outgrowth of aspirations many of which date back no more than 100 years.

8   What were the images of women that informed the life of a girl growing up 200 years ago? It's hard for us to imagine the world before it was wallpapered with ads, before it was inundated with all the visual "information" that comes our way in the course of an average day and competes with real people and events for our attention. There were no magazines, no photographs. In church, a girl would have seen renderings of the Virgin Mary and the saints. She may have encountered portraits of royalty, whose station, unless she'd been born an aristocrat, must have seemed even more unattainable than that of the saints. There were picturesque genre paintings depicting peasants and chambermaids, to be seen at the public salons, if anyone though to bring a girl to them. But the most ambitious artists concentrated on pagan goddesses and mythological women, who, being Olympian, inhabited a plane so lofty that they were presumably immune to quotidian concerns. History and fiction, for the girl who had access to them, contained tales of women whose lives had been somewhat more enterprising and action-packed than those of the women she saw around her, but her knowledge of most women's exploits in her own time would have been limited to hearsay: a woman had written a novel, a woman had played hostess to one of the greatest philosophers of the age and discussed ideas with him, a woman had disguised herself as a man and gone to war. Most likely, a girl would have modeled herself on a female relative, or on a woman in her community. The great beauty who set the standard by which others were measured would have been the one in their midst—the prettiest girl in town, whose fame was local.

9   Nineteenth-century icons like Sarah Bernhardt and George Sand would have imparted no more in the way of inspiration; their careers were predicated on their talents, which had been bestowed by God. It was Florence Nightingale who finally provided an example that was practicable, one to which well-born girls could aspire, and hundreds of women followed her into nursing.

10   Today, the images of women confronting a girl growing up in our culture are far more diverse, though not all of them can be interpreted as signs of progress. A woman who in former times might have served as the model for some painter's rendering of one or another pagan goddess is now deployed to sell us cars and soap. The great beauty has been chosen from an international field of contenders. At the movies, we see the stories of fictional women brought to life by real acresses whose own lives have become the stuff of fiction. In the news, we read about women running countries, directing corporations, and venturing into outer space.

11   The conditions that in our century have made possible this proliferation of female icons were of course brought on by the convergence of advances in women's rights and the growth of the media into an industry. As women accomplished the unprecedented, the press took them up and made them famous, trafficking in their accomplishments, their opinions, their fates. If, compared with the male icons of our time, our female icons seem to loom larger in our culture and to cast a longer shadow, perhaps it's because in so many cases their stories have had the urgency of history in the making.

12   When it comes to looking at women, we're all voyeurs, men and women alike. Does our urge to study the contours of their flesh and the changes in their faces stem from some primal longing to be reunited with the body that gave us life? Women

have been the immemorial repository of male fantasies—a lonesome role that many are nonetheless loath to relinquish, given the power it confers and the oblique satisfaction it brings. The curiousity and desire inherent in the so-called male gaze, deplored for the way it has objectified women in art and in films, are matched on women's part by the need to assess our own potential to be found beautiful and by the pleasure in putting ourselves in the position of the woman being admired.

13   Our contemporary images of women are descended from a centuries-old tradition and, inevitably, they are seen in its light. Women have often been universalized, made allegorical. The figure who represents Liberty, or Justice, to say nothing of Lust or Wrath, is a woman, not a man—a tradition that persists: there is no Mr. America. The unidentified woman in innumerable paintings—landscapes, genre scenes, mythological scenes—transcends her circumstances and becomes Woman. It's the particular that is customarily celebrated in men, and the general in woman. Even our collective notions of beauty reflect this: a man's idiosyncracies enhance his looks; a woman's detract from hers.

14   "I'm every woman, it's all in me," Chaka Khan sings, and the chords in the bass modulte optimistically upward, in a surge of possibility. Not all that long ago, the notion that any woman could be every woman would have been dismissed as blatantly absurd, but to our minds it makes evident sense, in keeping with the logic that we can be anything we want to be—the cardinal rule of the human-potential movement and an assumption that in America today is so widely accepted and dearly held that it might as well be written into the Constitution. Our icons are at this point sufficiently plentiful that to model ourselves on only one of them would seem arbitrary and limiting, when in fact we can take charge in the manner of Katharine Hepburn, strut in the way we learned by watching Tina Turner, flirt in the tradition of Rita Hayworth, grow old with dignity in the style of Georgia O'Keeffe. In the spirit of post-modernism, we piece ourselves together, assembling the examles of several women in a single personality—a process that makes for some unprecedented combinations, like Madonna: the siren who lifts weights and becomes a mother. We contemplate the women who have been singled out in our culture and the permutations of femininity they represent. About to move on to the next century, we call on various aspects of them as we reconfigure our lives, deciding which aspects of our selves we want to take with us and which aspects we want to leave behind.

QUESTIONS FOR DISCUSSION

1. What social and psychological factors cause certain women to become icons of popular culture? Can you think of other causes ?

2. How does Brubach define the term "icon," and what examples does she give to clarify her definition? Can you think of other examples or qualities of the icon?

3. How does Brubach contrast today's cultural icons for women and the ways that women relate to them to male cultural icons? Do you think the contrast she makes is a valid one?

4. How does Brubach contrast the female icons available to women today to those available two hundred years ago? Does the change she describes seem altogether desirable to you? Why or why not?

5. How does Brubach use the cliché of the human potential movement, "We can be anything that we want to be," to clarify the new way that women perceive themselves through relating to a variety of available iconic figures? Are the examples she uses to clarify her point effective?

CONNECTION

Compare Brubach's view of female role models with the classical myth "Pygmalion," in this chapter. How do both Brubach and the "Pygmalion" myth show us how our own identities and our views of the opposite gender are patterned on cultural icons and ideals?

IDEAS FOR WRITING

1. Write an essay about a media/cultural iconic figure (male or female) whom you admire or with whom you identify. Give examples of how the "icon" has helped you to pattern your sense of gender identity, including appearance, values, and/or lifestyle.

2. Write a response to Brubach in which you examine the desirability for women of identifying with and taking on qualities of iconic figures from the media and popular culture.

Sherry Turkle

Virtual Sex

Sherry Turkle was born in 1948 in New York City. She received a joint Ph.D. in Sociology and Personality Psychology at Harvard University and is a licensed clinical psychologist. Currently a Professor in the Science, Technology, and Society program at Massachusetts Institute of Technology, Turkle is particularly interested in the way computers and information technology influence our sense of identity and the way we relate to other people. She has received grants from the MacArthur Foundation, the Guggenheim Foundation, and the National Science Foundation. Turkle's books include Psychoanalytic Politics *(1978),* The Second Self: Computers and the Human Spirit *(1984), and* Life On The Screen: Identity in the Age of the Internet *(1995). In the following selection from* Life on the Screen, *Turkle examines the way gender identity changes when people begin to relate to and interact erotically with on-line correspondents.*

JOURNAL

Write a response to the concept of virtual sex. Does this sound like an interesting idea to you? Why or why not?

1   Virtual sex, whether in MUDs* or in a private room on a commercial online service, consists of two or more players typing descriptions of physical actions, verbal statements, and emotional reactions for their characters. In cyberspace, this activity is not only common but, for many people, it is the centerpiece of their online experience.

2   On MUDs, some people have sex as characters of their own gender. Others have sex as characters of the other gender. Some men play female personae to have netsex with men. And in the "fake-lesbian syndrome," men adopt online female personae in order to have netsex with women. Although it does not seem to be widespread, I have met several women who say they present as male characters in order to have netsex with men. Some people have sex as nonhuman characters, for example, as animals on FurryMUDs. Some enjoy sex with one partner. Some use virtual reality as a place to experiment with group situations. In real life, such behavior (where possible) can create enormous practical and emotional confusion. Virtual adventures may be eaiser to undertake, but they can also result in significant complications. Different people and different couples deal with them in very different ways.

3   Martin and Beth, both forty-one, have been married for nineteen years and have four children. Early in their marriage, Martin regretted not having had more time for sexual experimentation and had an extramarital affair. The affair hurt Beth deeply, and Martin decided he never wanted to do it again. When Martin discovered MUDs he was thrilled. "I really am monogamous. I'm really not interested in something outside my marriage. But being able to have, you know, a Tiny romance is kind of cool." Martin decided to tell Beth about his MUD sex life and she decided to tell him that she does not mind. Beth has made a conscius decision to consider Martin's sexual relationships on MUDs as more like his reading an erotic novel than like his having a rendezvous in a motel room. For Martin, his online affairs are a way to fill the gaps of his youth, to broaden his sexual experience without endangering his marriage.

4   Other partners of virtual adulterers do not share Beth's accepting attitude. Janet, twenty-four, a secretary at a New York law firm, is very upset by her husband Tim's sex life in cyberspace. After Tim's first online affair, he confessed his virtual infidelity. When Janet objected, Tim told her that he would stop "seeing" his online mistress. Janet says that she is not sure that he actually did stop.

> Look, I've got to say the thing that bothers me most is that he wants to do it in the first place. In some ways, I'd have an easier time understanding why he would want to have an affair in real life. At least there, I could say to myself, "Well, it is for someone with a better body, or just for the novelty." It's like the first kiss is always the best kiss. But in MUDding, he is saying that he wants

*Multi-user Dungeons—fantasy online chat rooms.

that feeling of intimacy with someone else, the "just talk" part of an encounter with a woman, and to me that comes closer to what is most important about sex.

First I told him he couldn't do it anymore. Then, I panicked and figured that he might do it anyway, because unlike in real life I could never find out. All these thousands of people all over the world with their stupid fake names . . . no way I would ever find out. So, I pulled back and said that talking about it was strictly off limits. But now I don't know if that was the right decision. I feel paranoid whenever he is on the computer. I can't get it off my mind, that he is cheating, and he probably is tabulating data for his thesis. It must be clear that this sex thing has really hurt our marriage.

5   This distressed wife struggles to decide whether her husband is unfaithful when his persona collaborates on writing real-time erotica with another persona in cyberspace. And beyond this, should it make a difference if unbeknownst to the husband his cyberspace mistress turns out to be a nineteen-year-old male college freshman? What if "she" is an infirm eighty-year-old man in a nursing home? And even more disturbing, what if she is a twelve-year-old girl? Or a twelve-year-old boy?

6   TinySex poses the question of what is at the heart of sex and fidelity. Is it the physical action? Is it the feeling of emotional intimacy with someone other than one's primary partner? Is infidelity in the head or in the body? Is it in the desire or in the action? What constitutes the violation of trust? And to what extent and in what ways should it matter who the virtual sexual partner is in the real world? The fact that the physical body has been factored out of the situation makes these issues both subtler and harder to resolve than before.

7   Janet feels her trust has been violated by Tim's "talk intimacy" with another woman. Beth, the wife who gave her husband Martin permission to have TinySex, feels that he violated her trust when he chose to play a female character having a sexual encounter with a "man." When Beth read the log of one of these sessions, she became angry that Martin had drawn on his knowledge of her sexual responses to play his female character.

8   For Rudy, thirty-six, what was most threatening about his girlfriend's TinySex was the very fact that she wanted to play a character of the opposite sex at all. He discovered that she habitually plays men and has sex with female characters in chat rooms on America Online (like MUDs in that people can choose their identities). This discovery led him to break off the relationship. Rudy struggles to express what bothers him about his ex-girlfriend's gender-bending in cyberspace. He is not sure of himself, he is unhappy, hesitant, and confused. He says, "We are not ready for the psychological confusion this technology can bring." He explains:

It's not the infidelity. It's the gnawing feeling that my girlfriend—I mean, I was thinking of marrying her—is a dyke. I know that everyone is bisexual, I know, I know . . . but that is one of those things that I knew but it never had anything to do with me. . . . It was just intellectual.

What I hate about the rooms on America Online is that it makes it so easy for this sort of thing to become real. Well, in the sense that the rooms are real. I mean, the rooms, real or not, make it too easy for people to explore these things. If she explored it in real life, well, it would be hard on me, but it would have been hard for her. If she really wanted to do it, she would do it, but it would have meant her going out and doing it. It seems like more of a statement. And if she had really done it, I would know what to make of it. Now, I hate her for what she does online, but I don't know if I'm being crazy to break up with her about something that, after all, is only words.

9   Rudy complained that virtual reality made it too easy for his girlfriend to explore what it might be like to have a sexual relationship with another woman, too easy for her to experience herself as a man, too easy to avoid the social consequences of her actions. MUDs provide a situation in which we can play out scenarios that otherwise might have remained pure fantasy. Yet the status of these fantasies-in-action in cyberspace is unclear. Although they involve other people and are no longer pure fantasy, they are not "in the world." Their boundary status offers new possibilities. TinySex and virtual gender-bending are part of the larger story of people using virtual spaces to construct identity.

10   Nowhere is this more dramatic than in the lives of children and adolescents as they come of age in online culture. Online sexual relationships are one thing for those of us who are introduced to them as adults, but quite another for twelve-year-olds who use the Internet to do their homework and then meet some friends to party in a MUD.

11 **Children and Netsex**   From around ten years of age, in those circles where computers are readily available, social life involves online flirting, necking, petting, and going all the way. I have already introduced a seventeen-year-old whose virtual affair was causing him to think more about the imaginative, emotional, and conversational aspects of sex. His experience is not unusual. A thirteen-year-old girl informs me that she prefers to do her sexual experimentation online. Her partners are usually the boys in her class at school. In person, she says, it "is mostly grope-y." Online, "They need to talk more." A shy fourteen-year-old, Rob, tells me that he finds online flirting easier than flirting at school or at parties. At parties, there is pressure to dance close, kiss, and touch, all of which he both craves and dreads. He could be reject or he could get physically excited, and "that's worse," he says. If he has an erection while online, he is the only one who will know about it.

12   In the grownup world of engineering, there is criticsm of text-based virtual reality as "low bandwidth," but Rob says he is able to get "more information" online than he would in person.

Face to face, a girl doesn't always feel comfortable either. Like about not saying "Stop" until they really mean *Stop there! Now!* But it would be less embarrassing if you got more signals like about more or less when to stop. I think girls online are more communicative.

13   And online, he adds, "I am able to talk with a girl all afternoon—and not even try anything [sexual] and it does not seem weird. It [online conversation] lends itself

to telling stories, gossiping; much more so than when you are trying to talk at a party."

14   A thirteen-year-old girl says that she finds it easier to establish relationships on-line and then pursue them offline. She has a boyfriend and feels closer to him when they send electronic mail or talk in a chat room than when they see each other in person. Their online caresses make real ones seem less strained. Such testimony supports Rob's descriptions of online adolescent sexual life as less pressured than that in RL. But here, as in other aspects of cyberlife, things can cut both ways. A twelve-year-old girl files this mixed report on junior high school cyberromance:

> Usually the boys are gross. Because you can't see them, they think they can say whatever they want. But other times, we just talk, or it's just [virtual] kissing and asking if they can touch your breast or put their tongue in your mouth.

15   I ask her if she thinks that online sexual activity has changed things for her. She says that she has learned more from "older kids" whom she wouldn't normally have been able to hang out with. I ask her if she has ever been approached by someone she believes to be an adult. She says no, but then adds: "Well, now I sometimes go online and say that I am eighteen, so if I do that more it will probably happen." I ask her if she is concerned about this. She makes it very clear that she feels safe because she can always just "disconnect."

16   There is no question that the Internet, like other environments where children congregate—playgrounds, scout troops, schools, shopping malls—is a place where they can be harassed or psychologically abused by each other and by adults. But parental panic about the dangers of cyberspace is often linked to their unfamilarity with it. As one parent put it, "I sign up for the [Internet] account, but I can barely use e-mail while my [fourteen-year-old] daughter tells me that she is finding neat home pages [on the World Wide Web] in Australia."

17   Many of the fears we have for our children—the unsafe neighborhoods, the drugs on the street, the violence in the schools, our inability to spend as much time with them as we wish to—are displaced onto those unknowns we feel we can control. Fifteen years ago, when children ran to personal computers with arms out-stretched while parents approached with hands behind their backs, there was much talk about computers as addicting and hypnotic. These days, the Internet is the new unknown.

18   Parents need to be able to talk to their children about where they are going and what they are doing. This same commonsense rule applies to their children's lives on the screen. Parents don't have to become technical experts, but they do need to learn enough about computer networks to discuss with their children what and who is out there and lay down some basic safety rules. The children who do best after a bad experience on the Internet (who are harassed, perhaps even propositioned) are those who can talk to their parents, just as children who best handle bad experiences in real life are those who can talk to a trusted elder without shame or fear of blame.

19 **Deception** Life on the screen makes it very easy to present oneself as other than one is in real life. And although some people think that representing oneself as other than one is is always a deception, many people turn to online life with the intention of playing it in precisely this way. They insist that a certain amount of shape-shifting is part of the online game. When people become intimate, they are particularly vulnerable; it is easy to get hurt in online relationships. But since the rules of conduct are unclear, it is also easy to believe that one does not have the right to feel wounded. For what can we hold ourselves and others accountable?

20   In cyberculture, a story that became known as the "case of the electronic lover" has taken on near-legendary status. Like many stories that become legends, it has several versions. There were real events, but some tellings of the legend conflate several similar incidents. In all the versions, a male psychiatrist usually called Alex becomes an active member of a CompuServe chat line using the name of a woman, usually Joan. In one version of the story, his deception began inadvertently when Alex, using the computer nickname Shrink, Inc., found that he was conversing with a woman who assumed he was a female psychiatrist. Alex was stunned by the power and intimacy of this conversation. He found that the woman was more open with him than were his female patients and friends in real life. Alex wanted more and soon began regularly logging on as Joan, a severly handicapped and disfigured Manhattan resident. (Joan said it was her embarrassment about her disfigurement that made her prefer not to meet her cyberfriends face to face.) As Alex expected, Joan was able to have relationships of great intimacy with "other" women on the computer service. Alex came to believe that it was as Joan that he could best help these women. He was encouraged in this belief by his online female friends. They were devoted to Joan and told her how central she had become to their lives.

21   In most versions of the story, Joan's handicap plays an important role. Not only did it provide her with an alibi for restricting her contacts to online communication, but it gave focus to her way of helping other people. Joan's fighting spirit and ability to surmount her handicaps served as an inspiration. She was married to a policeman and their relationship gave other disabled women hope that they, too, could be loved. Despite her handicaps, Joan was lusty, funny, a woman of appetites.

22   As time went on and relationships deepened, several of Joan's grateful online friends wanted to meet her in person, and Alex realized that his game was getting out of control. He decided that Joan had to die. Joan's "husband" got online and informed the community that Joan was ill and in the hospital. Alex was overwhelmed by the outpouring of sympathy and love for Joan. Joan's friends told her husband how important Joan was to them. They offered moral support, financial assistance, names of specialists who might help. Alex was in a panic. He could not decide whether to kill Joan off. In one account of the story, "For four long days Joan hovered between life and death." Finally, Alex had Joan recover. But the virtual had bled into the real. Joan's "husband" had been pressed for the name of the hospital where Joan was staying so that cards and flowers could be sent. Alex gave the name of the hospital where he worked as a psychiatrist. One member of the bulletin board

called the hospital to confirm its address and discovered that Joan was not there as a patient. The ruse began to unravel.

23   All the versions of the story have one more thing in common: The discovery of Alex's deception led to shock and outrage. In some versions of the story, the anger erupts because of the initial deception—that a man had posed as a woman, that a man had won confidences as a woman. The case presents an electronic version of the movie *Tootsie*, in which a man posing as a woman wins the confidence of another woman and then, when he is found out, her fury. In other versions, the anger centers on the fact that Joan had introduced some of her online women friends to lesbian netsex, and the women involved felt violated by Joan's virtual actions. These women believed they were making love with a woman, but in fact they were sharing intimacies with a man. In other accounts, Joan introduced online friends to Alex, a Manhattan psychiatrist, who had real-life affairs with several of them. In these versions, the story of the electronic lover becomes a tale of real-life transgression.

24   The con artist is a stock character who may be appreciated for his charm in fictional presentations, but in real life is more often reviled for his duplicity and exploitiveness. In this sense, Alex was operating as part of a long tradition. But when familiar phenomena appear in virtual form, they provoke new questions. Was the reclusive, inhibited Alex only pretending to have the personality of the sunny, outgoing, lusty Joan? What was his real personality? Did Joan help her many disabled online friends who became more active because of her inspiration? When and how did Alex cross the line from virtual friend and helper to con artist? Was it when he dated Joan's friends? Was it when he had sexual relations with them? Or was it from the moment that Alex decided to pose as a woman? At a certain point, traditional categories for sorting things out seem inadequate.

25   In the past fifteen years, I have noticed a distinct shift in people's way of talking about the case of the electronic lover. In the early 1980s, close to the time when the events first took place, people were most disturbed by the idea that a man had posed as a woman. By 1990, I began to hear more complaints about Joan's online lesbian sex. What most shocks today's audience is that Alex used Joan to pimp for him. The shock value of online gender-bending has faded. Today what disturbs us is when the shifting norms of the virtual world bleed into real life.

26   In 1993, the WELL computer network was torn apart by controversy over another electronic lover where the focus was on these shifting norms and the confusion of the real and the virtual. The WELL has a "Woman's Only" forum where several women compared notes on their love lives in cyberspace. They realized that they had been seduced and abandoned (some only virtually, some also in the flesh) by the same man, whom one called a "cyber-cad." As they discussed the matter with more and more women, they found out that Mr. X's activities were far more extensive and had a certain consistency. He romanced women via electronic mail and telephone calls, swore them to secrecy about their relationship, and even flew across the country to visit one of them in Sausalito, California. But then he dropped them. One of the women created a topic (area for discussion) on the WELL entitled "Do

You Know this Cyber ScamArtist?" Within ten days, nearly one thousand messages had been posted about the "outing" of Mr. X. Some supported the women, some observed that the whole topic seemed like a "high-tech lynching."

27   At the time of the incident and its widespread reporting in the popular media, I was interviewing people about online romance. The story frequently came up. For those who saw a transgression it was that Mr. X had confused cyberworld and RL.* It was not just that he used the relationships formed in the cyberworld to misbehave in RL. It was that he treated the relationships in the cyberworld as though they were RL relationships. A complex typology of relationships began to emerge from these conversations: real-life relationships, virtual relationships with the "real" person, and virtual relationships with a virtual other. A thirty-five-year-old woman real estate broker tried hard to make clear how these things needed to be kept distinct.

> In a MUD, or chat room, or on IRC, it might be OK to have different flings with other people hiding behind other handles. But this man was coming on to these women as though he was interested in them really—I mean he said he was falling in love with them, with the real women. And he even did meet—and dump—some. Do you see the difference, from the beginning he didn't respect that online is its own place.

28   Mr. X himself did not agree that he had done anything wrong. He told the computer network that although he had been involved in multiple, simultaneous consensual relationships, he believed that the rules of cyberspace permitted that. Perhaps they do. But even if they do, the boundaries between the virtual and real are staunchly protected. Having sex with several characters on MUDs is one thing, but in a virtual community such as the WELL, most people are creating an electronic persona that they experience as coextensive with their physically embodied one. There, promiscuity can be another thing altogether.

29   Once we take virtuality seriously as a way of life, we need a new language for talking about the simplest things. Each individual must ask: What is the nature of my relationships? What are the limits of my responsibility? And even more basic: Who and what am I? What is the connection between my physical and virtual bodies? And it is different in different cyberspaces? These questions are framed to interrogate an individual, but with minor modifications, they are equally central for thinking about community. What is the nature of our social ties? What kind of accountability do we have for our actions in real life and in cyberspace? What kind of society or societies are we creating, both on and off the screen?

QUESTIONS FOR DISCUSSION

1. According to Turkle, why are virtual adventures and TinySex so attractive? What problems can such adventures cause?

---

*RL: real life

2. What conflicting opinions does Turkle present of extra marital affairs on-
   line? Do you agree that such fantasy affairs are relatively harmless? Consider how you would answer Turkle's question: "Is infidelity in the head
   or in the body?"
3. What is gender-bending? What is Turkle's view of this tendency? What
   ethical problems are raised by gender deception in cyberspace? Are these
   problems different in essence from the ethical problems of gender decep-
   tions in real life, as in deceptive cross-dressing?
4. Why are children and adolescents especially vulnerable to virtual sexual
   adventures? How might "virtual sex" cause them problems? How might
   it possibly help them in handling their sexuality in later years?
5. How does Turkle use examples to present her main ideas? Do her examples seem representative? What other examples would you have
   liked to see?

CONNECTION

Compare Turkle's view of erotic relationships with strangers with those of Walt
Whitman as expressed in the poem "To a Stranger," included in this chapter.

IDEAS FOR WRITING

1. Write an essay in response to some of the key questions that Turkle asks
   in the final paragraph of her essay. What new responsibilities and ethical
   and gender issues of the age of the Internet are implied by these questions?
2. Although Turkle's position seems to support people of all ages becoming
   more aware of the responsible choices and pitfalls of on-line relationships,
   some politicians and groups have argued for regulation of the Internet to
   prevent sexual exploitation, particularly of children. Write an essay in
   which you present your view on regulation in the cyberspace "frontier."

Chitra Divakaruni

Nargis' Toilette

*Born in Calcutta, India, Chitra Divakaruni received a B.A. from the University of
Calcutta and a Ph.D. in English Literature from the University of California at
Berkeley in 1985. Divakaruni has taught English and creative writing at Foothill
College in California and at the University of Houston, Texas. She has had poetry
and stories published in literary magazines in both India and the United States. Her
poetry collections include* The Reason for Nasturtiums *(1990), and* Leaving

Yuba City (1997). Divakaruni also has written a collection of short stories, Arranged Marriages (1995) and two novels, Mistress of Spices (1997) and Sister of My Heart (1999). In the poem "Nargis' Toilette," from The Black Candle (1991), Divakaruni explores the world of a veiled Muslim woman.

JOURNAL

Write about a marriage ritual that you feel is erotic and dreamlike.

The uncovered face of a woman
is as a firebrand, inflaming men's
desires and reducing to ashes
the honor of her family.

Muslim saying

Powder to whiten skin
unsnagged as a just-ripe peach.
Kohl to underline the eye's mute deeps.
Attar of rose touched to the dip
5   behind the earlobe,
the shadow between the breasts,
the silk creases
of the crimson *kameez*.

In the women's courtyard
10 it is always quiet,
the carved iron gates locked.
The palm shivers by the marble fountain.
The *bulbul* sings to its crimson double
in the mirrored cage.

15 Satin *dupattas* rustle.
The women put henna
on Nargis' hands. They braid,
down her back,
the forest's long shadows,
20 their laughter like the silver anklets
they are tying to her feet.

Today the women will take Nargis
to visit the women of the Amin family.
They will drink chilled pomegranate juice,
25 nibble pistachio *burfis* green as ice.
The grandmothers will chew
betel leaves and discuss the heat.

Nargis will sit, eyes down,
tracing the peacock pattern
30 on the mosaic floor.
If Allah wills, a marriage
will be arranged
with the Amins' second son
whose face Nargis will see
35 for the first time
in the square wedding mirror
placed in the bride's lap.

It is time to go.
They bring her *burkha,*
40 slip it over her head.
Someone adjusts the lace slits to her eyes.
The *burkha* spills silk-black to her feet
and spreads, spreads,
over the land, dark wave
45 breaking over the women, quenching
their light.

Now all is ready.
Like a black candle
Nargis walks to the gate.

QUESTIONS FOR DISCUSSION

1. Why do you think the poem begins with an epigram from a Muslim saying? What is the relationship between the meaning of the saying and the meaning of the poem? How does the saying amplify the meaning of the poem?
2. From reading and thinking about the poem, explain your understanding of Muslim marriage traditions. What impact do you think that such traditions may have on the individual and on married couples?
3. Discuss several of the images and rituals in the poem that create the sense of sensuality woven into Nargis' preparation to meet the man selected to be her husband. What makes the preparation seem dreamlike?
4. Why is Nargis compared to a "black candle" as she walks to the gate to meet the man who may choose her to be his wife?
5. Although Nargis is the one chosen and not the one who makes the choice, she does have power. What is her power? Why is she dangerous? How does her veiled presence emphasize the theme of danger?

CONNECTION

Compare the function of the traditional marriage ritual in this poem with the comments made on the function of mythic patterns and ritual in Joseph Campbell's " Four Functions of Mythology" in Chapter Four.

1. Write an essay in which you compare and contrast the role and power of a wife in a traditional culture such as Pakistan or India to the role and power of a wife in a modern, less traditional culture such as modern America. What are the advantages and disadvantages of being a wife in each culture?

2. Develop your journal entry into an essay in which you discuss how marriage and sexuality are enhanced through traditional rituals that engage the imagination and the senses. Refer to literature and the popular media as well as to personal experience to support your main points.

Rosa Contreras

On Not Being a Girl

Rosa Contreras was born in Jalisco, Mexico, and raised in Half Moon Bay, California. She majored in Latin American studies and anthropology. Writing the following essay—a response to Julius Lester's selection in this chapter, "Being a Boy"—helped Contreras to think more analytically about the expectations that her family had for her when she was a young girl and about how both her expectations and those of her family changed as she prepared herself for college.

JOURNAL

Write about an experience during your teenage years in which you disagreed with your family over what your role or responsibilities should be as a girl or a boy.

1   As I grew into adolescence, I experienced constant conflict between being a girl and having what have been traditionally considered "masculine" qualities. At the same time that I wanted to be contemplative and artful, I also wanted to "take the initiative and all the responsibility," as Lester describes the typical male role. Like Lester in his essay "Being a Boy," I envied the opposite sex and their advantages and often found myself frustrated by my culture's traditional views of gender roles; unlike Lester, I tried actively to break away from the typical role of a girl as defined in the Mexican family. In fact, growing up in a Mexican household with strong cultural values while also experiencing American culture with its less clearly defined gender roles allowed me to criticize both cultures from different perspectives. This allowed me to take the ideals that I liked from both and reject those that I did not agree with. In this manner, I was able to build my own set of values, and naturally, I have tried to inculcate them into my family.

2   As the oldest child in my family, I was given by my parents responsibilities fit for an adult, while they insisted that I remain a little girl, innocent and oblivious to boys and sex. I in turn rebelled; I did not want to be seen as an obedient, subservient girl, with all the qualities that make for a good Mexican wife. Every day I pushed to assert myself as strong, able to take on anything and succeed. I wanted to show my father and every other male in my life that I could do everything a boy could, if not more.

3   By the time I was twelve, I was tired of being a girl. I was sick, not envious, as Lester was, of girls' activities: "sitting in the shades of porches, playing with dolls, toy refrigerators, and stoves." By this time I had accumulated five baby dolls, fourteen Barbie dolls, three Ken dolls, and four younger siblings. The fact that I was a girl, and the oldest one at that, burdened me with the responsibility of watching over my sisters and brother. If they hurt themselves, or strayed away from home, no one was blamed except me. I still remember one day when my little brother ran into the house, crying because he had slipped on the gravel while running. Upon hearing my brother's shrill cries, my father became irritated and turned towards me: "Look what happened! You're supposed to watch them!" I became angry. Why was I being blamed? Why did I have to watch them all the time?

4   One day I finally yelled out to my parents what I had been feeling for a while: "Why do I always get yelled at for the things they do? It's not my fault!—I can't always be watching THEM. THEY'RE your kids; you chose to have them! I wasn't even asked! I never asked to be born, much less asked to be born first!"

5   Looking back, I realize that those were extremely cruel and ungrateful words. Nevertheless, with this outcry, I opened my parents' eyes, and they saw that they were, in fact, being unreasonable when they expected me to watch four children all the time. Maybe they had already realized the unfairness of the situation I was in, because they did not protest or reprimand me for telling them how I felt. Afterwards, I was no longer blamed for my siblings' actions, and was given more independence from caring for them.

6   Along with protesting against the rules of watchdog and disciplinarian, which, in Mexican culture, are commonly reserved for girls, I did not like it that my family members disapproved of my love of reading. Nobody in my immediate or extended family gives books the importance that I do. Maybe the fact that I am a girl meant that books should not be very important to me. In old Mexican tradition, there exists the idea that it is not good for women to know too much. Not good for whom? For their husbands. A man was not a "real" man if his wife knew more than he did. However, I suspect that the main problem my family had with my reading books was that I often neglected my household chores because I would, literally, spend all day submerged in learning about other people, other worlds.

7   By the time I was twelve, I had disappointed my parents in their quest to make me a productive and useful young lady, according to what Mexican custom decrees. While the rest of the house was clean, my room was a mess. I had other things to do, like homework, studying for tests, reading, and playing basketball. And horror of horrors! I couldn't even cook a pot of beans. My mother was often distressed at my inability (and lack of desire) to cook and do housework, which simply did not interest me. I felt housework was a waste of time, and I'd rather be doing something else.

More importantly, though, I hated it because I associated it with the oppression and subservience of latina women, including those in my family.

8   The different roles of men and women in Mexican society are clearly marked and instilled in children from a very young age. While in first and third grade, I went to elementary school in Mexico. While the boys were encouraged to excel in athletics and academics, the girls competed in crocheting and embroidering. At the end of the year, there was a contest to see whose work was the most beautiful. Approximately once every two weeks, each girl had to help in either mopping, cleaning windows, or sweeping her classroom. Therefore, at a very young age, girls were taught to do housework and feminine things, like embroidery. My mother, all my aunts, and most Mexican women that I know were taught that the value of a woman consisted in keeping her family well-fed and a squeaky-clean house.

9   I realize that it was complicated for my mother to pass on these same values to me because we were no longer living in Mexico. But possibly because we were so far away from Mexico, it became very important for her to make this new home like her old one. Therefore, she tried to make sure that, although her daughters were being raised in a foreign country, we were still raised as she was taught. So when I refused to agree with the traditional Mexican ideals for raising a girl, she probably felt as though she had somehow failed. But I could not go along with what I truly felt was wrong. I could not please my older relatives in the way I was expected to because living in the United States, where the issue of women's rights is more openly debated, had opened my eyes to new and better possibilities for women.

10   From elementary school to high school, I went to school with a predominantly white population and came home to a Mexican household. At school I was taught what I liked. The teachers encouraged and praised me for my love of reading. Boys and girls were equally expected to do well in both sports and academics. Boys even took home economics! But often, when I brought home these ideas and chose to read rather than do housework or wait on my father and siblings, I was scolded. I was in a new environment that my parents had never experienced, so they did not understand why I felt so strongly about the way of life women had always led in Latin-American cultures.

11   From reading, which allowed me to learn a lot about other people, other lifestyles, and achieving excellent grades in school, I often felt that I knew it all. I became very outspoken. At first, I scolded my mother privately when I saw her being subservient to my father. When she waited up for him, I would become angry and tell her: "Why are you doing this? I can't believe you're waiting up for him to feed him dinner! It's not like he can't get it himself!" Later, I became bolder. For example, when I'd hear my dad ask my mother for tortillas, I would say: "They're on the stove. You can get them." By the time I was twelve, I had my future laid out for me. I would always say that when I got older, I would have a career and my husband would share in the household responsibilities. I was not about to go out and work and then come home to do even more work. I understood that the status of my mother as a housewife required that she do this kind of work, but I felt it was unfair that she had to work all day, while my father could come home and not do anything for the rest of the evening.

12　I know that the many outbursts and arguments I have had (and still do, although less often now than before) concerning women's equality were the cause for much conflict in my household. However, I realize today that because of my efforts, my parents have changed their ideas about what women can accomplish. As a young girl, I refused to mold myself to be good and docile, with traditional moral values and knowledge. I understand that these ideas are very ingrained in Mexican society and they will be hard to change, but I cannot stand by and watch the oppression of these women and keep myself quiet. Now, as a young woman, I'm on my way to defying the role traditionally designated for women. During my high school days, my mother often encouraged me to study hard so that I could have a career. She would tell me: "Study, so that you can have a better life." She wanted me to have the option of being someone else rather than a full-time housewife, who always depends on her husband. I believe I have shown my father that I am capable of succeeding, just like all men and women can if given the opportunity. He has grown to accept me as I am and to understand my way of thinking. I have earned my parents' respect, and today they are extremely proud of all that I have achieved.

QUESTIONS FOR DISCUSSION

1. What aspects of Mexican-American culture made it difficult for Contreras to feel comfortable in her family role?
2. What might have contributed to Contreras' mother's tendency to reinforce the old ways? How were her family's values undermined by living in the United States? How did her family respond to her rebellion?
3. How does Contreras use examples of her family's interactions and her responsibilities in the home to illustrate her thesis about not fitting into the mold of "proper" female behavior? Could she have provided other examples?
4. How effectively does Contreras use Julius Lester's essay "Being a Boy" and his position on gender roles to compare with her own perspective on being female? Could she have used other techniques or points made by Lester to extend her comparison?

Julie Bordner Apodaca

Gay Marriage: Why the Resistance?

Julie Bordner Apodaca was a student at the College of Alameda in California when she wrote the following essay. She is a native of Alameda and an aspiring writer who returned to college part-time after ten years out of school, working and starting a family. Ever since her elementary school days, Apodaca has enjoyed argumentation and has tried to encourage her fellow students and coworkers to see beyond biases and misconceptions about people whom society has labeled as "different." Thus,

when she was assigned to write a paper on a controversial issue for her critical think-
ing course, she chose to write on the subject of gay marriages and to examine the un-
derlying causes for bias against such relationships.

JOURNAL

What are your feelings about gay marriage? Is it such a controversial issue?

1   It has been over twenty years since the Stonewall riot triggered the civil rights movement in the gay and lesbian community. In the past two years, a good portion of the movement's focus has been on the issue of legalized marriage for homosexual couples, a move which many leaders in the gay community see as essentially conservative, as a sign that gays are opting for more traditional, stable life-styles and desire recognition as committed couples. Thus, American society has been asked to expand the traditionally heterosexual institution of marriage to include gay and lesbian couples. The response from mainstream America has been largely negative, due in part to the homophobic attitudes that permeate our society.

2   To understand why society continues to have a negative reaction to the idea of legalizing gay marriage, we must first understand homophobia. Webster's defines homophobia as "hatred or fear of homosexuals or homosexuality." Homophobic attitudes, which are generally emotional and lacking in factual foundation, have many origins, some of which are religious, some political and sociological, some psychological, some even medical in nature. In a general sense, it can be argued that the roots of homophobia in America can be found in the institutions and philosophy that are at the heart of our culture: our dominant religious tradition, our political and class systems, our moral perspective, and our psychological makeup.

3   Some of the most passionate arguments against legalization of gay and lesbian marriages stem from the Judaic and Christian fundamentalist religions in our society. A common belief is that homosexuality is a sin; not only is it morally wrong, but it mocks natural laws and the will of God. Marriage is a sanctified privilege of heterosexual union that constructs a foundation for the procreation and nurture of children. Despite the fact that many gays have dependent children from previous heterosexual unions, homosexuals are not seen by the religious fundamentalist as having the capacity for procreation within their relationships; thus sexual relations between homosexuals are viewed by many religious people as sinful and mocking, a way of undermining the essential meaning of marriage.

4   Some social thinkers hold views against homosexual marriage which coincide in some ways with those of the religious fundamentalists. Such individuals resist the legalization or wide acceptance of gay relationships, fearing the repercussions to the already threatened traditional family. With the stigma against homosexuality relaxed, perhaps the 20 percent of closeted homosexuals who marry heterosexual partners may instead choose gay partners. This could lead to a decline in the numbers of heterosexual marriages and even to the rise of other unusual social arrangements thought of as

destabilizing to our society, such as polygamy or group marriage (Hartinger 682). The traditional two-partner heterosexual marriage, already on the decline, could become a rarity, and our basic social structure, which historically was designed around this form of relationship, may crumble. The weakness of this type of causal reasoning is that it is based upon an assumption that it is somehow unhealthy for a society to change and evolve, as well as upon a view of the "stable nuclear family unit" that denies historical realities such as abusive families, alcoholism in the nuclear family, and other causes for the decline of the nuclear family, such as the high cost of maintaining a home, the high divorce rate, and the trend towards dual career families.

5   Despite the weaknesses in the reasoning, arguments against gay marriages as contributors towards the undermining of traditional families often have been used by politicians in order to win the support of the populace who feel that family values are endangered. Vice President Dan Quayle's attacks on the "cultural elite" during the 1992 presidential campaign could be seen as a veiled attack on homosexuals and their relationships. According to Quayle, the cultural elite are those who "respect neither tradition or standards. They believe that moral truths are relative and all 'life styles' are equal" (qtd. in Salter A15). Quayle's comments stirred both praise and rage throughout America in the summer of 1992; his ideas touched a sympathetic chord for many who are painfully aware of the increased fragility of the traditional nuclear, heterosexual family unit.

6   However, it is not only religious, conservative sociologists, and aspiring politicians who promote homophobia; our government and its official branches play a key role as well. For instance, the United States military continues to resist fully accepting homosexuals in the armed forces, despite any evidence that would suggest that these individuals generally are unfit for duty, disruptive, or that they pose a security threat. The discrimination against homosexual relationships in the military is instrumental in fostering and maintaining the psychological fears and stereotypes associated with homosexuals: that they are unstable, immoral, and, in some vague sense, a threat to the security of our nation.

7   The AMA does not classify homosexuality as a disease or a disorder, due to scientific experiments done in the 1950s that discredited the notion of the homosexual as any more neurotic or maladjusted than any other group in society. However, many people continue to cling to the outmoded belief that homosexuality is a psychological disorder. Some, including a minority in the psychiatric profession, believe that homosexuality should be therapeutically treated, rather than sanctioned by recognition of homosexual unions as the equivalent to "normal" married relationships. However, psychologist Richard Isay does not believe that the fear of homosexuality is simply a reaction to the idea of a "deviant" sex act; Isay considers that the fear and hatred for homosexuality is related intimately to "the fear and hatred of what is perceived as being 'feminine' in other men and in oneself" (qtd. in Alter 27). Thus, for some people, insecurity and mistrust of one's own sexuality may cause irrational anxiety about or contempt towards the homosexual. If homosexual marriages were legal, gay couples might feel free publicly and physically to express their affections. This possibility of overt display of homosexuality in turn adds to the homophobic indi-

vidual's fantasies that, rather than witnessing such encounters with "natural" revulsion, he or she could possibly experience an unwanted arousal.

8   Another common psychological concern about homosexual marriages, despite evidence that points to homosexuality as a quasi-biological sexual orientation rather than a learned or conditioned sexual response, is that legally sanctioned gay relationships will somehow influence children to become homosexual. The reasoning goes that adolescents and even younger children are often confused by the intense and unfamiliar sexual feelings stirring inside them; thus the adolescent confronted with the "normality" of homosexual relationships, in or out of their own family circle, might tend to gravitate toward this kind of sexual outlook. Furthermore, part of the stereotype of the homosexual as sexual deviant is that gays enjoy the company of young children and might, if not sufficiently isolated from mainstream society, take advantage of the vulnerability of naive and confused adolescents, encouraging such children to engage in gay sex.

9   A more recent fear that fuels the hostility to gay marriages is medically-based, but, as so many of the fears discussed above, based upon causal oversimplification. Consider AIDS; this disease is really a nightmare for our entire society, not just confined to the gay community, and it can be spread by both heterosexual sexual conduct and drug-related activity. Yet the fearful stereotype persists that AIDS is somehow a "gay" disease; in fact, some religious zealots have even spoken of AIDS as God's "divine retribution" against gays for their blasphemous behavior, despite the reality that gays didn't originate the disease and in spite of the fact that the gay community has made enormous progress in educating itself about AIDS and in discontinuing the unsafe sexual practices of the past. The legalization of homosexual marriage elicits the fear among those with a deep fear of both AIDS and homosexuality, that, along with the resulting increase in the numbers of homosexuals, such legalization will somehow cause the AIDS epidemic to become even more severe. This is truly an ironic misconception, when we consider that monogamous marriage, gay or heterosexual, is one of the most conservative sexual practices, one of the least likely to lead to a spread of disease beyond the bounds of matrimony.

10   As we have seen, there are many causes for the fear that surrounds the legalization of homosexual marriages. The cumulative effect of these causes has prevented legislation supporting such relationships in almost all parts of the country. Although some of the arguments against homosexual marriages may seem on the surface to have some justification, most are based on ignorance, irrationality, and fear. Perhaps, as Ernest Van Den Haag puts it, "nothing will persuade heterosexuals to believe that homosexuality is psychologically or morally as legitimate as their own heterosexuality" (38); however, despite the resistance that is likely to occur, it seems to me that a national effort should be made to dispel the misconceptions regarding homosexuality. What benefit is there in hiding behind irrational fears? Homosexuality is not going to disappear; history has proven that. Society would benefit from a better understanding of homosexuality, for if people were able to think more critically about the myths and the issues surrounding homosexuality, perhaps there would be a decrease in the nation's homophobia and an increased understanding

from which all people, gay and heterosexual alike, would benefit. We cannot expect a change overnight, but we can begin to educate the ignorant and break down some of the prejudice. As Martin Luther King, Jr., once said, "Take the first step in faith. You don't have to see the whole staircase, just take the first step."

WORKS CITED

Alter, Jonathan. "Degrees of Discomfort." *Newsweek* 12 March 1992: 27.
Hartinger, Brent. "A Case for Gay Marriage." *Commonweal* 22 Nov. 1991: 681–683.
Salter, Stephanie. "The 'Cultural Elite' and the Rest of Us." San Francisco *Chronicle* 14 June 1992: A15.
Van Den Haag, Ernest. "Sodom and Begorrah." *National Review* 29 April 1991: 35–38.

QUESTIONS FOR DISCUSSION

1. What are the major causes of the resistance to gay marriage as explored in the essay? Could the student have discussed other causes? Which ones?
2. Apodaca refutes the reasoning that underlies most of the "fears" she discusses. Is her refutation effective and fair?
3. What factual evidence does Apodaca use to support her general statements and conclusions? What additional evidence might she have used?
4. This essay includes some quotations from authorities or spokespersons to support some of the writer's ideas and conclusions about social attitudes. Were such citations of authorities handled appropriately, or would you have liked to see either more or less reliance on citation of authority?

Topics for Research and Writing

1. Develop an extended definition of masculinity. When relevant show how it relates to the ideas presented by Lester and Hemingway, as well as other writers whom you have read previously or done research on for this essay. Is masculinity primarily a cultural concept rather than a biological reality, or do definitions of the "masculine" appear more universal?
2. Review what you have learned about the limits and challenges of being born female in a patriarchal society from reading the selections such as those by Divakaruni, Hong Kingston, and Contreras; consider also your own experiences and outside readings in this area. Write up your findings in a documented essay.
3. Write an essay based on readings from the text, research, as well as your own thoughts and feelings about the role that sex plays in an individual's life, health, and sense of well-being. Consider if sex is primarily a "procreative" act, an expression of love, an erotic experience, or a combination of experiences. Does the importance of sex and the sexual act vary greatly from culture to culture?

4. Reread the selections in this chapter that reflect on the relationships among dreams, the unconscious, and sexuality, and do some further reading in this area. Write up your conclusions in the form of a documented essay.

5. Write a research essay that follows up on Turkle's comments on gender in her essay "Virtual Sex." How are definitions of male and female identity continuing to change in the era of cyberspace? In addition to doing some outside reading, you might interview some people you know who spend a lot of time in chatrooms and/or visit some chatrooms where gender identity role-playing is common.

6. In her essay "Swinging," Middlebrook comments that there may be as many as five different sexes, in terms of genital formation and appearance; yet often babies are operated upon at birth to make them more closely resemble societal norms of the "male" or "female" child. Do some further research into this controversial area. Do you think that it is humane and appropriate for doctors to do such "sex altering" surgery at birth? Why or why not?

7. Write about a film that portrays an issue of sexuality or gender. How does the film comment on certain issues raised in the readings in this chapter? You can select a film from the following list or one of your own choosing. *Incredible Adventure of Two Girls in Love, Oleanna, Working Girl, Baby Boom, Torch Song Trilogy, Fried Green Tomatoes, The Crying Game, The Wedding Banquet, The Bird Cage, Mrs. Doubtfire, Jeffrey, Orlando, In and Out, Serving in Silence, Elizabeth, Sex, Lies and Vidotape, Wilde*

8. The following URLs will lead you to web sites that focus on issues of gender and sexuality. They might be good sources for further research.

ACLU: Gay and Lesbian Rights
http://www.aclu.org/issues/gay/hmgl.html
This ACLU-sponsored page deals with legal and civil rights issues of discrimination related to gays, including marriage laws, domestic partnerships, parenting considerations, and transgender rights. Many links to news articles, databases, and other resources.

Cybersexual Addiction
http://www.netaddiction.com/resources/cybersexual_addiction_quiz.htm
Web page for the Center for On-line Addiction; includes a "virtual clinic" and list of other resources.

Love Addiction-Obsessive and Pathological Relationships
http://www.recovery-man.com/loveaddict.htm
Defines, indicates the symptoms, and offers possible treatments and resources for "love addiction," which is compared to other types of codependent relationships and to addictions such as chemical dependencies.

MYTH, STEREOTYPE, AND CROSS-GENDER IDENTITY
http://www.transgender.org/tg/gic/awptext.html
Overview of findings from the 21st Annual Feminist Psychology conference (1996), which critically analyzed diagnostic categories related to
transvestitism in the fourth edition of the *Diagnostic and Statistical Man-
ual of Mental Disorders*. Gender identity, transvestitism, myths and stereotypes about cross-dressing, and related cross-cultural issues are examined.

SIGMUND FREUD AND THE FREUD ARCHIVES
http://plaza.interport.net/nypsan/freudarc.html
This is one of the largest and most scholarly Freud pages, with links to
Freud's works on-line as well as the Freud Museum, biographical materials, and scholarly writings about Freud and his works.

STRENGTHS OF MIXED-RACE RELATIONSHIPS
http://www.apa.org/monitor/sep95/race.html
An article by Erin Burnette on how interracial couples often become
stronger in their relationship through overcoming "prejudice and cultural
differences."

7

The Double/The Other

Within each one of us there is another whom we do not know. He speaks to us in dreams and tells us how differently he sees us from how we see ourselves.

CARL JUNG

[The shadow] is exactly like any human being with whom one has to get along, sometimes by giving in, sometimes by resisting, sometimes by giving love—whatever the situation requires. The shadow becomes hostile only when he is ignored or misunderstood.

MARIE-LUISE VON FRANZ
The Realization of the Shadow in Dreams

Our challenge is to call forth the humanity within each adversary, while preparing for the full range of possible responses. Our challenge is to find a path between cynicism and naiveté.

FRAN PEAVEY
Us and Them

ARGUMENT AND DIALOGUE

Traditional Argument

Traditional argument begins by defining a problem or issue, then taking a position or stance. In this form of argument the advocate proceeds to develop a clear thesis and to demonstrate its validity through a series of convincing logical arguments, factual supports, and references to authority. Often the major aim of argument is seen as an attack on the ideas and positions of an opponent with an end to persuading the audience of the correctness of the proponent's position. Arguments that don't quite fit into the debater's viewpoint are sometimes ignored or are introduced to counter them more strongly in a process known as "refutation." Such traditional debate is frequently linked to political rhetoric, where only one candidate can be elected. A fundamental part of public life, oppositional argument at its best can be a powerful method of presenting one's own position and beliefs; at its worst, it can be manipulative and one-sided, leading people to believe that debate is more a matter of verbal warfare than a genuine form of communication. For examples of oppositional argument that leads to verbal warfare, visit some politically-oriented web sites on the Internet—or read the editorial page of your daily newspaper.

Dialogic Argument

Based on a thorough presentation of the facts and on the reasons supporting positions, the dialogic argument acknowledges the importance of creating a bridge between opposing viewpoints that are often rigidly separated in a traditional argument. This form of argument may remind you of the literary dialogue between opposites that we see at work in some of this chapter's stories and poems; it is best exemplified in expository form here in Fran Peavey's essay, "Us and Them"; it can also be seen in Ron Takaki's "A Different Mirror." The dialogic argument emphasizes the need for discussion and a genuine interchange of ideas, while making a conscious effort to bring together seemingly irreconcilable viewpoints in order to arrive at a type of synthesis of opposing perspectives that will allow the writer and his or her audience to learn more about themselves. Through the dialogic approach to argument, you can come to a new awareness of positions you may not have understood or considered. Working to understand these "opposite" positions does not necessarily imply that you totally accept them, or that you abandon your own ideas and viewpoint. What it does suggest is that you are beginning to consider the possibilities of strong arguments, positions, and value systems that are different from your own, and that you are making a real attempt to integrate these positions into your thinking.

Dialogue and Prewriting

An effective prewriting strategy for a balanced argument paper involves engaging your opponent in a dialogue. Begin by creating a dialogue that explores different positions relative to your subject, your thesis, and your supporting points. Following is an example of an excerpt from such a student dialogue on the subject of reading fairy tales to small children. We have labeled the two "sides" in the dialogue "I" and "Me." "I" stands for the position that the student really wants to present, while "Me" represents the side of the argument, perhaps a side of the self that the writer doesn't want to acknowledge and perceives as the "opponent."

I: I think all children should read fairy tales. I always loved hearing them as a kid; I liked the scary parts and the adventures. Fairy tales are so much more engrossing than the trash on the boob tube.

Me: I can see that you really like fairy tales. But wouldn't a lot of kids who get upset easily be frightened by reading stories about mean stepmothers and wicked witches, like in "Hansel and Gretel"?

I: I understand what you're saying; fairy tales might frighten some children, especially if they were very young or if they had had some really horrible things happen in their own lives that the stories reminded them of. Still, I think I can handle your objections. Kids should be read fairy tales by an adult who makes time to explain the issues in the story and who can reassure them if they think the story is too scary; after all, a fairy tale is "only a story."

Me: Well, I can see the point in having adults read the stories and explain them, but you're wrong about TV. There are some great programs for kids, like *Sesame Street* and *Barney*, that teach children to have positive values. And what about the values in those fairy tales? *Sesame Street* teaches you to love everyone and to give girls equal opportunities to succeed! Fairy tales are so old-fashioned and sexist, with all those beautiful sleeping princesses waiting around for Prince Charming.

I: I know what you mean. The values in fairy tales aren't always very modern. That's why it's really important that the adult who reads the stories to the kids discusses the old-fashioned way of life that is being presented and compares the world of the tale with our own values and life-styles. I can see letting kids watch TV, too. Fairy tales are only a part of the imaginative experience of childhood, but they're still a very important part!

In this short dialogue, you see the "I" and "Me" positions being brought closer together. "I"'s initial position is now more clearly stated, with some important, common-sense qualifications brought in through the interaction with the "Me."

Prewriting and the Audience

Before you begin to write your essay, try to establish a similar kind of dialogue with your imaginary audience as you did with the parts of yourself. As in traditional argument or in any type of writing situation, this involves trying to determine the interests and values of your audience. For example, the student writing about fairy tales would have to decide if his or her audience includes cautious parents of school-age children or liberal educators with a progressive philosophy of childrearing. Creating a clear "mental image" of the audience is essential before appropriate arguments can be selected. Once you have a clear image of the audience in mind, approach your readers directly and respectfully. Make the audience an integral part of your arguments; do not try to manipulate or dazzle them with your facts and figures; instead, establish a common ground with the audience, stating the positions you hold in common with them while designating areas of mutual agreement or possible compromise. This approach will remind you to keep your audience's point of view in mind and will facilitate meaningful communication.

Defining Key Terms

As in traditional argument, it is important for dialogic arguers to define their terms. Definitions support clear communication and help develop rapport in an argument. People feel more comfortable in a discussion when they understand what key terms refer to and mean. For example, if I am arguing for reading fairy tales to young children and am referring to fairy tales such as those of Hans Christian Andersen, while my audience thinks I am discussing modern fantasy children's stories such as those by Maurice Sendak, then we are really thinking about different definitions of a fairy tale and will be unlikely to come to a mutual understanding. In defining your terms, use simple, straightforward definitions; avoid connotative language designed to manipulate or trick your audience.

Evaluating "Facts"

If you have taken a statistics course or read articles in journals, you know that facts and statistics can be interpreted in a variety of ways. In reading the factual studies that will form an important part of the support in any argument paper, you need to consider a number of questions. Have the results of the social scientists or psychologists you are studying been confirmed by other researchers? Are the data current? Were they collected by qualified researchers using thorough and objective methods? Are they expressed in clear and unambiguous language? These and other questions should be asked about your sources of information so that you can create a sound factual base for the arguments you use in your paper. In doing research for your argument, you might look at web sites, even extremist ones, to get the feeling for some of the strong sentiments that different groups have about your issue—but don't rely on these partisan, advocacy sites to provide objective information. On the other hand, you do need to mention both widely believed facts and popular misconceptions that may *oppose* the argument you are making; you will need to show your audience respectfully how some of these beliefs are not factual, how others are not relevant, and concede that some are relevent and either can be dealt with by your proposed argument, or cannot and represent the practical limits of the situation at hand. Present your factual supports clearly; avoid overstating your conclusions in absolute, unqualified terms or overgeneralizing from limited data.

Feelings in Argument

Emotions play such a significant role in our lives that any argument that tried to be altogether rational, pretending that emotional concerns were unimportant and that only "facts" count, would be unrealistic and uninteresting. Emotions, both your own and those of your audience, are a central concern in argument. Although you need to present your ideas in ways that won't offend your readers, when feelings are a central issue in the argument itself, emotional issues do need to be directly confronted. For example, it would be impossible to discuss a subject such as abortion without acknowledging your own feelings and those of the audience relative to issues as emotionally involving as the life of a fetus. In this case, sharing such feelings will help to create an open and trusting relationship with your audience.

However, an important distinction must be made between acknowledging feelings and exploiting them to manipulate your readers. Often, strong arguments are based on emotions, which can be exaggerated in an attempt to strengthen a position and can cause you to overlook important issues. Avoid language that could ignite the emotional climate in a discussion. Bringing in irrelevant appeals for pity or fear can obscure the real issues involved in a discussion. Try to use language that is primarily emotionally neutral in describing the positions and ideas taken by their opposition. By doing so, you are more likely to keep the confidence of readers who might otherwise be offended by an adversarial position and manipulative language.

Argument can be one of the most satisfying forms of writing, but it can be one of the most difficult. To satisfy both the factual and emotional demands of shaping an effective argument, you can:

- Use the inner dialogue as an aid to prewriting and exploring different positions.
- Empathize with and acknowledge the assumptions and needs of your audience.
- Define key terms.
- Evaluate and use relevant factual supports.
- Be honest and direct in your treatment of the emotional aspects of an issue.

All of these strategies will be of use to you in your efforts to find a stance in argument that allows you to build bridges between your inner world and the worlds of others. This type of argument, when thoughtfully developed with an audience in mind, can be one of the most effective means of communication that a writer can draw upon, both in academic discourse and in private and community life.

T H E M A T I C   I N T R O D U C T I O N : T H E   D O U B L E / T H E   O T H E R

Many of us are conscious of having an alternate self, a self that, for whatever reasons, we do not make public. We sometimes see glimpses of an alternative or underground personality in a family member, friend, supervisor, colleague, or even in a media figure. From Greek myths to nursery rhymes and fairy tales, from Shakespearean doubles and disguises to Gothic tales of horror and revenge, from Victorian mysteries to the modern psychological short story, images of the double, of twins in spirit or twins in reality, have marked our developing understanding of the workings of the human mind.

The frequent recurrence and popularity of the image of the double in myth and literature is often attributed to the human need to explore, understand, and perhaps conquer divided feelings that individuals have about the parts of themselves that are in conflict. These conflicting parts of the self are revealed in many forms: the good self versus the evil self, the rational self versus the irrational self, the civilized self versus the antisocial or criminal self, the masculine self versus the feminine self, the physical self versus the spiritual self, the controlled, conventional self versus the wild self, the practical self versus the dreamy self.

Although literature and human experiences suggest that inward journeys into the mind's dual nature can lead to confusion, even neurosis or psychosis, at the same time, in literature and in life, there is the possibility of integrating and balancing the opposing parts of the self through developing an increased awareness of the inner self. In this way the main character of a poem or story, the writer, or a reader can experience a form of rebirth, emerging with a more balanced and confident sense of self and purpose. Your journey through this chapter will provide you with new insights into the dualities within the human personality.

The chapter opens with two selections that explore the double nature of the self. First, in Judith Ortiz Cofer's poem "The Other," the Hispanic-American speaker acknowledges the power of her "other," who is sensual, uninhibited, even dangerous, and more in touch with her cultural roots than her well-behaved public self. In "Updike and I," novelist John Updike explores the duality of his nature in the contrast between his everyday social self and his writer self.

The next three readings will help you to think about the importance of getting the oppositional sides of your mind and psyche to work together productively. In "The Realization of the Shadow in Dreams," psychoanalyst Marie-Louise von Franz offers a positive perspective on the inner division of the human psyche, showing ways in which the unconscious "shadow" self appears in dreams and myths and suggesting ways for the individual to come to a reconciliation with his or her shadow. The next two pieces by Robert Louis Stevenson examine contrasting ways that the dual aspects of human personality can work together creatively—or cause the mind to disintegrate altogether. In "A Chapter on Dreams," he demonstrates how he used the resources of his dreams and unconscious mind to help him create his classic tale, *The Strange Case of Dr. Jekyll and Mr. Hyde*. Following is the conclusion to Robert Louis Stevenson's classic double story, "Henry Jekyll's Full Statement of the Case," which illustrates the negative consequences of trying to separate the "good" or civilized side of the human character from its sensual and irrational side.

The next three selections discuss the crucial impact of inner conflict on political and social stances and decisions. Historian Ronald Takaki argues in "A Different Mirror" that Americans must go back and re-vision history in order to perceive themselves more accurately, terms of diversity, and the " common past." In "Being Black and Feeling Blue," Shelby Steele discusses the ways in which an African-American's negative self-concept, or internalized "anti-self," can make success more difficult. In "Us and Them," longtime peace activist Fran Peavey suggests a new approach to community organization and political action, which avoids dehumanizing and dismissing the opposition and instead encourages a balanced response to problem-solving.

The speaker in this chapter's final poem, "The Dream" by Pablo Neruda, shares the complexity of an intimate relationship to demonstrate how a sensitive association with a loved one can be similar to the relationship we sometimes experience with our shadow self." The two student essays that conclude the chapter offer new ways of thinking about how the double-sided nature of social issues can be internalized and affect the development of an individual's self-concept. The first student essay, "Mixed-Up," by Susan Voyticky, the daughter of an African-American father and a white mother, discusses some of the difficult decisions Voyticky had to make to create an identity that she could call her own. Jill Ho in "Affirmative Action: Perspectives From A Model Minority" reflects on the how Asian-Americans face a glass ceiling, a double-sided reward, after gaining entry to main stream jobs through affirmative action.

Exploring the duality of the human mind and spirit as reflected in the essays, stories, and poems included in this chapter, should prove to be provocative and enlightening. Becoming aware of the other voices that exist within you in addition to your dominant voice or persona can help you to understand yourself more fully and can provide you with additional resources to draw upon in your writing.

Jeanie Fan
Clown Mask

Student artist Jeanie Fan created the painting above, featuring a somber figure with a clown mask and a small clown image buttoned to his coat, to help herself deal with some of her feelings about self-deception, procrastination, and denial. Although she is perceived by many as a cheery and directed person, Fan makes the following comments about her relationship to the figure in the painting: "I always hide behind my mask and let that clown inside of me tell me that everything is all right."

Ideas for Drawing, Writing, and Discussion

1. Jeannie Fan's painting is about a person with a double self—one side of the self, that which is socially acceptable, is shown to the world, while another aspect remains hidden. Do a painting or drawing that reveals the relationship between the doubled quality in your own self, the inward versus the outward aspect.

2. Do a written description and explanation of what your visual depiction of the double self reveals about your personality and concerns.

3. Share your drawing and writing about your double self with members of your group. What different kind of double issues are revealed by the group members? In what ways did you and the other group members find it helpful to draw and then write about the double self?

Judith Ortiz Cofer

The Other

(See headnote on Judith Ortiz Cofer in Chapter 3) As a poet, Cofer often explores issues of cultural identity and heritage. In the following poem, notice how Cofer presents the inner conflict of identity experienced by the speaker through a series of progressively more disturbing images.

JOURNAL

Write about a part of yourself that you have difficulty accepting because the "other" in you seems too wild or irresponsible.

A sloe-eyed dark woman shadows me.
In the morning she sings
Spanish love songs in a high
falsetto filling my shower stall
5 with echoes.
She is by my side
in front of the mirror as I slip
into my tailored skirt and she
into her red cotton dress.
10 She shakes out her black mane as I
run a comb through my close-cropped cap.
Her mouth is like a red bull's eye
daring me.
Everywhere I go I must
15 make room for her: she crowds me
in elevators where others wonder
at all the space I need.
At night her weight tips my bed, and
it is her wild dreams that run rampant
20 through my head exhausting me. Her heartbeats,
like dozens of spiders carrying the poison
of her restlessness over the small
distance that separates us,
drag their countless legs
25 over my bare flesh.

QUESTIONS FOR DISCUSSION

1. How would you characterize the "other" that Cofer creates in this poem? Is it anything like your own "other"?
2. Describe the speaker's main self. How does the narrator's main self differ from the "other"?
3. Which part of the speaker is dominant? Which side do you think will eventually win out in the struggle?
4. Why do you think the two sides of the narrator's personality are in conflict? What different cultural and gender roles does each side reflect?
5. What images help to vividly portray the "other" and to contrast her with the speaker's main self?
6. What dreams and nocturnal fantasies of the narrator help to convey the struggle between the two sides of her personality? What do you think is meant by the fantasy image, "Her heartbeats, / like dozens of spiders carrying the poison / of her restlessness. . . "? In what sense is the restlessness a poison?

CONNECTION

Analyze this poem as a dream-narrative, using some of the insights to be found in Marie von Franz's "The Realization of the Shadow in Dreams," in this chapter.

IDEAS FOR WRITING

1. Write an essay about an inner struggle you have experienced that reflects a cultural conflict between the culture of your parents and that of friends or between that of your school and of your workplace or church. Include examples of ways in which your inner conflict is reflected in your dreams and fantasies.
2. Write an essay in which you explore arguments that will help you make an important decision in your life about which you feel inner conflict. You might want to discuss whether to change your position on issues and ways of relating to a marriage partner, friend, parent, supervisor at work, or teacher. After exploring your options, which choice seems preferable?

John Updike

Updike and I

(See headnote on John Updike in Chapter 2) In the brief fantasy "Updike and I" (1995), Updike reflects playfully on his creation of a literary "persona," a public double which sometimes gets confused with the "real" Updike.

JOURNAL

Write about the persona or self that is projected by your writing. How is the self that emerges in your writing different from your conversational "everyday" self?

1   I created Updike out of the sticks and mud of my Pennsylvania boyhood, so I can scarcely resent it when people, mistaking me for him, stop me on the street and ask me for his autograph. I am always surprised that I resemble him so closely that we can be confused. Meeting strangers, I must cope with an extra brightness in their faces, an expectancy that I will say something worthy of him; they do not realize that he works only in the medium of the written word, where other principles apply, and hours of time can be devoted to a moment's effect. Thrust into "real" time, he can scarcely function, and his awkward pleasantries and anxious stutter emerge through my lips. Myself, I am rather suave. I think fast, on my feet, and have no use for the qualifactory complexities and lame double entendres and pained exactations of language in which he is customarily mired. I move swiftly and rather blindly through life, spending the money he earns.

2   I early committed him to a search for significance, to philosophical issues that give direction and point to his verbal inventions, but I am not myself aware of much point or meaning to things. Things are, rather unsayably, and when I force myself to peruse his elaborate scrims of words I wonder where he gets it all—not from me, I am sure. The distance between us is so great that the bad reviews he receives do not touch me, though I treasure his few prizes and mount them on the walls and shelves of my house, where they instantly yellow and tarnish. That he takes up so much of my time, answering his cloying mail and reading his incessant proofs, I resent. I feel that the fractional time of day he spends away from being Updike is what feeds and inspires him, and yet, perversely, he spends more and more time being Updike, that monster of whom my boyhood dreamed.

3   Each morning I awake from my dreams, which as I age leave an ever more sour taste. Men once thought dreams to be messages from the gods, and then from something called the subconscious, as it sought a salubrious rearrangement of the contents of the day past; but now it becomes hard to believe that they partake of any economy. Instead, a basic chaos seems expressed: a random play of electricity generates images of inexplicable specificity.

4   I brush my teeth, I dress and descend to the kitchen, where I eat and read the newspaper, which has been dreaming its own dreams in the night. Postponing the moment, savoring every small news item and vitamin pill and sip of unconcentrated orange juice, I at last return to the upstairs and face the rooms that Updike has filled with his books, his papers, his trophies, his projects. The abundant clutter stifles me, yet I am helpless to clear away much of it. It would be a blasphemy. He has become a sacred reality to me. I gaze at his worn wooden desk, his boxes of dull pencils, his blank-faced word processor, with a religious fear. Suppose, some day, he fails to show up? I would attempt to do his work, but no one would be fooled.

QUESTIONS FOR DISCUSSION

1. From what materials has Updike created the persona "Updike"? Why does Updike not feel resentment about being mistaken for "Updike"? Why is he "surprised"?
2. Why does "Updike" have difficulty functioning in real time? How and why does he differ from his creator in terms of social skills?
3. How are "Updike" and Updike's values and beliefs different? Why does Updike refer to the persona "Updike" as a monster? Does he seem genuinely monstrous to you?
4. What view of dreams does Updike present? How does the emphasis on the dream state in "Updike and I" help you to understand the relationship between "Updike" and the "I" in the narrative?
5. The essay includes descriptions of the objects related to "Updike" and his career world. How do these objects help define the persona of "Updike," and why does the narrator, Updike, feel these objects constitute a "sacred reality"?

CONNECTION

Compare Updike's story of the creation of a literary persona with Robert Louis Stevenson's "A Chapter on Dreams," included in this chapter.

IDEAS FOR WRITING

1. Write an essay similar to "Updike and I" that explores the differences that exist between the part of yourself that writes and the part that exists in the everyday world. What have you learned about yourself from thinking about these differences?
2. Take an inventory of the objects you have accumulated in your home or room. How do these objects support and validate different selves within you? Write an essay that takes this inventory into account and explains how the different aspects of your personality and character developed and how these different personality traits support one another.

Marie-Louise von Franz

The Realization of the Shadow in Dreams

Marie-Louise von Franz (b. 1915), originally from Switzerland, is one of the world's most renowned analysts and a follower of Carl Jung. She has written such works as C. G. Jung *(1972),* Patterns of Creativity Mirrored in Creation Myths *(1972),* Shadow and Evil in Fairy Tales *(1974), and* Individuation in Fairy

Tales (1990). The following selection, on the psychological archetype of the shadow as it appears in dreams, is from Man and His Symbols *(1964), a book that von Franz wrote with Jung.*

JOURNAL

Write about a dream or fantasy that you have had about a figure who seemed to represent a quality of self that you had trouble accepting.

1   The shadow is not the whole of the unconscious personality. It represents unknown or little-known attributes and qualities of the ego—aspects that mostly belong to the personal sphere and that could just as well be conscious. In some aspects, the shadow can also consist of collective factors that stem from a source outside the individual's personal life.

2   When an individual makes an attempt to see his shadow, he becomes aware of (and often ashamed of) those qualities and impulses he denies in himself but can plainly see in other people—such things as egotism, mental laziness, and sloppiness; unreal fantasies, schemes, and plots; carelessness and cowardice; inordinate love of money and possessions—in short, all the little sins about which he might previously have told himself: "That doesn't matter; nobody will notice it, and in any case other people do it too."

3   If you feel an overwhelming rage coming up in you when a friend reproaches you about a fault, you can be fairly sure that at this point you will find a part of your shadow, of which you are unconscious. It is, of course, natural to become annoyed when others who are "no better" criticize you because of shadow faults. But what can you say if your own dreams—an inner judge in your own being—reproach you? That is the moment when the ego gets caught, and the result is usually embarrassed silence. Afterward the pain and lengthy work of self-education begins—a work, we might say, that is the psychological equivalent of the labors of Hercules. This unfortunate hero's first task, you will remember, was to clean up in one day the Augean Stables, in which hundreds of cattle had dropped their dung for many decades—a task so enormous that the ordinary mortal would be overcome by discouragement at the mere thought of it.

4   The shadow does no consist only of omissions. It shows up just as often in an impulsive or inadvertent act. Before one has time to think, the evil remarks pop out, the plot is hatched, the wrong decision is made, and one is confronted with results that were never intended or consciously wanted. Furthermore, the shadow is exposed to collective infections to a much greater extent than is the conscious personality. When a man is alone, for instance, he feels relatively all right; but as soon as "the others" do dark, primitive things he begins to fear that if he doesn't join in, he will be considered a fool. Thus he gives way to impulses that do not really belong to him at all. It is particularly in contacts with people of the same sex that one stumbles over both one's own shadow and those of other people. Although we do not see the shadow in a person of the opposite sex, we are usually much less annoyed by it and can more easily pardon it.

5   In dreams and myths, therefore, the shadow appears as a person of the same sex as that of the dreamer. The following dream may serve as an example. The dreamer was a man of forty-eight who tried to live very much for and by himself, working hard and disciplining himself, repressing pleasure and spontaneity to a far greater extent than suited his real nature.

> I owned and inhabited a very big house in town, and I didn't yet know all its different parts. So I took a walk through it and discovered, mainly in the cellar, several rooms about which I knew nothing and even exits leading into other cellars or into subterranean streets. I felt uneasy when I found that several of these exits were not locked and some had no locks at all. Moreover, there were some laborers at work in the neighborhood who could have sneaked in. . . .
>
> When I came back up again to the ground floor, I passed a back yard where again I discovered different exits into the street or into other houses. When I tried to investigate them more closely, a man came up to me laughing loudly and calling out that we were old pals from the elementary school. I remembered him too, and while he was telling me about his life, I walked along with him toward the exit and strolled with him through the streets.
>
> There was a strange chiaroscuro in the air as we walked through an enormous circular street and arrived at a green lawn where three galloping horses suddenly passed us. They were beautiful, strong animals, wild but well-groomed, and they had no rider with them. (Had they run away from military service?)

6   The maze of strange passages, chambers, and unlocked exits in the cellar recalls the old Egyptian representation of the underworld, which is a well-known symbol of the unconscious with its unknown possibilities. It also shows how one is "open" to other influences in one's unconscious shadow side, and how uncanny and alien elements can break in. The cellar, one can say, is the basement of the dreamer's psyche. In the back yard of the strange building (which represents the still unperceived psychic scope of the dreamer's personality) an old school friend suddenly turns up. This person obviously personifies another aspect of the dreamer himself—an aspect that had been part of his life as a child but that he had forgotten and lost. It often happens that a person's childhood qualities (for instance, gaiety, irascibility, or perhaps trustfulness) suddenly disappear, and one does not know where or how they have gone. It is such a lost characteristic of the dreamer that now returns (from the back yard) and tries to make friends again. This figure probably stands for the dreamer's neglected capacity for enjoying life and for his extroverted shadow side.

7   But we soon learn why the dreamer feels "uneasy" just before meeting this seemingly harmless old friend. When he strolls with him in the street, the horses break loose. The dreamer thinks they may have escaped from military service (that is to say, from the conscious discipline that has hitherto characterized his life). The fact that the horses have no rider shows that instinctive drives can get away from conscious control. In this old friend, and in the horses, all the positive force reappears that was lacking before and that was badly needed by the dreamer.

8   This is a problem that often comes up when one meets one's "other side." The shadow usually contains values that are needed by consciousness, but that exist in a form that makes it difficult to integrate them into one's life. The passages and the

large house in this dream also show that the dreamer does not yet know his own psychic dimensions and is not yet able to fill them out.

9   The shadow in this dream is typical for an introvert (a man who tends to retire too much from outer life). In the case of an extrovert, who is turned more toward outer objects and outer life, the shadow would look quite different.

10   A young man who had a very lively temperament embarked again and again on successful enterprises, while at the same time his dreams insisted that he should finish off a piece of private creative work he had begun. The following was one of those dreams:

> A man is lying on a couch and has pulled the cover over his face. He is a Frenchman, a desperado who would take on any criminal job. An official is accompanying me downstairs, and I know that a plot has been made against me: namely, that the Frenchman should kill me as if by chance. (That is how it would look from the outside.) He actually sneaks up behind me when we approach the exit, but I am on my guard. A tall, portly man (rather rich and influential) suddenly leans against the wall beside me, feeling ill. I quickly grab the opportunity to kill the official by stabbing his heart. "One only notices a bit of moisture"—this is said like a comment. Now I am safe, for the Frenchman won't attack me since the man who gave him his orders is dead. (Probably the official and the successful portly man are the same person, the latter somehow replacing the former.)

11   The desperado represents the other side of the dreamer—his introversion—which has reached a completely destitute state. He lies on a couch (i.e., he is passive) and pulls the cover over his face because he wants to be left alone. The official, on the other hand, and the prosperous portly man (who are secretly the same person) personify the dreamer's successful outer responsibilities and activities. The sudden illness of the portly man is connected with the fact that this dreamer had in fact become ill several times when he had allowed his dynamic energy to explode too forcibly in his external life. But this successful man has no blood in his veins—only a sort of moisture—which means that these external ambitious activities of the dreamer contain no genuine life and no passion, but are bloodless mechanisms. Thus it would be no real loss if the portly man were killed. At the end of the dream, the Frenchman is satisfied; he obviously represents a positive shadow figure who had turned negative and dangerous only because the conscious attitude of the dreamer did not agree with him.

12   This dream shows us that the shadow can consist of many different elements—for instance, of unconscious ambition (the successful portly man) and of introversion (the Frenchman). This particular dreamer's association to the French, moreover, was that they know how to handle love affairs very well. Therefore the two shadow figures also present two well-known drives: power and sex. The power drive appears momentarily in a double form, both as an official and as a successful man. The official, or civil servant, personifies collective adaptation, whereas the successful man denotes ambition; but naturally both serve the power drive. When the dreamer succeeds in stopping this dangerous inner force, the Frenchman is suddenly no longer hostile. In other words, the equally dangerous aspect of the sex drive has also surrendered.

13   Obviously, the problem of the shadow plays a great role in all political conflicts. If the man who had this dream had not been sensible about his shadow problem, he

could easily have identified the desperate Frenchman with the "dangerous Communists" of outer life, or the official plus the prosperous man with the "grasping capitalists." In this way he would have avoided seeing that he had within him such warring elements. If people observe their own unconscious tendencies in other people, this is called a "projection." Political agitation in all countries is full of such projections, just as much as the backyard gossip of little groups and individuals. Projections of all kinds obscure our view of our fellow men, spoiling its objectivity, and thus spoiling all possibility of genuine human relationships.

14   And there is an additional disadvantage in projecting our shadow. If we identify our own shadow with, say, the Communists or the capitalists, a part of our own personality remains on the opposing side. The result is that we shall constantly (though involuntarily) do things behind our own backs that support this other side, and thus we shall unwittingly help our enemy. If, on the contrary, we realize the projection and can discuss matters without fear or hostility, dealing with the other person sensibly, then there is a chance of mutual understanding—or at least a truce.

15   Whether the shadow becomes our friend or enemy depends largely upon ourselves. As the dreams of the unexplored house and the French desperado both show, the shadow is not necessarily always an opponent. In fact, he is exactly like any human being with whom one has to get along, sometimes by giving in, sometimes by resisting, sometimes by giving love—whatever the situation requires. The shadow becomes hostile only when he is ignored or misunderstood.

Questions for Discussion

1. Based on von Franz's discussion, how would you define the shadow? What inner and public qualities can the shadow represent?
2. How is the shadow related both to reproach and rage?
3. According to von Franz, why does the shadow usually appear to us in the form of a person of our own sex? Have you ever had a shadow figure appear in your dreams? What did the shadow figure mean to you?
4. In her essay, von Franz analyzes two dreams, one by a middle-aged, introverted man, one by a younger, "lively" individual. What are the differences between these two dreams? In what ways are they similar?
5. What role does the shadow play in political conflicts? How is this point illustrated by the second dream that von Franz analyzes? Can you apply von Franz's concept to your own experiences with politics?
6. How does von Franz suggest that the shadow can be made our "friend"? Is there anything else about the process of befriending your shadow that you would like to know more about?

Connection

Compare the kind of dreams von Franz analyzes here with the poem by Walt Whitman, "To a Stranger" in Chapter 6. How might von Franz's analysis of the shadow shed light on the fantasy experienced in Whitman's poem?

IDEAS FOR WRITING

1. Write an essay in which you reflect on ways that you could try to accommo-
    date or integrate the "shadow" side of your personality. Try creating a "dia-
    logue" with your shadow, or propose some compromises in your lifestyle
    that might please both sides of your personality.
2. Write an essay in which you argue for or against the concept of the need
    to integrate the "shadow" side of the personality as von Franz proposes.
    Support your main ideas with examples from your own dreams and expe-
    rience, readings, or films you have seen.

Robert Louis Stevenson

A Chapter on Dreams

*Robert Louis Stevenson (1850–1894) was born in Edinburgh, Scotland, and was
educated as a lawyer. Because he had congenital lung disease, Stevenson traveled extensively in search of a healthful climate and eventually settled in Samoa. He is remembered for his verses for children, his adventure novels, and his powerful novella
of horror,* The Strange Case of Dr. Jekyll and Mr. Hyde *(1886). In the following
excerpt from the essay "A Chapter on Dreams," which first appeared in* Across the
Plains *(1892), Stevenson explores the ways in which he used his dreams to help him
create his popular fiction such as* Dr. Jekyll and Mr. Hyde.

JOURNAL

Write about a dream that helped you to solve a problem in your waking life.

1   . . . This honest fellow had long been in the custom of setting himself to sleep with
tales, and so had his father before him; but these were irresponsible inventions, told
for the teller's pleasure, with no eye to the crass public or the thwart reviewer: tales
where a thread might be dropped, or one adventure quitted for another, on fancy's
least suggestion. So that the little people who manage man's internal theatre had
not as yet received a very rigorous training; and played upon their stage like children
who should have slipped into the house and found it empty, rather than like drilled
actors performing a set piece to a huge hall of faces. But presently my dreamer began
to turn his former amusement of story-telling to (what is called) account; by which I
mean that he began to write and sell his tales. Here was he, and here were the little
people who did that part of his business, in quite new conditions. The stories must
now be trimmed and pared and set upon all fours, they must run from a beginning to

an end and fit (after a manner) with the laws of life; the pleasure, in one word, had become a business; and that not only for the dreamer, but for the little people of his theatre. These understood the change as well as he. When he lay down to prepare himself for sleep, he no longer sought amusement, but printable and profitable tales; and after he had dozed off in his box-seat, his little people continued their evolutions with the same mercantile designs. All other forms of dream deserted him but two: he still occasionally reads the most delightful books, he still visits at times the most delightful places; and it is perhaps worthy of note that to these same places, and to one in particular, he returns at intervals of months and years, finding new field-paths, visiting new neighbours, beholding that happy valley under new effects of noon and dawn and sunset. But all the rest of the family of visions is quite lost to him: the common, mangled version of yesterday's affair, the raw-head-and-bloody-bones nightmare, rumoured to be the child of toasted cheese—these and their like are gone; and, for the most part, whether awake or asleep, he is simply occupied— he or his little people—in consciously making stories for the market. This dreamer (like many other persons) has encountered some trifling vicissitudes of fortune. When the bank begins to send letters and the butcher to linger at the back gate, he sets to belabouring his brains after a story, for that is his readiest money-winner; and, behold! at once the little people begin to bestir themselves in the same quest, and labour all night long, and all night long set before him truncheons of tales upon their lighted theatre. No fear of his being frightened now; the flying heart and the frozen scalp are things bygone; applause, growing applause, growing interest, growing exultation in his own cleverness (for he takes all the credit), and at last a jubilant leap to wakefulness, with the cry, "I have it, that'll do!" upon his lips: with such and similar emotions he sits at these nocturnal dramas, with such outbreaks, like Claudius in the play, he scatters the performance in the midst. Often enough the waking is a disappointment: he has been too deep asleep, as I explain the thing; drowsiness has gained his little people, they have gone stumbling and maundering through their parts; and the play, to the awakened mind, is seen to be a tissue of absurdities. And yet how often have these sleepless Brownies done him honest service, and given him, as he sat idly taking his pleasure in the boxes, better tales than he could fashion for himself. . . .

2   . . . The more I think of it, the more I am moved to press upon the world my question: Who are the Little People? They are near connections of the dreamer's, beyond doubt; they share in his financial worries and have an eye to the bank-book; they share plainly in his training; they have plainly learned like him to build the scheme of a considerate story and to arrange emotion in progressive order; only I think they have more talent; and one thing is beyond doubt, they can tell him a story piece by piece, like a serial, and keep him all the while in ignorance of where they aim. Who are they, then? and who is the dreamer?

3   Well, as regards the dreamer, I can answer that, for he is no less a person than myself;—as I might have told you from the beginning, only that the critics murmur over my consistent egotism;—and as I am positively forced to tell you now, or I

could advance but little farther with my story. And for the Little People, what shall I say they are but just my Brownies, God bless them! who do one-half my work for me while I am fast asleep, and in all human likelihood, do the rest for me as well, when I am wide awake and fondly suppose I do it for myself. That part which is done while I am sleeping is the Brownies' part beyond contention; but that which is done when I am up and about is by no means necessarily mine, since all goes to show the Brownies have a hand in it even then. Here is a doubt that much concerns my conscience. For myself—what I call I, my conscious ego, the denizen of the pineal gland unless he has changed his residence since Descartes, the man with the conscience and the variable bank-account, the man with the hat and the boots, and the privilege of voting and not carrying his candidate at the general elections—I am sometimes tempted to suppose he is no story-teller at all, but a creature as matter of fact as any cheesemonger or any cheese, and a realist bemired up to the ears in actuality; so that, by that account, the whole of my published fiction should be the single-handed product of some Brownie, some Familiar, some unseen collaborator, whom I keep locked in a back garret, while I get all the praise and he but a share (which I cannot prevent him getting) of the pudding. I am an excellent adviser, something like Molière's servant; I pull back and I cut down; and I dress the whole in the best words and sentences that I can find and make; I hold the pen, too; and I do the sitting at the table, which is about the worst of it; and when all is done, I make up the manuscript and pay for the registration; so that, on the whole, I have some claim to share, though not so largely as I do, in the profits of our common enterprise.

4   I can but give an instance or so of what part is done sleeping and what part awake, and leave the reader to share what laurels there are, at his own nod, between myself and my collaborators; and to do this I will first take a book that a number of persons have been polite enough to read, *The Strange Case of Dr. Jekyll and Mr. Hyde*. I had long been trying to write a story on this subject, to find a body, a vehicle, for that strong sense of man's double being which must at times come in upon and overwhelm the mind of every thinking creature. I had even written one, *The Travelling Companion*, which was returned by an editor on the plea that it was a work of genius and indecent, and which I burned the other day on the ground that it was not a work of genius, and that *Jekyll* had supplanted it. Then came one of those financial fluctuations to which (with an elegant modesty) I have hitherto referred in the third person. For two days I went about racking my brains for a plot of any sort; and on the second night I dreamed the scene at the window, and a scene afterward split in two, in which Hyde, pursued for some crime, took the powder and underwent the change in the presence of his pursuers. All the rest was made awake, and consciously, although I think I can trace in much of it the manner of my Brownies. The meaning of the tale is therefore mine, and had long pre-existed in my garden of Adonis, and tried one body after another in vain; indeed, I do most of the morality, worse luck! and my Brownies have not a rudiment of what we call a conscience. Mine, too, is the setting, mine the characters. All that was given me was the matter of three scenes, and the central idea of a voluntary change becoming involuntary.

Will it be thought ungenerous, after I have been so liberally ladling out praise to my unseen collaborators, if I here toss them over, bound hand and foot, into the arena of the critics? For the business of the powders, which so many have censured, is, I am relieved to say, not mine at all but the Brownies'. . . .

QUESTIONS FOR DISCUSSION

1. How does Stevenson contrast the way most people dream and fantasize with the way he as a professional writer uses his dreams? Have you ever been able to direct or utilize your dreams in the way Stevenson did? If so, provide examples.

2. According to Stevenson, who are the "Little People" and who is the dreamer? What part of his inner world do the "Brownies" represent? What popular mythology might they reflect?

3. How can either too much self-consciousness or too deep a level of sleep ruin the dreamer's literary creation?

4. How does Stevenson contrast "myself—what I call I" to the personalities and creativeness of the "Little People"? Do you think that this is a typical division of self for a writer to experience? If you feel a similar type of division within yourself, do you value one part of your mind over the other? Why?

5. After reading this selection, how do you understand the difference between the conscious and the unconscious mind?

6. How much of Stevenson's novella *The Strange Case of Dr. Jekyll and Mr. Hyde* actually came to him in a dream? What drawbacks does Stevenson suggest there might be in relying too extensively on the "Little People" or unconscious co-creators for crucial elements of a story? What does Stevenson's essay suggest about the importance of the revision process?

CONNECTION

How does reading this selection help you to understand *Dr. Jekyll and Mr. Hyde* in a different light? For instance, if you read "Henry Jekyll's Last Testament," in this chapter, what portions of the text allude to the kind of dualistic creative interaction between selves that this essay reflects upon?

IDEAS FOR WRITING

1. Write an essay in which you discuss the ways that you have found your dreams useful as insights into problem-solving, as ideas for stories or other forms of creative expression, or for their prophetic vision.

2. Stevenson suggests what modern brain researchers have discovered: that the brain really has two aspects that play a part in the writing process, the

creative and intuitive (right brain) and the logical, problem-solving (left brain). Write an essay in which you explain how you rely on the two parts of your brain when you write, providing examples from your writing experiences to support your point of view.

Robert Louis Stevenson

Henry Jekyll's Full Statement of the Case, from The Strange Case of Dr. Jekyll and Mr. Hyde

Robert Louis Stevenson wrote The Strange Case of Dr. Jekyll and Mr. Hyde *(1886), a short novel, at a time when he was very ill with tuberculosis. In the following selection, the conclusion to Stevenson's classic tale of good and evil, Henry Jekyll, a highly respected London physician, has chemically altered his own inner nature, constructing a morally depraved "second self," Mr. Hyde. The following "statement" of Dr. Jekyll, written just before his death, sets forth his reasons for and the fatal consequences of tampering with his inner world. The letter was found by his friends who discovered only the body of Mr. Hyde with a "crushed phial" of cyanide poison in his hand.*

JOURNAL

Write about experiencing your "other" or anti-self, through some change in your normal mental state, perhaps from an emotional crisis or chemical stimulation, or during an illness or extreme fatigue.

1   I was born in the year 18— to a large fortune, endowed besides with excellent parts, inclined by nature to industry, fond of the respect of the wise and good among my fellow-men, and thus, as might have been supposed, with every guarantee of an honourable and distinguished future. And indeed the worst of my faults was a certain impatient gaiety of disposition, such as has made the happiness of many, but such as I found it hard to reconcile with my imperious desire to carry my head high, and wear a more than commonly grave countenance before the public. Hence it came about that I concealed my pleasures; and that when I reached years of reflection, and began to look round me and take stock of my progress and position in the world, I stood already committed to a profound duplicity of life. Many a man would have even blazoned such irregularities as I was guilty of; but from the high views that I had set before me, I regarded and hid them with an almost morbid sense of shame. It was thus rather the exacting nature of my aspirations than any particular degradation in my

faults, that made me what I was, and, with even a deeper trench than in the majority of men, severed in me those provinces of good and ill which divide and compound man's dual nature. In this case, I was driven to reflect deeply and inveterately on that hard law of life, which lies at the root of religion and is one of the most plentiful springs of distress. Though so profound a double-dealer, I was in no sense a hypocrite; both sides of me were in dead earnest; I was no more myself when I laid aside restraint and plunged in shame, than when I laboured, in the eye of day, at the furtherance of knowledge or the relief of sorrow and suffering. And it chanced that the direction of my scientific studies, which led wholly towards the mystic and the transcendental, reacted and shed a strong light on this consciousness of the perennial war among my members. With every day, and from both sides of my intelligence, the moral and the intellectual, I thus drew steadily nearer to that truth, by whose partial discovery I have been doomed to such a dreadful shipwreck: that man is not truly one, but truly two. I say two, because the state of my own knowledge does not pass beyond that point. Others will follow, others will outstrip me on the same lines; and I hazard the guess that man will be ultimately known for a mere polity of multifarious, incongruous and independent denizens. I, for my part, from the nature of my life, advanced infallibly in one direction and in one direction only. It was on the moral side, and in my own person, that I learned to recognise the thorough and primitive duality of man; I saw that, of the two natures that contended in the field of my consciousness, even if I could rightly be said to be either, it was only because I was radically both; and from an early date, even before the course of my scientific discoveries had begun to suggest the most naked possibility of such a miracle, I had learned to dwell with pleasure, as a beloved daydream, on the thought of the separation of these elements. If each, I told myself, could be housed in separate identities, life would be relieved of all that was unbearable; the unjust might go his way, delivered from the aspirations and remorse of his more upright twin; and the just could walk steadfastly and securely on his upward path, doing the good things in which he found his pleasure, and no longer exposed to disgrace and penitence by the hands of his extraneous evil. It was the curse of mankind that these incongruous faggots were thus bound together—that in the agonised womb of consciousness, these polar twins should be continuously struggling. How, then, were they dissociated.

2   I was so far in my reflections when, as I have said, a side light began to shine upon the subject from the laboratory table. I began to perceive more deeply than it has ever yet been stated, the trembling immateriality, the mist-like transience, of this seemingly so solid body in which we walk attired. Certain agents I found to have the power to shake and pluck back that fleshy vestment, even as a wind might toss the curtains of a pavilion. For two good reasons, I will not enter deeply into this scientific branch of my confession. First, because I have been made to learn that the doom and burden of our life is bound for ever on man's shoulders, and when the attempt is made to cast it off, it but returns upon us with more unfamiliar and more awful pressure. Second, because, as my narrative will make, alas! too evident, my discoveries were incomplete. Enough, then, that I not only recognised my natural body from the mere aura and effulgence of certain of the powers that make up my spirit,

but managed to compound a drug by which these powers should be dethroned from their supremacy, and a second form and countenance substituted, none the less natural to me because they were the expression, and bore the stamp of lower elements in my soul.

3   I hesitated long before I put this theory to the test of practice. I knew well that I risked death; for any drug that so potently controlled and shook the very fortress of identity, might, by the least scruple of an overdose or at the least inopportunity in the moment of exhibition, utterly blot out that immaterial tabernacle which I looked to it to change. But the temptation of a discovery so singular and profound at last overcame the suggestions of alarm. I had long since prepared my tincture; I purchased at once, from a firm of wholesale chemists, a large quantity of a particular salt which I knew, from my experiments, to be the last ingredient required; and late one accursed night, I compounded the elements, watched them boil and smoke together in the glass, and when the ebullition had subsided, with a strong glow of courage, drank off the potion.

4   The most racking pangs succeeded: a grinding in the bones, deadly nausea, and a horror of the spirit that cannot be exceeded at the hour of birth or death. Then these agonies began swiftly to subside, and I came to myself as if out of a great sickness. There was something strange in my sensations, something indescribably new and, from its very novelty, incredibly sweet. I felt younger, lighter, happier in body; within I was conscious of a heady recklessness, a current of disordered sensual images running like a millrace in my fancy, a dissolution of the bonds of obligation, an unknown but not an innocent freedom of the soul. I knew myself, at the first breath of this new life, to be more wicked, tenfold more wicked, sold a slave to my original evil; and the thought, in that moment, braced and delighted me like wine. I stretched out my hands, exulting in the freshness of these sensations; and in the act, I was suddenly aware that I had lost in stature.

5   There was no mirror, at that date, in my room; that which stands beside me as I write, was brought there later on and for the very purpose of these transformations. That night, however, was far gone into the morning—the morning, black as it was, was nearly ripe for the conception of the day—the inmates of my house were locked in the most rigorous hours of slumber, and I determined, flushed as I was with hope and triumph, to venture in my new shape as far as to my bedroom. I crossed the yard, wherein the constellations looked down upon me, I could have thought, with wonder, the first creature of that sort that their unsleeping vigilance had yet disclosed to them; I stole through the corridors, a stranger in my own house; and coming to my room, I saw for the first time the appearance of Edward Hyde.

6   I must here speak by theory alone, saying not that which I know, but that which I suppose to be most probable. The evil side of my nature, to which I had now transferred the stamping efficacy, was less robust and less developed than the good which I had just deposed. Again, in the course of my life, which had been, after all, nine tenths a life of effort, virtue and control, it had been much less exercised and much less exhausted. And hence, as I think, it came about that Edward Hyde was so much smaller, slighter and younger than Henry Jekyll. Even as good shone upon the countenance of

the one, evil was written broadly and plainly on the face of the other. Evil besides (which I must still believe to be the lethal side of man) had left on that body an imprint of deformity and decay. And yet when I looked upon that ugly idol in the glass, I was conscious of no repugnance, rather of a leap of welcome. This, too, was myself. It seemed natural and human. In my eyes it bore a livelier image of the spirit, it seemed more express and single, than the imperfect and divided countenance I had been hitherto accustomed to call mine. And in so far I was doubtless right. I have observed that when I wore the semblance of Edward Hyde, none could come near to me at first without a visible misgiving of the flesh. This, as I take it, was because all human beings, as we meet them, are commingled out of good and evil: and Edward Hyde, alone in the ranks of mankind, was pure evil.

7   I lingered but a moment at the mirror: the second and conclusive experiment had yet to be attempted; it yet remained to be seen if I had lost my identity beyond redemption and must flee before daylight from a house that was no longer mine; and hurrying back to my cabinet, I once more prepared and drank the cup, once more suffered the pangs of dissolution, and came to myself once more with the character, the stature and the face of Henry Jekyll.

8   That night I had come to the fatal crossroads. Had I approached my discovery in a more noble spirit, had I risked the experiment while under the empire of generous or pious aspirations, all must have been otherwise, and from these agonies of death and birth, I had come forth an angel instead of a fiend. The drug had no discriminating action; it was neither diabolical nor divine; it but shook the doors of the prisonhouse of my disposition; and like the captives of Phillipi, that which stood within ran forth. At that time my virtue slumbered; my evil, kept awake by ambition, was alert and swift to seize the occasion; and the thing that was projected was Edward Hyde. Hence, although I had now two characters as well as two appearances, one was wholly evil, and the other was still the old Henry Jekyll, that incongruous compound of whose reformation and improvement I had already learned to despair. The movement was thus wholly toward the worse.

9   Even at that time, I had not conquered my aversion to the dryness of a life of study. I would still be merrily disposed at times; and as my pleasures were (to say the least) undignified, and I was not only well known and highly considered, but growing toward the elderly man, this incoherency of my life was daily growing more unwelcome. It was on this side that my new power tempted me until I fell in slavery. I had but to drink the cup, to doff at once the body of the noted professor, and to assume, like a thick cloak, that of Edward Hyde. I smiled at the notion; it seemed to me at the time to be humorous; and I made my preparations with the most studious care. I took and furnished that house in Soho, to which Hyde was tracked by the police; and engaged as a housekeeper a creature whom I knew well to be silent and unscrupulous. On the other side, I announced to my servants that a Mr. Hyde (whom I described) was to have full liberty and power about my house in the square; and to parry mishaps, I even called and made myself a familiar object, in my second character. I next drew up that will to which you so much objected; so that if anything befell me in the person of Dr. Jekyll, I could enter on that of Edward Hyde without

pecuniary loss. And thus fortified, as I supposed, on every side, I began to profit by the strange immunities of my position.

10   Men have before hired bravoes to transact their crimes, while their own person and reputation sat under shelter. I was the first that ever did so for his pleasures. I was the first that could plod in the public eye with a load of genial respectability, and in a moment, like a schoolboy, strip off these lendings and spring headlong into the sea of liberty. But for me, in my impenetrable mantle, the safety was complete. Think of it—I did not even exist! Let me but escape into my laboratory door, give me but a second or two to mix and swallow the draught that I had always standing ready; and whatever he had done, Edward Hyde would pass away like the stain of breath upon a mirror; and there in his stead, quietly at home, trimming the midnight lamp in his study, a man who could afford to laugh at suspicion, would be Henry Jekyll.

11   The pleasures which I made haste to seek in my disguise were, as I have said, undignified; I would scarce use a harder term. But in the hands of Edward Hyde, they soon began to turn toward the monstrous. When I would come back from these excursions, I was often plunged into a kind of wonder at my vicarious depravity. This familiar that I called out of my own soul, and sent forth alone to do his good pleasure, was a being inherently malign and villainous; his every act and thought centered on self; drinking pleasure with bestial avidity from any degree of torture to another; relentless like a man of stone. Henry Jekyll stood at times aghast before the acts of Edward Hyde; but the situation was apart from ordinary laws, and insidiously relaxed the grasp of conscience. It was Hyde, after all, and Hyde alone, that was guilty. Jekyll was no worse; he woke again to his good qualities seemingly unimpaired; he would even make haste, where it was possible, to undo the evil done by Hyde. And thus his conscience slumbered.

12   Into the details of the infamy at which I thus connived (for even now I can scarce grant that I committed it) I have no design of entering; I mean but to point out the warnings and the successive steps with which my chastisement approached. I met with one accident which, as it brought on no consequence, I shall no more than mention. An act of cruelty to a child aroused against me the anger of a passerby, whom I recognised the other day in the person of your kinsman; the doctor and the child's family joined him; there were moments when I feared for my life; and at last, in order to pacify their too just resentment, Edward Hyde had to bring them to the door, and pay them in a cheque drawn in the name of Henry Jekyll. But this danger was easily eliminated from the future, by opening an account at another bank in the name of Edward Hyde himself; and when, by sloping my own hand backward, I had supplied my double with a signature, I thought I sat beyond the reach of fate.

13   Some two months before the murder of Sir Danvers, I had been out for one of my adventures, had returned at a late hour, and woke the next day in bed with somewhat odd sensations. It was in vain I looked about me; in vain I saw the decent furniture and tall proportions of my room in the square; in vain that I recognised the pattern of the bed curtains and the design of the mahogany frame; something still kept insisting that I was not where I was, that I had not wakened where I seemed to

be, but in the little room in Soho where I was accustomed to sleep in the body of Edward Hyde. I smiled to myself, and, in my psychological way, began lazily to inquire into the elements of this illusion, occasionally, even as I did so, dropping back into a comfortable morning doze. I was still so engaged when, in one of my more wakeful moments, my eyes fell upon my hand. Now the hand of Henry Jekyll (as you have often remarked) was professional in shape and size: it was large, firm, white and comely. But the hand which I now saw, clearly enough, in the yellow light of a mid-London morning, lying half shut on the bedclothes, was lean, corded, knuckly, of a dusky pallor and thickly shaded with a swart growth of hair. It was the hand of Edward Hyde.

14   I must have stared upon it for near half a minute, sunk as I was in the mere stupidity of wonder, before terror woke up in my breast as sudden and startling as the crash of cymbals; and bounding from my bed, I rushed to the mirror. At the sight that met my eyes, my blood was changed into something exquisitely thin and icy. Yes, I had gone to bed Henry Jekyll, I had awakened Edward Hyde. How was this to be explained? I asked myself; and then, with another bound of terror—how was it to be remedied? It was well on in the morning; the servants were up; all my drugs were in the cabinet—a long journey down two pairs of stairs, through the back passage, across the open court and through the anatomical theatre, from where I was then standing horror-struck. It might indeed be possible to cover my face; but of what use was that, when I was unable to conceal the alteration in my stature? And then with an overpowering sweetness of relief, it came back upon my mind that the servants were already used to the coming and going of my second self. I had soon dressed, as well as I was able, in clothes of my own size; had soon passed through the house, where Bradshaw stared and drew back at seeing Mr. Hyde at such an hour and in such a strange array; and ten minutes later, Dr. Jekyll had returned to his own shape and was sitting down, with a darkened brow, to make a feint of breakfasting.

15   Small indeed was my appetite. This inexplicable incident, this reversal of my previous experience, seemed, like the Babylonian finger on the wall, to be spelling out the letters of my judgment; and I began to reflect more seriously than ever before on the issues and possibilities of my double existence. That part of me which I had the power of projecting, had lately been much exercised and nourished; it had seemed to me of late as though the body of Edward Hyde had grown in stature, as though (when I wore that form) I were conscious of a more generous tide of blood, and I began to spy a danger that, if this were much prolonged, the balance of my nature might be permanently overthrown, the power of voluntary change be forfeited, and the character of Edward Hyde become irrevocably mine. The power of the drug had not been always equally displayed. Once, very early in my career, it had totally failed me; since then I had been obliged on more than one occasion to double, and once, with infinite risk of death, to treble the amount; and these rare uncertainties had cast hitherto the sole shadow on my contentment. Now, however, and in the light of that morning's accident, I was led to remark that whereas, in the beginning, the difficulty had been to throw off the body of Jekyll, it had of late gradually but decid-

edly transferred itself to the other side. All things therefore seemed to point to this: that I was slowly losing hold of my original and better self, and becoming slowly incorporated with my second and worse.

16   Between these two, I now felt I had to choose. My two natures had memory in common, but all other faculties were most unequally shared between them. Jekyll (who was composite) now with the most sensitive apprehensions, now with a greedy gusto, projected and shared in the pleasures and adventures of Hyde; but Hyde was indifferent to Jekyll, or but remembered him as the mountain bandit remembers the cavern in which he conceals himself from pursuit. Jekyll had more than a father's interest; Hyde had more than a son's indifference. To cast in my lot with Jekyll, was to die to those appetites which I had long secretly indulged and had of late begun to pamper. To cast it in with Hyde, was to die to a thousand interests and aspirations, and to become, at a blow and forever, despised and friendless. The bargain might appear unequal; but there was still another consideration in the scales; for while Jekyll would suffer smartingly in the fires of abstinence, Hyde would be not even conscious of all that he had lost. Strange as my circumstances were, the terms of this debate are as old and commonplace as man; much the same inducements and alarms cast the die for any tempted and trembling sinner; and it fell out with me, as it falls with so vast a majority of my fellows, that I chose the better part and was found wanting in the strength to keep to it.

17   Yes, I preferred the elderly and discontented doctor, surrounded by friends and cherishing honest hopes; and bade a resolute farewell to the liberty, the comparative youth, the light step, leaping impulses and secret pleasures, that I had enjoyed in the disguise of Hyde. I made this choice perhaps with some unconscious reservation, for I neither gave up the house in Soho, nor destroyed the clothes of Edward Hyde, which still lay ready in my cabinet. For two months, however, I was true to my determination; for two months, I led a life of such severity as I had never before attained to, and enjoyed the compensations of an approving conscience. But time began at last to obliterate the freshness of my alarm; the praises of conscience began to grow into a thing of course; I began to be tortured with throes and longings, as of Hyde struggling after freedom; and at last, in an hour of moral weakness, I once again compounded and swallowed the transforming draught.

18   I do not suppose that, when a drunkard reasons with himself upon his vice, he is once out of five hundred times affected by the dangers that he runs through his brutish, physical insensibility; neither had I, long as I had considered my position, made enough allowance for the complete moral insensibility and insensate readiness to evil, which were the leading characters of Edward Hyde. Yet it was by these that I was punished. My devil had been long caged, he came out roaring. I was conscious, even when I took the draught, of a more unbridled, a more furious propensity to ill. It must have been this, I suppose, that stirred in my soul that tempest of impatience with which I listened to the civilities of my unhappy victim; I declare, at least, before God, no man morally sane could have been guilty of that crime upon so pitiful a provocation; and that I struck in no more reasonable spirit than that in which a sick

child may break a plaything. But I had voluntarily stripped myself of all those bal-ancing instincts by which even the worst of us continues to walk with some degree of steadiness among temptations and in my case, to be tempted, however slightly, was to fall.

19   Instantly the spirit of hell awoke in me and raged. With a transport of glee, I mauled the unresisting body, tasting delight from every blow; and it was not till weariness had begun to succeed, that I was suddenly, in the top fit of my delirium, struck through the heart by a cold thrill of terror. A mist dispersed; I saw my life to be forfeit; and fled from the scene of these excesses, at once glorying and trembling, my lust of evil gratified and stimulated, my love of life screwed to the topmost peg. I ran to the house in Soho, and (to make assurance doubly sure) destroyed my papers; thence I set out through the lamplit streets, in the same divided ecstasy of mind, gloating on my crime, light-headedly devising others in the future, and yet still has-tening and still hearkening in my wake for the steps of the avenger. Hyde had a song upon his lips as he compounded the draught, and as he drank it, pledged the dead man. The pangs of transformation had not done tearing him, before Henry Jekyll, with streaming tears of gratitude and remorse, had fallen upon his knees and lifted his clasped hands to God. The veil of self-indulgence was rent from head to foot. I saw my life as a whole: I followed it up from the days of childhood, when I had walked with my father's hand, and through the self-denying toils of my professional life, to arrive again and again, with the same sense of unreality, at the damned hor-rors of the evening. I could have screamed aloud; I sought with tears and prayers to smother down the crowd of hideous images and sounds with which my memory swarmed against me; and still, between the petitions, the ugly face of my iniquity stared into my soul. As the acuteness of this remorse began to die away, it was suc-ceeded by a sense of joy. The problem of my conduct was solved. Hyde was thence-forth impossible; whether I would or not, I was now confined to the better part of my existence; and O, how I rejoiced to think of it! with what willing humility I em-braced anew the restrictions of natural life! with what sincere renunciation I locked the door by which I had so often gone and come, and ground the key under my heel!

20   The next day, came the news that the murder had been overlooked, that the guilt of Hyde was patent to the world, and that the victim was a man high in public esti-mation. It was not only a crime, it had been a tragic folly. I think I was glad to know it; I think I was glad to have my better impulses thus buttressed and guarded by the terrors of the scaffold. Jekyll was now my city of refuge; let but Hyde peep out an in-stant, and the hands of all men would be raised to take and slay him.

21   I resolved in my future conduct to redeem the past; and I can say with honesty that my resolve was fruitful of some good. You know yourself how earnestly, in the last months of the last year, I laboured to relieve suffering; you know that much was done for others, and that the days passed quietly, almost happily for myself. Nor can I truly say that I wearied of this beneficent and innocent life; I think instead that I daily enjoyed it more completely; but I was still cursed with my duality of purpose; and as the first edge of my penitence wore off, the lower side of me, so long indulged,

so recently chained down, began to growl for licence. Not that I dreamed of resuscitating Hyde; the bare idea of that would startle me to frenzy; no, it was in my own person that I was once more tempted to trifle with my conscience; and it was as an ordinary secret sinner that I at last fell before the assaults of temptation.

22   There comes an end to all things; the most capacious measure is filled at last; and this brief condescension to my evil finally destroyed the balance of my soul. And yet I was not alarmed; the fall seemed natural, like a return to the old days before I had made my discovery. It was a fine, clear, January day, wet under foot where the frost had melted, but cloudless overhead; and the Regent's Park was full of winter chirrupings and sweet with spring odours. I sat in the sun on a bench; the animal within me licking the chops of memory; the spiritual side a little drowsed, promising subsequent penitence, but not yet moved to begin. After all, I reflected, I was like my neighbours; and then I smiled, comparing myself with other men, comparing my active goodwill with the lazy cruelty of their neglect. And at the very moment of that vainglorious thought, a qualm came over me, a horrid nausea and the most deadly shuddering. These passed away, and left me faint; and then, as in its turn faintness subsided, I began to be aware of a change in the temper of my thoughts, a greater boldness, a contempt of danger, a solution of the bonds of obligation. I looked down; my clothes hung formlessly on my shrunken limbs; the hand that lay on my knee was corded and hairy. I was once more Edward Hyde. A moment before I had been safe of all men's respect, wealthy, beloved—the cloth laying for me in the dining-room at home; and now I was the common quarry of mankind, hunted, house-less, a known murderer, thrall to the gallows.

23   My reason wavered, but it did not fail me utterly. I have more than once observed that, in my second character, my faculties seemed sharpened to a point and my spirits more tensely elastic; thus it came about that, where Jekyll perhaps might have succumbed, Hyde rose to the importance of the moment. My drugs were in one of the presses of my cabinet; how was I to reach them? That was the problem that (crushing my temples in my hands) I set to myself to solve. The laboratory door I had closed. If I sought to enter by the house, my own servants would consign me to the gallows. I saw I must employ another hand, and thought of Lanyon. How was he to be reached? how persuaded? Suppose that I escaped capture in the streets, how was I to make my way into his presence? and how should I, an unknown and displeasing visitor, prevail on the famous physician to rifle the study of his colleague, Dr. Jekyll? Then I remembered that of my original character, one part remained to me: I could write my own hand; and once I had conceived that kindling spark, the way that I must follow became lighted up from end to end.

24   Thereupon, I arranged my clothes as best I could, and summoning a passing hansom, drove to an hotel in Portland Street, the name of which I chanced to remember. At my appearance (which was indeed comical enough, however tragic a fate these garments covered) the driver could not conceal his mirth. I gnashed my teeth upon him with a gust of devilish fury; and the smile withered from his face—happily for him—yet more happily for myself, for in another instant I had certainly dragged

him from his perch. At the inn, as I entered, I looked about me with so black a countenance as made the attendants tremble; not a look did they exchange in my presence; but obsequiously took my orders, led me to a private room, and brought me wherewithal to write. Hyde in danger of his life was a creature new to me; shaken with inordinate anger, strung to the pitch of murder, lusting to inflict pain. Yet the creature was astute; mastered his fury with a great effort of the will; composed his two important letters, one to Lanyon and one to Poole; and that he might receive actual evidence of their being posted, sent them out with directions that they should be registered. Thenceforward, he sat all day over the fire in the private room, gnawing his nails; there he dined, sitting alone with his fears, the waiter visibly quailing before his eye; and thence, when the night was fully come, he set forth in the corner of a closed cab, and was driven to and fro about the streets of the city. He, I say— I cannot say, I. That child of Hell had nothing human; nothing lived in him but fear and hatred. And when at last, thinking the driver had begun to grow suspicious, he discharged the cab and ventured on foot, attired in his misfitting clothes, an object marked out for observation, into the midst of the nocturnal passengers, these two base passions raged within him like a tempest. He walked fast, hunted by his fears, chattering to himself, skulking through the less frequented thoroughfares, counting the minutes that still divided him from midnight. Once a woman spoke to him, offering, I think, a box of lights. He smote her in the face, and she fled.

25   When I came to myself at Lanyon's, the horror of my old friend perhaps affected me somewhat: I do not know; it was at least but a drop in the sea to the abhorrence with which I looked back upon these hours. A change had come over me. It was no longer the fear of the gallows, it was the horror of being Hyde that racked me. I received Lanyon's condemnation partly in a dream; it was partly in a dream that I came home to my own house and got into bed. I slept after the prostration of the day, with a stringent and profound slumber which not even in the nightmares that wrung me could avail to break. I awoke in the morning shaken, weakened, but refreshed. I still hated and feared the thought of the brute that slept within me, and I had not of course forgotten the appalling dangers of the day before; but I was once more at home, in my own house and close to my drugs; and gratitude for my escape shone so strong in my soul that it almost rivalled the brightness of hope.

26   I was stepping leisurely across the court after breakfast, drinking the chill of the air with pleasure, when I was seized again with those indescribable sensations that heralded the change; and I had but the time to gain the shelter of my cabinet, before I was once again raging and freezing with the passions of Hyde. It took on this occasion a double dose to recall me to myself; and alas! six hours after, as I sat looking sadly in the fire, the pangs returned, and the drug had to be re-administered. In short, from that day forth it seemed only by a great effort as of gymnastics, and only under the immediate stimulation of the drug, that I was able to wear the countenance of Jekyll. At all hours of the day and night, I would be taken with the premonitory shudder; above all, if I slept, or even dozed for a moment in my chair, it was always as Hyde that I awakened. Under the strain of this continually impending doom and by the sleeplessness to which I now condemned myself, ay, even beyond

what I had thought possible to man, I became, in my own person, a creature eaten up and emptied by fever, languidly weak both in body and mind, and solely occupied by one thought: the horror of my other self. But when I slept, or when the virtue of the medicine wore off, I would leap almost without transition (for the pangs of transformation grew daily less marked) into the possession of a fancy brimming with images of terror, a soul boiling with causeless hatreds, and a body that seemed not strong enough to contain the raging energies of life. The powers of Hyde seemed to have grown with the sickliness of Jekyll. And certainly the hate that now divided them was equal on each side. With Jekyll, it was a thing of vital instinct. He had now seen the full deformity of that creature that shared with him some of the phenomena of consciousness, and was co-heir with him to death: and beyond these links of community, which in themselves made the most poignant part of his distress, he thought of Hyde, for all his energy of life, as of something not only hellish but inorganic. This was the shocking thing; that the slime of the pit seemed to utter cries and voices; that the amorphous dust gesticulated and sinned; that what was dead, and had no shape, should usurp the offices of life. And this again, that that insurgent horror was knit to him closer than a wife, closer than an eye; lay caged in his flesh, where he heard it mutter and felt it struggle to be born; and at every hour of weakness, and in the confidence of slumber, prevailed against him, and deposed him out of life. The hatred of Hyde for Jekyll was of a different order. His terror of the gallows drove him continually to commit temporary suicide, and return to his subordinate station of a part instead of a person; but he loathed the necessity, he loathed the despondency into which Jekyll was now fallen, and he resented the dislike with which he was himself regarded. Hence the apelike tricks that he would play me, scrawling in my own hand blasphemies on the pages of my books, burning the letters and destroying the portrait of my father; and indeed, had it not been for his fear of death, he would long ago have ruined himself in order to involve me in the ruin. But his love of life is wonderful; I go further: I, who sicken and freeze at the mere thought of him, when I recall the abjection and passion of this attachment, and when I know how he fears my power to cut him off by suicide, I find it in my heart to pity him.

27   It is useless, and the time awfully fails me, to prolong this description; no one has ever suffered such torments, let that suffice; and yet even to these, habit brought— no, not alleviation—but a certain callousness of soul, a certain acquiescence of despair; and my punishment might have gone on for years, but for the last calamity which has now fallen, and which has finally severed me from my own face and nature. My provision of the salt, which had never been renewed since the date of the first experiment, began to run low. I sent out for a fresh supply and mixed the draught; the ebullition followed, and the first change of colour, not the second; I drank it and it was without efficacy. You will learn from Poole how I have had London ransacked; it was in vain; and I am now persuaded that my first supply was impure, and that it was that unknown impurity which lent efficacy to the draught.

28   About a week has passed, and I am now finishing this statement under the influence of the last of the old powders. This, then, is the last time, short of a miracle,

that Henry Jekyll can think his own thoughts or see his own face (now how sadly altered!) in the glass. Nor must I delay too long to bring my writing to an end; for if my narrative has hitherto escaped destruction, it has been by a combination of great prudence and great good luck. Should the throes of change take me in the act of writing it, Hyde will tear it in pieces; but if some time shall have elapsed after I have laid it by, his wonderful selfishness and circumscription to the moment will probably save it once again from the action of his ape-like spite. And indeed the doom that is closing on us both has already changed and crushed him. Half an hour from now, when I shall again and forever reindue that hated personality, I know how I shall sit shuddering and weeping in my chair, or continue, with the most strained and fearstruck ecstasy of listening, to pace up and down this room (my last earthly refuge) and give ear to every sound of menace. Will Hyde die upon the scaffold? or will he find courage to release himself at the last moment? God knows; I am careless; this is my true hour of death, and what is to follow concerns another than myself. Here then, as I lay down the pen and proceed to seal up my confession, I bring the life of that unhappy Henry Jekyll to an end.

QUESTIONS FOR DISCUSSION

1. What strengths, faults, and inner divisions of character does Jekyll describe in the first paragraph of the narrative? Why does he feel a need to conceal his "pleasures"?

2. Upon what fantasy or "beloved daydream" does Jekyll come to dwell? Why does he become so obsessed with this fantasy? What does he invent to make his fantasy a reality? Is his invention a success?

3. What are the differences in appearance, stature, power, and age between Dr. Jekyll and Mr. Hyde? How do these physical distinctions underscore symbolically the differences in their characters as well as the flaws in Dr. Jekyll's original character and the folly of artificially separating the two parts of the self?

4. How does Jekyll first respond to the changes in his character? How does his response and the nature of the control over the "double" personality gradually change? What difficulty does he experience in deciding which of his sides to finally repress?

5. Why is Jekyll unable to stick with his decision to refrain from "doubling" his personality? When he again reverts to Hyde, how has Hyde changed? What crime does Hyde perform, and how does Jekyll react to the crime? How does he attempt to reform himself? Under what circumstances does Hyde emerge a final time? How would you explain the mutual loathing that each side now feels for the other?

6. From the evidence in the letter, which side of the personality would you conclude killed Mr. Hyde: Hyde himself, in an act of suicide, or Jekyll, in an act of combined murder/suicide of both sides of his personality? Explain your response using references to the text.

CONNECTION

Analyze this story as a dream narrative, using some of the insights contained in Marie von Franz's "The Realization of the Shadow in Dreams," included in this chapter.

IDEAS FOR WRITING

1. After reading the entire text of *The Strange Case of Doctor Jekyll and Mr. Hyde*, write an essay in which you interpret the story as a criticism of rigid social conventions and moral standards of "acceptable" or "unacceptable," "good" or "bad" behavior. In what ways does the story suggest that such strict standards can heighten the division between an individual's good and bad side, the main self and the double or shadow self? Or, write an interpretation of your own that you can support through reference to the story.
2. This story concerns the dual nature of the human psyche, the struggle between our "good" side and our "bad" side, between the conscious mind and the unthinking appetites of the body. What do you think can be done to ease such a struggle? Write a paper in which you argue for an approach to life that would help to heal the split between potential "Jekyll and Hyde" personalities within the human psyche.

Ronald Takaki

A Different Mirror

Ronald Takaki (b.1939), regarded as one of America's leading scholars in race relations, was born in Honolulu to a family that emigrated from Japan in the late 1800s to work in the sugar cane fields of Hawaii. Takaki attended Wooster College and has taught at the University of California, Los Angeles; he is currently a Professor of Ethnic Studies at the University of California, Berkeley. Takaki has commented about his academic work that "my scholarship seeks not to separate our diverse groups but to show how our experiences were different but . . . . not disparate. Multicultural history, as I write and present it, leads not to what Schlesinger calls the 'disuniting of America' but rather to the re-uniting of America." Takaki's books include Iron Cages: Race and Culture in 19th Century America *(1990),* A Different Mirror: A History of Multicultural America *(1993),* From Different Shores : Perspectives On Race And Ethnicity In America *(1994) and* A Larger Memory: A History of Our Diversity With Voices *(1998). The essay included here, "A Different Mirror," presents ideas designed to enable the American people to overcome racial divisions in order to "see themselves and each other in our common past."*

Write about an incident when another person made stereotypical statements about you because of your race or gender. How did you feel and how did you respond?

1 I had flown from San Francisco to Norfolk and was riding in a taxi to my hotel to attend a conference on multiculturalism. Hundreds of educators from across the country were meeting to discuss the need for greater cultural diversity in the curriculum. My driver and I chatted about the weather and the tourists. The sky was cloudy, and Virginia Beach was twenty minutes away. The rearview mirror reflected a white man in his forties. "How long have you been in this country?" he asked. "All my life," I replied, wincing. "I was born in the United States." With a strong southern drawl, he remarked: "I was wondering because your English is excellent!" Then, as I had many times before, I explained: "My grandfather came here from Japan in the 1880s. My familiy has been here, in America, for over a hundred years." He glanced at me in the mirror. Somehow I did not look "American" to him; my eyes and complexion looked foreign.

2   Suddenly, we both became uncomfortably conscious of a racial divide separating us. An awkward silence turned my gaze from the mirror to the passing landscape, the shore where the English and the Powhatan Indians first encountered each other. Our highway was on land that Sir Walter Raleigh had renamed "Virginia" in honor of Elizabeth I, the Virgin Queen. In the English cultural appropriation of America, the indigenous peoples themselves would become outsiders in their native land. Here, at the eastern edge of the continent, I mused, was the site of the beginning of multicultural America. Jamestown, the English settlement founded in 1607, was nearby: the first twenty Africans were brought here a year before the Pilgrims arrived at Plymouth Rock. Several hundred miles offshore was Bermuda, the "Bermoothes" where Williams Shakespeare's Prospero had landed and met the native Caliban in *The Tempest*. Earlier, another voyage has made an Atlantic crossing and unexpectedly bumped into some islands to the south. Thinking he had reached Asia, Christopher Columbus mistakenly identified one of the islands as "Cipango" (Japan). In the wake of the admiral, many peoples would come to America from different shores, not only from Europe but also Africa and Asia. One of them would be my grandfather. My mental wandering across terrain and time ended abruptly as we arrived at my destination. I said good-bye to my driver and went into the hotel, carrying a vivid reminder of why I was attending this conference.

3   Questions like the one my taxi driver asked me are always jarring, but I can understand why he could not see me as an American. He had a narrow but widely shared sense of the past—a history that has viewed American as European in ancestry. "Race," Toni Morrison explained, has functioned as a "metaphor" necessary to the "construction of Americanness": in the creation of our national identity, "American" has been defined as "white."

4   But America has been racially diverse since our very beginning on the Virginia shore, and this reality is increasingly becoming visible and ubiquitous. Currently, one-third of the American people do not trace their origins to Europe; in California, minorities are fast becomig a majority. They already predominate in major cities across the country—New York, Chicago, Atlanta, Detroit, Philadelphia, San Francisco, and Los Angeles.

5   This emerging demographic diversity has raised fundamental questions about America's identity and culture. In 1990, *Time* published a cover story on "America's Changing Colors." "Someday soon," the magazine announced, "white Americans will become a minority group." How soon? By 2056, most Americans will trace their descent to "Africa, Asia, the Hispanic world, the Pacific Islands, Arabia—almost anywhere but white Europe." This dramatic change in our nation's ethnic composition is altering the way we think about ourselves. "The deeper significance of America's becoming a majority nonwhite society is what it means to the national psyche, to individuals' sense of themselves and their nation—their idea of what it is to be American."

6   Indeed, more than ever before, as we approach the time when whites become a minority, many of us are perplexed about our national identity and our future as one people. This uncertainty has provoked Allan Bloom to reaffirm the preeminence of Western civilization. Author of *The Closing of the American Mind*, he has emerged as a leader of an intellectual backlash against cultural diversity. In his view, students entering the university are "uncivilized," and the university has the responsibility to "civilize" them. Bloom claims he knows what their "hungers" are and "what they can digest." Eating is one of his favorite metaphors. Noting the "large black presence" in major universities, he laments the "one failure" in race relations—black students have proven to be "indigestible." They do not "melt as have *all* other groups." The problem, he contends, is that "blacks have become blacks": they have become "ethnic." This separatism has been reinforced by an academic permissiveness that has befouled the curriculum with "Black Studies" along with "Learn Another Culture." The only solution, Bloom insists, is "the good old Great Books approach."

7   Similarly, E. D. Hirsch worries that America is becoming a "tower of Babel," and that this multiplicity of cultures is threatening to rend our social fabric. He, too, longs for a more cohesive culture and a more homogeneous America: "If we *had* to make a choice between the *one* and the *many*, most Americans would choose the principle of unity, since we cannot function as a nation without it." The way to correct this fragmentization, Hirsch argues, is to acculturate "disadvantaged children." What do they need to know? "Only by accumulating shared symbols, and the shared information that symbols represent," Hirsch answers, "can we learn to communicate effectively with one another in our national community." Though he concedes the value of multicultural education, he quickly dismisses it by insisting that it "should not be allowed to supplant or interfere with our schools' responsibility to ensure our children's mastery of American literate culture." In *Cultural Literacy: What Every American Needs to Know*, Hirsch offers a long list of terms that excludes much of the history of minority groups.

8   While Bloom and Hirsch are reacting defensively to what they regard as a vexatious balkanization of America, many other educators are responding to our diversity

as an opportunity to open American minds. In 1990, the Task Force on Minorities for New York emphasized the importance of a culturally diverse education. "Essentially," the *New York Times* commented, "the issue is how to deal with both dimensions of the nation's motto: 'E pluribus unum'—'Out of many, one.' " Universities from New Hampshire to Berkeley have established American cultural diversity graduation requirements. "Every student needs to know," explained University of Wisconsin's chancellor Donna Shalala, "much more about the origins and history of the particular cultures which, as Americans, we will encounter during our lives." Even the University of Minnesota, located in a state that is 98 percent white, requires its students to take ethnic studies courses. Asked why multiculturalism is so important, Dean Fred Lukermann answered: As a national university, Minnesota has to offer a national curriculum—one that includes all of the peoples of America. He added that after graduation many students move to cities like Chicago and Los Angeles and thus need to know about racial diversity. Moreover, many educators stress, multiculturalism has an intellectual purpose. By allowing us to see events from the viewpoints of different groups, a multicultural curriculum enables us to reach toward a more comprehensive understanding of American history.

9   What is fueling this debate over our national identity and the content of our curriculum is America's intensifying racial crisis. The alarming signs and symptoms seem to be everywhere—the killing of Vincent Chin in Detroit, the black boycott of a Korean grocery store in Flatbush, the hysteria in Boston over the Carol Stuart murder, the battle between white sportsmen and Indians over tribal fishing rights in Wisconsin, the Jewish-black clashes in Brooklyn's Crown Heights, the black-Hispanic competition for jobs and educational resources in Dallas, which *Newsweek* described as "a conflict of the have-nots," and the Willie Horton campaign commercials, which widened the divide between the suburbs and the inner cities.

10   This reality of racial tension rudely woke America like a fire bell in the night on April 29, 1992. Immediately after four Los Angeles police officers were found not guilty of brutality against Rodney King, rage exploded in Los Angeles. Race relations reached a new nadir. During the nightmarish rampage, scores of people were killed, over two thousand injured, twelve thousand arrested, and almost a billion dollars' worth of property destroyed. The live television images mesmerized America. The rioting and the murderous melee on the streets resembled the fighting in Beirut and the West Bank. The thousands of fires burning out of control and the dark smoke filling the skies brought back images of the burning oil fields of Kuwait during Desert Storm. Entire sections of Los Angeles looked like a bombed city. "Is this America?" many shocked viewers asked. "Please, can we get along here," pleaded Rodney King, calling for calm. "We all can get along. I mean, we're all stuck here for a while. Let's try to work it out."

11   But how should "we" be defined? Who are the people "stuck here" in America? One of the lessons of the Los Angeles explosion is the recognition of the fact that we are a multiracial society and that race can no longer be defined in the binary terms of white and black. "We" will have to include Hispanics and Asians. While

blacks currently constitute 13 percent of the Los Angeles population, Hispanics represent 40 percent. The 1990 census revealed that South Central Los Angeles, which was predominantly black in 1965 when the Watts rebellion occurred, is now 45 percent Hispanic. A majority of the first 5,438 people arrested were Hispanic, while 37 percent were black. Of the fifty-eight people who died in the riot, more than a third were Hispanic, and about 40 percent of the businesses destroyed were Hispanic-owned. Most of the other shops and stores were Korean-owned. The dreams of many Korean immigrants went up in smoke during the riot: two thousand Korean-owned businesses were damaged or demolished, totaling about $400 million in losses. There is evidence indicating they were targeted. "After all," explained a black gang member, "we didn't burn our community, just *their* stores."

12   "I don't feel like I'm in America anymore," said Denisse Bustamente as she watched the police protecting the firefighters. "I feel like I am far away." Indeed, Americans have been witnessing ethnic strife erupting around the world—the rise of neo-Nazism and the murder of Turks in Germany, the ugly "ethnic cleansing" in Bosnia, the terrible and bloody clashes between Muslims and Hindus in India. Is the situation here different, we have been nervously wondering, or do ethnic conflicts elsewhere represent a prologue for America? What is the nature of malevolence? Is there a deep, perhaps primordial, need for group identity rooted in hatred for the other? Is ethnic pluralism possible for America? But answers have been limited. Television reports have been little more than thirty-second sound bites. Newspaper articles have been mostly superficial descriptions of racial antagonisms and the current urban malaise. What is lacking is historical context; consequently, we are left feeling bewildered.

13   How did we get to this point, Americans everywhere are anxiously asking. What does our diversity mean, and where is it leading us? *How* do we work it out in the post-Rodney King era?

14   Certainly one crucial way is for our society's various ethnic groups to develop a greater understanding of each other. For example, how can African Americans and Korean Americans work it out unless they learn about each other's cultures, histories, and also economic situations? This need to share knowledge about our ethnic diversity has acquired new importance and has given new urgency to the pursuit for a more accurate history.

15   More than ever before, there is a growing realization that the established scholarship has tended to define America too narrowly. For example, in his prize-winning study *The Uprooted,* Harvard historian Oscar Handlin presented—to use the book's subtitle—"the Epic Story of the Great Migrations That Made the American People." But Handlin's "epic story" excluded the "uprooted" from Africa, Asia, and Latin America—the other "Great Migrations" that also helped to make "the American People." Similarly, in *The Age of Jackson,* Arthur M. Schlesinger, Jr., left out blacks and Indians. There is not even a mention of two marker events—the Nat Turner insurrection and Indian removal, which Andrew Jackson himself would have been surprised to find omitted from a history of his era.

16   Still, Schlesinger and Handlin offered us a refreshing revisionism, paving the way
      for the study of common people rather than princes and presidents. They inspired
      the next generation of historians to examine groups such as the artisan laborers of
      Philadelphia and the Irish immigrants of Boston. "Once I thought to write a history
      of the immigrants in America," Handlin confided in his introduction to *The Up-
      rooted*. "I discovered that the immigrants *were* American history." This door, once
      opened, led to the flowering of a more inclusive scholarship as we began to recognize
      that ethnic history was American history. Suddenly, there was a proliferation of
      seminal works such as Irving Howe's *World of Our Fathers: The Journey of the East
      European Jews to America*, Dee Brown's *Bury My Heart at Wounded Knee: An Indian
      History of the American West*, Albert Camarillo's *Chicanos in a Changing Society*,
      Lawrence Levine's *Black Culture and Black Consciousness*, Yuji Ichioka's *The Issei:
      The World of the First Generation Japanese Immigrants*, and Kerby Miller's *Emigrants
      and Exiles: Ireland the Irish Exodus to North America*.

17   But even this new scholarship, while it has given us a more expanded under-
      standing of the mosaic called America, does not address our needs in the post-Rod-
      ney King era. These books and others like them fragment American society,
      studying each group separately, in isolation from the other groups and the whole.
      While scrutinizing our specific pieces, we have to step back in order to see the rich
      and complex portrait they compose. What is needed is a fresh angle, a study of the
      American past from a comparative perspective. . . .

18   The signs of America's ethnic diversity can be discerned across the continent—Ellis
      Island, Angel Island, Chinatown, Harlem, South Boston, the Lower East Side, places
      with Spanish names like Los Angeles and San Antonio or Indian names like Massachu-
      setts and Iowa. Much of what is familiar in America's cultural landscape actually has
      ethnic origins. The Bing cherry was developed by an early Chinese immigrant named
      Ah Bing. American Indians were cultivating corn, tomatoes, and tobacco long before
      the arrival of Columbus. The term *okay* was derived from the Choctaw word *oke*, mean-
      ing "it is so." There is evidence indicating that the name *Yankee* came from Indian
      terms for the English—from *eankke* in Cherokee and *Yankwis* in Delaware. Jazz and
      blues as well as rock and roll have African-American origins. The "Forty-Niners" of the
      Gold Rush learned mining techniques from the Mexicans; American cowboys acquired
      herding skills from Mexican *vaqueros* and adopted their range terms—such as *lariat* from
      la reato, *lasso* from *lazo*, and *stampede* from *estampida*. Songs like "God Bless America,"
      "Easter Parade," and "White Christmas" were written by a Russian-Jewish immigrant
      named Israel Baline, more popularly known as Irving Berlin.

19   Furthermore, many diverse ethnic groups have contributed to the building of
      the American economy, forming what Walt Whitman saluted as a "vast, surging,
      hopeful army of workers." They worked in the South's cotton fields, New England's
      textile mills, Hawaii's canefields, New York's garment factories, California's or-
      chards, Washington's salmon canneries, and Arizon's copper mines. They built
      the railroad, the great symbol of America's industrial triumph. Laying railroad
      ties, black laborers sang:

Down the railroad, um-huh
Well, raise the iron, um-huh
Raise the iron, um-huh.

Irish railroad workers shouted as they stretch an iron ribbon across the continent:

Then drill, my Paddies, drill—
Drill, my heroes, drill,
Drill all day, no sugar in your tay
Workin' on the U.P. railway.

Japanese laborers in the Northwest chorused as their bodies fought the fickle weather:

A railroad worker—
That's me!
I am great.
Yes, I am a railroad worker.
Complaining:
"It is too hot!"
"It is too cold!"
"It rains too often!"
"It snows too much!"
They all ran off.
I alone remained.
I am a railroad worker!

Chicano workers in the Southwest joined in as they swore at the punishing work:

Some unloaded rails
Others unloaded ties,
And others of my companions
Threw out thousands of curses.

20   Moreover, our diversity was tied to America's most serious crisis: the Civil War was fought over a racial issue—slavery. In his "First Inaugural Address," presented on March 4, 1861, President Abraham Lincoln declared: "One section of our country believes slavery is *right* and ought to be extended, while the other believes it is *wrong* and ought not to be extended." Southern secession, he argued, would be anarchy. Lincoln sternly warned the South that he had a solemn oath to defend and preserve the Union. Americans were one people, he explained, bound together by "the mystic chords of memory, stretching from every battlefield and patriot grave to every living heart and hearthstone all over this broad land." The struggle and sacrifices of the War for Indpendence had enabled Americans to create a new nation out of thirteen separate colonies. But Lincoln's appeal for unity fell on deaf ears in the South. And the war came. Two and a half years later, at Gettysburg, President Lincoln declared that "brave men" had fought and "consecrated" the ground of this battlefield

in order to preserve the Union. Among the brave were black men. Shortly after this bloody battle, Lincoln acknowledged the military contributions of blacks. "There will be some black men," he wrote in a letter to an old friend, James C. Conkling, "who can remember that with silent tongue, and clenched teeth, and steady eye, and well-poised bayonet, they have helped mankind on to this great consummation . . . . " Indeed, 186,000 blacks served in the Union Army, and one-third of them were listed as missing or dead. Black men in blue, Frederick Douglass pointed out, were "on the battlefield mingling their blood with that of white men in one common effort to save the country." Now the mystic chords of memory stretched across the new battlefields of the Civil War, and black soldiers were buried in "patriot graves." They, too, had given their lives to ensure that the "government of the people, by the people, for the people shall not perish from the earth." . . .

21   In his recent study of Spain and the New World, *The Buried Mirror*, Carlos Fuentes points out that mirrors have been found in the tombs of ancient Mexico, placed there to guide the dead through the underworld. He also tells us about the legend of Quetzalcoatl, the Plumed Serpent: when this god was given a mirror by the Toltec deity Tezcatlipoca, he saw a man's face in the mirror and realized his own humanity. For us, the "mirror" of history can guide the living and also help us recognize who we have been and hence are. In *A Distant Mirror*, Barbara W. Tuchman finds "phenomenal parallels" between the "calamitous 14th century" of European society and our own era. We can, she observes, have "greater fellow-feeling for a distraught age" as we painfully recognize the "similar disarray," "collapsing assumptions," and "unusual discomfort."

22   But what is needed in our own perplexing times is not so much a "distant" mirror, as one that is "different." While the study of the past can provide collective self-knowledge, it often reflects the scholar's particular perspective or view of the world. What happens when historians leave out many of America's peoples? What happens, to borrow the words of Adrienne Rich, "when someone with the authority of a teacher" describes our society, and "you are not in it?" Such an experience can be disorienting—"a moment of psychic disequilibrium, as if you looked into a mirror and saw nothing."

23   Through their narratives about their lives and circumstances, the people of America's diverse groups are able to see themselves and each other in our common past. They celebrate what Ishmael Reed had described as a society "unique" in the world because "the world is here"—a place "where the cultures of the world crisscross." Much of America's past, they point out, has been riddled with racism. At the same time, these people offer hope, affirming the struggle for equality as a central theme in our country's history. At its conception, our nation was dedicated to the proposition of equality. What has given concreteness to this powerful national principle has been our coming together in the creation of a new society. "Stuck here" together, workers of different backgrounds have attempted to get along with each other.

People harvesting
Work together unaware
Of racial problems,

wrote a Japanese immigrant describing a lesson learned by Mexican and Asian farm laborers in California.

24   Finally, how do we see our prospects for "working out" America's racial crisis? Do we see it as through a glass darkly? Do the televised images of racial hatred and violence that riveted us in 1992 during the days of rage in Los Angeles frame a future of divisive race relations—what Arthur Schlesinger, Jr., has fearfully denounced as the "disunitng of America"? Or will Americans of diverse races and ethnicities be able to connect themselves to a larger narrative? Whatever happens, we can be certain that much of our society's future will be influenced by which "mirror" we choose to see ourselves. America does not belong to one race or one group, the people in this study remind us, and Americans have been constantly redefining their national identity from the moment of first contact on the Virginia shore. By sharing their stories, they invite us to see ourselves in a different mirror.

QUESTIONS FOR DISCUSSION

1. Why is the narrative of Takaki's conversation with the taxi driver on the way to a multiculturalism conference that opens the selection especially ironic and effective? How does Takaki develop the significance of the setting where the conversation takes place?
2. What is Takaki's thesis? What types of evidence does he include to show that American history needs to be seen from a different perspective?
3. How does Takaki refute his opponents, Allan Bloom and E. D. Hirsch?
4. How does Takaki begin to answer his own questions: "How should 'we' be defined? Who are the people 'stuck here' in America? "
5. How does Takaki develop the concept of seeing ourselves in a different mirror as a metaphorical and literal means of beginning to solve the racial crisis in America today?
6. What is Takaki saying about the inner worlds of citizens who do not see themselves reflected in the current standard history books? How are they damaged by being left out? What contribution have these citizens and their ancestors made to American history and language?

CONNECTION

Compare and contrast Shelby Steele's and Takaki's perspectives on how social change takes place. Why do both feel that re-visioning what we have seen in the mirrors of history is crucial?

IDEAS FOR WRITING

1. Write an essay that speculates on how increasing immigrant populations and cultural diversity will influence American education and values in the near future.

2. Do research into your family background. Contrast the reality of your own family's struggle with the way that your family's nationality, race, gender and/or religious perspective have been presented in standard history textbooks and in the popular imagination. How would you like to see history books and the media changed to reflect a more accurate sense of your family's struggle here in the United States?

Shelby Steele

Being Black and Feeling Blue

Shelby Steele was born in Chicago in 1946. His parents were active in the civil rights movement, and Steele grew up with a keen sense of the realities of racial conflict and injustice. He received a Ph.D. in English at the University of Utah in 1974, and is a professor of English at San Jose State University in California. His essays on self-esteem and social status among African-Americans have appeared in many magazines and newspapers. His first book The Content of Our Character: A New Vision of Race in America *(1990) has been a controversial bestseller because of its focus on what Steele perceives as a sort of victim complex, based on past racism, that makes it more difficult for African-Americans to achieve success. Steele's most recent book,* A Dream Deferred: The Second Betrayal of Black Freedom in America *(1998), continues and updates his critique of contemporary race relations in America. The following excerpt from* The Content of Our Character *explores how many African-Americans experience an "anti-self" as a result of generations of racial oppression.*

JOURNAL

Steele develops the concept of an "anti-self" in his selection. Before reading it, think about whether you feel you have an anti-self. Present an example to illustrate the power of that side of your personality.

1   In the early seventies when I was in graduate school, I went out for a beer late one afternoon with another black graduate student whom I'd only known casually before. This student was older than I—a stint in the army had interrupted his education—and he had the reputation of being bright and savvy, of having applied street smarts to the business of getting through graduate school. I suppose I was hoping for what would be called today a little mentoring. But it is probably not wise to drink with someone when you are enamored of his reputation, and it was not long before we stumbled into a moment that seemed to transform him before my very eyes. I asked him what he planned to do when he finished his Ph.D., fully expecting to hear of

high aspirations matched with shrewd perceptions on how to reach them. But before he could think, he said with a kind of exhausted sincerity, "Man, I just want to hold on, get a job that doesn't work me too hard, and do a lot of fishing." Was he joking, I asked. "Hell, no," he said with exaggerated umbrage. "I'm not into it like the white boys. I don't need what they need."

2   I will call this man Henry and report that, until five or six years ago when I lost track of him, he was doing exactly as he said he would do. With much guile and little ambition he had moved through a succession of low-level administrative and teaching jobs, mainly in black studies programs. Of course, it is no crime to just "hold on," and it is hardly a practice limited to blacks. Still, in Henry's case there was truly a troubling discrepancy between his ambition and a fine intelligence recognized by all who knew him. But in an odd way this intelligence was more lateral than vertical, and I would say that it was rechanneled by a certain unseen fear into the business of merely holding on. It would be easy to say that Henry had simply decided on life in a slower lane than he was capable of traveling in, or that he was that rare person who had achieved ambitionless contentment. But if this was so, Henry would have had wisdom rather than savvy, and he would not have felt the need to carry himself with more self-importance than his station justified. I don't think Henry was uninterested in ambition; I think he was afraid of it.

3   It is certainly true that there is a little of Henry in most people. My own compulsion to understand him informs me that I must have seen many elements of myself in him. And though I'm sure he stands for a universal human blockage, I also believe that there is something in the condition of being black in America that makes the kind of hesitancy he represents one of black America's most serious and debilitating problems. As Henry reached the very brink of expanded opportunity, with Ph.D. in hand, he diminished his ambition almost as though his degree delivered him to a kind of semiretirement. I don't think blacks in general have any illusions about semiretirement, but I do think that, as a group, we have hesitated on the brink of new opportunities that we made enormous sacrifices to win for ourselves. The evidence of this lies in one of the most tragic social ironies of late twentieth-century American life: as black Americans have gained in equality and opportunity, we have also declined in relation to whites, so that by many socioeconomic measures we are further behind whites today than before the great victories of the civil rights movement. By one report, even the black middle class, which had made great gains in the seventies, began to lose ground to its white counterpart in the eighties. Most distressing of all, the black underclass continues to expand rather than shrink.

4   Of course, I don't suggest that Henry's peculiar inertia singularly explains social phenomena so complex and tragic. I do believe, however, that blacks in general are susceptible to the same web of attitudes and fears that kept Henry beneath his potential, and that our ineffectiveness in taking better advantage of our greater opportunity has much to do with this. I think there is a specific form of racial anxiety that all blacks are vulnerable to that can, in situations where we must engage the mainstream society, increase our self-doubt and undermine our confidence so that we often back

away from the challenges that, if taken, would advance us. I believe this hidden racial anxiety may well now be the strongest barrier to our full participation in the American mainstream; that it is as strong or stronger even than the discrimination we still face. To examine this racial anxiety, allow me first to look at how the Henry was born in me.

5   Until the sixth grade, I attended a segregated school in a small working-class black suburb of Chicago. The school was a dumping ground for teachers with too little competence or mental stability to teach in the white school in our district. In 1956, when I entered the sixth grade, I encountered a new addition to the menagerie of misfits that was our faculty—an ex-Marine whose cruelty was suggested during our first lunch hour when he bit the cap off his Coke bottle and spit it into the wastebasket. Looking back I can see that there was no interesting depth to the cruelty he began to show us almost immediately—no consumptive hatred, no intelligent malevolence. Although we were all black and he was white, I don't think he was even particularly racist. He had obviously needed us to like him though he had no faith that we would. He ran the class like a gang leader, picking favorites one day and banishing them the next. And then there was a permanent pool of outsiders, myself among them, who were made to carry the specific sins that he must have feared most in himself.

6   The sin I was made to carry was the sin of stupidity. I misread a sentence on the first day of school, and my fate was sealed. He made my stupidity a part of the classroom lore, and very quickly I in fact became stupid. I all but lost the ability to read and found the simplest math beyond me. His punishments for my errors rose in meanness until one day he ordered me to pick up all of the broken glass on the playground with my bare hands. Of course, this would have to be the age of the pop bottle, and there were sections of this playground that glared like a mirror in sunlight. After half an hour's labor I sat down on strike, more out of despair than rebellion.

7   Again, cruelty was no more than a vibration in this man, and so without even a show of anger he commandeered a bicycle, handed it to an eighth-grader—one of his lieutenants—and told the boy to run me around the school grounds "until he passes out." The boy was also given a baseball bat to "use on him when he slows down." I ran two laps, about a mile, and then pretended to pass out. The eighth-grader knew I was playing possum but could not bring himself to hit me and finally rode off. I exited the school yard through an adjoining cornfield and never returned.

8   I mention this experience as an example of how one's innate capacity for insecurity is expanded and deepened, of how a disbelieving part of the self is brought to life and forever joined to the believing self. As children we are all wounded in some way and to some degree by the wild world we encounter. From these wounds a disbelieving *anti-self* is born, an internal antagonist and saboteur that embraces the world's negative view of us, that believes our wounds are justified by our own unworthiness, and that entrenches itself as a lifelong voice of doubt. This anti-self is a hidden aggressive force that scours the world for fresh evidence of our unworthiness. When

the believing self announces its aspirations, the anti-self always argues against them, but never on their merits (this is a healthy function of the believing self). It argues instead against our worthiness to pursue these aspirations and, by its lights, we are never worthy of even our smallest dreams. The mission of the anti-self is to deflate the believing self and, thus, draw it down into inertia, passivity, and faithlessness.

9   The anti-self is the unseen agent of low self-esteem; it is a catalytic energy that tries to induce low self-esteem in the believing self as though it were the complete truth of the personality. The anti-self can only be contained by the strength of the believing self, and this is where one's early environment becomes crucial. If the childhood environment is stable and positive, the family whole and loving, the schools good, the community safe, then the believing self will be reinforced and made strong. If the family is shattered, the schools indifferent, the neighborhood a mine field of dangers, the anti-self will find evidence everywhere with which to deflate the believing self.

10   This does not mean that a bad childhood cannot be overcome. But it does mean—as I have experienced and observed—that one's *capacity* for self-doubt and self-belief are roughly the same from childhood on, so that years later when the believing self may have strengthened enough to control the anti-self, one will still have the same capacity for doubt whether or not one has the *actual* doubt. I think it is this struggle between our capacities for doubt and belief that gives our personalities one of their peculiar tensions and, in this way, marks our character.

11   My own anti-self was given new scope and power by this teacher's persecution, and it was so successful in deflating my believing self that I secretly vowed never to tell my parents what was happening to me. The anti-self had all but sold my believing self on the idea that I was stupid, and I did not want to feel that shame before my parents. It was my brother who finally told them, and his disclosure led to a boycott that closed the school and eventually won the dismissal of my teacher and several others. But my anti-self transformed even this act of rescue into a cause of shame— if there wasn't something wrong with me, why did I have to be rescued? The anti-self follows only the logic of self-condemnation.

12   But there was another dimension to this experience that my anti-self was only too happy to seize upon. It was my race that landed me in this segregated school and, as many adults made clear to me, my persecution followed a timeless pattern of racial persecution. The implications of this were rich food for the anti-self—my race was so despised that it had to be segregated; as a black my education was so unimportant that even unbalanced teachers without college degrees were adequate; ignorance and cruelty that would be intolerable in a classroom of whites was perfectly all right in a classroom of blacks. The anti-self saw no injustice in any of this, but instead took it all as confirmation of a racial inferiority that it could now add to the well of personal doubt I already had. When the adults thought they were consoling me— "*Don't worry. They treat all blacks this way*"—they were also deepening the wound and expanding my capacity for doubt.

13   And this is the point. The condition of being black in America means that one will likely endure more wounds to one's self-esteem than others and that the capacity

for self-doubt born of these wounds will be compounded and expanded by the black race's reputation of inferiority. The anti-self will most likely have more ammunition with which to deflate the believing self and its aspirations. And the universal human struggle to have belief win out over doubt will be more difficult.

14   More than difficult, it is also made inescapable by the fact of skin color, which, in America, works as a visual invocation of the problem. Black skin has more dehumanizing stereotypes associated with it than any other skin color in America, if not the world. When a black presents himself in an integrated situation, he knows that his skin alone may bring these stereotypes to life in the minds of those he meets and that he, as an individual, may be diminished by his race before he has a chance to reveal a single aspect of his personality. By the symbology of color that operates in our culture, black skin accuses him of inferiority. Under the weight of this accusation, a black will almost certainly doubt himself on some level and to some degree. The ever-vigilant anti-self will grab this racial doubt and mix it into the pool of personal doubt, so that when a black walks into an integrated situation—a largely white college campus, an employment office, a business lunch—he will be vulnerable to the entire realm of his self-doubt before a single word is spoken.

15   This constitutes an intense and lifelong racial vulnerability and anxiety for blacks. Even though a white American may have been wounded more than a given black, and therefore have a larger realm of inner doubt, his white skin, with its connotations of privilege and superiority, will actually help protect him from that doubt and from the undermining power of his anti-self, at least in relations with blacks. In fact, the larger the realm of doubt, the more he may be tempted to rely on his white skin for protection from it. Certainly in every self-avowed white racist, whether businessman or member of the Klan, there is a huge realm of self-contempt and doubt that hides behind the mythology of white skin. The mere need to pursue self-esteem through skin color suggests there is no faith that it can be pursued any other way. But if skin color offers whites a certain false esteem and impunity, it offers blacks vulnerability.

16   This vulnerability begins for blacks with the recognition that we belong, quite simply, to the most despised race in the human community of races. To be a member of such a group in a society where all others gain an impunity by merely standing in relation to us is to live with a relentless openness to diminishment and shame. By the devious logic of the anti-self, one cannot be open to such diminishment without in fact being inferior and therefore deserving of diminishment. For the anti-self, the charge verifies the crime, so that racial vulnerability itself is evidence of inferiority. In this sense, the anti-self is an internalized racist, our own subconscious bigot, that conspires with society to diminish us.

17   So when blacks enter the mainstream, they are not only vulnerable to society's racism but also to the racist within. This internal racist is not restricted by law, morality, or social decorum. It cares nothing about civil rights and equal opportunity. It is the self-doubt born of the original wound of racial oppression, and its mission is to establish the justice of that wound and shackle us with doubt.

18   Of course, the common response to racial vulnerability, as to most vulnerabilities, is denial—the mind's mechanism for ridding itself of intolerable possibilities. For blacks to acknowledge a vulnerability to inferiority anxiety, in the mist of a society that has endlessly accused us of being inferior, feels nothing less than intolerable—as if we were agreeing with the indictment against us. But denial is not the same as eradication, since it only gives unconscious life to what is intolerable to our consciousness. Denial reassigns rather than vanquishes the terror of racial vulnerability. This reassignment only makes the terror stronger by making it unknown. When we deny, we always create a dangerous area of self-ignorance, an entire territory of the self that we cannot afford to know. Without realizing it, we begin to circumscribe our lives by avoiding those people and situations that might breach our denial and force us to see consciously what we fear. Though the denial of racial vulnerability is a human enough response, I think it also makes our public discourse on race circumspect and unproductive, since we cannot talk meaningfully about problems we are afraid to name.

19   Denial is a refusal of painful self-knowledge. When someone or something threatens to breach this refusal, we receive an unconscious shock of the very vulnerability we have denied—a shock that often makes us retreat and more often makes us intensify our denial. When blacks move into integrated situations or face challenges that are new for blacks, the myth of black inferiority is always present as a *condition* of the situation, and as such it always threatens to breach our denial of racial vulnerability. It also threatens to make us realize consciously what is intolerable to us—that we have some anxiety about inferiority. We feel this threat unconsciously as a shock of racial doubt delivered by the racist anti-self (always the inner voice of the myth of black inferiority). Consciously, we feel this shock as a sharp discomfort or a desire to retreat from the situation. Almost always we will want to intensify our denial.

20   I will call this *integration shock*, since it occurs most powerfully when blacks leave their familiar world and enter the mainstream. Integration shock and denial are mutual intensifiers. The stab of racial doubt that integration shock delivers is a pressure to intensify denial, and a more rigid denial means the next stab of doubt will be more threatening and therefore more intense. The symbiosis of these two forces is, I believe, one of the reasons black Americans have become preoccupied with racial pride, almost to the point of obsession over the past twenty-five or so years. With more exposure to the mainstream, we have endured more integration shock, more jolts of inferiority anxiety. And, I think, we have often responded with rather hyperbolic claims of black pride by which we deny that anxiety. In this sense, our self-consciousness around pride, our need to make a point of it, is, to a degree, a form of denial. Pride becomes denial when it ceases to reflect self-esteem quietly and begins to compensate loudly for unacknowledged inner doubt. Here it also becomes dangerous since it prevents us from confronting and overcoming that doubt.

21   I think the most recent example of black pride-as-denial is the campaign (which seems to have been launched by a committee) to add yet another name to the litany

of names that blacks have given themselves over the past century. Now we are to be African-Americans instead of, or in conjunction with, being black Americans. This self-conscious reaching for pride through nomenclature suggests nothing so much as a despair over the possibility of gaining the less conspicuous pride that follows real advancement. In its invocation of the glories of a remote African past and its wistful suggestion of homeland, this name denies the doubt black Americans have about their contemporary situation in America. There is no element of self-confrontation in it, no facing of real racial vulnerabilities, as there was with the name "black." I think "black" easily became the name of preference in the sixties, precisely because it was not a denial but a confrontation of inferiority anxiety, with the shame associated with the color black. There was honest self-acceptance in this name, and I think it diffused much of our vulnerability to the shame of color. Even between blacks, "black" is hardly the drop-dead fighting word it was when I was a child. Possibly we are ready now for a new name, but I think "black" has been our most powerful name yet because it so frankly called out our shame and doubt and helped us (and others) to accept ourselves. In the name "African-American" there is too much false neutralization of doubt, too much looking away from the caldron of our own experience. It is a euphemistic name that hides us even from ourselves.

22   I think blacks have been more preoccupied with pride over the past twenty-five years because we have been more exposed to integration shock since the 1964 Civil Rights Act made equal opportunity the law of the land (if not quite the full reality of the land). Ironically, it was the inequality of opportunity and all the other repressions of legal segregation that buffered us from our racial vulnerability. In a segregated society we did not have the same accountability to the charge of racial inferiority since we were given little opportunity to disprove the charge. It was the opening up of opportunity—anti-discrimination laws, the social programs of the Great Society, equal opportunity guidelines and mandates, fair housing laws, affirmative action, and so on—that made us individually and collectively more accountable to the myth of black inferiority and therefore more racially vulnerable.

23   This vulnerability has increased in the same proportion that our freedom and opportunity have increased. The exhilaration of new freedom is always followed by a shock of accountability. Whatever unresolved doubt follows the oppressed into greater freedom will be inflamed since freedom always carries a burden of proof, always throws us back on ourselves. And freedom, even imperfect freedom, makes blacks a brutal proposition: if you're not inferior, prove it. This is the proposition that shocks us and makes us vulnerable to our underworld of doubt. The whispers of the racist anti-self are far louder in the harsh accountability of freedom than in subjugation, where the oppressor is so entirely to blame.

24   The bitter irony of all this is that our doubt and the hesitancy it breeds now help limit our progress in America almost as systematically as segregation once did. Integration shock gives the old boundaries of legal segregation a regenerative power. To avoid the shocks of doubt that come from entering the mainstream, or plunging more deeply into it, we often pull back at precisely those junctures where segrega-

tion once pushed us back. In this way we duplicate the conditions of our oppression and reenact our role as victims even in the midst of far greater freedom and far less victimization. Certainly there is still racial discrimination in America, but I believe that the unconscious replaying of our oppression is now the greatest barrier to our full equality.

25   The way in which integration shock regenerates the old boundaries of segregation for blacks is most evident in three tendencies—the tendency to minimalize or avoid real opportunities, to withhold effort in areas where few blacks have achieved, and to self-segregate in integrated situations.

26   If anything, it is the presence of new opportunities in society that triggers integration shock. If opportunity is a chance to succeed, it is also a chance to fail. The vulnerability of blacks to hidden inferiority anxiety makes failure a much more forbidding prospect. If a black pursues an opportunity in the mainstream—opens a business, goes up for a challenging job or difficult promotion—and fails, that failure can be used by the anti-self to confirm both personal and racial inferiority. The diminishment and shame will tap an impersonal, as well as personal, source of doubt. When a white fails, he alone fails. His doubt is strictly personal, which gives him more control over the failure. He can discover *his* mistakes, learn the reasons *he* made them, and try again. But the black, laboring under the myth of inferiority, will have this impersonal, culturally determined doubt with which to contend. This form of doubt robs him of a degree of control over his failure since he alone cannot eradicate the cultural myth that stings him. There will be a degree of impenetrability to his failure that will constitute an added weight of doubt.

27   The effect of this is to make mainstream opportunity more intimidating and risky for blacks. This is made worse in that blacks, owing to past and present deprivations, may come to the mainstream in the first place with a lower stock of self-esteem. High risk and low self-esteem is hardly the best combination with which to tackle the challenges of a highly advanced society in which others have been blessed by history with very clear advantages. Under these circumstances, opportunity can seem more like a chance to fail than a chance to succeed. All this makes for a kind of opportunity aversion that I think was behind the hesitancy I saw in Henry, in myself, and in other blacks of all class backgrounds. It is also, I believe, one of the reasons for the sharp decline in the number of black students entering college, even as many colleges launch recruiting drives to attract more black students.

28   This aversion to opportunity generates a way of seeing that minimalizes opportunity to the point where it can be ignored. In black communities the most obvious entrepreneurial opportunities are routinely ignored. It is often outsiders or the latest wave of immigrants who own the shops, restaurants, cleaners, gas stations, and even the homes and apartments. Education is a troubled area in black communities for numerous reasons, but certainly one of them is that many black children are not truly imbued with the idea that learning is virtually the same as opportunity. Schools—even bad schools—were the opportunity that so many immigrant

groups used to learn the workings and the spirit of American society. In the very worst inner-city schools there are accredited teachers who teach the basics, but too often to students who shun those among them who do well, who see studying as a sucker's game and school itself as a waste of time. One sees in many of these children almost a determination not to learn, a suppression of the natural impulse to understand, which cannot be entirely explained by the determinism of poverty. Out of school, in the neighborhood, these same children learn everything. I think it is the meeting with the mainstream that school symbolizes that clicks them off. In the cultural ethos from which they come, it is always these meetings that trigger the aversion to opportunity, behind which lies inferiority anxiety. Their parents and their culture send them a double message: go to school but don't really apply yourself. The risk is too high.

29   This same pattern of avoidance, this unconscious circumvention of possibility, is also evident in our commitment to effort—the catalyst of opportunity. Difficult, sustained effort—in school, career, or family life—will be riddled with setbacks, losses, and frustrations. Racial vulnerability erodes effort for blacks by exaggerating the importance of these setbacks, by recasting them as confirmation of racial inferiority rather than the normal pitfalls of sustained effort. The racist anti-self greets these normal difficulties with an I-told-you-so attitude, and the believing self, unwilling to risk seeing that the anti-self is right, may grow timid and pull back from the effort. As with opportunity, racial vulnerability makes hard effort in the mainstream a high-risk activity for blacks.

30   But this is not the case in those areas where blacks have traditionally excelled. In sports and music, for example, the threat of integration shock is effectively removed. Because so many blacks have succeeded in these areas, a black can enter them without being racially vulnerable. Failure carries no implication of racial inferiority, so the activity itself is far less risky than those in which blacks have no record of special achievement. Certainly, in sports and music one sees blacks sustain the most creative and disciplined effort and then seize opportunities where one would have thought there were none. But all of this changes the instant racial vulnerability becomes a factor. Across the country thousands of young black males take every opportunity and make every effort to reach the elite ranks of the NBA or NFL. But in the classroom, where racial vulnerability is a hidden terror, they and many of their classmates put forth the meagerest effort and show a virtual indifference to the genuine opportunity that is education.

31   But the most visible circumvention that results from integration shock is the tendency toward self-segregation that, if anything, seems to have increased over the last twenty years. Along with opportunity and effort, it is also white people themselves who are often avoided. I hear young black professionals say they do not socialize with whites after work unless at some "command performance" that comes with the territory of their career. On largely white university campuses where integration shock is particularly intense, black students often try to enforce a kind of neo-separatism that includes black "theme" dorms, black student unions, Afro-houses, black cultural centers, black student lounges, and so on. There is a geopolitics involved in this activity,

where race is tied to territory in a way that mimics the whites only/colored only designations of the past. Only now these race spaces are staked out in the name of pride.

32   I think this impulse to self-segregate, to avoid whites, has to do with the way white people are received by the black anti-self. Even if the believing self wants to see racial difference as essentially meaningless, the anti-self, that hidden perpetrator of racist doubt, sees white people as better than black people. Its mission is to confirm black inferiority, and so it looks closely at whites, watches the way they walk, talk, and negotiate the world, and then grants these styles of being and acting superiority. Somewhere inside every black is a certain awe at the power and achievement of the white race. In every barbershop gripe session where whites are put through the grinder of black anger, there will be a kind of backhanded respect—"Well, he might be evil, but that white boy is smart." True or not, the anti-self organizes its campaign against the believing self's faith in black equality around this supposition. And so, for blacks (as is true for whites in another way), white people in the generic sense have no neutrality. In themselves, they are stimulants to the black anti-self, deliverers of doubt. Their color slips around the deepest need of blacks to believe in their own immutable equality and communes directly with their self-suspicion.

33   So it is not surprising to hear black students on largely white campuses say that they are simply more comfortable with other blacks. Nor is it surprising to see them caught up in absurd contradictions—demanding separate facilities for themselves even as they protest apartheid in South Africa. Racial vulnerability is a species of fear and, as such, it is the progenitor of countless ironies. More freedom makes us more vulnerable so that in the midst of freedom we feel the impulse to carve our segregated comfort zones that protect us more from our own doubt than from whites. We balk before opportunity and pull back from effort just as these things would bear fruit. We reconstitute the boundaries of segregation just as they become illegal. By averting opportunity and curbing effort for fear of awakening a sense of inferiority, we make inevitable the very failure that shows us inferior.

34   One of the worst aspects of oppression is that it never ends when the oppressor begins to repent. There is a legacy of doubt in the oppressed that follows long after the cleanest repentance by the oppressor, just as guilt trails the oppressor and makes his redemption incomplete. These themes of doubt and guilt fill in like fresh replacements and work to duplicate the oppression. I think black Americans are today more oppressed by doubt than by racism and that the second phase of our struggle for freedom must be a confrontation with that doubt. Unexamined, this doubt leads us back into the tunnel of our oppression where we reenact our victimization just as society struggles to end its victimization of us. We are not a people formed in freedom. Freedom is always a call to possibility that demands an overcoming of doubt. We are still new to freedom, new to its challenges, new even to the notion that self-doubt can be the slyest enemy of freedom. For us freedom has so long meant the absence of oppression that we have not yet realized it also means the conquering of doubt.

35   Of course, this does not mean that doubt should become a lake we swim in, but it does mean that we should begin our campaign against doubt by acknowledging it, by

outlining the contours of the black anti-self so that we can know and accept exactly what it is that we are afraid of. This is knowledge that can be worked with, knowledge that can point with great precision to the actions through which we can best mitigate doubt and advance ourselves. This is the sort of knowledge that gives the believing self a degree of immunity against the anti-self and that enables it to pile up little victories that, in sum, grant even more immunity.

36   Certainly inferiority has long been the main theme of the black anti-self, its most lethal weapon against our capacity for self-belief. And so, in a general way, the acceptance of this piece of knowledge implies a mission: to show *ourselves* and (only indirectly) the larger society that we are not inferior in any dimension. That this should already be assumed goes without saying. But what "should be" falls within the province of the believing self, where it has no solidity until the doubt of the anti-self is called out and shown false by demonstrable action in the real world. This is the proof that grants the "should" its rightful solidity, that transforms it from a well-intentioned claim into a certainty.

37   The temptation is to avoid so severe a challenge, to maintain a black identity, painted in the colors of pride and culture, that provides us with a way of seeing ourselves apart from this challenge. It is easier to be "African-American" than to organize oneself on one's own terms and around one's own aspirations and then, through sustained effort and difficult achievement, put one's insidious anti-self quietly to rest. No black identity, however beautifully conjured, will spare blacks this challenge that, despite its fairness or unfairness, is simply in the nature of things. But then I have faith that in time we will meet this challenge since this, too, is in the nature of things.

QUESTIONS FOR DISCUSSION

1. Explain Steele's concept of the anti-self. What are its origins and what type of "wounds" contribute to it? What does the anti-self argue for and against?
2. Steele begins his essay with his friend Henry's decision not to choose an ambitious career. How does Steele's next example about his own elementary school days reveal "how the Henry was born in me"? Are these two examples convincing? Why or why not?
3. How do black adults who tell their children, "Don't worry. They treat all blacks that way," contribute to the anti-self? Do you agree?
4. Steele claims that the anti-self is "an internalized racist, our own unconscious bigot, that conspires with society to diminish us," and that, in today's world, "the unconscious replaying of our oppression is now the greatest barrier to our full equality." What evidence does Steele present to back up these assertions? Is his evidence convincing?
5. What does Steele mean by "integration shock," "self-segregation," and "black pride as denial"? How does the anti-self lead to these responses?
6. What methods does Steele use to argue for his perspective on black culture and identity? Does his argument seem to be "dialogic," that is, does

he take the arguments and feelings of his opposition into account? Is his approach effective and appropriate?

Compare Steele's idea of the shadowy anti-self that holds back one's potential with the struggle and the shadow as described in Marie von Franz's "The Realization of the Shadow in Dreams."

1. Steele argues against the "self-segregation" of blacks today. What is your response to the new black separatist movement? Do you agree with Steele that it is a sign of "integration shock" and self-doubt, or do you see it as a genuine cultural affirmation, a positive step forward for African-Americans? Write an essay in which you take a position on this issue.
2. Steele's argument rests on a consideration of the psychological responses of blacks to the injustices of the past. Write an essay in support of his position or refute it.

Fran Peavey (with Myrna Levy and Charles Varon)

Us and Them

Fran Peavey is a long-time California peace activist, ecologist, and community organizer. Peavey's books include Heart Politics *(1984)*, A Shallow Pool of Time: One Woman Grapples with the Aids Epidemic *(1989)*, By Life's Grace: Musings on the Essence of Social Change *(1994)*, and (with Radmila Manojlovic Zarkovic) the anthology I Remember: Writings by Bosnian Women Refugees *(1996)*. Peavey has also written articles for a number of alternative-press publications, and has served as a long-time observer of the Balkans struggle and the war in Kosovo. As you read her essay "Us and Them," from* Heart Politics, *consider how the people whom we feel are different from us politically or socially can be mistakenly perceived as alien beings with whom we have nothing in common, and how accepting the "other" outside of ourselves is something like accepting the rejected parts of our own identity.*

JOURNAL

Write about someone with whom you have trouble communicating because this individual is "different" from you in some way. What do you have in common with this person that could form the basis for better communication?

1   Time was when I knew that the racists were the lunch-counter owners who re-
      fused to serve blacks, the warmongers were the generals who planned wars and
ordered the killing of innocent people, and the polluters were the industrialists
whose factories fouled the air, water and land. I could be a good guy by boycotting,
marching, and sitting in to protest the actions of the bad guys.

2   But no matter how much I protest, an honest look at myself and my relationship with the rest of the world reveals ways that I too am part of the problem. I notice that on initial contact I am more suspicious of Mexicans than of whites. I see
that I'm addicted to a standard of living maintained at the expense of poorer people around the world—a situation that can only be perpetuated through military
force. And the problem of pollution seems to include my consumption of resources
and creation of waste. The line that separates me from the bad guys is blurred.

3   When I was working to stop the Vietnam War, I'd feel uneasy seeing people in
military uniform. I remember thinking, "How could that guy be so dumb as to have
gotten into that uniform? How could he be so acquiescent, so credulous as to have
fallen for the government's story in Vietnam?" I'd get furious inside when I imagined
the horrible things he'd probably done in the war.

4   Several years after the end of the war, a small group of Vietnam veterans wanted
to hold a retreat at our farm in Watsonville. I consented, although I felt ambivalent
about hosting them. That weekend, I listened to a dozen men and women who had
served in Vietnam. Having returned home only to face ostracism for their involvement in the war, they were struggling to come to terms with their experiences.

5   They spoke of some of the awful things they'd done and seen, as well as some things
they were proud of. They told why they had enlisted in the army or cooperated with
the draft: their love of the United States, their eagerness to serve, their wish to be
brave and heroic. They felt their noble motives had been betrayed, leaving them with
little confidence in their own judgment. Some questioned their own manhood or
womanhood and even their basic humanity. They wondered whether they had been a
positive force or a negative one overall, and what their buddies' sacrifices meant. Their
anguish disarmed me, and I could no longer view them simply as perpetrators of evil.

6   How had I come to view military people as my enemies? Did vilifying soldiers
serve to get me off the hook and allow me to divorce myself from responsibility for
what my country was doing in Vietnam? Did my own anger and righteousness keep
me from seeing the situation in its full complexity? How had this limited view affected my work against the war?

7   When my youngest sister and her husband, a young career military man, visited
me several years ago, I was again challenged to see the human being within the soldier. I learned that as a farm boy in Utah, he'd been recruited to be a sniper.

8   One night toward the end of their visit, we got to talking about his work. Though
he had also been trained as a medical corpsman, he could still be called on at any
time to work as a sniper. He couldn't tell me much about this part of his career—
he'd been sworn to secrecy. I'm not sure he would have wanted to tell me even if he
could. But he did say that a sniper's work involved going abroad, "bumping off" a
leader, and disappearing into a crowd.

9   When you're given an order, he said, you're not supposed to think about it. You feel alone and helpless. Rather than take on the Army and maybe the whole country himself, he chose not to consider the possibility that certain orders shouldn't be carried out.

10   I could see that feeling isolated can make it seem impossible to follow one's own moral standards and disobey an order. I leaned toward him and said, "If you're ever ordered to do something that you know you shouldn't do, call me immediately and I'll find a way to help. I know a lot of people would support your stand. You're not alone." He and my sister looked at each other and their eyes filled with tears.

11   How do we learn whom to hate and fear? During my short lifetime, the national enemies of the United States have changed several times. Our World War II foes, the Japanese and the Germans, have become our allies. The Russians have been in vogue as our enemy for some time, although during a few periods relations improved somewhat. The North Vietnamese, Cubans, and Chinese have done stints as our enemy. So many countries seem capable of incurring our national wrath—how do we choose among them?

12   As individuals, do we choose our enemies based on cues from national leaders? From our schoolteachers and religious leaders? From newspapers and TV? Do we hate and fear our parents' enemies as part of our family identity? Or those of our culture, subculture, or peer group?

13   Whose economic and political interests does our enemy mentality serve?

14   At a conference on holocaust and genocide I met someone who showed me that it is not necessary to hate our opponents, even under the most extreme circumstances. While sitting in the hotel lobby after a session on the German holocaust, I struck up a conversation with a woman named Helen Waterford. When I learned she was a Jewish survivor of Auschwitz, I told her how angry I was at the Nazis. (I guess I was trying to prove to her that I was one of the good guys.)

15   "You know," she said, "I don't hate the Nazis." This took me aback. How could anyone who had lived through a concentration camp not hate the Nazis?

16   Then I learned that Helen does public speaking engagements with a former leader of the Hitler Youth movement: they talk about how terrible facism is as viewed from both sides. Fascinated, I arranged to spend more time with Helen and learn as much as I could from her.

17   In 1980, Helen read an intriguing newspaper article in which a man named Alfons Heck described his experiences growing up in Nazi Germany. When he was a young boy in Catholic school, the priest would come in every morning and say, "Heil Hitler," and then "Good Morning," and finally, "In the name of the Father and the Son and the Holy Spirit . . ." In Heck's mind, Hitler came before God. At ten, he volunteered for the Hitler Youth, and he loved it. It was in 1944, when he was sixteen, that Heck first learned that the Nazis were systematically killing the Jews. He thought, "This can't be true." But gradually he came to believe that he had served a mass murderer.

18   Heck's frankness impressed Helen, and she thought, "I want to meet that man." She found him soft-spoken, intelligent and pleasant. Helen had already been speaking publicly about her own experiences of the holocaust, and she asked Heck to share a podium with her at an upcoming engagement with a group of four-hundred schoolteachers.

They spoke in chronological format, taking turns telling their own stories of the Nazi period. Helen told of leaving Frankfurt in 1934 at age twenty-five.

19   She and her husband, an accountant who had lost his job when the Nazis came to power, escaped to Holland. There they worked with the underground Resistance, and Helen gave birth to a daughter. In 1940 the Nazis invaded Holland. Helen and her husband went into hiding in 1942. Two years later, they were discovered and sent to Auschwitz. Their daughter was hidden by friends in the Resistance. Helen's husband died in the concentration camp.

20   Heck and Waterford's first joint presentation went well, and they decided to continue working as a team. Once, at an assembly of eight-hundred high school students, Heck was asked, "If you had been ordered to shoot some Jews, maybe Mrs. Waterford, would you have shot them?" The audience gasped. Heck swallowed and said, "Yes. I obeyed orders. I would have." Afterward he apologized to Helen, saying he hadn't wanted to upset her. She told him, "I'm glad you answered the way you did. Otherwise, I would never again believe a word you said."

21   Heck is often faced with the "once a Nazi, always a Nazi" attitude. "You may give a good speech," people will say, "but I don't believe any of it. Once you have believed something, you don't throw it away." Again and again, he patiently explains that it took years before he could accept the fact that he'd been brought up believing falsehoods. Heck is also harassed by neo-Nazis, who call him in the middle of the night and threaten: "We haven't gotten you yet, but we'll kill you, you traitor."

22   How did Helen feel about the Nazis in Auschwitz? "I disliked them. I cannot say that I wished I could kick them to death—I never did. I guess that I am just not a vengeful person." She is often denounced by Jews for having no hate, for not wanting revenge. "It is impossible that you don't hate," people tell her.

23   At the conference on the holocaust and genocide and in subsequent conversations with Helen, I have tried to understand what has enabled her to remain so objective and to avoid blaming individual Germans for the holocaust, for her suffering and for her husband's death. I have found a clue in her passionate study of history.

24   For many people, the only explanation of the holocaust is that it was the creation of a madman. But Helen believes that such an analysis only serves to shield people from believing that a holocaust could happen to them. An appraisal of Hitler's mental health, she says, is less important than an examination of the historical forces at play and the ways Hitler was able to manipulate them.

25   "As soon as the war was over," Helen told me, "I began to read about what had happened since 1933, when my world closed. I read and read. How did the 'S.S. State' develop? What was the role of Britain, Hungary, Yugoslavia, the United States, France? How can it be possible that the holocaust really happened? What is the first step, the second step? What are people searching for when they join fanatical movements? I guess I will be asking these questions until my last days."

26   Those of us working for social change tend to view our adversaries as enemies, to consider them unreliable, suspect, and generally of lower moral character. Saul Alinsky, a brilliant community organizer, explained the rationale for polarization this way:

> One acts decisively only in the conviction that all the angels are on one side and all the devils are on the other. A leader may struggle toward a decision and weigh the merits and demerits of a situation which is 52 percent positive and 48 percent negative, but once the decision is reached he must assume that his cause is 100 percent positive and the opposition 100 percent negative. . . . Many liberals, during our attack on the then-school superintendent [in Chicago], were pointing out that after all he wasn't a 100-percent devil, he was a regular churchgoer, he was a good family man, and he was generous in his contributions to charity. Can you imagine in the arena of conflict charging that so-and-so is a racist bastard and then diluting the impact of the attack with qualifying remarks? This becomes political idiocy.

27   But demonizing one's adversaries has great costs. It is a strategy that tacitly accepts and helps perpetuate our dangerous enemy mentality.

28   Instead of focusing on the 52-percent "devil" in my adversary, I choose to look at the other 48 percent, to start from the premise that within each adversary I have an ally. That ally may be silent, faltering, or hidden from my view. It may be only the person's sense of ambivalence about morally questionable parts of his or her job. Such doubts rarely have a chance to flower because of the overwhelming power of the social context to which the person is accountable. My ability to be *their* ally also suffers from such pressures. In 1970, while the Vietnam War was still going on, a group of us spent the summer in Long Beach, California, organizing against a napalm factory there. It was a small factory that mixed the chemicals and put the napalm in canisters. An accidental explosion a few months before had spewed hunks of napalm gel onto nearby homes and lawns. The incident had, in a real sense, brought the war home. It spurred local residents who opposed the war to recognize their community's connection with one of its most despicable elements. At their request, we worked with and strengthened their local group. Together we presented a slide show and tour of the local military-industrial complex for community leaders, and we picketed the napalm factory. We also met with the president of the conglomerate that owned the factory.

29   We spent three weeks preparing for this meeting, studying the company's holdings and financial picture and investigating whether there were any lawsuits filed against the president or his corporation. And we found out as much as we could about his personal life: his family, his church, his country club, his hobbies. We studied his photograph, thinking of the people who loved him and the people he loved, trying to get a sense of his worldview and the context to which he was accountable.

30   We also talked a lot about how angry we were at him for the part he played in killing and maiming children in Vietnam. But though our anger fueled our determination, we decided that venting it at him would make him defensive and reduce our effectiveness.

31   When three of us met with him, he was not a stranger to us. Without blaming him personally or attacking his corporation, we asked him to close the plant, not to bid for the contract when it came up for renewal that year, and to think about the consequences of his company's operations. We told him we knew where his corporation was vulnerable (it owned a chain of motels that could be boycotted), and said we intended to continue working strategically to force his company out of the business of

burning people. We also discussed the company's other war-related contracts, because changing just a small part of his corporation's function was not enough; we wanted to raise the issue of economic dependence on munitions and war.

32   Above all, we wanted him to see us as real people, not so different from himself. If we had seemed like flaming radicals, he would have been likely to dismiss our concerns. We assumed he was already carrying doubts inside himself, and we saw our role as giving voice to those doubts. Our goal was to introduce ourselves and our perspective into his context, so he would remember us and consider our position when making decisions.

33   When the contract came up for renewal two months later, his company did not bid for it.

34   Working for social change without relying on the concept of enemies raises some practical difficulties. For example, what do we do with all the anger that we're accustomed to unleashing against an enemy? Is it possible to hate actions and policies without hating the people who are implementing them? Does empathizing with those whose actions we oppose create a dissonance that undermines our determination?

35   I don't delude myself into believing that everything will work out for the best if we make friends with our adversaries. I recognize that certain military strategists are making decisions that raise the risks for us all. I know that some police officers will rough up demonstrators when arresting them. Treating our adversaries as potential allies need not entail unthinking acceptance of their actions. Our challenge is to call forth the humanity within each adversary, while preparing for the full range of possible responses. Our challenge is to find a path between cynicism and naivete.

QUESTIONS FOR DISCUSSION

1. Why does Peavey no longer find it easy to feel clear about the distinctions between the "good guys" and the "bad guys"? What elements of the bad guys does she now perceive in herself?
2. What was Peavey's rationale for being angry at soldiers? What did Peavey learn from her experience hosting a group of Vietnam veterans on her farm?
3. What did Peavey learn from the visit with her sister and her sister's husband, a military sniper? Does Peavey feel that the husband should be forgiven? Do you agree?
4. How does Peavey's friendship with Helen Waterford break down preconceptions Peavey holds about Nazis and concentration camp survivors? Do you agree with Waterford and Peavey's new perspective on Nazis?
5. Through providing an example of her own successful organizing technique against a napalm factory, Peavey attempts to refute an argument by organizer Saul Alinsky against the folly of "qualifying" our attacks on our enemies. Is Peavey's argument a convincing one?
6. How effective is Peavey's conclusion in anticipating and resolving objections readers might have to her position? What point does she concede? Does her concession weaken or strengthen her argument?

CONNECTION

Compare Peavey's view on effective activism which works toward accepting the socially defined "other" or antagonist with the views of Ron Takaki on effective multicultural practice in his essay "A Different Mirror."

IDEAS FOR WRITING

1. After reading Peavey's essay and the discussion by the editors at the beginning of this chapter on the dialogic argument, write an essay in which you argue either for or against Peavey's approach to resolving political differences. If you see her approach as working better in some situations than in others, provide examples of areas of conflict where the approach might or might not work.

2. One of Peavey's points that relates to how "anger and righteousness" sometimes prevent us from seeing the perspective of our opponents, or from seeing them as human, like ourselves. Write an essay about an experience in which you separated yourself from another person or an opposed group of people because of your anger or righteousness but later were able to understand and identify with their behavior and to accept their difference.

Pablo Neruda

The Dream

Pablo Neruda (1904–1973) was born and educated in Chile. When he was twenty-five, Neruda began his long career in politics as a Chilean consul in Ceylon and East Asia and went on to serve at the Chilean Embassy in Mexico City. Neruda was a member of the World Peace Council from 1950 to 1973 and received many international peace prizes. He is considered one of the greatest of the 20th Century poets; his work has been translated into over twenty different languages. In 1971 he received the Nobel Prize in Literature. Critics have noted that Neruda's poetry "structures itself on emotive association like the subconscious, and worlds in the flux of sensation and thought." These qualities are apparent in "The Dream," which appears in The Captain's Verses *(1952 in Spanish; 1972 in English translation).*

JOURNAL

Write about a time when you thought about ending a relationship that you felt was getting too intimate, weighing you down, to the point that the other person had become too much a part of yourself. Alternatively, write about a time when you decided you had to "erase" an aspect of your personality that you found troublesome.

Walking on the sands
I decided to leave you.
I was treading a dark clay
that trembled
5   and I, sinking and coming out,
decided that you should come out
of me, that you were weighing me down
like a cutting stone,
and I worked out your loss
10 step by step:
to cut off your roots,
to release you alone into the wind.
Ah in that minute,
my dear, a dream
15 with its terrible wings
was covering you.
You felt yourself swallowed by the clay,
and you called to me and I did not come,
you were going, motionless,
20 without defending yourself
until you were smothered in the quicksand.
Afterwards
my decision encountered your dream,
and from the rupture
25 that was breaking our hearts
we came forth clean again, naked,
loving each other
without dream, without sand,
29 complete and radiant,
sealed by fire.

Questions for Discussion

1. What is significant about the quicksand the speaker walks on in the poem? How do the speaker and the "you" in the poem both change in relation to the sand as the poem develops?
2. What leads the "I" in the poem to decide to leave the "you"?
3. In the third stanza, what is the meaning of the dream "with its terrible wings" that covers the "you"? How does the "you" feel about the relationship?
4. What causes the "I" to change his or her mind about leaving the "you"?
5. Why and how do the two reintegrate and renew their relationship?
6. Although this poem can be read as a love poem, another perspective is to see the "I" and "you" as two parts of a person who is experiencing an inner conflict. If the poem is seen in this way, what might the conflict be and how is it resolved?

CONNECTION

Compare the dualism between warring selves (and their final resolution) in Neruda's poem to that described in Fran Peavey's essay in this chapter. How does each work draw on the healing power of love to draw antagonists into a more harmonious relationship?

IDEAS FOR WRITING

1. Write an essay in which you interpret and discuss the definition of a relationship (either with one's own self or with a lover) implicit in the poem's final lines: "loving each other / without dream, without sand, / complete and radiant, / sealed by fire."
2. Write an essay in which you develop your journal entry about a relationship in which you felt "trapped" or, like the speaker in the poem, as if you were sinking in emotional quicksand. How did you change the relationship?

Susan Voyticky

Mixed-Up

Susan Voyticky grew up in Brooklyn, New York. She enjoys traveling, studying genetics, and writing poetry. The following essay was written for her freshman English class in response to a question that asked students to reflect on an aspect of their ethnic heritage about which they have conflicting feelings.

1   Having parents from different ethnic groups and growing up mixed is not easy in this country; in fact, it can really mix a person up, culturally as well as socially. Often, mixed children are confused about the cultural group to which they belong, and sometimes these children are alienated from half or even all of their cultural background. Other times children exposed to two distinct cultures feel pressured by society to choose one culture and social group to fit into and to define themselves through. However, as a person of mixed background, I try, despite the pressures that society puts on me, to relate to both my European and to my African heritage. I realize that I have a unique and independent cultural identity.

2   My lack of wanting to identify with a particular culture defines who I am. For instance, I remember going shopping in a store when I was ten years old that had black and white floor tiles. I decided to play with two children, a boy and a girl who were my age. After a while the girl said, "We'll [she and the boy] step on the white tiles, and you [pointing to me] step on the black tiles 'cause you're black." I couldn't believe what she had said. Even at that age, I found the idea insulting to my existence—she was ignoring half of me. I replied indignantly, "You two can

step on the white tiles, I'll step anywhere I want because I'm both." Then I quickly returned to my mother.

3   As a child, I quickly grew to realize that I was not ethnically "identifiable." During recess at my elementary school I often would try to play with the few African-American girls at my school. Usually the game was double-dutch, but I didn't know how to play, and the African-Americans kids said I turned the rope "like a white girl." To whites, I was black, and to blacks, I was less than black. I refused to be either; my ethnicity is an entirely different color—gray. If my mother is black and my father is white, then I most certainly must be gray. What else does one get by mixing black and white? Some would consider gray a "drab" color, but often one forgets gray comes in an infinite number of shades.

4   Because I have not chosen to identify with only one of my parents' cultures, I'll never know the comfort of belonging to a specific group of people with ancient customs and rituals. This society does not recognize my unique cross-cultural heritage of African-American, Irish, Russian, Polish, and Czechoslovakian. Few people choose to be mixed, to accept everything about themselves, and sometimes they are not given the choice. I have lost something in not being "white"; I also have lost something in not being "black." However, I have gained something important: my cultural independence. My brother puts it best when he says, "God was making a bunch of cookies. The white people he took out of the oven too soon. The black people he took out too late. We are the perfect cookies. One day everyone will be perfect, like us."

5   I struggle to be accepted in this society for what I am and not for what others would make of me. The longer I live, the more I feel pressured by society to "label" myself. When standardized forms were handed out in school, I would ask the teachers, "What should I fill out?" Most replied that I could fill whichever I wished. Most of the time that's what I did. One year I was black, the next year I was white, the next year I'd fill out two ovals. In high school, I was told I was black, because the federal government has a rule that if one is one fourth black, one is black. I ignored this and continued to fill out forms in my usual way.

6   Finally the true test of my "grayness" arrived—college applications. My mother said that I should fill out African-American, for the ethnic question, considering that it would improve my chances of being accepted. I didn't listen to her, for it's not in my nature to lie. How could I not be honest about who I was? On half of my applications I wrote "Black-Caucasian"; on the other half I wrote, "White African-American." My mother was not amused by what seemed to her a completely inane act. She didn't understand that I can't be told what I am, because I know who I am. In my blood run the tears of slaves torn from their homeland and the sweat of poor farmers looking for a better life. Their struggle is part of my identity.

7   A large part of one's culture is internal and cannot be represented simply by the color of one's skin. In this society it is difficult to be accepted for anything more than face value, but each person must try to be who he or she is within, not simply in the eyes of society. I am proud of my choice of identity with both of my ethnic backgrounds. Although being mixed often means being "mixed-up," being mistaken for something you are not by people too ignorant to care. Identity is more than skin deep.

QUESTIONS FOR DISCUSSION

1. What aspects of her mixed ethnic background cause Voyticky the most difficulty? How has she tried to resolve her problem of identity?
2. Compare Voyticky's view of the consequences of a mixed cultural and ethnic background with that presented in the poem by Judith Ortiz Cofer, "The Other."
3. Do you agree with Voyticky's approach to choosing an ethnicity for her college applications, or do you think that she should have taken fuller advantage of the opportunities afforded her?
4. Voyticky illustrates her essay with several examples drawn from her experience of being of mixed heritage at different stages of her life. What does each add to her essay's persuasiveness and its portrait of the dilemmas faced in our society by individuals from backgrounds similar to Voyticky's? What other kinds of evidence or examples would have helped to persuade you?

Jill Ho

Affirmative Action: Perspectives from a Model Minority

Born in Taipei, Taiwan in 1979, Jill Ho immigrated to the United States with her family and was educated in this country. In high school she was involved in many student organizations and was the co-founder of the first Asian-American Student Organization in Wichita, Kansas. She plans to complete a biology major and to pursue a career in medicine. In her spare time, she enjoys rollerblading, doing crossword puzzles, keeping up with current events, and designing web pages. Ho wrote the following essay as a response to a professional essay by Dinesh D'Souza that criticized affirmative action and hiring quotas.

1   *Intelligent. Hardworking. Compliant.* These three words are used frequently to describe Asian-Americans who succeed in educational and occupational spheres. When I hear these words, they make me cringe because they mask my individuality and define my identity according to stereotypical expectations. A widespread belief referred to by Asian-American scholars as the Model Minority Myth holds that Asian-Americans are more successful than other minority groups. This stereotype has led to the distorted perspective that Asian-Americans do not really need affirmative action and racial preference programs for education and employment; thus, in practice, such programs for the most part do not benefit and often completely ignore Asians.

2   Being Asian was just a minor part of my identity until high school, when I realized that my "Asianness" affected how people perceived me, regardless of how I perceived myself. Since ninth grade, I have chosen to leave the racial background bubble blank

on my standardized tests, because I strongly believe that my identity cannot be summarized in the three short words *Asian/Pacific Islander*. I am proud of my cultural background, which is similar to that of many other Asians who have grown up in the United States and who experience their culture not as all-Asian or all-American, nor as a combination of "partly Asian" and "partly American," but rather as something unique.

3   Despite my pride in my identity, being Asian-American has forced me to deal with situations which have made me feel excluded from both Asian *and* American cultures through pervasive stereotyping. For example, I am currently enrolled in a first year Chinese language class because my relatives tease me for not being able to speak my native tongue. On the first day of class, a student who apparently assumed I was already fluent in Chinese asked me why I was enrolled in the introductory class. It was strange that my relatives would think I wasn't "Asian enough" until I had learned how to speak Chinese while my classmate thought I was "too Asian" to be in the beginners class. My classmate's harmless question suggested that she thought most Asian-Americans were bilingual. Other common misperceptions include the stereotypes of Asians as hardworking, highly intelligent, socially awkward or even "nerdy," modest and passive, interested in math and science, and deficient in their command of spoken English (Cheng 278). While many traits associated with the Model Minority are positive, the myth supports a powerful stereotype that many Asians feel pressured to fit.

4   Not only does the Model Minority Myth tell Asians how they should behave, it also silences the unique experiences of Asian Americans. Dinesh D'Souza points out how ludicrous it would be to "abolish racial preferences for all groups except African-Americans" (28). In a country as multi-ethnic as the United States, it would seem extremely unfair to propose affirmative action plans, which only focus on one minority group; yet Asians are already invisible minorities, excluded by most if not all racial preference programs, even though they are the fastest growing minority group in the United States. In 1980, 3.5 million Asian Americans were living in the United States; by 1990 that figure had doubled to 7.3 million and numbers are still increasing (Cheng and Thatchenkery 270). Part of the reason Asians are frequently not considered as minorities for preferences is the widespread belief that Asians are successful without benefiting from racial preferences; therefore they aren't disadvantaged enough. While Asian-Americans include the same spectrum of demographic diversity as any other minority group, the Model Minority Myth leads people to believe that most Asians are Ivy League overachievers, despite the fact that many live in poverty in the inner city.

5   Because people generally refuse to acknowledge their minority status, Asian-Americans are often unfairly treated in the workplace. The Model Minority Myth frequently appears to give Asians an initial advantage in getting hired when compared to other groups; however, Asians are actually at a disadvantage if we consider their job-related qualifications. Even when more educated than white applicants, Asians are often underpaid and occupy positions lower than would be expected for their level of education and training. Because people generally believe Asians are intelligent and industrious, many Asians feel they have to prove they are extra qualified to be considered for a position; once hired, they have to be exceptional to be promoted. When education and experience are accounted for, Asian-American

high school graduates "earn 26 percent less than comparably educated white high school graduates, and Asian-American college graduates earn 11 percent less than white college graduates" (Narasaki 5). While other applicants need only prove they are well-qualified, Asians are forced to prove they are qualified above and beyond the already high expectations the Model Minority Myth sets for them.

6   However, despite the problems Asian-Americans have in the workplace, I agree with D'Souza that forcing companies to meet racial quotas may unfairly result in consideration of issues entirely unrelated to who is most qualified. Selecting the less competent over better qualified applicants who do not benefit from racial preference programs is not only unfair towards qualified candidates denied positions at that company, but also unfair for the companies forced to absorb the economic costs of rejecting the best applicants (D'Souza 30). Furthermore, as D'Souza explains, companies would be unlikely to reject a highly qualified minority applicant for racial reasons because it would make no economic sense to do so; in fact, it would only hurt companies trying to compete in the market-place to ignore talented minority applicants (30).

7   At the same time, affirmative action programs are essential to help minorities combat promotion discrimination. While it is reasonable to assume that companies are unlikely to discriminate blatantly against minorities in the hiring process, D'Souza fails to recognize that minority employees are far less likely to receive promotions or pay increases. This glass ceiling effect is common for all members of minority groups, but especially so for Asian-Americans, who are victims of the Model Minority Myth. Since the stereotype portrays Asians as diligent, hardworking, and compliant, many employers believe that Asians are ideal employees because they are non-confrontational. After his 1992 interviews with human resource managers in the Silicon Valley, Edward Park concluded that "Asian-Americans are seen as expendable workers who may be hired and fired at will because they will take what is offered and are too passive to complain, let alone file wrongful termination lawsuits" (163).

8   The same notion that Asians are unlikely to complain makes it more difficult for Asians to receive promotions or pay raises. The glass ceiling which prevents minority members from advancing to upper management positions especially affects Asian-Americans. In top management fewer than 1 percent are minority members and even in companies where there are numerous overqualified Asian employees in lower positions, fewer than .3 percent of senior level positions are held by Asian-Americans (Cheng 285). One possible explanation is that the same passive nature thought to prevent Asians from complaining if not promoted would also make them ineffective managers. Additionally, another aspect of the Model Minority Myth, poor English skills, may lead employers to believe that Asian supervisors would be unable to communicate clearly to employees. For many minorities, especially Asian-Americans, discrimination within companies for promotions is a bigger problem than possible discrimination in initial hiring.

9   Eric Foner points out that we cannot pretend that "eliminating affirmative action will produce a society in which rewards are based on merit" because race is still an issue (925). Although few companies today would openly refuse to hire minority employees, the unusually low number of minorities with equal seniority and/or equal

pay in companies still reflects the effects of promotion discrimination. To remedy this situation, racial preference programs should strive to create equal access to higher education for all minorities so anyone can have the training to be well qualified for the workplace. Furthermore, employers need to focus on breaking down barriers that limit opportunities for minority promotion to senior-level positions so anyone can break through the glass ceiling. All people, regardless of race, gender, religion, or sexual orientation should be accepted in the workplace for who they are and rewarded for their competency and hard work on the job.

WORKS CITED

Cheng, Cliff. "Are Asian American Employees a Model Minority or Just a Minority?" *Journal of Applied Behavioral Sciences* Sep. 1997: 277–90.
Cheng, Cliff and Tojo Joseph Thatchenkery. "Why is There a Lack of Workplace Diversity Research on Asian Americans?" *Journal of Applied Behavioral Sciences* Sep. 1997: 270–76.
D'Souza, Dinesh. "Beyond Affirmative Action." *National Review* 9 Dec. 1996: 26–30.
Foner, Eric. "Hiring Quotas for White Males Only." *The Nation* 26 June 1995: 924–25.
Narasaki, K.K. "Separate But Equal? Discrimination and the Need for Affirmative Action Legislation." *Perspectives on Affirmative Action.* Los Angeles: Asian Pacific American Public Policy Institute, 1995. 5–8.
Park, Edward. "Asians Matter: Asian American Entrepreneurs in the Silicon Valley High Technology Industry." *Reframing the Immigration Debate.* B. Hing and R. Lee, Eds. Los Angeles: UCLA Asian American Studies Center, 1996. 155–77.

QUESTIONS FOR DISCUSSION

1. What is the Model Minority Myth? How do the traits of the "model" influence the lives of Asian-Americans?
2. What examples from her own experiences does Ho provide? Are they effective?
3. What position does this essay take on Dinesh D'Souza's "Beyond Affirmative Action"? How does Ho both agree and disagree with D'Souza?
4. What solutions does Ho offer for improving work opportunities for Asian-Americans? Do you think her solutions are clearly stated and adequate?

Topics for Research and Writing

1. Do some research into the use of the double in Stevenson's *Dr. Jekyll and Mr. Hyde.* You should read the complete text, preferably an annotated version, and find some biographical information about Stevenson's life and the world he lived in order to see how the values of his society played a role in his creation of Jekyll and Hyde. How does the double of Jekyll/Hyde reveal typical preoccupations of Victorian England such as sexual repression and the hypocrisy of maintaining the façade of proper behavior in a society whose moral standards ignored the realities of violence, illegitimacy, drug use, and rampant prostitution? In what ways does the struggle Stevenson portrays seem relevant to the struggles people go through today?

2. Before Stevenson wrote *Jekyll and Hyde*, the double had had a long history as a literary subject, particularly in the Romantic era (late 18th and early 19th Centuries). Do some research into classic doubles stories by writers like Hoffmann, Mary Shelley, and Poe. Try to formulate some conclusions about the enduring popularity of this theme in literature.

3. At its most extreme, inability to incorporate the shadow self into one's dominant personality reveals itself in mental illness and breakdown. Do some research into a type of mental illness such as schizophrenia or multiple personality disorder in which the individual's personality tends to fragment into portions which cannot acknowledge one another or function together as a unified self. What are the causes of the particular disorder you have chosen to study? What treatments have been tried in the past and which are currently available?

4. Although the double is often seen as having a primarily psychological origin, there are often social and practical reasons why someone may choose to lead a literal "double life." Do some research into those who have chosen to pass as the "other," such as women like Billy Tipton who choose to disguise themselves as men, blacks who choose to pass for white, gays who are "closeted" or pass for "straight," etc. What are the social causes of this type of self-concealment? What are the psychological effects of having to conceal one's true self in society?

5. Takaki's "A Distant Mirror" examines the way our society fails to acknowledge the contributions of ethnic and cultural minorities in America, despite the fact that this is in theory a multicultural society. Do some research into the psychological impact of being perceived by the dominant society as the "other," as a sort of shadowy outsider, less than a "real" American. You might also consider here Shelby Steele's "Being Black and Feeling Blue" and other research into the impact of racism on the self-esteem of many African-Americans.

6. People have long been fascinated by identical twins as literal doubles. Do some research on the inner world of identical twins, concerning some of the following issues: In what ways does each twin see himself/herself in the "other"? How are twins bonded with one another for life? What happens when identical twins are reared apart and later reunited? How does a surviving twin respond psychologically to the death of his or her sibling?

7. Write an analysis of a film that dramatically portrays the double or divided personality. How does this film echo insights provided by one or more of the authors in this chapter? You might consider a film such as one of the following: *Three Faces of Eve, Dr. Jekyll and Mr. Hyde* (several versions of this film exist, each with a different view of the doube), *Mary Reilly* (still another perspective on Jekyll and Hyde), *Ringers, The Double Life of Veronique, La Femme Nikita, Superman, True Lies, American Beauty*.

8. To help get you started with some Internet research into the divided self, we have provided the folowing URLS:

CONFLICT RESOLUTION RESOURCE CENTER
http://www.conflict-resolution.net/
Resources and addresses of mediation/conflict resolution practitioners in various areas: business/workplace, parent/children, civil liberties, environment, etc.

ROMANCING THE SHADOW: AN INTERVIEW WITH CONNIE ZWEIG
http://www.west.net/~insight/zweig.htm
This on-line interview from *Kindred Spirit* with author and psychotherapist Connie Zweig defines the Jungian concept of the shadow, discusses celebrity and the public fascination with the idea of the shadow-self, and raises the question of how best to integrate self and shadow.

SCHIZOPHRENIA.ORG - THE HUXLEY INSTITUTE FOR BIOSOCIAL RESEARCH
http://www.schizophrenia.org/
The site of the Huxley Institute provides definitions and links to articles and other resources about schizophrenia and the divided self.

R.L. STEVENSON – RECENT STUDIES
http://www.unibg.it/rls/biblio2.htm
A large annotated bibliography for further research on Robert Louis Stevenson and his works such as *Doctor Jekyll and Mr. Hyde*, this site includes several studies on-line as well as many current articles and books.

TWINS IN LITERATURE
http://www.modcult.brown.edu/students/angell/twinslit.html
This page provides historical background on the roles that twins and the theme of the double have played in literature and film.

TWINSPACE
http://www.twinspace.com/
This web site provides information about research topics, books and articles, bookstores, and organizations devoted to twins and their identity issues.

VIEWING RACE WEB SITE
http://www.viewingrace.org/project/index.html
The web site of the project Viewing Race is devoted to helping overcome racial misunderstanding through providing grassroots groups with ready access to powerful films, videos, and other resources, both print and on-line, designed to promote racial harmony.

Society's Dreams

8

When we wake
the news of the world embraces us. . .
>   STEPHEN DUNN
>   Middle Class Poem

We would not have to insist that images reflect life, except that all
too often we ask life to reflect images.
>   GISH JEN
>   Challenging the Asian Illusion

"Who controls the past," ran the Party slogan, "controls the future:
who controls the present controls the past.". . . ."Reality control,"
they called it; in Newspeak, "doublethink."
>   GEORGE ORWELL
>   1984

RESEARCH WRITING

More so than any other type of writing, the research paper is a journey
outward, into the worlds of many other writers past and present who have
thought and articulated their views on a subject of public interest. The
challenge in developing a research paper is the synthesizing and harmonizing
of a number of diverse voices that you encounter and respond to in the
course of your research, while at the same time interspersing your own
voice and arguments with those of the writers whom you introduce into
your text. This writing process, if successful, can lead to a document that is
clearly your own, yet which properly introduces and fairly credits the ideas
and language of your sources.

The new skills needed to integrate and document facts and a variety of intellectual perspectives often overwhelm students just beginning a research paper.
To minimize the anxiety, try to maintain a balance between the creative and

437

the rational sides of your mind. The steps that follow will provide your rational side with a map to keep you on the main trail, but you should also allow your curious and creative mind to explore the many side paths and research possibilities that you will discover as you compose your paper. Above all, start early and pace yourself. A research paper needs to be completed in stages; it takes time to gather and to absorb, both intellectually and emotionally, the materials that will be used.

For many students, being assigned a research paper raises a number of practical questions and issues: "How many sources will I be expected to use?" "What procedure should I follow in taking notes and doing a bibliography?" "How does the computer in the library catalogue information?" "How can I access and evaluate information on the World Wide Web?" While these concerns are essential parts of the research paper writing process, we do not discuss specific techniques of finding, quoting, and documenting source information in the library or on the World Wide Web because these issues are thoroughly covered in most standard rhetorics and handbooks; librarians are also available and willing to help you. We will discuss the process involved in producing a research paper and the importance of maintaining a sense of voice and control over the information and point of view that you are presenting.

Research is more than a catalogue of interesting facts and quotations; it should help writers understand and evaluate their own perspectives and see their topic in relationship to their personal values as well as to broader issues. Professional writers naturally turn to outside sources of knowledge to deepen their own personal perspective and to better inform and engage their readers. Because their writing is thoughtfully constructed and thoroughly revised, their source material becomes an integral part of their writer's voice and stance; what was originally research doesn't sound strained, dry, or "tacked on," even though they may have used numerous brief quotations and paraphrases of their source material.

To minimize the anxiety involved in composing a research paper, try to maintain a balance between the creative and the rational sides of your mind. While it is natural to think about how your paper will be evaluated, it is more important to remain curious and to have fun discovering your sources and learning about your subject. It is helpful to keep a regular log of your process, making journal entries as you move through each stage of your paper, as you gather new insights into your topic and new understanding about how your mind works under the pressure of research paper deadlines.

Finding a Topic

Spend some time exploring possible topics for your paper; writing brief summaries of several different topics may help you to decide on the topic that interests you most. The best research papers are produced by students who are thoroughly engaged in their topic and in communicating what they have learned to their readers. This enthusiasm and intellectual curiosity will help you work through the inevitable frustrations associated with learning how to use a library and tracking down information that may not be easily available. After you complete some preliminary research, reevaluate and narrow your general topic further, if necessary, so that it can be covered within the scope and limits of the assignment. Notice, for instance, how Jason Glickman in his essay "Technology and the Future of American Wilderness" in this chapter has narrowed the focus of his essay down from the general topic of wilderness to American wilderness. He further narrows the scope of his research by choosing to focus only on digital technology—cellular telephones and laptop computers— that connect us with the Internet. Thus, by focusing on a particular country and media that he had special concerns about and knowledge of, he made his topic more manageable.

Timetable and Process

Make a timetable for your project and follow it. For example, you might allow yourself two to three weeks to establish a working bibliography and do research. Then schedule several work sessions to write the first draft, and several more days to complete your research and revise the draft. Also plan to give yourself sufficient time to complete the final draft, check your documentation, and do the final proofreading. At every stage in this process you should seek out as much useful feedback and advice as you possibly can. Tell your family and friends about your topic; they may have ideas about where to find sources. Read your first draft to peers and give your teacher a copy. Make sure that your readers clearly understand your paper's purpose and examples and that your writing holds their interest. Don't feel discouraged if you find that you need to do several revisions to clarify your ideas. This is a natural part of the research paper writing process.

Your Voice and the Voices of Your Sources

Practice careful reading and accurate note-taking as you prepare to write your paper. To avoid becoming overwhelmed by the sources you are working with, treat them as outside voices, as people with whom you want to conduct a dialogue. Take every quotation you intend to use in your paper and paraphrase it carefully into your own language to make sure that you really understand it. If you feel confused or intimidated by a source, freewriting may help you to get in touch with your feelings and responses to the authority. Is this "authority" really correct in his or her assertions, or do your experiences suggest that some of his or her comments are questionable or simply incorrect? Throughout this text we've created models of these types of questions in our study questions; now it is time for you to begin posing and answering your own questions about your sources. Undigested sources often produce a glorified book report, a rehash of ideas that you have not fully absorbed and integrated with your own point of view. For further information on evaluating sources and the facts they present, both from print and electronic media such as web sites, newsgroups, and listservs, see the section on argument in Chapter 7 of *Dreams and Inward Journeys* as well as any of a number of recent texts such as *Researching Online* (Longman, 1999).

Purpose and Structure

Always keep focused on the purpose and structure in your essay. Your research paper should express an original central purpose and have a compelling thesis. Each major idea must be introduced by a clear topic sentence and supported by evidence and examples. While using an outline is very helpful, feel free to revise the outline as you do further research and also to make changes in your original view of your material and topic. A research paper brings together many different ideas into a unified, original vision of a subject that, as the writer, only you can provide.

Language and Style

As you write your first draft, and particularly as you work through later stages of the paper, continue to express your own writer's voice. Your point of view should be communicated in language with which you feel comfortable and should always be your paper's guide. Read your paper aloud periodically. Is it tedious to listen to? Do you sound like yourself in this essay? Check your vocabulary and compare it with the sense of language in your previous papers. Are you using more multisyllabic words than usual or a specialized jargon that even you can hardly understand, one that is too derivative of your sources? Are your sentences more convoluted than usual? Have you lost touch with your own personal voice? If the answer to any of these questions is yes, try returning to the feelings and thoughts that inspired you in the first place.

The Computer as a Research Partner

Whether you work on a personal computer at home or store files on floppy discs and use the computers in your library's resource center, please consider the advantage of using a computer at all stages of your research writing process. The Internet can help you to identify and refine topics; you also can keep a record of your writing timetable and progress on your computer files. It is also helpful to gather and store information from different sources on the computer to save the time of re-copying information. When it comes time to draft your research paper you can just get started writing and integrating the information you have already saved; moving major portions of the paper around and fine editing are done more efficiently with the use of a computer. There are even computer programs such as *Endnote* (Niles software, Berkeley, Ca. <http://www.niles.com>), that allows you to search hundreds of libraries and databases and automatically formats your data into different bibliographic formats, including the MLA Works Cited format required for most English classes.

Writing a research paper is a challenge that provides you with the opportunity to develop, to utilize, and to integrate your research and writing skills as well as your creativity. A well-written research paper is a genuine accomplishment, a milestone on your inward journey.

THEMATIC INTRODUCTION: SOCIETY'S DREAMS

Who creates and monitors the dreams of our society and our own dreams? The readings in this chapter suggest different ways in which social customs; mass media such as film, television, and advertising; and political ideology influence our dreams and self-concepts. Although it would be naive to imagine that we could have total control over our own dreams, creating them without assistance from our culture, many of us aspire to be individualistic, first valuing our inner feelings and thoughts while forming impressions and evaluations of our social and political worlds. In modern society, however, individualism and developing an inner life are too often undermined and threatened by social forces that seek to mold us into loyal citizens, passive consumers, productive and compliant workers. Eager to escape temporarily from our immediate problems, feeling a strong need to belong to our social world, we allow ourselves to ignore the impact that overexposure to the mass media and the steady barrage of consumerist and political propaganda can have on the development and integrity of our private selves as well as on our sense of its power to shape us.

One of the most common ways that society enters our minds and creates distorted pictures of the external world and its values is through the news. Television newscasts, radio talk shows, and newspaper stories select and present reports of human events and natural disasters that are disturbing, full of uncontrollable dangers, disasters, and violence. These reports, while sometimes accurate, often intensify the negative, especially in contrast to what usually occurs in day-to-day life. To the extent that we internalize these nightmarish pictures of the world, our inner lives and private dream worlds are affected.

Our first two selections explore different ways that we process what we learn from the media. In Stephen Dunn's "Middle Class Poem," the speaker provides us with one perspective on how peoples' waking lives and dreams are haunted by images from the evening news. In "Pictures in Our Heads," Anthony Pratkanis and Elliot Aronson discuss surveys that reveal the exaggerated impressions held by heavy television viewers of the level of violence and risk in society. Their selection asks us to question why we allow the news media to define the questions and issues that concern us; they urge us to take more responsibility in selecting what is newsworthy.

Perhaps our deepest fear is that one day the media and political propaganda will control our minds and our lives completely. In order to change a society dominated by the media, counter-cultural groups and those who desire to create political change need to create their own propaganda, to find creative ways to bring their message to a massive public audience. In his classic work of negative utopian fiction, *1984*, George Orwell addresses the fear of total media control by the government, portraying a future world where it is almost impossible to entertain a private dream or memory. In the reading selected for this chapter, "Winston Was Dreaming," the central character attempts to capture and interpret a precious childhood dream only to be struck by a sense of tragic loss, realizing that such concepts as tragedy and love belong to an "ancient time," a time when inner worlds and the individual imagination were treasured.

Despite Orwell's warning of a time in which media may be controlled from the top down, our next selection, Martin Luther King, Jr.'s famous speech "I Have A Dream," shows us the power of a grass-roots political campaign such as King's Civil Rights Movement of the 1960s to upset the status quo and to force access to mainstream media by becoming truly newsworthy. King's memorable address was delivered before a massive crowd of 300,000 civil rights marchers at the Lincoln Memorial in Washington D.C., but his actual audience was in the millions because of extensive coverage of this "media event" by national and international radio and television networks.

In addition to the impact of news coverage of public events and political activities, our inner worlds are also strongly influenced by popular fiction, dream-like escapist films, and other forms of mass entertainment. We do not always realize the extent of the significance of such "fictional" fare, often dismissing it as a form of relaxation and escape into someone else's mass-produced fantasy. Philosopher Sissela Bok, in "Aggression: The Impact of Media Violence" examines the impact of the violence in television and films on children's abilities to control their own aggression. Next, novelist and poet Jessica Hagedorn traces the changing images of Asian women in film "Asian Women in Film: No Joy, No Luck." She concludes that "we [female Asians] have learned. . . to accept the fact that we are either decorative, invisible or one dimensional." In our next selection, sports journalist Joan Ryan shows in her essay, "Little Girls in Pretty Boxes," how our cultural and media fixation on beauty, slenderness, and youth have shaped gymnastics and figure skating into sports where young girls are sometimes driven to self-destructive behavior.

A broader criticism of the dangers of electronic culture as an influence on our thinking and values is seen in our next two selections. Umberto Eco in his essay "The City of Robots" is critical of the superficial promises that are sometimes offered in social dreams; he asks us to think about why the totally fake, robotic and ever-cheerful theme park, as best exemplified by Disneyland, has become a national place of worship where our true national values are enshrined. Work in an age of cybernetic machines also has its dangers, as the workers are encouraged to think and perform like the thinking machines they build and program, as can be seen in software engineer Ellen Ullman's "Getting Close to the Machine." In her essay, Ullman reflects on her intense experience of writing computer code and communicating with programmers who cannot tolerate normal human interactions.

The final selections in the chapter explore the ways that our fantasies of the wilderness and American history are being affected by the media and technology. In "Dear John Wayne," Louise Erdrich asks us to question the fantasies we have about the settling of the West and our stereotypes of Native Americans. The student research essay, "Technology and the Future of the American Wilderness," by Jason Glickman, examines the historic concept of the wilderness in American culture and explores the impact of digital technology on the wilderness experience.

We hope that reading the selections in this chapter will help you to think more deeply about the ways that your dreams and beliefs are shaped by the mass media, social conventions, and political ideology. An important part of a writer's inward journey involves value clarification. Unraveling one's own genuine dreams and values from those that are artificial and mass-produced can be both liberating and life-affirming.

Brady Beaubien
"Interface"

Like Ellen Ullman's "Close to the Machine" in the "Society's Dreams" chapter, the student drawing above portrays a future world in which we will be called on increasingly to express ourselves through computers and to view our thought processes and identities using computing and Internet-based analogies.

Ideas for Drawing, Writing, and Discussion

1. Create a drawing representing how modern computing and communications technology have influenced your thinking and imagination. If you wish, use images and situations from one of the readings in this chapter or elsewhere in the text.
2. Write a short explanation of your drawing, indicating the major effects you were trying to portray. Which effects were negative? Which were positive?
3. In a small group, share your drawing and discuss some of the different and intersecting views of technology expressed by other group members.

Stephen Dunn

Middle Class Poem

Stephen Dunn (b. 1939) was born in New York City and studied at the New School for Social Research at Syracuse University. Dunn has worked as a copywriter for an advertising company and as a basketball player. Currently he is poet in residence at Stockton State College in New Jersey. His books of poetry include Not Dancing *(1984),* Landscape at the End of the Century: Poems *(1991),* Loosestrife: Poems *(1996),* New & Selected Poems: (1974–1994), *and a book of prose reflections,* Walking Light: Essays & Memoirs *(1993.) In "Middle Class Poem," Dunn explores the impact of television news and consumerism on people's dreams and emotional life.*

JOURNAL

Write about a time when your sleep was disturbed by thoughts, fantasies, or dreams related to stories or issues raised in the newspaper or on the radio or television news.

In dreams, the news of the world
comes back, gets mixed up
with our parents and the moon.
We can't help but thrash.
5   Those with whom we sleep, never equally,
roll away from us and sigh.

When we wake
the news of the world embraces us,

pulls back. Who let go first?—
10 a lover's question, the lover
who's most alone.
We purchase a little forgetfulness
at the mall. We block the entrance
to our hearts.

15 Come evening, the news of the world
is roaming the streets
while we bathe our children,
while we eat what's plentiful
and scarce. We know what we need
20 to keep out, what's always there—
painful to look at, bottomless.

QUESTIONS FOR DISCUSSION

1. What does the speaker in the poem believe "comes back" in dreams?
2. Why is there a "thrashing" in the beds of the sleepers in the poem? What disturbs their sleep and causes them to "sigh"?
3. In the second stanza of the poem, the speaker refers to the "news of the world" as a lover. If the news is a lover, what sort of lover is it? How does the news betray us? Why does the news make us feel like the lover who is "most alone"?
4. In lines 12–14, the speaker is buying "forgetfulness at the mall." How does shopping help people to forget and to wall off emotions? Do you think that this is a common reason for going shopping? Do most people whom you know simply shop when they need to buy something?
5. The last stanza of the poem personifies the news, referring to it as "roaming the streets," like an animal or a dangerous criminal. What kinds of feelings does this comparison evoke? Do you think that such feelings about the news and its subject matter are typical ones for middle-class people?
6. The last three lines of the poem refer to that which the middle-class people in the poem prefer "to keep out, what's always there—painful to look at, bottomless." What exactly is it in the news that causes people so much pain and anxiety? To what extent is what they fear real? To what extent is what they fear just a creation of their own over stimulated imaginations?

CONNECTION

Compare fears and anxiety created in the middle-class consumers portrayed in Dunn's poem with the responses of Native American viewers to the violence against Native people portrayed in the John Wayne Westerns as seen in Louise Erdrich's "Dear John Wayne." Which group seems more deeply disturbed by the distortions and violence of the media, and why?

IDEAS FOR WRITING

1. "Middle Class Poem" suggests that the news alarms people, perhaps even disrupting sleeping patterns and causing nightmares. Write an essay about the ways you think the news, particularly television news, influences people's dreams and emotional life. To support your ideas draw on your own experiences, interview friends, or read relevant articles.

2. The poem explores the effects of consumerism and compulsive shopping. Write an essay on compulsive shopping: What causes people to want to "shop till they drop"? Can overshopping become an addictive form of behavior?

Anthony Pratkanis and Elliot Aronson

Pictures in Our Heads

Anthony Pratkanis and Elliot Aronson are professors of psychology at the University of California, Santa Cruz. Pratkanis has taught courses in consumerism and advertising at Carnegie Mellon. He has written many articles for both popular and scholarly journals and is an editor of Attitude Structure and Function*(1989) and, with Aronson,* Social Psychology *(1993). Aronson is one of the world's most highly regarded social psychologists. He is the author of many books, including* The Social Animal *(1972, 7th ed. 1995) and* The Jigsaw Classroom *(1978, 1997). The following article is from Pratkanis and Aronson's* The Age of Propaganda *(1992), which focuses on the ways people's views of the world are influenced and molded by the constant barrage of media propaganda.*

JOURNAL

Write about an attitude you have toward a certain political or social issue that you believe was influenced by the images provided by television news.

1   In *Public Opinion*, the distinguished political analyst Walter Lippmann tells the story of a young girl, brought up in a small mining town, who one day went from cheerfulness into a deep spasm of grief.[1] A gust of wind had suddenly cracked a kitchen windowpane. The young girl was inconsolable and spoke incomprehensibly for hours. When she finally was able to speak intelligibly, she explained that a broken pane of glass meant that a close relative had died. She was therefore mourning her father, whom she felt certain had just passed away. The young girl remained disconsolate until, days later, a telegram arrived verifying that her father was still alive. It appears that the girl had constructed a complete fiction based on a simple external fact (a broken window), a superstition (broken window means death), fear, and love for her father.

2   The point of Lippmann's story was not to explore the inner workings of abnormal personality, but to ask a question about ourselves: To what extent do we, like the young girl, let our fictions guide our thoughts and actions? Lippmann believed that we are much more similar to that young girl than we might readily admit. He contended that the mass media paint an imagined world and that the "pictures in our heads" derived from the media influence what men and women will do and say at any particular moment. Lippmann made these observations in 1922. Seven decades later, we can ask: What is the evidence for his claim? To what extent do the pictures we see on television and in other mass media influence how we see the world and set the agenda for what we view as most important in our lives?

3   Let's look at the world we see on television. George Gerbner and his associates have conducted the most extensive analysis of television to date.[2] Since the late 1960s, these researchers have been videotaping and carefully analyzing thousands of prime-time television programs and characters. Their findings, taken as a whole, indicate that the world portrayed on television is grossly misleading as a representation of reality. Their research further suggests that, to a surprising extent, we take what we see on television as a reflection of reality.

4   In prime-time programming, males outnumber females by 3 to 1, and the women portrayed are younger than the men they encounter. Nonwhites (especially Hispanics), young children, and the elderly are underrepresented; and members of minority groups are disproportionately cast in minor roles. Moreover, most prime-time characters are portrayed as professional and managerial workers: Although 67 percent of the work force in the United States are employed in blue-collar or service jobs, only 25 percent of TV characters hold such jobs. Finally, crime on television is ten times more prevalent than it is in real life. The average 15-year-old has viewed more than 13,000 TV killings. Over half of TV's characters are involved in a violent confrontation each week; in reality, fewer than 1 percent of people in the nation are victims of criminal violence in any given year, according to FBI statistics. David Rintels, a television writer and former president of the Writers' Guild of America, summed it up best when he said, "From 8 to 11 o'clock each night, television is one long lie."[3]

5   To gain an understanding of the relationship between watching television and the pictures in our heads, Gerbner and his colleagues compared the attitudes and beliefs of heavy viewers (those who watch more than four hours a day) and light viewers (those who watch less than two hours a day). They found that heavy viewers (1) express more racially prejudiced attitudes; (2) overestimate the number of people employed as physicians, lawyers, and athletes; (3) perceive women as having more limited abilities and interests than men; (4) hold exaggerated views of the prevalence of violence in society; and (5) believe old people are fewer in number and less healthy today than they were twenty years ago, even though the opposite is true. What is more, heavy viewers tend to see the world as a more sinister place than do light viewers; they are more likely to agree that most people are just looking out for themselves and would take advantage of you if they had a chance. Gerbner and

his colleagues conclude that these attitudes and beliefs reflect the inaccurate portrayals of American life provided to us by television.

6   Let's look at the relationship between watching television and images of the world by looking more closely at how we picture criminal activity. In an analysis of "television criminology," Craig Haney and John Manzolati point out that crime shows dispense remarkably consistent images of both the police and criminals.[4] For example, they found that television policemen are amazingly effective, solving almost every crime, and are absolutely infallible in one regard: The wrong person is never in jail at the end of a show. Television fosters an illusion of certainty in crime-fighting. Television criminals generally turn to crime because of psychopathology or insatiable (and unnecessary) greed. Television emphasizes criminals' personal responsibility for their actions and largely ignores situational pressures correlated with crime, such as poverty and unemployment.

7   Haney and Manzolati go on to suggest that this portrayal has important social consequences. People who watch a lot of television tend to share this belief system, which affects their expectations and can cause them to take a hard-line stance when serving on juries. Heavy viewers are likely to reverse the presumption of innocence, believing that defendants must be guilty of something, otherwise they wouldn't be brought to trial.

8   A similar tale can be told about other "pictures painted in our heads." For example, heavy readers of newspaper accounts of sensational and random crimes report higher levels of fear of crime. Repeated viewing of R-rated violent "slasher" films is associated with less sympathy and empathy for victims of rape. When television is introduced into an area, the incidence of theft increases, perhaps due partly to television's promotion of consumerism, which may frustrate and anger economically deprived viewers who compare their life-styles with those portrayed on television.[5]

9   It should be noted, however, that the research just described—that done by Gerbner and colleagues and by others—is correlational; that is, it shows merely an association, not a causal relation, between television viewing and beliefs. It is therefore impossible to determine from this research whether heavy viewing actually causes prejudiced attitudes and inaccurate beliefs or whether people already holding such attitudes and beliefs simply tend to watch more television. In order to be certain that watching TV causes such attitudes and beliefs, it would be necessary to perform a controlled experiment in which people are randomly assigned to conditions. Fortunately, some recent experiments do allow us to be fairly certain that heavy viewing does indeed determine the pictures we form of the world.

10   In a set of ingenious experiments, the political psychologists Shanto Iyengar and Donald Kinder varied the contents of evening news shows watched by their research participants.[6] In their studies, Iyengar and Kinder edited the evening news so that participants received a steady dose of news about a specific problem facing the United States. For example, in one of their experiments, some participants heard about the weaknesses of U.S. defense capabilities; a second group watched shows emphasizing pollution concerns; a third group heard about inflation and economic matters.

11   The results were clear. After a week of viewing the specially edited programs, participants emerged from the study more convinced than they were before viewing the shows that the target problem—the one receiving extensive coverage in the shows they had watched—was a more important one for the country to solve. What is more, the participants acted on their newfound perceptions, evaluating the current president's performance on the basis of how he handled the target issue and evaluating more positively than their competitors those candidates who took strong positions on those problems.

12   Iyengar and Kinder's findings are not a fluke. Communications researchers repeatedly find a link between what stories the mass media cover and what viewers consider to be the most important issues of the day.[7] The content of the mass media sets the public's political and social agenda. As just one example, in a pioneering study of an election in North Carolina, researchers found that the issues that voters came to consider to be most important in the campaign coincided with the amount of coverage those issues received in the local media.[8] Similarly, the problems of drug abuse, NASA incompetence, and nuclear energy were catapulted into the nation's consciousness by the coverage of dramatic events such as the drug-related death of basketball star Len Bias, the *Challenger* explosion, and the nuclear-reactor accidents at Three Mile Island and Chernobyl. Former Secretary of State Henry Kissinger clearly understood the power of the news media in setting agendas. He once noted that he never watched the content of the evening news but was only interested in "what they covered and for what length of time, to learn what the country was getting."[9]

13   Of course, each of us has had extensive personal contact with many people in a myriad of social contexts; the media are just one source of our knowledge about political affairs and different ethnic, gender, and occupational groups. The information and impressions we receive through the media are relatively less influential when we can also rely on firsthand experience. Thus those of us who have been in close contact with several women who work outside the home are probably less susceptible to the stereotypes of women portrayed on television. On the other hand, regarding issues with which most of us have had limited or no personal experience, such as crime and violence, television and the other mass media are virtually the only vivid source of information for constructing our image of the world.

14   The propaganda value of the mass media in painting a picture of the world has not been overlooked by would-be leaders. Such social policy as a "get tough on crime" program, for example, can be easily sold by relating it to the prime-time picture of crime as acts committed by the psychopathic and the greedy, rather than dealing with situational determinants such as poverty and unemployment. In a similar vein, it is easier to sell a "war on drugs" after the drug-related death of a prominent basketball star or to promote an end to nuclear power after a fatal tragedy at a nuclear reactor.

15   It is even more important for a would-be leader to propagate his or her own picture of the world. The political scientist Roderick Hart notes that since the early

1960s, U.S. presidents have averaged over twenty-five speeches per month—a large amount of public speaking.[10] Indeed, during 1976, Gerald Ford spoke in public once every six hours, on average. By speaking frequently on certain issues (and gaining access to the nightly news), a president can create a political agenda—a picture of the world that is favorable to his or her social policies. Indeed, one of President Bush's key advisors is Robert Teeter, a pollster who informs the president on what Americans think and what issues should be the topic of his speeches. This can be of great importance in maintaining power. According to Jeffery Pfeffer, an expert on business organizations, one of the most important sources of power for a chief executive officer is the ability to set the organization's agenda by determining what issues will be discussed and when, what criteria will be used to resolve disputes, who will sit on what committees, and, perhaps most importantly, which information will be widely disseminated and which will be selectively ignored.[11]

16   Why are the pictures of the world painted by the mass media so persuasive? For one thing, we rarely question the picture that is shown. We seldom ask ourselves, for example, "Why are they showing me this story on the evening news rather than some other one? Do the police really operate in this manner? Is the world really this violent and crime-ridden?" The pictures that television beams into our homes are almost always simply taken for granted as representing reality.

17   Once accepted, the pictures we form in our heads serve as fictions to guide our thoughts and actions. The images serve as primitive social theories—providing us with the "facts" of the matter, determining which issues are most pressing, and decreeing the terms in which we think about our social world. As the political scientist Bernard Cohen observed, the mass media

> may not be successful much of the time in telling people *what to think,* but it is stunningly successful in telling its readers *what to think about...* The world will look different to different people, depending... on the map that is drawn for them by writers, editors, and publishers of the papers they read.[12]

END NOTES

1. Lippmann, W. (1922). *Public opinion.* New York: Harcourt, Brace.
2. Gerbner, G., Gross, L., Morgan, M., & Signorielli, N. (1986). "Living with television: The dynamics of the cultivation process." In J. Bryant & D. Zillman (Eds.), *Perspectives on media effects* (pp. 17–40). Hillsdale, NJ: Erlbaum.
3. Quoted in *Newsweek*, December 6, 1982, p. 40.
4. Haney, C., & Manzolati, J. (1981). "Television criminology: Network illusions on criminal justice realities." In E. Aronson (Ed.), *Readings about the social animal* (3rd ed.; pp. 125–136). New York: W. H. Freeman.
5. See Heath, L. (1984). "Impact of newspaper crime reports on fear of crime: Multimethodological investigation." *Journal of Personality and Social Psychology,* 47, 263–276; Linz, D. G., Donnerstein, E., & Penrod, S. (1988). "Effects of long-term exposure to violent and sexually degrading depictions of women." *Journal of Personality and Social Psychology,* 55, 758–768; Henningan, K., Heath, L., Wharton, J. D., Del Rosario, M., Cook, T. D., & Calder, B. (1982). "Impact of the introduction of television on crime in the United States: Empirical findings and theoretical implications." *Journal of Personality and Social Psychology,* 42, 461–477.

6. Iyengar, S., & Kinder, D. R. (1987). *News that matters*. Chicago: University of Chicago Press.

7. Rogers, E. M., & Dearing, J. W. (1988). "Agenda-setting research: Where has it been, Where is it going?" In J. A. Anderson (Ed.), *Communication Yearbook* 11 (pp. 555–594). Beverly Hills, CA: Sage.

8. McCombs, M. E., & Shaw, D. L. (1972). "The agenda setting function of mass media." *Public Opinion Quarterly*, 36, 176–187.

9. Dilenschneider, R. L. (1990). *Power and influence*. New York: Prentice-Hall.

10. Hart, R. P. (1987). *The sound of leadership*. Chicago: University of Chicago Press.

11. Pfeffer, J. (1981). *Power in organizations*. Cambridge, MA: Ballinger.

12. Cited in Rogers and Dearing (1988). See note 7.

QUESTIONS FOR DISCUSSION

1. What is the point of Walter Lippmann's story of the young girl who superstitiously mourned her father? Why is this an effective way to begin the essay?

2. What are the "pictures in our heads" that Lippmann and the authors of the essay comment on? How do these "pictures" both resemble and differ from dreams and fantasies?

3. What conclusions can be drawn from George Gerbner's television program analysis? What comparisons did Gerbner and his associates make between different kinds of viewers and their beliefs?

4. How are criminals usually portrayed on television? What impact does this portrayal have on our attitudes and beliefs? How have politicians used stereotypical portrayals of criminals and crime to "sell" their programs to the public?

5. What flaw can be found in Gerbner's research? How have the experiments of Iyengar and Kinder on evening news shows and their viewers helped to correct and support Gerbner's research?

6. Explain Bernard Cohen's distinction between the media's telling us what to think as opposed to telling us "what to think about." What does Cohen consider the media's most stunning success? What examples does he provide?

CONNECTION

Compare the fearfulness that results from seeing the world through television news with the attitudes and emotions expressed by the characters in Stephen Dunn's "Middle Class Poem."

IDEAS FOR WRITING

1. Do some research into recent intensive media coverage of a political event or a controversial issue. Discuss the media's impact on the public's perceptions of the "reality" of the situation. You might take a look at some

public opinion polls that were taken during the period you are discussing and examine typical stories aired on television and in the newspapers.

2. Write about your attitudes toward a political issue covered extensively by the mass media; explain to what degree your political views and social outlook were influenced by the media in contrast to direct experience and conversation.

George Orwell

Winston Was Dreaming

Named Eric Blair, George Orwell (1903–1950) was born in India. His family struggled to send him to be educated at Eton College in England. Orwell had a life rich in experiences. He served with the Imperial Police in Burma, fought in the Spanish Civil War, as a member of the Home Guard, and as a writer for the BBC during World War II. As a journalist, essayist, and novelist, Orwell was "the conscience of his generation" because he confronted the political nightmares of his age in his books; some of the most widely read include Burmese Days *(1934),* Homage to Catalonia *(1938), and* A Collection of Essays *(1946). Orwell is best known for his two brilliantly satirical novels,* Animal Farm *(1945) and* 1984 *(1949), from which the following selection is excerpted. In both of his novels Orwell condemns totalitarianism and big government's lust for power, believing that "like certain wild animals" the imagination "will not breed in captivity."*

JOURNAL

Write about how you felt during a time when your mind and your life were being controlled by a person or institution that had political power over you.

1 Winston was dreaming of his mother.

2 He must, he thought, have been ten or eleven years old when his mother had disappeared. She was a tall, statuesque, rather silent woman with slow movements and magnificent fair hair. His father he remembered more vaguely as dark and thin, dressed always in neat dark clothes (Winston remembered especially the very thin soles of his father's shoes) and wearing spectacles. The two of them must evidently have been swallowed up in one of the first great purges of the Fifties.

3 At this moment his mother was sitting in some place deep down beneath him, with his young sister in her arms. He did not remember his sister at all, except as a tiny, feeble baby, always silent, with large, watchful eyes. Both of them were looking up at him. They were down in some subterranean place—the bottom of a well, for instance, or a very deep grave—but it was a place which, already far below him, was

itself moving downwards. They were in the saloon of a sinking ship, looking up at him through the darkening water. There was still air in the saloon, they could still see him and he them, but all the while they were sinking down, down into the green waters which in another moment must hide them from sight forever. He was out in the light and air while they were being sucked down to death, and they were down there *because* he was up here. He knew it and they knew it, and he could see the knowledge in their faces. There was no reproach either in their faces or in their hearts, only the knowledge that they must die in order that he might remain alive, and that this was part of the unavoidable order of things.

4   He could not remember what had happened, but he knew in his dream that in some way the lives of his mother and his sister had been sacrificed to his own. It was one of those dreams which, while retaining the characteristic dream scenery, are a continuation of one's intellectual life, and in which one becomes aware of facts and ideas which still seem new and valuable after one is awake. The thing that now suddenly struck Winston was that his mother's death, nearly thirty years ago, had been tragic and sorrowful in a way that was no longer possible. Tragedy, he perceived, belonged to the ancient time, to a time when there were still privacy, love, and friendship, and when the members of a family stood by one another without needing to know the reason. His mother's memory tore at his heart because she had died loving him, when he was too young and selfish to love her in return, and because somehow, he did not remember how, she had sacrificed herself to a conception of loyalty that was private and unalterable. Such things, he saw, could not happen today. Today there were fear, hatred, and pain, but no dignity of emotion, no deep or complex sorrows. All this he seemed to see in the large eyes of his mother and his sister, looking up at him through the green water, hundreds of fathoms down and still sinking.

5   Suddenly he was standing on short springy turf, on a summer evening when the slanting rays of the sun gilded the ground. The landscape that he was looking at recurred so often in his dreams that he was never fully certain whether or not he had seen it in the real world. In his waking thoughts he called it the Golden Country. It was an old, rabbit-bitten pasture, with a foot track wandering across it and a molehill here and there. In the ragged hedge on the opposite side of the field the boughs of the elm trees were swaying very faintly in the breeze, their leaves just stirring in dense masses like women's hair. Somewhere near at hand, though out of sight, there was a clear, slow-moving stream where dace were swimming in the pools under the willow trees.

6   The girl with dark hair was coming toward him across the field. With what seemed a single movement she tore off her clothes and flung them disdainfully aside. Her body was white and smooth, but it aroused no desire in him; indeed, he barely looked at it. What overwhelmed him in the instant was admiration for the gesture with which she had thrown her clothes aside. With its grace and carelessness it seemed to annihilate a whole culture, a whole system of thought, as though Big Brother and the Party and the Thought Police could all be swept into nothingness by a single splendid movement of the arm. That too was a gesture belonging to the ancient time. Winston woke up with the word "Shakespeare" on his lips.

7   The telescreen was giving forth an ear-splitting whistle which continued on the same note for thirty seconds. It was nought seven fifteen, getting-up time for office workers. Winston wrenched his body out of bed—naked, for a member of the Outer Party received only three thousand clothing coupons annually, and a suit of pajamas was six hundred—and seized a dingy singlet and a pair of shorts that were lying across a chair. The Physical Jerks would begin in three minutes. The next moment he was doubled up by a violent coughing fit which nearly always attacked him soon after waking up. It emptied his lungs so completely that he could only begin breathing again by lying on his back and taking a series of deep gasps. His veins had swelled with the effort of the cough, and the varicose ulcer had started itching.

8   "Thirty to forty group!" yapped a piercing female voice. "Thirty to forty group! Take your places, please. Thirties to forties!"

9   Winston sprang to attention in front of the telescreen, upon which the image of a youngish woman, scrawny but muscular, dressed in tunic and gum shoes, had already appeared.

10   "Arms bending and stretching!" she rapped out. "Take your time by me. *One,* two, three, four! *One,* two, three four! Come on, comrades, put a bit of life into it! *One,* two, three, four! *One,* two, three, four! . . . "

11   The pain of the coughing fit had not quite driven out of Winston's mind the impression made by his dream, and the rhythmic movements of the exercise restored it somewhat. As he mechanically shot his arms back and forth, wearing on his face the look of grim enjoyment which was considered proper during the Physical Jerks, he was struggling to think his way backward into the dim period of his early childhood. It was extraordinarily difficult. Beyond the late Fifties everything faded. When there were no external records that you could refer to, even the outline of your own life lost its sharpness. You remembered huge events which had quite probably not happened, you remembered the detail of incidents without being able to recapture their atmosphere, and there were long blank periods to which you could assign nothing. Everything had been different then. Even the names of countries, and their shapes on the map, had been different. Airstrip One, for instance, had not been so called in those days: it had been called England or Britain, though London, he felt fairly certain, had always been called London.

12   Winston could not definitely remember a time when his country had not been at war, but it was evident that there had been a fairly long interval of peace during his childhood, because one of his early memories was of an air raid which appeared to take everyone by surprise. Perhaps it was the time when the atomic bomb had fallen on Colchester. He did not remember the raid itself, but he did remember his father's hand clutching his own as they hurried down, down, down into some place deep in the earth, round and round a spiral staircase which rang under his feet and which finally so wearied his legs that he began whimpering and they had to stop and rest. His mother, in her slow dreamy way, was following a long way behind them. She was carrying his baby sister—or perhaps it was only a bundle of blankets that she was carrying: he was not certain whether his sister had been born then. Finally they had emerged into a noisy, crowded place which he had realized to be a Tube station.

13   There were people sitting all over the stone-flagged floor, and other people, packed tightly together, were sitting on metal bunks, one above the other. Winston and his mother and father found themselves a place on the floor, and near them an old man and an old woman were sitting side by side on a bunk. The old man had on a decent dark suit and a black cloth cap pushed back from very white hair; his face was scarlet and his eyes were blue and full of tears. He reeked of gin. It seemed to breathe out of his skin in place of sweat, and one could have fancied that the tears welling from his eyes were pure gin. But though slightly drunk he was also suffering under some grief that was genuine and unbearable. In his childish way Winston grasped that some terrible thing, something that was beyond forgiveness and could never be remedied, had just happened. It also seemed to him that he knew what it was. Someone whom the old man loved, a little granddaughter perhaps, had been killed. Every few minutes the old man kept repeating:

14   "We didn't ought to 'ave trusted 'em. I said so, Ma, didn't I? That's what come of trusting 'em. I said so all along. We didn't ought to 'ave trusted the buggers."

15   But which buggers they didn't ought to have trusted Winston could not now remember.

16   Since about that time, war had been literally continuous, though strictly speaking it had not always been the same war. For several months during his childhood there had been confused street fighting in London itself, some of which he remembered vividly. But to trace out the history of the whole period, to say who was fighting whom at any given moment, would have been utterly impossible, since no written record, and no spoken word, ever made mention of any other alignment than the existing one. At this moment, for example, in 1984 (if it was 1984), Oceania was at war with Eurasia and in alliance with Eastasia. In no public or private utterance was it ever admitted that the three powers had at any time been grouped along different lines. Actually, as Winston well knew, it was only four years since Oceania had been at war with Eastasia and in alliance with Eurasia. But that was merely a piece of furtive knowledge which he happened to possess because his memory was not satisfactorily under control. Officially the change of partners had never happened. Oceania was at war with Eurasia: therefore Oceania had always been at war with Eurasia. The enemy of the moment always represented absolute evil, and it followed that any past or future agreement with him was impossible.

17   The frightening thing, he reflected for the ten thousandth time as he forced his shoulders painfully backward (with hands on hips, they were gyrating their bodies from the waist, an exercise that was supposed to be good for the back muscles)—the frightening thing was that it might all be true. If the Party could thrust its hand into the past and say of this or that event, *it never happened*—that, surely, was more terrifying than mere torture and death.

18   The Party said that Oceania had never been in alliance with Eurasia. He, Winston Smith, knew that Oceania had been in alliance with Eurasia as short a time as four years ago. But where did that knowledge exist? Only in his own consciousness, which in any case must soon be annihilated. And if all others accepted the lie which

the Party imposed—if all records told the same tale—then the lie passed into history and became truth. "Who controls the past," ran the Party slogan, "controls the future: who controls the present controls the past." And yet the past, though of its nature alterable, never had been altered. Whatever was true now was true from everlasting to everlasting. It was quite simple. All that was needed was an unending series of victories over your own memory. "Reality control," they called it; in Newspeak, "doublethink."

19   "Stand easy!" barked the instructress, a little more genially.

20   Winston sank his arms to his sides and slowly refilled his lungs with air. His mind slid away into the labyrinthine world of doublethink. To know and not to know, to be conscious of complete truthfulness while telling carefully constructed lies, to hold simultaneously two opinions which canceled out, knowing them to be contradictory and believing in both of them, to use logic against logic, to repudiate morality while laying claim to it, to believe that democracy was impossible and that the Party was the guardian of democracy, to forget whatever it was necessary to forget, then to draw it back into memory again at the moment when it was needed, and then promptly to forget it again, and above all, to apply the same process to the process itself—that was the ultimate subtlety: consciously to induce unconsciousness, and then, once again, to become unconscious of the act of hypnosis you had just performed. Even to understand the word "doublethink" involved the use of doublethink.

21   The instructress had called them to attention again. "And now let's see which of us can touch our toes!" she said enthusiastically. "Right over from the hips, please, comrades. One–two! One–two! . . . "

22   Winston loathed this exercise, which sent shooting pains all the way from his heels to his buttocks and often ended by bringing on another coughing fit. The half-pleasant quality went out of his meditations. The past, he reflected, had not merely been altered, it had been actually destroyed. For how could you establish even the most obvious fact when there existed no record outside your own memory? He tried to remember in what year he had first heard mention of Big Brother. He thought it must have been at some time in the Sixties, but it was impossible to be certain. In the Party histories, of course, Big Brother figured as the leader and guardian of the Revolution since its very earliest days. His exploits had been gradually pushed backwards in time until already they extended into the fabulous world of the Forties and the Thirties, when the capitalists in their strange cylindrical hats still rode through the streets of London in great gleaming motor cars or horse carriages with glass sides. There was no knowing how much of this legend was true and how much invented. Winston could not even remember at what date the Party itself had come into existence. He did not believe he had ever heard the word Ingsoc before 1960, but it was possible that in its Oldspeak form—"English Socialism," that is to say—it had been current earlier. Everything melted into mist. Sometimes, indeed, you could put your finger on a definite lie. It was not true, for example, as was claimed in Party history books, that the Party had invented airplanes. He remembered airplanes since his earliest childhood. But you could prove nothing. There was never any evidence. Just

once in his whole life he had held in his hands unmistakable documentary proof of the falsification of a historical fact. And on that occasion—

23   "Smith!" screamed the shrewish voice from the telescreen. "6079 Smith W! Yes, *you!* Bend lower, please! You can do better than that. You're not trying. Lower, please! *That's* better, comrade. Now stand at ease, the whole squad, and watch me."

24   A sudden hot sweat had broken out all over Winston's body. His face remained completely inscrutable. Never show dismay! Never show resentment! A single flicker of the eyes could give you away. He stood watching while the instructress raised her arms above her head and—one could not say gracefully, but with remarkable neatness and efficiency—bent over and tucked the first joint of her fingers under her toes.

25   "*There,* comrades! *That's* how I want to see you doing it. Watch me again. I'm thirty-nine and I've had four children. Now look." She bent over again. "You see *my* knees aren't bent. You can all do it if you want to," she added as she straightened herself up. "Anyone under forty-five is perfectly capable of touching his toes. We don't all have the privilege of fighting in the front line, but at least we can all keep fit. Remember our boys on the Malabar front! And the sailors in the Floating Fortresses! Just think what *they* have to put up with. Now try again. That's better, comrade, that's *much* better," she added encouragingly as Winston, with a violent lunge, succeeded in touching his toes with knees unbent, for the first time in several years.

QUESTIONS FOR DISCUSSION

1. What is the significance of Winston's dream about his last memory of his family? What does the "darkening water" through which they look up to him represent?

2. At the time the story takes place, why is death no longer "tragic and sorrowful"?

3. Why does Winston admire the "gesture" of the girl in his fantasy? What does the gesture suggest?

4. Why does Winston wake up with the word "Shakespeare" on his lips? Why would there be no place for writers like Shakespeare in a world such as the one introduced in the story?

5. What is the function of the telescreen? Compare and contrast its function and impact to that of television in our society.

6. Why is it so difficult for Winston to "think his way back" into the world of his childhood?

CONNECTION

Compare the media-saturated, helpless, captive yet uneasy mentality of the citizens portrayed in "Winston Was Dreaming" with the American consumers in Stephen Dunn's "Middle Class Poem."

IDEAS FOR WRITING

1. Develop your journal entry about being controlled by an institution into an essay. Emphasize the nature of the control and the impact this had on you. Did you rebel or acquiesce to the control?
2. Write an essay in which you explain "doublethink." Refer to the way Winston thinks and uses language and provide examples in our own world of political "doublethink." Consider also how history has been rewritten in many countries to accommodate shifting ideologies.

Martin Luther King, Jr.

I Have a Dream

Martin Luther King, Jr. (1928–1968), who came from a family of ministers, graduated from Morehouse University and received a Ph.D. in theology from Boston University. After graduation, King became a pastor and founded the Southern Christian Leadership Conference, developing the concept, derived from the teachings of Thoreau and Gandhi, of nonviolent civil disobedience resistance to obtain civil rights and an end to segregation. King won the Nobel Peace Prize in 1964. Although his life ended in a tragic assassination, King wrote many speeches and essays on race and civil rights, which are collected in books such as I Have A Dream: Writings and Speeches That Changed the World *(1992) and* The Papers of Martin Luther King, Jr. *(1992). "I Have a Dream," King's most famous speech, was originally delivered in 1963 in front of the Lincoln Memorial in Washington, D.C., before a crowd estimated at 300,000. Notice how King uses powerful language, images, and comparisons to move his massive, diverse audience and to express his idealistic dream for America's future.*

JOURNAL

Write about a time when you found yourself moved by a persuasive public speaker, either in a speech you heard live or saw on television. What skills of rhetoric and/or delivery do you remember as contributing to your strong feelings in response to this speech? If you saw it on television, what elements of video editing and soundtrack (music, applause, etc.) contributed to your response?

1   I am happy to join with you today in what will go down in history as the greatest demonstration for freedom in the history of our nation.

2   Five score years ago, a great American, in whose symbolic shadow we stand today, signed the Emancipation Proclamation. This momentous decree came as a great beacon light of hope to millions of Negro slaves who had been seared in the flames

of withering injustice. It came as a joyous daybreak to end the long night of their captivity.

3   But one hundred years later, the Negro still is not free; one hundred years later, the life of the Negro is still sadly crippled by the manacles of segregation and the chains of discrimination; one hundred years later, the Negro lives on a lonely island of poverty in the midst of a vast ocean of material prosperity; one hundred years later, the Negro is still languished in the corners of American society and finds himself in exile in his own land.

4   So we've come here today to dramatize a shameful condition. In a sense we've come to our nation's capital to cash a check. When the architects of our republic wrote the magnificent words of the Constitution and the Declaration of Independence, they were signing a promissory note to which every American was to fall heir. This note was the promise that all men, yes, black men as well as white men, would be guaranteed the unalienable rights of life, liberty, and the pursuit of happiness.

5   It is obvious today that America has defaulted on this promissory note in so far as her citizens of color are concerned. Instead of honoring this sacred obligation, America has given the Negro people a bad check, a check which has come back marked "insufficient funds." But we refuse to believe that the bank of justice is bankrupt. We refuse to believe that there are insufficient funds in the great vaults of opportunity of this nation. And so we've come to cash this check, a check that will give us upon demand the riches of freedom and the security of justice.

6   We have also come to this hallowed spot to remind America of the fierce urgency of now. This is no time to engage in the luxury of cooling off or to take the tranquilizing drug of gradualism. Now is the time to make real the promises of democracy; now is the time to rise from the dark and desolate valley of segregation to the sunlit path of racial justice; now is the time to lift our nation from the quicksands of racial injustice to the solid rock of brotherhood; now is the time to make justice a reality for all of God's children. It would be fatal for the nation to overlook the urgency of the moment. This sweltering summer of the Negro's legitimate discontent will not pass until there is an invigorating autumn of freedom and equality.

7   Nineteen sixty-three is not an end, but a beginning. And those who hope that the Negro needed to blow off steam and will now be content, will have a rude awakening if the nation returns to business as usual. There will be neither rest nor tranquility in America until the Negro is granted his citizenship rights. The whirlwinds of revolt will continue to shake the foundations of our nation until the bright day of justice emerges.

8   But there is something that I must say to my people, who stand on the worn threshold which leads into the palace of justice. In the process of gaining our rightful place, we must not be guilty of wrongful deeds. Let us not seek to satisfy our thirst for freedom by drinking from the cup of bitterness and hatred. We must forever conduct our struggle on the high plain of dignity and discipline. We must not allow our creative protests to degenerate into physical violence. Again and again we must rise to

the majestic heights of meeting physical force with soul force. The marvelous new militancy, which has engulfed the Negro community, must not lead us to a distrust of all white people. For many of our white brothers, as evidenced by their presence here today, have come to realize that their destiny is tied up with our destiny. And they have come to realize that their freedom is inextricably bound to our freedom. We cannot walk alone. And as we walk, we must make the pledge that we shall always march ahead. We cannot turn back.

9   There are those who are asking the devotees of Civil Rights, "When will you be satisfied?" We can never be satisfied as long as the Negro is the victim of the unspeakable horrors of police brutality; we can never be satisfied as long as our bodies, heavy with the fatigue of travel, cannot gain lodging in the motels of the highways and the hotels of the cities; we cannot be satisfied as long as the Negro's basic mobility is from a smaller ghetto to a larger one; we can never be satisfied as long as our children are stripped of their selfhood and robbed of their dignity by signs stating "For Whites Only"; we cannot be satisfied as long as the Negro in Mississippi cannot vote and a Negro in New York believes he has nothing for which to vote. No! No, we are not satisfied, and we will not be satisfied until "justice rolls down like waters and righteousness like a mighty stream."

10   I am not unmindful that some of you have come here out of great trials and tribulations. Some of you have come fresh from narrow jail cells. Some of you have come from areas where your quest for freedom left you battered by the storms of persecution and staggered by the winds of police brutality. You have been the veterans of creative suffering. Continue to work with the faith that unearned suffering is redemptive. Go back to Mississippi. Go back to Alabama. Go back to South Carolina. Go back to Georgia. Go back to Louisiana. Go back to the slums and ghettos of our Northern cities, knowing that somehow this situation can and will be changed. Let us not wallow in the valley of despair.

11   I say to you today, my friends, so even though we face the difficulties of today and tomorrow, I stillhave a dream. It is a dream deeply rooted in the American dream. I have a dream that one day this nation will rise up and live out the true meaning of its creed, "We hold these truths to be self-evident, that all men are created equal." I have a dream that one day on the red hills of Georgia, sons of former slaves and the sons of former slaves owners will be able to sit down together at the table of brotherhood. I have a dream that one day even the state of Mississippi, a state sweltering with the heat of injustice, sweltering with the heat of oppression, will be transformed into an oasis of freedom and justice. I have a dream that my four little children will one day live in a nation where they will not be judged by the color of their skin, but by the content of their character.

12   I HAVE A DREAM TODAY!

13   I have a dream that one day down in Alabama—with its vicious racists, with its Governor having his lips dripping with the words of interposition and nullifcation—one day right there in Alabama, little black boys and black girls will be able to join hands with little white boys and white girls as sisters and brothers.

14   I HAVE A DREAM TODAY!

15   I have a dream today that one day every valley shall be exalted, and every hill and mountain shall be made low. The rough places will be plain and the crooked places will be made straight, "and the glory of the Lord shall be revealed, and all flesh shall see it together."

16   This is our hope. This is the faith that I go back to the South with. With this faith we will be able to hew out of the mountain of despair a stone of hope. With this faith we will be able to transform the jangling discords of our nation into a beautiful symphony of brother-hood. With this faith we will be able to work together, to pray together, to struggle together, to go to jail together, to stand up for freedom together, knowing that we will be free one day. And this will be the day. This will be the day when all of God's children will be able to sing with new meaning, "My country 'tis of thee, sweet land of liberty, of thee I sing. Land where my fathers died, land of the pilgrims' pride, from every mountainside, let freedom ring." And if America is to be a great nation, this must become true.

17   So let freedom ring from the prodigious hilltops of New Hampshire; let freedom ring from the mighty mountains of New York; let freedom ring from the heightening Alleghenies of Pennsylvania; let freedom ring from the snow-capped Rockies of Colorado; let freedom ring from the curvaceous slopes of California. But not only that. Let freedom ring from Stone Mountain of Georgia; let freedom ring from Lookout Mountain of Tennessee; let freedom ring from every hill and mole hill of Mississippi. "From every mountainside, let freedom ring." And when this happens, and when we allow freedom to ring, when we let it ring from every village and every hamlet, from every state and every city, we will be able to speed up that day when all of God's children, black men and white men, Jews and Gentiles, Protestants and Catholics, will be able to join hands and sing in the words of the old Negro spiritual: "Free at last. Free at last. Thank God Almighty, we are free at last."

QUESTIONS FOR DISCUSSION

1. What is the "dream" to which the title of the essay refers? What techniques or strategies does King use to define his dream? Is his definition effective? Why or why not?
2. What does King mean by his analogy of a "promissory note"? Is this an effective metaphor?
3. Who is the primary audience of King's speech, the "we" to whom he refers in paragraph 4, the "you" in paragraph 10? How does King try to appeal to the needs and concerns of this audience?
4. Who is the secondary audience for the speech, other than those to whom he refers as having "come to our nation's capital to cash a check"? What rhetorical strategies in the speech are designed to stretch its message beyond the immediate needs and expectations of the present audience and to appeal to other audiences, including those who might see the speech on television or hear it on radio?

5. What does King mean by "creative suffering" in paragraph 10? How does this expression reflect different aspects of his vision of nonviolent resistance?
6. How does King use repetition of images, phrases, and entire sentences to help convey his dream to his audience? Provide examples.

CONNECTION

Compare King's dream of wanting people to be judged by the "content of their character" rather than skin color with Shelby Steele's views in "Being Black and Feeling Blue" (Chapter 7). Note that Steele takes King's words for the title of the book that "Being Black" originally appeared in. How do you think that King might react to Steele's observations about the behavior of today's young African-Americans, the beneficiaries of the Civil Rights movement and Affirmative Action? Would he agree with Steele's critique of the "anti-self"?

IDEAS FOR WRITING

1. Write a speech in the form of an essay and/or multi-media presentation that discusses a dream that you have for your society. Express your dream in emotional and persuasive language and imagery (including, if you desire, a description of slides, audio clips, or other multi-media features) in order to appeal to a specific audience that you understand well. Indicate your intended audience.
2. Based on your understanding and reading about the current state of civil rights in America, write an essay in which you reflect on whether King, if he were alive today, would feel that his dream for African-Americans had "come true." What aspects of his dream might King feel still remain to be accomplished?

Sissela Bok

Aggression: The Impact of Media Violence

Sissela Bok has made a major contribution to the contemporary debate over values and ethical issues in society. Born in Sweden to liberal economists and peace activists Alva and Gunnar Myrdal, Bok was influenced by her parents' devotion to public causes, and in 1992, she wrote a biography of her mother, Alva Myrdal: A Daughter's Memoir. Bok left Sweden at an early age to study abroad; she received her Ph.D. in philosophy from Harvard University in 1970. She has been a Professor of Philosophy at Brandeis University and is currently a Distinguished Fellow at the Harvard Center for Population and Development Studies. Bok's writings on ethical issues include Lying: Moral Choice in Public and Private Life *(1978),* Secrets: On the Ethics of Concealment and Revelation *(1983),* A Strategy for Peace: Human*

Values and the Threat of War *(1989)*, Common Values *(1995)*, *and, most re-cently*, Mayhem: Violence as Public Entertainment *(1998)*, *which contains the following essay on the relationship between media and aggression.*

JOURNAL

Do you believe that media violence can cause a significant amount of actual vio-lence in children? How could you prove your belief to be a fact?

1   Even if media violence were linked to no other debilitating effects, it would re-main at the center of public debate so long as the widespread belief persists that it glamorizes aggressive conduct, removes inhibitions toward such conduct, arouses viewers, and invites imitation. It is only natural that the links of media vi-olence to aggression should be of special concern to families and communities. Whereas increased fear, desensitization, and appetite primarily affect the viewers themselves, aggression directly injures others and represents a more clear-cut vio-lation of standards of behavior. From the point of view of public policy, therefore, curbing aggression, has priority over alleviating subtler psychological and moral damage.

2   Public conern about a possible link between media violence and societal violence has further intensified in the past decade, as violent crime reached a peak in the early 1990s, yet has shown no sign of downturn, even after crime rates began drop-ping in 1992. Media coverage of violence, far from declining, has escalated since then, devoting ever more attention to celebrity homicides and copycat crimes. The latter, explicitly modeled on videos or films and sometimes carried out with meticu-lous fidelity to detail, are never more relentlessly covered in the media than when they are committed by children and adolescents. Undocumented claims that violent copycat crimes are mounting in number contribute further to the ominous sense of threat that these crimes generate. Their dramatic nature drains away the public's at-tention from other, more mundane forms of aggression that are much more com-monplace, and from. . . other. . . harmful effects of media violence.

3   Media analyst Ken Auletta reports that, in 1992, a mother in France sued the head of a state TV channel that carried the American series *MacGyver*, claiming that her son was accidentally injured as a result of having copied MacGyver's recipe for making a bomb. At the time, Auletta predicted that similar lawsuits were bound to become a weapon against media violence in America's litigious culture. By 1996, novelist John Grisham had sparked a debate about director Oliver Stone's film *Natural Born Killers*, which is reputedly linked to more copycat assaults and murders than any other movie to date. Grisham wrote in protest against the film after learning that a friend of his, Bill Savage, had been killed by nineteen-year-old Sarah Edmondson and her boyfriend Benjamin Darras, eighteen: after repeated viewings of Stone's film on video, the two had gone on a killing spree with the film's murderous, gleeful heroes expressly in mind. Characterizing the film as "a horrific movie that glamorized casual mayhem and blood-lust," Grisham proposed legal action:

Think of a film as a product, something created and brought to market, not too dissimilar from breast implants. Though the law has yet to declare movies to be products, it is only a small step away. If something goes wrong with the product, either by design or defect, and injury ensues, then its makers are held responsible. . . . It will take only one large verdict against the like of Oliver Stone, and his production company, and perhaps the screenwriter, and the studio itself, and then the party will be over. The verdict will come from the heartland, far away from Southern California, in some small courtroom with no cameras. A jury will finally say enough is enough; that the demons placed in Sarah Edmondson's mind were not solely of her own making.

4   As a producer of books made into lucrative movies—themselves hardly devoid of violence—and as a veteran of contract negotiations within the entertainment industry, Grisham may have become accustomed to thinking of films in industry terms as "products." As a seasoned courtroom lawyer, he may have found the analogy between such products and breast implants useful for invoking product liability to pin personal responsibility on movie producers and directors for the lethal consequences that their work might help unleash.

5   Oliver Stone retorted that Grisham was drawing "upon the superstition about the magical power of pictures to conjure up the undead spectre of censorship." In dismissing concerns about the "magical power of pictures" as merely superstitious, Stone sidestepped the larger question of responsibility fully as much as Grisham had sidestepped that of causation when he attributed liability to filmmakers for anything that "goes wrong" with their products so that "injury ensues."

6   Because aggression is the most prominent effect associated with media violence in the public's mind, it is natural that it should also remain the primary focus of scholars in the field. The "aggressor effect" has been studied both to identify the short-term, immediate impact on viewers after exposure to TV violence, and the long-term influences. . . . There is near-unanimity by now among investigators that exposure to media violence contributes to lowering barriers to aggression among some viewers. This lowering of barriers may be assisted by the failure of empathy that comes with growing desensitization, and intensified to the extent that viewers develop an appetite for violence—something that may lead to still greater desire for violent programs and, in turn, even greater desensitization.

7   When it comes to viewing violent pornography, levels of aggression toward women have been shown to go up among male subjects who view sexualized violence against women. "In explicit depictions of sexual violence," a report by the American Psychological Association's Commission on Youth and Violence concludes after surveying available research data, "it is the message about violence more than the sexual nature of the materials that appears to affect the attitudes of adolescents about rape and violence toward women." Psychologist Edward Donnerstein and colleagues have shown that if investigators tell subjects that aggression is legitimate, then show them violent pornography, their aggression toward women increases. In slasher films, the speed and ease with which "one's feelings can be transformed from sensuality into viciousness may surprise even those quite conversant with the links between sexual and violent urges."

8   Viewers who become accustomed to seeing violence as an acceptable, common, attractive way of dealing with problems find it easier to identify with aggressors and to suppress any sense of pity or respect for victims of violence. Media violence has been found to have stronger effects of this kind when carried out by heroic, impressive, or otherwise exciting figures, especially when they are shown as invulnerable and are rewarded or not punished for what they do. The same is true when the violence is shown as justifiable, when viewers identify with the aggressors rather than with their victims, when violence is routinely resorted to, and when the programs have links to how viewers perceive their own environment.

9   While the consensus that such influences exist grows among investigators as research accumulates, there is no consensus whatsoever about the size of the correlations involved. Most investigators agree that it will always be difficult to disentangle the precise effects of exposure to media violence from the many other factors contributing to societal violence. No reputable scholar accepts the view expressed by 21 percent of the American public in 1995, blaming television more than any other factor for teenage violence. Such tentative estimates as have been made suggest that the media account for between 5 and 15 percent of societal violence. Even these estimates are rarely specific enough to indicate whether what is at issue is all violent crime, or such crimes along with bullying and aggression more generally.

10   One frequently cited investigator proposes a dramatically higher and more specific estimate than others. Psychiatrist Brandon S. Centerwall has concluded from large-scale epidemiological studies of "white homicide" in the United States, Canada, and South Africa in the period from 1945 to 1974, that it escalated in these societies within ten to fifteen years of the introduction of television, and that one can therefore deduce that television has brought a doubling of violent societal crime:

> Of course, there are many factors other than television that influence the amount of violent crime. Every violent act is the result of a variety of forces coming together—poverty, crime, alcohol and drug abuse, stress—of which childhood TV exposure is just one. Nevertheless, the evidence indicates that if hypothetically, television technology had never been developed, there would today be 10,000 fewer homicides each year in the United States, 70,000 fewer rapes, and 700,000 fewer injurious assaults. Violent crime would be half of what it now is.

11   Centerwall's study, published in 1989, includes controls for such variables as firearm possession and economic growth. But his conclusions have been criticized for not taking into account other factors, such as population changes during the time period studied, that might also play a role in changing crime rates. Shifts in policy and length of prison terms clearly affect these levels as well. By now, the decline in levels of violent crime in the United States since Centerwall's study was conducted, even though television viewing did not decline ten to fifteen years before, does not square with his extrapolations. As for "white homicide" in South Africa under apartheid, each year brings more severe challenges to official statistics from that period.

12   Even the lower estimates, however, of around 5 to 10 percent of violence as correlated with television exposure, point to substantial numbers of violent crimes

in a population as large as America's. But if such estimates are to be used in discussions of policy decisions, more research will be needed to distinguish between the effects of television in general and those of particular types of violent programming, and to indicate specifically what sorts of images increase the aggressor effect and by what means; and throughout to be clearer about the nature of the aggressive acts studied.

13   Media representatives naturally request proof of such effects before they are asked to undertake substantial changes in programming. In considering possible remedies for a problem, inquiring into the reasons for claims about risks is entirely appropriate. It is clearly valid to scrutinize the research designs, sampling methods, and possible biases of studies supporting such claims, and to ask about the reasoning leading from particular research findings to conclusions. But to ask for some demonstrable pinpointing of just when and how exposure to media violence affects levels of aggression sets a dangerously high threshold for establishing risk factors.

14   We may never be able to trace, retrospectively, the specific set of television programs that contributed to a particular person's aggressive conduct. The same is true when it comes to the links between tobacco smoking and cancer, between drunk driving and automobile accidents, and many other risk factors presenting public health hazards. Only recently have scientists identified the specific channels through which tobacco generates its carcinogenic effects. Both precise causative mechanisms and documented occurrences in individuals remain elusive. Too often, media representatives formulate their requests in what appear to be strictly polemical terms, raising dismissive questions familiar from debates over the effects of tobacco: "How can anyone definitively pinpoint the link between media violence and acts of real-life violence? If not, how can we know if exposure to media violence constitutes a risk factor in the first place?"

15   Yet the difficulty in carrying out such pinpointing has not stood in the way of discussing and promoting efforts to curtail cigarette smoking and drunk driving. It is not clear, therefore, why a similar difficulty should block such efforts when it comes to media violence. The perspective of "probabilistic causation". . . is crucial to public debate about the risk factors in media violence. The television industry has already been persuaded to curtail the glamorization of smoking and drunk driving on its programs, despite the lack of conclusive documentation of the correlation between TV viewing and higher incidence of such conduct. Why should the industry not take analogous precautions with respect to violent programming?

16   Americans have special reasons to inquire into the causes of societal violence. While we are in no sense uniquely violent, we need to ask about all possible reasons why our levels of violent crime are higher than in all other stable industrialized democracies. Our homicide rate would be higher still if we did not imprison more of our citizens than any society in the world, and if emergency medical care had not improvedd so greatly in recent decades that a larger proportion of shooting victims survive than in the past. Even so, we have seen an unprecedented rise not only in child and adolescent violence, but in levels of rape, child abuse, domestic violence, and every other form of assault.

17   Although America's homicide rate has declined in the 1990s, the rates for suicide, rape, and murder involving children and adolescents in many regions have too rarely followed suit. For Americans aged fifteen to thirty-five years, homicide is the second leading cause of death, and for young African Americans, fifteen to twenty-four years, it is *the* leading cause of death. In the decade following the mid-1980s, the rate of murder committed by teenagers fourteen to seventeen more than doubled. The rates of injury suffered by small children are skyrocketing, with the number of seriously injured children nearly quadrupling from 1986 to 1993; and a proportion of these injuries are inflicted by children upon one another. Even homicides by children, once next to unknown, have escalated in recent decades.

18   America may be the only society on earth to have experienced what has been called an "epidemic of children killing children," which is ravaging some of its communities today. As in any epidemic, it is urgent to ask what it is that makes so many capable of such violence, victimizes so many others, and causes countless more to live in fear. Whatever role the media are found to play in this respect, to be sure, is but part of the problem. Obviously, not even the total elimination of media violence would wipe out the problem of violence in the United States or any other society. The same can be said for the proliferation and easy access to guns, or for poverty, drug addiction, and other risk factors. As Dr. Deborah Prothrow-Stith puts it, "It's not an either or. It's not guns or media or parents or poverty."

19   We have all witnessed the four effects that I have discussed. . . —fearfulness, numbing, appetite, and aggressive impulses—in the context of many influences apart from the media. Maturing involves learning to resist the dominion that these effects can gain over us; and to strive, instead, for greater resilience, empathy, self-control, and respect for self and others. The process of maturation and growth in these respects is never completed for any of us; but it is most easily thwarted in childhood, before it has had chance to take root. Such learning calls for nurturing and education at first; then for increasing autonomy in making personal decisions about how best to confront the realities of violence.

20   Today, the sights and sounds of violence on the screen affect this learning process from infancy on, in many homes. The television screen is the lens through which most children learn about violence. Through the magnifying power of this lens, their everyday life becomes suffused by images of shootings, family violence, gang warfare, kidnappings, and everything else that contributes to violence in our society. It shapes their experiences long before they have had the opportunity to consent to such shaping or developed the ability to cope adequately with this knowledge. The basic nurturing and protection to prevent the impairment of this ability ought to be the birthright of every child.

Questions for Discussion

1. What question does Bok believe John Grisham and Oliver Stone avoid in their debate over the impact of films on "copycat" violent crimes? Do their arguments seem reasonable to you, as she presents them here?

2. According to the research that Bok discusses, what circumstances tend to have the greatest impact on viewers' tendency to find violence acceptable?
3. According to Bok, what further research remains to be done before we can draw more definitive conclusions about the impact of such violence on actual patterns of aggression?
4. Bok points out the difficulty in making a clear-cut connection between smoking and cancer, even though we presume there is a cause. How effective is her analogy with media violence as a presumed cause of actual violence among heavy viewers? Do her conclusions here seem clear and reasonable?
5. What does Dr. Deborah Prothrow-Stith mean when she states, "It's not an either or. It's not guns or media or parents or poverty"? What conclusions does Bok suggest can be drawn from this statement about causes and solutions for the "problem" of media violence?
6. How, according to Bok, might excessive exposure to media violence thwart a child's ability to learn to resist aggression and to acquire such traits as empathy, respect, and self-control? Do you agree?

CONNECTION

Compare the way Bok tries to demonstrate a connection between TV violence and violence in the life of children with the efforts of Anthony Pratkanis and Elliot Aronson to show a relationship between viewing of violence in the media and beliefs about violence in society.

IDEAS FOR WRITING

1. Write an essay in which you consider some alternative causes for the current outbreak of youth violence. For instance, what about parental neglect and abuse, the decay of our educational system, or the violence of war?
2. If you accept Bok's argument that there is too much media violence and that this can lead to more youth aggression, how do we cut back on the media violence that young people are currently being exposed to? Write an essay in the form of a proposal for change, considering some ideas that have been suggested and that are currently being tried on a limited basis.

Jessica Hagedorn

Asian Women in Film: No Joy, No Luck

Poet, performance artist, and novelist, Jessica Hagedorn was born in the Philippines and immigrated with her mother to San Francisco. Hagedorn currently lives in New York. Influenced by popular culture and the writers of the Beat Generation, Hagedorn's work explores a wide range of characters who are estranged from the dominant culture of both

Asia and the United States and who attempt to create their own sense of cultural values. Her work includes Dangerous Music *(1975),* Danger and Beauty *(1993), the novel* Dogeater *(l990),* Charlie Chan Is Dead: An Anthology of Contemporary Asian American Fiction *(1993), and the novel* The Gangster of Love *(1996). In her essay "Asian Women in Film," (1994), Hagedorn discusses stereotypical images of Asian women in recent films.*

JOURNAL

Write about a film or television show you have seen featuring Asian women. Were these women presented realistically or in a stereotyped fashion?

Pearl of the Orient. Whore. Geisha. Concubine. Whore. Hostess. Bar Girl. Mamasan. Whore. China Doll. Tokyo Rose. Whore. Butterfly. Whore. Miss Saigon. Whore. Dragon Lady. Lotus Blossom. Gook. Whore. Yellow Peril. Whore. Bangkok Bombshell. Whore. Hospitality Girl. Whore. Comfort Woman. Whore. Savage. Whore. Sultry. Whore. Faceless. Whore. Porcelain. Whore. Demure. Whore. Virgin. Whore. Mute. Whore. Model Minority. Whore. Victim. Whore. Woman Warrior. Whore. Mail-Order Bride. Whore. Mother. Wife. Lover. Daughter. Sister.

1   As I was growing up in the Philippines in the 1950s, my fertile imagination was colonized by thoroughly American fantasies. Yellowface variations on the exotic erotic loomed larger than life on the silver screen. I was mystified and enthralled by Hollywood's skewed representations of Asian women: sleek, evil goddesses with slanted eyes and cunning ways, or smiling, sarong-clad South Seas "maidens" with undulating hips, kinky black hair, and white skin darkened by makeup. Hardly any of the "Asian" characters were played by Asians. White actors like Sidney Toler and Warner Oland played "inscrutable Oriental detective" Charlie Chan with taped eyelids and a singsong, chop suey accent. Jennifer Jones was a Eurasian doctor swept up in a doomed "interracial romance" in *Love Is a Many Splendored Thing.* In my mother's youth, white actor Luise Rainer played the central role of the Patient Chinese Wife in the 1937 film adaptation of Pearl Buck's novel *The Good Earth.* Back then, not many thought to ask why; they were all too busy being grateful to see anyone in the movies remotely like themselves.

2   Cut to 1960: *The World of Suzie Wong,* another tragic East/West affair. I am now old enough to be impressed. Sexy, sassy Suzie (played by Nancy Kwan) works out of a bar patronized by white sailors, but doesn't seem bothered by any of it. For a hardworking girl turning nightly tricks to support her baby, she manages to parade an astonishing wardrobe in damn near every scene, down to matching handbags and shoes. The sailors are also strictly Hollywood, sanitized and not too menacing. Suzie and all the other prostitutes in this movie are cute, giggling, dancing sex machines with hearts of gold. William Holden plays an earnest, rather prim, Nice Guy painter

seeking inspiration in The Other. Of course, Suzie falls madly in love with him. Typically, she tells him, "I not important," and "I'll be with you until you say— Suzie, go away." She also thinks being beaten by a man is a sign of true passion, and is terribly disappointed when Mr. Nice Guy refuses to show his true feelings.

3   Next in Kwan's short-lived but memorable career was the kitschy 1961 musical *Flower Drum Song,* which, like *Suzie Wong,* is a thoroughly American commercial product. The female roles are typical of Hollywood musicals of the times: women are basically airheads, subservient to men. Kwan's counterpart is the Good Chinese Girl, played by Miyoshi Umeki, who was better playing the Loyal Japanese Girl in that other classic Hollywood tale of forbidden love, *Sayonara.* Remember? Umeki was so loyal, she committed double suicide with actor Red Buttons. I instinctively hated *Sayonara* when I first saw it as a child; now I understand why. Contrived tragic resolutions were the only way Hollywood got past the censors in those days. With one or two exceptions, somebody in these movies always had to die to pay for breaking racial and sexual taboos.

4   Until the recent onslaught of films by both Asian and Asian American filmmakers, Asian Pacific women have generally been perceived by Hollywood with a mixture of fascination, fear, and contempt. Most Hollywood movies either trivialize or exoticize us as people of color and as women. Our intelligence is underestimated, our humanity overlooked, and our diverse cultures treated as interchangeable. If we are "good," we are childlike, submissive, silent, and eager for sex (see France Nuyen's glowing performance as Liat in the film version of *South Pacific*) or else we are tragic victim types (see *Causalities of War,* Brian De Palma's graphic 1989 drama set in Vietnam). And if we are not silent, suffering doormats, we are demonized dragon ladies—cunning, deceitful, sexual provocateurs. Give me the demonic any day— Anna May Wong as a villain slithering around in a slinky gown is at least gratifying to watch, neither servile nor passive. And she steals the show from Marlene Dietrich in Josef von Sternberg's *Shanghai Express.* From the 1920s through the '30s, Wong was our only female "star." But even she was trapped in limited roles, in what filmmaker Renee Tajima has called the dragon lady/lotus blossom dichotomy.

5   Cut to 1985: There is a scene toward the end of the terribly dishonest but weirdly compelling Michael Cimino movie *Year of the Dragon* (cowritten by Oliver Stone) that is one of my favorite twisted movie moments of all time. If you ask a lot of my friends who've seen that movie (especially if they're Asian), it's one of their favorites too. The setting is a crowded Chinatown nightclub. There are two very young and very tough Jade Cobra gang girls in a shoot-out with Mickey Rourke, in the role of a demented Polish American cop who, in spite of being Mr. Ugly in the flesh—an arrogant, misogynistic bully devoid of any charm—wins the "good" Asian American anchorwoman in the film's absurd and implausible ending. This is a movie with an actual disclaimer as its lead-in, covering its ass in advance in response to anticipated complaints about "stereotypes."

6   My pleasure in the hard-edged power of the Chinatown gang girls in *Year of the Dragon* is my small revenge, the answer to all those Suzie Wong "I want to be your

slave" female characters. The Jade Cobra girls are mere background to the white male foreground/focus of Cimino's movie. But long after the movie has faded into video-rental heaven, the Jade Cobra girls remain defiant, fabulous images in my memory, flaunting tight metallic dresses and spiky cock's-comb hairdos streaked electric red and blue.

> *Mickey Rourke looks down with world-weary pity at the unnamed Jade Cobra girl (Doreen Chan) he's just shot who lies sprawled and bleeding on the street: "You look like you're gonna die, beautiful."*
> *Jade Cobra girl: "Oh yeah? [blood gushing from her mouth] I'm proud of it."*
> *Rourke: "You are? You got anything you wanna tell me before you go, sweetheart?"*
> *Jade Cobra girl: "Yeah. [pause] Fuck you."*

7   Cut to 1993: I've been told that like many New Yorkers, I watch movies with the right side of my brain on perpetual overdrive. I admit to being grouchy and overcritical, suspicious of sentiment, and cynical. When a critic like Richard Corliss of *Time* magazine gushes about *The Joy Luck Club* being "a fourfold *Terms of Endearment*," my gut instinct is to run the other way. I resent being told how to feel. I went to see the 1993 eight-handkerchief movie version of Amy Tan's best-seller with a group that included my ten-year-old daughter. I was caught between the sincere desire to be swept up by the turbulent mother-daughter sagas and my own stubborn resistance to being so obviously manipulated by the filmmakers. With every flashback came tragedy. The music soared; the voice-overs were solemn or wistful; tears, tears, and more tears flowed onscreen. Daughters were reverent; mothers carried dark secrets.

8   I was elated by the grandness and strength of the four mothers and the luminous actors who portrayed them, but I was uneasy with the passivity of the Asian American daughters. They seemed to exist solely as receptors for their mothers' amazing life stories. It's almost as if by assimilating so easily into American society, they had lost all sense of self.

9   In spite of my resistance, my eyes watered as the desperate mother played by Kieu Chinh was forced to abandon her twin baby girls on a country road in war-torn China. (Kieu Chinh resembles my own mother and her twin sister, who suffered through the brutal Japanese occupation of the Philippines.) So far in this movie, an infant son had been deliberately drowned, a mother played by the gravely beautiful France Nuyen had gone catatonic with grief, a concubine had cut her flesh open to save her dying mother, an insecure daughter had been oppressed by her boorish Asian American husband, another insecure daughter had been left by her white husband, and so on. . . . The overall effect was numbing as far as I'm concerned, but a man sitting two rows in front of us broke down sobbing. A Chinese Philipino writer even more grouchy than me later complained, "Must ethnicity only be equated with suffering?"

10   Because change has been slow, *The Joy Luck Club* carries a lot of cultural baggage. It is a big-budget story about Chinese American women, directed by a Chinese American man, cowritten and coproduced by Chinese American women. That's a lot to be thankful for. And its box office success proves that an immigrant narrative told from female perspectives can have mass appeal. But my cynical side tells me

that its success might mean only one thing in Hollywood: more weepy epics about Asian American mother-daughter relationships will be planned.

11   That the film finally got made was significant. By Hollywood standards (think white male; think money, money, money), a movie about Asian Americans even when adapted from a best-seller was a risky proposition. When I asked a producer I know about the film's rumored delays, he simply said, "It's still an *Asian* movie," surprised I had even asked. Equally interesting was director Wayne Wang's initial reluctance to be involved in the project; he told the New York *Times*, "I didn't want to do another Chinese movie."

12   Maybe he shouldn't have worried so much. After all, according to the media, the nineties are the decade of "Pacific Overtures" and East Asian chic. Madonna, the pop queen of shameless appropriation, cultivated Japanese high-tech style with her music video, "Rain," while Janet Jackson faked kitschy orientalia in hers, titled "If." Critical attention was paid to movies from China, Japan, and Vietnam. But that didn't mean an honest appraisal of women's lives. Even on the art house circuit, filmmakers who should know better took the easy way out. Takehiro Nakajima's 1992 film *Okoge* presents one of the more original film roles for women in recent years. In Japanese, "okoge" means the crust of rice that sticks to the bottom of the rice pot; in pejorative slang, it means fag hag. The way "okoge" is used the film seems a reappropriation of the term: the portrait Nakajima creates of Sayoko, the so-called fag hag, is clearly an affectionate one. Sayoko is a quirky, self-assured woman in contemporary Tokyo who does voice-overs for cartoons, has a thing for Frida Kahlo paintings, and is drawn to a gentle young gay man named Goh. But the other women's roles are disappointing, stereotypical "hysterical females" and the movie itself turns conventional halfway through. Sayoko sacrifices herself to a macho brute Goh desires, who rapes her as images of Frida Kahlo paintings and her beloved Goh rising from the ocean flash before her. She gives birth to a baby boy and endures a terrible life of poverty with the abusive rapist. This sudden change from spunky survivor to helpless victimized woman is baffling. Whatever happened to her job? Or that arty little apartment of hers? Didn't her Frieda Kahlo obsession teach her anything?

13   Then there was Tiana Thi Thanh Nga's *From Hollywood to Hanoi*, a self-serving but fascinating documentary. Born in Vietnam to a privileged family that included an uncle who was defense minister in the Thieu government and an idolized father who served as press minister, Nga (a.k.a. Tiana) spent her adolescence in California. A former actor in martial arts movies and fitness teacher ("Karaticize with Tiana"), the vivacious Tiana decided to make a record of her journey back to Vietnam.

14   *From Hollywood to Hanoi* is at times unintentionally very funny. Tiana includes a quick scene of herself dancing with a white man at the Metropole hotel in Hanoi, and breathlessly announces: "That's me doing the tango with Oliver Stone!" Then she listens sympathetically to a horrifying account of the My Lai massacre by one of its few female survivors. In another scene, Tiana cheerfully addresses a food vendor on the streets of Hanoi: "Your hairdo is so pretty." The unimpressed, poker-faced woman gives a brusque, deadpan reply: "You want to eat, or what?" Sometimes it is hard to tell the difference between Tiana Thi Thanh Nga and her Hollywood persona: the real

Tiana still seems to be playing one of her B-movie roles, which are mainly fun because they're fantasy. The time was certainly right to explore postwar Vietnam from a Vietnamese woman's perspective; it's too bad this film was done by a Valley Girl.

15   1993 also brought Tran Anh Hung's *The Scent of Green Papaya*, a different kind of Vietnamese memento—this is a look back at the peaceful, lush country of the director's childhood memories. The film opens in Saigon, in 1951. A willowy ten-year-old girl named Mui comes to work for a troubled family headed by a melancholy musician and his kind, stoic wife. The men of this bourgeois household are idle, pampered types who take naps while the women do all the work. Mui is a male fantasy: she is a devoted servant, enduring acts of cruel mischief with patience and dignity; as an adult, she barely speaks. She scrubs floors, shines shoes, and cooks with loving care and never a complaint. When she is sent off to work for another wealthy musician, she ends up being impregnated by him. The movie ends as the camera closes in on Mui's contented face. Languid and precious, *The Scent of Green Papaya* is visually haunting, but it suffers from the director's colonial fantasy of women as docile, domestic creatures. Steeped in highbrow nostalgia, it's the arty Vietnamese version of *My Fair Lady* with the wealthy musician as Professor Higgins, teaching Mui to read and write.

16   And then there is Ang Lee's tepid 1993 hit, *The Wedding* Banquet—a clever culture-clash farce in which traditional Chinese values collide with contemporary American sexual mores. The somewhat formulaic plot goes like this: Wai-Tung, a yuppie landlord, lives with his white lover, Simon, in a chic Manhattan brownstone. Wai-Tung is an only child and his aging parents in Taiwan long for a grandchild to continue the family legacy. Enter Wei-Wei, an artist who lives in a grungy loft owned by Wai-Tung. She slugs tequila straight from the bottle as she paints and flirts boldly with her young, uptight landlord, who brushes her off. "It's my fate. I am always attracted to handsome gay men," she mutters. After this setup, the movie goes downhill, all edges blurred in a cozy nest of happy endings. In a refrain of Sayoko's plight in *Okoge*, a pregnant, suddenly complacent Wei-Wei gives in to family pressures—and never gets her life back.

"It takes a man to know what it is to be a real woman."
                                              —Song Liling in *M. Butterfly*

17 Ironically, two gender-bending films in which men play men playing women reveal more about the mythology of the prized Asian woman and the superficial trappings of gender than most movies that star real women. The slow-moving M. *Butterfly* presents the ultimate object of Western male desire as the spy/opera diva Song Liling, a Suzie Wong/Lotus Blossom played by actor John Lone with a five o'clock shadow and bobbing Adam's apple. The best and most profound of these forays into cross-dressing is the spectacular melodrama *Farewell My Concubine*, directed by Chen Kaige. Banned in China, *Farewell My Concubine* shared the prize for Best Film at the 1993 Cannes Film Festival with Jane Campion's *The Piano*. Sweeping through fifty years of tumultuous history in China, the story revolves around the lives of two male Beijing Opera stars

and the woman who marries one of them. The three characters make an unforget-table triangle, struggling over love, art, friendship, and politics against the bloody backdrop of cultural upheaval. They are as capable of casually betraying each other as they are of selfless, heroic acts. The androgynous Dieyi, doomed to play the same female role of concubine over and over again, is portrayed with great vulnerability, wit, and grace by male Hong Kong pop star Leslie Cheung. Dieyi competes with the prostitute Juxian (Gong Li) for the love of his childhood protector and fellow opera star, Duan Xiaolou (Zhang Fengyi).

18   Cheung's highly stylized performance as the classic concubine-ready-to-die-for-love in the opera within the movie is all about female artifice. His sidelong glances, restrained passion, languid stance, small steps, and delicate, refined gestures say everything about what is considered desirable in Asian women—and are the an-tithesis of the feisty, outspoken woman played by Gong Li. The characters of Dieyi and Juxian both see suffering as part and parcel of love and life. Juxian matter-of-factly says to Duan Xiaolou before he agrees to marry her: "I'm used to hardship. If you take me in, I'll wait on you hand and foot. If you tire of me, I'll. . . kill myself. No big deal." It's an echo of Suzie Wong's servility, but the context is new. Even with her back to the wall, Juxian is not helpless or whiny. She attempts to manipu-late a man while admitting to the harsh reality that is her life.

19   Dieyi and Juxian are the two sides of the truth of women's lives in most Asian countries. Juxian in particular—wife and ex-prostitute—could be seen as a thankless and stereotypical role. But like the characters Gong Li has played in Chinese direc-tor Zhang Yimou's films, *Reg Sorghum*, *Raise the Red Lantern*, and especially *The Story of Qiu Ju*, Juxian is tough, obstinate, sensual, clever, oafish, beautiful, infuriating, cowardly, heroic, and banal. Above all, she is resilient. Gong Li is one of the few Asian Pacific actors whose roles have been drawn with intelligence, honesty, and depth. Nevertheless, the characters she plays are limited by the possibilities that ex-ist for real women in China.

20   "Let's face it. Women still doesn't mean shit in China," my friend Meeling re-minds me. What she says so bluntly about her culture rings painfully true, but in less obvious fashion for me. In the Philippines, infant girls aren't drowned, nor were their feet bound to make them more desirable. But sons were and are cherished. To this day, men of the bourgeois class are coddled and prized, much like the spoiled men of the elite household in *The Scent of Green Papaya*. We do not have a geisha tradition like Japan, but physical beauty is overtreasured. Our daughters are pro-tected virgins or primed as potential beauty queens. And many of us have bought into the image of the white man as our handsome savior: G. I. Joe.

21   BUZZ magazine recently featured an article entitled "Asian Women/L.A. Men," a report on a popular hangout that caters to white men's fantasies of nubile Thai women. The lines between movies and real life are blurred. Male screenwriters and cinematographers flock to this bar-restaurant, where the waitresses are eager to "au-dition" for roles. Many of these men have been to Bangkok while working on film crews for Vietnam War movies. They've come back to L.A., but for them, the movie never ends. In this particular fantasy the boys play G.I. Joe on a rescue mission in

the urban jungle, saving the whore from herself. "A scene has developed here, a kind of R-rated *Cheers*," author Alan Rifkin writes. "The waitresses audition for sitcoms. The customers date the waitresses or just keep score."

22   Colonization of the imagination is a two-way street. And being enshrined on a pedestal as someone's Pearl of the Orient fantasy doesn't seem so demeaning, at first; who wouldn't want to be worshiped? Perhaps that's why Asian women are the ultimate wet dream in most Hollywood movies; it's no secret how well we've been taught to play the role, to take care of our men. In Hollywood vehicles, we are objects of desire or derision; we exist to provide sex, color, and texture in what is essentially a white man's world. It is akin to what Toni Morrison calls "the Africanist presence" in literature. She writes: "Just as entertainers, through or by association with blackface, could render permissible topics that otherwise would have been taboo, so American writers were able to employ an imagined Africanist persona to articulate and imaginatively act out the forbidden in American culture." The same analogy could be made for the often titillating presence of Asian women in movies made by white men.

23   Movies are still the most seductive and powerful of artistic mediums, manipulating us with ease by a powerful combination of sound and image. In many ways, as females and Asians, as audiences or performers, we have learned to settle for less—to accept the fact that we are either decorative, invisible, or one-dimensional. When there are characters who look like us represented in a movie, we have also learned to view between the lines, or to add what is missing. For many of us, this way of watching has always been a necessity. We fill in the gaps. If a female character is presented as a mute, willowy beauty, we convince ourselves she is an ancestral ghost—so smart she doesn't have to speak at all. If she is a whore with a heart of gold, we claim her as a tough feminist icon. If she is a sexless, sanitized, boring nerd, we embrace her as a role model for our daughters, rather than the tragic whore. And if she is presented as an utterly devoted saint suffering nobly in silence, we lie and say she is just like our mothers. Larger than life. Magical and insidious. A movie is never just a movie, after all.

QUESTIONS FOR DISCUSSION

1. After the opening list of stereotyped images of Asian women in film, Hagedorn reveals that she grew up in the Philippines in the 1950s. How does the juxtaposition of this comment with the list prepare you for her point of view on film?

2. According to the essay, why did certain stereotypes of Asian women prevail in the 1950s and 1960s ? What conclusions does Hagedorn draw as she develops her historical account?

3. How does the film *Year of the Dragon* (1985) go beyond previous dehumanized film images of Asian-American women?

4. Hagedorn sees the film version of *The Joy Luck Club* as a turning point in the presentation of Asian women in film. Why? What flaws does she see in this film?

5. How does Hagedorn interpret the impact of the "gender bending" films *The Wedding Banquet* and *M. Butterfly*? What are the strengths and weaknesses of these films, in her view?
6. Does Hagedorn believe that the presentation of Asian women in the film media is more accurate and less dehumanizing than it was in the 1950s?

CONNECTION

Compare Hagedorn's presentation of images of Asian women in film to Ron Takaki's ideas in "A Different Mirror" (Chapter 7) on racial stereotypes and the general level of ignorance about the minority contribution to American culture. What response would Takaki have to the examples of film images of Asian women presented by Hagedorn?

IDEAS FOR WRITING

1. Write an essay in which you examine the impact that media images of Asian women (or women of some other group) have had on your perception of the roles that they typically assume in "real life." Have these film presentations influenced your perceptions negatively or positively?
2. Watch one or two of the films that Hagedorn discusses; then write your own interpretation of the films' presentations of Asian women. Compare your conclusions about the impact of these media presentations to Hagedorn's views.

Joan Ryan

Little Girls in Pretty Boxes

A nationally known sportswriter and a sport columnist for the San Francisco Examiner *since 1985, Joan Ryan (b. 1959) has won many awards for her journalism. Her most recent book is a collaboration with Tara VanDerveer, coach of the Stanford women's basketball team,* Shooting From The Outside *(1997). Ryan was given the Associated Press Sports Editors' Award for Enterprise Reporting, and the Women's Sports Foundation's Journalism Award for the research gathered for the selection that follows, which is included in her book on young women athletes,* Little Girls in Pretty Boxes: The Making and Breaking of Elite Gymnasts and Figure Skaters *(1995).*

JOURNAL

Write about a time when you played sports yet felt that your coaches and/or your parents were pushing you too hard to compete like a "professional."

1   The little girls marched into the Atlanta arena in single file, heads high, shoulders
     back, bare toes pointed. Under hair ribbons and rouged cheeks, their balletic
bodies flowed past bleachers where expectant fathers craned forward with videocam-
eras. Small and pretty in their shimmery leotards, the girls looked like trinkets from a
Tiffany box. They lined up facing the crowd, and when the announcer summoned
the winners of the Peachtree Classic, the gymnasts stepped forward and bowed their
heads as soberly as Nobel laureates to receive their medals. Mothers with scoresheets
tucked under their arms clapped until their hands hurt, shooting hopeful glances at
the ESPN cameras roving among the girls. Along velvet ropes strung across the base
of the bleachers, awetruck seven- and eight-year-olds stretched toward the winning
gymnasts clutching programs and gym bags for them to sign.

2   On the opposite coast, at a skating rink in Redwood City, California, one fifteen-
year-old skater—in a ponytail, braces and baby-blue sequins—stood at the edge of the
rink, eyes wide, listening to her coach's last-minute instructions as her parents held
hands in the bleachers, packed solid for the Pacific Coast Sectional Championships.
She glided to the center of the ice. Then, as her music began, she spun like a jewel-
box ballerina, executing the intricate choreography of leaps and footwork she had
practiced nearly every day for as long as she could remember. On her 1/4-inch skate
blades rode her hopes of qualifying for the U.S. Figure Skating Championships,
moving her one step closer to the Winter Olympic Games.

3   In gyms and rinks across the country, the air is thick with the scent of the Olympics.
And the parents, coaches and young athletes chase it like hounds, impatient for the rewards of the sports that captivate American audiences as no others do. Gymnasts and
figure skaters hold a unique and cherished place among American athletes. Gymansts
are the darlings of the Summer Games, figure skaters the ice princesses of the Winter
Games. Every four years they keep us glued to our televisions for two weeks with their
grace, agility, youth and beauty. They land on magazine covers, Wheaties boxes, the
"Today" show. Television ratings for Olympic gymnastics and figure skating events rank
among the highest for any sport on television. Helped by the Tonya Harding–
Nancy Kerrigan saga, the women's technical program at the 1994 Winter Games drew
the fourth-highest rating of any show in the history of television, placing it up there
with the final episode of "M*A*S*H." But even at the controversy-free 1992 Winter
Games, women's figure skating attracted a larger television audience than either the final game of the 1992 World Series or the 1992 National Collegiate Athletic Association basketball championship game between Michigan and Duke. Americans are so
enchanted by gymnasts and figure skaters that in a 1991 survey they chose gymnast
Mary Lou Retton and skater Dorothy Hamill—both long retired—as their favorite athletes, beating out the likes of Chris Evert, Michael Jordan and Magic Johnson.

4   Yet while gymnastics and figure skating are among the most-watched sports in
the country, the least is known about the lives of their athletes (with the exceptions,
of course, of Harding and Kerrigan). We watch thirteen-year-old Michelle Kwan, an
eighth grader, land six triple jumps to finish second at the 1994 U.S. Figure Skating
Championships. We see sixteen-year-old Shannon Miller soar above the balance
beam as if it were a trampoline to win a silver medal at the 1992 Olympics. But we

know little about how they achieve so much at such a young age or what becomes of them when they leave their sport.

5   Unlike women's tennis, a sport in which teenage girls rise to the highest echelon year after year in highly televised championships, gymnastics and figure skating flutter across our screens as ephemerally as butterflies. We know about tennis burnout, about Tracy Austin, Andrea Jaeger, Mary Pierce and, more recently, about Jennifer Capriati, who turned pro with $5 million in endorsement contracts at age thirteen and ended up four years later in a Florida motel room, blank-eyed and disheveled, sharing drugs with runaways. But we hear precious little about the young female gymnasts and figure skaters who perform magnificent feats of physical strength and agility, and even less about their casualties. How do the extraordinary demands of their training shape these young girls? What price do their bodies and psyches pay?

6   I set out to answer some of these questions during three months of research for an article that ran in the *San Francisco Examiner*, but when I finished I couldn't close my notebook. I took a year's leave to continue my research, focusing this time on the girls who never made it, not just on the champions.

7   What I found was a story about legal, even celebrated, child abuse. In the dark troughs along the road to the Olympics lay the bodies of the girls who stumbled on the way, broken by the work, pressure and humiliation. I found a girl whose father left the family when she quit gymnastics at age thirteen, who scraped her arms and legs with razors to dull her emotional pain and who needed a two-hour pass from a psychiatrict hospital to attend her high school graduation. Girls who broke their necks and backs. One who so desperately sought the perfect, weightless gymanstics body that she starved herself to death. Others—many—who became so obsessive about controlling their weight that they lost control of themselves instead, falling into the potentially fatal cycle of bingeing on food, then purging by vomiting or taking laxatives. One who was sexually abused by her coach and one who was sodomized for four years by the father of a teammate. I found a girl who felt such shame at not making the Olympic team that she slit her wrists. A skater who underwent plastic surgery when a judge said her nose was distracting. A father who handed custody of his daughter over to her coach so she could keep skating. A coach who fed his gymnasts so little that federation officials had to smuggle food into their hotel rooms. A mother who hid her child's chicken pox with makeup so she could compete. Coaches who motivated their athletes by calling them imbeciles, idiots, pigs, cows.

8   I am not suggesting that gymnastics and figure skating in and of themselves are destructive. On the contrary, both sports are potentially wonderful and enriching, providing an arena of competition in which the average child can develop a sense of mastery, self-esteem and healthy athleticism. But this book isn't about recreational sports or the average child. It's about the elite child athlete and the American obsession with winning that has produced a training environment wherein results are bought at any cost, no matter how devastating. It's about how our cultural fixation on beauty and weight and youth has shaped both sports and driven the athletes into a sphere beyond the quest for physical performance.

9   The well-known story of Tonya Harding and Nancy Kerrigan did not happen in a vacuum; it symbolizes perfectly the stakes now involved in elite competition—itself a reflection of our national character. We created Tonya and Nancy not only by our hunger for winning but by our criterion for winning, an exaggeration of the code that applies to ambitious young women everywhere: Talent counts, but so do beauty, class, weight, clothes and politics. The anachronistic lack of ambivalence about femininity in both sports is part of their attraction, hearkening back to a simpler time when girls were girls, when women were girls for that matter: coquettish, malleable, eager to please. In figure skating especially, we want our athletes thin, graceful, deferential and cover-girl pretty. We want eyeliner, lipstick and hair ribbons. Makeup artists are fixtures backstage at figure skating competitions, primping and polishing. In figure skating, costumes can actually affect a score. They are so important that skaters spend $1500 and up on one dress—more than they spend on their skates. Nancy Kerrigan's dresses by designer Vera Wang cost upward of $5000 each.

10   Indeed, the costumes fuel the national fairy tale of Tonya and Nancy. Nancy wore virginal white. She was the perfect heroine, a good girl with perfect white teeth, a 24-inch waist and a smile that suggested both pluck and vulnerability. She remained safely within skating's pristine circle of grace and femininity. Tonya, on the other hand, crossed all the lines. She wore bordello red-and-gold. She was the pefect villainess, a bad girl with truck-stop manners, a racy past and chunky thighs. When she became convinced Nancy's grace would always win out over her own explosive strength, Tony crossed the final line, helping to eliminate Nancy from competition. The media frenzy tapped into our own inner wranglings about the good girl/bad girl paradox, about how women should behave, about how they should look and what they should say. The story touched a cultural nerve about women crossing societal boundaries—of power, achievement, violence, taste, appearance—and being ensnared by them. In the end, both skaters were trapped, Tonya by her ambition and Nancy by the good-girl image she created for the ice—an image she couldn't live up to. The public turned on Nancy when foolish comments and graceless interviews made it clear she wasn't Snow White after all.

11   Both sports embody the contradiction of modern womanhood. Society has allowed women to aspire higher, but to do so a woman must often reject that which makes her female, including motherhood. Similarly, gymnastics and figure skating remove the limits of a girl's body, teaching it to soar beyond what seems possible. Yet they also imprison it, binding it like the tiny Victorian waist or the Chinese woman's foot. The girls aren't allowed passage into adulthood. To survive in the sports, they beat back puberty, desperate to stay small and thin, refusing to let their bodies grow up. In this way the sports pervert the very femininity they hold so dear. The physical skills have become so demanding that only a body shaped like a missile—in other words, a body shaped like a boy's—can excel. Breasts and hips slow the spins, lower the leaps and disrupt the clean, lean body lines that judges reward. "Women's gymnastics" and "ladies' figure skating" are misnomers today. Once the athletes become women, their elite careers wither.

12   In the meantime, their childhoods are gone. But they trade more than their childhoods for a shot at glory. They risk serious physical and psychological problems that can linger long after the public has turned its attention to the next phenom in pigtails. The intensive training and pressure heaped on by coaches, parents and federation officials—the very people who should be protecting the children—often result in eating disorders, weakened bones, stunted growth, debilitating injuries and damaged psyches. In the last six years two U.S. Olympic hopefuls have died as a result of their participation in elite gymnastics.

13   Because they excel at such a young age, girls in these sports are unlike other elite athletes. They are world champions before they can drive. They are the Michael Jordans and Joe Montanas of their sports before they learn algebra. Unlike male athletes their age, who are playing quarterback in high school or running track for the local club, these girls are competing on a worldwide stage. If an elite gymnast or figure skater fails, she fails globally. She sees her mistake replayed in slow motion on TV and captured in bold headlines in the newspaper. Adult reporters crowd around, asking what she has to say to a country that had hung its hopes on her thin shoulders. Tiffany Chin was seventeen when she entered the 1985 U.S. Figure Skating Championships as the favorite. She was asked at the time how she would feel if she didn't win. She paused, as if trying to consider the possibility. "Devastated," she said quietly. "I don't know. I'd probably die."

14   Chin recalled recently that when she did win, "I didn't feel happiness. I felt relief. Which was disappointing." Three months before the 1988 Olympics, Chin retired when her legs began to break down. Some, however, say she left because she could no longer tolerate the pressure and unrelenting drive of her stern mother. "I feel I'm lucky to have gotten through it," she said of skating. "I don't think many people are that lucky. There's a tremendous strain on people who don't make it. The money, the sacrifices, the time. I know people emotionally damaged by it. I've seen nervous breakdowns, psychological imbalances."

15   An elite gymnast or figure skater knows she takes more than her own ambition into a competition. Her parents have invested tens of thousands of dollars in her training, sometimes hundreds of thousands. Her coach's reputation rides on her performance. And she knows she might have only one shot. By the next Olympics she might be too old. By the next *year* she might be too old. Girls in these sports are under pressure not only to win but to win quickly. They're running against a clock that eventually marks the lives of all women, warning them they'd better hurry up and get married and have children before it's too late. These girls hear the clock early. They're racing against puberty.

16   Boys, on the other hand, welcome the changes that puberty brings. They reach their athletic peak after puberty when their bodies grow and their muscles strengthen. In recent years Michael Chang and Boris Becker won the French Open and Wimbledon tennis titles, respectively, before age eighteen, but in virtually every male sport the top athletes are men, not boys. Male gymnastics and figure skating champions are usually in their early to mid twenties; female champions are usually

fourteen to seventeen years old in gymnastics and sixteen to early twenties in figure skating.

17   In staving off puberty to maintain the "ideal" body shape, girls risk their health in ways their male counterparts never do. They starve themselves, for one, often in response to their coaches' belittling insults about their bodies. Starving shuts down the menstrual cycle—the starving body knows it cannot support a fetus—and thus blocks the onset of puberty. It's a dangerous strategy to save a career. If a girl isn't menstruating, she isn't producing estrogen. Without estrogen, her bones weaken. She risks stunting her growth. She risks premature osteoporosis. She risks fractures in all bones, including her vertebrae, and she risks curvature of the spine. In several studies over the last decade, young female athletes who didn't mensturate were found to have the bone densities of postmenopausal women in their fifties, sixties and seventies. Most elite gymnasts don't begin to menstruate until they retire. Kathy Johnson, a medalist in the 1984 Olympics, didn't begin until she quit the sport at age twenty-five.

18   Our national obsession with weight, our glorification of thinness, have gone completely unchecked in gymnastics and figure skating. The cultural forces that have produced extravagantly bony fashion models have taken their toll on gymnasts and skaters already insecure about their bodies. Not surprisingly, eating disorders are common in both sports, and in gymnastics they're rampant. Studies of female college gymnasts show that most practice some kind of disordered eating. In a 1994 University of Utah study of elite gymnasts—those training for the Olympics—59 percent admitted to some form of disordered eating. And in interviewing elites for this book, I found only a handful who had not tried starving, throwing up or taking laxatives or diuretics to control their weight. Several left the sport because of eating disorders. One died. Eating disorders among male athletes, as in the general male population, are virtually unknown.

19   "Everyone goes through it, but nobody talks about it, because they're embarrassed," gymnast Kristie Phillips told me. "But I don't put the fault on us. It's the pressures that are put on us to be so skinny. It's mental cruelty. It's not fair that all these pressures are put on us at such a young age and we don't realize it until we get older and we suffer from it."

20   Phillips tooks laxatives, thyroid pills and diuretics to lose weight. She had been the hottest gymnast in the mid-1980s, the heir apparent to 1984 Olympic superstar Mary Lou Retton. But she not only didn't win a medal at the 1998 Summer Games, she didn't even make the U.S. team. She left the sport feeling like a failure. She gained weight, then became bulimic, caught in a cycle of bingeing and vomiting. Distraught, she took scissors to her wrists in a botched attempt to kill herself. "I weighed ninety-eight pounds and I was being called [by her coach] an overstuffed Christmas turkey," Phillips said in our interview. "I was told I was never going to make it in life because I was going to be fat. I mean, in *life*. Things I'll never forget."

21   Much of the direct blame for the young athletes' problems falls on the coaches and parents. Obviously, no parent wakes up in the morning and plots how to ruin his or her child's life. But the money, the fame and the promise of great achievement

can turn a parent's head. Ambition gets perverted. The boundaries of parents and coaches bloat and mutate, with the parent becoming the ruthless coach and coach becoming the controlling parent. One father put gymnastics equipment in his living room and for every mistake his daughter made at the gym she had to repeat the skill hundreds of times at home. He moved the girl to three gyms around the country, pushing her in the sport she came to loathe. He said he did it because he wanted the best for her.

22   Coaches push because they are paid to produce great gymnasts. They are relentless about weight because physically round gymnasts and skaters don't win. Coaches are intolerant of injuries because in the race against puberty, time off is death. Their job is not to turn out happy, well-adjusted young women; it is to turn out champions. If they scream, belittle or ignore, if they prod an injured girl to forget her pain, if they push her to drop out of school, they are only doing what the parents have paid them to do. So, sorting out the blame when a girl falls apart is a messy proposition; everyone claims he was just doing his job.

23   The sports' national governing bodies, for their part, are mostly impotent. They try to do well by the athletes, but they, too, often lose their way in a tangle of ambition and politics. They're like small-town governments: personal, despotic, paternalistic and absolutely without teeth. The federations do not have the power that the commissioner's offices in a professional baseball, football and basketball do. They cannot revoke a coach's or an athlete's membership for anything less than criminal activity. (Tonya Harding was charged and sentenced by the courts before the United States Figure Skating Association expelled her.) They cannot fine or suspend a coach whose athletes regularly leave the sport on stretchers.

24   There simply is no safety net protecting these children. Not the parents, the coaches or the federations.

25   Child labor laws prohibit a thirteen-year-old from punching a cash register for forty hours a week, but that same child can labor for forty hours or more inside a gym or an ice skating rink without drawing the slightest glance from the government. The U.S. government requires the licensing of plumbers. It demands that even the tiniest coffee shop adhere to a fastidious health code. It scrutinizes the advertising claims on packages of low-fat snack food. But it never asks a coach, who holds the lives of his young pupils in his hands, to pass a minimum safety and skills test. Coaches in this country need no license to train children, even in a high-injury sport like elite gymnastics. The government that forbids a child from buying a pack of cigarettes because of health concerns never checks on the child athlete who trains until her hands bleed or her knees buckle, who stops eating to achieve the perfect body, who takes eight Advils a day and offers herself up for another shot of cortisone to dull the pain, who drinks a bottle of Ex-Lax because her coach is going to weigh her in the morning. The government never takes a looks inside the gym or the rink to make sure these children are not being exploited or abused or worked too hard. Even college athletes—virtually all of whom are adults—are restricted by the NCAA to just twenty hours per week of formal training. But no laws, no agencies, put limits on the number of hours a child can train or the methods a coach can use.

26   Some argue that extraordinary children should be allowed to follow extraordinary
paths to realize their potential. They argue that a child's wants are no less important
than an adult's and thus she should not be denied her dreams just because she is still a
child. If pursuing her dream means training eight hours a day in a gym, withstanding
abusive language and tolerating great pain, and if the child wants to do it and the
parents believe it will build character, why not let her? Who are we to tell a child
what she can and cannot do with her life?

27   In fact, we tell children all the time what they can and cannot do with their lives.
Restricting children from certain activities is hardly a revolutionary concept. Laws
prohibit children from driving before sixteen and drinking before twenty-one. They
prohibit children from dropping out of school before fifteen and working full-time
before sixteen. In our society we put great value on protecting our children from
physical harm and exploitation, and sometimes that means protecting them from
their own poor judgment and their parents' poor judgment. No one questions the
wisdom of the government in forbidding a child to work full-time, so why is it all
right for her to train full-time with no rules to ensure her well-being? Child labor
laws should address all labor, even that which is technically nonpaid, though top
gymnasts and figure skaters *do* labor for money.

28   In recent years the federations have begun to pay their top athletes a stipend
based on their competition results. The girls can earn bonuses by representing the
United States in certain designated events. Skaters who compete in the World Figure Skating Championships and the Olympic Games, for example, receive $15,000.
They earn lesser amounts for international competitions such as Skate America.
They also earn money from corporate sponsors and exhibitions. The money might
not cover much more than their training expenses, which can run $75,000 for a top
skater and $20,000 to $30,000 per year for a top gymnast, but it's money—money
that is paid specifically for the work the athletes do in the gym and the skating rink.

29   The real payoff for their hard work, however, waits at the end of the road. That's
what the parents and athletes hope anyway. When Mary Lou Retton made millions
on Madison Avenue after winning the gold medal at the 1984 Olympics, she
changed gymnastics forever. "Kids have agents now before they even make it into
their teens," Retton says. Now the dream is no longer just about medals but about
Wheaties boxes and appearance fees, about paying off mom and dad's home equity
loans and trading in the Toyota for a Mercedes. It doesn't seem to matter that only
six girls every four years reach the Olympics and that winning the gold once they get
there is the longest of long shots. Even world champion Shannon Miller didn't win
the all-around Olympic gold in 1992.

30   Figure skating, even more than gymnastics, blinds parents and athletes with the
glittering possibilities, and for good reason. Peggy Fleming and Dorothy Hamill are
still living off gold medals won decades ago. Nancy Kerrigan landed endorsements
with Reebok, Evian, Seiko and Campbell's soup with only a bronze medal in 1992.
With glamorous and feminine stars like Kerrigan and Kristi Yamaguchi to lead the
way, the United States Figure Skating Association has seen the influx of corporate
sponsorship climb 2000 percent in just five years. Money that used to go to tennis is

now being shifted to figure skating and gymanstics as their popularity grows. The payoff in money and fame now looms large enough to be seen from a distance, sparkling like the Emerald City, driving parents and children to extremes to reach its doors.

31   I'm not suggesting that all elite gymnasts and figure skaters emerge from their sports unhealthy and poorly adjusted. Many prove that they can thrive under intense pressure and physical demands and thus are stronger for the experience. But too many can't. There are no studies that establish what percentage of elite gymnasts and figure skaters are damaged by their sports and in what ways. So the evidence I've gathered for this book is anecdotal, the result of nearly a hundred interviews and more than a decade of covering both sports as a journalist.

32   The bottom line is clear. There have been enough suicide attempts, enough eating disorders, enough broken bodies, enough regretful parents and enough bitter young women to warrant a serious reevaluation of what we're doing in this country to produce Olympic champions. Those who work in these sports know this. They know the tragedies all too well. If the federations and coaches truly care about the athletes and not simply about the fame and prestige that come from trotting tough little champions up to the medal stand, they know it is past time to lay the problems on the table, examine them and figure out a way to keep their sports from damaging so many young lives. But since those charged with protecting young athletes so often fail in their responsibility, it is time the government drops the fantasy that certain sports are merely games and takes a hard look at legislation aimed at protecting elite child athletes.

33   It is also my hope that by dramatizing the particularly intense subculture of female gymnastics and figure skating, we can better understand something of our own nature as a country bent on adulating, and in some cases sacrificing, girls and young women in a quest to fit them into our pretty little boxes.

QUESTIONS FOR DISCUSSION

1. According to Ryan, why do female figure skaters and gymnasts hold a "unique and cherished place" while the public continues to know so little about their physical and psychological problems?
2. How might the extensive media coverage of the female figure skaters and gymnasts contribute to the physical and psychological pressures they experience?
3. According to Ryan, how does the story of Tonya Harding and Nancy Kerrigan, along with its extensive media coverage, reflect our national character and the contradictory images and expectations we have for modern American women?
4. Why do gymnastics and figure skating impede the healthy development of young women while male athletes are strengthened by the course of their training? Do you think that women athletes are more vulnerable to manipulation and exploitation than male athletes? Explain your response.

5. How does Ryan think that the training of young girls for the Olympics should be changed? What does she think we can do to protect them? How do you think they should be protected?
6. Do you agree with Ryan that our culture glorifies the female as a little girl with doll-like qualities, but not for her achievements as a woman or a mother? Explain your point of view.

CONNECTION

Compare Ryan's ideas on the effects of media exposure and excessive "professionalism" on young female athletes with Ellen Ullman's ideas on the impact of the programmer's lifestyle on young people in the computing industry.

IDEAS FOR WRITING

1. Ryan argues that the story of gymnasts and figure skaters training for the Olympics is a story of child abuse. Write an essay in which you explain why you agree or disagree with her.
2. Write an essay about the ways in which excessive media exposure and publicity in a particular sport with which you are familiar can have a negative influence on younger athletes.

Umberto Eco

The City of Robots

Umberto Eco was born in 1932 in Alessandria, Italy, and earned his Ph.D. in 1954 from the University of Turin. He is currently a professor at the University of Bologna in Italy and has taught at universities all over the world. He is world-renowned for his work in semiotics, a discipline that studies the ways culture is communicated through signs, and is also considered an expert on literature and history. His novels include The Name of the Rose *(1980), which became an international bestseller, and* The Island of the Day Before *(1995). Eco's books of cultural criticism and philosophy include* Faith In Fakes *(1986),* Apocalypse Postponed *(1994) and* Serendipities: Language & Lunacy *(1998). In the following selection from* Travels in Hyperreality *(1983), Eco reflects on the role of the theme park in American culture.*

JOURNAL

Write about a visit to a theme park such as Disneyland, Marriott's Great America, or Seven Flags over Texas. What were your impressions of the theme park? What did you learn about your own values and the values of American popular culture from your visit?

1   In Europe, when people want to be amused, they go to a "house" of amusement (whether a cinema, theater, or casino); sometimes a "park" is created, which may seem a "city," but only metaphorically. In the United States, on the contrary, as everyone knows, there exist amusement cities. Las Vegas is one example; it is focused on gambling and entertainment, its architecture is totally artificial, and it has been studied by Robert Venturi as a completely new phenomenon in city planning, a "message" city, entirely made up of signs, not a city like the others, which communicate in order to function, but rather a city that functions in order to communicate. But Las Vegas is still a "real" city, and in a recent essay on Las Vegas, Giovanni Brino showed how, though born as a place for gambling, it is gradually being transformed into a residential city, a place of business, industry, conventions. The theme of our trip—on the contrary—is the Absolute Fake; and therefore we are interested only in absolutely fake cities. Disneyland (California) and Disney World (Florida) are obviously the chief examples, but if they existed alone they would represent a negligible exception. The fact is that the United States is filled with cities that imitate a city, just as wax museums imitate painting and the Venetian palazzos or Pompeiian villas imitate architecture. In particular there are the "ghost towns," the Western cities of a century and more ago. Some are reasonably authentic, and the restoration or preservation has been carried out on an extant, "archeological" urban complex; but more interesting are those born from nothing, out of pure imitative determination. They are "the real thing."

2   There is an embarrassment of riches to choose from: You can have fragments of cities, as at Stone Mountain near Atlanta, where you take a trip on a nineteenth-century train, witness an Indian raid, and see sheriffs at work, against the background of a fake Mount Rushmore. The Six Guns Territory, in Silver Springs, also has train and sheriffs, a shoot-out in the streets and French can-can in the saloon. There is a series of ranchos and Mexican missions in Arizona; Tombstone with its OK Corral, Old Tucson, Legend City near Phoenix. There is the Old South Bar-b-Q Ranch at Clewison, Florida, and so on. If you venture beyond the myth of the West, you have cities like the Magic Mountain in Valencia, California, or Santa Claus Village, Polynesian gardens, pirate islands, Astroworlds like the one in Kirby, Texas, and the "wild" territories of the various Marinelands, as well as ecological cities, which we will discuss elsewhere.

3   There are also the ship imitations. In Florida, for example, between Tampa and St. Petersburg, you can board the *Bounty*, anchored at the edge of a Tahitian village, faithfully reconstructed according to the drawings preserved by the Royal Society in London, but with an eye also on the old film with Charles Laughton and Clark Gable. Many of the nautical instruments are of the period, some of the sailors are waxworks, one officer's shoes are those worn by the actor who played the part, the historical information on the various panels is credible, the voices that pervade the atmosphere come from the sound track of the movie. But we'll stick to the Western myth and take as a sample city the Knott's Berry Farm of Buena Park, Los Angeles.

4   Here the whole trick seems to be exposed; the surrounding city context and the iron fencing (as well as the admission ticket) warn us that we are entering not a real

city but a toy city. But as we begin walking down the first streets, the studied illusion takes over. First of all, there is the realism of the reconstruction: the dusty stables, the sagging shops, the offices of the sheriff and the telegraph agent, the jail, the saloon are life size and executed with absolute fidelity; the old carriages are covered with dust, the Chinese laundry is dimly lit, all the buildings are more or less practical, and the shops are open, because Berry Farm, like Disneyland, blends the reality of trade with the play of fiction. And if the dry-goods store is fake 19th-century and the shopgirl is dressed like a John Ford heroine, the candies, the peanuts, the pseudo-Indian handicrafts are real and are sold for real dollars, just as the soft drinks, advertised with antique posters, are real, and the customer finds himself participating in the fantasy because of his own authenticity as a consumer; in other words, he is in the role of the cowboy or the gold-prospector who comes into town to be fleeced of all he has accumulated while out in the wilds.

5   Furthermore the levels of illusion are numerous, and this increases the hallucination—that is to say, the Chinese in the laundry or the prisoner in the jail are wax dummies, who exist, in realistic attitudes, in settings that are equally realistic, though you can't actually enter them; but you don't realize the room in question is a glass display case, because it looks as if you could, if you chose, open the door or climb through the window; and then the next room, say, which is both the general store and the justice of the peace's office, looks like a display case but is actually practical, and the justice of the peace, with his black alpaca jacket and his pistols at his hips, is an actual person who sells you his merchandise. It should be added that extras walk about the streets and periodically stage a furious gun battle, and when you realize that the average American visitor is wearing blue jeans not very different from the cowboys', many of the visitors become confused with the extras, increasing the theatricality of the whole. For example, the village school, reconstructed with hyperrealistic detail, has behind the desk a schoolmarm wearing a bonnet and an ample checked skirt, but the children on the benches are little passing visitors, and I heard one tourist ask his wife if the children were real or "fake" (and you could sense his psychological readiness to consider them, at will, extras, dummies, or moving robots of the sort we will see in Disneyland).

6   Apparently ghost towns involve a different approach from that of wax museums or museums for copies of works of art. In the first nobody expects the wax Napoleon to be taken for real, but the hallucination serves to level the various historical periods and erase the distinction between historical reality and fantasy; in the case of the works of art what is culturally, if not psychologically, hallucinatory is the confusion between copy and original, and the fetishization of art as a sequence of famous subjects. In the ghost town, on the contrary, since the theatricality is explicit, the hallucination operates in making the visitors take part in the scene and thus become participants in that commercial fair that is apparently an element of the fiction but in fact represents the substantial aim of the whole imitative machine.

7   In an excellent essay on Disneyland as "degenerate utopia" ("a degenerate utopia is an ideology realized in the form of myth"), Louis Marin analyzed the

structure of that 19th-century frontier city street that receives entering visitors and distributes them through the various sectors of the magic city. Disneyland's Main Street seems the first scene of the fiction whereas it is an extremely shrewd commercial reality. Main Street—like the whole city, for that matter—is presented as at once absolutely realistic and absolutely fantastic, and this is the advantage (in terms of artistic conception) of Disneyland over the other toy cities. The houses of Disneyland are full-size on the ground floor, and on a two-thirds scale on the floor above, so they give the impression of being inhabitable (and they are) but also of belonging to a fantastic past that we can grasp with our imagination. The Main Street façades are presented to us as toy houses and invite us to enter them, but their interior is always a disguised supermarket, where you buy obsessively, believing that you are still playing.

8   In this sense Disneyland is more hyperrealistic than the wax museum, precisely because the latter still tries to make us believe that what we are seeing reproduces reality absolutely, whereas Disneyland makes it clear that within its magic enclosure it is fantasy that is absolutely reproduced. The Palace of Living Arts presents its Venus de Milo as almost real, whereas Disneyland can permit itself to present its reconstructions as masterpieces of falsification, for what it sells is, indeed, goods, but genuine merchandise, not reproductions. What is falsified is our will to buy, which we take as real, and in this sense Disneyland is really the quintessence of consumer ideology.

9   But once the "total fake" is admitted, in order to be enjoyed it must seem totally real. So the Polynesian restaurant will have, in addition to a fairly authentic menu, Tahitian waitresses in costume, appropriate vegetation, rock walls with little cascades, and once you are inside nothing must lead you to suspect that outside there is anything but Polynesia. If, between two trees, there appears a stretch of river that belongs to another sector, Adventureland, then that section of stream is so designed that it would not be unrealistic to see in Tahiti, beyond the garden hedge, a river like this. And if in the wax museums wax is not flesh, in Disneyland, when rocks are involved, they are rock, and water is water, and a baobab a baobab. When there is a fake—hippopotamus, dinosaur, sea serpent—it is not so much because it wouldn't be possible to have the real equivalent but because the public is meant to admire the perfection of the fake and its obedience to the program. In this sense Disneyland not only produces illusion, but—in confessing it—stimulates the desire for it: A real crocodile can be found in the zoo, and as a rule it is dozing or hiding, but Disneyland tells us that faked nature corresponds much more to our daydream demands. When, in the space of twenty-four hours, you go (as I did deliberately) from the fake New Orleans of Disneyland to the real one, and from the wild river of Adventureland to a trip on the Mississippi, where the captain of the paddle-wheel steamer says it is possible to see alligators on the banks of the river, and then you don't see any, you risk feeling homesick for Disneyland, where the wild animals don't have to be coaxed. Disneyland tells us that technology can give us more reality than nature can.

10   In this sense I believe the most typical phenomenon of this universe is not the
more famous Fantasyland—an amusing carousel of fantastic journeys that take the
visitor into the world of Peter Pan or Snow White, a wondrous machine whose fascination and lucid legitimacy it would be foolish to deny—but the Caribbean Pirates
and the Haunted Mansion. The pirate show lasts a quarter of an hour (but you lose
any sense of time, it could be ten minutes or thirty); you enter a series of caves, carried in boats over the surface of the water, you see first abandoned treasures, a captain's skeleton in a sumptuous bed of moldy brocade, pendent cobwebs, bodies of
executed men devoured by ravens, while the skeleton addresses menacing admoni-
tions to you. Then you navigate an inlet, passing through the crossfire of a galleon
and the cannon of a fort, while the chief corsair shouts taunting challenges at the
beleaguered garrison; then, as if along a river, you go by an invaded city which is being sacked, with the rape of the women, theft of jewels, torture of the mayor; the city
burns like a match, drunken pirates sprawled on piles of kegs sing obscene songs;
some completely out of their heads, shoot at the visitors; the scene degenerates,
everything collapses in flames, slowly the last songs die away, you emerge into the
sunlight. Everything you have seen was on human scale, the vault of the caves became confused with that of the sky, the boundary of this underground world was that
of the universe and it was impossible to glimpse its limits. The pirates moved,
danced, slept, popped their eyes, sniggered, drank—really. You realize that they are
robots, but you remain dumbfounded by their verisimilitude. And, in fact, the "Audio-
Animatronic" technique represented a great source of pride for Walt Disney, who
had finally managed to achieve his own dream and reconstruct a fantasy world more
real than reality, breaking down the wall of the second dimension, creating not a
movie, which is illusion, but total theater, and not with anthropomorphized animals, but with human beings. In fact, Disney's robots are masterpieces of electronics;
each was devised by observing the expressions of a real actor, then building models,
then developing skeletons of absolute precision, authentic computers in human
form, to be dressed in "flesh" and "skin" made by craftsmen, whose command of realism is incredible. Each robot obeys a program, can synchronize the movements of
mouth and eyes with the words and sounds of the audio, repeating ad infinitum all
day long his established part (a sentence, one or two gestures) and the visitor,
caught off guard by the succession of events, obliged to see several things at once, to
left and right and straight ahead, has no time to look back and observe that the robot he has just seen is already repeating his eternal scenario.

11   The "Audio-Animatronic" technique is used in many other parts of Disneyland
and also enlivens a review of presidents of the United States, but in the pirates'
cave, more than anywhere else, it demonstrates all its miraculous efficacy. Humans
could do no better, and would cost more, but the important thing is precisely the
fact that these are not humans and we know they're not. The pleasure of imitation,
as the ancients knew, is one of the most innate in the human spirit; but here we not
only enjoy a perfect imitation, we also enjoy the conviction that imitation has
reached its apex and afterwards reality will always be inferior to it.

12   Similar criteria underlie the journey through the cellars of the Haunted Mansion, which looks at first like a rundown country house, somewhere between Edgar Allan Poe and the cartoons of Charles Addams; but inside, it conceals the most complete array of witchcraft surprises that anyone could desire. You pass through an abandoned graveyard, where skeletal hands raise gravestones from below, you cross a hill enlivened by a witches' sabbath complete with spirits and beldams; then you move through a room with a table all laid and a group of transparent ghosts in 19th century costume dancing while diaphanous guests, occasionally vanishing into thin air, enjoy the banquet of a barbaric sovereign. You are grazed by cobwebs, reflected in crystals on whose surface a greenish figure appears, behind your back; you encounter moving candelabra. . . . In no instance are these the cheap tricks of some tunnel of love; the involvement (always tempered by the humor of the inventions) is total. As in certain horror films, detachment is impossible; you are not witnessing another's horror, you are inside the horror through complete synesthesia; and if there is an earthquake the movie theater must also tremble.

13   I would say that these two attractions sum up the Disneyland philosophy more than the equally perfect models of the pirate ship, the river boat, and the sailing ship *Columbia*, all obviously in working order. And more than the Future section, with the science-fiction emotions it arouses (such as a flight to Mars experienced from inside a spacecraft, with all the effects of deceleration, loss of gravity, dizzying movement away from the earth, and so on). More than the models of rockets and atomic submarines, which prompted Marin to observe that whereas the fake Western cities, the fake New Orleans, the fake jungle provide life size duplicates of organic but historical or fantastic events, these are reduced-scale models of mechanical realities of today, and so, where something is incredible, the full-scale model prevails, and where it is credible, the reduction serves to make it attractive to the imagination. The Pirates and the Ghosts sum up all Disneyland, at least from the point of view of our trip, because they transform the whole city into an immense robot, the final realization of the dreams of the 18th-century mechanics who gave life to the Writer of Neuchâtel and the Chess-playing Turk of Baron von Kempelen.

14   Disneyland's precision and coherence are to some extent disturbed by the ambitions of Disney World in Florida. Built later, Disney World is a hundred fifty times larger than Disneyland, and proudly presents itself not as a toy city but as the model of an urban agglomerate of the future. The structures that make up California's Disneyland form here only a marginal part of an immense complex of construction covering an area twice the size of Manhattan. The great monorail that takes you from the entrance to the Magic Kingdom (the Disneyland part proper) passes artificial bays and lagoons, a Swiss village, a Polynesian village, golf courses and tennis courts, an immense hotel: an area dedicated, in other words, to organized vacationing. So you reach the Magic Kingdom, your eyes already dazzled by so much science fiction that the sight of the high medieval castle (far more Gothic than Disneyland: a Strasbourg Cathedral, let's say, compared to a San Miniato) no longer stirs the imagination. Tomorrow, with its violence, has made the colors fade from the stories of

Yesterday. In this respect Disneyland is much shrewder; it must be visited without anything to remind us of the future surrounding it. Marin has observed that, to enter it, the essential condition is to abandon your car in an endless parking lot and reach the boundary of the dream city by special little trains. And for a Californian, leaving his car means leaving his own humanity, consigning himself to another power, abandoning his own will.

15   An allegory of the consumer society, a place of absolute iconism, Disneyland is also a place of total passivity. Its visitors must agree to behave like its robots. Access to each attraction is regulated by a maze of metal railings which discourages any individual initiative. The number of visitors obviously sets the pace of the line; the officials of the dream, properly dressed in the uniforms suited to each specific attraction, not only admit the visitor to the threshold of the chosen sector, but, in successive phases, regulate his every move ("Now wait here please, go up now, sit down please, wait before standing up," always in a polite tone, impersonal, imperious, over the microphone). If the visitor pays this price, he can have not only "the real thing" but the abundance of the reconstructed truth. Like the Hearst Castle, Disneyland also has no transitional spaces; there is always something to see, the great voids of modern architecture and city planning are unknown here. If America is the country of the Guggenheim Museum or the new skyscrapers of Manhattan, then Disneyland is a curious exception and American intellectuals are quite right to refuse to go there. But if America is what we have seen in the course of our trip, then Disneyland is its Sistine Chapel, and the hyperrealists of the art galleries are only the timid voyeurs of an immense and continuous "found object."

QUESTIONS FOR DISCUSSION

1. According to Eco, what is the distinction between an "amusement city," a "real" city, and a "total fake"? What examples does he give? Can you think of others?

2. How do "fake" cities blend and at times confuse "the reality of trade with the play of fiction"? What role do the "extras" play in this confusion?

3. Why does the author Louis Marin see Disneyland as a "degenerate utopia"? What ideology and what myth does Disneyland exploit?

4. Why is it so important for the spectators' enjoyment that the "total fake" appear to be "totally real" in each of Disneyland's dream-like lands? How does this creation of the appearance of reality lead us to the impression that "technology can give us more reality than nature can?"

5. How do Eco's extensive descriptions of the Pirates of the Caribbean and the Haunted Mansion help to support and clarify the points he makes about pleasure, illusion, and seeming reality through robotic techniques in Disneyland?

6. Why does Eco believe Disneyland to be an "allegory of the consumer society"? In what sense must the visitors "behave like its [Disneyland's] robots"?

CONNECTION

Compare Bok's discussion of the way people behave in response to the "fake world" created by the mass media, which appears like our real world but is much more violent, with Eco's view of the public response to the fake world created in Disneyland and other family theme parks. Does Disneyland, which is relatively non-violent, serve visiting families as a sort of false antidote for the real-seeming, ultra-violent media world of film and TV?

IDEAS FOR WRITING

1. Write an essay in response to Eco's claim at the end of the essay that Disneyland, more so than other American architectural masterpieces and museums such as the Guggenheim, is America's "Sistine Chapel"—that is, a place of worship where our true national values are enshrined in a culturally appropriate artistic form. What true American values (if any) can be found in the form and contents of Disneyland?
2. If you have traveled to another amusement park or entertainment facility which attempts to make the "total fake" appear "totally real," describe the environment created there and evaluate its success at emulating a nonexistent or vanished reality.

Ellen Ullman

Getting Close to the Machine

Ellen Ullman was born and raised in New York City, where her father owned a business and commercial real estate. She currently lives in San Francisco, where she has been a software engineer and computer programmer and consultant since 1978. Ullman has written programming and software related articles for publications such as Byte magazine, PC World, and Datamation. In 1995 an article she wrote for Harper's, "Getting Close to the Machine," led to a book-length work entitled Close to the Machine (1997), a personal examination of the lifestyle and work habits of young people intimately involved in the world of creative programming. In the following essay, "Getting Close to the Machine," Ullman examines the obsessive communication and thinking styles of those whose demanding technical work takes them "close to the machine"—but a long way from ordinary people.

Write about a time when you or someone you know became overly involved in working on computers or surfing the Internet, to the detriment of interactions with other people.

1   People imagine that computer programming is logical, a process like fixing a clock. Nothing could be further from the truth. Programming is more like an illness, a fever, an obsession. It's like riding a train and never being able to get off.

2   The problem with programming is not that the computer is illogical—the computer is terribly logical, relentlessly literal. It demands that the programmer explain the world on its terms; that is, as an algorithm that must be written down in order, in a specific syntax, in a strange language that is only partially readable by regular human beings. To program is to translate between the chaos of human life and the rational, line-by-line world of computer language.

3   When you program, reality presents itself as thousands of details, millions of bits of knowledge. This knowlege comes at you from one perspective and then another, then comes a random thought, then you remember something else important, then you reconsider that idea with a what-if attached. For example, try to think of everything you know about something as simple as an invoice. Now try to tell an idiot how to prepare one. That is programming.

4   I used to have dreams in which I was overhearing conversations I had to program. Once I dreamed I had to program two people making love. In my dream they sweated and tumbled while I sat looking for the algorithm. The couple went from gentle caresses to ever-deepening passion, and I tried desperately to find a way to express the act of love in the C computer language.

5   When you are programming, you must not let your mind wander. As the human-world knowledge tumbles about in your head, you must keep typing. You must not be interrupted. Any break in your concentration causes you to lose a line here or there. Some bit comes, then—oh no, it's leaving, please come back. But it may not come back. You may lose it. You will create a bug and there's nothing you can do about it.

6   People imagine that programmers don't like to talk because they prefer machines to people. This is not completely true. Programmers don't talk because they must not be interrupted.

7   This need to be uninterrupted leads to a life that is strangely asynchronous to the one lived by other human beings. It's better to send e-mail to a programmer than to call. It's better to leave a note on the chair than to expect the programmer to come to a meeting. This is because the programmer must work in mind time while the phone rings and the meetings happen in real time. It's not just ego that prevents programmers from working in groups—it's the synchronocity problem. Synchronizing with other people (or their representations in telephones, buzzers, and doorbells) can only mean interrupting the thought train. Interruptions mean bugs. You must not get off the train.

8   I once had a job in which I didn't talk to anyone for two years. Here was the arrangement: I was the first engineer to be hired by a start-up software company. In exchange for large quantities of stock that might be worth something someday, I was supposed to give up my life.

9   I sat in a large room with two other engineers and three workstations. The fans in the machines whirred, the keys on the keyboards clicked. Occasionally one of us would grunt or mutter. Otherwise we did not speak. Now and then I would have an outburst in which I pounded the keyboard with my fists, setting off a barrage of beeps. My colleagues might have looked up, but they never said anything.

10   Real time was no longer compelling to me. Days, weeks, months, and years came and went without much change in my surroundings. Surely I was aging. My hair must have grown, I must have cut it, it must have slowly become grayer. Gravity must have been working on my late-thirties body, but I didn't pay attention.

11   What was compelling was the software. I was making something out of nothing, I thought, and I admit that the software had more life for me during those years than a brief love affair, my friends, my cat, my house, or my neighbor who was stabbed and nearly killed by her husband. One day I sat in a room by myself, surrounded by computer monitors. I remember looking at the screens and saying, "Speak to me."

12   I was creating something called a device-independent interface library. ("Creating"—that is the word we used, each of us a genius in the attic.) I completed the library in two years and left the company. Five years later, the company's stock went public, and the original arrangement was made good: the engineers who stayed—the ones who had given seven years of their lives to the machine—became very, very wealthy.

13   If you want money and prestige, you need to write code that only machines or other programmers understand. Such code is called "low." In regular life, "low" usually signifies something bad. In programming, "low" is good. Low means that you are close to the machine.

14   If the code creates programs that do useful work for regular human beings, it is called "high." Higher-level programs are called "applications." Applications are things that people use. Although it would seem that usefulness is a good thing, direct people-use is bad from a programmer's point of view. If regular people, called "users," can understand the task accomplished by your program, you will be paid less and held in lower esteem.

15   A real programmer wants to stay close to the machine. The machine means midnight dinners of Diet Coke. It means unwashed clothes and bare feet on the desk. It means anxious rides through mind time that have nothing to do with the clock. To work on things used only by machines or other programmers—that's the key. Programmers and machines don't care how you live. They don't care when you live. You can stay, come, go, sleep—or not. At the end of the project looms a deadline, the terrible place where you must get off the train. But in between, for years at a stretch, you are free: free from the obligations of time.

16   I once designed a graphical user interface with a man who wouldn't speak to me. My boss hired him without letting anyone else sit in on the interview. My boss lived to regret it.

17   I was asked to brief my new colleague with the help of the third member of our team. We went into a conference room, where my co-worker and I filled two white boards with lines, boxes, circles, and arrows while the new hire watched. After about a half hour, I noticed that he had become very agitated.

18   "Are we going too fast?" I asked him.

19   "Too much for the first day?" asked my colleague.

20   "No," said our new man, "I just can't do it like this."

21   "Do what?" I asked. "Like what?"

22   His hands were deep in his pockets. He gestured with his elbows. "Like this," he said.

23   "You mean design?" I asked.

24   "You mean in a meeting?" asked my colleague.

25   No answer from the new guy. A shrug. Another elbow motion.

26   Something terrible was beginning to occur to me. "You mean talking?" I asked.

27   "Yeah, talking," he said. "I can't do it by talking."

28   By this time in my career, I had met many strange software engineers. But here was the first one who wouldn't talk at all. We had a lot of design work to do. No talking was certainly going to make things difficult.

29   "So how *can* you do it?" I asked.

30   "Mail," he said. "Send me e-mail."

31   Given no choice, we designed a graphical user interface by e-mail. Corporations across North America and Europe are still using a system designed by three people in the same office who communicated via computer, one of whom barely spoke at all.

32   Pretty graphical interfaces are commonly called "user-friendly." But they are not really your friends. Underlying every user-friendly interface is terrific contempt for the humans who will use it.

33   The basic idea of a graphical inteface is that it will not allow anything alarming to happen. You can pound on the mouse button, your cat can run across it, your baby can punch it, but the system should not crash.

34   To build a crash-proof system, the designer must be able to imagine—and disallow—the dumbest action possible. He or she has to think of every single stupid thing a human being could do. Gradually, over months and years, the designer's mind creates a construct of the user as an imbecile. The image is necessary. No crash-proof system can be built unless it is made for an idiot.

35   The designer's contempt for your intelligence is mostly hidden deep in the code. But now and then the disdain surfaces. Here's a small example: You're trying to do something simple such as copying files onto a diskette on your Mac. The program proceeds for a while, then encounters an error. Your disk is defective, says a message, and below the message is a single button. You absolutely must click this button. If you don't click it, the program will hang there indefinitely. Your disk is defective, your files may be bollixed up, but the designer leaves you only one possible reply. You must say, "OK."

36   The prettier the user interface, and the fewer replies the system allows you to make, the dumber you once appeared in the mind of the designer. Soon, everywhere we look, we will see pretty, idiot-proof interfaces designed to make us say, "OK." Telephones, televisions, sales kiosks will all be wired for "interactive," on-demand services. What power—demand! See a movie, order seats to a basketball game, make hotel reservations, send a card to mother—all of these services will be waiting for us on our televisions or computers whenever we want them, midnight, dawn, or day. Sleep or order a pizza: it no longer matters exactly what we do when. We don't need to involve anyone else in the satisfaction of our needs. We don't even have to talk. We get our services when we want them, free from the obligations of regularly scheduled time. We can all live, like programmers, close to the machine. "Interactivity" is misnamed. It should be called "asynchrony": the engineering culture come to everyday life.

37   The very word "interactivity" implies something good and wonderful. Surely a response, a reply, an answer is a positive thing. Surely it signifies an advance over something else, something bad, something that doesn't respond. There is only one problem: what we will be interacting with is a machine. We will be "talking" to programs that are beginning to look surprisingly alike; each has little animated pictures we are supposed to choose from, like push buttons on a toddler's toy. The toy is meant to please us. Somehow it is supposed to replace the rewards of fumbling for meaning with a mature human being, in the confusion of a natural language, together, in a room, within touching distance.

38   As the computer's pretty, helpful face (and contemptuous underlying code) penetrates deeper into daily life, the cult of the engineer comes with it. The engineer's assumptions and presumptions are in the code. That's the purpose of the program, after all: to sum up the intelligence and intentions of all the engineers who worked on the system over time—tens and hundreds of people who have learned an odd and highly specific way of doing things. The system reproduces and re-enacts life as engineers know it: alone, out of time, disdainful of anyone far from the machine.

QUESTIONS FOR DISCUSSION

1. What point is Ullman making through discussing her dream about having to program a couple making love?
2. Why does programming require such intense concentration? Can you think of other activities that require similarly strict and focused concentration?
3. What was your response to Ullman's statement: "I once had a job in which I didn't talk to anyone for two years." What compels Ullman to work on her project in such abject solitude? How does programming influence a person's sense of time?
4. How does Ullman distinguish between low code, high code, and applications? Why does a real programmer want to stay "close to the machine"? Why does Ullman introduce this computer jargon into her essay?

5. What is the aim of a crash proof program? Why does Ullman characterize computer code as contemptuous? What is ironic about the term "interactivity" as it is used by engineers?
6. How does Ullman contrast computer code language and every day human language?

CONNECTION

Compare Ullman's reflections on the alienating effects of computer technology with the ideas on gender relations expressed in Sherry Turkle's "Virtual Sex" (Chapter 6).

IDEAS FOR WRITING

1. Write an essay that explores the anti-social effects of long hours spent working on a computer. What are the costs of getting *too* close to the machine?
2. Write an essay about how people's attitude towards language and conversation is changing as a result of computer-mediated interactions such as e-mail and chat-rooms.

Louise Erdrich

Dear John Wayne

Louise Erdrich (b. 1954) was raised in Wahlpeton, North Dakota, as a member of the Turtle Mountain Chippewa tribe. Her parents encouraged her to write, and her culture valued story telling. Erdrich attended Dartmouth College where she studied with Michael Dorris, whom she later married. She earned a B.A. from Dartmouth in 1976 and an M.F.A. in creative writing from Johns Hopkins University several years later. Her first novel Love Medicine *(1984, expanded edition 1993), which won the National Book Critics Circle Award, introduces many of the characters and clan histories that are developed in her later novels,* The Beet Queen *(1986),* Tracks *(1988), and* The Bingo Palace *(1994). Her most recent work includes a memoir,* The Blue Jay's Dance *(1994), and a novel,* Antelope Woman *(1998). The poem that follows, "Dear John Wayne," is included in* Jacklight *(1984).*

JOURNAL

Write about a film that influenced your view of a particular cultural, ethnic, or national group.

August and the drive-in picture is packed.
We lounge on the hood of the Pontiac
surrounded by the slow-burning spirals they sell
at the window, to vanquish the hordes of mosquitoes.
5 Nothing works. They break through the smoke-screen
for blood.

Always the look-out spots the Indians first,
spread north to south, barring progress.
The Sioux, or Cheyenne, or some bunch
10 in spectacular columns, arranged like SAC missiles,
their feathers bristling in the meaningful sunset.

The drum breaks. There will be no parlance.
Only the arrows whining, a death-cloud of nerves
swarming down on the settlers
15 who die beautifully, tumbling like dust weeds
into the history that brought us all here
together: this wide screen beneath the sign of the bear.

The sky fills, acres of blue squint and eye
that the crowd cheers. His face moves over us,
20 a thick cloud of vengeance, pitted
like the land that was once flesh. Each rut,
each scar makes a promise: *It is*
not over, this fight, not as long as you resist.
Everything we see belongs to us.

25 A few laughing Indians fall over the hood
slipping in the hot spilled butter.
The eye sees a lot, John, but the heart is so blind.
How will you know what you own?
He smiles, a horizon of teeth
30 the credits reel over, and then the white fields
again blowing in the true-to-life dark.
The dark films over everything.
We get into the car
scratching our mosquito bites, speechless and small
35 as people are when the movie is done.
We are back in ourselves.

How can we help but keep hearing his voice,
the flip side of the sound-track, still playing:
Come on, boys, we've got them
40 *where we want them, drunk, running.*
They will give us what we want, what we need:
The heart is a strange wood inside of everything
we see, burning, doubling, splitting out of its skin.

1. What is the ironic significance of the setting of the poem: a drive-in movie in August, where "hordes of mosquitoes" attack Indian patrons?
2. How are the Native Americans characterized in the second stanza? How does Erdrich use ironic images and details to create a critique of the stereotypical attitudes of Native Americans that the film reflects? Are Native Americans characterized differently in contemporary films?
3. What image of the "history that brought us all here together" is presented in the poem? How would the Native Americans have told the film's story?
4. What is the impact of the huge close-up face and eye of John Wayne described in the fourth stanza? What attitude toward Native Americans does Wayne's face portray? Why is the poem addressed to Wayne?
5. What criticisms of Wayne's values and the values of the western film genre are made through the italicized lines in stanzas five and six? Who is speaking in these lines?
6. Who is describing the heart in these lines: "the heart is so blind. . . ." and "The heart is a strange wood. . . ."? Interpret the meaning of these lines.

CONNECTION

Compare the tone of this poem about racist stereotypes of Native Americans to Jessica Hagedorn's essay about images of Asian women in recent films; which work seems more "serious"? Does Hagedorn seem more or less concerned than Erdrich about the impact of media-based stereotypes on minority groups?

IDEAS FOR WRITING

1. Write a critique of a particular film that you believe exploits racist stereotypes and could possibly influence the public negatively against a particular group of people.
2. Write about a film that you believe challenges stereotypes and presents a positive or original, revealing view of a group of people who have been stereotyped negatively.

Jason Glickman

Technology and the Future of the American Wilderness

Jason Glickman, who enjoys working with computers as well as canoeing, hiking, and backpacking in wilderness areas, wrote the following research paper for his introductory writing course. Glickman critiques the dependence on communication technology such as cell phones and lap-tops because this "portable" communications technology makes it difficult for people to experience the quiet and solitude of the wilderness. Notice how Glickman uses extensive historical and contemporary research to build his case for a wilderness experience free of technological and media intrusion.

1   When one finally arrives at the point where schedules are forgotten, and becomes immersed in ancient rhythms, one begins to live. —Sigurd Olson

2   In Olson's home—the vast lakeland wilderness of Northern Minnesota—schedules are forgotten with ease. Air and water engage in a fanciful dance tenderly embraced by lush forest. A canoe glides through the water with the slice of a razor, yet disturbs nothing. It has no motor; this vessel is propelled by the paddle's whisper.

3   In the wilderness I am at home. In the wilderness America is at home; since its birth, the nation's identity has been deeply rooted in its wilderness. First formulated by Henry David Thoreau and popularized by John Muir, the *wilderness experience* has become classically American. The Wilderness Act, which outlawed motor vehicles in designated backcountry areas, validated Muir's efforts. In the thirty-five years since its passage, the Act has been very effective in fostering wilderness appreciation. But will this success continue into the 21st-Century?

4   Today, the wilderness experience is again threatened by technology. Devices like global positioning system (GPS) receivers, cellular phones, and palmtop computers deaden the wilderness experience. If the traditional wilderness experience is defined by a disconnection from society, how can America reconcile the growing use of information technology in the outdoors? How can America reconcile the potential loss of the wilderness experience, heretofore crucial to her identity? Legislation will not suffice, for it cannot evolve as rapidly as information technology does. To ensure the wilderness experience's long-term viability, backcountry users must champion a new outdoor ethics. Developing a technology-directed clone of Leave No Trace (the most successful minimum impact program to date) is the best way to preserve the wilderness experience.

5   In contrast to contemporary concerns, America's earliest colonists thought little of preserving wilderness. They imported a utilitarian view of wilderness, measuring its value in economic terms. The wilderness was not to be enjoyed, but subjugated in the name of human progress. As poet and naturalist Gary Snyder observes, in early America, "wild is associated with unruliness," and represented a disorder that ought to be controlled (5). The driving vision of pioneer ideology was the taming of Western wilderness for human benefit.

6   In the 19th-Century, however, a new attitude emerged that wilderness could be enjoyed for its mere existence (Nash 67). Thinkers like Ralph Waldo Emerson initiated a gradual appreciation of the beauty and solitude of the backcountry. As Emerson noted, "[T]he sky, the mountain, the tree, the animal, give us a delight in and for themselves" (531). In a statement that would become a mantra for wilderness advocates, Emerson's friend and fellow transcendenalist, Henry David Thoreau, decreed that "in wildness is the preservation of the world" (qtd. in Nash 84). In attaching this degree of divinity to wilderness, Emerson and Thoreau hoped to remove its stigma.

7   Thoreau's influence upon the popular conception of "wilderness" cannot be overlooked. His quest for refuge from the stress of industrial society led him deep into the
Canadian backcountry, yet he still clung to the threads of civilization. Hoping to
strike a balance, Thoreau authored a vision of the wilderness as a refresher—a sort of
spiritual vacation. His idea was deeply influential, as he "led the intellectual revolution that was beginning to invest wilderness with attractive rather than repulsive
qualities" (Nash 95).

8   Thoreau's view of wilderness as an idyllic respite from industrial civilization soon
bore a new idea: *the wilderness experience.* Central to the wilderness experience was
one's willingness to blend into the landscape rather than dominate it. Though
Thoreau first conceived these ideals, John Muir is credited with entering "the wilderness experience" into the national lexicon. In his *Wilderness and The American Mind,*
Roderick Nash writes, " Wild country needed a champion, and in. . . John Muir it
found one" (122). Muir's ideals borrowed heavily from transcendentalism, but di-
verged in their unabashed enthusiasm. This zeal propagated itself in his writing,
which enjoyed a greater audience than any wilderness or conservation issues had ever
before (Nash 131). Muir's notion of walking into the high Sierra with only what he
could carry on his back and emerging at his fancy ". . . demanded dependency on self
rather than on society" (Nash 253). Others would soon adopt this notion, crafting it
into the archetypal wilderness experience.

9   In Muir's lifetime, straddling the turn of the century, it was possible for one to
simply "run away" from industrial society into the wilderness. This was ensured by
the remoteness, harshness, and sheer scale of much of the American landscape.
Nash notes, "For a time in the history of the West, lack of technology held in check
human desire to modify the land" (276). Without efficient transportation, it would
be impossible for industrial society to encroach upon the deepest wilderness. However, in the 20th Century, all but the most unforgiving wilderness was threatened by
the advent of the automobile. The question, "What is technology's place in the
wilderness?" moved into the foreground. Here, more philosophical questions at the
root of the issue emerge. At what level are beauty, solitude, independence, and one-
ness with nature jeopardized? When does the progress of man directly encroach
upon the wilderness experience? Can we let the wilderness experience change, or
must we preserve it as Thoreau and Muir envisioned it?

10   Early 20th Century conservationists, in the mold of Thoreau and Muir, argued for
the maintenance of the traditional wilderness experience through the protection of
land. Aldo Leopold, borrowing from Thoreau, developed a "land ethic," which
"changes the role of Homo sapiens from conqueror of the land-community to plain
member and citizen of it" (qtd. in Watkins 3). In this decree, Leopold reinforced the
foundation for the traditional wilderness experience. For if man could adopt such a
land ethic, he could ensure that the solitude and beauty of the wilderness would remain intact for ages.

11   Strong efforts to legislate Leopold's vision took root after World War II. In
September 1964, the U.S. Congress passed "The Wilderness Act," designating

some 9 million acres as "wilderness areas." The Act stipulated that ". . . there shall be no commercial enterprise and no permanent road within any wilderness area. . . there shall be no temporary road, no use of motor vehicles, motorized equipment or motorboats, no landing of aircraft, no other form of mechanical transport, and no structure or installation within any such area" (Section 4c). For both wilderness advocates and opponents, this was a striking measure. In anointing a wilderness area as land free of the combustion engine—arguably the foremost symbol of post-Industrial Revolution progress—the Wilderness Act offered a barrier to the relentless onslaught of progress (Borrie and Friemund 1).

12   Preserving the land so that future generations could enjoy it in its original state was the Wilderness Act's central concern. It specified that wilderness areas "shall be administered for the use and enjoyment of the American people in such manner as will leave them unimpaired for future use and enjoyment as wilderness" (Sec. 2a). In theory, the Act allowed one to experience the Sierra Nevada exactly as Muir had done seventy-five years earlier. Muir's exploration of the Sierra was at its time unmatched in scope; he pioneered first ascents on many of the range's most forbidding peaks. The illusion that one is the *first* to climb a distant peak or paddle a raging river is key to the wilderness experience. Whether or not others have done so is mostly irrelevant; the beauty of the moment comes in that one is able to share it with nature alone. The degree of importance the Wilderness Act attached to such a feat was a major victory for backcountry enthusiasts, for it validated the intangible value of the wilderness experience.

13   However, because of its position in technological history, the Wilderness Act was ill-suited to be the wilderness experience's ultimate protector. Its passage stood at a pivotal point: after the close of the Industrial Revolution, but at the brink of the computer age. In 1965, few could have fathomed the potential for information technology. Especially in the last decade, computing has become smaller, faster, and cheaper. Powerful laptop computers can now be had in packages well under five pounds. Cellular towers dot the landscape, allowing one to place a call from nearly anywhere. Satellite phones allow one to literally talk to *anyone* on the globe from *anywhere* on the globe. GPS units permit one to pinpoint their location to within 100 yards—*anywhere on earth*. While contemporary society lauds these technological miracles, they also pose a direct threat to the wilderness experience.

14   The wilderness experience hinges on a *disconnection* from society—the lack of dependency that Nash cites. Information technology works directly against this ideal. In theory, one might stay connected to the Internet for the entire duration of a backcountry stay. This, of course, is currently impossible due to battery limitations, but, with solar energy and superior batteries, can it be long before it is a reality? The traditional wilderness experience minimizes the gap between man and nature. Modern information technology just does the opposite; it erects a barrier between humans and the wilderness. Man is shielded from nature's vitality by his technology, precluding one from becoming "immersed in ancient rhythms," as Olson wrote. It

follows that successive generations of technology will further this trend, further numbing the reality of a backcountry trip.

15   With every new device will come "more shallow contact and superficial understandings," writes David Strong in *Crazy Mountains: Using Wilderness to Weigh Technology* (163). For an experience whose meaning lay in its spiritual depth, Strong's contention is ominous. Traveling in the wilderness is a relatively simple affair—technology brings unnecessary complexity to the wilderness. "The beauty of backpacking is its simplicity," I was once told, "it's nothing more than walking." Not having anything to focus on but *walking* facilitates incredible self-reflection and natural appreciation. The spirituality of the wilderness experience is marred by the presence of technology. Recognizing and dispatching technology's imposition has become a focal point for wilderness advocates in the last half-decade.

16   Accordingly, a wealth of discussion has sprung up to find an appropriate role for information technology in the wilderness. In an article entitled "Tech overload victims, unite!," Dan McMillan argues that modern computing devices have no place in the wilderness:

> I read about this wondrous little [cellular phone and e-mail] device the morning after returning from a week-long backpacking trip in Idaho's Seven Devils Wilderness Area. The entire point of said trip being to get away from anything more technologically advanced than a water filter. (1)

17   McMillan's objection is shared by a variety of wilderness users. In an interview of six Stanford students (whose trail time ranged from one to over one hundred nights) about technology's impact upon the wilderness, information technology was unanimously stigmatized. Galen Weston, a freshman with extensive experience in the Sierra backcountry, laments, "The more you bring, it cheapens [the experience]." Wary of this type of reaction, magazines like *Backpacker* and *Outside* have been reluctant to take a stance on the use of information technology in the wilderness.

18   In this fashion, the March 1999 issue of *Outside* reviewed cellular phones, handheld computers, and satellite phones in an aptly named article: "Always in Touch (If, That is, You Want to Be)." The title's qualification lends credence to the argument that information technology's role in the wilderness ought to be determined by the individual user. However, the *Outside* article also included a sidebar reviewing a protective case for cell phones, noting that it ". . . is lined with enough padding to take a good licking but not so much that you won't hear an incoming call" (Hurtig 1).

19   Receiving a call in the backcountry clearly violates the wilderness experience—it's an obvious connection to society. But, some might argue, isn't it an individual's *right* to receive a call? If one wishes *not* to have a traditional wilderness experience, isn't that permissible? Absolutely. But a cell-phone-toting visitor's right to receive calls should not infringe upon others' right to the magnificently rich silence of a backcountry jaunt. In nature's comparatively quiet sound-scape, a cell phone's digital whine carries much farther than in an urban environment. Many wilderness users

consider it a disappointment to see any other humans while in the backcountry—
how will they react when they hear or see a cellular phone in use? For wilderness advocates, the chief virtue of the wilderness experience—the enjoyment of nature's
unbridled power—is threatened by information technology. How, then, to guarantee that the traditional wilderness experience remains intact? The Wilderness Act,
while safeguarding against the technology of yesteryear, lacks provisions for the
technology of tomorrow. An act whose basis is the outlaw of specific technologies
cannot protect the wilderness experience in an ever-advancing society. Will the
Act's failure mark the end of the wilderness experience as we know it? To address
this question, one must further examine the character of the wilderness experience.

20   The wilderness experience is fundamentally aesthetic; it is highly dependent on
sensory impulse: the bite of an alpine breeze; the smell of a pine forest; the soft lap-
ping of water against a canoe. Therefore, this aesthetic must be the standard for the
maintenance of the wilderness experience. In the two decades following the Wilderness Act, this aesthetic was threatened by the rapidly growing ranks of wilderness
users. To combat this trend, wilderness advocates initiated "minimum impact"
movements. Leave No Trace (LNT), begun in the early '80s, is one such program.
Originally conceived by a Forest Service ranger, LNT is today spearheaded by the
National Outdoor Leadership School (NOLS). While some of LNT's guidelines directly protect the *wilderness* itself (i.e. depositing human waste away from water
sources), others are aesthetically-oriented—designed solely to preserve the *wilderness experience*. The NOLS *Wilderness Guide* offers this snippet:

> NOLS issues tents and backpacks in earth tones of blue, brown, and green, rather
> than bright Day-Glo colors, to help ensure that we fade into beauty and solitude
> which our students, instructors, and other backpackers are in the wilderness to
> enjoy. (Simer and Sullivan 24)

21   Such a guideline is wholly visual; the physical impact of a bright orange parka upon
the land is non-existent. LNT's success in this sort of outdoor ethic has garnered it a
wide network of support: four federal partnerships, heavy corporate backing, and
NOLS' influence as the leading outdoor education program in the world ("Leave No
Trace: Questions and Answers"). Much of LNT's success may be attributable to the
fact that it is not legislation and is thus endlessly adaptable. As new threats to the
wilderness experience have emerged, LNT has been able to compensate appropriately.

22   Such a revision occurred on February 24th as LNT added a new principle to the six
it had already established. The seventh, "Be Considerate of Other Visitors," is necessarily broad to reflect LNT's overall mission ("Principles of Leave No Trace"). But this
principle may also be applied to the role of information technology in the wilderness.
Implicit in the principle is the assurance that visitors may have a traditional wilderness
experience; it could be amended to read "Be Considerate of Other Visitors *so as Not to
Disturb Their Wilderness Experience*" without betraying its original meaning. The added
clause is actually a concise statement of LNT's true purpose: maintaining the viability
of the wilderness so that the wilderness experience remains intact.

23 LNT has demonstrated an ability to successfully engender respect for the wilderness and its occupants. If articulated properly, a new outdoor ethics in the mold of LNT would effectively counter high-tech's threat to the wilderness experience. As LNT does, such a program would *educate* rather than *regulate*. In lieu of declaring a role for information technology in the wilderness, it would inform people as to *why* technology threatens the wilderness experience. Appreciation for the wilderness experience would grow in turn; once something is threatened—e.g. an endangered species—it draws more attention.

24 This new ethics might even be designed as a subset of LNT so as to use the latter's name recognition. Wilderness and technology advocates alike are desperately looking for ways to make these two American fixtures coexist; a tech-directed outdoor ethics would encourage the productive dialogue that's just beginning. As technology becomes more and more advanced, this exchange of ideas will become increasingly crucial. Wilderness advocates must voice their displeasure with technology that infringes upon the wilderness experience.

25 To be sure, the American wilderness is at a crossroads. The looming technological threat will continue to mount; how does America respond? Does she place a higher valuation on her wilderness, or does she let the Wilderness Act become just another wayward roadblock in the progress of man? The goal for wilderness users must not be the condemnation of technology, but finding a way to blend the traditional wilderness experience with new technology. This synergy will become even more critical for America's identity in the years ahead. In an increasingly tech-driven society, Americans will need a way to escape. Hopefully, that way will continue to be among the snow-capped peaks, cold mountain streams, and sheer magnificence of *their wilderness*.

WORKS CITED

Borrie, William T. and Wayne A. Friemund. *Wilderness in the 21st Century: Are There Technical Solutions to our Technical Solutions?* Oct. 1997. University of Montana. 2 Feb. 1999 <http://www.forestry.umt.edu/people/borrie/papers/techno>.

Daniel, John. "Toward Wild Heartlands." *Audobon* Sept .–Oct. 1994: 38–47.

Emerson, Ralph Waldo. *The Works of Ralph Waldo Emerson.* New York: Black Reader's Service. 1929.

Hurtig, Brent. "Review: Always in Touch (If, That Is, You Want to Be)." *Outside.* Mar. 1999. 28 Feb. 1999 <http://outside.starwave.com:80/magazine/0399/9903review.html>.

"Leave No Trace: Questions and Answers." *Leave No Trace Home Page.* 1998. 1 Mar. 1999 <http://www.lnt.org/LNT_FAQ.html>.

McMillan, Dan. "Tech Overload Victims, Unite!" *The Business Journal of Portland* 12 Oct. 1998. 1 Feb. 1999 <http://www.amcity.com/portland/stories/101298/editorial2.html>.

Nash, Roderick. *Wilderness and the American Mind.* New Haven, Connecticut: Yale University Press, 1982.

"Principles of Leave No Trace." *Leave No Trace Home Page.* 1998. 1 Mar. 1999 <http://www.lnt.org/LNTPrinciples/LNTPrinciples.update.html>.

Simer, Peter and John Sullivan. *The National Outdoor Leadership School's Wilderness Guide.* New York: Simon and Schuster, 1983.

Snyder, Gary. *The Practice of the Wild.* San Francisco: North Point Press, 1990.

Strong, David. *Crazy Mountains: Learning From Wilderness to Weigh Technology.* Albany, New York: State University of New York Press, 1995.

Watkins, T.H. "The Hundred-Million-Acre Understanding." *Audobon.* Sep.–Oct. 1994: 36–39.

Weston, Galen. Interview on Technology. Stanford, California. 19 Feb. 1999.

QUESTIONS FOR DISCUSSION

1. Why does Glickman begin his essay with the quotation and introductory paragraph on Sigurd Olson?
2. How does Glickman define both the wilderness experience and the Wilderness Act ? How do these two definitions help prepare us for the contemporary problem he wants to discuss?
3. How have technological advances affected the wilderness experience? Why is the Wilderness Act unable to cope with current technology?
4. What solution does Glickman present for the problems related to technology that he explores in his essay? Does his solution seem adequate? Is a solution to this problem possible?

Topics for Research and Writing

1. Many critics have commented that mass communications media often portray a biased or stereotyped image of minority groups, sometimes excluding certain groups altogether. Do research into the media coverage of one ethnic group and write up your conclusions in the form of a documented research essay.
2. Write a research paper that discusses the media's coverage and influence on the outcome of a significant event in your community, city, or state.
3. After doing some outside reading and Internet research, write an essay that focuses on the ways that computers and the electronic environment have influenced modern life and perceptions of reality. Consider whether communication through computers and the World Wide Web is more positive than negative or more negative than positive in its influences.
4. Examine the current television schedule (cable as well as network TV) for programs that you think encourage imagination, creativity, and a concern for the inner life; then read some media reviews of these programs in print media or the Internet. Write an evaluative review of several such programs, trying to draw some conclusions about the potential the television medium has for improving the quality of modern life.
5. Write a research paper that addresses the negative impact of a particular mass medium or aspect of a medium on the values and self-concept of citizens in our society. Define and present examples of the problem, then suggest solutions such as legislation or citizen action. You could discuss issues such as children's TV programs, MTV, subliminal persuasion, or other forms of manipulative advertising, or excessive sex and violence in the media.
6. Write a research essay that discusses the way that images of roles and behavior for women are created and reinforced by the mass media. To narrow your topic, you might focus on women of a certain age group,

ethnic, or cultural background, as Hagedorn does in her essay in this chapter.

7. Although she is convinced that media violence has a negative impact on children's behavior maturation, Bok points out the difficulty of collecting accurate statistics and drawing clear-cut causal relations in these areas. Write an essay in which you examine studies done in this area, pointing out limitations and suggesting avenues for further research into the causes and effects of media violence.

8. Write about a film that examines issues of advertising, propaganda, or mass media on society, politics, and the inner life of the individual. Watch the film and take notes on the dialogue and any other details that can be used to support the conclusions you draw; also read some critical responses to the film, both in popular journals and in specialized magazines that critique films. You might select a film from the following list: *Day of the Locust, Network, Broadcast News, 1984, Closet Land, The Kiss of the Spider Woman, The Celluloid Closet, Hoop Dreams, Pulp Fiction, To Die For, Johnny Mnemonic, Glengarry Glen Ross, Truman Show, Wag the Dog, Bullworth, Pleasantville.*

9. The following URLs are good sources for research into the impact of the mass media and the Internet on society and the individual:

ASIAN AMERICAN MEDIAWATCH
http://www.tmiweb.com/cgi-bin/imagemap/~tweb2/Maps/media.map?74,14
A site providing an "Asian Awareness Report Card" and guidelines for activism in relation to presence and portrayals of Asians in the media.

GENDER AND RACE IN MEDIA
http://www.uiowa.edu/~commstud/resources/GenderMedia/index.html
This is a set of links to resources and indexes on media images of women, African-Americans, Asian-Americans, Latin Americans, Native Americans, and gays. Site is from the University of Iowa and maintained by Karla Tonella.

MEDIA AND SOCIETY
http://www.bctv.net/telcom/tel12links.html
A collection of links prepared for an on-line class at Butte College in California, this site contains a great many links to propaganda sites, sites on race and gender issues in media, sites on advertising analysis, as well as the corporate control of media.

MEDIA LITERACY ON-LINE PROJECT
http://interact.uoregon.edu/MediaLit/HomePage

Provides information on international conferences and organizations devoted to media literacy as well as a very large index of articles and resource, including links to on-line broadcasts.

Media Theory Site
http://www.theory.org.uk/about.htm
This wittily designed and accessible web site, by David Gauntlett of the Institute of Communications Studies, University of Leeds, England, contains media theory by many modern thinkers and theoretical analysis on the impact of media. Also contains links to theories on alternative media in a related site, New Media Studies.

Propaganda Page
http://www.webexpert.net/vasilios/propag.htm
This set of links, part of the larger site Hellenism of the Greater New York Area, maintained by Vasilios Apostolopoulos, provides an enormous collection of links to all aspects of propaganda and many examples from the history of political propaganda around the world.

Violence on Television
http://www.apa.org/pubinfo/violence.html
This document, contained on the web site of the American Psychological Association Office of Public Affairs, contains valuable information on the impact of media violence on children, as well as possible alternatives and interventions for parents.

9

Visions of Nature

It was as if this plant with its hosts of lives was a society, one in which moment by moment, depending on light and moisture, there was great and diverse change.

LINGA HOGAN
Walking

*His vision, from the constantly passing bars,
has grown so weary that it cannot hold
anything else. . . .*

RAINER MARIA RILKE
The Panther

Efforts to change the environment and to change the individual are both necessary, but it is difficult to change the environment if individuals are not in a state of equilibrium.

THICH NHAT HANH
Love in Action

CREATIVITY, PROBLEM SOLVING, AND SYNTHESIS

Creativity involves combining information and experience into a new form that solves problems and/or produces something that a person can take pride in, such as a piece of writing that is humanely and aesthetically satisfying, both to oneself and to others. While many people are inspired by the examples of creative visionaries in different fields and can learn from studying their techniques, creativity is in large part a generative rather than an imitative and technical process, a process of discovery that often originates in the unconscious mind, sometimes without a clear goal or defined "product" in mind—at least at the beginning. An open, receptive mental attitude encourages the initiation of the creative process.

Everyone is potentially creative; in fact, all people are creative for a part of each night when they dream, whether or not they are consciously aware of the process. As author John Steinbeck noted, a problem is often "resolved in the morning after the committee of sleep has worked it out." In waking life people are creative in a more conscious, directed manner, seeking solutions to problems in order to survive and to make their lives more comfortable and rewarding. For example, when you redecorate your room, look for a better job, or select a new course of study in school, you are working on creative solutions for the problems that you have recognized in your life, just as you are when you write a proposal for your job or for one of your classes at school, as student Sheila Walsh did in her imaginative project at the end of this chapter, "Visualizing Our Environment." You may see what you are doing at work or school as competing for a raise or completing a course requirement—but there is room for creative solutions in every environment, and it is usually the creative ideas that get the most attention.

Although it is true that everyone exercises some degree of creativity, it is equally true that most people have the potential to be far more creative in many aspects of their lives than they are. Writers, psychologists, and social scientists have identified patterns of behavior that are likely to block an individual's creativity. Understanding how these mental traps work may help you find a way to release yourself from nonproductive behavior and become more creative.

Habit Versus Risk

Habit and self-image can be major blocks to creativity. If your inner self-image is that of a person stuck in a round of repetitive daily tasks and rituals, it is unlikely that you will feel that you have the capacity to be creative. You may have come to believe that you really need to follow a ritualized pattern in performing your job, relating to people, or writing. This type of thinking also protects you from taking risks: the risk of an original expression of a feeling or situation, the risk of a controversial solution to a problem, the risk of not being understood by others.

Furthermore, creative risk-taking approaches to problem solving can be quite time-consuming. Many people convince themselves that they don't have the time to explore a new and creative approach, that it is more efficient to follow a method that has worked (or "sort of" worked) in the past. This inclination to play it safe and to be overly concerned with time management is typical of workers, managers, students, teachers, and writers who fear change and are wary of embarking on a new direction in their lives. Even if you see yourself as a non-risk-taking person, it is never too late to change; fantasizing about new approaches and thinking about alternatives is a positive first step toward finding creative solutions. Try to develop your alternative fantasies as do many of the writers in this chapter.

Reason Versus Intuition

You may be building another obstacle to uncovering your creativity if you value a linear, rational approach to handling problems to the extent that you ignore the imaginative, emotional, and intuitive side of the mind and the solutions that your imagination might suggest. Did you know that many landmark solutions to creative problems, both in the arts and in the sciences, were born in the unconscious mind and some specifically in dreams: Descartes' philosophical system, the invention of the sewing machine needle, the pattern of the benzene ring, as well as the basic concepts for classic works of literature such as Mary Shelley's *Frankenstein*, Samuel Taylor Coleridge's "Kubla Khan," and Robert Louis Stevenson's *The Strange Case of Dr. Jekyll and Mr. Hyde*.

While we do not want you to think that all you have to do is to take a nap and allow your problems to solve themselves or that if you sleep long enough, you will discover the seeds of great art and great ideas, we do encourage you to look to your dream mind for ideas and feelings and to allow your unconscious mind to have time to process and integrate ideas that are being developed by your rational mind. For example, after you have finished the first draft of a paper, go for a walk, or a swim, or listen to some music, or take a nap. Let your unconscious mind have a chance to think about what you have written. When you return to your first draft, you may find that your unconscious mind has sent you new ideas to work with or that you have a solution to a problem in your paper that was concerning you.

Developing Self-Confidence: Learning to Trust Your Own Processes

Another barrier to the creative process can be built by an overeagerness to please an authority such as a teacher or employer. If you focus your energy on trying to please your teacher at the expense of what you think or believe, an inner conflict may keep you from writing your paper altogether. If you become overly reliant on your instructor's assignment and approval, you will not be developing your own working style and sense of independence, which every writer must possess. Finally, if you rush to produce a finished paper in one draft, you will miss the excitement of discovery, the potential for personal involvement that is an essential part of the writing process; it is always preferable to relax and work within a writing project rather than to become overly concerned with what it is supposed to be.

Evaluation and Application

The creative problem-solving process does include evaluation and application— but only after you give free expression to a range of imaginative solutions and ideas. Once you have finished the creative or generative part of your writing project, you will want to think about whether or not you have accomplished your goals. To evaluate your work you need to establish clear standards so that you can compare your work with that of others. Always try to formulate standards that are challenging and yet realistic.

Peer sharing can be a useful comparative and evaluative process that will help you to create realistic standards for assessing your own writing in relationship to your classmates'. Through sharing your work as well as reading and editing the work of your classmates, you will begin to develop realistic standards for the style, structure, and content of your writing. Learn to ask questions of yourself and of your peers. Develop criteria for evaluating papers as you go along. Soon you will find that you have established a vocabulary that allows you to talk about one anothers' papers and that you have defined some standards for effective writing.

Synthesis

Synthesis, the final step in the creative process, involves bringing a number of different ideas or solutions, which you may have considered separately, together to form an integrated solution. For example, if you are trying to decide on a method for presenting an essay on "How to Make Your Dreams Work for You," you will need to evaluate and then synthesize or integrate the different points of view of experts as well as your own on the subject of dream power. Synthesis is an excellent metaphor for the gathering and unifying of information from diverse sources that can produce a lively research proposal such as Sheila Walsh's "Visualizing our Environment." Sheila brought together for her paper research into 19th Century artists, modernist painters like Picasso, Chicano muralists, and accounts of detailed paintings of plants and plies effected by doses of radiation; she also comments on episodes of *Dateline* and *ER*. Out of her synthesis of diverse, seemingly discordant materials, she arrives at a solution that is complex and nuanced. In a sense, synthesis also defines the writing process itself, as writing involves bringing together a number of different skills to solve a variety of problems: engaging your reader's interest, persuading your reader, developing an overall structure and pattern, supporting your main ideas, and using language that is both appropriate and creative.

Writing is a rewarding activity that can help you discover your thoughts and feelings and combine them in new ways. In performing any type of writing, you work through the stages and difficulties inherent in the creative process as a whole.

THEMATIC INTRODUCTION: VISIONS OF NATURE

Visions of nature provide valuable insights into the human spirit at its most creative, courageous, and hopeful. From ancient times to the present, people have discovered solutions to personal, aesthetic, social, and scientific problems as well as spiritual healing through paying heed to the messages from their unconscious minds and their dreams, messages that often come to us more intensely and clearly when we experience nature. The selections in this chapter present a variety of natural dreams of vision or prophecy from different cultures. We hope that reading and reflecting on these dreams and visions will help you develop insight into possible alternatives to the spiritual and social dilemmas we face today.

The chapter begins with two works that examine the connection between humans and animals. First, Rainer Maria Rilke's poem, "The Panther," captures imaginatively and concretely the inner and outer worlds of a caged panther. In our next selection, poet and scholar Gary Snyder in his short essay from "The Etiquette of Freedom" reflects on the connections between human and animal behavior and language, asking us to think about how instinctual or unconscious behavior has been integrated into formal language.

How is nature connected to our sense of change and community? This is a question that all of us ask and that politicians, writers, and religious leaders often try to help us answer through speculative or reflective writing and through direct calls to change. We see political values, natural imagery, and spiritual visions integrated in John G. Neihardt and Black Elk's "The Great Vision." As a Sioux Indian medicine man, he writes of his vision of Native American solidarity and cultural renewal that became the cornerstone of his life, moving him to help his community change their destiny. In a contrasting vision of time in nature, the essay "Walking" by Native American poet Linda Hogan encourages us to think about the way nature reveals itself to us over a long cycle of time and seasonal change. She creates a representative micro-community around a sunflower that she observes repeatedly over a year of walking in nature.

The next selection asks us to think about how we feel about our relationship to the divine or ultimate ground of being as revealed in the quiet world of nature. Annie Dillard's "A Field of Silence" captures a moment of intense illumination; while living a life of solitude on a farm, she is taken by the power of God and the unknown. Finally, Dillard must turn away from the intensity of her vision, yet she is changed by her insight. We hope that reading Dillard's reflection will encourage you to think for a time about the natural world in its immensity, the world beyond the day-to-day routines and struggles that mark your rational journey.

Our next three works present new ways for revisioning our relationship with nature and reorganize our society to make our visions real. E. M. Forster's story "The Other Side of the Hedge" presents a pastoral agrarian world that stands in contrast to the values of progress and the work ethic that propel those of us who accept life on the road as we know it in a capitalistic world. Following tradition of political and religious visions of the future, Terry Tempest Williams in "The Clan of One-Breasted Women" addresses a fundamental ethical issue: the morality of United States nuclear bomb testing in the Utah desert since the early 1970s, which continues to cause deaths from nuclear fallout. Williams sees women as the mothers of the earth who have a new responsibility: "A contract had been made and broken between human beings and the land. A new contract was being drawn by the women, who understood the fate of the earth as their own." In the third of these selections, Thich Nhat Hanh's essay "Love in Action," a Buddhist monk and peace activist, advises environmentalists, psychotherapists, and those whom they can influence to heal themselves through meditating on the connections between the mind, the spirit, nature, and the human family.

Our last poem is an anonymous Zuni prayer, "Offering." This Native American prayer calls upon the earth gods to sustain the cyclic, nurturing pattern of the nature and to assure a good harvest for the community. Two student writings follow. The first, "Jerusalem's Spring," is by a student living abroad, Michael Noah Ford, and resembles the Zuni prayer that precedes it in terms of its focus on the beauty and sacredness of the natural patterns. Our final student essay is a researched proposal by Sheila Walsh, "Visualizing our Environment." In this imaginative proposal, the student writer presents examples of art projects that have promoted an awareness of ecological systems as well as a proposal that urges a heightened level of public awareness and support for such projects in the future.

Powerful writing is nurtured through connections: between the inner world of dreams and the imagination, between the world of experience and knowledge, between one's own feeling for and mastery of the conventions of language and written expression. As you gain more experience expressing and crafting your ideas about yourself, the natural world around you, and your hopes for the future, we hope that writing will become a vital and versatile means for expressing your thoughts, feelings, hopes, and visions.

Cathy Young (1946-)
"Underneath the Oak"

Like Annie Dillard in "Field of Silence," Cathy Young, a professional artist, offers us a glimpse of the spiritual through her creative work. A meditation on the sun shining through the branches of an oak tree revealed for Young a vision of the eternal in nature which she tried to capture in oils.

Ideas for Drawing, Writing, and Discussion

1. Draw a scene from nature that you find inspiring.
2. Express the meaning of the experience that your drawing reflects through words, either in a descriptive narrative, a poem, or a simple freewriting.
3. Working in a group of other students, share your drawing and writing. Has your understanding of the experience changed through sharing it with others? If so, how?

Rainer Maria Rilke

The Panther
translated by Stephen Mitchell

See headnote for "Letters to a Young Poet" in Chapter 1. Rilke wrote the poem "The Panther" for his collection New Poems (1907–1908), while working with the sculptor Rodin. In this book Rilke attempted to form in language "not feelings but the things [he] had felt." His effort produced some of his most memorable poems, as in the case of the "The Panther," in which he brings a trapped zoo animal's perceptions alive in an intense, imaginative way.

JOURNAL

Closely observe a pet or zoo animal and write a paragraph or poem in which you try to capture in words the perceptions and "feelings" of the animal.

In the Jardin des Plantes, Paris

His vision, from the constantly passing bars,
has grown so weary that it cannot hold
anything else. It seems to him there are
a thousand bars; and behind the bars, no world.

5 As he paces in cramped circles, over and over,
the movement of his powerful soft strides
is like a ritual dance around a center
in which a mighty will stands paralyzed.

Only at times, the curtain of the pupils
10 lifts, quietly—. An image enters in,
rushes down through the tensed, arrested muscles,
plunges into the heart and is gone.

Im Jardin des Plantes, Paris

Sein Blick ist vom Vorübergehn der Stäbe
so müd geworden, daß er nichts mehr hält.
Ihm ist, als ob es tausend Stäbe gäbe
und hinter tausend Stäben keine Welt.

5 Der weich Gang geschmeidig starker Schritte,
der sich im allerkleinsten Kreise dreht,
ist wie ein Tanz von Kraft um eine Mitte,
in der betäubt ein großer Wille steht.

Nur manchmal schiebt der Vorhang der Pupille
10 sich lautlos auf—. Dangeht ein Bild hinein,

geht durch der Glieder angespannte Stille—
und hört im Herzen auf zu sein.

QUESTIONS FOR DISCUSSION

1. Rilke tries to capture the "vision" of the panther. What does the animal see ordinarily? What limits his vision?
2. How does Rilke describe the panther's movements? Why does he compare them to a "ritual dance"?
3. How and why does Rilke develop the metaphor of paralysis of will in describing the panther?
4. How does Rilke use contrast to emphasize the wild, powerful potential of the trapped panther?
5. Examine the final stanza of the poem. What is the significance of the description beginning "an image enters in"? Why is it significant that the image "plunges into the heart and is gone"?
6. Although the poem is clearly sympathetic to the captive status of zoo animals, it also can be seen as a critique of modern human life. Which words and images seem to compare the captive panther to a human being?

CONNECTION

Compare the comments on the human-animal connection made by Gary Snyder in "The Etiquette of Freedom" with the sad image of the captive panther created by Rilke. How would Snyder criticize the attitude toward nature implicit in the caging and display of this beast?

IDEAS FOR WRITING

1. Making references back to Rilke's image of the trapped panther, develop question six into an essay critiquing modern life in terms of our alienation from nature and our natural impulses.
2. Write an essay in which you argue whether or not zoos serve a useful function in our society, or if they can be considered useless, a form of cruelty to animals. Can you imagine a more natural zoo in which animals would not feel as confined and degraded as the panther in the Rilke poem?

Gary Snyder

The Etiquette of Freedom

Gary Snyder (b. 1930) grew up in the Pacific Northwest. He earned his B.A. at Reed College and did graduate work at the University of California at Berkeley, where he studied Asian languages, culture, and poetry. Eastern thought and religion have been fundamental to his work since the 1950s, when he lived for several years in Japan and

*associated with the writers of the Beat Generation. Snyder's poetry explores the relation-
ships between the spiritual and natural worlds. During the 1960s, Snyder was intensely
involved in a variety of liberal causes and protest events; he continues to write and speak
out on peace and environmental awareness. In 1975, he won the Pulitzer Prize in poetry for* Turtle Island. *Snyder and his family have been living in the foothills of the
Sierra Nevada in northern California for more than twenty years. Currently he teaches
at the University of California at Davis. Snyder has written many books of poetry and
prose. His most recent collections include* No Nature: New and Selected Poems
(1992); A Place in Space: Ethics, Aesthetics and Watersheds: New and Selected
Prose *(1995), and* Mountains and Rivers Without End *(1996). The selection that
follows is excerpted from "The Etiquette of Freedom" that appears in the prose collection*
The Practice of the Wild *(1991).*

JOURNAL

Write about your feelings of relationship to animals. How are you alienated from
them? In what way do you find kinship with them?

1   Do you really believe you are an animal? We are now taught this in school. It is a
wonderful piece of information: I have been enjoying it all my life and I come
back to it over and over again, as something to investigate and test. I grew up on a
small farm with cows and chickens, and with a second-growth forest right at the
back fence, so I had the good fortune of seeing the human and animal as in the same
realm. But many people who have been hearing this since childhood have not absorbed the implications of it, perhaps feel remote from the nonhuman world, are not
sure they are animals. They would like to feel they might be something better than
animals. That's understandable: other animals might feel they are something different than "just animals" too. But we must contemplate the shared ground of our common biological being before emphasizing the differences.

2   Our bodies are wild. The involuntary quick turn of the head at a shout, the ver-
tigo at looking off a precipice, the heart-in-the-throat in a moment of danger, the
catch of the breath, the quiet moments relaxing, staring, reflecting—all universal responses of this mammal body. They can be seen throughout the class. The body does
not require the intercession of some conscious intellect to make it breathe, to keep
the heart beating. It is to a great extent self-regulating, it is a life of its own. Sensation and perception do not exactly come from outside, and the unremitting thought
and image flow are not exactly outside. The world is our consciousness, and it surrounds us. There are more things in mind, in the imagination, than "you" can keep
track of—thoughts, memories, images, anger, delights, rise unbidden. The depths of
mind, the unconscious, are our inner wilderness areas, and that is where a bobcat is
right now. I do not mean personal bobcats in personal psyches, but the bobcat that
roams from dream to dream. The conscious agenda-planning ego occupies every tiny
territory, a little cubicle somewhere near the gate, keeping track of some of what
goes in and out (and sometimes making expansionistic plots), and the rest takes care
of itself. The body is, so to speak, in the mind. They are both wild.

3   Some will say, so far so good. "We are mammal primates. But we have language, and the animals don't." By some definitions perhaps they don't. But they do communicate extensively, and by call systems we are just beginning to grasp.

4   It would be a mistake to think that human beings got "smarter" at some point and invented first language and then society. Language and culture emerge from our biological-social natural existence, animals that we were/are. Language is a mind-body system that coevolved with our needs and nerves. Like imagination and the body, language rises unbidden. It is of a complexity that eludes our rational intellectual capacities. All attempts at scientific description of natural languages have fallen short of completeness, as the descriptive linguists readily confess, yet the child learns the mother tongue early and has virtually mastered it by six.

5   Language is learned in he house and in the fields, not at school. Without having ever been taught formal grammar we utter syntactically correct sentences, one after another, for all the waking hours of the years of our life. Without conscious device we constantly reach into the vast word-hoards in the depths of the wild unconscious. We cannot as individuals or even as a species take credit for this power. It came from someplace else: from the way clouds divide and mingle (and the arms of energy that toil first back and then forward), from the way the many flowerets of a composite blossom divide and redivide, from the gleaming calligraphy of the ancient riverbeds under present riverbeds of the Yukon River streaming out the Yukon flats, from the wind in the pine needles, from the chuckles of grouse in the ceanothus bushes.

6   Language teaching in schools is a matter of corralling off a little of the language-behavior territory and cultivating a few favorite features—culturally defined elite forms that will help you apply for a job or give you social credibility at a party. One might even learn how to produce the byzantine artifact known as the professional paper. There are many excellent reasons to master these things, but the power, the *virtu*, remains on the side of the wild.

7   Social order is found throughout nature—long before the age of books and legal codes. It is inherently part of what we are, and its patterns follow the same foldings, checks and balances, as flesh or stone. What we call social organization and order in government is a set of forms that have been appropriated by the calculating mind from the operating principles in nature.

QUESTIONS FOR DISCUSSION

1. What personal experiences led Snyder to find kinship with animals? Why do many people find this a difficult concept to accept, despite the evidence of evolutionary biology?
2. Why does Snyder assert that "the body is, so to speak, in the mind. They are both wild"? Explain why you agree or disagree with Snyder.
3. According to Snyder, what role does the unconscious mind play in monitoring and integrating one's animal and conscious self?

4. Why does Snyder argue that animals have language? How do they learn their languages?
5. How does Snyder believe that humans learn language? Explain why you agree or disagree with him.
6. Why does Snyder conclude that "what we call social organization and order in government is a set of forms that have been appropriated by the calculating mind from the operating principles in nature"? What evidence does he provide for this assertion?

CONNECTION

Compare Snyder's ideas about mind/body connections to those of Thich Nhat Hanh in "Love in Action" in this chapter.

IDEAS FOR WRITING

1. Using your own observations of animals and the political process, develop an argument essay around Snyder's final claim that our social organization and governmental forms derive from the "operating principles in nature."
2. Develop your journal entry about your sense of kinship with animals into an extended narrative essay or story.

Black Elk and John G. Neihardt

The Great Vision

Black Elk (1963–1950) was a visionary Oglala Sioux medicine man whose life and teachings are recorded in The Sacred Pipe: Black Elk's Account of the Seven Rites of the Oglala Sioux, *in William S. Lyon's* Black Elk : The Sacred Ways of a Lakota *(1990), and in John G. Neihardt's* Black Elk Speaks *(1932; 1963), which retells the story of Black Elk's life and his vision quests. Neihardt (1881–1973) was the Poet Laureate of Nebraska and a student of American Indian history and folklore. "The Great Vision" from* Black Elk Speaks *relates a vision Black Elk had as a child during a time of sickness. His vision, with its natural imagery of the revitalization of the Indian nation, gave a purpose and direction to Black Elk's life and inspired his community.*

JOURNAL

Write about a vision or dream of nature you had in childhood that helped to shape the values and choices of your later life.

1 I entered the village, riding, with the four horse troops behind me—the blacks, the whites, the sorrels, and the buckskins; and the place was filled with moaning and with mourning for the dead. The wind was blowing from the south like fever, and when I looked around I saw that in nearly every tepee the women and the children and the men lay dying with the dead.

2 So I rode around the circle of the village, looking in upon the sick and dead, and I felt like crying as I rode. But when I looked behind me, all the women and the children and the men were getting up and coming forth with happy faces.

3 And a Voice said: "Behold, they have given you the center of the nation's hoop to make it live."

4 So I rode to the center of the village, with the horse troops in their quarters round about me, and there the people gathered. And the Voice said: "Give them now the flowering stick that they may flourish, and the sacred pipe that they may know the power that is peace, and the wing of the white giant that they may have endurance and face all winds with courage."

5 So I took the bright red stick and at the center of the nation's hoop I thrust it in the earth. As it touched the earth it leaped mightily in my hand and was a waga chun, the rustling tree,* very tall and full of leafy branches and of all birds singing. And beneath it all the animals were mingling with the people like relatives and making happy cries. The women raised their tremolo of joy, and the men shouted all together: "Here we shall raise our children and be as little chickens under the mother sheo's† wing."

6 Then I heard the white wind blowing gently through the tree and singing there, and from the east the sacred pipe came flying on its eagle wings, and stopped before me there beneath the tree, spreading deep peace around it.

7 Then the daybreak star was rising, and a Voice said: "It shall be a relative to them; and who shall see it, shall see much more, for thence comes wisdom; and those who do not see it shall be dark." And all the people raised their faces to the east, and the star's light fell upon them, and all the dogs barked loudly and the horses whinnied.

8 Then when the many little voices ceased, the great Voice said: "Behold the circle of the nation's hoop, for it is holy, being endless, and thus all powers shall be one power in the people without end. Now they shall break camp and go forth upon the red road, and your Grandfathers shall walk with them." So the people broke camp and took the good road with the white wing on their faces, and the order of their going was like this:

9 First, the black horse riders with the cup of water; and the white horse riders with the white wing and the sacred herb; and the sorrel riders with the holy pipe; and the buckskins with the flowering stick. And after these the little children and the youths and maidens followed in a band.

10 Second, came the tribe's four chieftains, and their band was all young men and women.

11 Third, the nation's four advisers leading men and women neither young nor old.

12 Fourth, the old men hobbling with their canes and looking to the earth.

*The cottonwood
†Prairie hen

13 Fifth, old women hobbling with their canes and looking to the earth.

14 Sixth, myself all alone upon the bay with the bow and arrows that the First Grandfather gave me. But I was not the last; for when I looked behind me there were ghosts of people like a trailing fog as far as I could see—grandfathers of grandfathers and grandmothers of grandmothers without number. And over these a great Voice—the Voice that was the South—lived, and I could feel it silent.

15 And as we went the Voice behind me said: "Behold a good nation walking in a sacred manner in a good land!"

16 Then I looked up and saw that there were four ascents ahead, and these were generations I should know. Now we were on the first ascent, and all the land was green. And as the long line climbed, all the old men and women raised their hands, palms forward, to the far sky yonder and began to croon a song together, and the sky ahead was filled with clouds of baby faces.

17 When we came to the end of the first ascent we camped in the sacred circle as before, and in the center stood the holy tree, and still the land about us was all green.

18 Then we started on the second ascent, marching as before, and still the land was green, but it was getting steeper. And as I looked ahead, the people changed into elks and bison and all four-footed beings and even into fowls, all walking in a sacred manner on the good red road together. And I myself was a spotted eagle soaring over them. But just before we stopped to camp at the end of that ascent, all the marching animals grew restless and afraid that they were not what they had been, and began sending forth voices of trouble, calling to their chiefs. And when they camped at the end of that ascent, I looked down and saw that leaves were falling from the holy tree.

19 And the Voice said: "Behold your nation, and remember what your Six Grandfathers gave you, for thenceforth your people walk in difficulties."

20 Then the people broke camp again, and saw the black road before them towards where the sun goes down and black clouds coming yonder; and they did not want to go but could not stay. And as they walked the third ascent, all the animals and fowls that were the people ran here and there, for each one seemed to have his own little vision that he followed and his own rules; and all over the universe I could hear the winds at war like wild beasts fighting.*

21 And when we reached the summit of the third ascent and camped, the nation's hoop was broken like a ring of smoke that spreads and scatters and the holy tree seemed dying and all its birds were gone. And when I looked ahead I saw that the fourth ascent would be terrible.

22 Then when the people were getting ready to begin the fourth ascent, the Voice spoke like someone weeping, and it said: "Look there upon your nation." And when I looked down, the people were all changed back to human, and they were thin,

---

*At this point Black Elk remarked: "I think we are near that place now, and I am afraid something very bad is going to happen all over the world." He cannot read and knows nothing of world affairs.

their faces sharp, for they were starving. Their ponies were only hide and bones, and the holy tree was gone.

23   And as I looked and wept, I saw that there stood on the north side of the starving camp a sacred man who was painted red all over his body, and he held a spear as he walked into the center of the people, and there he lay down and rolled. And when he got up, it was a fat bison standing there, and where the bison stood a sacred herb sprang up right where the tree had been in the center of the nation's hoop. The herb grew and bore four blossoms on a single stem while I was looking— a blue,* a white, a scarlet, and a yellow—and the bright rays of these flashed to the heavens.

24   I know now what this meant, that the bison were the gift of a good spirit and were our strength, but we should lose them, and from the same good spirit we must find another strength. For the people all seemed better when the herb had grown and bloomed, and the horses raised their tails and neighed and pranced around, and I could see a light breeze going from the north among the people like a ghost; and suddenly the flowering tree was there again at the center of the nation's hoop where the four-rayed herb had blossomed.

25   I was still the spotted eagle floating, and I could see that I was already in the fourth ascent and the people were camping yonder at the top of the third long rise. It was dark and terrible about me, for all the winds of the world were fighting. It was like rapid gun-fire and like whirling smoke, and like women and children wailing and like horses screaming all over the world.

26   I could see my people yonder running about, setting the smoke-flap poles and fastening down their tepees against the wind, for the storm cloud was coming on them very fast and black, and there were frightened swallows without number fleeing before the cloud.

27   Then a song of power came to me and I sang it there in the midst of that terrible place where I was. It went like this:

A good nation I will make live.
This the nation above has said.
They have given me the power to make over.

    And when I had sung this, a Voice said: "To the four quarters you shall run for help, and nothing shall be strong before you. Behold him!"

28   Now I was on my bay horse again, because the horse is of the earth, and it was there my power would be used. And as I obeyed the Voice and looked, there was a horse all skin and bones yonder in the west, a faded brownish black. And a Voice there said: "Take this and make him over"; and it was the four-rayed herb that I was holding in my hand. So I rode above the poor horse in a circle, and as I did this I could hear the people yonder calling for spirit power, "A-hey! a-hey! a-hey!

---

*Blue as well as black may be used to represent the power of the west.

a-hey!" Then the poor horse neighed and rolled and got up, and he was a big, shiny, black stallion with dapples all over him and his mane about him like a cloud. He was the chief of all the horses; and when he snorted, it was a flash of lightning and his eyes were like the sunset star. He dashed to the west and neighed, and the west was filled with a dust of hoofs, and horses without number, shiny black, came plunging from the dust. Then he dashed toward the north and neighed, and to the east and to the south, and the dust clouds answered, giving forth their plunging horses without number—whites and sorrels and buckskins, fat, shiny, rejoicing in their fleetness and their strength. It was beautiful, but it was also terrible.

29   Then they all stopped short, rearing, and were standing in a great hoop about their black chief at the center, and were still. And as they stood, four virgins, more beautiful than women of the earth can be, came through the circle, dressed in scarlet, one from each of the four quarters, and stood about the great black stallion in their places; and one held the wooden cup of water, and one the white wing, and one the pipe, and one the nation's hoop. All the universe was silent, listening; and then the great black stallion raised his voice and sang. The song he sang was this:

"My horses, prancing they are coming.
My horses, neighing they are coming;
Prancing, they are coming.
All over the universe they come.
They will dance; may you behold them.   (4 times)

A horse nation, they will dance. May you behold them."   (4 times)

His voice was not loud, but it went all over the universe and filled it. There was nothing that did not hear, and it was more beautiful than anything can be. It was so beautiful that nothing anywhere could keep from dancing. The virgins danced, and all the circled horses. The leaves on the trees, the grasses on the hills and in the valleys, the waters in the creeks and in the rivers and the lakes, the four-legged and the two-legged and the wings of the air—all danced together to the music of the stallion's song.

30   "And when I looked down upon my people yonder, the cloud passed over, blessing them with friendly rain, and stood in the east with a flaming rainbow over it.

31   Then all the horses went singing back to their places beyond the summit of the fourth ascent, and all things sang along with them as they walked.

32   And a Voice said: "All over the universe they have finished a day of happiness." And looking down, I saw that the whole wide circle of the day was beautiful and green, with all fruits growing and all things kind and happy.

33   Then a Voice said: "Behold this day, for it is yours to make. Now you shall stand upon the center of the earth to see, for there they are taking you."

34   I was still on my bay horse, and once more I felt the riders of the west, the north, the east, the south, behind me in formation, as before, and we were going east. I looked ahead and saw the mountains there with rocks and forests on them, and

from the mountains flashed all colors upward to the heavens. Then I was standing on the highest mountain of them all, and round about beneath me was the whole hoop of the world.* And while I stood there I saw more than I can tell and I understood more than I saw; for I was seeing in a sacred manner the shapes of all things in the spirit, and the shape of all shapes as they must live together like one being. And I saw that the sacred hoop of my people was one of the many hoops that made one circle, wide as daylight and as starlight, and in the center grew one mighty flowering tree to shelter all the children of one mother and one father. And I saw that it was holy.

35   Then as I stood there, two men were coming from the east, head first like arrows flying, and between them rose the daybreak star. They came and gave a herb to me and said: "With this on earth you shall undertake anything and do it." It was the day-break-star herb, the herb of understanding, and they told me to drop it on the earth. I saw it falling far, and when it struck the earth it rooted and grew and flowered, four blossoms on one stem, a blue, a white, a scarlet, and a yellow; and the rays from these streamed upward to the heavens so that all creatures saw it and in no place was there darkness.

36   Then the Voice said: "Your Six Grandfathers—now you shall go back to them."

37   I had not noticed how I was dressed, until now, and I saw that I was painted red all over, and my joints were painted black, with white stripes between the joints. My bay had lightning stripes all over him, and his mane was cloud. And when I breathed, my breath was lightning.

38   Now two men were leading me, head first like arrows slanting upward—the two that brought me from the earth. And as I followed on the bay, they turned into four flocks of geese that flew in circles, one above each quarter, sending forth a sacred voice as they flew: Br-r-r-p, br-r-r-p, br-r-r-p, br-r-r-p!

39   Then I saw ahead the rainbow flaming above the tepee of the Six Grandfathers, built and roofed with cloud and sewed with thongs of lightning; and underneath it were all the wings of the air and under them the animals and men. All these were rejoicing, and thunder was like happy laughter.

40   As I rode in through the rainbow door, there were cheering voices from all over the universe, and I saw the Six Grandfathers sitting in a row, with their arms held toward me and their hands, palms out; and behind them in the cloud were faces thronging, without number, of the people yet to be.

41   "He has triumphed!" cried the six together, making thunder. And as I passed before them there, each gave again the gift that he had given me before—the cup of water and the bow and arrows, the power to make live and to destroy; the white wing of cleansing and the healing herb; the sacred pipe; the flowering stick. And each one spoke in turn from west to south, explaining what he gave as he had done before, and as each one spoke he melted down into the earth and rose again; and as each did this, I felt nearer to the earth.

*Black Elk said the mountain he stood upon in his vision was Harney Peak in the Black Hills. "But anywhere is the center of the world," he added.

42   Then the oldest of them all said: "Grandson, all over the universe you have seen. Now you shall go back with power to the place from whence you came, and it shall happen yonder that hundreds shall be sacred, hundreds shall be flames! Behold!"

43   I looked below and saw my people there, and all were well and happy except one, and he was lying like the dead—and that one was myself. Then the oldest Grandfather sang, and his song was like this:

"There is someone lying on earth in a sacred manner.
There is someone—on earth he lies.
In a sacred manner I have made him to walk."

44   Now the tepee, built and roofed with cloud, began to sway back and forth as in a wind, and the flaming rainbow door was growing dimmer. I could hear voices of all kinds crying from outside: "Eagle Wing Stretches is coming forth! Behold him!"

45   When I went through the door, the face of the day of earth was appearing with the daybreak star upon its forehead; and the sun leaped up and looked upon me, and I was going forth alone.

46   And as I walked alone, I heard the sun singing as it arose, and it sang like this:

"With visible face I am appearing.
In a sacred manner I appear.
For the greening earth a pleasantness I make.
The center of the nation's hoop I have made pleasant.
With visible face, behold me!
The four-leggeds and two-leggeds, I have made them to walk;
The wings of the air, I have made them to fly.
With visible face I appear.
My day, I have made it holy."

47   When the singing stopped, I was feeling lost and very lonely. Then a Voice above me said: "Look back!" It was a spotted eagle that was hovering over and spoke. I looked, and where the flaming rainbow tepee, built and roofed with cloud, had been, I saw only the tall rock mountain at the center of the world.

48   I was all alone on a broad plain now with my feet upon the earth, alone but for the spotted eagle guarding me. I could see my people's village far ahead, and I walked very fast, for I was homesick now. Then I saw my own tepee, and inside I saw my mother and my father, bending over a sick boy that was myself. And as I entered the tepee, someone was saying: "The boy is coming to; you had better give him some water."

49   Then I was sitting up; and I was sad because my mother and my father didn't seem to know I had been so far away.

QUESTIONS FOR DISCUSSION

1. What is the significance of the Nation's hoop, the flowering stick, the sacred pipe, and the giant wing? What importance do these symbols have in the American Indian culture and universally?

2. What are the "four ascents" that Black Elk and the Indian nation climb in the vision? Why are the four ascents significant?

3. How would you interpret the images and symbols in each of the first three ascents: the holy tree, the people turned to animals, the broken hoop, and starving people?

4. Does the fourth ascent suggest a solution to the problems implied by the first three? What strengths of the Indian culture are implied through the images of the "sacred man . . . painted red," the black stallion, and the four virgins bearing the sacred symbols?

5. What is Black Elk's final vision at the peak of the fourth ascent? What force of unification does he find amongst humanity?

6. Why do the Grandfathers tell Black Elk to return "whence you came," to the home of his parents?

CONNECTION

Compare the transformative, natural vision of Black Elk to the vision of the narrator in E. M. Forster's "The Other Side of the Hedge." What are the "stages" of each vision, and how is each man transformed ?

IDEAS FOR WRITING

1. Write an essay in which you try to interpret Black Elk's vision in terms of the struggle of the Native Americans to reassert their cultural heritage after the coming of the white settlers.

2. Create your own vision of a future or an afterlife in which your people (friends, family, community) are strong and united. Try to use symbols that are especially meaningful to you and to your cultural heritage.

Linda Hogan

Walking

Linda Hogan (b. 1947), a member of the Chickasaw tribe, was raised in Denver, Colorado. She completed her M.A. at the University of Colorado at Boulder in 1978. Hogan began her career teaching creative writing and Native American literature at the University of Colorado at Boulder and went on to teach poetry and literature in outreach programs in Colorado and Oklahoma. Since 1989 she has been an associate professor of English at the University of Colorado at Boulder. Her most recent writing includes Mean Spirit: A Novel *(1990),* Book of Medicines: Poems *(1993),* Solar Storms *(1995), and* Power *(1998). The following selection,*

"Walking," a chronicle of observation in nature over a period of time, is excerpted from her essay collection, Dwellings (1995).

JOURNAL

Write about a solitary walk that you took repeatedly in a nature area. What changes did you notice in the environment over time?

1 It began in dark and underground weather, a slow hunger moving toward light. It grew in a dry gulley beside the road where I live, a place where entire hillsides are sometimes yellow, windblown tides of sunflower plants. But this plant was different. It was alone and larger than the countless others that had established their lives farther up the hill. This one was a traveler, a settler, and like a dream beginning in conflict, it grew where the land had been disturbed.

2 I saw it first in early summer. It was a green and sleeping bud, raising itself toward the sun. Ants worked around the unopened bloom, gathering aphids and sap. A few days later, it was a tender young flower, soft and new, with a pale green center and a troop of silver-gray insects climbing up and down the stalk. Over the summer this sunflower grew into a plant of incredible beauty, turning its face daily toward the sun in the most subtle of ways, the black center of it dark and alive with a deep blue light, as if flint had sparked an elemental fire there, in community with rain, mineral, mountain air, and sand.

3 As summer changed from green to yellow there were new visitors daily, the lace-winged insects, the bees whose legs were fat with pollen, and grasshoppers with their clattering wings and desperate hunger. There were other lives I missed, those too small or hidden to see. It was as if the plant with its host of lives was a society, one in which moment by moment, depending on light and moisture, there was great and diverse change.

4 There were changes in the next larger world around the plant as well. One day I rounded a bend in the road to find the disturbing sight of a dead horse, black and still against a hillside, eyes rolled back. Another day I was nearly lifted by a wind and sandstorm so fierce and hot that I had to wait for it to pass before I could return home. On this day the faded dry petals of the sunflower were swept across the land. That was when the birds arrived to carry the new seeds to another future.

5 In this one plant, in one summer season, a drama of need and survival took place. Hungers were filled. Insects coupled. There was escape, exhaustion, and death. Lives touched down a moment and were gone.

6 I was an outsider. I only watched. I never learned the sunflower's golden language or the tongues of its citizens. I had a small understanding, nothing more than a shallow observation of the flower, insects, and birds. But they knew what to do, how to live. An old voice from somewhere, gene or cell, told the plant how to evade the pull of gravity and find its way upward, how to open. It was instinct, intuition,

necessity. A certain knowing directed the seed-bearing birds on paths to ancestral homelands they had never seen. They believed it. They followed.

7   There are other summons and calls, some even more mysterious than those commandments to birds or those survival journeys of insects. In bamboo plants, for instance, with their thin green canopy of light and golden stalks that creak in the wind. Once a century, all of a certain kind of bamboo flower on the same day. Neither the plants' location, in Malaysia or in a greenhouse in Minnesota, nor their age or size make a difference. They flower. Some current of an inner language passes among them, through space and separation, in ways we cannot explain in our language. They are all, somehow, one plant, each with a share of communal knowledge.

8   John Hay, in *The Immortal Wilderness*, has written: "There are occasions when you can hear the mysterious language of the Earth, in water, or coming through the trees, emanating from the mosses, seeping through the undercurrents of the soil, but you have to be willing to wait and receive."

9   Sometimes I hear it talking. The light of the sunflower was one language, but there are others more audible. Once, in the redwood forest, I heard a beat, something like a drum or heart coming from the ground and trees and wind. That underground current stirred a kind of knowing inside me, a kinship and longing, a dream barely remembered that disappeared back to the body. Another time, there was the booming voice of an ocean storm thundering from far out to sea, telling about what lived in the distance, about the rough water that would arrive, wave after wave revealing the disturbance at center.

10   Tonight I walk. I am watching the sky. I think of the people who came before me and how they knew the placement of stars in the sky, watched the moving sun long and hard enough to witness how a certain angle of light touched a stone only once a year. Without written records, they knew the gods of every night, the small, fine details of the world around them and of immensity above them.

11   Walking, I can almost hear the redwoods beating. And the oceans are above me here, rolling clouds, heavy and dark, considering snow. On the dry, red road, I pass the place of sunflower, that dark and secret location where creation took place. I wonder if it will return this summer, if it will multiply and move up to the other stand of flowers in a territorial struggle.

12   It's winter and there is smoke from the fires. The square, lighted windows of houses are fogging over. It is a world of elemental attention, of all things working together, listening to what speaks in the blood. Whichever road I follow, I walk in the land of many gods, and they love and eat one another. Walking, I am lisening to a deeper way. Suddenly all my ancestors are behind me. Be still, they say. Watch and listen. You are the result of the love of thousands.

QUESTIONS FOR DISCUSSION

1. Why does the essay begin by anticipating the birth of the sunflower? Explain the logic behind Hogan's organization of her ideas in this essay.

2. Why does Hogan personify the sunflower is a "traveler, a settler, like a dream beginning in conflict"?

3. Hogan describes herself as an outsider and an observer: "I never learned the sunflower's golden language or the tongues of its citizens." How and why does she believe that those within the sunflower's world communicated? What does their ability to communicate exemplify for Hogan?

4. What relationship between life and death, love and hate is Hogan developing in this essay?

5. What does Hogan believe that observers and walkers can learn from the natural world? Explain why you agree or disagree with her assumptions.

6. Why is the essay entitled "Walking"? Discuss several different ways that walking is a meaningful activity in this essay.

CONNECTION

Compare and contrast how Gary Snyder and Hogan see non-verbal language systems at work in the natural world.

IDEAS FOR WRITING

1. Hogan concludes, "Walking, I am listening to a deeper way." Write an essay that is developed from observational walks in which you try to be aware of what Hogan describes about the changes in nature over time.

2. Hogan quotes from John Hay's *Immortal Wilderness* "There are occasions when you can hear the mysterious language of the Earth, in water, or coming through the trees, . . . but you have to be willing to wait and receive." Write an essay about a time when you heard or sensed one form of the mysterious language of the earth.

Annie Dillard

A Field of Silence

Poet, essayist, and naturalist Annie Dillard (b. 1945) was raised in Pittsburgh, Pennsylvania. She received an M.A. in 1968 from Hollins College in Virginia. Dillard has worked as an editor and college teacher and has written many essays and books, including Pilgrim at Tinker Creek *(1974), for which she received a Pulitzer Prize,* An American Childhood *(1987),* The Writing Life *(1989),* The Living: A Novel *(1992),* Mornings Like These: Found Poems *(1995), and* For the Time Being *(1999). In her essay "A Field of Silence" (1978), Dillard explores a powerful vision she once had on a remote farm and reflects on the difficulty she has in accepting and sharing this kind of experience in a world that values rationality and scientific progress.*

JOURNAL

Write about a moment in which you were alone in nature and felt you made an abrupt break from your familiar perception of reality and began to experience the world from a new perspective.

1 There is a place called "the farm" where I lived once, in a time that was very lonely. Fortunately I was unconscious of my loneliness then, and felt it only deeply, bewildered, in the half-bright way that a puppy feels pain.

2   I loved the place, and still do. It was an ordinary farm, a calf-raising, haymaking farm, and very beautiful. Its flat, messy pastures ran along one side of the central portion of a quarter-mile road in the central part of an island, an island in Puget Sound, so that from the high end of the road you could look west toward the Pacific, to the Sound and its hundred islands, and from the other end—and from the farm—you could see east to the water between you and the mainland, and beyond it the mainland's mountains slicked smooth with snow.

3   I liked the clutter about the place, the way everything blossomed or seeded or rusted; I liked the hundred half-finished projects, the smells, and the way the animals always broke loose. It is calming to herd animals. Often a regular rodeo breaks out—two people and a clever cow can kill a morning—but still, it is calming. You laugh for a while, exhausted, and silence is restored; the beasts are back in their pastures, the fences not fixed but disguised as if they were fixed, ensuring the animals' temporary resignation; and a great calm descends, a lack of urgency, a sense of having to invent something to do until the next time you must run and chase cattle.

4   The farm seemed eternal in the crude way the earth does—extending, that is, a very long time. The farm was as old as earth, always there, as old as the island, the Platonic form of "farm," of human society itself and at large, a piece of land eaten and replenished a billion summers, a piece of land worked on, lived on, grown over, plowed under, and stitched again and again, with fingers or with leaves, in and out and into human life's thin weave. I lived there once.

5   I lived there once and I have seen, from behind the barn, the long roadside pastures heaped with silence. Behind the rooster, suddenly, I saw the silence heaped on the fields like trays. That day the green hayfields supported silence evenly sown; the fields bent just so under the even pressure of silence, bearing it, even, palming it aloft: cleared fields, part of a land, a planet, they did not buckle beneath the heel of silence, nor split up scattered to bits, but instead lay secret, disguised as time and matter as though that were nothing, ordinary—disguised as fields like those which bear the silence only because they are spread, and the silence spreads over them, great in size.

6   I do not want, I think, ever to see such a sight again. That there is loneliness here I had granted, in the abstract—but not, I thought, inside the light of God's presence, inside his sanction, and signed by his name.

7   I lived alone in the farmhouse and rented; the owners, Angus and Lynn, in their twenties, lived in another building just over the yard. I had been reading and restless for two or three days. It was morning. I had just read at breakfast an Updike story, "Packed Dirt, Churchgoing, A Dying Cat, A Traded Car," which moved me. I heard our own farmyard rooster and two or three roosters across the street screeching. I quit the house, hoping at heart to see Lynn or Angus, but immediately to watch our rooster as he crowed.

8   It was Saturday morning late in the summer, in early September, clear-aired and still. I climbed the barnyard fence between the poultry and the pastures; I watched the red rooster, and the rooster, reptilian, kept one alert and alien eye on me. He pulled his extravagant neck to its maximum length, hauled himself high on his legs, stretched his beak as if he were gagging, screamed, and blinked. It was a ruckus. The din came from everywhere, and only the most rigorous application of reason could persuade me that it proceeded in its entirety from this lone and maniac bird.

9   After a pause, the roosters across the street would start, answering the proclamation, or cranking out another round, arrhythmically, interrupting. In the same way there is no pattern nor sense to the massed stridulations of cicadas; their skipped beats, enjambments, and failed alterations jangle your spirits, as though each of those thousand insects, each with identical feelings, were stubbornly deaf to the others, and loudly alone.

10 I shifted along the fence to see if Lynn or Angus was coming or going. To the rooster I said nothing, but only stared. And he stared at me: we were both careful to keep the wooden fence slat from our line of sight, so that this profiled eye and my two eyes could meet. From time to time I looked beyond the pastures to learn if anyone might be seen on the road.

11 When I was turned away in this manner, the silence gathered and struck me. It bashed me broadside from nowhere, as if I'd been hit by a plank. It dropped from the heavens above me like yard goods; ten acres of fallen, invisible sky choked the fields. The pastures on either side of the road turned green in a surrealistic fashion, monstrous, impeccable, as if they were holding their breath. The roosters stopped. All the things of the world—the fields and the fencing, the road, a parked orange truck—were stricken and self-conscious. A world pressed down on their surfaces, a world battered just within their surfaces, and that real world, so near to emerging, had got struck.

12 There was only silence. It was the silence of matter caught in the act and embarrassed. There were no cells moving, and yet there were cells. I could see the shape of the land, how it lay holding silence. Its poise and its stillness were unendurable, like the ring of the silence you hear in your skull when you're little and notice you're living, the ring which resumes later in life when you're sick.

13 There were flies buzzing over the dirt by the henhouse, moving in circles and buzzing, black dreams in chips off the one long dream, the dream of the regular

world. But the silent fields were the real world, eternity's outpost in time, whose look I remembered but never like this, this God-blasted, paralyzed day. I felt myself tall and vertical, in a blue shirt, self-conscious, and wishing to die. I heard the flies again; I looked at the rooster who was frozen looking at me.

14   Then at last I heard whistling, human whistling far on the air, and I was not able to bear it. I looked around, heartbroken; only at the big yellow Charolais farm far up the road was there motion—a woman, I think, dressed in pink, and pushing a wheelbarrow easily over the grass. It must have been she who was whistling and heaping on top of the silence those hollow notes of song. But the slow sound of the music—the beautiful sound of the music ringing the air like a stone bell—was isolated and detached. The notes spread into the general air and became the weightier part of silence, silence's last straw. The distant woman and her wheelbarrow were flat and detached, like mechanized and pink-painted properties for a stage. I stood in pieces, afraid I was unable to move. Something had unhinged the world. The houses and roadsides and pastures were buckling under the silence. Then a Labrador, black, loped up the distant driveway, fluid and cartoonlike, toward the pink woman. I had to try to turn away. Holiness is a force, and like the others can be resisted. It was given, but I didn't want to see it, God or no God. It was as if God had said, "I am here, but not as you have known me. This is the look of silence, and of loneliness unendurable: it too has always been mine, and now will be yours." I was not ready for a life of sorrow, sorrow deriving from knowledge I could just as well stop at the gate.

15   I turned away, willful, and the whole show vanished. The realness of things disassembled. The whistling became ordinary, familiar; the air above the fields released its pressure and the fields lay hooded as before. I myself could act. Looking to the rooster I whistled to him myself, softly, and some hens appeared at the chicken house window, greeted the day, and fluttered down.

16   Several months later, walking past the farm on the way to a volleyball game, I remarked to a friend, by way of information, "There are angels in those fields." Angels! That silence so grave and so stricken, that choked and unbearable green! I have rarely been so surprised at something I've said. Angels! What are angels! I had never thought of angels, in any way at all.

17   From that time I began to think of angels. I considered that sights such as I had seen of the silence must have been shared by the people who said they saw angels. I began to review the thing I had seen that morning. My impression now of those fields is of thousands of spirits—spirits trapped, perhaps, by my refusal to call them more fully, or by the paralysis of my own spirit at that time—thousands of spirits, angels in fact, almost discernible to the eye, and whirling. If pressed I would say they were three or four feet from the ground. Only their motion was clear (clockwise, if you insist); that, and their beauty unspeakable.

18   There are angels in those fields, and I presume, in all fields, and everywhere else. I would go to the lions for this conviction, to witness this fact. What all this means about perception, or language, or angels, or my own sanity, I have no idea.

QUESTIONS FOR DISCUSSION

1. How does the loneliness Dillard experiences on the farm help to set the stage for her vision?
2. What causes Dillard's vision? Why does her vision end?
3. How does Dillard make the abstract notion of absolute silence concrete and alive? Why does she create such a vibrant image of the silence? How do you respond to her image?
4. Why is the stillness "unendurable"? What similes does Dillard use to express her concept? Why does she "try to turn away" from her vision? Why is her vision one of sorrow?
5. Why does Dillard reverse an accepted assumption by referring to the "regular world" as a "dream"? What does she mean by "regular" and "dream" in the context of her essay?
6. After having time to reflect, Dillard decides, "There are angels in those fields." How do you imagine the angels? Why is it significant that Dillard, usually so precise and perceptive, has "no idea" about the meaning of her vision and has difficulty talking about it? How do you interpret her vision of nature?

CONNECTION

Compare Dillard's visionary experience in nature with that of Black Elk in this chapter. What different values and conclusions does each come to based upon visions?

IDEAS FOR WRITING

1. Write a reflective essay on a vision or an intense moment of natural insight you have had. Was it difficult for you to share this experience? Were you able to do so? In what form?
2. Write an essay in which you attempt to interpret Dillard's vision, based on what you know about her from reading this essay. What does Dillard's vision reveal about her personality, values, and response to the natural world?

E. M. Forster

The Other Side of the Hedge

E. M. Forster (1879–1970) was born in London and educated at Cambridge. Individualistic and liberal in his political views, Forster was a member of the Bloomsbury group, a distinguished coterie of writers and critics that included Virginia Woolf and Roger Frye.

A prolific author of critical essays, stories, and social novels such as A Room with a View *(1908) and* Passage to India *(1924), Forster wrote the utopian fantasy "The Other Side of the Hedge" (1903) during a transitional period in his early life, shortly after his graduation from Cambridge and after a trip to Greece and Italy. The story presents an alternative vision to competitive, technologically oriented modern lifestyles.*

JOURNAL

Write about an experience, fantasy, or dream you have had in which you found yourself exhausted by your current lifestyle and imagined or ventured into an alternate, more natural world where you could relax and not be pressured to compete.

1   My pedometer told me that I was twenty-five; and, though it is a shocking thing to stop walking, I was so tired that I sat down on a milestone to rest. People outstripped me, jeering as they did so, but I was too apathetic to feel resentful, and even when Miss Eliza Dimbleby, the great educationist, swept past, exhorting me to persevere, I only smiled and raised my hat.

2   At first I thought I was going to be like my brother, whom I had had to leave by the roadside a year or two round the corner. He had wasted his breath on singing, and his strength on helping others. But I had travelled more wisely, and now it was only the monotony of the highway that oppressed me—dust under foot and brown crackling hedges on either side, ever since I could remember.

3   And I had already dropped several things—indeed, the road behind was strewn with the things we all had dropped; and the white dust was settling down on them, so that already they looked no better than stones. My muscles were so weary that I could not even bear the weight of those things I still carried. I slid off the milestone into the road, and lay there prostrate, with my face to the great parched hedge, praying that I might give up.

4   A little puff of air revived me. It seemed to come from the hedge; and, when I opened my eyes, there was a glint of light through the tangle of boughs and dead leaves. The hedge could not be as thick as usual. In my weak, morbid state, I longed to force my way in, and see what was on the other side. No one was in sight, or I should not have dared to try. For we of the road do not admit in conversation that there is another side at all.

5   I yielded to the temptation, saying to myself that I would come back in a minute. The thorns scratched my face, and I had to use my arms as a shield, depending on my feet alone to push me forward. Halfway through I would have gone back, for in the passage all the things I was carrying were scraped off me, and my clothes were torn. But I was so wedged that return was impossible, and I had to wiggle blindly forward, expecting every moment that my strength would fail me, and that I should perish in the undergrowth.

6   Suddenly cold water closed round my head, and I seemed sinking down for ever. I had fallen out of the hedge into a deep pool. I rose to the surface at last, crying for

help, and I heard someone on the opposite bank laugh and say: "Another!" And then I was twitched out and laid panting on the dry ground.

7   Even when the water was out of my eyes, I was still dazed, for I had never been in so large a space, nor seen such grass and sunshine. The blue sky was no longer a strip, and beneath it the earth had risen grandly into hills—clean, bare buttresses, with beech trees in their folds, and meadows and clear pools at their feet. But the hills were not high, and there was in the landscape a sense of human occupation—so that one might have called it a park, or garden, if the words did not imply a certain triviality and constraint.

8   As soon as I got my breath, I turned to my rescuer and said:

9   "Where does this place lead to?"

10 "Nowhere, thank the Lord!" said he, and laughed. He was a man of fifty or sixty—just the kind of age we mistrust on the road—but there was no anxiety in his manner, and his voice was that of a boy of eighteen.

11 "But it must lead somewhere!" I cried, too much surprised at his answer to thank him for saving my life.

12 "He wants to know where it leads!" he shouted to some men on the hill side, and they laughed back, and waved their caps.

13 I noticed then that the pool into which I had fallen was really a moat which bent round to the left and to the right, and that the hedge followed it continually. The hedge was green on this side—its roots showed through the clear water, and fish swam about in them—and it was wreathed over with dog-roses and Traveller's Joy. But it was a barrier, and in a moment I lost all pleasure in the grass, the sky, the trees, the happy men and women, and realized that the place was but a prison, for all its beauty and extent.

14 We moved away from the boundary, and then followed a path almost parallel to it, across the meadows. I found it difficult walking, for I was always trying to out-distance my companion, and there was no advantage in doing this if the place led nowhere. I had never kept step with anyone since I left my brother.

15 I amused him by stopping suddenly and saying disconsolately, "This is perfectly terrible. One cannot advance: one cannot progress. Now we of the road—"

16 "Yes. I know."

17 "I was going to say, we advance continually."

18 "I know."

19 "We are always learning, expanding, developing. Why, even in my short life I have seen a great deal of advance—the Transvaal War, the Fiscal Question, Christian Science, Radium. Here for example—"

20 I took out my pedometer, but it still marked twenty-five, not a degree more.

21 "Oh, it's stopped! I meant to show you. It should have registered all the time I was walking with you. But it makes me only twenty-five."

22 "Many things don't work in here," he said. "One day a man brought in a Lee-Metford, and that wouldn't work."

23 "The laws of science are universal in their application. It must be the water in the moat that has injured the machinery. In normal conditions everything works.

Science and the spirit of emulation—those are the forces that have made us what we are."

24   I had to break off and acknowledge the pleasant greetings of people whom we passed. Some of them were singing, some talking, some engaged in gardening, hay-making, or other rudimentary industries. They all seemed happy; and I might have been happy too, if I could have forgotten that the place led nowhere.

25   I was startled by a young man who came sprinting across our path, took a little fence in fine style, and went tearing over a ploughed field till he plunged into a lake, across which he began to swim. Here was true energy, and I exclaimed: "A cross-country race! Where are the others?"

26   "There are no others," my companion replied; and, later on, when we passed some long grass from which came the voice of a girl singing exquisitely to herself, he said again: "There are no others." I was bewildered at the waste in production, and murmured to myself, "What does it all mean?"

27   He said: "It means nothing but itself"—and he repeated the words slowly, as if I were a child.

28   "I understand," I said quietly, "but I do not agree. Every achievement is worthless unless it is a link in the chain of development. And I must not trespass on your kind-ness any longer. I must get back somehow to the road and have my pedometer mended."

29   "First, you must see the gates," he replied, "for we have gates, though we never use them."

30   I yielded politely, and before long we reached the moat again, at a point where it was spanned by a bridge. Over the bridge was a big gate, as white as ivory, which was fitted into a gap in the boundary hedge. The gate opened outwards, and I exclaimed in amazement, for from it ran a road—just such a road as I had left—dusty under foot, with brown crackling hedges on either side as far as the eye could reach.

31   "That's my road!" I cried.

32   He shut the gate and said: "But not your part of the road. It is through this gate that humanity went out countless ages ago, when it was first seized with the desire to walk."

33   I denied this, observing that the part of the road I myself had left was not more than two miles off. But with the obstinacy of his years he repeated: "It is the same road. This is the beginning, and though it seems to run straight away from us, it doubles so often, that it is never far from our boundary and sometimes touches it." He stooped down by the moat, and traced on its moist margin an absurd figure like a maze. As we walked back through the meadows, I tried to convince him of his mistake.

34   "The road sometimes doubles to be sure, but that is part of our discipline. Who can doubt that its general tendency is onward? To what goal we know not—it may be to some mountain where we shall touch the sky, it may be over precipices into the sea. But that it goes forward—who can doubt that? It is the thought of that that makes us strive to excel, each in his own way, and gives us an impetus which is lack-ing with you. Now that man who passed us—it's true that he ran well, and jumped

well, and swam well; but we have men who can run better, and men who can jump better, and who can swim better. Specialization has produced results which would surprise you. Similarly, that girl—"

35   Here I interrupted myself to exclaim: "Good gracious me! I could have sworn it was Miss Eliza Dimbleby over there, with her feet in the fountain!"

36   He believed that it was.

37   "Impossible! I left her on the road, and she is due to lecture this evening at Tunbridge Wells. Why, her train leaves Cannon Street in—of course my watch has stopped like everything else. She is the last person to be here."

38   "People always are astonished at meeting each other. All kinds come through the hedge, and come at all times—when they are drawing ahead in the race, when they are lagging behind, when they are left for dead. I often stand near the boundary listening to the sounds of the road—you know what they are—and wonder if anyone will turn aside. It is my great happiness to help someone out of the moat, as I helped you. For our country fills up slowly, though it was meant for all mankind."

39   "Mankind have other aims," I said gently, for I thought him well-meaning; "and I must join them." I bade him good evening, for the sun was declining, and I wished to be on the road by nightfall. To my alarm, he caught hold of me, crying: "You are not to go yet!" I tried to shake him off, for we had no interests in common, and his civility was becoming irksome to me. But for all my struggles the tiresome old man would not let go; and, as wrestling is not my specialty, I was obliged to follow him.

40   It was true that I could have never found alone the place where I came in, and I hoped that, when I had seen the other sights about which he was worrying, he would take me back to it. But I was determined not to sleep in the country, for I mistrusted it, and the people too, for all their friendliness. Hungry though I was, I would not join them in their evening meals of milk and fruit, and, when they gave me flowers, I flung them away as soon as I could do so unobserved. Already they were lying down for the night like cattle—some out on the bare hillside, others in groups under the beeches. In the light of an orange sunset I hurried on with my unwelcome guide, dead tired, faint from want of food, but murmuring indomitably: "Give me life, with its struggles and victories, with its failures and hatreds, with its deep moral meaning and its unknown goal!"

41   At last we came to a place where the encircling moat was spanned by another bridge, and where another gate interrupted the line of the boundary hedge. It was different from the first gate; for it was half transparent like horn, and opened inwards. But through it, in the waning light, I saw again just such a road as I had left—monotonous, dusty, with brown crackling hedges on either side, as far as the eye could reach.

42   I was strangely disquieted at the sight, which seemed to deprive me of all self-control. A man was passing us, returning for the night to the hills, with a scythe over his shoulder and a can of some liquid in his hand. I forgot the destiny of our race. I forgot the road that lay before my eyes, and I sprang at him, wrenched the can out of his hand, and began to drink.

43   It was nothing stronger than beer, but in my exhausted state it overcome me in a moment. As in a dream, I saw the old man shut the gate, and heard him say: "This is where your road ends, and through this gate humanity—all that is left of it—will come in to us."

44   Though my senses were sinking into oblivion, they seemed to expand ere they reached it. They perceived the magic song of nightingales, and the odour of invisible hay, and stars piercing the fading sky. The man whose beer I had stolen lowered me down gently to sleep off its effects, and, as he did so, I saw that he was my brother.

QUESTIONS FOR DISCUSSION

1. What type of person is the narrator? Do you like him? How does he feel about competition? What is his attitude toward his brother? Does he find pleasure in his life?

2. What is the meaning of the road and the runners on it? What does the hedge suggest? What does it hide from view?

3. What is suggested by the narrator's closing his eyes just before seeing the light through the hedge? What is the significance of his difficult passage through the hedge ("all the things I was carrying were scraped off me . . . I had to wiggle blindly forward")?

4. What are the main qualities of life on "the other side of the hedge"? How is the landscape different? In what type of activities do the citizens participate? How do they feel about progress and achievement?

5. What is your response to the narrator's initial reaction to the world on the other side of the hedge? Do you agree that this world is "but a prison," that "the place led nowhere"? Are the narrator's arguments about the advantages of the road convincing?

6. Who is the man with the scythe? What choice does the narrator make at the close of the story? Why? Do you find the ending of the story hopeful or disturbing?

CONNECTION

Compare the experience of spiritual insight and renewal in this story with Annie Dillard's experience with silence in nature in "A Field of Silence" in this chapter.

IDEAS FOR WRITING

1. Write an extended comparison between your own vision of a relaxed, noncompetitive lifestyle and the other side of the hedge presented in Forster's story. How is your perspective similar to and/or different from that of Forster's narrator? How much of your life do you feel should be spent in non-competitive activities?

2. Based on evidence given in the story, write an essay in which you interpret the narrator's final gesture. Do you believe that the narrator has changed his perspective and that he will stay on the other side, or do you think he will return to life on the road? In your view, has he made the right decision?

Terry Tempest Williams

The Clan of One-Breasted Women

Terry Tempest Williams (b. 1959) was raised in Nevada and attended Teton Science School where she earned a B.A. in English and an M.A. in environmental education. She now works as a naturalist for the Utah Museum of Natural History and lives with her husband in the mountains outside of Salt Lake City, Utah. She is a well-respected nature writer; some of her better known published works include Pieces of White Shell *(1984),* Coyote's Canyon *(1989),* Desert Quartet *(1995), and* A Love that is Wild *(1998). "The Clan of One-Breasted Women" is excerpted from* Refuge: An Unnatural History of Family and Place *(1992). In this selection, Williams describes her protest against radiation poisoning resulting from nuclear testing.*

JOURNAL

Write about an event you have witnessed, learned about, or participated in that involved a protest against some form of environmental violation or social injustice.

1 I belong to a Clan of One-Breasted Women. My mother, my grandmothers, and six aunts have all had mastectomies. Seven are dead. The two who survive have just completed rounds of chemotherapy and radiation.

2 I've had my own problems: two biopsies for breast cancer and a small tumor between my ribs diagnosed as a "borderline malignancy."

3 This is my family history.

4 Most statistics tell us breast cancer is genetic, hereditary, with rising percentages attached to fatty diets, childlessness, or becoming pregnant after thirty. What they don't say is living in Utah may be the greatest hazard of all.

5 We are a Mormon family with roots in Utah since 1847. The "word of wisdom" in my family aligned us with good foods—no coffee, no tea, tobacco, or alcohol. For the most part, our women were finished having their babies by the time they were thirty. And only one faced breast cancer prior to 1960. Traditionally, as a group of people, Mormons have a low rate of cancer.

6 Is our family a cultural anomaly? The truth is, we didn't think about it. Those who did, usually the men, simply said, "bad genes." The women's attitude was stoic.

Cancer was part of life. On February 16, 1971, the eve of my mother's surgery, I accidentally picked up the telephone and overheard her ask my grandmother what she could expect.

7   "Diane, it is one of the most spiritual experiences you will ever encounter."

8   I quietly put down the receiver.

9   Two days later, my father took my brothers and me to the hospital to visit her. She met us in the lobby in a wheelchair. No bandages were visible. I'll never forget her radiance, the way she held herself in a purple velvet robe, and how she gathered us around her.

10   "Children, I am fine. I want you to know I felt the arms of God around me."

11   We believed her. My father cried. Our mother, his wife, was thirty-eight years old.

12   A little over a year after Mother's death, Dad and I were having dinner together. He had just returned from St. George, where the Tempest Company was completing the gas lines that would service southern Utah. He spoke of his love for the country, the sandstoned landscape, bare-boned and beautiful. He had just finished hiking the Kolob trail in Zion National Park. We got caught up in reminiscing, recalling with fondness our walk up Angel's Landing on his fiftieth birthday and the years our family had vacationed there.

13   Over dessert, I shared a recurring dream of mine. I told my father that for years, as long as I could remember, I saw this flash of light in the night in the desert—that this image had so permeated my being that I could not venture south without seeing it again, on the horizon, illuminating buttes and mesas.

14   "You did see it," he said.

15   "Saw what?"

16   "The bomb. The cloud. We were driving home from Riverside, California. You were sitting on Diane's lap. She was pregnant. In fact, I remember the day, September 7, 1957. We had just gotten out of the Service. We were driving north, past Las Vegas. It was an hour or so before dawn, when this explosion went off. We not only heard it, but felt it. I thought the oil tanker in front of us had blown up. We pulled over and suddenly, rising from the desert floor, we saw it, clearly, this golden-stemmed cloud, the mushroom. The sky seemed to vibrate with an eerie pink glow. Within a few minutes, a light ash was raining on the car."

17   I stared at my father.

18   "I thought you knew that," he said. "It was a common occurrence in the fifties."

19   It was at this moment that I realized the deceit I had been living under. Children growing up in the American Southwest, drinking contaminated milk from contaminated cows, even from the contaminated breasts of their mothers, my mother—members, years later, of the Clan of One-Breasted Women.

20   It is a well-known story in the Desert West, "The Day We Bombed Utah," or more accurately, the years we bombed Utah: above ground atomic testing in Nevada took place from January 27, 1951 through July 11, 1962. Not only were the winds blowing north covering "low-use segments of the population" with fallout and leaving sheep dead in their tracks, but the climate was right. The United States of the

1950s was red, white, and blue. The Korean War was raging. McCarthyism was rampant. Ike was it, and the cold war was hot. If you were against nuclear testing, you were for a communist regime.

21   Much has been written about this "American nuclear tragedy." Public health was secondary to national security. The Atomic Energy Commissioner, Thomas Murray, said, "Gentlemen, we must not let anything interfere with this series of tests, nothing."

22   Again and again, the American public was told by its government, in spite of burns, blisters, and nausea, "It has been found that the tests may be conducted with adequate assurance of safety under conditions prevailing at the bombing reservations." Assuaging public fears was simply a matter of public relations. "Your best action," an Atomic Energy Commission booklet read, "is not to be worried about fallout." A news release typical of the times stated, "We find no basis for concluding that harm to any individual has resulted from radioactive fallout."

23   On August 30, 1970, during Jimmy Carter's presidency, a suit was filed, *Irene Allen v. The United States of America*. Mrs. Allen's case was the first on an alphabetical list of twenty-four test cases, representative of nearly twelve hundred plaintiffs seeking compensation from the United States government for cancers caused by nuclear testing in Nevada.

24   Irene Allen lived in Hurricane, Utah. She was the mother of five children and had been widowed twice. Her first husband, with their two oldest boys, had watched the tests from the roof of the local high school. He died of leukemia in 1956. Her second husband died of pancreatic cancer in 1978.

25   In a town meeting conducted by Utah Senator Orrin Hatch, shortly before the suit was filed, Mrs. Allen said, "I am not blaming the government, I want you to know that, Senator Hatch. But I thought if my testimony could help in any way so this wouldn't happen again to any of the generations coming up after us . . . I am happy to be here this day to bear testimony of this."

26   God-fearing people. This is just one story in an anthology of thousands.

27   On May 10, 1984, Judge Bruce S. Jenkins handed down his opinion. Ten of the plaintiffs were awarded damages. It was the first time a federal court had determined that nuclear tests had been the cause of cancers. For the remaining fourteen test cases, the proof of causation was not sufficient. In spite of the split decision, it was considered a landmark ruling. It was not to remain so for long.

28   In April 1987, the Tenth Circuit Court of Appeals overturned Judge Jenkins's ruling on the ground that the United States was protected from suit by the legal doctrine of sovereign immunity, a centuries-old idea from England in the days of absolute monarchs.

29   In January 1988, the Supreme Court refused to review the Appeals Court decision. To our court system it does not matter whether the United States government was irresponsible, whether it lied to its citizens, or even that citizens died from the fallout of nuclear testing. What matters is that our government is immune: "The King can do no wrong."

30   In Mormon culture, authority is respected, obedience is revered, and independent thinking is not. I was taught as a young girl not to "make waves" or "rock
the boat."

31   "Just let it go," Mother would say. "You know how you feel, that's what counts."

32   For many years, I have done just that—listened, observed, and quietly formed my
own opinions, in a culture that rarely asks questions because it has all the answers.
But one by one, I have watched the women in my family die common, heroic
deaths. We sat in waiting rooms hoping for good news, but always receiving the bad.
I cared for them, bathed their scarred bodies, and kept their secrets. I watched beautiful women become bald as Cytoxan, cisplatin, and Adriamycin were injected into
their veins. I held their foreheads as they vomited green-black bile, and I shot them
with morphine when the pain became inhuman. In the end, I witnessed their last
peaceful breaths, becoming a midwife to the rebirth of their souls.

33   The price of obedience has become too high.

34   The fear and inability to question authority that ultimately killed rural communities in Utah during atmospheric testing of atomic weapons is the same fear I saw in
my mother's body. Sheep. Dead sheep. The evidence is buried.

35   I cannot prove that my mother, Diane Dixon Tempest, or my grandmothers, Let-
tie Romney Dixon and Kathryn Blackett Tempest, along with my aunts developed
cancer from nuclear fallout in Utah. But I can't prove they didn't.

36   My father's memory was correct. The September blast we drove through in 1957
was part of Operation Plumbbob, one of the most intensive series of bomb tests to be
initiated. The flash of light in the night in the desert, which I had always thought
was a dream, developed into a family nightmare. It took fourteen years, from 1957 to
1971, for cancer to manifest in my mother—the same time, Howard L. Andrews, an
authority in radioactive fallout at the National Institutes of Health, says radiation
cancer requires to become evident. The more I learn about what it means to be a
"downwinder," the more questions I drown in.

37   What I do know, however, is that as a Mormon woman of the fifth-generation
of Latter-day Saints, I must question everything, even if it means losing my faith,
even if it means becoming a member of a border tribe among my own people.
Tolerating blind obedience in the name of patriotism or religion ultimately takes
our lives.

38   When the Atomic Energy Commission described the country north of the
Nevada Test Site as "virtually uninhabited desert terrain," my family and the birds
at Great Salt Lake were some of the "virtual uninhabitants."

39   One night, I dreamed women from all over the world circled a blazing fire in
the desert. They spoke of change, how they hold the moon in their bellies and wax
and wane with its phases. They mocked the presumption of even-tempered beings
and made promises that they would never fear the witch inside themselves. The
women danced wildly as sparks broke away from the flames and entered the night
sky as stars.

40   And they sang a song given to them by Shoshone grandmothers:

Ah ne nah, nah	Consider the rabbits
nin nah nah—	How gently they walk on the earth—
ah ne nah, nah	Consider the rabbits
nin nah nah—	How gently they walk on the earth—
Nyaga mutzi	We remember them
oh ne nay—	We can walk gently also—
Nyaga mutzi	We remember them
oh ne nay—	We can walk gently also—

The women danced and drummed and sang for weeks, preparing themselves for what was to come. They would reclaim the desert for the sake of their children, for the sake of the land.

41   A few miles downwind from the fire circle, bombs were being tested. Rabbits felt the tremors. Their soft leather pads on paws and feet recognized the shaking sands, while the roots of mesquite and sage were smoldering. Rocks were hot from the inside out and dust devils hummed unnaturally. And each time there was another nuclear test, ravens watched the desert heave. Stretch marks appeared. The land was losing its muscle.

42   The women couldn't bear it any longer. They were mothers. They had suffered labor pains but always under the promise of birth. The red hot pains beneath the desert promised death only, as each bomb became a stillborn. A contract had been made and broken between human beings and the land. A new contract was being drawn by the women, who understood the fate of the earth as their own.

43   Under the cover of darkness, ten women slipped under a barbed-wire fence and entered the contaminated country. They were trespassing. They walked toward the town of Mercury, in moonlight, taking their cues from coyote, kit fox, antelope squirrel, and quail. They moved quietly and deliberately through the maze of Joshua trees. When a hint of daylight appeared they rested, drinking tea and sharing their rations of food. The women closed their eyes. The time had come to protest with the heart, that to deny one's genealogy with the earth was to commit treason against one's soul.

44   At dawn, the women draped themselves in mylar, wrapping long streamers of silver plastic around their arms to blow in the breeze. They wore clear masks, that became the faces of humanity. And when they arrived at the edge of Mercury, they carried all the butterflies of a summer day in their wombs. They paused to allow their courage to settle.

45   The town that forbids pregnant women and children to enter because of radiation risks was asleep. The women moved through the streets as winged messengers, twirling around each other in slow motion, peeking inside homes and watching the easy sleep of men and women. They were astonished by such stillness and periodically would utter a shrill note or low cry just to verify life.

46   The residents finally awoke to these strange apparitions. Some simply stared. Others called authorities, and in time, the women were apprehended by wary soldiers dressed in desert fatigues. They were taken to a white, square building on the other

edge of Mercury. When asked who they were and why they were there, the women replied, "We are mothers and we have come to reclaim the desert for our children."

47   The soldiers arrested them. As the ten women were blindfolded and handcuffed, they began singing:

> *You can't forbid us everything*
> *You can't forbid us to think—*
> *You can't forbid our tears to flow*
> *And you can't stop the songs that we sing.*

The women continued to sing louder and louder, until they heard the voices of their sisters moving across the mesa:

> *Ah ne nah, nah*
> *nin nah nah—*
> *Ah ne nah, nah*
> *nin nah nah—*
> *Nyaga mutzi*
> *oh ne nay—*
> *Nyaga mutzi*
> *oh ne nay—*

"Call for reinforcements," one soldier said.

48   "We have," interrupted one woman, "we have—and you have no idea of our numbers."

49   I crossed the line at the Nevada Test Site and was arrested with nine other Utahns for trespassing on military lands. They are still conducting nuclear tests in the desert. Ours was an act of civil disobedience. But as I walked toward the town of Mercury, it was more than a gesture of peace. It was a gesture on behalf of the Clan of One-Breasted Women.

50   As one officer cinched the handcuffs around my wrists, another frisked my body. She found a pen and a pad of paper tucked inside my left boot.

51   "And these?" she asked sternly.

52   "Weapons," I replied.

53   Our eyes met. I smiled. She pulled the leg of my trousers back over my boot.

54   "Step forward, please," she said as she took my arm.

55   We were booked under an afternoon sun and bused to Tonopah, Nevada. It was a two-hour ride. This was familiar country. The Joshua trees standing their ground had been named by my ancestors, who believed they looked like prophets pointing west to the Promised Land. These were the same trees that bloomed each spring, flowers appearing like white flames in the Mojave. And I recalled a full moon in May, when Mother and I had walked among them, flushing out mourning doves and owls.

56   The bus stopped short of town. We were released.

57   The officials thought it was a cruel joke to leave us stranded in the desert with no way to get home. What they didn't realize was that we were home, soul-centered and strong, women who recognized the sweet smell of sage as fuel for our spirits.

QUESTIONS FOR DISCUSSION

QUESTIONS FOR DISCUSSION

1. Why did the author's grandmother believe that a mastectomy is "one of the most spiritual experiences you will ever encounter"? Why do you think that the author's mother looks radiant after her mastectomy and tells her children, "I felt the arms of God around me"?

2. What is the meaning of Williams' recurring dream of a "flash of light" in the desert night? What real-world physical event does the dream recall? What are the long-term, hidden consequences of this event?

3. Why does Williams believe that "to deny one's genealogy with the earth was to commit treason against one's soul"? Why does Williams participate in the ritual protest in Mercury? Why are the protesters arrested for civil disobedience? With whose position are you in agreement?

4. What weapons does Williams have with her during the protest? In what ways do her weapons have more and less power than nuclear bombs that are being tested?

5. How does the officials' "cruel joke" on the protesters turn out differently from what they had expected? In what sense are the women victorious, despite the physical defeat of their protest?

6. What is Williams' purpose in writing this essay, both in terms of her family legacy of cancer and in terms of her larger audience?

CONNECTION

Compare the type of physical protest recommended by Williams with the non-violent, "mindful" approach recommended by Hahn. Which approach do you prefer, and why? In what circumstances would a person choose one approach or the other?

IDEAS FOR WRITING

1. Develop your journal entry into an essay on your experience with social protest. Did you find your protest action to be effective, and if so, how?

2. Do some research into theatrical and creative approaches to social protests. Are these approaches effective, and if so, why?

Thich Nhat Hanh

Love in Action

Teacher, writer, spiritual leader, and political activist, Thich Nhat Hanh (b. 1926) was born in Vietnam and became a Buddhist monk at the age of sixteen. Later he studied in the United States and attended Princeton University. Hanh was exiled from Vietnam because of his nonviolent resistance against the war; he then began publishing his writing about the Vietnam conflict and was nominated for the Nobel Peace Prize in 1967. Hanh participated in the Paris peace talks that brought about the end of American involvement in Vietnam and helped refuges and dissenters after the war. He helped to found the mindfulness community of Plum Village in south-western France for activists, artists, and Vietnam veterans, and continues to give public lectures and participate in retreats. Many of Hanh's books are published by the Community of Mindful Living in Berkeley, California, one of numerous non-profit organizations based on his teachings. His works include Call Me by My True Names: The Collected Poems of Thich Nhat Hanh *(1993),* Love in Action: Writings on Nonviolent Social Change *(1993),* Moment by Moment: The Art and Practice of Mindfulness *(1997), and* A Buddhist Life in America *(1998). The following selection in excerpted from* Love in Action.

JOURNAL

Write about a quiet time in nature that you spent in thought and meditation. How did your perceptions of yourself and of nature change through this experience?

1   In 1951, I went with a few brother monks to a remote mountain in the Dai Lao region of Vietnam to build a meditation center. We asked some native mountain people for their help, and two Montagnards from the Jarai tribe joined us in clearing the forest, cutting trees into lumber, and gathering other materials for construction. They were hard workers, and we were grateful for their assistance. But after working with us only three days, they stopped coming. Without their help, we had many difficulties, as we were not familiar with the ways of the forest. So we walked to their village and asked what had happened. They said, "Why should we return so soon? You already paid us enough to live for a month! We will come again when we run out of rice." At the time, it was a common practice to underpay the Montagnards, to avoid just this kind of thing. We had paid them properly, and, surely enough, they stopped coming.

2   Many people criticized the Montagnards for this ethic. They said that this laziness could only lead to trouble, and they listed four reasons to support their claim: (1) The Montagnards would be happier and more comfortable if they would work harder. (2) They would earn more money, which they could save for difficult periods. (3) The Montagnards should work harder in order to help others. (4) If they would work harder, they would have the means to defend themselves from invasions and the exploitation of others. There may be some validity to each of these points, but if we look closely at the lives of the Montagnards, we will come to understand them, and ourselves, better.

3   *1. The Montagnards would be happier and more comfortable if they would work harder.* The Montagnards lived simply. They did not store much food at all. They had no bank accounts. But they were much more serene and at peace with themselves,

nature, and other people, than almost anyone in the world. I am not suggesting that we all return to primitive lifestyles, but it is important that we see and appreciate the wisdom contained in a lifestyle like this, a wisdom that those of us immersed in modernization and economic growth have lost.

4   How much stuff do we need to be happy and comfortable? Happiness and comfort vary according to taste. Some people think they need three or four houses—one on the Riviera, one in New York, one in Tokyo, and perhaps one in Fiji. Others find that a two or three-room hut is quite enough. In fact, if you own a dozen luxurious houses, you may rarely have time to enjoy them. Even when you have the time, you may not know how to sit peacefully in one place. Always seeking distraction—going to restaurants, the theater, or dinner parties, or taking vacations that exhaust you even more, you can't stand being alone and facing yourself directly.

5   In former times, people spent hours drinking one cup of tea with dear friends. A cup of tea does not cost much, but today, we go to a cafe and take less than five minutes to drink our tea or coffee, and even during that short time, we are mostly thinking and talking about other things, and we never even notice our tea. We who own just one house barely have the time to live in it. We leave home early in the morning after a quick breakfast and go off to work, spending an hour in the car or the train and the rest of the day in the office. Then we return home exhausted, eat dinner, watch TV, and collapse so we can get up early for work. Is this "progress"?

6   The Montagnards were quite content to live in simple bamboo and palm-leaf huts and wash their clothes by hand. They refused to be slaves to economic pressures. Content with just a few possessions, they rarely needed to spend their time or money seeing doctors or psychotherapists for stress-related ailments.

7   *2. They would earn more money, which they could save for difficult periods.*
How much do we need to save? We do not save air, because we trust that it will be available to us when we need it. Why must we stockpile food, money, or other things for our own private use, while so many others are hungry?

8   People who accumulate a house, a car, a position, and so forth, identify themselves with what they own, and they think that if they lose their house, their car, or their position, they would not be themselves. To me, they are already lost. By accumulating and saving, they have constructed a false self, and in the process they have forgotten their truest and deepest self. Psychotherapists can try to help, but the cause of this illness is in their way of life. One way to help such a person would be to place him in an "underdeveloped" country where he could grow his own food and make his own clothes. Sharing the fate and simple life of peasants might help him heal quickly.

9   We have enough resources and know-how to assure every human being of adequate shelter and food every day. If we don't help others live, we ourselves are not going to be able to live either. We are all in the same boat—the planet earth. Why not put our efforts into trying to help each other and save our boat instead of accumulating savings only for ourselves and our own children?

550 Visions of Nature

10   *3. The Montagnards should work harder in order to help others.*

Of course, the Montagnards could have spent more time working in order to send aid to people who were starving in other parts of the world. If they did not do so, it was because they didn't know much about the existence of other nations. They certainly did help their own tribal members whenever they got sick or when a crop was destroyed by some natural disaster. But let us reflect for a moment on what the Montagnard people did not do.

11   They did not harm or exploit others. They grew their own food and exchanged some of their products with other people. They did not do violence to nature. They cut only enough wood to build their houses. They cleared only enough land to plant their crops. Because of their simple lifestyle, they did not overconsume natural resources. They did not pollute the air, water, or soil. They used very little fuel and no electricity. They did not own private cars, dishwashers, or electric razors. The way they lived enabled natural resources to continually renew themselves. A lifestyle like theirs demonstrates that a future for humankind is possible, and this is the most helpful thing anyone can do to help others.

12   *4. If they would work harder, they would have the means to defend themselves from invasion and the exploitation of others.*

It is true that the Montagnards were exploited by others and were often victims of social injustice. They lived in remote mountain areas. If others settled nearby, they risked losing land due to a lack of means with which to defend themselves.

13   People said that if the rest of us in Vietnam worked as little as they did, our country would never be able to resist foreign intervention and exploitation. It seems clear that the Montagnards and others like them had to do something more. But what? If the Montagnards would have moved down to the more populated areas, they would have seen men and women working extremely hard and getting poorer. They would have seen how expensive food, lodging, electricity, water, clothing, and transportation were. Their civilized countrymen were working all day long and could barely pay for the most basic items they consumed. The Montagnards in the forest did not need to spend any money. If they would have lived and worked in the cities, how would that have helped Vietnam resist foreign intervention? All they would have learned is that in the so-called developed nations, resources are used to make bombs and other elaborate weapons, while many citizens live in misery. The Montagnards might well need nuclear weapons to resist foreign intervention if they were to catch up with their more "developed" brothers and sisters. Will social injustice ever be abolished before all people wake up and realize that unless we let others live, we ourselves will not be able to live?

14   Economic growth may be necessary for the welfare of people, but the present rate of economic growth is destroying humanity and nature. Injustice is rampant. We humans are part of nature, and doing harm to nature only harms us. It is not just the poor and oppressed who are victims of environmental damage. The affluent are just as much victims of pollution and the exploitation of resources. We must

look at the whole picture and ask, "Does our way of life harm nature? Does our way of life harm our fellow humans? Do we live at the expense of others, at the expense of the present, and at the expense of the future?" If we answer truthfully, we will know how to orient our lives and our actions. We have much to learn from the Montagnards and others like them. We must learn to live in a way that makes a future possible.

15 *THE HUMAN FAMILY*   Although human beings are a part of nature, we single ourselves out and classify other animals and living beings as "nature," while acting as if we were somehow separate from it. Then we ask, "How should we deal with nature?" We should deal with nature the way we should deal with ourselves! Nonviolently. We should not harm ourselves, and we should not harm nature. To harm nature is to harm ourselves, and vice versa. If we knew how to deal with ourselves and our fellow human beings, we would know how to deal with nature. Human beings and nature are inseparable. By not caring property for either, we harm both.

16   We can only be happy when we accept ourselves as we are. We must first be aware of all the elements within us, and then we must bring them into harmony. Our physical and mental well-being are the result of understanding what is going on in ourselves. This understanding helps us respect nature in ourselves and also helps us bring about healing.

17   If we harm another human being, we harm ourselves. To accumulate wealth and our own excessive portions of the world's natural resources is to deprive our fellow humans of the chance to live. To participate in oppressive and unjust social systems is to widen the gap between rich and poor and thereby aggravate the situation of social injustice. Yet we tolerate excess, injustice, and war, while remaining unaware that the human race as a family is suffering. While some members of the human family are suffering and starving, for us to enjoy false security and wealth is a sign of insanity.

18   The fate of each individual is inextricably linked to the fate of the whole human race. We must let others live if we ourselves want to live. The only alternative to co-existence is co-nonexistence. A civilization in which we kill and exploit others for our own aggrandizement is sick. For us to have a healthy civilization, everyone must be born with an equal right to education, work, food, shelter, world citizenship, and the ability to circulate freely and settle on any part of the earth. Political and economic systems that deny one person these rights harm the whole human family. We must begin by becoming aware of what is happening to every member of the human family if we want to repair the damages already done.

19   To bring about peace, we must work for harmonious coexistence. If we continue to shut ourselves off from the rest of the world, imprisoning ourselves in our narrow concerns and immediate problems, we are not likely to make peace or to survive. It is difficult for one individual to preserve harmony among the elements within himself, and it is even more difficult to preserve harmony among the members of the human family. We have to understand the human race to bring it into harmony.

Cruelty and disruption destroy the harmony of the family. We need legislation that keeps us from doing violence to ourselves or nature, and prevents us from being disruptive and cruel.

20   We have created a system that we cannot control. This system imposes itself on us, and we have become its slaves. Most of us, in order to have a house, a car, a refrigerator, a TV, and so on, must sacrifice our time and our lives in exchange. We are constantly under the pressure of time. In former times, we could afford three hours for one cup of tea, enjoying the company of our friends in a serene and spiritual atmosphere. We could organize a party to celebrate the blossoming of one orchid in our garden. But today we can no longer afford these things. We say that time is money. We have created a society in which the rich become richer and the poor become poorer, and in which we are so caught up in our own immediate problems that we cannot afford to be aware of what is going on with the rest of the human family. We see images on TV, but we do not really understand our Third World brothers and sisters.

21   The individual and all humanity are both a part of nature and should be able to live in harmony with nature. Nature can be cruel and disruptive and therefore, at times, needs to be controlled. To control is not to dominate or oppress but to harmonize and equilibrate. We must be deep friends with nature in order to control certain aspects of it. This requires a full understanding of nature. Typhoons, tornadoes, droughts, floods, volcanic eruptions, and proliferations of harmful insects all constitute danger and destruction to life. Although parts of nature, these things disrupt the harmony of nature. We should be able to prevent to a large degree the destruction that natural disasters cause, but we must do it in a way that preserves life and encourages harmony.

22   The excessive use of pesticides that kill all kinds of insects and upset the ecological balance is an example of our lack of wisdom in trying to control nature.

23   The harmony and equilibrium in the individual, society, and nature are being destroyed. Individuals are sick, society is sick, and nature is sick. We must reestablish harmony and equilibrium, but how? Where can we begin the work of healing? Would we begin with the individual, society, or the environment? We must work in all three domains. People of different disciplines tend to stress their particular areas. For example, politicians consider an effective rearrangement of society necessary for the salvation of humans and nature, and therefore urge that everyone engage in the struggle to change political systems.

24   We Buddhist monks are like psychotherapists in that we tend to look at the problem from the viewpoint of mental health. Meditation aims at creating harmony and equilibrium in the life of the individual. Buddhist mediation uses the breath as a tool to calm and harmonize the whole human being. As in any therapeutic practice, the patient is placed in an environment that favors the restoration of harmony. Usually psychotherapists spend their time observing and then advising their patients. I know of some, however, who, like monks, observe themselves first, recognizing the need to free their own selves from the fears, anxieties, and despair that exist in each of us. Many therapists seem to think that they themselves have no mental problems, but

the monk recognizes in himself the susceptibility to fears and anxieties, and to the mental illness that is caused by the inhuman social and economic systems that prevail in today's world.

25   Buddhists believe that the reality of the individual, society, and nature's integral being will reveal itself to us as we recover, gradually ceasing to be possessed by anxiety, fear, and the dispersion of mind. Among the three—individual, society, and nature— it is the individual who begins to effect change. But in order to effect change, he or she must have personally recovered, must be whole. Since this requires an environment favorable to healing, he or she must seek the kind of lifestyle that is free from destructiveness. Efforts to change the environment and to change the individual are both necessary, but it is difficult to change the environment if individuals are not in a state of equilibrium. From the mental health point of view, efforts for us to recover our humanness should be given priority.

26   Restoring mental health does not mean simply helping individuals adjust to the modern world of rapid economic growth. The world is sick, and adapting to an unwell environment will not bring real health. Many people who seek the help of a psychotherapist are really victims of modern life, which separates human beings from the rest of nature. One way to help such a person may be to move him or her to a rural area where he can cultivate the land, grow his own food, wash his clothes in a clear river, and live simply, sharing the same life as millions of peasants around the world. For psychotherapy to be effective, we need environmental change, and psychotherapists must participate in efforts to change the environment. But that is only half their task. The other half is to help individuals be themselves, not by helping them adapt to an ill environment, but by providing them with the strength to change it. To tranquilize them is not the way. The explosion of bombs, the burning of napalm, the violent deaths of relatives and neighbors, the pressures of time, noise, and pollution, the lonely crowds have all been created by the disruptive course of our economic growth. They are all sources of mental illness, and they must end. Anything we can do to bring them to an end is preventive medicine. Political activities are not the only means to this end.

27   While helping their particular patients, psychotherapists must, at the same time, recognize their responsibility to the whole human family. Their work must also prevent others from becoming ill. They are challenged to safeguard their own humanness. Like others, psychotherapists and monks need to observe first themselves and their own ways of life. If they do, I believe they will seek ways to disengage themselves from the present economic systems in order to help reestablish harmony and balance in life. Monks and psychotherapists are human beings. We cannot escape mental illness if we do not apply our disciplines to ourselves. Caught in forgetfulness and acquiescence to the status quo, we will gradually become victims of fear, anxiety, and egotism of all kinds. But if psychotherapists and monks, through mutual sharing, help each other apply our disciplines to our own lives, we will rediscover the harmony in ourselves and thereby help the whole human family.

28   A tree reveals itself to an artist when he or she can establish a genuine relationship with it. If a human is not a real human being, he may look at his fellow humans

and not see them; he may look at a tree and not see it. Many of us cannot see things because we are not wholly ourselves. When we are wholly ourselves, we can see how one person by living fully demonstrates to all of us that life is possible, that a future is possible. But the question, "Is a future possible?" is meaningless without seeing the millions of our fellow humans who suffer, live, and die around us. Only when we really see them will we be able to see ourselves and see nature.

29 **THE SUN MY HEART**   When I first left Vietnam, I had a dream in which I was a young boy, smiling and at ease, in my own land, surrounded by my own people, in a time of peace. There was a beautiful hillside, lush with trees and flowers, and on it was a little house. But each time I approached the hillside, obstacles prevented me from climbing it, and then I woke up.

30   The dream recurred many times. I continued to do my work and to practice mindfulness, trying to be in touch with the beautiful trees, people, flowers, and sunshine that surrounded me in Europe and North America. I looked deeply at these things, and I played under the trees with the children exactly as I had in Vietnam. After a year, the dream stopped. Seeds of acceptance and joy had been planted in me, and I began to look at Europe, America, and other countries in Asia as also my home. I realized that my home is the earth. Whenever I felt homesick for Vietnam, I went outside into a backyard or a park, and found a place to practice breathing, walking, and smiling among the trees.

31   But some cities had very few trees, even then. I can imagine someday soon a city with no trees in it at all. Imagine a city that has only one tree left. People there are mentally disturbed, because they are so alienated from nature. Then one doctor in the city sees why people are getting sick, and he offers each person who comes to him the prescription: "You are sick because you are cut off from Mother Nature. Every morning, take a bus, go to the tree in the center of the city, and hug it for fifteen minutes. Look at the beautiful green tree and smell its fragrant bark."

32   After three months of practicing this, the patient will feel much better. But because many people suffer from the same malady and the doctor always gives the same prescription, after a short time, the line of people waiting their turn to embrace the tree gets to be very long, more than a mile, and people begin to get impatient. Fifteen minutes is now too long for each person to hug the tree, so the city council legislates a five-minute maximum. Then they have to shorten it to one minute, and then only a few seconds. Finally there is no remedy at all for the sickness.

33   If we are not mindful, we might be in that situation soon. We have to remember that our body is not limited to what lies within the boundary of our skin. Our body is much more immense. We know that if our heart stops beating, the flow of our life will stop, but we do not take the time to notice the many things outside of our bodies that are equally essential for our survival. If the ozone layer around our earth were to disappear for even an instant, we would die. If the sun were to stop shining, the flow of our life would stop. The sun is our second heart, our heart outside of our body. It gives all life on earth the warmth necessary for existence. Plants live thanks to the sun. Their leaves absorb the sun's energy, along with carbon dioxide from the

air, to produce food for the tree, the flower, the plankton. And thanks to plants, we and other animals can live. All of us—people, animals, plants, and minerals—"consume" the sun, directly and indirectly. We cannot begin to describe all the effects of the sun, that great heart outside of our body.

34   When we look at green vegetables, we should know that it is the sun that is green and not just the vegetables. The green color in the leaves of the vegetables is due to the presence of the sun. Without the sun, no living being could survive. Without sun, water, air, and soil, there would be no vegetables. The vegetables are the coming-together or many conditions near and far.

35   There is no phenomenon in the universe that does not intimately concern us, from a pebble resting at the bottom of the ocean, to the movement of a galaxy millions of light years away. Walt Whitman said, "I believe a blade of grass is no less than the journey-work of the stars. . . . " These words are not philosophy. They come from the depths of his soul. He also said, "I am large, I contain multitudes."

36   This might be called a meditation on "interbeing endlessly interwoven." All phenomena are interdependent. When we think of a speck of dust, a flower, or a human being, our thinking cannot break loose from the idea of unity, of one, of calculation. We see a line drawn between one and many, one and not one. But if we truly realize the interdependent nature of the dust, the flower, and the human being, we see that unity cannot exist without diversity. Unity and diversity interpenetrate each other freely. Unity is diversity, and diversity is unity. This is the principle of interbeing.

37   If you are a mountain climber or someone who enjoys the countryside or the forest, you know that forests are our lungs outside of our bodies. Yet we have been acting in a way that has allowed millions of square miles of land to be deforested, and we have also destroyed the air, the rivers, and parts of the ozone layer. We are imprisoned in our small selves, thinking only of some comfortable conditions for this small self, while we destroy our large self. If we want to change the situation, we must begin by being our true selves. To be our true selves means we have to *be* the forest, the river, and the ozone layer. If we visualize ourselves as the forest, we will experience the hopes and fears of the trees. If we don't do this, the forests will die, and we will lose our chance for peace. When we understand that we inter-are with the trees, we will know that it is up to us to make an effort to keep the trees alive. In the last twenty years, our automobiles and factories have created acid rain that has destroyed so many trees. Because we inter-are with the trees, we know that if they do not live, we too will disappear very soon.

38   We humans think we are smart, but an orchid, for example, knows how to produce noble, symmetrical flowers, and a snail knows how to make a beautiful, well-proportioned shell. Compared with their knowledge, ours is not worth much at all. We should bow deeply before the orchid and the snail and join our palms reverently before the monarch butterfly and the magnolia tree. The feeling of respect for all species will help us recognize the noblest nature in ourselves.

39   An oak tree is an oak tree. That is all an oak tree needs to do. If an oak tree is less than an oak tree, we will all be in trouble. In our former lives, we were rocks, clouds, and trees. We have also been an oak tree. This is not just Buddhist; it is scientific.

We humans are a young species. We were plants, we were trees, and now we have become humans. We have to remember our past existences and be humble. We can learn a lot from an oak tree.

40   All life is impermanent. We are all children of the earth, and, at some time, she will take us back to herself again. We are continually arising from Mother Earth, being nurtured by her, and then returning to her. Like us, plants are born, live for a period of time, and then return to the earth. When they decompose, they fertilize our gardens. Living vegetables and decomposing vegetables are part of the same reality. Without one, the other cannot be. After six months, compost becomes fresh vegetables again. Plants and the earth rely on each other. Whether the earth is fresh, beautiful, and green, or arid and parched depends on the plants.

41   It also depends on us. Our way of walking on the earth has a great influence on animals and plants. We have killed so many animals and plants and destroyed their environments. Many are now extinct. In turn, our environment is now harming us. We are like sleepwalkers, not knowing what we are doing or where we are heading. Whether we can wake up or not depends on whether we can walk mindfully on our Mother Earth. The future of all life, including our own, depends on our mindful steps.

42   Birds' songs express joy, beauty, and purity, and evoke in us vitality and love. So many beings in the universe love us unconditionally. The trees, the water, and the air don't ask anything of us; they just love us. Even though we need this kind of love, we continue to destroy them. By destroying the animals, the air, and the trees, we are destroying ourselves. We must learn to practice unconditional love for all.

43   Our earth, our green beautiful earth is in danger, and all of us know it. Yet we act as if our daily lives have nothing to do with the situation of the world. If the earth were your body, you would be able to feel many areas where she is suffering. Many people are aware of the world's suffering, and their hearts are filled with compassion. They know what needs to be done, and they engage in political, social, and environmental work to try to change things. But after a period of intense involvement, they become discouraged, because they lack the strength needed to sustain a life of action. Real strength is not in power, money, or weapons, but in deep, inner peace.

44   If we change our daily lives—the way we think, speak, and act—we change the world. The best way to take care of the environment is to take care of the environmentalist.

45   Many Buddhist teachings help us understand our interconnectedness with our mother, the earth. One of the deepest is the Diamond Sutra, which is written in the form of a dialogue between the Buddha and his senior disciple, Subhuti. It begins with this question by Subhuti: "If daughters and sons of good families wish to give rise to the highest, most fulfilled, awakened mind, what should they rely on and what should they do to master their thinking?" This is the same as asking, "If I want to use my whole being to protect life, what methods and principles should I use?"

46   The Buddha answers, "We have to do our best to help every living being cross the ocean of suffering. But after all beings have arrived at the shore of liberation, no being at all has been carried to the other shore. If you are still caught up in the idea of a self,

a person, a living being, or a life span, you are not an authentic bodhisattva." Self, person, living being, and life span are four notions that prevent us from seeing reality.

47   Life is one. We do not need to slice it into pieces and call this or that piece a "self." What we call a self is made only of non-self elements. When we look at a flower, for example, we may think that it is different from "non-flower" things. But when we look more deeply, we see that everything in the cosmos is in that flower. Without all of the non-flower elements—sunshine, clouds, earth, minerals, heat, rivers, and consciousness—a flower cannot be. That is why the Buddha teaches that the self does not exist. We have to discard all distinctions between self and non-self. How can anyone work to protect the environment without this insight?

48   The second notion that prevents us from seeing reality is the notion of a person, a human being. We usually discriminate between humans and non-humans, thinking that we are more important than other species. But since we humans are made of non-human elements, to protect ourselves we have to protect all of the non-human elements. There is no other way. If you think, "God created man in His own image and He created other things for man to use," you are already making the discrimination that man is more important than other things. When we see that humans have no self, we see that to take care of the environment (the non-human elements) is to take care of humanity. The best way to take good care of men and women so that they can be truly healthy and happy is to take care of the environment.

49   I know ecologists who are not happy in their families. They worked hard to improve the environment, partly to escape family life. If someone is not happy within himself, how can he help the environment? That is why the Buddha teaches that to protect the non-human elements is to protect humans, and to protect humans is to protect non-human elements.

50   The third notion we have to break through is the notion of a living being. We think that we living beings are different from inanimate objects, but according to the principle of interbeing, living beings are comprise of non-living-being elements. When we look into ourselves, we see minerals and all other non-living-being elements. Why discriminate against what we call inanimate? To protect living beings, we must protect the stones, the soil, and the oceans. Before the atomic bomb was dropped on Hiroshima, there were many beautiful stone benches in the parks. As the Japanese were rebuilding their city, they discovered that these stones were dead, so they carried them away and buried them. Then they brought in live stones. Do not think these things are not alive. Atoms are always moving. Electrons move at nearly the speed of light. According to the teaching of Buddhism, these atoms and stones are consciousness itself. That is why discrimination by living beings against non-living beings should be discarded.

51   The last notion is that of a life span. We think that we have been alive since a certain point in time and that prior to that moment, our life did not exist. This distinction between life and non-life is not correct. Life is made of death, and death is made of life. We have to accept death; it makes life possible. The cells in our body are dying every day, but we never think to organize funerals for them. The death of

one cell allows for the birth of another. Life and death are two aspects of the same reality. We must learn to die peacefully so that others may live. This deep meditation brings forth non-fear, non-anger, and non-despair, the strengths we need for our work. With non-fear, even when we see that a problem is huge, we will not burn out. We will know how to make small, steady steps. If those who work to protect the environment contemplate these four notions, they will know how to be and how to act.

52   In another Buddhist text, the Avatamsaka (Adoring the Buddha with Flowers) Sutra, the Buddha further elaborates his insights concerning our "interpenetration" with our environment. Please meditate with me on the "Ten Penetrations":

53   The first is, "All worlds penetrate a single pore. A single pore penetrates all worlds." Look deeply at a flower. It may be tiny, but the sun, the clouds, and everything else in the cosmos penetrates it. Nuclear physicists say very much the same thing: one electron is made by all electrons; one electron is in all electrons.

54   The second penetration is, "All living beings penetrate one body. One body penetrates all living beings." When you kill a living being, you kill yourself and everyone else as well.

55   The third is, "Infinite time penetrates one second. One second penetrates infinite time." A *ksana* is the shortest period of time, actually much shorter than a second.

56   The fourth penetration is, "All Buddhist teachings penetrate one teaching. One teaching penetrates all Buddhist teaching." As a young monk, I had the opportunity to learn that Buddhism is made of non-Buddhist elements. So, whenever I study Christianity or Judaism, I find the Buddhist elements in them, and vice versa. I always respect non-Buddhist teachings. All Buddhist teachings penetrate one teaching, and one teaching penetrates all Buddhist teachings. We are free.

57   The fifth penetration is, "Innumerable spheres enter one sphere. One sphere enters innumerable spheres." A sphere is a geographical space. Innumerable spheres penetrate into one particular area, and one particular area enters into innumerable spheres. It means that when you destroy one area, you destroy every area. When you save one area, you save all areas. A student asked me, "Thây, there are so many urgent problems, what should I do?" I said, "Take one thing and do it very deeply and carefully, and you will be doing everything at the same time."

58   The sixth penetration is, "All sense organs penetrate one organ. One organ penetrates all sense organs"—eye, ear, nose, tongue, body, and mind. To take care of one means to take care of many. To take care of your eyes means to take care of the eyes of innumerable living beings.

QUESTIONS FOR DISCUSSION

1. Why does Hanh begin with the example of the Montagnards' work ethic? Do you agree with his views on the Montagnards?
2. Why does Hanh believe that when we harm nature we harm ourselves both physically and psychologically? Explain why you agree or disagree with his point of view.

3. Explain why you agree or disagree with Hanh's claim, "While some members of the human family are suffering and starving, for us to enjoy false security and wealth is a sign of insanity."
4. What is the meaning of the dream that Hanh had when he first left Vietnam: What helped him to resolve the dream and his feelings of homesickness?
5. How does Hanh think that monks and psychotherapists can help their patients and the human family to establish a genuine relationship with nature and with other human beings? How can therapists and environmentalists help themselves to better mental health?
6. In the latter part of his essay, Hanh provides contemporary examples and explanation of the Buddha's "four notions that prevent us from seeing reality: the notions of self, person, living being, and life span." How does he clarify the importance of seeing beyond these deceptive notions in order to attain happiness and harmony with the environment?

CONNECTION

Compare Gary Snyder's views on people and animals in "Etiquette of Freedom" with Hanh's ideas on improving the relationship of humans to nature.

IDEAS FOR WRITING

1. Write an essay in response to Hanh's discussion of the importance of seeing beyond the four notions mentioned above. Do you agree or disagree that these notions damage our relation with the environment, with the human family, and with ourselves?
2. Although Hanh believes in political action to improve our relationship with nature and the human family, his emphasis in this essay is on mindful meditation, particularly the meditation on "interbeing endlessly interwoven." Explain what Hanh means by mindful meditation of this type (you might do some outside reading on the concept of "mindfulness"); then write an essay in which you discuss the advantages and/or disadvantages of this approach to psychological, social, ecological problems.

Offering (Traditional; Zuni People)

Adapted by Robert Bly from the translation by Ruth Bunzel

Anthropologists have traced Zuni habitation to A.D. 700 in an area between New Mexico and Arizona on the Zuni River. Around 1680, the Spanish relocated the Zuni in their current reservation area after an unsuccessful Pueblo rebellion. The

Zuni are a peaceful agricultural people; their staple crop has always been corn. Until recently, they lived close to the fields they farmed in the summer, using a traditional runoff system of farming that spread water from summer rains into the fields rather than storing water in modern reservoirs that can cause soil erosion. The Zuni hold the earth and their ceremonies sacred. They thank supernatural and natural forces for the fertility of the land and health of the community.

JOURNAL

Write a brief "offering" poem in which you make several wishes that you hope will come true through performing a magical ceremony that you describe in the poem.

This is what I want to happen: that our earth mother
may be clothed in ground corn four times over;
that frost flowers cover her over entirely;
that the mountain pines far away over there
5   may stand close to each other in the cold;
that the weight of snow crack some branches!
In order that the country may be this way
I have made my prayer sticks into something alive.

QUESTIONS FOR DISCUSSION

1. What does the speaker in the poem hope will occur in the natural world? Does the speaker seem confident that the wishes will be made real?
2. The speaker makes four wishes, each beginning with the word "that." How does the use of parallel structure and line breaks (probably emphasized by drumming in the "performed" version of the offering) help to emphasize each of the wishes?
3. How do images and metaphors enhance the statement of the four wishes? Examine each of the metaphors and explain its sensory impact and meaning.
4. What is the nature of the "offering," or exchange of powers in the poem, and to whom or what does the speaker address the offering?
5. What does it mean to make one's "prayer sticks into something alive"? What are several alternative meanings of "alive" in this context?

CONNECTION

Compare the sense of communion with nature seen in this poem with that of the imaginary culture described in E. M. Forster's "The Other Side of the Hedge." What do these two societies have in common? How are they different?

IDEAS FOR WRITING

1. Although modern technology allows us to remain indoors at about the same temperature all year round, earlier cultures embraced the changing seasons and the advantages brought by each. Using some of the images from "Offering," write an essay in defense of living through the four seasons—what do we derive from each, practically speaking and in spiritual terms?

2. Write a poem based on this Zuni offering that describes your ideal vision of nature.

Michael Noah Ford

Jerusalem's Spring

The following poem began in Jerusalem, where Michael Ford studies the Hebrew and Aramaic languages as well as Talmudic and Hasidic thought. After a period of sadness and loss during a long winter, Ford welcomed the return of spring both as a student of the Jewish religion and as a lover of nature. In "Jerusalem's Spring" the masculine aspect of Divinity is alluded to as "It" while the feminine aspect (associated with the coming of spring) is referred to using the feminine pronoun, and is paralleled with the unrestrained giving and renewal of the Divine spirit in nature.

With small red explosions all surrounding me
And even smaller yellow flashes—splattered
In the bright, twinkling greens of spring's time,
That squish, softly, silently, beneath
5   My feet, that have been—till now—so tired.
Here, jewels are seen of baby blue and purple
Sparkling their inner joy out to these eyes,
Revealing again the much needed face of
Divinity's mask, that interface between It and us—
10 Through the seasons' four-step beat It uses.

Treasures now are shown in this new beginning,
After that dark turning away of winter—
When the light concealed from time and place
Causes one to call out in truthful yearning:
15 To show us, despite the fact we may forget,
The gift will be given, continually, always . . .
With the blooming lights, the flowers open,
And It again, allows Her to return—
To us.

1. Comment on the sensory images in the first seven lines. How do the strong, repeated colors, sounds and rhythms in these lines help to create the direct impression of a spring day?
2. What is meant by "the much needed face of Divinity's mask"? How does the mask function as an "interface"? What is the "four-step beat"?
3. What is the "gift"? In what sense is it given to us "continually"?
4. Compare the view of nature, the changing seasons, and spiritual renewal in this poem with "Offering," the Zuni poem that immediately precedes it in this chapter.

Sheila Walsh

Visualizing Our Environment: Communication of Environmental Issues Through Visual Arts

Sheila Walsh was a first year student majoring in biology and minoring in studio art when she wrote the following research proposal for her introductory composition course. As an undergraduate doing research at the campus Center for Conservation Biology, Walsh became interested in ways to make the conservation of the environment a public issue. Because of her interest in art, she decided to focus on public art as a way to change the way that people think about nature and environmental issues.

1   The nation is ready to make the environment the key issue for 2000. Recent evidence of climate change is too drastic for anyone to ignore. . . . [W]ho can doubt that our climate is changing severely?

—*Sierra Club Action Daily*, 26 Feb. 1999

2   If articulated properly, the environment can be the central issue of the next decade.

—Dick Morris, *The Hill*, 24 Feb. 1999

3   The face of our planet is changing rapidly as a result of ecotastrophes such as global warming, pollution, and deforestation, but the average person cannot see it happening, even though scientists generate data everyday to support the reality of the changes. The problem is not how many facts and figures we receive about global warming, habitat destruction, and diversity loss—but how we perceive these facts. Frightening information about the degradation of our environment is ignored as it flows over TV waves into nightly news programs and hides amongst editorial columns in newspapers. The current form of communication has made people

entirely apathetic to the destruction of the world that we live in. To change the way that people and whole societies treat the environment, the communication of environmental issues must change. Communicating environmental issues through visual arts will force people to actually *see* the change in their environment. Public murals, photography, and billboards will make environmental issues immediate, changing apathy into urgency and catalyzing environmental action on local and global scales.

4   The current mode of communication to the public has led to the stagnation of the environmental movement; emphatic, public visual arts will re-energize it. Murals, photographs, and billboards actively engage people on a personal and emotional level. Images activate the vivid memory bank of experiences that each person has. The images of these experiences create the mental landscape that we live our lives on; the contents of those images in turn can influence our actions. As one looks at photographs of cracked, dry earth from the *Water in the West Project*, a model for communication through visual arts, the images become part of the person's mental landscape. Later, when she sees a lush green lawn in Arizona or her tap water left running, she will give it a second thought.

5   However, every person has a different collection of experiences and, consequently, a different level of visual literacy. "Visual literacy does not apply to our society as a whole," regrets Margaret Moulton, professor of photography at Stanford University. Even though we are constantly bombarded with images, people do not have a sophisticated level of literacy with visual images (Moulton). Public images, though, are uniquely democratic. Every person who passes by a mural in a park, regardless of her level of visual literacy, has the same opportunity to stop for a moment and think about it. Art breaks cultural and literacy boundaries that limit many people's abilities to communicate in other media.

6   The art must be displayed in public to be successful. It must be in city and county parks, on the side of high rises and parking structures, and plastered on the billboards that create a forest around expressways. Margaret Moulton agrees that all people have the ability to respond to art but not all people have the ability to see art because it is not in public. Art of this type cannot be in museums or galleries because it will become as esoteric as the conventional texts that it is trying to improve upon. Many artists who are dealing with environmental issues display their art in places like The Ansel Adams Center for Photography. Sadly enough, the majority of the public does not go to The Ansel Adams Center for Photography, but global warming still affects us all.

7   Social and political issues have already been communicated through visual arts to the public outside of museums. Images have been intentionally and unintentionally changing the way that people live since pictographs first appeared on rock faces. In modern times, despite the advent of the printing press, a few specific images have dramatically changed people's perceptions of society more than headlines. Visual images have made radical social and political change and will make radical environmental change.

8   Environmental degradation is as much of a social and political issue as war, oppression, and eating disorders. Picasso changed people's perceptions of World War II more than most newspaper headlines with his painting *Guernica*. The twisted faces

and contorted bodies scream out Picasso's message. *Guernica* embodies all that is corrupt, ugly, atrocious, and unbearable that now defines war for a person of the twentieth century. The Chicano movement forced people to recognize the more subtle forms of oppression occurring during peacetime using public murals. Murals and poster making became the emphasis of the movement's activism because they informed the literate and non-literate masses. A Chicano/a could "read" the message of the mural and be able to see "the social, economic, and political conditions forced onto the Chicano community" differently ("Brief History of Chicano Murals"). Through the Chicano Movement, visual arts became a tool for inciting people to take action. Robin Lasser and Catherine Sylva have proved that visual arts can also be a tool for educating people about themselves. They use billboards located in Sacramento to inform the commuters about the eating disorders that affect the majority of women today. The project, *Consuming Landscapes and Other Eating Disorders*, shows images of distorted bodies, flaming silver ware, and barbequed meat. The billboards are provocative because of their imagery and their ability to talk about a subject that most people are silent about. Public murals, photography, and billboards about any social, political, or environmental issue are provocative because they force the viewer to question the world in which they are viewing the art. When an environmental image forces the viewer to question the world around her, the answer she will find is that something has to change.

9   The success with social and political issues will be easily transferred to environmental issues because they are often more visual than social and political issues. Oppression of people can be silent and invisible; however, the destruction of old growth forests is loud and visible. Yet, environmental issues are still ignored because of our anthropomorphic sense of progress. Public displays of visual arts that use the affective characteristics of *Guernica*, the murals of the Chicano Movement, and the billboards of *Consuming Landscapes* will demand attention for environmental issues by questioning our progress.

10   Despite the inherent visual quality of environmental issues, visual arts have still not been addressed as seriously as a medium for communicating environmental issues as they have been for social and political issues. Fleeting television programs have been devoted to global warming or El Niño. However, television, a type of visual art, has a way of turning real problems into fantasies. The viewers of *Dateline* or *20/20* do not often leave the couch between these news shows and the next episode of *ER*. The real problems of global warming presented on *Dateline* special edition are then ignored because they seem as fantastic and distant as the people dying of multiple gun shot wounds on *ER*. These problems are also ignored because environmental issues are generally thought of as being strictly scientific. In between fantasy and science fiction, visual arts need to show reality. Murals, photography, and billboards have shown the reality of social and political issues and now they will show the reality of the destruction of our environment because it is a social and political issue.

11   During the Industrial Revolution, J.M.W. Turner (1775–1851) and John Ruskin (1819–1900) recognized the environmental degradation of London as a social issue in their watercolor paintings. Through default, they made the first steps toward

communicating environmental issues through visual arts. Clouds, smoke, and steam fill their work. Although the Turner and Ruskin's images were similar, the messages that they were trying to communicate were quite different: "where Turner celebrates the destructive energy of industrialization, Ruskin fears its affects on Nature" (Danahay 62). In Ruskin's work pollution is "a sign of social and spiritual disorder, a symptom of the blurring of the boundaries between the natural and the abominable, the sacred and the profane" (Danahay 63). The connection of social ills to pollution made him a forerunner of the contemporary ecological movement. He was one of a group of experts who were just realizing the negative affects of what we call "pollution" (Danahay 68). Connecting a change in environment to a social issue caused him difficulty when trying to reach his audience in lectures. Consequently, "Rather than exhort his audience to action, Ruskin frequently. . . [left] questions hanging and his points unarticulated" (Danahay 70). If Ruskin had been successful in articulating his concerns about the trends in London's environment, it may not have taken until the 1970s to recognize the drastic changes in the environment that began in the 1870s.

12   If scientists and the general public could have learned from art at the turn of the century, can they learn from art now at the turn of the millennium? According to Cornelia Hesse-Honegger, the answer is yes. She began drawing *Dropsophilia* flies in the late 1960s at the Zoological Institute of the University of Zurich to supplement scientific research. In 1987, she upset the scientific community because her detailed paintings of insects and plants affected by radioactive emissions revealed mutations greater than those expected by scientists. When Hesse-Honegger published this in the Swiss periodical, *Das Magazine*, she received criticism from scientists who did not believe that such small doses of radiation could cause the mutations that Hesse-Honegger had recorded in her drawings. Dr. William Thompson, formerly a Professor of the humanities and social sciences at MIT, describes how "disorder broke out in Switzerland when Hesse-Honegger moved out of her place to use her art as a means of scientific analysis and political description of the modern technical world" (Hesse-Honegger and Thompson 18). In Hesse-Honegger's work, the role of art was to portray "an image: an image which reflects that which we actually have but do not want." She showed how we "destroy, poison and mutate" (18). Then, "we are faced with the awkward question, why does the gap between environmental destruction and taking action against it grow?" (17).

13   Hesse-Honegger's work shows how provocative communication of environmental issues through visual arts can be. She showed that "if we wish to think with art about science, we may find. . . a realism that is aesthetically unsettling precisely because it is neither horrific nor natural, but it is what we have made of a nature we once thought of as given" (19). Although it might be unsettling, the general public needs to be forced to *see* how we have changed nature as they walk through a park, down a side walk, or drive on the expressway. Artists are recognizing that their work can force this change where conventional forms of communication have failed to.

14   Successful work has come in a great variety of purpose and form. Artist's purposes range from simple environmental awareness to a call for specific action. Their forms range from public murals to photographic documentation. There is still not a perfect

model. However, the current work is creating the guidelines for successful communication. Two examples with very different purposes and forms provide the foundation of these guidelines.

15   The popular ocean artist, Wyland, has been successful in promoting environmental awareness. He has confronted thousands of people with their relationship to oceanic animals through the life-size murals that he has painted in major cities all over the world. His sixty-seven, and counting, *Whaling Walls* represent an attempt to change attitudes on a large scale. Wyland says that "By painting them life-sized in public places, I hope to raise people's consciousness and get them involved in protecting the whales. . . . These murals will be seen by tens of millions of people each year. You can choose not to go into an art gallery or museum, but you can't ignore a giant mural" ("Wyland Whaling Wall"). His majestic whales have become regular features in the lives of the people who live in those cities. Passersby recognize the beauty in the arc of a whale as it breeches up through aqua painted water on the side of their office building. The mural is an especially effective medium because it can be "'consumed' over and over again by the same person, it also can be 'consumed' simultaneously by many viewers" (Walker 74).

16   Wyland's *Whaling Walls* suggest change; the photographs of the *Water in the West* demand it. The *Water in the West* is a "photographic response to the growing water crisis that exists because our culture thinks of water as a commodity or an abstract legal right, rather than the most basic physical source of life" (Manchester i). Photographers Mark Wett, Terry Evans, Laurie Brown, Robert Dawson, Martin Stupich, Gregory Coniff, Wanda Hammerback, and Peter Goin wanted to answer the question: How can photography contribute to the urgent public debate over water use, allocation, and privilege? These photographers recognized that their medium is "uniquely qualified to offer information and visual insight" (Manchester i). Goin recalls that "A significant amount of our time was devoted to discussing the relationship of the photograph as a creative object to the photograph as a tool for political change. After a consensus, the project's goal was to create a collection of photos and related visual material that will contribute significantly to the dialogue about the future and quality of life on earth as sustained by increasingly limited natural resources such as water" (Manchester 15).

17   At the same time as the *Water and the West Project* was formulating its plans, the Nevada Humanities Committee was sponsoring a conference entitled "Water in the Arid West." The two groups collaborated in their efforts to bring together historians, writers, ranchers, politicians, lawyers, students and community members to discuss the water issue. The scholars were able to realize what the photographers had realized through their work: "The irony in the American West today is that we have no water, yet seem to have plenty to drink" (Manchester 1). *Water and the West* continues to be displayed, affecting change and serving as a model for the communication of environmental issues through visual arts.

18   Wyland and the *Water in the West* show the range of the current work with visual arts to communicate environmental issues. In between these examples are the violent images of the Headwaters campaign and the serene landscapes of Adams. They

are all models for how visual images can create change. Wyland and Ansel Adams have changed the way that tens of thousands of people *see* nature. The Headwaters campaign and *Water in the West* have made their issues immediate and have been catalysts for change. To improve upon these individual efforts, their strengths have to be combined. Communication of environmental issues through visual arts must address the issues that are being ignored despite sufficient scientific data, then portray the issue so that people can *see* it differently, make sure the image accessible to the public, and emphasize the immediacy of the issue and the need for action. These four guidelines will make the communication of environmental issues through visual arts a catalyst for local and global action. The environmental movement desperately needs visual arts as a catalyst to propel it into the 21st Century. A commitment of significant amounts of federal money should be made to sponsor independent, local artists to create murals, photography, and billboards that would become permanent fixtures in communities nation-wide. The conventional means of communication have led to the stagnation of the popular environmental movement. This radical, grass-root form of communication through visual arts will re-energize the movement for the new millennium.

WORKS CITED

"A Brief History of Chicano Murals." L.A. Murals Home Page. Sep 1996. 13 Jan 1999 <http://latino.sscnet.ucla.edu/murals/Sparc/muralhis.html>.

Danahay, Martin A. "Matter Out of Place: The Politics of Pollution in Ruskin and Turner." *CLIO* 21.1 (Fall, 1991): 61.

Hesse-Honegger, Cornelia and William Thompson. "Painting Mutations." *Geographical Magazine* 64.11 (Nov. 1992): 15.

Lasser, Robin. Telephone interview. 12 Feb. 1999.

Manchester, Ellen. *Arid Waters: Photographs From the Water and The West Project.* Ed. Peter Goin. Reno: University of Nevada Press, 1992.

Moulton, Margaret. Telephone interview. 14 Jan. 1999.

Walker, John A. and Sarah Chaplin. *Visual Culture: An Introduction.* Manchester, NY: Manchester U. P., 1997.

"Wyland Brings Whaling Wall to San Diego." *San Diego Earth Times* Aug. 1994. 3 March 1999. <http://www.sdearthtimes.com/et0894/et0894s6.html>.

QUESTIONS FOR DISCUSSION

1. How do Walsh's comments on environmental change and perceptions of change in the first paragraph help to establish a problem that needs to be solved? At what point does Walsh state, in general terms, her proposed solution to the problem?

2. What examples of the way the media present environmental problems. does Walsh provide, and what flaws and limits does she see in them? What are the limitations of some current venues for displaying environmental art, such as the Ansel Adams Center? How do the critical points Walsh makes about the media and the current places of exhibition help to strengthen her thesis and proposal?

3. How effectively does Walsh present past and current examples of effective environmental and protest art in order to strengthen her proposal? Could she have provided other examples?
4. Walsh originally used a number of visual illustrations to present her points more forcefully. Which of her points and references do you think could have been effectively reinforced by visuals? Does the essay make its points well without them?
5. Evaluate Walsh's specific proposal for change which she develops on her final paragraphs. Is the proposal clear and convincing? Would her plan (assuming it were to get governmental funding) really engage people's understanding and concern about environmental degradation? Why or why not?

Topics for Research and Writing

1. In essay or story form, create a utopian community based on a theme of ecological balance and integration of people with nature. Conclude with an explanation of the choices you made in setting up your utopian world, and an analysis of problems your utopian citizens might face as well as ideas for how they might handle the problems.
2. Do some research into the kind of mindful, nonviolent study and action espoused by Hanh, Matthew Fox, Thomas Berry, and other followers of the "deep ecology" movement for integrating Eastern and Western spiritual practices with ecological activism. Write an essay in which you discuss this movement's effectiveness and its future.
3. Develop an ideal program for educating today's children to live in harmony with nature. What emphasis would you put on science and technology? How would you introduce dreams, myths, and imaginative literature? How would you present history, social science, and politics? What books would you assign, and why? Discuss several particular projects and field trip experiences that you might have your students complete to give your readers a sense of how you would teach.
4. Write a proposal based on Snyder's "Etiquette of Freedom," Rilke's "Panther," and other research you do about zoos. How would you design a zoo environment that encourages people to learn about the ecosystems that animals exist within in the wild and that also allows animals some of the freedom and privacy they enjoy in their native environments?
5. The vision of nature of the ethnic and cultural groups in the United States vary greatly due to their histories and prior successes or failures in attaining the "American Dream." Compare the visions of nature or attitudes toward ecology and wilderness areas of two or three different ethnic groups represented in this chapter or elsewhere in the text—Asian-Americans,

African-Americans, Native Americans, Hispanic-Americans. Discuss the historical origins of the view of nature each group has.

6. Snyder in "Etiquette of Freedom" as well as many modern biologists argues that the way we pattern our societies, our personal interactions, and even our languages have close parallels in the animal world. Do some research into some of these parallels and write a research paper detailing your findings and conclusions.

7. A number of films have been made that attempt to provide visions of possible futures for the environment or to comment on some aspect of nature. Select and view a film that presents a vision of nature; then discuss the vision of the filmmaker. You might select a film from the following list: *Dreams (Kurosawa), Strange Days, The Last Wave, Mindwalk, What Dreams May Come, Kundun, Dances with Wolves*

8. For further research into our relationship with nature and ecological activism that stems from a deep appreciation of natural patterns, try the following URLs:

ANTHROPOCENTRISM AND DEEP ECOLOGY
http://www.uq.oz.au/philosophy/anthropocentrism.html#ade
This essay by philosopher William Grey, which appeared originally in the *Australiasian Journal of Philosophy* in 1993, presents a critique of the anti-anthropocentric bias in the Deep Ecology movement.

BUDDHISM & SCIENCE: PROBING THE BOUNDARIES OF FAITH AND REASON
http://online.sfsu.edu/~rone/Buddhism/VerhoevenBuddhism
Science
This essay by Martin J. Verhoeven, from a talk given at the Berkeley Buddhist Monastery in 1997, discusses the history of philosophical inter-relations between science and religion with a special focus on Buddhist beliefs about nature.

DEEP ECOLOGY AND ENVIRONMENTAL ETHICS
http://www.msue.msu.edu/msue/imp/modej/10169571.html
This site from Michigan State University Extension provides a selected and annotated bibliography of materials published since 1980 on the subject of Deep Ecology and Environmental Ethics.

ENVIRONMENTAL JUSTICE—NATIVE AMERICANS AND THE ENVIRONMENT
http://www.indians.org/library/subenv1.html
This site, sponsored by the American Indian Heritage Foundation, presents links to organizations, articles and databases concerned with environmental injustice to and environmental activism by Native Americans.

INTERNATIONAL RIVERS NETWORK POETRY AND ART CONTEST FOR CHILDREN
http://www.irn.org/row/index.shtml

Part of the International Rivers Network web site and co-sponsored by the Library of Congress and former United States Poet Laureate Robert Hass, this page presents an innovative example of using creativity to get children and their families involved with environmental action.

NEW DIMENSIONS DEEP ECOLOGY LINKS
http://newdimensions.org/html/delinks.html
This site, maintained by the ecology group New Dimensions, includes links to organizations and media devoted to deep ecology and environmentalism.

SMITHSONIAN MUSEUM NATURAL HISTORY WEB: LINKS TO HERE AND THERE
http://www.nmnh.si.edu/links.html
The Smithsonian Museum of Natural History maintains this large set of helpful links to natural history and anthropological museum sites around the world.

TECHNIQUES FOR CREATIVE THINKING
http://www.ozemail.com.au/~caveman/Creative/Techniques/index.html
From the large web site Creativity Web, the techniques listed here are linked to further explanation and advice on stimulating creative thought and writing.

CREDITS

and Contemporary Culture. Used by permission of Dutton, a division of Penguin Putnam, Inc.

Sheila Chanani, "Whirling Through: My Writing Process as a Tornado Within." Reprinted by permission of the author

Joyce Chang, "Drive Be Carefully." Reprinted by permission of the author.

Judith Ortiz Cofer, "Silent Dancing." Reprinted with permission from the publisher of *Silent Dancing: A Partial Remembrance of a Puerto Rican Childhood* (Houston: Arte Publico Press-University of Houston, 1990).

Judith Ortiz Cofer, "The Other" from *Reaching for the Mainland and Selected New Poems*. Copyright 1995. Reprinted by permission of Bilingual Press/Editorial Bilingue, Arizona State University, Tempe, Arizona.

Rosa Contreras, "On Not Being a Girl." Reprinted by permission of the author.

Annie Dillard, "A Field of Silence" from *Teaching a Stone to Talk*. Copyright © 1982 by Annie Dillard. Reprinted by permission of HarperCollins Publishers, Inc.

Chitra Divakaruni, "Nargis' Toilette" from *The Black Candle*. Copyright © 1990 by CALYX Books. Reprinted by permission of the publisher.

Stephen Dunn, "Middle Class Poem" from *Not Dancing*. Copyright © 1984 by Stephen Dunn. Reprinted by permission of Carnegie Mellon University Press.

Umberto Eco, "City of Robots" from *Travel in Hyperreality*. Copyright © 1983 by Gruppo Editoriale Fabbri-Bompiani, Sonzogno, Etas S.p.A, English translation copyright © 1986 by Harcourt, Inc. Reprinted by permission of Harcourt, Inc.

Peter Elbow, "Teaching Two Kinds of Thinking by Teaching Writing" from *Embracing Contraries*. Copyright © 1986 by Peter Elbow. Used by permission of Oxford University Press, Inc.

Naomi Epel, Steven King intview from *Writers Dreaming*. Copyright © 1993 by Naomi Epel. Reprinted by permission of Carol Southern Books, a division of Random House, Inc.

Louise Erdrich, "Dear John Wayne" from *Jacklight*. Copyright © 1984 by Louise Erdrich. Reprinted by permission of Henry Holt and Company, LLC.

Michael Noah Ford, "Jerusalem's Spring." Reprinted by permission of the author.

E. M. Forster, "The Other Side of the Hedge" from *Collected Tales*. Published 1947 by Alfred A. Knopf, Inc. Reprinted by permission of Alfred Knopf, Inc. a division of Random House, Inc.

Sigmund Freud, from *On Dreams*, translated by James Strachey. Copyright © 1952 by W.W. Norton & Company, Inc., renewed © 1980 by Alix S. Strachey. Used by permission of W. W. Norton & Company, and Sigmund Freud Copyrights, The Institute of Psycho-Analysis and The Hogarth Press from The Standard Edition of the Complete Psychological Works of Sigmund Freud.

James Finn Garner, "The Politically Correct Cinderella" from *Politically Correct Holiday Stories*, 1995.

Nikki Giovanni, "Ego Tripping" from *The Women and the Men*. Copyright © 1970, 1974, 1975 by Nikki Giovanni. By permission of William Morrow and Company, Inc.

Jason Glickman, "Technology and the Future of the American Wilderness." Reprinted by permission of the author.

Lissy Goralnik, "The Sandstorm of Time and Knowledge." Reprinted by permission of the author.

Stephen Jay Gould, "Muller Bros. Moving & Storage." Copyright © 1990 American

INDEX